MW00803922

20
4B

# Educational Psychology

## A COGNITIVE VIEW

### Second Edition

**DAVID P. AUSUBEL**
Graduate School and University Center
City University of New York

**JOSEPH D. NOVAK**
Cornell University

**HELEN HANESIAN**
Brooklyn College
City University of New York

**Holt, Rinehart
and Winston**

New York   Chicago   San Francisco   Dallas
Montreal   Toronto   London   Sydney

Library of Congress Cataloging in Publication Data
Ausubel, David Paul.
Educational psychology.
Bibliography: p. 631
Includes indexes.
1. Educational psychology.    I.  Novak, Joseph
Donald, joint author.    II.    Hanesian, Helen, joint author.    III.    Title.
LB1051.A747    1978    370.15    77-26093
ISBN 0-03-089951-6

*Dedicated—*

To my wife, Pearl   (D.P.A.)

To my wife, Joan   (J.D.N.)

To my parents, Vahan and Anna   (H.H.)

*If I had to reduce all of educational psychology to just one principle, I would say this: The most important single factor influencing learning is what the learner already knows. Ascertain this and teach him accordingly.*

# PREFACE TO THE
# SECOND EDITION

The second edition of this book is generally congruous with the senior author's conception (expressed in the first edition) of educational psychology as an independent applied discipline dealing with the nature, outcomes, and evaluation of school (subject-matter) learning, and with the various variables of cognitive structure, development, intellectual ability, practice, motivation, personality, instructional material, society, and teachers that influence it. Like the first edition, it is almost exclusively concerned with meaningful learning, particularly meaningful reception learning. However, learning by discovery, problem solving, concept formation, and creativity are fully discussed. We do not by any means discount the importance of discovery learning. Rather we believe that students acquire large bodies of subject matter primarily through meaningful reception learning that is facilitated by appropriately designed expository teaching and instructional materials. We make a clear distinction between the rote ↔ meaningful dimension of learning and the reception ↔ discovery dimension.

The major change in the organization of the book was to place the chapter on concept formation immediately after the chapter on meaning and meaningful learning, instead of considering it in the latter portion of the book devoted to discovery learning. The rationale for this change is that even though concept *formation* is a form of discovery learning, the major type of concept acquisition in school settings is concept *assimilation* (which is one type of meaningful reception learning).

The theory of cognitive learning first developed in *The Psychology of Meaningful Verbal Learning* (1963), and expanded in the earlier edition of this book (1968), has been modified somewhat in the present edition on the basis of research and feedback from students and colleagues. We have chosen to label this theory of learning as *assimilation* theory to emphasize a major characteristic; the important interactive role that existing cognitive structures play in the process of new learning. We have explicitly described the elements of assimilation theory, including an emphasis on the concepts of subsumption, progressive differentiation, and integrative reconciliation.

In revising the first edition, therefore, we paid selective attention to new developments in educational psychology that were relevant to our non-eclectic view of the nature of educational psychology as a whole, as well as to our patricular theoretical view of the nature of subject-matter learning. Because of the virtual demise of the curriculum reform movements, we have chiefly emphasized in Chapter 10 the various ways of presenting instructional materials, and the advantages and disadvantages of each, in accordance with assimilation theory. Similarly, since the mediational theory of meaning is now a dead issue, it is not discussed in the present edition.

The chapter on individual differences in intellectual ability has been expanded to include both the retarded child and the child with learning disabilities. The discussion of the nature–nurture problem in the growth of intellectual abilities also reflects recent controversial developments regarding the relative influence of each factor, particularly in the determination of "racial" and social-class differences in intellectual ability, as well as differences attributable to cultural disadvantage. In the sociocultural area, numerous changes in the attitudes and self-concepts of black children and of students' attitudes toward the school have been explored. The relatively recent emergence of performance/competency-based teaching has been included in the chapters on teacher characteristics and principles of measurement and evaluation.

The ways in which this book is different from more traditional eclectic text books in educational psychology, and the rationale for excluding much of the material customarily found in these books, are fully discussed in the Preface to the First Edition (following this preface) and need not be repeated here. In the interest of clarifying many complex ideas, however, we have made use of schematic diagrams. The organization of the book, however, is still deliberately consistent with the principles of progressive differentiation and integrative reconciliation, which, we believe, are of great importance in promoting meaningful learning of subject matter.

The many changes in the second edition that enhances its readability— a glossary of terms used in assimilation theory; the use of organizer-like introductions* to each of the chapters (which provide ideational scaffolding for the material that follows and integrate the chapter with preceding and succeeding chapters); the use of schematic diagrams; a livelier (if less precise) prose style; and the wider use of examples illustrating assimilation theory that are applicable to the classroom—all make this edition suitable for undergraduate as well as graduate students in educational psychology.

It is an integral part of our theoretical view of school learning that a body of subject matter is much easier to understand and remember if it is relatable (anchorable) to organizing and explanatory ideas derived from a

---

* See footnote on p. 171 for a discussion of why these introductions are not true organizers as we define the term. Hence, they should not be used as models of genuine advance organizers (see Glossary).

*single* theoretical stance with face plausibility than if it is a mere compendium of discrete, unintegrated and unexplained facts related at best to a wide variety of contradictory and often irreconcilable theoretical views. This has been the case particularly with the typical eclectic textbooks in educational psychology. Such books still adhere primarily to a psychology of learning that is more applicable to rats in a maze than to pupils in a classroom. Sometimes it is combined with an information theory or a cybernetic model (without any attempt to bridge the gap between these theories) that is only 15 years out of date in contrast to the 25 years in the case of rote (behavioristic) learning theory.

We are indebted to Pearl Ausubel for critical reading of the manuscript and for many helpful suggestions in the organization and presentation of ideas.

We gratefully acknowledge permission to use illustrations and materials from Chapters 5 and 6 of *A Theory of Education* (J. D. N.), published by Cornell University Press.

One of us (H. H.) wishes to express her thanks to Ruth Birnbaum for her valuable assistance in the preparation of the manuscript.

D. P. A.
*New York City*                                                       J. D. N.
*Ithaca, N.Y.*                                                         H. H.

# PREFACE TO THE
# FIRST EDITION

THE BASIC PREMISE UNDERLYING THIS BOOK is that educational psychology is primarily concerned with the nature, conditions, outcomes, and evaluation of classroom learning. Unlike most of its predecessors in the field, it does not conceive of educational psychology as an amalgam of learning theory, developmental psychology, mental hygiene, and educational and psychological measurement. More specifically this text differs from these other works in the following six respects:

First, it does not consider such topics as child development, adolescent psychology, the psychology of adjustment, mental hygiene, personality, and group dynamics as ends in themselves. It considers them only insofar as they bear on and are *directly* relevant to classroom learning. This criterion of relevance has, of course, also been adopted by other textbooks in the field, but more in theory than in actuality. I have endeavored to include in this volume only psychological theory, evidence, problems, and issues that are of direct concern either to the serious student of education or to the future teacher in his role as facilitator of school learning.

Second, it eliminates *entirely* many normally covered topics drawn from general and developmental psychology which bear little or no relation to classroom learning. Examples include the nature and development of needs, general determinants of behavior, reactions to frustration, developmental tasks, mechanisms of adjustment, parent-child relationships, noncognitive development during infancy and the preschool years, and physical development. It is true, for example, that physical development during childhood affects motor coordination, writing, and popularity in the peer group, and that physical changes in adolescence affect the self-concept, emotional stability, peer relations, and athletic skills. But an educational psychology textbook cannot cover everything. Prospective primary-school teachers will presumably have a course in child development, and prospective secondary-school teachers will presumably have a course in adolescent psychology. Similarly, certain aspects of motivation *are* obviously relevant for classroom learning, but a general discussion of needs, their nature, function, development, and classification, such as would be appropriate in a course in general psychology, hardly seems necessary.

Third, this text is principally concerned with the kinds of learning that take place in the classroom; that is, meaningful symbolic learning—both reception and discovery. Some kinds of learning, such as rote learning and motor learning, are considered so inconsequential a part of school learning as to warrant no systematic treatment in a textbook on educational psychology. Other kinds of learning, for example, the learning of values and attitudes, are not considered indigenous to the primary or distinctive function of the school, and are treated only insofar as they affect or are part of the learning of subject matter. Their more general aspects are left to such courses as general and social psychology. And still other kinds of learning, for example, animal learning, conditioning, instrumental learning, and simple discrimination learning, are considered irrelevant for most learning tasks in school, despite the fact that wildly extrapolated findings in these areas quite commonly pad the learning chapters of many educational psychology textbooks.

Fourth, this work is not eclectic in theoretical orientation, but proceeds from a consistent point of view based on a cognitive theory of meaningful verbal learning.

Fifth, greater stress is placed on cognitive development than in most other educational psychology texts, and the material is integrated with related aspects of cognitive functioning.

Finally, a level of discourse is employed that is appropriate for prospective teachers and mature students of education. Oversimplified explanations, language, and presentation of ideas are avoided. Educational psychology is a complex rather than a simple subject. Hence to oversimplify it is to render the beginning student a serious disservice. Clarity and incisiveness of presentation do not require reversion to a kindergarten level of writing and illustration. In fact, it is the writer's firm conviction that much of the thinly disguised contempt many prospective teachers have for courses in pedagogy and educational psychology stems from watered-down, repetitive content and an unnecessarily elementary level of vocabulary, sentence structure, illustration, and example. Illustrations, tables, and figures, therefore, are used in this text only where it is felt they could convey meanings more effectively and succinctly than could language; they are not used to provide relief, diversion, sentimental atmosphere, or an aura of scientific precision. For the same reason, and also because they are so space-consuming and so frequently accepted as evidence rather than as interesting illustrative matter, case histories and anecdotal material are not included in this volume.

In short, the aim of this book is to furnish the prospective teacher with the basic psychological sophistication he will need for classroom teaching. It should be supplemented by courses in general, developmental, and social psychology and cannot attempt to serve as a substitute for any or all of these subjects.

My decision to restrict the discussion of learning to meaningful verbal learning points up the unfortunate paucity of experimental evidence in this area. This situation is a reflection of the prevailing tendency, over the past three or more decades, for educational psychologists to extrapolate findings from animal, rote, and perceptual-motor learning experiments rather than to conduct research on meaningful verbal learning. But presenting certain significant theoretical propositions without definitive empirical support was considered preferable to leaving large gaps in theory or filling them by means of unwarranted extrapolation. In certain instances, however, where abundant confirmatory research was available, considerations of space made judicious selection necessary. Cited evidence, therefore, should be considered more illustrative than exhaustive.

To be consistent with the pedagogic principles of progressive differentiation and integrative reconciliation (see Chapter 4), the book is organized in such a way that early chapters present an overview of later chapters, and the introductory material in each chapter performs the same function in relation to the material that follows. Furthermore, when similar material is encountered again in a different context, deliberate repetition, explicitly delineating similarities and differences, is considered pedagogically superior to expecting the student to perform the necessary cross-referencing of related concepts and propositions by himself. These devices render chapter summaries superfluous. Unlike a summary, an overview orients the reader in advance. When used as an "organizer," it presents (at a higher level of abstraction, generality, and inclusiveness) an ideational scaffolding for the detailed material to follow. It is also a well-known fact that students frequently abuse summaries by using them as the *sole* basis for review.

Several other familiar textbook features are missing in this book. First, specific questions are not posed at the end of each chapter. This degree of explicit guidance in review is considered more appropriate at the elementary- and high-school levels of instruction. The use of an accompanying workbook was rejected for the same reason. Second, chapter reading lists are not offered since it is believed that most students simply ignore suggested readings selected by the author. The student who is genuinely interested in exploring original sources of particular interest to *him* can easily do so by identifying them in the text and then turning to the bibliography at the end of the book. Lastly, a file of test items is not made available to instructors using this text. Evaluation of student learning is considered to lie within the latter's responsibility.

I am indebted to my wife, Pearl Ausubel, and to Mrs. Mary Stager for critical reading of the manuscript and for many helpful suggestions that have materially increased its clarity and readability. Mrs. Margaret Brengle and Miss Irene Pysanchyn were particularly helpful in preparing the manuscript for publication.

Finally I owe a special debt of gratitude to the publishers of my previous works, and especially to Grune & Stratton, Inc., for generously permitting me to incorporate previously published material into this volume.

D. P. A.

*Toronto, Ontario*
*January 1968*

# CONTENTS

## PART TWO    Cognitive Factors in Learning

# PART ONE

## INTRODUCTION

# 1

# THE ROLE AND SCOPE
# OF EDUCATIONAL
# PSYCHOLOGY

The role of educational psychology in teacher education is based on the premise that there are general principles of meaningful classroom learning that can be derived from a plausible theory of such learning. These principles can be both empirically validated and effectively communicated to prospective teachers. They provide a psychological rationale for teachers both for discovering more efficacious teaching methods on their own and for choosing more intelligently among the new teaching methods that are constantly being thrust upon them. Valid theories and methods of teaching must be related to the nature of the learning process in the classroom and to both the cognitive and the affective-social factors that influence it.

In the past, psychological principles of learning bore little or no relationship to actual classroom teaching because they were uncritically extrapolated from research on rote and animal learning (or from other simpler kinds of learning, such as conditioning and instrumental learning) all of which are intrinsically unrelated to most subject-matter learning.

All classroom learning can be located along two independent dimensions—the rote–meaningful dimension and the reception–discovery dimension. Much confusion has been generated in the past *by axiomatically regarding all reception learning (that is, based on expository teaching) as rote, and all discovery learning as meaning- ful. Actually, discovery and reception learning can both be mean- ingful, (1) if the student employs a meaningful learning set (a disposition to relate new learning material meaningfully to his existing structure of knowledge), and (2) if the learning task itself is potentially meaningful (if it itself consists of plausible or sensible material and if it can be related in a nonarbitrary and substantive fashion to the particular student's cognitive structure). In reception learning, the principal content of the learning task is merely pre- sented to the learner; and he is only required to relate it actively and meaningfully to relevant aspects of his cognitive structure and to retain it for later recall or recognition, or as a basis for learning related new material. In discovery learning, on the other hand, the principal content of what is to be learned must be discovered inde- pendently before it can be assimilated into cognitive structure.*

*As shown in Figure 1.1, neither meaningful nor discovery learning is an absolute. Rather, each can be located on rote–meaningful and reception–discovery continua. For logistical reasons, most classroom learning, especially in older pupils, is meaningful reception learn- ing. However, for certain kinds of learning, and in younger learners, some degree of rote and discovery learning is indicated. This problem is discussed at length in succeeding chapters.*

*The learning of most subject-matter material assumes that the acquisition of knowledge is an end in itself. This is the case because most classroom learning, apart from basic intellectual and voca- tional skills, has little or no relevance for later utilitarian purposes. It also assumes that although students must, in the final analysis, assume responsibility for their own learning, the school cannot abdi- cate responsibility for the guided direction of learning. It must assume the burden both for presenting students with learning mate- rials that are substantively valid and pedagogically appropriate, and for devising learning materials and teaching methods that are appropriately located on the rote–meaningful and reception– discovery continua.*

In the preface to the first edition we made explicit our conception of the nature, scope, and function of educational psychology in education and of six significant ways in which this book differs from other textbooks in the field. We also indicated that this book as a whole, and each chapter as well, has been organized to conform to certain pedagogic principles (for example, progressive differentiation, integrative reconciliation, advance organizer)[1] that are consistent with our theoretical view of meaningful subject-matter learning. The preface to the second edition specifies the important developments in the field since the first edition was published in 1968 and how the present edition has been written to take these changes into account. Thus, if the reader has not already done so, he is strongly advised to read both prefaces so that he can appreciate the thrust of this book, the rationale underlying the choice of material, and why it was written and organized the way it was. As already stated, it is our view that the basic role of educational psychology, in the educational enterprise, is to deal with the nature, conditions, and evaluation of classroom or subject-matter learning along with the factors that influence it.

In considering the role and scope of educational psychology in modern education, we shall want to consider a number of important questions.

1. What justification is there for advocating that educational psychology constitute part of the preparation of all prospective teachers? Does knowledge of subject matter suffice in teaching a given subject effectively? Are teachers born rather than made?

2. What contributions can psychology make to education, or in what ways can psychological principles be applied to educational practice? Does educational psychology have anything to offer that is not implicit in common-sense notions of teaching, and how do its legitimate concerns differ from those of psychology proper?

3. Why has classroom learning theory undergone a serious decline over the past half century? Is there room for both theories of learning and theories of teaching? If so, what should be the relationship between them?

4. What part does research strategy play in educational psychology? Is educational psychology a field in its own right with its own basic theory, research problems, and methodology, or does it merely consist of the direct application of general psychological principles and methods to educational problems? Should research workers in educational psychology follow a "basic-science" or an applied approach?

5. Are there qualitatively different kinds of learning, or can all manifestations of learning be explained by the same basic principles? From the standpoint of what is learned in school, what distinctions are most helpful in classifying the various kinds of learning?

6. What are the principal factors influencing school learning, and what is the most useful way of categorizing them?

7. What current trends in educational thought are consonant with the thesis of this book—that educational psychology should focus primarily on the nature and facilitation of subject-matter learning?

---

[1] See glossary at the end of the book for a brief definition of these terms, which are also considered at length in many of the chapters that follow.

## Why Educational Psychology for Prospective Teachers?

Any justification for educational psychology as a science rests on two fundamental premises: first, the nature of classroom learning and the factors influencing such learning can be reliably identified; second, such knowledge can be both systematized and transmitted effectively to prospective teachers. These premises, however, are in conflict with two widely held propositions about the nature of teaching. One is that knowledge of a given subject automatically confers competence in the teaching of that subject. The second states that if teaching skill apart from knowledge of subject matter does exist, it is innate—"teachers are born, not made."

Everyday experience undermines the validity of the first proposition. The highly competent scholar who is utterly incapable of transmitting his or her knowledge to students is a familiar phenomenon in everyone's experience; conversely, many less competent scholars are eminently more successful as teachers.

The second proposition also has limited validity. Nobody would deny that native aptitude for teaching varies. People differ in at least two respects—in ability to discover intuitively or to learn from others valid principles of learning and teaching and in ability to implement such principles successfully. Nevertheless, it is reasonable to expect that most persons of normal intelligence can profit from systematic instruction in logically and empirically validated propositions about the nature and facilitation of the learning process. Those who are less gifted can at least become passably good teachers, and those who have more innate aptitude can better develop whatever latent capacities they possess. Ideally, of course, the selection process in teacher education should be such that educational psychology largely performs the latter function. In any case, instruction in the principles of classroom learning is a necessary but hardly a sufficient condition for becoming a good teacher. Other prerequisites, in addition to initial aptitude, include interest, commitment, and motivation. Equally important are training in the methodology of teaching a particular subject-matter content and age level of pupils, and adequately supervised practice in such teaching.

## The Role of Psychological Principles in Education

In the absence of valid psychological principles dealing with classroom learning, teachers can adopt only two alternative procedures in searching for successful teaching practices. They can rely on the traditional prescriptions available in the educational folklore and on the precepts and examples of their own teachers and older colleagues. Or they can attempt to discover effective techniques of teaching through trial and error. It is true that some traditional "rules of teaching" have withstood the test of time and are probably valid. Nevertheless, their application varies as educational conditions and objectives change, and thus not even the most venerable rules can be followed blindly. Rules must always be reexamined in the light of changing conditions. Further, since by definition rules are stated in general terms, there cannot be a rule for each situation a teacher is likely to encounter. Principles are more flexible than rules because, being less prescriptive, they can be adapted to individual differences between persons and situations. In addition, most educational situations require the balancing of several pertinent principles rather than the arbitrary application of a single rule. With a set of psychological principles, a resourceful teacher can improvise solutions to new problems as they arise instead of blindly following simple rules of thumb.

Discovering effective teaching methods through trial and error is also a blind and therefore wasteful procedure. If, on the contrary, a teacher starts with established principles of classroom learning, he or she can rationally choose new teaching techniques instead of relying on vague intuitions or on the current fads endorsed by prestigious persons in the educational profession. Valid psychological principles not only suggest many new approaches to teaching but also eliminate many proposed practices from consideration. They narrow the field of practices deserving trial, since many proposals can be summarily dismissed as inconsistent with previously established principles.

A network of related principles constituting a comprehensive theory of classroom learning is obviously superior to a collection of discrete principles since more than one consideration applies to most educational situations. It is also self-evident that more than one kind of practice or method of teaching may be consistent with any given principle. One method may be appropriate under one set of educational conditions and teacher personality traits, whereas a quite different technique may be equally suitable under different instructional circumstances or in the hands of another teacher. This state of affairs hardly negates the principles in question.

Principles of learning are applicable to all classroom practices such as grouping, marking, the use of instructional aids, "look–say" versus phonic methods of teaching reading, lecture versus discussion techniques, essay versus objective tests, and "direct" versus "indirect" methods of teaching foreign languages. They are applicable to these educational issues because they are derived from relevant psychological theory and from relevant psychological research conducted in an educational context. Psychologists can make a contribution to many pedagogic issues by bringing to bear their knowledge of learning capacities, processes, and aspirations. Examples of such issues are the education of gifted, retarded, and culturally disadvantaged children; reception versus discovery learning; meaningful versus rote learning; and the grade placement of subject matter (such as whether foreign-language instruction should take place in the elementary school).

*Applying Psychological Principles to Educational Practice*

Although principles of classroom learning have an important place in education, they cannot be translated directly and immediately into classroom teaching practices. They merely give general direction to the search for such practices. Much intervening research of an applied nature is necessary before principles of learning can be transformed into principles of teaching. In formulating principles of teaching, it is essential to take into account complexities arising from the classroom situation. These include the presence of many pupils of unequal aptitude, readiness, and motivation; the difficulties of teacher-pupil communication; the particular characteristics of the subject matter being taught; and the age-level characteristics of the pupils.

Furthermore, in applying a given psychological principle to any particular teaching situation, teachers must exercise considerable professional judgment. They must weigh the claims of one pertinent principle against another; consider relevant aspects of their own preparation and personality; evaluate the momentary situation in the classroom, for example, the pupils' state of readiness, motivation, attentiveness, fatigue, and current understanding; appraise the adequacy of ongoing communication; and take into account differential factors of sex, ability, personality, aspiration, and social-class membership among pupils. Principles, although more flexible and less dogmatic than rules, are also no more than generalizations. Applying them effectively to particular situations is more of an art than a science.

Teaching, like medicine, requires a long period of practical apprenticeship as well as particular sensitivities, diagnostic skills, and the ability to prescribe and implement suitable practices. These competencies go beyond what is learned in applied-science courses such as educational psychology and child development (or medical physiology and pathology), or in clinical courses such as methodology and student teaching (or clinical diagnosis and clinical clerkship). Also, the individual skilled in appraising an educational situation (or in diagnosing a patient's condition) is not necessarily equally skilled in proposing and putting into practice effective measures for learning (or treatment). But judgment without knowledge of principles is no more effective than knowledge of principles without judgment. Neither is it any more likely to be free of error. Hence there is little warrant for the popularly held belief that given good judgment and native common sense, any teacher of good will, irrespective of training in pedagogy, can be depended upon to make the right decisions in the classroom.

*Educational Psychology and Common Sense*

Is there really anything more to classroom learning principles than can be derived intuitively from common sense? Although all psychology should be consistent with common sense, common sense is not always in accord with scientific fact as represented by psychological findings. Many common-sense "truths" are plausible in the sense that they could be true but just don't happen to be so. There are many alternative theories about natural phenomena that are equally plausible, such as the Lamarckian and Darwinian theories of evolution and the phlogiston and oxidation theories of combustion. In each case, however, one theory is closer to the truth than the other. Nevertheless, the incorrect alternatives, especially if backed by the weight of authority, tradition, or persuasive language, often masquerade as common-sense truisms. Some truisms in educational practice, because of their seeming "naturalness" and familiarity, may tend to impress us as eternal verities. Among these we might cite the traditional grade placement of subject matter; the traditional methods of teaching arithmetic, science, reading, and foreign languages; the traditional elementary and high-school curriculums; and the postponement of the lecture method of instruction until the university level. Actually, these practices are merely particular products of time-bound educational conditions and objectives, based on the prevailing common-sense notions of the day.

Common-sense principles, therefore, are not necessarily wrong, but neither are they necessarily correct. (The earth is obviously flat unless one can see it from space.) Many psychological theories in education are equally plausible, and hence the issue in each case can be resolved only by empirical test. Examples of such issues include mass versus distributed practice, part versus whole methods of learning, early versus delayed review, intermittent versus continuous reinforcement, drill versus learning in natural settings, homogeneous versus heterogeneous learning tasks, prompting versus confirmation, and constructed versus multiple-choice test items. Additionally, even though consistent with common sense, some psychological principles, far from being obvious truisms, can be derived only from a systematic body of theoretical principles and from the empirical findings inspired by these principles. Thus, although common sense obviously plays an important role in the discovery and application of psychological principles in education, it cannot serve as a substitute for such principles. Neither in terms of their functions in educational theory and practice nor in terms of their distribution in the population at large are common sense and psychological knowledge conflicting or mutually exclusive. A knowledgeable teacher is not necessarily devoid of common sense, and a teacher richly endowed with common sense still has much need of and can readily acquire psychological knowledge.

Psychology versus Educational Psychology

Since both psychology and educational psychology deal with the problem of learning, how can we distinguish between the special theoretical and
research interests of each? As an applied science, educational psychology is
not concerned with general laws of learning in themselves. Rather, its focus
is on those properties of learning that can be related to effective ways  of
*deliberately* bringing about stable cognitive changes that have social value
(Ausubel, 1953). Education, therefore, refers to guided or manipulated
learning directed toward specific practical ends. These ends may be defined
as the long-term acquisition of stable bodies of knowledge and of the
capacities needed for acquiring such knowledge.

The interest of psychologists in learning, on the other hand, is much
more general. They are concerned with many aspects of learning other than
the efficient achievement of designated competencies and capacities for
growth in a directed context. More typically, the psychologist investigates
the nature of simple, fragmentary, or short-term learning experiences,
which are presumably representative of learning, rather than the long-
term learning involved in assimilating organized bodies of knowledge.

*The Subject Matter of Educational Psychology*

Psychoeducational research tends to study the following kinds of learning problems:

1. Discovery of the nature of those aspects of the learning process that
affect the acquisition and long-term retention of organized bodies of
knowledge
2. Long-range improvement of learning and problem-solving capacities
3. Discovery of which cognitive and personality characteristics of the
learner, and of which interpersonal and social aspects of the learning environment, affect subject-matter learning outcomes, motivation for learning,
and typical ways of assimilating material
4. Discovery of appropriate and maximally efficient ways of organizing
and presenting learning materials and of deliberately motivating and directing learning toward specific goals

We might say that *general* aspects of learning interest the psychologist,
whereas *classroom* learning, or deliberately guided learning of subject
matter in a social context, is the special province of the educational psychologist. The subject matter of educational psychology, therefore, can be
inferred directly from the problems facing the classroom teacher. The latter
must generate interest in subject matter, inspire commitment to learning,
motivate pupils, and help induce realistic aspirations for educational
achievement. Teachers must decide what is important for pupils to learn,

ascertain what learnings they are ready for, pace instruction properly, and decide on the appropriate size and difficulty level of learning tasks. They are expected to organize subject matter expeditiously, present materials clearly, simplify learning tasks at initial stages of mastery, and integrate current and past learnings. Teachers have the responsibility of arranging practice schedules and reviews; offering confirmation, clarification, and correction; asking critical questions; providing suitable rewards; evaluating learning and development; and, where feasible, promoting discovery learning and problem-solving ability. Finally, since teachers are concerned with teaching groups of students in a social environment, they must grapple with problems of group instruction, individualization, communication, and discipline.

Thus the scope of educational psychology as an applied science is exceedingly broad, and the potential rewards it offers in terms of the social value of facilitating the subject-matter learning of pupils are proportionately great.

## The Decline of Classroom Learning Theory

The serious decline in knowledge and theorizing about school learning that has taken place over the past half century, accompanied by the steady retreat of educational psychologists from the classroom, has not been without adequate cause. Much of this deliberate avoidance can be attributed to the scientific disrepute into which studies of school learning fell as a result of two factors: glaring deficiencies in conceptualization and research design and excessive concern with the improvement of narrowly conceived academic skills and techniques of instruction rather than with the discovery of general principles affecting the improvement of overall classroom learning and instruction. The majority of studies in the field of school learning, after all, have been conducted by teachers and other school personnel who often have not received training in research development. In contrast, laboratory studies of simple learning tasks have been invested with the growing glamour and prestige of the experimental sciences. In addition, such an approach also makes possible the investigation of general learning variables under rigorously controlled conditions.

### Emphasis of Recent Research

Thus the more scientifically conducted research in learning theory has been undertaken largely by psychologists unconnected with the educational enterprise. Understandably then, this research has investigated problems quite remote from the type of learning that goes on in the classroom. The focus has been on animal learning or on short-term and fragmentary rote or nonverbal forms of human learning rather than on the learning of organized bodies of meaningful material. Experimental psychologists, of course, can hardly be criticized if laboratory studies of nonverbal and rote verbal learning have had little applicability to the classroom. Like all pure research efforts in the basic sciences, these studies were designed to yield only general scientific laws as ends in themselves, quite apart from any practical utility. The blame—if any is to be assigned—must certainly fall upon educational psychologists. In general, they have failed to conduct the necessary applied research and have succumbed to the temptation of extrapolating the theories and findings of their experimental colleagues to problems of classroom learning.

Finally, for the past three decades, educational psychologists have been preoccupied with measurement and evaluation, personality development, mental hygiene, group dynamics, and counseling. Despite the importance of classroom learning and cognitive development for the psychological aspects of education, these areas were ignored, both theoretically and empirically (Ausubel, 1963a).

Although the withdrawal of educational psychologists from problems of meaningful classroom learning was temporarily expedient, in the long run it was highly unfortunate on both theoretical and research grounds. The materials for rote learning and meaningful learning are represented and organized quite differently in the student's psychological structure of knowledge (cognitive structure) and hence conform to quite different principles of learning and retention. Not only are the respective learning processes dissimilar, but the significant variables involved in the two processes are also markedly different, or, where similar, have very different effects. A distinction must be made between two kinds of learning tasks. One involves the short-term acquisition of single, somewhat contrived concepts, the solution of artificial problems, or the learning of arbitrary associations— in a laboratory setting. The other consists of the long-term acquisition and retention of the complex network of interrelated ideas characterizing an organized body of knowledge that learners must incorporate into their cognitive structures. Recently there has been a research trend toward studying potentially meaningful verbal learning material as opposed to rote learning material, even though the learning process is explained in rote learning terms (Anderson & Myrow, 1971).

The emphasis on the extrapolation of rote learning theory and evidence to school learning problems has had many disastrous consequences. It perpetuated erroneous conceptions about the nature and conditions of classroom learning and led educational psychologists to neglect research on factors influencing meaningful learning. Hence it delayed the discovery of more effective techniques of verbal exposition. It also convinced some educators to question the relevance of learning theory for the educational enterprise and to formulate teaching theories that attempt to conceptualize the nature, purposes, and effects of instruction independently of its rela-tionship to learning. Finally, it encouraged many teachers to perceive and present potentially meaningful materials as if they were rote in character. At the same time, it persuaded others that since educational psychologists conceptualize all verbal learning as a rote process, meaningful learning could be achieved only through the use of nonverbal and problem-solving methods (Ausubel, 1963a).

## Theories of Learning versus Theories of Teaching

Disillusionment regarding the relevance of learning theory for educa-tional practice has been partially responsible for the recent emergence of "theories of teaching" that are avowedly independent of theories of learn-ing. The justification of such theories has been advanced on both historical and logical grounds.

### The Historical Argument

Gage cites the historical record to argue that theories of learning have had very little applicability to and influence on educational practice, whether in educational psychology textbooks, methods courses, or everyday class-room teaching. He argues further that theories of learning are inherently irrelevant to problems of instruction and should therefore be replaced by theories of teaching. For example, he states that

> while theories of learning deal with the ways an organism learns, theories of teaching deal with the ways in which a person influences an organism to learn. . . . To satisfy the practical demands of education, theories of learn-ing must be "stood on their head" so as to yield theories of teaching (Gage, 1964, pp. 268–269).

This argument is based essentially on the historical failure of learning theory to provide a psychologically relevant basis for pedagogic practice. But this undeniable shortcoming of learning theory to date is by no means a necessary or inherent limitation in the applicability of such theory to education. It is merely characteristic of the prevailing brand of school learn-ing theory, which in general does not deal with the kind of learning that occurs in the classroom but rather has been uncritically extrapolated from laboratory learning theory. A truly realistic and scientifically viable theory of classroom learning, in contrast, would be primarily concerned with the complex and meaningful types of verbal and symbolic learning that take place in school and similar learning environments. It would also give a prominent place to those variable factors that affect it. There is a close relationship between knowing how a pupil learns and understanding the changeable variables influencing learning, on the one hand, and knowing what to do to help the pupil learn better, on the other. By teaching we mean primarily the deliberate guidance of learning processes along lines suggested by relevant classroom learning theory. It would seem reasonable to suppose, therefore, that the discovery of the most effective methods of teaching would be dependent upon and related to the status of learning theory.

Of course, only general principles for facilitating school learning could be considered the domain of educational psychology. The applied aspects of pedagogy derived from these principles would constitute a theory of instruction and would continue to be taught in methods courses—an aspect of preparation comparable to the clinical phase of a medical student's training. The methods courses would delve into the many complexities of the classroom teaching process, both generally and for particular age groups and subject matters.

## The Logical Argument

Smith's (1960) logical rationale for formulating theories of teaching is in sharp contrast to Gage's historical argument that focuses on the failure of learning theory to prove relevant to educational practice. Smith advocates formulating theories of teaching that are wholly independent of, rather than complementary to, theories of learning. He bases his case on the propositions that learning and teaching are not inseparable and that a theory of learning cannot tell us how to teach.

### Learning versus Teaching

Smith's insistence that learning and teaching are different and separately identifiable phenomena does more than belabor the obvious. It clears up some widely prevalent semantic confusion—since, in Smith's own words, it is frequently implied that "if the child has not learned, the teacher has not taught," or else has taught incompetently. Teaching and learning are not coextensive—teaching is only one of the conditions which may influence learning. Thus pupils can learn without being taught, that is, by teaching themselves. And even if teaching is competent, it does not necessarily lead to learning if the pupils concerned are inattentive, unmotivated, or cognitively unprepared.

Nevertheless, once these unwarranted inferences about the coextensiveness of learning and teaching are discarded, it is useful to focus on those aspects of teaching and learning that are related to each other. These reciprocal relationships include the purposes, effects, and evaluation of teaching. Thus, although it is true that teaching is logically distinct from learning and can be analyzed independently of what pupils learn, what would be the practical advantage of this separate analysis? The facilitation of learning is the only proper end of teaching. We do not teach as an end in itself but only so that pupils will learn; even though the failure of pupils to learn does not necessarily indict the competence of the teacher, learning is still the only feasible measure of teaching merit. Further, as was just pointed out, teaching itself is effective only to the extent that it manipulates effectively those psychological variables that govern learning.

### The Role of Learning Theory for Teaching

Even though a valid theory of learning cannot tell us how to teach in a prescriptive sense, it does offer us the most feasible point of departure for discovering general principles of teaching that can be formulated in terms of both intervening psychological processes and cause-effect relationships. It is largely from a theory of learning that we can develop defensible notions of how crucial factors in the learning-teaching situation can most effectively be manipulated. The only other possible approaches are to vary teaching factors at random or to rely on intuition. Not only are these approaches more time-consuming, they can also yield only purely empirical laws that cannot be formulated in general terms with respect to the psychological conditions and relevant cognitive processes involved.

Of course, an adequate theory of learning is not a sufficient condition for the improvement of instruction. Valid principles of teaching are necessarily based on relevant principles of learning, but, as we know, they are not simple and direct application of these principles. Laws of classroom learning merely provide general direction for discovering effective teaching principles; they do not identify these principles. The formulation of teaching principles requires much supplementary research that takes account of practical problems and new instructional variables not implicit in the learning principles themselves. In other words, one can consider the basic principles of teaching as applied derivatives of school learning theory. These principles are products of an engineering type of research and are based on such modifications of learning theory as are necessitated by the practical difficulties or the additional new variables involved in the task of teaching.

Smith (1960) asserts that simply by knowing "the cause of a phenomenon" one does not thereby acquire control of it "for practical ends." For example, we can know the cause of a disease without knowing how to treat it, and we can treat a disease successfully without knowing its cause. Undeniably, many practical and useful inventions come about accidentally without the inventor understanding how or why they work. But who would advocate this as a *deliberate* research strategy? Ordinarily, scientists search for practical methods of control that can be related to general statements of relationship among the relevant variables involved. The superiority of this approach inheres in the fact that methods of control that can be related to general principles not only are understandable and capable of being interpreted but also are more widely transferable to other practical problems. We could, for example, discover as an empirical fact that using teaching method X facilitates learning. But the practical value of such knowledge is quite limited. Would it not be preferable to formulate the research problem so that we could ascertain in what ways method X influences relevant psychologic variables and intervening cognitive states in the course of facilitating learning? It is wasteful of time and effort to search for more efficient methods of teaching that can be described only in terms of characteristics of the teaching act and cannot be related to laws of learning. Even when scientists do stumble accidentally on useful empirical laws, they immediately launch new hypothesis-oriented research to explain in more general terms the underlying basis of the discovery.

### The Interdependence of Theories of Learning and Theories of Teaching

Although knowledge of causation does not imply immediate discovery of control procedures, it aids in the search for such procedures. For one thing, it narrows the field; for another, it enables one to try procedures that have proved successful in controlling related conditions. Knowing that tuberculosis was caused by a microorganism, for example, did not immediately provide us with a cure or a preventative. But it enabled us to try approaches—such as vaccines, immune sera, antisepsis, quarantine, and chemotherapy—that had been used successfully in treating other infectious diseases. In the same sense, knowledge of the cause of cancer would help immeasurably in discovering a cure, and knowledge of the nature and relevant variables involved in concept acquisition would be of invaluable assistance in devising effective methods of teaching concepts.

As Hilgard points out, however, scientific practices in instruction need not necessarily wait upon agreement among learning theorists.

> If one were unable to proceed without a learning theory upon which all agreed, the situation would indeed be frightening. At least two things need be said. For one thing, the disagreement among theorists may be in respect to the interpretation of a set of facts upon which, as facts, all agree; in this case, the issue often is not one to trouble the practical person at all. Thus rewards may control learning in a given situation and be interpreted in contiguity terms, in reinforcement terms, or in information terms. While eventually the correct interpretation might make some difference, it often makes little difference at the present stage of technology. . . . Second, the technology of instruction rests on much more than learning theory (Hilgard, 1964, pp. 402–403).

In conclusion, therefore, theories of learning and theories of teaching are interdependent rather than mutually exclusive. Both are needed for a complete science of pedagogy, and neither one is an adequate substitute for the other. Theories of teaching must be based on theories of learning and also must have a more applied focus; that is, they must be concerned to a greater extent with engineering kinds of problems.


## Research Strategy in Educational Psychology

Few persons would take issue with the proposition that education is an applied or engineering science. It is an applied[2] science because it is concerned with the realization of certain practical ends which have social value. The precise nature of these ends is highly controversial in terms of both substance and relative emphasis. To some individuals the function of education is to transmit the ideology of the culture and a core body of knowledge and intellectual skills. To others education is primarily concerned with the optimal development of potentiality for growth and achievement—not only with respect to cognitive abilities but also with respect to personality goals and adjustment. Disagreement with respect to ends, however, neither removes education from the category of science nor makes it any less of an applied branch of knowledge. It might be mentioned that automobile engineers are also not entirely agreed as to the characteristics of the "ideal" car, and physicians disagree violently concerning a definition of health.

Regardless of the ends it chooses to adopt, an applied discipline becomes a science only when it seeks to base proposed means to ends on propositions that can be empirically validated. The operations involved in such an undertaking are commonly subsumed under the term "research." The question under discussion here relates to the nature of research in applied science, or, more specifically, in education. Is educational research a field in its own right, with theoretical problems and a methodology of its own, or does it merely involve the operation of applying knowledge from "pure" scientific disciplines to practical problems of pedagogy?

Even though education is an applied science, educational psychologists have tended to extrapolate research findings uncritically from laboratory studies of simplified learning situations to the classroom learning environment. This tendency reflects the fascination of many research workers for the "basic-science" approach to research in the applied sciences, as well as their failure to appreciate its inherent limitations. They argue that progress in educational psychology is made more rapidly by focusing indirectly on basic-science problems in general psychology than by trying to come to grips directly with the applied problems that are more indigenous to the

---

[2] The term "applied" is used here to distinguish between sciences that are oriented toward practical ends, as opposed to "basic" sciences, which do not have this orientation. Applied does not imply that the content of the practical disciplines consists of applications from the "basic" disciplines. The problems rather than the knowledge of applied sciences are "applied."

field. Spence (1959), for example, perceives classroom learning as much too complex to permit the discovery of general laws of learning. He advocates a straightforward application to the classroom situation of the laws of learning discovered in the laboratory. There is, however, very little scope, in his view, for applying the latter laws to problems of educational practice. Hilgard (1964) and Melton (1959) take a more eclectic position. They would search for basic-science laws of learning in both laboratory and classroom contexts and would leave to the educational technologist the task of conducting the research necessary for implementing these laws in the classroom.

The position we have adopted thus far in this book is that the principles governing the nature and conditions of school learning can be discovered only through an applied or engineering type of research. Such research must take into account both the kinds of learning that occur in the classroom and the salient characteristics of the learners. We cannot merely extrapolate to classroom learning general basic-science laws that are derived from the laboratory study of qualitatively different and vastly simpler instances of learning. Attempts to do so are extremely tortuous. For example, Mandler (1962) attempts to explain complex cognitive functioning in terms of the laws of association, while Sheffield (1961) explains the hierarchical learning of sequentially organized materials in terms of the principle of contiguous conditioning.

Educational technologists need laws of classroom learning at an *applied*[3] level before they can conduct the research preparatory to effecting scientific changes in teaching practices. They can be aided further by general principles of teaching that are intermediate, in level of generality and prescriptiveness, between laws of classroom learning and the technological problems that confront them. Contrary to Spence's (1959) contention, the greater complexity and number of determining variables involved in classroom learning does not preclude the possibility of discovering precise laws with wide generality from one educational situation to another. It simply means that such research demands experimental ingenuity and sophisticated use of modern techniques of research design.

## Basic Science versus Applied Approach

Three different kinds of research orientations have been adopted by those who are concerned with scientific progress in applied disciplines such as medicine and education: basic-science research, extrapolated research in the basic sciences, and research at an applied level (Ausubel, 1953).

---

[3] These laws are just as "basic" as basic-science laws. The terms "basic" and "applied" refer to the distinction between basic (pure) and applied (practical) sciences made earlier. "Basic" does not mean "fundamental." In the latter sense, applied research is just as "basic" for its domain as research in the pure sciences.

*Basic-Science Research*

The approach of basic-science research is predicated on the very defensible proposition that applied sciences are ultimately related to knowledge in the underlying sciences. Progress in medicine, for example, is intimately related to progress in general biochemistry and bacteriology; progress in engineering is tied to progress in physics and chemistry; and progress in education is dependent upon advances in general psychology, statistics, and sociology.

**Some Qualifications**

Two important qualifications have to be placed on the value of basic-science research for the applied sciences: a qualification óf purpose or relevance and a qualification of level of applicability.

By definition, basic-science research is concerned with the discovery of general laws of physical, biological, or sociological phenomenology. Researchers in these fields have no objection, of course, if their findings are applied to practical problems which have social value; in fact, there is reason to believe that they are motivated to some extent by this consideration. But the design of basic-science research bears no intended relation to problems in the applied disciplines—the sole aim is advancement of knowledge. Ultimately, of course, such knowledge is applicable in a very broad sense to practical problems, but since the research design is not oriented toward solving these problems, applicability is apt to be quite indirect and unsystematic. In addition, research findings may be relevant only over a span that is too long to be meaningful in terms of the short-range needs of the applied disciplines.

The second qualification has to do with the level at which findings in the basic sciences can be applied once their relevance has been established. Such findings, of course, exhibit a much higher level of generality than the problems to which they can be applied. At the applied level, specific ends and conditions are added which demand additional research to indicate the precise way in which the general law operates in the specific case. That is, the applicability of general principles to specific problems is not given in the statement of the general principle, but must be worked out explicitly for each individual problem. Knowledge about nuclear fission, for example, does not tell us how to make an atomic bomb or an atomic-powered airplane.

In fields such as education, the problem of generality is further complicated by the fact that practical problems often exist at higher levels of complexity with respect to the order of phenomenology involved than do the basic-science findings requiring application. That is, new variables added may qualitatively alter the general principles from the basic science to such an extent that at the applied level they have substrate validity but lack explanatory or predictive value. For example, antibiotic reactions that take place in test tubes do not necessarily take place in living systems, and methods of learning that children employ in the laboratory to master lists of nonsense syllables by rote do not necessarily correspond to methods of learning children use in classrooms to acquire a meaningful grasp of subject matter.

The basic-science approach in educational research, therefore, is subject to many serious disadvantages. Its relevance is remote and indirect because it is not oriented toward solving educational problems. Its findings, if relevant, are applicable only if much additional research is performed to translate general principles into the more specific form required in the complex contexts of the classroom.

Naivete with respect to immediate applicability is particularly common and has led to serious distortions in our knowledge of those aspects of the psychology of learning that are relevant for pedagogy. The psychology of learning studied by teachers is based on findings in general psychology that have been borrowed wholesale without much attempt to test their applicability to learning situations in classrooms. It would be a shocking situation indeed if a comparable procedure were practiced in medicine, that is, if physicians employed therapeutic techniques validated only in the test tube or by animal experimentation.

### Extrapolated Research in the Basic Sciences

The second general research approach in the applied disciplines is extrapolated basic-science research. Unlike pure basic-science research, it is oriented toward the solution of practical or applied problems. It starts out by identifying significant problems in the applied field and designs experiments pointed toward their solution on a highly simplified basic-science level. Such an approach satisfies the important criterion of relevance, but must still contend with the problem of level of applicability. The rationale of this approach is that many practical problems are so complex that they must be reduced to simpler terms and patterned after simpler models before one can develop fruitful hypotheses leading to their solution. Once the problems are simplified, control and measurement become more manageable.

Depending on the nature of the problem under investigation, this approach may have genuine merit. The resulting research findings, of course, must be regarded only as "leads" or hypotheses to be tested in the applied situation rather than as definitive answers to problems in pedagogy. As already noted, however, educational researchers have a tendency to extrapolate basic-science findings to pedagogical problems without conducting the additional research necessary to bridge the gap between the two levels of generality involved.

*Research at the Applied Level*

The third approach to educational research, research at the applied level, is the most relevant and direct of the three kinds of research orientations, yet paradoxically it is the least utilized by professional research workers in the field. When research is performed in relation to the actual problems of education at the level of complexity at which they exist, and under the conditions in which they are actually found, the problems of relevance and extrapolation do not arise.[4]

Although applied research presents greater difficulties with respect to research design, control, and measurement, the rewards are correspondingly greater when these problems are solved. If any applied discipline with unique and distinctive problems of its own is to survive as a science it is obliged to develop such research methodologies.

Many of the better-known generalizations in educational psychology— the principle of readiness, the effects of overlearning, the concrete to abstract trend in conceptualizing the environment—illustrate the pitfalls of the basic-science approach to educational research. These ideas are interesting and potentially useful to curriculum specialists and educational technologists, but have little utility in educational practice until they are *particularized* at an applied level. The prevailing lack of practical particularization damages the "image" of educational psychology insofar as it induces many beginning teachers to nurture unrealistic expectations about the current usefulness of these principles. These teachers, after undergoing acute disillusionment, may lose whatever original confidence they may have felt in the value of a psychological approach to educational problems.

The need for applied research in these areas is well illustrated by the principles of readiness. At present we can only speculate on the form that curriculum sequences might take if they took into account precise and detailed (but currently unavailable) research findings on the emergence of readiness for different subject-matter areas, subareas, and levels of difficulty within areas. Such sequences would also have to take into account different methods of teaching the same material. Because of the unpredictability of readiness—as shown, for example, by the fact that four- and five-year-olds can profit from training in pitch but not in rhythm (Jersild & Bienstock, 1931, 1935)—valid answers to questions such as those of readiness cannot be derived from logical extrapolation; they require meticulous empirical research in a school setting. The next step involves the development of teaching methods and materials appropriate for taking optimal advantage of existing degrees of readiness and for increasing readiness

---

[4] Applied research is also directed toward the discovery of general laws within the framework of its applied ends. Therefore, the generalizations it discovers exist at a different plane of generality than those of basic-science research.

wherever necessary and desirable. But since we generally do not have this research data available, except perhaps in the field of reading, we can pay only lip service to principles of readiness in curriculum planning.

In conclusion, educational psychology is unequivocally an applied discipline, but it is *not* general psychology applied to educational problems—no more so than mechanical engineering is general physics applied to problems of designing machinery or medicine is general biology applied to problems of diagnosing, curing, and preventing human diseases. In these latter applied disciplines, general laws from the parent discipline are not applied to a domain of practical problems; rather, separate bodies of applied theory have evolved that are just as basic as the theory underlying the parent disciplines. These laws, however, are stated at a lower level of generality and have more direct relevance and applicability to the applied problems in their respective fields.

The time-bound and particular properties of knowledge in the applied sciences have also been exaggerated. Such knowledge involves more than technological applications of basic-science generalizations to current practical problems. Although less generalizable than the basic sciences, they are also disciplines *in their own right*, with distinctive and relatively enduring bodies of theory and methodology that cannot simply be derived or extrapolated from the basic sciences to which they are related. It is simply not true that only basic-science knowledge can be related to and organized around general principles. Each of the applied biological sciences (for example, medicine or agronomy) possesses an independent body of general principles underlying the detailed knowledge in its field, in addition to being related in a still more general way to basic principles in biology. In the same way, educational psychology must evolve as an autonomous discipline, with its own theory and methodology, but must obviously continue to be influenced by the parent discipline of psychology—as an independent adult peer rather than as a dependent child with a wholly derivative status.

## Types of Learning

Much of the current confusion regarding the nature of learning is a reflection of the fact that, for a long time, most psychologists have tended to subsume many *qualitatively* different kinds of learning under a single explanatory model. It has been assumed that "the nature of the change called learning must in some fundamental sense be the same, regardless of what is being learned." But:

> [A]lthough the verification of general laws is surely a desirable objective, the assumption that the kind of change in capability being studied is always

somehow "the same" may be unjustified. How much similarity is there, actually, between the kind of change represented by a child learning to say his first word, and that represented by a more experienced child learning to read printed English sentences? Or between learning to distinguish triangles from rectangles and learning to demonstrate that the sum of the internal angles of a triangle is the same as a straight angle? How much similarity is there between the learning of new "facts" by a beginning chemistry student from a textbook, and the learning of new "facts" by his chemistry professor from a technical journal? All of these are surely examples of learning; that is, they involve a change in capability which can be inferred from a before-and-after comparison of performance. But are they the same kind of change?

Despite the prevailing emphasis on fundamental similarities of process in various learning situations, investigators of learning have always recognized certain "types" of learning. There is "trial-and-error learning," "discrimination learning," "paired associate learning," "concept learning," "conditioned response learning," and so on. . . . But these varieties of learning have tended to be identified with certain kinds of stimulus situations generated by particular equipment or materials, like the bar-pressing apparatus, or the memory drum with verbal syllables, or the maze with choice points. The tendency has not been for these types of learning to be distinguished in terms of the kind of change in capability they imply.

The existence of differentiable performances as outcomes of learning naturally leads to the inference that different kinds of capabilities are established by learning; . . . [and] the identification of these different kinds of performance, together with the different kinds of capability they imply, suggests that there may be at least as many different kinds of learning. And if this is so, it may be supposed that there exist an equal number of conditions of effective learning to correspond with each variety. A theory of instruction, then, cannot be maximally useful if it concerns itself with only those conditions that are general to all classes of learning. Instead, such a theory must concern itself in an individual manner with each of the types of learning (Gagné, 1967, pp. 296–300).

Thus, from the standpoint of enhancing school learning, no theoretical concern is more relevant or urgent in the present state of our knowledge than the need for distinguishing clearly among the principal kinds of learning (rote and meaningful learning, concept formation, and verbal and nonverbal problem solving) that can take place in the classroom (Ausubel, 1961). The most significant way of differentiating among these types of classroom learning is to make two crucial process distinctions that cut across all of them. We can make a distinction between reception and discovery learning and another between rote and meaningful learning. The first distinction is significant because most of the understandings that learners acquire both in and out of school are presented rather than discovered. And since most learning material is presented verbally, it is equally important to appreciate that verbal reception learning is not necessarily rote in character and can be meaningful without prior nonverbal or problem-solving experience.

### Reception versus Discovery Learning

In reception learning (rote or meaningful) the entire content of what is to be learned is presented to the learner in final form. The learning task does not involve any independent discovery on the student's part. The learner is required only to internalize or incorporate the material (a list of nonsense syllables or paired adjectives; a poem or geometrical theorem) that is presented so that it is available or reproducible at some future date. In the case of meaningful reception learning, the potentially meaningful task or material is comprehended or made meaningful in the process of internalization. In the case of rote reception learning, the learning task either is not potentially meaningful or is not made meaningful in the process of internalization.

Much of the confusion in discussions of school learning arises from the failure to recognize that rote and meaningful learning are not completely dichotomous. Although they are *qualitatively* discontinuous in terms of the psychological processes underlying *each* and therefore cannot be placed at opposite poles of the same continuum, there are transitional types of learning that share some of the properties of both rote and meaningful learning (for example, representational learning or learning the names of objects, events, and concepts). Further, both types of learning can take place concomitantly in the same learning task. This same qualification also holds true for the distinction between reception and discovery learning. In somewhat simplified terms, these relationships are shown in diagrammatic form in Figure 1.1, in which these two dimensions of learning are viewed as orthogonal to each other.[5]

The essential feature of discovery learning, whether concept formation or rote problem solving, is that the principal content of what is to be learned is not given but must be discovered by the learner before it can be meaningfully incorporated into the student's cognitive structure. The distinctive and prior learning task, in other words, is to discover something —which of two maze alleys leads to the goal, the precise nature of the relationship between two variables, the common attributes of a number of diverse instances, and so forth. The first phase of discovery learning involves a process quite different from that of reception learning. The learner must rearrange information, integrate it with existing cognitive structure, and reorganize or transform the integrated combination in such a way as to

---

[5] In Chapter 2 we shall discuss these concepts in greater detail and provide examples of such transitional stages and of the concomitant operation of both types of learning in a single learning task.

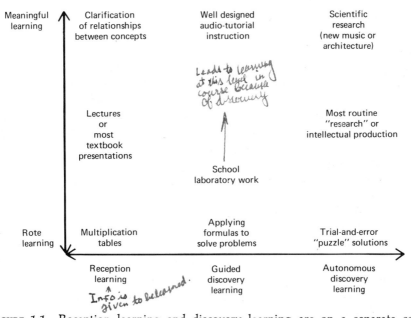

Meaningful learning

Clarification of relationships between concepts

Well designed audio-tutorial instruction

Scientific research (new music or architecture)

*Leads to learning at this level in course because of discovery*

Lectures or most textbook presentations

Most routine "research" or intellectual production

School laboratory work

Rote learning

Multiplication tables

Applying formulas to solve problems

Trial-and-error "puzzle" solutions

Reception learning

Guided discovery learning

Autonomous discovery learning

*Info is given to be learned.*

FIGURE 1.1    Reception learning and discovery learning are on a separate continuum from rote learning and meaningful learning.

generate a desired end-product or discover a missing means-end relationship. After discovery learning itself is completed, the discovered content is made meaningful in much the same way that presented content is made meaningful in reception learning.

Reception and discovery learning are thus two quite different kinds of processes. It will be shown later that most classroom instruction is organized along the lines of reception learning. The next section will point out that verbal reception learning is not necessarily rote in character. Much ideational material (concepts, generalizations) can be internalized and retained meaningfully without prior problem-solving experience. And at no stage of development does the learner have to discover principles independently in order to be able to understand and use them meaningfully.

It is important to note at this point that reception and discovery learning also differ with respect to their respective principal roles in intellectual development and functioning (Ausubel, 1961). For the most part, large bodies of subject matter are acquired through reception learning, whereas the everyday problems of living are solved through discovery learning. Nevertheless, some overlap of function obviously exists. Knowledge acquired through reception learning is also used in everyday problem solving, and discovery learning is commonly used in the classroom both to apply, extend, clarify, integrate, and evaluate subject-matter knowledge and to test comprehension. In laboratory situations, discovery learning provides insight into scientific method and also leads to the contrived rediscovery of known propositions. When employed by gifted persons it may generate significant new knowledge. In the more typical classroom situation, however, the discovery of original propositions through problem-solving activity is not a conspicuous feature in the acquisition of new concepts or information. As far as the formal education of the individual is concerned, the educational agency largely transmits ready-made concepts, classifications, and propositions. In any case, discovery methods of teaching hardly constitute an efficient *primary* means of transmitting the *content* of an academic discipline.

One can justifiably argue that the school is also concerned with developing the student's ability to use acquired knowledge in solving particular problems systematically, independently, and critically in various fields of inquiry. But this function of the school, although constituting a legitimate objective of education in its own right, is less central than its related transmission-of-knowledge function. This is true in terms of the amount of time that can be reasonably allotted to this function, in terms of the objectives of education in a democratic society and in terms of what can be reasonably expected from most students.

From the standpoint of psychological process, meaningful discovery learning is obviously more complex than meaningful reception learning. It involves an antecedent problem-solving stage before meaning emerges and can be internalized (Ausubel, 1961). Generally speaking, however, reception learning, although phenomenologically simpler than discovery learning, paradoxically emerges later developmentally and, particularly in its more advanced and pure verbal forms, implies a higher level of cognitive maturity. Greater intellectual maturity in this case makes possible a simpler and more efficient mode of cognitive functioning in the acquisition of knowledge.

Thus concepts and propositions are typically acquired during the post-infancy, preschool, and early elementary-school years. This comes about as a result of inductive processing of verbal and nonverbal concrete-empirical experience—typically through autonomous problem solving or discovery. The young child, for example, acquires the concept of a chair by abstracting the common features of the concept from multiple incidental encounters with chairs of many different sizes, shapes, and colors, and then generalizing these attributes. Reception learning, on the other hand, although also occurring early, does not become a prominent feature of intellectual functioning until the child is cognitively mature enough to comprehend verbally presented concepts and propositions in the absence of

concrete, empirical experience—until, for example, he or she can comprehend the meaning of "democracy" or "acceleration" from their dictionary
definitions. In other words, inductive concept *formation* based on nonverbal, concrete, empirical problem-solving experience exemplifies early
developmental phases of information processing. Concept *assimilation*
through meaningful verbal reception learning exemplifies later stages.

### Meaningful versus Rote Learning

Although the distinction between reception and discovery learning discussed above has absolutely nothing to do with the rote-meaningful dimension of the learning process, the two dimensions of learning were
commonly confused. This confusion is partly responsible for the widespread but unwarranted twin beliefs that reception learning is invariably
rote and that discovery learning is inherently and necessarily meaningful.
Both assumptions, of course, reflect the long-standing belief in many educational circles that the only knowledge one *really* possesses and understands is knowledge that one discovers by oneself. Actually, each distinction (rote versus meaningful learning and reception versus discovery learning) constitutes an entirely independent dimension of learning. Hence a
much more defensible proposition is that *both* reception *and* discovery
learning can be *either* rote *or* meaningful depending on the conditions
under which learning occurs (Ausubel, 1961). The relationships between
rote and meaningful learning, as well as their orthogonal relationship
to the reception-discovery dimension are shown diagrammatically in
Figure 1.1.

In both instances meaningful learning takes place if the learning task
can be related in nonarbitrary, substantive (nonverbatim) fashion to what
the learner already knows, and if the learner adopts a corresponding learning set to do so. Rote learning, on the other hand, occurs if the learning
task consists of purely arbitrary associations, as in paired-associate, puzzle-
box, maze, or serial learning, if the learner lacks the relevant prior knowledge necessary for making the learning task potentially meaningful, and
also (regardless of how much potential meaning the task has) if the learner
adopts a set merely to internalize it in an arbitrary, verbatim fashion (that
is, as an arbitrary series of words).

Insofar as classroom and similar kinds of learning are concerned, it is
evident that meaningful learning is as preponderant with respect to rote
learning as reception learning is with respect to discovery learning. Both
within and outside the classroom, meaningful verbal learning is the principal means of acquiring large bodies of knowledge. Rote learning of lists
of nonsense syllables or of arbitrarily paired adjectives may be characteristic of many research studies in the psychological laboratory, but is representative of few actual tasks in modern classrooms. It is difficult, indeed,

to find supportive evidence for Underwood's assertion that "much of our educational effort is devoted to making relatively meaningless verbal units meaningful" (Underwood, 1959, p. 11). To be sure, some classroom learning does somewhat approach the rote level, such as the letter symbols in reading, foreign language vocabulary, the names of particular objects and concepts, and the symbols used to represent the chemical elements. This is so because the words or symbols chosen to represent the objects, sounds, or abstractions in question are purely arbitrary. There is no good reason, for example, why the particular combination of sounds in "chair" should have been chosen to represent the object it does. Such learning, however, tends to form a very small part of the curriculum, especially once children have mastered the basic letter and number symbols in the elementary-school years.

Furthermore, it is much less arbitrary to learn that a particular foreign-language word is equivalent in meaning to a word or an idea that is already meaningful—that *garçon* represents the meaning of already meaningful "boy"—than to learn a list of paired adjectives such as "unctuous–previous," "arduous–reversible." In the first case one is relating in some comprehensible fashion (on the basis of proposed equivalence) a new symbol to an already established and meaningful symbol in the learner's psychological structure of knowledge. In the second case, one is trying to establish a wholly arbitrary association between two already meaningful words that the learner very well knows are neither equivalent nor otherwise reasonably related to each other. The learning of representational equivalents, in other words, may more properly be considered a primitive form of meaningful learning than a true variety of rote learning.

It is true that much potentially meaningful knowledge taught by verbal exposition results in rotely learned verbalisms. This rote outcome, however, is not inherent in the expository method, but rather in such abuses of this method as fail to satisfy the criteria of meaningful learning (Ausubel, 1961).

There is much greater reluctance, on the other hand, to acknowledge that the conditions of meaningful learning just mentioned also apply to problem-solving methods. Performing laboratory experiments in cookbook fashion without understanding the underlying substantive and methodological principles involved confers little appreciation of scientific method. Neither does "discovering" correct answers to problems in mathematics and science, without really understanding what one is doing, add to knowledge or problem-solving ability. Students accomplish this latter feat merely by rotely memorizing "type problems" and mechanical procedures for manipulating algebraic symbols. Nevertheless, it must be recognized that laboratory work and problem-solving are not genuinely meaningful experiences unless they meet two conditions. First, they must be built on a foundation of clearly understood concepts and principles; second, the constituent operations must themselves be meaningful.

As indicated previously, we shall be concerned in this volume only with meaningful kinds of learning, both reception and discovery. Excluded from consideration, in addition to rote learning, are such noncognitive (non-intellectual) kinds of learning as classical and instrumental conditioning and motor skills learning and such less complex kinds of cognitive learning as perceptual and simple discrimination learning. The latter types of learning have only indirect, tangential, and occasional relevance to what is learned in the classroom. We shall be concerned, therefore, with the complex varieties of meaningful, cognitive learning. This learning encompasses the less immediate kinds of knowing, understanding, and problem solving that are dependent on the "higher mental processes" and comprises most intellectual activity in the school environment. The psychology of specific school subjects, however, is not considered except by way of example, since this book deals only with general principles of learning applicable to all variables and grade levels of subject matter. The former topic is more indigenous to the "clinical" aspects of the pedagogic curriculum.

## Classification of Learning Variables and the Organization of the Book

Inasmuch as instruction involves the manipulation of those variables (factors) influencing learning, a rational classification of learning variables can help to clarify both the nature of the learning process and the conditions that affect it. Such a classification also provides, in a sense, an organizational preview of this book, since any textbook in educational psychology must be organized around the factors that influence classroom learning.

### Interpersonal and Situational Categories

One obvious way of classifying learning variables is to divide them into *intrapersonal* (factors within the learner) and *situational* (factors in the learning situation) categories.

#### Intrapersonal Category

The category of factors within the learner includes the following variables:

1. *Cognitive structure variables*—substantive and organizational properties of previously acquired knowledge in a particular subject-matter field that are relevant for the assimilation of another learning task in the same field. Since subject-matter knowledge tends to be organized in sequential

and hierarchical fashion, what one already knows in a given field, and how well one knows it, obviously influences one's readiness for related new learnings.

2. *Developmental readiness*—the particular kind of readiness that reflects the learner's stage of intellectual development and the intellectual capacities and modes of intellectual functioning characteristic of that stage. The cognitive equipment of the 15-year-old learner obviously makes the pupil ready for different kinds of learning tasks than does the equipment of the 6- or 10-year-old learner.

3. *Intellectual ability*—the individual's relative degree of general scholastic aptitude (general intelligence or brightness level), and his or her relative standing with respect to particular more differentiated or specialized cognitive abilities. How well a pupil learns subject matter in science, mathematics, or literature obviously depends on general intelligence, verbal and quantitative abilities, and problem-solving ability.

4. *Motivational and attitudinal factors*—desire for knowledge, need for achievement and self-enhancement, and ego involvement (interest) in a particular kind of subject matter. These general variables affect such relevant conditions of learning as alertness, attentiveness, level of effort, persistence, and concentration.

5. *Personality factors*—individual differences in level and kind of motivation, personal adjustment, other personality characteristics, and level of anxiety. Subjective factors such as these have profound effects on quantitative and qualitative aspects of the learning process.

**Situational Category**

The situational category includes the following learning variables:

1. *Practice*—its frequency, distribution, method, and general conditions (including feedback or knowledge of results).

2. *The arrangement of instructional materials*—in terms of amount, difficulty, step size, underlying logic, sequence, pacing, and the use of instructional aids.

3. *Certain group and social factors*—classroom climate, cooperation and competition, social-class stratification, cultural disadvantage, and racial segregation.

4. *Characteristics of the teacher*—cognitive abilities, knowledge of subject matter, pedagogic competence, personality, and behavior.

Gagné states that intrapersonal and situational variables undoubtedly have interactive effects upon learning. . . .

> The external variables cannot exert their effects without the presence in the learner of certain states derived from motivation and prior learning and development. Nor can the internal capabilities of themselves generate learning without the stimulation provided by external events. . . . As a problem

for research, the learning problem is one of finding the necessary relationships which must obtain among internal and external variables in order for a change in capability to take place. Instruction may be thought of as the institution and arrangement of the external conditions of learning in ways which will optimally interact with internal capabilities of the learner, so as to bring about change in these capabilities (Gagné, 1967a, p. 295).

### Cognitive and Affective-Social Categories

Another useful way of classifying the same set of learning variables is to group them into cognitive and affective-social categories. The former group includes the relatively objective intellectual factors, whereas the latter group includes the subjective and interpersonal determinants of learning. Since this scheme of categorization is somewhat more convenient for the researcher, and is also more familiar to the classroom teacher than is the intrapersonal-situational scheme, it has been adopted in this book. Part II, "Cognitive Factors in Learning" (Chapters 5–10), considers cognitive structure variables, developmental readiness, intellectual ability, practice, and instructional materials. Part III, "Affective and Social Factors in Learning" (Chapters 11–14), considers motivational and attitudinal variables, personality factors, group and social factors, and teacher characteristics. The two other principal parts of the book deal with learning processes, themselves: Part I, "Meaning and Meaningful Learning" (Chapters 2–4), which confines itself to reception learning, and Part IV, "Discovery Learning" (Chapters 15–16). Part V, "Evaluation and Measurement" (Chapter 17), is the final section of the book.

Just as intrapersonal and situational factors interact in their effects on learning, cognitive and affective-social variables also influence the learning process concomitantly, and undoubtedly interact in various ways. Classroom learning does not take place in a social vacuum, but only in relation to other individuals who both generate personal emotional reactions and serve as impersonal representatives of the culture. During the course of personality development the individual also acquires a characteristic motivational orientation to learning. This affects not only the person's mode of acquiring new value judgments, but also the scope, depth, and efficiency of the learning process. Nevertheless, for purposes of theoretical analysis or empirical investigation, either set of factors can be systematically varied while the other is held constant.

## Convergent Current Trends in Educational Thought

Consistent with the emphasis in this book that educational psychology should focus primarily on the nature and facilitation of subject-matter learning are three related trends in educational thought. These are greater concern with the importance and quality of intellectual training in the school, greater stress on the acquisition of knowledge as an end in itself, and greater willingness on the part of the school to assume responsibility for the direction of learning and for the preparation of suitable instructional materials. Indeed, wholesome concern with these issues seems almost to have replaced futile public disputes concerning such pseudo-issues as whether the curriculum has become "softer," whether students today learn as much in school as did prior generations of students, whether Johnny can read at all or as well as Ivan, whether intellectual development should be the *sole* concern of the school, and whether training in pedagogy should constitute a major or minor aspect of teacher education.

### Greater Concern with Intellectual Training

There are many indications that persons connected with the educational process are manifesting increasing concern with development of basic skills, intellectual content, and quality of the curriculum. Underlying this concern is the current goal of equality of educational opportunity, which has led to a diverse student population in schools and colleges. First, in teacher education, there is a trend toward an articulation process and working partnership between schools and colleges for the development of basic skills. In addition, the subject-matter preparation and competence of teachers are receiving greater attention in the form of fifth-year teacher education programs, performance/competency-based education for teacher certification and continued in-service training for the career teacher. Second, in the area of classroom organization and administration various experiments continue to be conducted. All of these aim at development of basic skills for those who need it and more effective teaching of subject matter for students who are more capable. Experiments include the use of specialist teachers in reading, mathematics, and science, team teaching, ungraded schools, the organization of special programs for students who are gifted or delayed in development, the use of teachers' aides, and the more flexible scheduling of classes in terms of the number of pupils and the amount of time allotted to each. The open classroom, on the other hand, places less emphasis on academic training, but it is not opposed in theory to the goal of more concern for intellectual training. In the open classroom situation, importance is placed on the pupil's own discovery of knowledge with the teacher as facilitator; this approach is more suitable to the elementary school than to junior and senior high school. Third, the subject-matter content of the curriculum is being increased through such devices as the longer school day and year, introduction of foreign languages in elementary school, more advanced mathematics and science instruction, and greater emphasis on homework. At the high-school level, the unit requirements for graduation are less mandatory, with more opportunity for elective subjects through specialized magnet programs (for example, criminal justice, science) and offering of college-level courses to superior high school students. Fourth, greater use has been made of teaching aids, including educational films and television, programmed instruction, schematic models, and electronic aids.

Finally, and perhaps most important, scholars, curriculum experts, psychologists, and educational technologists are collaborating in a wide variety of curriculum reform movements. These movements seek greater emphasis on the basic, unifying principles of the different academic disciplines, on more efficient sequencing and pacing of subject-matter content, on more adequate depth of coverage, on consonance with recent advances in knowledge, and on more valid measurement of learning outcomes. Such movements flourished in the 1960s and are much less prominent today.

By calling attention to these recent developments in educational practice, we do not wish to imply that the mainstream of American education had previously rejected intellectual training as the primary function of the school. Undeniably, of course, this has often *appeared* to be the case—but only because of the articulateness and persuasiveness of the more extreme advocates of the child-centered point of view in education who tended to be somewhat ambivalent about the goal of intellectual competence. These extremists placed major emphasis upon optimal personality development and social adjustment in a maximally permissive school environment. Frequently they seemed to derogate knowledge of subject matter, and they advocated using children's current interests as the principal guideline for constructing the curriculum.

Most teachers and school administrators, however, have always agreed that the *distinctive* function of the school in our society is to foster intellectual growth and to transmit subject-matter knowledge. The child-centered versus the subject-matter approach to education constitutes a pseudo-dichotomy that causes serious disagreement only among extremists at either end of the continuum. No realistic advocate of the subject-matter approach suggests that the school should disregard the personality development and social adjustment of pupils or that subject matter should be taught without regard for such relevant factors as readiness, motivation, and individual differences in intellectual ability. Similarly, constructive proponents of the child-centered approach largely emphasize noncognitive determinants and outcomes of learning because of their importance in mastering subject matter.

Of course, greater emphasis upon intellectual competence can be made to serve undesirable purposes. To begin with, higher standards, more advanced content, and longer assignments are not ends in themselves. They are valueless and even pernicious unless they fulfill two requirements.

First, the subject-matter content must be worthwhile, lead to meaningful knowledge, and be consonant with contemporary scholarship. Second, the standards themselves need to be differentially applied so as to demand from each pupil what he or she can actually do and the best of which he or she is capable. Raised standards must never be used as a means of eliminating from school those pupils in the lower range of intellectual ability. Rather, new ways must be found to motivate such pupils adequately and to teach them academic subject matter more effectively. Second, excellence is not synonymous with high examination scores; one must consider the way in which such scores are achieved, the kind of knowledge they reflect, and the motivation underlying them.

More important than what pupils know at the end of the sixth, eighth, and twelfth grades is the extent of their knowledge at ages 25, 40, and 60, as well as their ability and desire both to learn more and to apply their knowledge fruitfully in adult life. In setting our academic goals, therefore, we must be concerned with the *ultimate* intellectual objectives of schooling; namely, these are the long-term acquisition of valid and usable bodies of knowledge and intellectual skills and the development of ability to think critically, systematically, and independently.

## Knowledge as an End in Itself

Related to the greater emphasis on intellectual training is an encouraging recent trend to place higher value on the acquisition of knowledge as a significant end in itself. It is true that the school cannot and dare not ignore totally the current concerns and the future family, vocational, and civic problems of high-school students, particularly those who have no intention of attending college. The danger of disregarding these latter concerns is that adolescents tend to lose interest in academic studies if they perceive the school as indifferent to their problems. Some extreme proponents of the "life-adjustment" movement, however, carried this approach too far by adopting an antiintellectual and overly utilitarian attitude toward secondary-school education. They tended to dismiss summarily as a waste of time any subject-matter knowledge that had no immediate application to problems of everyday living. In some instances, they diluted the curriculum by giving students a choice between academic subjects and various recreational frills and trivia.

Learning tasks, however, need not necessarily be concerned with problems of adolescent adjustment in order to motivate and interest high-school students. Meaningfully organized subject matter taught by competent teachers can generate considerable drive for learning as an end in itself. The value of much school learning, after all, can be defended only on the grounds that it enhances pupils' understanding of important ideas in their culture—not because it has, even remotely, any practical uses or implications. Nevertheless, some aspects of academic training do constitute, in a general way, just as important a preparation for adult living as education that is explicitly directed toward vocational and family adjustment.

## Responsibility for Directing Education

One extreme point of view associated with the child-centered approach to education is the notion that children are innately equipped in some mysterious fashion for knowing precisely what is best for them. This idea is obviously an outgrowth of predeterministic theories (for example, those of Rousseau and Gesell), which conceive of development as a series of internally regulated sequential steps that unfold in accordance with a prearranged design. According to these theorists, the environment facilitates development best by providing a maximally permissive field that does not interfere with the predetermined processes of spontaneous maturation. From these assumptions it is but a short step to the claim that children themselves are in the most strategic position to select those components of the environment that correspond most closely to their current developmental needs. Empirical "proof" of this proposition is adduced from the fact that nutrition is adequately maintained and existing deficiency conditions are spontaneously corrected when infants are permitted to select their own diets. If children can successfully choose their diets, they must certainly know what is best for them in all areas of growth and should therefore be permitted to select everything, including their curriculum.

Several arguments refute this theory. First, even if development were primarily a matter of internal ripening, there would still be no good reason for supposing that children are axiomatically equipped to make the choices that will best facilitate their development. Because individuals are sensitive in early childhood to internal cues of physiological need, we cannot conclude that they are similarly sensitive to cues reflective of psychological and other developmental needs; even in the area of nutrition, self-selection is a reliable criterion of need only during early infancy.

Second, unless one assigns a sacrosanct status to children's own motivations, there is little warrant for believing that they alone are truly reflective of children's genuine developmental requirements. Neither is there reason to believe that environmentally derived needs are "imposed," authoritarian in spirit, and inevitably fated to thwart the actualization of the pupil's developmental potentialities. Actually, most needs originate from without, in response to appropriate stimulation and successful experience. They become internalized in the course of children's interaction and identification with significant persons in their families and cultural environments.

Third, one can never assume that children's spontaneously expressed interests and activities are completely reflective of all of their important needs and capacities. Just because capacities can potentially provide their own motivation does not mean that they always or necessarily do so. It is not the possession of capacities per se that is motivating but the anticipation of future satisfactions once they have been successfully exercised. But because of such factors as inertia, lack of opportunity, lack of appreciation, and preoccupation with other activities, many capacities may never be exercised in the first place. Thus, children typically develop only some of their capacities, and their expressed interests cannot be considered coextensive with the potential range of interests they are capable of developing with appropriate stimulation.

In conclusion, therefore, the current interest and spontaneous desires of immature pupils can hardly be considered reliable guideposts and adequate substitutes for specialized knowledge and seasoned judgment in designing a curriculum. Recognizing the role of pupil needs in school learning does not mean that the syllabus should be restricted to the concerns and interests that happen to be present in a group of children growing up under particular social and intellectual conditions. In fact, a primary function of education should be to stimulate the development of motivations and interests that are currently nonexistent. It is true that academic achievement is greater when pupils manifest felt needs to acquire knowledge as an end in itself. Such needs, however, do not come from within but are acquired—largely through exposure to provocative, meaningful, and developmentally appropriate instruction. Hence, while it is reasonable to consider the views of pupils and even, under certain circumstances, to solicit their participation in the planning of the curriculum, it makes little developmental or administrative sense to entrust them with responsibility for significant policy or operational decisions.

The school, of course, can never assume complete responsibility for the student's learning. The latter must also bear his or her full share by learning actively and critically, seeking persistently to understand and retain what is taught, integrating new learning tasks with previously acquired knowledge and idiosyncratic experience, translating new propositions into his or her own language, putting forth the necessary effort to master difficult new subject matter, asking significant questions, and conscientiously undertaking the problem-solving exercises that are assigned. All of this, however, is a far cry from demanding that pupils take complete charge of their own learning. It does not mean that pupils must discover everything they learn for themselves, locate and interpret their own instructional materials from primary sources, design their own experiments, and merely use the teacher as a consultant and critic.

The very nature of education as adequately guided instruction implies knowledgeable selection, organization, interpretation, and sequential arrangement of learning materials and experiences by academically and pedagogically competent persons rather than a trial-and-error process of self-instruction. True, since education does not end when students leave school, they must also be taught to learn by themselves; but these two aspects of education are by no means mutually preclusive. Acknowledgment of the desirability of students devoting part of the school day to acquiring skills in locating, interpreting, and organizing information by themselves does not in any way relieve the educational establishment of the primary responsibility of structuring subject-matter content. Leading educators are currently returning to the more traditional educational view that the content of the curriculum is the school's, not the student's, responsibility.

# 2

# MEANING AND
# MEANINGFUL LEARNING

*In Chapter 1 we considered the difference between rote and mean-*
*ingful learning and between reception and discovery learning. We*
*concluded that in each case we are dealing with orthogonal (inde-*
*pendent) dimensions of school learning tasks, and specified the*
*conditions under which meaningful learning (reception or discovery)*
*occurs.*

*Meaningful reception learning involves the acquisition of new*
*meanings. It requires both a meaningful learning set and the pre-*
*sentation of potentially meaningful material to the learner. The*
*latter condition, in turn, presupposes (1) that the learning material*
*itself can be nonarbitrarily (plausibly, sensibly, and nonrandomly)*
*and substantively (nonverbatimly) related to any appropriate cog-*
*nitive structure (possesses "logical" meaning) and (2) that the par-*
*ticular learner's cognitive structure contains relevant anchoring*
*idea(s) to which the new material can be related. The interaction*
*between potentially new meanings and relevant ideas in the*
*learner's cognitive structure gives rise to actual or psychological*
*meanings. Because each learner's cognitive structure is unique, all*
*acquired new meanings are perforce themselves unique.*

*Meaningful learning is not synonymous with the learning of*
*meaningful material. First, the learning material is only potentially*
*meaningful. Second, a meaningful learning set must be present.*
*Learning material may consist of already meaningful components*
*(such as paired adjectives), but the learning task as a whole (learn-*

ing a list of arbitrarily linked meaningful words) is not "logically" meaningful. And even logically meaningful material may be learned by rote if the learner's learning set is not meaningful.

Three kinds of meaningful reception learning may be distinguished:

Representational learning (such as naming), is closest to rote learning. It occurs when arbitrary symbols are equated in meaning with their referents (objects, events, concepts) and signify to the learner whatever meaning their referents do. Representational learning is meaningful because such propositions of representational equivalence can be nonarbitrarily related as exemplars to a generalization present in almost everyone's cognitive structure at about the first year of life—that everything has a name and that the name signifies whatever its referent means to the particular learner.

Concept learning is discussed in detail in Chapters 3 and 6 and in their respective organizers.

Propositional learning can be either subordinate (subsumptive), superordinate, or combinatorial. Subsumptive learning occurs when a "logically" meaningful proposition in a particular discipline (plausible, but not necessarily logically or empirically valid in the philosophical sense) is related meaningfully to specific superordinate propositions in the pupil's cognitive structure. Such learning may be called derivative if the learning material simply exemplifies or supports an idea already existing in cognitive structure. It is called correlative if it is an extension, elaboration, modification, or qualification of previously learned propositions.

Superordinate propositional learning occurs when a new proposition is relatable to specific subordinate ideas in existing cognitive structure but is relatable to a broad background of generally rele- structure that can be subsumed under it. Finally, combinational propositional learning refers to instances where a potentially meaningful proposition cannot be related to specific superordinate or subordinate ideas in the learner's cognitive structure but is relatable to a broad background of generally relevant content in such structure.

Meaningful reception learning is important in education because it is the human mechanism par excellence for acquiring and storing the vast quantity of ideas and information represented by any field of knowledge. The acquisition and retention of large bodies of subject matter is really a very impressive phenomenon, considering that, first, human beings, unlike computers, can apprehend, and immediately remember, only a few discrete items of information that are presented a single time, and second, that memory for rotely learned lists receiving multiple presentations is notoriously limited

*both over time and with respect to length of list, unless greatly over-
learned and frequently reproduced. The tremendous efficiency of
meaningful learning inheres in its two principal characteristics—
nonarbitrariness and substantiveness.*

*As typical classroom examples of meaningful reception learning,
we discuss in some detail: (1) the learning of syntax (by concept
formation and propositional discovery learning of syntactical rules)
(the preschool period); (2) learning how to read, by equating the
meaning of printed letters, words, phrases, and syntactical rules
with their established spoken counterparts in cognitive structure
(elementary school); and (3) the learning of a second language by
establishing the same kind of representational equivalence between
second-language words and already established words in the
learner's native language, and by the meaningful reception learning
of new syntactical propositions (secondary school).*

*Language is an important facilitator of meaningful reception and
discovery learning. By increasing the manipulability of concepts
and propositions through the representational properties of words,
and by refining emerging subverbal understandings in meaningful
reception and discovery learning, it both clarifies such meanings
and makes them more precise and transferable. Contrary to Piaget's
position, language, therefore, plays an integral and operative
(process) role in thinking rather than merely a communicative role.*

Classroom learning, we believe, is concerned primarily with the acquisition,
retention, and use of large bodies of potentially meaningful information.
Therefore it is important that we make very explicit at the outset what is
meant by the psychology of meaning and meaningful learning. In this
chapter we shall explore the nature of meaning and consider the relationship of meaning to meaningful verbal learning. In so doing, we shall also
be concerned with such issues as the general significance of meaningful
learning in acquiring knowledge; how words, concepts, and propositions
acquire meaning; the distinction between logical and psychological meaning; and the relationship between perception and cognition. Finally, we
shall discuss problems of language acquisition and the importance of meaning and meaningful learning for understanding how we learn the syntax
of our native language, how we learn to read, and how we learn second
languages.

## The Nature of Meaning

Meaningful learning involves the acquisition of new meanings, and
new meanings, conversely, are the products of meaningful learning. That

is, the emergence of new meanings in the learner reflects the completion of a meaningful learning process. After indicating in some detail what is involved in this process, we shall examine more explicitly both the nature of meaning itself and its relationship to meaningful learning.

### The Conditions of Meaningful Learning

The essence of the meaningful learning process is that symbolically expressed ideas are related in a nonarbitrary and substantive (nonverbatim) fashion to what the learner already knows. By substantive and nonarbitrary relatedness we mean that the ideas are related to some *specifically relevant existing aspect* of the learner's cognitive structure, such as an image, an already meaningful symbol, a concept or a proposition. Meaningful learning presupposes *both* that the learner manifest a meaningful learning set— that is, a disposition to relate the new material nonarbitrarily and substantively to his or her cognitive structure—and that the material learned be potentially meaningful to him or her—namely, relatable to his or her structure of knowledge on a nonarbitrary and nonverbatim basis (Ausubel, 1961) (see A in Table 2.1). Thus, irrespective of how much potential meaning may inhere in a particular proposition, if the learner's intention is to memorize it arbitrarily and verbatim (as a series of arbitrarily related words), both the learning process and the learning outcome must be rote or meaningless. And, conversely, no matter how meaningful the learner's set may be, neither the process nor the outcome of learning can possibly be meaningful if the learning task is not potentially meaningful—if it is not nonarbitrarily and substantively relatable to his cognitive structure.

This is illustrated by rote memorization of definitions of concepts or propositions without recognition of the meaning of the words in the definition. A student could learn Ohm's law, which indicates that current in a circuit is directly proportional to voltage. However, this proposition will not be *meaningfully learned* unless the student already has meanings for the concepts of current, voltage, resistance, direct and inverse proportion, *and* unless he or she tries to relate these meanings as indicated by Ohm's law.

One reason why pupils commonly develop a rote learning set in relation to potentially meaningful subject matter is because they learn from sad experience that substantively correct answers lacking in verbatim correspondence to what they have been taught receive no credit whatsoever from certain teachers. Another reason is that because of a generally high level of anxiety or because of chronic failure experience in a given subject (reflective, in turn, of low aptitude or poor teaching), they lack confidence in their ability to learn meaningfully, and hence perceive no alternative to panic apart from rote learning. (This phenomenon is very familiar to mathematics teachers because of the widespread prevalence of "number shock" or "number anxiety.") Moreover, pupils may develop a rote learning set

**TABLE 2.1**  Relationships Between Meaningful Learning, Potential Meaningfulness, Logical Meaningfulness, and Psychological Meaning

| | | (1) | | (2) |
|---|---|---|---|---|
| A  MEANINGFUL LEARNING or THE ACQUISITION OF MEANINGS | requires | Potentially Meaningful Material | and | Meaningful Learning Set |
| B  POTENTIAL MEANINGFULNESS | depends on | *Logical Meaningfulness* (the nonarbitrary and substantive relatability of the learning material to correspondingly relevant ideas that lie within the realm of human learning capability) | and | The availabiilty of such relevant ideas in the *particular* learner's cognitive structure |
| C  PSYCHOLOGICAL MEANING (IDIOSYNCRATIC, PHENOMENOLOGICAL MEANING) | is the product of | Meaningful Learning | or of | Potential Meaningfulness and Meaningful Learning Set |

if they are under excessive pressure to exhibit glibness, or to conceal, rather than admit and gradually remedy, original lack of genuine understanding. Under these circumstances it seems easier and more important to create a spurious impression of facile comprehension, by rotely memorizing a few key terms or sentences, than to try to understand what they mean. Teachers frequently forget that pupils become very adept at using abstract terms with apparent appropriateness—when they have to—even though their understanding of the underlying concepts is virtually nonexistent.

Whether the learning task is potentially meaningful (nonarbitrarily and substantively relatable to the learner's structure of knowledge) is a somewhat more complex matter than meaningful learning. At the very least, it obviously depends on the two principal factors involved in establishing this kind of relationship, that is, both on the nature of the materials to be learned and on the nature of the *particular* learner's cognitive structure (see Table 2.1 and note especially B and C. The ideas in this table are very important and should be studied carefully.) Turning first to the nature of the material, it must itself be sufficiently nonarbitrary or nonrandom that it could be related on a nonarbitrary and substantive basis to correspondingly relevant ideas that lie within the realm of human learning capability (to correspondingly relevant ideas that at least *some* human beings are capable of learning if given the opportunity to do so). This property of the learning task itself that determines whether or not it is potentially meaningful is referred to as logical[1] meaningfulness. It seldom, if ever, is lacking in school learning tasks since subject-matter content, almost by definition, is logically meaningful. School subject matter nearly always represents our cultural interpretation of some aspect of the real world or some logical constructions (such as mathematics) and hence necessarily has logical meaningfulness. Such is not the case, however, with respect to many psychology laboratory tasks and some everyday learning tasks (for example, telephone numbers, paired adjectives, scrambled sentences, lists of nonsense syllables) that are relatable to anyone's cognitive structure on only an arbitrary and verbatim basis. Much experimentation in psychology laboratories has used nonsense syllables for the express purpose of providing *meaningless* learning material. It is now recognized by many learning theorists that most of the "laws" or theories based on such experimentation have little or no relevance to an understanding of classroom learning.

The second factor determining whether learning material is potentially meaningful is a function of the learner's cognitive structure rather than of the learning material. The acquisition of meanings as a natural phenomenon occurs in *particular* human beings—not in mankind generally. Hence, for meaningful learning to occur in fact, it is not sufficient that the new mate-

---

[1] We recognize that our use of the term *logical* to denote a kind of meaning inherent in knowledge to be learned is not the same usage employed in philosophy, but rather represents a restricted meaning.

rial simply be nonarbitrarily and substantively relatable to correspondingly relevant ideas in the abstract sense of the term (to correspondingly relevant ideas that *some* human beings *could* learn under appropriate circumstances); it is also necessary that such relevant ideational content be available in the cognitive structure of the *particular* learner. It is apparent, therefore, that insofar as meaningful learning outcomes in the classroom are concerned, the availability, and other significant properties, of *relevant content* in different *learners' cognitive structures* constitute the most crucial and variable determinants of potential meaningfulness. Thus it follows that the potential meaningfulness of learning materials varies not only with prior educational background, but also with such factors as age, IQ, occupation, and social class and cultural membership. The ideas presented in this paragraph and in Table 2.1 are fundamental to understanding the model for learning presented in this book and will be of continuing concern throughout the book.

### Criteria for Learning Material

What, precisely, is meant by the statement that for learning material to be logically meaningful it must be nonarbitrarily and substantively relatable to correspondingly relevant ideas that lie within human learning capacity? The first criterion—nonarbitrary relatability—simply implies that if the material *itself* exhibits sufficient nonarbitrariness (or nonrandomness), an adequate and almost self-evident basis exists for relating it in nonarbitrary fashion to the kinds of correspondingly relevant ideas that human beings are capable of learning. Logically meaningful learning material could thus be nonarbitrarily relatable to *specifically* relevant ideas as examples, derivatives, special cases, extensions, elaborations, modifications, qualifications and more inclusive generalizations; or it could be relatable to a *wider array* of relevant ideas in the sense of being generally congruent with them. For example, data on mean monthly temperatures for cities meaningfully relates to a concept of climate, and these data also relate to ideas about solar radiation, the earth's orbital position, and so on, in a generally congruent way.

The second criterion—substantive relatability—implies that if the learning material again is sufficiently nonarbitrary, an ideationally equivalent symbol or group of symbols could be related to cognitive structure without any resulting change in meaning. In other words, neither meaningful learning nor emergent meaning are dependent on the *exclusive* use of *particular* signs and no others; the same concept or proposition could be expressed in synonymous language and would convey precisely the same meaning. Thus, for example, "canine," "Hund," and "chien" would elicit the same meanings as "dog" in a person who has a fair command of English, German, and French; and "The sum of the internal angles of a triangle equals a straight angle" would mean the same to most geometry students as "The sum of the interior angles of a triangle equals 180 degrees."

Rote learning tasks, of course, are not mastered in a cognitive vacuum. They *are* relatable to cognitive structure but *only* in an arbitrary, verbatim fashion that does not result in the acquisition of any meanings. Since, for example, the particular stimulus and response members of a given pair of adjectives in paired-associate learning are linked together in purely arbitrary fashion, there is no possible basis for nonarbitrarily relating the learning task to anyone's cognitive structure, and the learner must also remember verbatim the response to each stimulus word (he cannot use synonyms). This arbitrary and verbatim relatability of rote learning tasks to cognitive structure does, of course, have certain significant consequences for learning. First, since human cognitive equipment, unlike a computer, cannot handle information very efficiently that is related to it on an arbitrary and verbatim basis, only relatively short learning tasks can be internalized in this fashion, and these can be retained for only short periods of time unless greatly overlearned. Second, arbitrary and verbatim relatability to cognitive structure makes rote learning tasks highly vulnerable to interference from previously learned and concurrently encountered similar materials. As we shall see later, it is this basically different kind of relatability to cognitive structure (arbitrary and verbatim versus nonarbitrary and substantive) that accounts for the fundamental difference between rote and meaningful learning processes. (Refer again to Figure 1.1.)

It is also true that *already meaningful component* elements of a rote learning task can be related to cognitive structure in ways that do not involve any learning of the elements themselves, but nevertheless facilitate the rote learning of the task as a whole. It is by virtue of such relatability, for example, that the component letters of nonsense syllables are *perceived* meaningfully, and that the syllables as a whole evoke associations to similar meaningful words (and are thus perceived as partly meaningful themselves). For similar reasons—by enhancing the familiarity of the material, by obviating the need for prior learning of the component elements, and by making possible the combination of these elements into larger units (thereby reducing the total number of discrete associations to be established)—the use of already meaningful component elements in learning material facilitates rote learning. So-called "memory experts" employ a variety of strategies to add meaning to what others perceive as prodigious rote memory feats.

## Relationship of Meaning to Meaningful Learning

It should be evident by now that *meaning itself* is a product of the meaningful learning process. The question naturally arises: how does the whole process get started? The next chapter will deal with the process of *concept formation* more systematically, but we should recognize at this point that meanings of signs or symbols for concepts or groups of concepts must be acquired gradually and idiosyncratically by each learner. Once initial meanings are established for signs or symbols of concepts in the process of concept formation, new meaningful learning will give additional meanings to the signs or symbols, and new relationships between previously learned concepts will be acquired. We will see how concept labels for specific concepts, like "dog" or "red," become differentiated further and develop new relationships to concepts such as animal or color as meaningful learning progresses. Although learners acquire meanings for signs or symbols in their own idiosyncratic way, these meanings have sufficient commonality in any given culture to allow use of the symbols to exchange information. If this were not so, schooling or any other form of organized exchange of knowledge would be impossible, and meaningful learning would also be impossible except through discovery learning methods.

### Types of Meaningful Learning

The most basic type of meaningful learning, upon which all other meaningful learning depends, is *representational* learning, which involves learning the meanings of single symbols (typically words) or learning what they represent. Single words in any language, after all, are conventional or socially shared symbols, each of which represents a unitary object, situation, concept, or other symbol in the physical, social, and ideational worlds (Cassirer, 1957). To any *uninitiated* individual, however, what a given symbol means, or represents, is at first something completely unknown to him; it is something that he has to learn. The process whereby he learns this, called representational learning, is coextensive with the process whereby new words come to represent for him the corresponding objects or ideas to which the words refer (their referents). The new words come to signify to him the same things that the referents do or to elicit the same differentiated cognitive content that they do.

For example, when a child is first learning the meaning of the word "dog," it is proposed that the sound of the word (which is potentially meaningful but as yet has no meaning for the child) represents, or is equivalent to, a particular dog-object that he or she is perceiving at the moment, and hence that it signifies the same thing (an image of this dog-object) that the object itself does. The child, in turn, actively relates—in relatively nonarbitrary and substantive fashion—this proposition of representational equivalence to relevant content in his or her cognitive structure. Thus, when meaningful learning is completed, the word "dog" is reliably capable of eliciting a composite image of the various dogs in his experience which is approximately equivalent to that elicited by particular dog-objects. Once the more generic meaning for the word "dog" is acquired, this symbol also serves as a concept label for the cultural concept "dog."

How representational learning actually occurs, and how children develop a capacity for such learning, will be discussed later in this chapter. At this point we wish only to distinguish between three basic kinds of meaningful learning: *representational learning, concept learning*, and *propositional learning. Representational learning* concerns the meanings of unitary symbols or words and propositional learning concerns the meanings of ideas expressed by groups of words combined into propositions or sentences. In the first instance (as in naming, labeling, and defining activities), learning the meanings of single words involves learning what they represent (Lennenberg, 1967). It means learning that particular symbols represent or are equivalent in meaning to particular referents.

Another type of meaningful learning that is prominent in the acquisition of subject matter consists of *concept learning*. Concepts (unitary generic or categorical ideas) are also represented by single symbols just as other unitary referents are. Except in very young learners, the individual words that are commonly combined in sentence form to constitute propositions actually represent concepts rather than objects or situations, and hence propositional learning largely involves learning the meaning of a composite idea generated by combining into a sentence single words each of which represents a concept.

In *propositional learning*, the meaningful learning task is not to learn what words singly, or in combination, represent, but rather to learn the meaning of new ideas expressed in propositional form. In true propositional learning, in other words, the object is not to learn propositions of representational equivalence but to learn the meaning of verbal propositions that express ideas other than those of representational equivalence. That is, the meaning of the proposition is not simply the sum of meanings of the component words.

In true verbal propositional learning, one is learning the meaning of a new composite idea in the sense that: (1) the proposition itself is generated by combining or relating to each other multiple individual words, each representing a unitary referent; and (2) the individual words are combined in such a way (usually, in sentence form) that the resulting new idea is more than just the sum of the meanings of the component individual words. Obviously, before one can learn the meanings of verbal propositions one must first know the meanings of their component terms, or what the terms represent. Thus representational learning is basic to, or a prerequisite for, true propositional learning when propositions are expressed in verbal form.

At this point, we should indicate how concept learning is related to representational learning. Since concepts, as well as objects and situations, are represented by words or names, learning what *concept words* mean (learning which concept is represented by a given new concept word, or learning that the new concept word is equivalent in meaning to whatever the concept itself means) is a major type of *representational* learning. It typically follows concept learning itself, inasmuch as it is very convenient to be able to represent a newly learned concept by a single word that is equivalent to it in meaning. But learning what the concept *itself* means—which, in effect, consists of learning what its criterial (distinguishing or identifying) attributes are—involves a very different type of meaningful learning. Like propositional learning, this type of learning is substantive in nature and intent rather than nominalistic or representational (Lennenberg, 1971). These two types of meaningful learning (conceptual and propositional) are different. In the former instance the *criterial attributes* of a new concept are related to cognitive structure to yield a new generic but *unitary* meaning, whereas in the latter instance a new *proposition* (or composite idea) is related to cognitive structure to yield a new *composite* meaning. They are *both* very different from representational learning, even though concept learning is typically followed by a form of representational learning in which the newly learned concept is equated in meaning with the concept word that represents it. In the example given earlier, Ohm's law is a proposition that can be learned meaningfully only after the component concepts have been learned. In terms of the rote → meaningful learning continuum (see Figure 1.1), representational learning usually would be closer to the rote form, and concept or propositional learning may extend to the highest (most complex) forms of meaningful learning. A person can rotely learn that Ohm's law states that the current in a circuit is equal to the voltage divided by the resistance in the circuit. As noted earlier, this proposition cannot be meaningfully learned unless the component concepts are available with a sufficient degree of clarity.

## Logical and Psychological Meaning

The preceding discussion distinguished between the *potential* meaning inherent for particular learners in certain symbolic expressions and in the statement of certain propositions, on the one hand, and *actual* (phenomenological or psychological) meaning, which is the product of a meaningful learning process, on the other. Actual meaning, according to this view, emerges when this potential meaning becomes converted into new, differentiated, and idiosyncratic cognitive content within a *particular* individual as a result of being nonarbitrarily and substantively related to, and interacting with, relevant ideas in his cognitive structure. Our task in this section is simply to make explicit the analogous distinction between logical and psychological meaning (see Table 2.1). Psychological meaning is identical with actual or phenomenological meaning as defined above, whereas logical meaning corresponds to the meaning that learning material exhibits if it meets the *general* or nonidiosyncratic requirements for potential meaningfulness. In short, logical meaning depends *only* on the "nature of the material." It is one of the two prerequisites that together determine whether learning material is potentially meaningful to a particular learner. The other prerequisite is the availability of the appropriate relevant content in this *particular* learner's cognitive structure.

*Logical* meaning, therefore, refers to the meaning that is inherent in certain kinds of symbolic material by virtue of the very nature of this material. Such material manifests logical meaning if it can be related on a nonarbitrary and substantive basis to correspondingly relevant ideas that lie within the realm of human learning capability. For example, if propositional material itself consists of generally nonarbitrary relationships, then it is also, almost by definition, nonarbitrarily and substantively relatable to the cognitive structure of some persons in a given culture and thus is logically meaningful. Obviously excluded, therefore, from the domain of logical meaning is the almost infinite number of possible relationships between concepts that can be formulated on the basis of purely *random* or arbitrary pairings. This does not necessarily mean that all propositions with logical meaning are empirically *valid* or even logically defensible. The questions of empirical and logical validity are issues that simply do not enter into the determination of logical meaning. Propositions based on unvalidated premises or on faulty logic may conceivably abound in logical meaning. For example, for centuries the proposition that the earth is flat was considered to be both logical and valid, but we now know that this proposition is invalid.

*Psychological* (actual or phenomenological) meaning, on the other hand, is a wholly *idiosyncratic* cognitive experience. Corresponding to the distinction between the logical and the psychological structure of knowledge, there is an equally important distinction between logical and psychological meaning. Subject-matter content can, at best, have logical meaning. It is the nonarbitrary and substantive relatability of logically meaningful propositions to a *particular* learner's cognitive structure that makes them potentially meaningful to him and thereby creates the possibility of transforming logical into psychological meaning in the course of meaningful learning. Thus the emergence of psychological meaning depends not only on presenting the learner with material manifesting logical meaning, but also on the latter's actual possession of the necessary ideational background. The proposition that adverbs are words that modify verbs has psychological meaning only to individuals who already have to some degree meaningful concepts of words, modifiers, and verbs.

When an individual learns logically meaningful propositions, therefore, they automatically lose their nonidiosyncratic flavor. Psychological meaning is always an idiosyncratic phenomenon. Its idiosyncratic nature, however, does not rule out the possibility of social or shared meanings. The various individual meanings that different members of a given culture have for the same concepts and propositions are ordinarily sufficiently similar to permit interpersonal communication and understanding. As noted earlier, this homogeneity of shared meanings within a particular culture, and even between related cultures, reflects the same logical meaning inherent in logically meaningful concepts and propositions and the many common aspects of ideational background in different learners' cognitive structures.

### Meaningful Learning versus the Learning of Meaningful Material

Meaningful learning is not to be interpreted simply as the learning of meaningful material. In meaningful learning, the materials are only *potentially* meaningful. If they were *already* meaningful, the goal of meaningful learning—that is, the acquisition of new meanings—would be already accomplished, by definition, before any learning was ever attempted. It is true, of course, that in most potentially meaningful learning tasks, the *component parts* of the material are already meaningful; but in these instances the *task as a whole* is only potentially meaningful. For example, in learning a new geometrical theorem each of the component words is already meaningful, but the learning task as a whole (learning the meaning of the theorem) is yet to be accomplished. Thus *already* meaningful material, just like its already meaningful component parts, may be *perceived* or otherwise reacted to meaningfully, but it cannot be meaningfully *learned.*

This brings us to the important distinction between the *meaningful* learning of *potentially* meaningful material and the *rote* learning of tasks that contain *already meaningful* components. There are innumerable examples of rote or nonmeaningful learning. When a list of paired adjectives is to be learned, for example, each adjective is already meaningful, but the learning task itself is not potentially meaningful because these wholly arbitrary associations between adjectives cannot be related to the learner's existing knowledge in a nonarbitrary, nonverbatim fashion. In learning a geometrical theorem, on the other hand, each component word is not only already meaningful but the learning task as a whole is also potentially meaningful. However, unless the learner manifests a meaningful learning set in this latter instance, no meaning will emerge: he or she will merely learn rotely a series of arbitrarily related words. Thus, it is important to distinguish between the *meaningful* learning of *potentially* meaningful material, on the one hand, and on the other, the *rote* learning of already meaningful component elements that, taken together, either may or may not constitute potentially meaningful learning tasks.

In the course of meaningful learning, a student must relate the component elements to his or her idiosyncratic cognitive structure. The result is almost always some minor variation between how the learner internalizes the information and how the teacher perceives the information. Thus in later recall of statements or propositions, the student's answer may vary somewhat from that expected by the teacher even when the student's answer is substantively correct. Unfortunately, such responses often are scored wrong and students learn to use rote (verbatim) learning approaches rather than to learn meaningfully.

### Meaning versus Meaningfulness

What do investigators of rote verbal learning mean when they talk about the *meaningfulness* of the units (nonsense syllables, words) they employ in their learning tasks? In using this term they do not refer to the substantive meaning of a given symbol (the differential cognitive content it evokes in the learner after being meaningfully learned), but rather to the *relative degree* of meaning it manifests as compared to that manifested by other symbols. The meaningfulness of a word, for example, depends on whether it has a concretely identifiable referent (such as "book") or merely serves a transactional function (such as "since") (Epstein, Rock, & Zuckerman, 1960), and also on such factors as the frequency and variety of the contexts in which it is encountered (Björgen, 1964; Noble, 1953; Underwood & Schulz, 1960). A highly meaningful word, therefore, tends to be subjectively more familiar (Noble, 1953) and to evoke more associations (Glaze, 1928; Noble, 1952) than a less meaningful word—but these are indices of its meaningfulness rather than explanations of how it becomes meaningful in the first place. One must be careful, in other words, not to confuse the mechanism whereby a word acquires meaning with the factors accounting for the relative degree of meaning it exhibits. Reference has already been made to the reasons why meaningfulness facilitates rote learning.

### The Acquisition of Meanings

In this section we propose to discuss more systematically some of the problems involved in the acquisition of word and propositional meanings. Thus far, the acquisition of these latter types of meanings has just been considered illustratively in clarifying the nature of meaning. The acquisition of concept meanings will be considered here only insofar as such learning must be distinguished from the learning of what concept words mean. More definitive treatment of concept learning will be presented in the next chapter.

*Vocabulary or Representational Learning*

We have already indicated that learning the meanings of single words, or learning what single words represent, involves the meaningful learning of particular propositions of representational equivalence—learning that particular words represent and thereby signify psychologically the same things that their referents do. It was also pointed out that as a result of such learning, words come to elicit approximately the same differentiated cognitive content that their referents do. Our task at this point is to relate representational learning to the previously presented discussion of the meaningful learning process and to the nature of meaning itself. In other words, how do human beings acquire vocabulary? How do they actually learn what single words mean? How does such learning exemplify meaningful learning in general?

To begin with, there is the matter of genic endowment, without which no amount of appropriate experience would suffice. Human beings have a genically determined potentiality for representational learning (Ausubel, 1963a; Cassirer, 1957; Werner & Kaplan, 1963). As stated earlier, representational learning is learning that a given pattern of stimulation (such as the distinctive pattern of sounds in the symbol "dog" or even a graphic symbol, such as a drawing or sketch) represents and thereby signifies approximately the same thing (a dog-image) that an entirely unrelated pattern of stimulation (such as the referent dog-object) signifies. (When a given referent actually signifies something to a particular learner it is conventionally referred to as a "significate.") The principal step in actualizing this potentiality for representational learning is typically taken near the end of the first year of life, when the child acquires the *general insight* that it is possible to use a symbol to represent any significate. The child acquires this insight by generalizing, subverbally and intuitively, from multiple exposures to the two complementary forms of the proposition of representational equivalence that more proficient users of his or her native language have arranged—that different referents have different names and that different exemplars of the same referent have the same name.

Once this insight is firmly established in cognitive structure, it lays the necessary foundation for all subsequent representational learning. Thereafter, when a particular new proposition of representational equivalence is presented (that "dog" is representationally equivalent to different dog-objects and, hence, to their corresponding dog-images), the child is able nonarbitrarily and substantively to relate such a proposition to the already established and more generalized version of the same proposition in his or her cognitive structure. The resulting product of the interaction between the two propositions is the differentiated cognitive content that "dog" signifies, or is representationally equivalent to, a composite dog-image; and presentation of the word "dog" will subsequently elicit this image. At this stage of the game, a particular proposition of representational equivalence may often be learned and retained for a surprisingly long time, even though it is put to the child only once and in connection with a single exemplar of the significate in question, provided of course, that the significate is familiar to him or her.

### Types of Vocabulary Learning

In the early stages of vocabulary learning, words tend to represent actual and noncategorical objects and events, and hence to be equated in meaning with the relatively concrete and specific images such referents signify. Thus "naming," the earliest form of vocabulary learning in children, involves the establishment of representational equivalence between first-order symbols and concrete images. Later on, as words begin to represent concepts or generic ideas, they become concept names and are equated in meaning with more abstract, generalized, and categorical cognitive content. The word "dog" to a toddler may just signify a composite image of his own pet and of the particular dogs in his neighborhood; to the older preschool child, however, it signifies the *criterial attributes* of a composite dog-image that the child has discovered inductively from his or her own concrete-empirical experience with dogs. (This latter discovery process is called "concept formation" and is discussed in detail in the next chapter.) Correlated with the *denotative* meaning of "dog" that emerges when the criterial attributes of this concept are meaningfully learned are various idiosyncratic affective and attitudinal reactions that the term elicits in each child depending on his or her particular experience with the species. These reactions constitute the *connotative* meaning of "dog." It should be noted, however, that in older children the connotations of most words, for instance, "divorce," "alcohol," "communism," are not acquired through firsthand experience, but are assimilated from prevailing evaluative attitudes in their immediate cultural environment.

After the preschool years the meanings of most new words are learned by definition or by being encountered in appropriate and relatively explicit contexts. In this case representational equivalence is established in cognitive structure between synonyms and already meaningful words or between new concept words and the meanings conveyed by their respective definitions or contexts. An adequate definition or context furnishes, in turn, the criterial attributes of the new concept expressed in already meaningful words or combinations of such words. For example, in learning the meaning of the new concept *word* "president" (a form of representational learning typically following concept learning itself), a pupil equates the word in meaning to whatever "chief of state or chief executive in a republic" means to him or her. The pupil does so *after* learning what these attributes presented in the definition[2] mean (concept learning). However, only the representational learning that *follows* concept learning—namely, the process of equating the concept word in meaning with what the concept itself means—can be legitimately considered part of vocabulary learning since, by any reasonable standard, vocabulary learning is synonymous with representational learning. According to the generally accepted meaning, acquiring a vocabulary consists of learning a body of word meanings; by definition, this expression refers to learning what the words mean and not to learning what their referents mean. Thus, using the term "vocabulary learning" to encompass concept learning as well as learning what concept words mean, although very commonly done, only generates confusion (Deese, 1967).

Learning what concept words mean obviously demands more sophisticated *prior* knowledge about their corresponding referents than do other forms of representational learning, since learning the meaning of concept words differs in one important respect from learning the meaning of words that do not represent concepts. Where the referent of a given word is an *actual* object or event, learning that the word signifies the same thing as the referent does not really involve a prior *substantive* task of *learning* what the referent itself signifies. Getting to know what an object or event signifies is a simple matter of perception. An object simply signifies the corresponding perceptual image it evokes when present, or the corresponding memory image that remains, and can be otherwise evoked when the object is no longer present. However, when the referent of a word is a concept (an abstraction or a generic idea that does not actually exist), learning that the concept word signifies the same thing as the referent *does* involve a prior substantive task of learning what the referent signifies. One can get to know what the concept itself signifies only by *learning* what its criterial attributes are and what they mean. This, by definition, is a substantive form of meaningful learning. Thus learning the meaning of a concept word always presupposes that the learner *first meaningfully learn* what its referent (the concept) signifies, even though the actual *representational* learning process involved is essentially no different from that involved in learning the meaning of words that do not represent concepts (words like "the," "when," and so on).

The practical importance of distinguishing carefully between learning the meanings of concepts and learning the meanings of concept words can be illustrated by citing several everyday and educational examples. First, it not infrequently happens that pupils acquire particular concepts mean-

---

[2] When the criterial attributes of a concept are presented to the learner by definition or context, rather than discovered by him as in the case of concept formation, concept learning is referred to as "concept assimilation." In both instances, however, whether the criterial attributes are discovered or presented, they must be meaningfully related to cognitive structure before concept meanings emerge.

ingfully without learning for quite some time what their names are; thus simply because they do not know what particular concept words mean, it cannot be assumed that they necessarily do not know the corresponding concept meanings. For example, we found in one of our studies that children did not recognize the importance of *soil* to plant growth. The difficulty later proved to be that we chose a word for the significate that was technically correct, but children in our group only recognized *dirt* as the representational word for the concept more appropriately labeled *soil*. Second, it is very possible either to forget what a given concept word means but to remember its corresponding concept meaning, or to remember a concept word but to forget its meaning. Third, in teaching native-language synonyms or foreign-language equivalents to native-language words, it is important to appreciate that pupils only have to learn new concept words— not new concepts. Thus it is only necessary for them to equate in meaning the old concept words and the corresponding new synonyms or foreign-language equivalents; it is superfluous and wasteful of time for them to equate in meaning the new concept words and the referents to the old concept words.

Finally, if concepts are rotely learned as a result of failure to relate their criterial attributes to cognitive structure substantively and nonverbatimly, it necessarily follows that the labeling concept words are also rotely learned. It is unlikely that a learner will nonarbitrarily relate a concept word to other relevant concept words so acquired in his cognitive structure, and hence both the concept definition and its symbol concept word will have been rotely learned. Knowing about the two separate kinds of rote learning involved here helps one understand why rotely learned concept words that have been equated with rotely learned concepts have such little utility and are forgotten so quickly.

### Vocabulary Learning as Meaningful Learning

It is clear from the foregoing that vocabulary learning, or the acquisition of word meanings, is not regarded in this text as a manifestation of conditioning or rote verbal learning. It reflects, rather, a meaningful and active cognitive process involving the establishment in cognitive structure of representational equivalence between a new symbol and the idiosyncratic, specifically relevant cognitive content its referent signifies. It is true, of course, that most verbal symbols do represent their significates on a somewhat arbitrary and verbatim basis; there is no nonarbitrary reason why a given word is chosen to represent the corresponding object or idea to which it refers.[3] Verbatim reproducibility is also essential if representa-

---

[3] In some instances, where new words are derived from already meaningful roots, either native or foreign, the representational relationship between word and referent is not arbitrary provided that the individuals learning such words are aware of the derivations in question.

tional symbols are to function as surrogates of the referents, since only a very slight change (a single letter of a word) may drastically change or even reverse the meaning. On both counts, therefore, vocabulary (representational) learning is the kind of meaningful learning that lies close to the rote end of the rote–meaningful continuum.

Nevertheless, representational learning still meets the minimum criterion of nonarbitrary, substantive relatability of the learning task to cognitive structure that is required for meaningful learning. First of all, any particular proposition of representational equivalence can be nonarbitrarily related to a more general proposition of the same nature that is typically established in cognitive structure quite early in childhood. Moreover, even quite young children growing up in a bilingual environment seem implicitly to appreciate that second-language symbols manifest the same representational relationship that the first-language symbols do, both to the referents in question and to what the referents signify. In any case, the learning of representational equivalence between new symbols and what their referents signify is a much less arbitrary learning task than either the serial learning of nonsense syllables or the learning of paired associates. The type of meaningful cognitive process involved in representational learning is obviously basic to and accounts for the learning of all units of meaning in any symbolic system. Furthermore, it is only because the meanings of single words can be learned in this way that, by combining such meanings, it becomes possible to generate verbally both conceptual and propositional ideas that are inherently less arbitrary and can therefore be learned more meaningfully.

### Concept Learning

We shall define concepts as objects, events, situations or properties that possess common criterial attributes and are designated by some sign or symbol. In Chapter 3 we will describe two methods of concept learning: (1) concept formation, which takes place primarily in young children; and (2) concept assimilation, which is the dominant form of concept learning in school children and adults. In concept formation the criterial attributes of the concept are acquired through direct experience, through successive stages of hypothesis generation and testing and generalization. Thus young children come to know the concept "dog" through successive encounters with dogs, cats, cows, and so on, until they can generalize those criterial attributes that constitute the cultural concept of "dog." In this case the sign "dog" (or "doggie") is usually acquired before the concept, but the reverse may occur for other concepts, such as "argument" or "mammal."

As a child's vocabulary increases, new concepts can be acquired through the process of concept assimilation since the criterial attributes of new concepts can be defined by use in new combinations of existing referents available in the child's cognitive structure. While concrete-empirical props may also aid concept assimilation in young children, it is possible to use existing relevant concepts to accelerate the process of defining the criterial attributes of new concepts. In older children and adults, very few new concepts are learned by the process of concept formation. Much of this book is therefore devoted to discussion of the processes and conditions that facilitate concept assimilation.

## Propositional Learning

The meaningful learning of verbal propositions, though somewhat more complex than learning the meaning of words, is similar to representational learning in that new meanings emerge after a potentially meaningful learning task is related to, and interacts with, relevant ideas in cognitive structure. In this case, however, the learning task, or potentially meaningful proposition, consists of a composite idea that is expressed verbally in a sentence containing both denotative and connotative word meanings and the syntactic functions[4] of and relations between words. The differentiated cognitive content resulting from the meaningful learning process, and constituting its meaning, is an interactional product of the *particular* way in which the content of the new proposition is related to the content of relevant established ideas in cognitive structure. The relationship in question may be either subordinate, superordinate, or a combination of the two.

## Anchorage of New Information to Existing Ideas

It is important to recognize that meaningful learning does not mean that new information forms a kind of simple bond with preexisting elements of cognitive structure. On the contrary, only in rote learning does a simple arbitrary and nonsubstantive linkage occur with preexisting cognitive structure. In meaningful learning the very process of acquiring information results in a modification of both the newly acquired information and the specifically relevant aspect of cognitive structure to which the new information is linked. In most instances new information is linked to a relevant concept or proposition. As a matter of convenience, we will refer to concepts or propositions as relevant *ideas* in cognitive structure. In order to connote that meaningful learning involves an interaction between new information and preexisting ideas in cognitive structure, we will employ the term *anchorage* to suggest the role of the preexisting idea. For example, in subsumption, preexisting ideas provide anchorage for meaningful learning of new information

---

[4] The learning of syntax itself and the apprehension of syntactic relationships will be discussed in later sections of this chapter.

*Subsumption*

In both concept learning and propositional learning, new information is frequently linked or anchored to *relevant* aspects of an individual's existing cognitive structure. This process of linking new information to pre-existing segments of cognitive structure is referred to as *subsumption*. Since cognitive structure itself tends to be hierarchically organized with respect to level of abstraction, generality, and inclusiveness of ideas, the emergence of *new* propositional meanings most typically reflects a *subordinate* relationship of the new material to existing cognitive structure. This involves the subsumption of potentially meaningful propositions under more inclusive and general ideas in existing cognitive structure, and this in turn results in the hierarchical organization of cognitive structure. The efficiency of subsumptive learning can probably be attributed to the fact that once subsuming ideas are themselves adequately established in cognitive structure:

1. They have maximally specific and direct relevance for subsequent learning tasks.

2. They possess enough explanatory power to render otherwise arbitrary factual detail potentially meaningful.

3. They possess sufficient inherent stability to provide the firmest type of anchorage for newly learned detailed meanings.[5]

4. They organize related new facts around a common theme, thereby integrating the component elements of new knowledge, both with each other and with existing knowledge.

It is necessary to distinguish between two basically different kinds of subsumption that occur in the course of meaningful learning and retention. *Derivative* subsumption takes place when learning material is understood as a specific example of an established concept in cognitive structure or is supportive or illustrative of a previously learned general proposition. In either case the new material to be learned is directly and self-evidently derivable from or implicit in an already established and more inclusive concept or proposition in cognitive structure. Under these circumstances, the meaning of the derivative material emerges quickly and *relatively* effortlessly.

An example would be to recognize that scarlet, aqua, and lavender are names for colors, albeit less common than red, blue, or purple.

More typically, however, new subject matter is learned by a process of *correlative* subsumption. The new learning material in this case is an exten-

---

[5] The superior inherent stability of superordinate or inclusive ideas in cognitive structure is demonstrated by their greater resistance to forgetting over protracted time intervals, as shown by qualitative analysis of subject-matter forgetting.

sion, elaboration, modification, or qualification of previously learned propositions. It is incorporated by and interacts with relevant and more inclusive subsumers, but its meaning is not implicit in, and cannot be adequately represented by, these latter subsumers. For example, recognition that displaying the American flag is an act of patriotism would be a common example of correlative subsumption. And more recently we have come to regard conservation of fuel as an act of patriotism.

### Superordinate and Combinatorial Learning

New learning bears a _superordinate_ relationship to cognitive structure when one learns an inclusive new proposition under which several established ideas may be subsumed. Superordinate learning takes place in the course of inductive reasoning or when presented material is organized inductively or involves the synthesis of component ideas. The acquisition of superordinate meanings occurs more commonly in _conceptual_ than in propositional learning as, for example, when children learn that the familiar concepts of carrots, peas, beans, beets, and spinach may all be subsumed under the new term "vegetable."

The meaningful learning of new propositions that bear neither a subordinate nor a superordinate relationship to _particular_ relevant ideas in cognitive structure—those that cannot be subsumed under particular established propositions or cannot themselves subsume particular established ideas—gives rise to _combinatorial_ meanings. The learning of many new propositions, as well as concepts, leads to this category of meaning. They are potentially meaningful because they consist of sensible combinations of previously learned ideas that can be nonarbitrarily related to a _broad background_ of _generally_ relevant content in cognitive structure by virtue of their _general congruence_ with such content as a whole. Unlike subordinate or superordinate propositions, they are not relatable to _particular_ relevant ideas within cognitive structure. This availability of only generally and nonspecifically relevant content presumably makes combinatorial propositions less relatable or anchorable to previously acquired knowledge and hence, at least initially, more difficult to learn and remember than subordinate or superordinate propositions. This latter inference follows directly from the previously described conditions of meaningful learning and from evidence indicating that the availability of appropriately relevant content in cognitive structure is a crucial variable in meaningful learning.

Most of the _new_ generalizations that students learn in science, mathematics, social studies, and the humanities are examples of combinatorial learnings, for example, relationships between mass and energy, heat and volume, genic structure and variability, demand and price. Although acquired with greater difficulty than subordinate or superordinate propositions, they manifest, once adequately established, the same inherent stability as any inclusive or superordinate (subsuming) idea in cognitive structure. Further elaboration of these ideas typically results in derivative or correlative subsumption (analysis, differentiation) and less commonly in superordinate learning (generalization, synthesis).

Since propositions can presumably be learned and retained most readily when they are subsumable under specifically relevant ideas and since the hierarchical organization of cognitive structure is itself illustrative of the subsumptive principle, it seems reasonable to suggest that the subsumptive mode of meaningful learning be utilized wherever possible. We will elaborate on the importance of subsumption for school learning in later chapters.

Some school learning that is frequently labeled "rote learning" (and under many circumstances *is* purely rote) is actually intended to be a simple form of meaningful propositional learning—for example, certain aspects of the learning of addition and multiplication facts. It is true that some rote learning may be encouraged as a means of accelerating speed of response and calculation; but in most modern schools the multiplication table, for instance, is learned *after* a clear understanding of number ideas and relationships is acquired. Since this type of learning—relating pairs of numbers to their product—can be nonarbitrarily and substantively related to existing concepts of number relationships in cognitive structure, it is hardly analogous to the rote learning of paired associates of nonsense syllables. It is much more comparable to an actor's verbatim memorization of his lines after he acquires a meaningful grasp of the story or plot. Learning sets, therefore, need not be purely rote or purely meaningful. Learners may simultaneously or successively choose to learn both meaningfully and rotely.

### Discovery Learning

Propositional learning, as described earlier, is typical of the situation prevailing in reception learning when substantive propositions are *presented* to the learner, who is required only to learn and remember their meaning. It is important to realize, however, that propositional learning is also a major type of verbal problem solving or discovery learning. The main differance between propositional learning as found in reception-learning situations, on the one hand, and in discovery-learning situations, on the other, inheres in whether the principal content of what is to be learned is discovered by or is presented to the learner. In reception learning this content is presented in the form of a substantive or non-problem-setting proposition that the learner need only understand and remember. In discovery learning, on the other hand, the learner must first discover this content by generating propositions that represent either solutions to the problems set or successive steps in their solution.

Actually, the reception and discovery varieties of propositional learning are involved successively at different stages in the problem-solving process.

To begin with, problem-solving propositions are not generated anew. Their generation involves, rather, a transformation (restructuring, reorganization, synthesis, integration) of relevant and available *substrate* propositions (propositions undergoing transformation). Substrate propositions, in turn, are of two main types: (1) *problem-setting* propositions, defining the nature and conditions of the current problem situation; and (2) *background* propositions, consisting of relevant aspects of previously acquired knowledge (information, principles) that bear on the problem.

The meaningful learning of problem-setting propositions, in school and similar learning environments, typically involves only reception learning.[6] That is, the learner need only learn and remember what the propositions mean by relating them nonarbitrarily and substantively to his or her cognitive structure. However, unlike *substantive* reception learning situations that *end* with the learning and retention of the propositions in question, the meaningful internalization of *problem-setting* propositions sets in motion a discovery learning process. A new *problem-solving* proposition, embodying a potentially meaningful means-end relationship, is then generated through various transformation operations on the internalized problem-setting and background propositions. The final step in this meaningful learning sequence, namely, learning and retaining the meaning of the newly generated problem-solving proposition, is again a matter of meaningful reception learning. In fact, the only real discovery aspect of this entire sequence consists of the actual process of transforming the substrate propositions into a potentially meaningful problem-solving proposition.

Thus in meaningful discovery learning, as opposed to the more typical (substantive) instances of meaningful reception learning, the learner nonarbitrarily and substantively relates problem-setting propositions to his cognitive structure—not for the purpose of understanding and remembering what they mean *as an end in itself*, but for the purpose of transforming them (in conjunction with and with the benefit of previously acquired relevant background knowledge) into new problem-solving propositions that are potentially meaningful to him.

## Cognition versus Perception in Meaningful Verbal Learning

The distinction between perceptual and cognitive processes in meaningful verbal learning is particularly difficult to define because both kinds of processes involve interaction between verbal stimulus input and cognitive

---

[6] In more informal learning situations and in research laboratories (where discovery is genuinely autonomous) the learner formulates problem-setting propositions through a preliminary type of discovery learning followed by meaningful reception learning of the products of discovery.

structure. We both perceive verbal messages *and* cognitively learn their meaning as a result of interpreting them in the light of existing knowledge. The difference between the two processes is one of immediacy and complexity. Perception involves an *immediate* content of awareness *before* the intervention of such complex cognitive processes as are even involved in reception learning. Cognition involves such processes as relating the new material to relevant aspects of existing cognitive structure, ascertaining how the resulting new meaning can be reconciled with established knowledge, and recoding it in more familiar and idiosyncratic language.

Hence, if verbal meaning results when potentially meaningful verbal materials are related to and incorporated within existing cognitive structure (thereby generating new and differentiated cognitive content), and if this process of learning (acquiring) meanings is conceded to be *cognitive* in nature, when and how in this sequence of events does *perception* play a role in meaningful verbal learning? Whether a given intellectual operation involves an immediate content of awareness (perception), on the one hand, or more complex intellectual processes (cognition), on the other, depends to a great extent on the complexity of the learning task relative to the learner's cognitive maturity, and on whether the new material is first being learned or is *already* meaningful (Ausubel, 1965f). Learning that particular auditory symbols (words) represent particular objects is a *cognitive* problem to a child learning the meanings of words. Similarly, understanding functionally the distinctive syntactic properties of words in a sentence is also a cognitive problem to the same child. It presupposes both minimal mastery of the syntactic code and of the ability to apply such knowledge in syntactically decoding the sentence at hand. Later on, however, when both the spoken words and the syntax are *already* thoroughly mastered, the child is able to grasp their denotative meanings and syntactic functions on a purely *perceptual* basis. This sequence of events with regard to cognition and perception is then repeated as the child learns to *read* words and sentences in school. In other words, once the symbols, spoken or written, are encountered many times and become meaningful, they become immediately and effortlessly (that is, perceptually) apprehensible (meaningful) on subsequent encounters.

The situation is somewhat more complicated in understanding propositions expressed in sentence form. In this case the proposition itself is always a new learning task whose meaning remains to be acquired, even if the meanings and syntactic functions of the component words are already known and can thus be apprehended (understood) perceptually. The understanding of a sentence is thus a two-stage process involving perception and cognition successively. The first stage involves the perception of the potentially meaningful material, and the second stage involves relating perceived potential meanings to relevant existing propositions in cognitive structure. In the first stage the learner perceives what the message is, or what is to be learned. In the second stage the child understands what he or she perceives; that is, acquires the meaning. Thus perception precedes cognition. The product of the perceptual process is not propositional meaning itself; rather, it is the immediate content of awareness that follows from preliminary interpretation of the *sensory* input (visual or aural) furnished by the potentially meaningful learning task. This perceptual content of awareness is intermediate, both temporally and in terms of complexity of process, between primitive sensation and the actual emergence of meanings. It consists of awareness both of the separate meanings of the component words and of the syntactic relations among them, but stops short of apprehension of the meaning of the propositional message as a whole.

Hence, in order to understand a sentence, one must first be able to perceive the potential propositional meaning it communicates (understand the denotative meanings and the syntactical functions of its *component* words) and then be able to incorporate this perceived potential meaning within existing cognitive structure. The first step implies both adequate knowledge of vocabulary and a functional, if not a formal, grasp of syntax. The second step implies relating the perceived proposition to relevant anchoring ideas in cognitive structure.

Repeated encounters with, or exposure to, the *same* potentially meaningful propositions change the above-specified relationship between cognition and perception. During the first encounter the potentially meaningful message is first perceived, and the perceived content is then incorporated into cognitive structure to yield a corresponding meaning. But once the message becomes meaningful, perhaps as early as on the second presentation, the two processes, cognition and perception, become telescoped into one. That is, as a result of the initial emergence of meaning and the concomitant change in cognitive structure, the learner becomes sensitized to the potential meaning in the message on subsequent encounters with it. Its meaning having already been grasped, the message no longer presents a cognitive problem; it *immediately* (without the intervention of any cognitive processes) conveys actual rather than merely potential meaning when next perceived.[7] Hence, although the *acquisition* of meanings is a cognitive process, it is proper to refer to the cognitive content evoked by an *already* meaningful proposition as a product of perception rather than of learning.

To summarize, once the syntactical code and a basic vocabulary are mastered, the only cognitive aspects of understanding a sentence are associated with relating the ideas it contains to a relevant existing proposition in cognitive structure. The denotative meanings and syntactical functions of

---

[7] Partly because of this telescoping effect (the immediate or perpetual emergence of meaning), repetition, as will be pointed out later, has a particularly consolidating effect on learning and retention: The learner does not have to grasp meanings on subsequent trials and can concentrate solely on trying to remember them.

the component words are already meaningful and can therefore be apprehended perceptually. Even the grasping of the propositional meaning itself becomes a purely perceptual process after the message is repeated one or more times.

One of the difficulties we observe in children learning to read is that much of the lesson material used is essentially *meaningless* to the child. In consequence, component words do not form propositions that are meaningful to him and he cannot *comprehend* the phrases or sentences through his usual cognitive processes. In attempting to prepare reading materials that are "easy" for the beginner, we have produced essentially nonsense materials that negate the power of meaningful learning and associated perception as a tool for unraveling the printed code.

## The Significance of Meaningful Learning in Acquiring Knowledge

We have already indicated the importance of existing relevant knowledge in cognitive structure for the facilitation of meaningful learning. New knowledge is linked substantively and nonarbitrarily to existing concepts and propositions in cognitive structure. When, on the other hand, learning material is *arbitrarily* related to cognitive structure, no *direct* use can be made of established knowledge in internalizing the learning task. At the very best, already meaningful *components* of the learning task can be related to existing *unitary* ideas in cognitive structure (thereby facilitating indirectly the rote learning of the task as a whole); but this in no way either makes the newly internalized arbitrary associations *themselves* relatable as a whole to established content in cognitive structure or makes them usable in acquiring new knowledge. And because the human mind is not efficiently designed to interiorize and store arbitrary associations, this approach permits only limited amounts of material to be internalized and retained, and then only after much effortful repetition. We have already noted the problem this approach creates for children learning to read.

Also, the very fact that a new idea becomes *meaningful* after it is meaningfully learned presumably makes it intrinsically less vulnerable than internalized arbitrary associations are to interference from other arbitrary associations, and hence makes it more retainable. In addition, the maintenance of this same *nonarbitrary relatability* advantage (through the *anchorage* of the new meaning to its corresponding established idea during the storage period) further extends the span of retention.

Moreover, the *substantive* or *nonverbatim* nature of thus relating new material to, and incorporating it within, cognitive structure circumvents the drastic limitations imposed by the short item retention and time spans of rote memory on the processing and storing of information. Much more can be apprehended and retained if the learner is required only to assimilate the substance of ideas rather than the precise words used in expressing them.

The distinctively human capacity for meaningful verbal learning is dependent, of course, upon such cognitive capabilities as symbolic representation, abstraction, categorization, and generalization. It is the possession of these latter abilities that ultimately makes possible the original discovery and subsequent learning of generic concepts and propositions, and hence the later acquisition of the more detailed, relatable information and ideas comprising the bulk of knowledge.

Another means of. compensating for the information-processing and -storing limitations of the human brain has been described by Miller (1956). It is called "chunking" and is derived from information theory. "Chunking" refers to the process of rearranging the stimulus input successively into a smaller and more efficiently organized "sequence of chunks." Miller suggests that linguistic recoding is the most powerful device that human beings possess for extending the amount of information they can process and remember, and thus for acquiring large bodies of knowledge.

Miller and Selfridge argue against the importance of meaning in learning by applying this type of information-theory analysis to the problem of explaining why meaningless connected discourse is remembered better than strings of linguistically unconnected words and as well as meaningful prose. In this instance, chunking is accomplished by grouping a series of words that are sequentially dependent on each other into larger units (phrases), and then remembering the phrases rather than individual words. The recoding scheme under these circumstances is derived from the contextual constraints that characterize linguistically connected discourse and are both built into the structure of language and implicitly learned by all those who use it. These contextual constraints are defined in terms of "dependent probabilities," that is, the statistical dependency of the choice of a particular word upon the words that precede it, or the extent to which the choice of a given word is determined by the preceding words. As degree of contextual constraint or order of approximation to English increases in a given sequence of words, learning is progressively facilitated. This is so because the message "preserves the short range associations of the English language that are so familiar to us" (Miller & Selfridge, 1950, p. 183), and hence permits chunking or phrasing. "In fact, when short range contextual dependencies are preserved in nonsense material, the nonsense is as readily recalled as is meaningful material. From this it is argued that contextual dependencies extending over five or six words permit positive transfer, and that it is these familiar dependencies rather than the meaning that facilitates learning" (Miller & Selfridge, 1950, p. 184).

It is evident from careful analysis of these findings, however, that compensatory mechanisms such as chunking merely increase the learner's *rote* capacity for apprehending and retaining information. For example, although

Miller and Selfridge demonstrated unequivocally that nonsense material manifesting the same contextual constraints as potentially meaningful prose is recalled just as readily as meaningful prose, it is important to 'bear in mind that they demanded *verbatim* recall of the prose material. Such verbatim or *rote* learning of potentially meaningful connected discourse obviously precludes all of the information-processing and -storing advantages of meaningful verbal learning; it is superior (in the same way that the rote learning of connected *nonsense* material is also superior) to the rote learning of linguistically *unconnected* words solely because the sequential flow of the connected material conforms to the familiar contextual constraints of the language that make phrasing possible. True meaningful learning, on the other hand, presupposes *both* that the learning task is potentially meaningful and that the learner exhibit a meaningful learning set. Thus, irrespective of how much potential meaning may inhere in a given passage of connected discourse, the material is still rotely learned as long as the learner's set is to assimilate it verbatim. In short, because of their *rote learning set*, the subjects of this experiment never had a fair opportunity to demonstrate that *meaningful* learning of prose material is superior to the *rote* learning of linguistically connected nonsense.

Consequently, one cannot apply Miller's conclusion that "it is these familiar dependencies rather than the meaning that facilitates learning" to any situation other than the artificial one involved in verbatim or rote learning. The acquisition of large bodies of knowledge is simply impossible in the absence of meaningful learning. By making "chunking" possible, the connectedness of discourse undoubtedly facilitates learning and retention; but unless learning is meaningful, very little knowledge, organized or otherwise, can be assimilated.

It is gratifying to see a growing awareness on the part of psychologists who were trained in behaviorist theory that *meaning* is an important variable influencing both the rate of learning and the amount of learning. In a more recent paper by Simon (1974), Miller's (1956) concept of a memory "chunk" is reexamined, together with the methodological problems that have been encountered in traditional research on memory. Simon reports on a number of studies including data showing that size of a memory "chunk" is a function of the experimental procedure, the prior experience of the subjects, and the meaning of the material. For example, chess grand masters and masters can recall the position of chess pieces (20 to 25) almost without error after a 5- to 10-second exposure, whereas ordinary persons can only place half a dozen pieces correctly. However, the latter is true only when *actual* game positions are used. Grand masters and masters do no better than amateurs when pieces are placed *randomly* on the chessboard. These studies clearly demonstrate the importance of cognitive structure variables in learning and in "chunk" size whenever the learning task has the potential for meaningful learning. If verbatim recall were not required in these studies, the importance of individual variation in cognitive structure would bear even stronger relationship to success in learning.

### Assimilation Theory

Throughout this book we shall emphasize the process of meaningful learning, for this is the most important process to be achieved in school learning. Since these ideas were first described in *The Psychology of Meaningful Verbal Learning* (Ausubel, 1963) many persons interested in the application of learning theory to school learning have found the concepts to be useful. It is somewhat surprising, therefore, that recent books on theories of learning do not make mention of the theory presented in the 1963 book or the first edition of this book. In part, the explanation must lie in the "conceptual goggles" (to borrow a term from Kuhn, 1962) many psychologists in North America wear and the consequent inability to understand or to accept learning theories that are not rooted in earlier behavioristic concepts. Therefore, we are placing greater stress on the specific description of the *assimilation* theory of learning that forms the basis of this book.

Assimilation theory belongs to the family of cognitive learning theories that reject the behaviorist's dictum that one should not speculate on the internal mechanisms of the mind. Behaviorist psychology is *peripheralist* (cf. Strike, 1974) in nature, and only the stimuli applied and resultant *observable behavior* are legitimate components for study. In contrast, cognitive psychologies deal with processes such as concept formation and the nature of human understanding of structure and syntax in language. Behaviorist psychological theories had their origins primarily in research on animal behavior or with human studies where the learning tasks were largely *rote* in nature. Since animals do not form genuine concepts and since concept learning is at the very core of human understanding (cf. Toulmin, 1972), it should be evident that earlier behavioristic theories may have value for the interpretation of learning in infrahuman species, but much more must be considered in a theory of learning that can underpin educational practices in schools.

Up to this point we have tried to clarify the differences between meaningful learning and rote learning. The processes of subsumption, superordinate learning, and combinatorial learning are *internal cognitive processes* and hence not part of behaviorist theories of learning. We have emphasized that the acquisition of new information is highly dependent on the relevant ideas already in cognitive structure and that meaningful learning in humans occurs through an *interaction* of new information with relevant existing ideas in cognitive structure. The result of the interaction that takes place between the new material to be learned and the existing cognitive structure is an *assimilation* of old and new meanings to form a more highly differentiated cognitive structure. In subsequent sections we will elaborate further the processes involved in the assimilation of new meanings as meaningful learning proceeds. The ideas presented up to this point are summarized in Table 2.2.

TABLE 2.2    Forms of Meaningful Learning as Viewed in Assimilation Theory

1.  Subordinate Learning:                                    Established idea

    *A. Derivative*                                              *A*
        *subsumption*

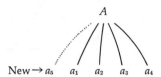

                   New → $a_5$   $a_1$   $a_2$   $a_3$   $a_4$

      In derivative subsumption, new information $a_5$ is linked to superordinate idea *A* and represents another case or extension of *A*. The criterial attributes of the concept *A* are not changed, but new examples are recognized as relevant.

    *B. Correlative*                                             Established idea
        *subsumption*                                           *X*

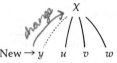

              New → $y$   $u$   $v$   $w$

      In correlative subsumption, new information $y$ is linked to idea *X*, but is an extension, modification, or qualification of *X*. The criterial attributes of the subsuming concept may be extended or modified with the new correlative subsumption.

2.  Superordinate Learning:                                  New idea $A → A$

                Established ideas   $a_1$   $a_2$   $a_3$

      In superordinate learning, established ideas $a_1$, $a_2$, and $a_3$ are recognized as more specific examples of new idea *A* and become linked to *A*. Superordinate idea *A* is defined by a new set of criterial attributes that encompass the subordinate ideas.

3.  Combinatorial Learning:                                  New idea $A → B - C - D$

                                 Established ideas

      In combinatorial learning new idea *A* is seen as related to existing ideas *B*, *C*, and *D* but is neither more inclusive nor more specific than ideas *B*, *C*, and *D*. In this case, new idea *A* is seen to have some criterial attributes in common with preexisting ideas.

4.  Assimilation Theory:

      New information is linked to *relevant, preexisting* aspects of cognitive structure and both the newly acquired information and the preexisting structure are modified in the process. All of the above forms of learning are examples of assimilation. Most meaningful learning is essentially the assimilation of new information.

## Acquiring Meanings: Informal Learning of Syntax

Linguistically speaking, grammar largely consists of the particular set of syntactic rules that are generally accepted by the users of a language for inflecting words and combining them into sentences. It is, in effect, a syntactic code consisting, among other things, of: (1) connecting words (prepositions, conjunctions); (2) designative words (articles, demonstrative adjectives); (3) inflections indicating number, gender, person, case, tense, mode, and mood; and (4) word-order rules adding relational meaning to connected discourse. From a psychological standpoint, however, syntactical rules primarily serve the *transactional* function of bringing verbally expressed ideas (images and concepts) into relationship with each other in a reliable fashion for the purpose of generating and understanding new ideas. Hence, when words in a group are appropriately inflected and combined according to the designated rules, the resulting sequence is not only grammatically correct, but also communicates the idea that the speaker or writer intends to convey. Typically, therefore, a given word in a sentence both conveys a distinctive denotative meaning and, by virtue of its particular syntactical function in the sentence (subject, object, verb), furnishes additional *semantic* information that contributes to the understanding of propositional meaning. As a matter of fact, one often needs to know the syntactical function of a word before its denotative meaning can be apprehended, as in the case of words of different meaning that sound alike, or of certain words that can serve as both nouns and verbs.

The principal psychological problems with respect to grammar, then, are to specify the cognitive processes involved in generating and understanding sentences, and to discover how children learn to identify and appropriately use different syntactic categories. Selected aspects of the first problem have already been discussed in some detail earlier in this chapter. The second problem will be considered briefly below.

Assimilation theory holds that the genic influence on language learning is primarily on the *capacity* with which children acquire concepts and propositions, and this can obviously be influenced substantially by experience. Some prominent linguists such as Chomsky (1957, 1972), Katz (1966), Lenneberg (1967), and McNeill (1970) maintain that genes control the development of *innate* grammar. Chomsky (1972, p. 9) asserts that: "They cannot know at birth which language he is to learn, but he must know that its *grammar must be of a predetermined form* that excludes many imaginable languages" (emphasis added). Chomsky (1959) tramples Skinner's arguments when the latter attempts (Skinner, 1957) to enter the linguist's turf and to use examples from grammar to support his (Skinner's) brand of behavioristic theory. We believe that Chomsky and his colleagues have only demolished what is now generally recognized as a straw man—that is, behavioristic explanations of human verbal learning. In terms of assimilation theory, all that a child requires to understand a new sentence is that it can be related nonarbitrarily and substantively to existing concepts and propositions in his or her cognitive structure, including concepts of syntactic structure and function acquired through repeated exposure to multiple examples in adult language.

Similarly, the child can generate an infinite variety of statements that represent meaningful verbal statements of concepts, propositions, or relationships. The nativistic propositions of Chomsky and others represent in our opinion an unparsimonious, preformationist view of human language behavior that is not required in the explanation of how individuals acquire, use, and comprehend the language. Syntactical functions are acquired like any concept in early childhood (through concept formation). And there is no paradox, as some linguists assert, in understanding how individuals can comprehend and generate an infinite number of sentences from a finite vocabulary if one simply applies the basic principles of assimilation theory.

The informal learning of syntax is a gradual and extended learning process that is comparable to other forms of meaningful learning and retention. In this case, however, the structure of the language itself is the learning task or object of learning. The grammar used by young children is obviously different from that of adults, but nevertheless manifests a distinctive structure of its own at each particular stage—a structure that is related in some "reduced" fashion to the adult structure from which it is derived (Brown & Fraser, 1963). A complete psychological analysis of the successive syntactic structures that evolve during early childhood would require specification of the cognitive processes involved, of the relevant variables influencing these processes, and of the role played by general characteristics of the prevailing stage of cognitive development. But since the informal acquisition of syntax is generally completed about two years before children enter school, detailed analysis along these lines is obviously beyond the scope of a textbook in educational psychology. In any case, the various stages in the acquisition of syntax are still not completely understood.[8] It may be noted, however, that functional mastery of the syntactic code of one's native language is acquired *inductively* through extensive practice in decoding the meaning of sentences. Hence, once the code is mastered at various levels of sophistication, there is really little further problem in applying such knowledge either to understanding (decoding) sentences or to generating (encoding) them.

[8] The interested reader may consult Bellugi (1971); Braine (1936a, 1936b); Brown & Fraser (1963); Chomsky (1957, 1972); Cocking (1972); Erwin & Miller (1963); McNeill (1970a, 1970b); Menyuk (1963, 1971); Nelson (1973). While most children acquire the major portion of the syntax of their native language before they are 5 years of age, it is important to realize that important syntactical development occurs during the elementary-school years (Laban, 1966; O'Donnell, 1967; Palermo & Molfese, 1972; Slobin, 1966).

Acquiring Meanings: Learning to Read[9]

Learning to read is essentially a matter of learning to *perceive* the potential meaning in *written* messages and then relating the perceived potential meaning to cognitive structure so as to comprehend it. The beginning reader, who is already able to perceive the potential meaning in *spoken* messages, must now acquire the same ability in relation to written messages. Because the denotative meanings and syntactic functions of the component words the reader will encounter are *already* known in their corresponding spoken forms, learning to read obviously constitutes a less significant cognitive accomplishment than the original learning of the spoken language. In other words, beginning readers are not really learning a *completely new* symbolic code, but rather a written equivalent of a familiar spoken code whose basic vocabulary and syntax they have already mastered.

The most salient psychological characteristic of learning to read, therefore, is the dependence of the learning process on the previously acquired mastery of the spoken language, and on the use of this mastery as a medium for perceiving the potential meaning in written messages. In fact, children learn to read their native language by reconstructing written into spoken messages. They try to establish representational equivalence between new written words and their already meaningful spoken counterparts. In view of this important mediating function of the spoken language in learning to decipher the meaning of written messages, it is theoretically indefensible to teach reading by seeking to establish *direct* equivalences between the new visual symbols and their significates (objects or pictures). The common elementary-school practice of showing pictures and printed words of a specific cat, house, or chair and using these words to represent a more generic concept often serves as a source of confusion to a child for whom other significates better represent his verbally labeled concept. Thus the printed concept label with the teacher-presented significates can lead to substantial cognitive dissonance.

Learning to reconstruct written into spoken messages involves at least two major component steps. First, there is the problem of converting written words into spoken words. This problem is rendered less difficult, however, by the alphabetic basis of structuring most written languages. Thus, written words are not just configurations of visual symbols that *arbitrarily* represent their auditory counterparts. Rather, there is a more or less lawful relationship between the combination of distinguishable sounds (phonemes)

[9] Portions of this section have been excerpted, with permission, from Ausubel's article, "Cognitive Structure: Learning to Read," in *Education*, 1967, *87*, 544–548. Copyright 1967 by The Bobbs-Merrill Company, Inc., Indianapolis, Indiana. See also Chall (1967) and Gibson and Levin (1975).

constituting the spoken word and the analogous combination of letters (graphemes) constituting the corresponding written word. The beginning reader must, therefore, learn how to convert graphemes and combinations of graphemes into their phonemic equivalents, and then learn how to coalesce several graphemic combinations and reconstruct them into spoken words. In this latter process of word recognition he is aided by such cues as knowledge of common graphemic combinations (prefixes and suffixes) and awareness of the wider context in which the written message is presented.

The second step in reconstructing the wirtten message is learning how to combine and convert groups of written words into spoken phrases and sentences. Here knowledge of the syntactic code of the spoken language can be utilized in perceiving the potential meaning of the written message. The beginning reader, in other words, is unable to apprehend directly the syntactic functions of the words in the written message. In order to perceive its potential propositional meaning, therefore, the beginner reconstructs it into a spoken message, relying on his or her intuitive knowledge of the syntax of the spoken language.

However, once a certain facility in reading is acquired, it seems reasonable to suppose that the spoken language no longer plays a mediating role in the perception of potential meaning from written messages. It is implausible to suppose, therefore, that even in skilled silent reading, "the reader does not respond solely to visual symbols . . . [but] also to some sort of reconstruction of a spoken message which he derives from the written message" (Carroll, 1964, p. 338). The skilled reader, rather, perceives *directly* both the denotative meanings of words in a sentence and their syntactic functions without any prior need for reconstructing words or phrases into their spoken counterparts; once the reconstructive process is dispensed with, these meanings emerge as an immediate (perceptual) content of awareness. Thus, *current* skilled reading capability becomes functionally autonomous of its previous association with the spoken language. It goes without saying, however, that the directly perceived denotative and syntactic meanings first have to be related to relevant ideas in cognitive structure before they yield actual propositional meaning.

We can compare the acquisition of the ability to perceive denotative and syntactic meanings directly from written messages to the ability, eventually acquired by experienced students of a foreign language, to speak and understand that language without first translating it into their native tongue. In both instances, dependence on the mediating function of an already meaningful code is restricted to the *learning* phase of the new language capability. In short, a cognitive process characterizing the acquisition of a new ability does not necessarily apply to the later exercise of that ability.

Actually, although native readers of a language *typically* go through the stage of reconstructing written into spoken messages, this reconstructive stage is not absolutely necessary in learning to read. Deaf mutes, for example, can learn to read without being able to use or understand the spoken language. One can also learn to read a second language—without first learning to speak or understand it—simply by converting foreign-language written words and phrases into their native-language equivalents. This does not mean, of course, that one should not take advantage of the normal child's mastery of the spoken language in teaching him to read his native tongue. By the same token, once he already knows how to read, there is no point in insisting that he is *currently* dependent on the mediating function of the spoken language.

### Phonetic versus Wholistic Methods of Teaching Reading

In terms of the foregoing analysis of the cognitive processes involved in learning to read, the so-called phonetic or phonic method of teaching reading (that is, prior emphasis on letter recognition and grapheme–phoneme correspondences before actual reading practice) makes more psychological sense than teaching children to recognize words as wholes from the outset (the "look–say" method). The phonetic approach makes the problem of word recognition less arbitrary by giving the child a lawful code with which to reconstruct currently meaningless but potentially meaningful written words into their already meaningful spoken equivalents. Word recognition thus becomes more a matter of rational problem solving than of random guessing; that is, it becomes a process of lawfully decoding the unknown written word by applying existing knowledge of grapheme–phoneme correspondences with the aid of such additional cues as context. The "look–say" method, on the other hand, renders written English, based for the most part on regular and learnable correspondences between graphemes and phonemes, into a pictorial, nonalphabetic written language like Chinese. In short, the "look–say" method corresponds most closely to the rote end of our learning continuum, whereas the use of graphemes and phonemes employs representational meaningful learning. It is true, of course, that children who learn to read by the "look–say" method tend spontaneously to develop some impressions about grapheme–phoneme correspondence, and to use these impressions in deciphering unfamiliar words. But this haphazard, incidental, and unguided discovery learning of grapheme–phoneme correspondence can hardly be considered a defensible instructional procedure when such knowledge can be transmitted much more efficiently on a systematic, suitably programmed, and guided reception basis.

The learning of grapheme–phoneme correspondence does not imply that pupils must learn a set of formal rules. This would hardly be practicable at the age of initial reading instruction. Rather, it means providing guided practice in responding phonically to the more frequently encountered letter combinations in words so that the child acquires an intuitive grasp of grapheme–phoneme correspondence. He thus eventually becomes capable of responding automatically with the correct phonemic equivalents of the different graphemes and graphemic combinations.

Wholistic methods of teaching reading are sometimes defended on the grounds that mature readers perceive whole words and even phrases at a time rather than individual letters or syllables. This, of course, is true, but it is totally irrelevant to the point at issue. What applies to skilled readers does not necessarily apply to pupils who are first learning to read. The techniques employed by an expert in performing a complex skill can hardly be recommended as suitable practice exercises for the novice. The beginning student of Morse code, for example, thinks in terms of letter units, not in terms of larger word and phrase units characterizing the transmitting and receiving operations of the skilled telegraphist.

Finally, it is important to bear in mind that phonetic and wholistic approaches need not be mutually exclusive procedures, either in theory or in practice. Advocates of the phonetic method ordinarily teach whole-word recognition of some of the more common words as a means of making possible earlier reading of simple meaningful text, and thereby of enhancing the beginning reader's interest, self-confidence, and motivation; and "look–say" advocates typically introduce varying degrees of phonic analysis *after* their pupils acquire some reading fluency. The difference between the two schools of thought today is largely one of timing and relative emphasis. Nevertheless, this difference is still important both theoretically and practically; and although definitive empirical evidence is still lacking, the arguments of the phonetic school, in our opinion, rest on theoretically more tenable ground.


### Acquiring Meanings: Second-Language Learning

"Learning a foreign language consists fundamentally in the acquisition of an *additional set of symbols* for old, familiar meanings" according to Bernard. Just as we learn to read by establishing representational equivalence between new written symbols and familiar, already meaningful spoken symbols, and by reconstructing written into spoken messages, so do we learn a new language by establishing representational equivalence between new foreign-language symbols (both spoken and written) and their already meaningful native-language counterparts, and by reconstructing foreign-language into native-language messages. It is evident, therefore, that the second-language learner is in a much different psychological position from that of the native-language learner. In the first place, he has already mastered the basic vocabulary and the syntactic code of one language. Second, he is generally able to read this latter language. Moreover, he is capable of comprehending and applying formally stated syntactical propositions. Thus "the learner . . . approaches the second language with the mechanism of a first language already fixed in his thought and speech, and he is by no means expected to discard or even neglect his native tongue" (Bernard, 1951, p. 89).

## The Audiolingual Approach

The great popularity of audiolingual methods in second-language learning today is more than just an overreaction to previous pedogogic techniques that concentrated almost exclusively on reading, translation, and composition skills and neglected oral comprehension and speaking ability. In part, it is also a reflection of the widespread cultural belief that, because children learn language the "natural" (audiolingual) way and are apparently much more successful in this enterprise than are older learners who are subjected to more formal reading and grammatical instructional procedures, the audiolingual approach must obviously be the most effective method of acquiring new languages and should be used by older learners in second-language learning.

This line of argument, in our opinion, is vulnerable on two counts. In the first place, on either research or theoretical grounds, it is difficult to substantiate the thesis that children, in learning a native or second language, are, in fact, superior to adolescents and adults in learning second languages. Second, even if this were the case, there would still be no good reason for believing that methods that yield satisfactory results with children must necessarily be appropriate for adults. These latter methods are used, after all, not because they are demonstrably more efficacious under *all* conditions, but because children's cognitive immaturity and lack of certain intellectual skills preclude many approaches that are feasible for older age groups.

Naturalness is a slippery argument because what is natural for one age group is not necessarily natural for another. The point about naturalness would be tenable only if the respective cognitive equipment of second-language and native-language learners were comparable. Since this is not the case, however, what is natural for one learner is quite unnatural for the other. Because of the aforementioned highly significant changes in cognitive readiness that take place as a result of the learner's mastery of his native language, certain features of the audiolingual approach are psychologically incompatible with effective learning processes in adults. These features include: (1) "direct" learning of second-language meanings and syntactical functions, that is, avoidance of the mediational role of the native language; (2) rote learning of phrases; (3) inductive rather than deductible learning of grammatical generalizations; (4) extensive presentation of the spoken

form of the language before the written form; and (5) insistence on exposing the beginner to the "natural-speed rendition" of the spoken language
(Ausubel, 1964a).

### Avoidance of the Native Language

The audiolingual method seeks in all possible ways to avoid the mediating role of the native language in second-language learning. It attempts
to accomplish this objective through the rote learning of phrases and
through the inductive learning of syntactic rules; through direct association
of second-language words and phrases with objects, pictures, and situations
rather than with native-language words; by giving second-language instruction in the target language itself; and by proscribing translation practice.

Actually, it is both unrealistic and inefficient for the learner to try to
circumvent the mediating role of his native language when learning a second language. In the first place, after early childhood, even the

> greater part of our own language is learned . . . not by the direct method,
> i.e., not by the direct association of words and things, but *indirectly* through
> old, known symbols, e.g., by way of synonyms, antonyms, definition, or
> context in speech or reading matter. . . . Hence it is clear that . . . the direct
> association of . . . [new] symbols with their respective objects is, of neces-
> sity, totally inadequate for the learning of a new language. . . . Indeed . . .
> even where the possibility is offered for a direct association between the
> new symbol and the object, the old symbols at first always involuntarily
> intervene (Bernard, 1951, pp. 91–92).

In addition, it is important to recognize that we learn the new syntactic
code by using native-language syntax as a model and then noting similarities and differences between the two codes. This type of analysis is also
best conducted in the native language. Thus, numerous aspects of first-
language knowledge—the meanings of most concepts, the understanding
of syntactical categories and functions, facility in using many structural
patterns that are nearly identical in the two languages—are directly transferable to second-language learning. It would, therefore, be not only impracticable but also impossible not to make use of this knowledge in
acquiring the second language.

Avoidance of the mediating function of the student's native language
in second-language learning is customarily justified on two grounds. First,
it is argued that children do not learn their native language through the
mediation of another language. This argument, however, is completely beside the point because the native-language learner does not possess another
set of meaningful symbols and hence could not avail himself of their mediating influence even if he wanted to. When such a set is available, however,
it is unrealistic not to make use of it, irrespective of whether the new task
is learning to read or learning a second language. Second, it is pointed out

that the truly bilingual individual thinks directly in the second language rather than translating from his native tongue. It must be realized, however, that although this latter state of affairs is generally true, it is a reflection of a *terminal* state of second-language proficiency and does not describe the learning situation when the bilingual individual is a beginning student.

> What is usually lost sight of by those who argue for the direct method and for immediate, direct reading is that "to grasp the thought directly from the written page without the intervention of the mother tongue" presents already an *advanced stage* of achievement and that the fundamental thing is *first to learn the meaning* of the numerous individual words or phrases that constitute the page. There is the obvious confusion here of the means with the end: of the immediate with the ultimate objective. True, we want our students to read the foreign language directly and fluently with the least possible interference from the mother tongue. But this is, or ought to be, the *final result*, the goal and aim of our teaching and not necessarily the means of achieving it. How can we expect learners to read a foreign language directly and fluently when this is the *very thing* we expect them to acquire *as a result* of our teaching? (Bernard, 1951, p. 95)

### Rote Learning of Phrases

Because young children are explicitly unaware of syntactic functions and categories, it is often assumed that their language capability consists of *rote verbal habits*. Actually, however, the ability to understand and generate sentences implies, even in children, a meaningful learning process in which there is at least some implicit awareness of the denotative and syntactical contributions of component words to the total meaning of the sentence. The latter is clearly recognized in British "infant" schools, where reading and writing are taught in the context of special activities pursued by the student. In older learners this awareness, particularly in second-language learning, exists on a much more explicit and abstract basis, and hence meaningful learning is an even more important consideration in teaching them than in teaching children.

The audiolingual approach, however, tends to assume that second-language learning, both in children and adults, is largely a process of rote verbal learning. Both in "pattern practice" drills and memorized dialogue practice[10] there is either no awareness of phrase meaning whatsoever or, at the very best, awareness of *total* phrase meaning. Thus the learner

---

[10] Pattern practice drills consist of practice in repeating phrases illustrative of a particular grammatical construction and in making simple substitutions and transformations in such phrases that further exemplify the same construction with only slight changes in meaning. In memorized dialogue practice, students rotely learn and practice the phrases they use in carrying on a conversation.

understands neither the syntactic functions of the component words nor the denotative and syntactical contributions of the *individual* words to the total meaning of the phrase. A purely arbitrary (rote) rather than lawful or meaningful relationship prevails between phrase meaning and component elements of the phrase.

Under these circumstances, it is hardly surprising that particular grammatical patterns can be emitted perfectly in a familiar and structurally limited context, or that simple substitutions, transformations, and elaborations can be made, but that new words in a wider, unfamiliar context cannot be fitted into the learned pattern, or that the same words and syntactical categories cannot be recombined in different patterns to express different ideas. In contrast, the principal transferable objective that truly *meaningful* pattern practice should aim to achieve is precise knowledge of the syntactical function of each word and of its semantic contribution to total phrase meaning. In manifesting this knowledge, the learner is able: (1) to construct a structurally comparable phrase expressive of an entirely different idea, in which each component word bears a syntactical relationship to total phrase meaning that is analogous to the set of relationships prevailing between component words and total phrase meaning in the learned model phrase; and (2) to recombine familiar words and known syntactic functions in the learning of new grammatical patterns.

The remedy, therefore, is not to eliminate pattern practice drills but to make them more meaningful. Second-language learning obviously requires overlearning of the basic and characteristic structural patterns of the language. But unless the learner appreciates the precise relationship between the verbal manipulations he practices and the changes in meaning that he induces by such manipulation, the practice is not very transferable.

### Inductive Learning of Grammatical Rules

Pattern practice drills seek to duplicate in second-language learning the process whereby children attain syntactical mastery of their native language. What is primarily striven for is a functional, intuitive grasp of syntax after inducing much manipulative experience with the major structural patterns of the language. Grammatical generalizations are provided, if at all, only after the principles in question are acquired on an inductive, intuitive basis and are rendered virtually automatic.

Young children, of course, *have* to learn syntactical rules through an inductive process of discovering various linguistic regularities in the multiform language patterns to which they are repetitively exposed. Grammatical generalizations would make absolutely no sense whatsoever to them, since they are manifestly incapable of understanding complex relationships between abstractions. This type of discovery learning, however, is exceedingly wasteful and unnecessary when we deal with older learners who are perfectly capable of comprehending abstract syntactic propositions. It takes a long time to discover grammatical rules autonomously and inductively; and until the correct discovery is made, practice is not transferable. Furthermore, as long as these rules are known only intuitively and implicitly, their transferability to comparable situations is restricted to what is analogically quite similar and obvious.

Deductive use of grammatical generalizations, on the other hand, is decidedly more efficient in second-language learning. No time is wasted in discovery, and both the generalization and the experience of applying it to appropriate exemplars are transferable from the very beginning of practice. As a precisely, explicitly, and abstractly stated proposition, a grammatical generalization also has wider transferability to new situations.

### Prior Presentation of Materials in Spoken Form

A cardinal principal of the audiolingual approach is that instructional materials should be presented in their spoken form before they are presented in their written form and that listening and speaking skills should be acquired before reading and writing skills.

The major rationale offered for this order of skill acquisition is that it is the "natural" order in which children learn their native language. But because a child *has* to learn how to speak and understand his native tongue before he can read it, it does not necessarily follow that once he knows how to read, he has to observe the same sequence of events in learning a second language. Once any new skill such as reading is learned, it can obviously be used as a tool in acquiring new knowledge. It is unnatural to expect that after an individual becomes literate, he will learn in the same way as when he was illiterate.

A second reason for advocating this order of learning is the belief that it can lead to "direct reading" in the second language. It is maintained that if various items of second-language material can be understood and spoken, they can also be read without any explicit practice in reading as such. This would have the additional presumed advantage of avoiding any tendency to translate the material as it was being read. The available research evidence (Agard & Dunkel, 1948) indicates, however, that audiolingual and reading skills are separate, independently developed capabilities. Although practice in one is partly transferable to the other, especially at higher levels of proficiency, considerable specific training in each skill is required for the acquisition of competence.[11]

[11] Evidence from the same investigation indicates that the audiolingual approach also fails to accomplish its other principal objective, namely, to enable students to acquire higher levels of speaking and oral comprehension skills than are customarily acquired in conventional foreign-language courses. In a more recent and better-controlled study, however, Scherer and Wertheimer (1964) found that the audiolingual method does enhance ability to speak and think in German, although traditionally trained students are superior in writing skills and in translating from German into English. No lasting differences were found in reading and listening skills or in ability to translate from English into German.

Still a third reason for advocating prior presentation of materials in spoken form is the possibility that the written form of the second language will generate phonological interference from the native language because the same graphemes often have different phonemic values. On the other hand, it can be plausibly argued that the individual sooner or later has to learn to associate graphemes in the second language with their phonemic equivalents and that he may as well confront this first-language interference and learn to overcome it from the very beginning.[12]

Turning now to the other side of the argument, two defensible reasons can be advanced for presenting written and spoken materials in the second language both alternately and concomitantly. First, in our culture, adolescents and adults are habituated to learning most new ideas and subject-matter content by reading rather than by listening. Thus a pure audiolingual approach deprives the older learner of his principal learning tool and of the instructional medium in which he feels most comfortable and confident. This is particularly unfortunate during the early phases of instruction when learning stresses tend to be greatest.

Second, prior familiarization with and simultaneous exposure to the written form of the material can serve as helpful props in the early stages of acquiring oral comprehension skills. Because of unfamiliarity with new sounds, with atypical sequences of sounds, and with the characteristic word order and syntactical patterns of the second language, it is very difficult for the beginner to distinguish individual words, inflectional forms, and groups of words from listening alone. Hence, he often fails not only to grasp the meaning of the spoken material, but also to appreciate its syntactical structure well enough for purposes of transfer. Simultaneous reading can furnish the necessary cues for meaning and grasp of syntactic structure while listening skills are being developed. As oral comprehension increases, particular passages can be omitted in the written lesson and eventually the written material will not be needed at all.

### "Natural-Speed Rendition" of the Spoken Language

In the audiolingual approach, beginners are typically exposed to the "natural rendition" of the spoken language—presumably to accustom them to the "natural rhythm" of the language. It is pointed out that children eventually learn to understand their native tongue under comparable circumstances. In terms of gain per unit of learning time; however, it should be self-evident that practice in listening improves oral comprehension ability primarily insofar as what is heard is also understood. Thus, if the sam-

---

[12] The only direct evidence bearing on this issue is a study by Pyper (1964) indicating that oral prepractice with various phonemic sequences in beginning Spanish, prior to the presentation of written materials, does *not* significantly enhance initial pronunciation ability.

ple of speech presented is too rapid for the learner to understand, it does little to enhance his or her ability to comprehend the spoken language. Furthermore, even if the learner is able to understand the material in a general way, he or she may still not be able to distinguish the major structural patterns well enough to transfer them to speaking and other listening situations.

Hence, since learning to comprehend the spoken language is a very gradual process, it should undoubtedly be assisted in the beginning by means of a slower rate of speech that is progressively accelerated as oral comprehension improves. Artificial simplification is always justifiable during the early stages of any learning process. When any given passage of material is presented, the beginner can, of course, be exposed to a sloweddown version and then to a normal-speed rendition.

## Language and Cognitive Functioning

Although preverbal cognitive functioning does exist and characterizes the behavior and thought of infrahuman organisms and of young children, it plays a relatively minor role in school learning.[13] For all practical purposes, the acquisition of subject-matter knowledge depends on verbal and other forms of symbolic learning. In fact, it is largely because of language and symbolization that most complex forms of cognitive functioning become possible.

> Translation of experience into symbolic form, with its attendant means of achieving remote reference, transformation, and combination, opens up realms of intellectual possibility that are orders of magnitude beyond the most powerful image-forming system. . . . Once the child has succeeded in internalizing language as a cognitive instrument, it becomes possible for him to represent and systematically transform the regularities of experience with greater power and flexibility than before (Bruner, 1964a, pp. 13–14).

Evidence from various sources indicates that somewhere between the fourth and fifth years of life, language assumes a dominant role in cogni-

[13] According to Piaget (1951, 1952) the sensorimotor stage of representation (those early images "which serve as symbols before the advent of language") are derivatives of internalized, deferred imitation, and are qualitatively discontinuous from true verbal signs. Unlike mediational theory of meaning, once verbal symbolization arises, Piaget ceases to regard images as having a symbolic function. He considers verbal symbols as signifiers representing objects or events rather than as the organismic bases of meaning. "Piaget regards the internalized action as a symbol signifying the object or event it represents, and not, as Osgood asserts (Osgood, Suci, & Tannenbaum, 1957), as the *meaning* of the symbol" (Ausubel, 1965). "Piaget's action theory of thought, however, does incongruously have much in common with neobehavioristic formulations of relational thought (Ausubel, 1965). See Chapter 16.

tive functioning. Luria (1959) has shown that the "internalization" of speech at this age (that is, the ability of the child to manifest speech on a nonvocal and noncommunicative basis) coincides with the emergence of language as the principal directive factor in instigating, controlling, and organizing behavior. The same shift from stimulus to verbal-cognitive control of behavior is exhibited in discrimination learning (Kendler, 1963) and in the ability to transpose a learned relationship to an analogous pair of stimuli (Alberts & Ehrenfreund, 1951; Kuenne, 1946). For example, after the "verbal" child learns to choose the larger member of a pair of two blocks, he can transfer this learned relationship to similar pairs of *any* absolute size. Experimental findings in discrimination learning (Kendler & Kendler, 1961; Spiker, 1963), transposition learning (Spiker & Terrell, 1955) and concept formation (Lacey, 1961; Weir & Stevenson, 1959) suggest that the superiority of verbal learning to preverbal cognitive functioning is attributable to the fact that symbolic learnings can be identified, transformed, and differentially responded to much more efficiently than can the stimuli or situations represented by the symbols.[14] Finally, by this age, the child has also mastered the syntax of language sufficiently well to understand and generate fairly complex propositional statements.

Parallel analysis of the development of language and thought (Inhelder & Piaget, 1958; Vygotsky, 1962) also suggests that growth in logical thinking is, in large measure, tied to growth in language capability. On purely theoretical grounds, it would be difficult indeed to deny some degree of causal relationship between (1) such linguistic developments as symbolical representation, the mastery of syntax, the internalization of language, and the acquisition of more abstract and relational terms, and (2) such developments in cognitive functioning as the internalization of logical operations, emergence of the ability to understand and manipulate relationships between abstractions without the benefit of current or recent concrete-empirical experience, and attainment of the capacity to think in terms of hypothetical relations between variables (see Chapter 6).

Much of the failure to appreciate the important facilitative role of language in cognitive functioning is, of course, a reflection of the view popularized by the "progressive education" movement that verbal learning necessarily consists of rotely memorized glib verbalisms. In large part, however, it also *reflects confusion between the labeling and process functions of language*. Hendrix, for example, argues that "in the natural order of events, the abstraction comes first and *then* a name for it is invented"

---

[14] As we shall see later (Chapters 5 and 15) in discussing the relevant research, verbalization is an important factor in transferring learned principles to new problem-solving situations, even those of a motor or mechanical nature. These findings challenge the widely accepted tenet of "progressive education" that verbal learning is necessarily rote in character and that only nonrepresentational experience is transferable from one problem-solving situation to another.

(Hendrix, 1950, p. 335). According to her, the understanding and discovery of ideas is completely a "subverbal, internal process"; the *entire* substance of an idea purportedly inheres in subverbal insight. Language only enters the picture because of the need to attach a symbol or label to the emerging subverbal insight so that it can be recorded, verified, classified, and communicated to others. Verbalization, she asserts further (1947), is not only unnecessary for the generation and transfer of ideas and understanding, but is also positively harmful when used for *these* purposes. "The resulting problem then becomes one of how to plan and execute teaching so that language can be used for its necessary *secondary* (labeling) functions without damage to the dynamic quality of the learning itself" (Hendrix, 1961, p. 292).

How plausible are these propositions? Let us grant at the outset that a subverbal type of insight exists and that this type of insight is displayed by rats, monkeys, and chimpanzees in experimental learning situations, and by household pets, saddle horses, barnyard animals, wild beasts, children, and adults in a wide variety of everyday problem-solving situations. But is it because of *this* type of insight that human beings have created cultures and are able to discover and assimilate knowledge in such fields as physics, chemistry, biology, mathematics, and philosophy quite beyond anything yet approached by horses, chickens, or apes? Or is it because of the qualitatively superior transfer power of *verbal* or symbolic generalization?

What Hendrix is referring to, of course, is simply the labeling or naming function of language in thought. The choice of a particular arbitrary symbol to represent a *new* abstraction obviously comes *after* the process of abstraction and is not organically related to it. But this is not the *only* role of language in the abstraction process, nor is it the *first* time that it is used in this process. Verbalization does more than verbally gild the lily of subverbal insight; it does more than just attach a symbolic handle to an idea so that one can record, verify, classify, and communicate it more readily. It constitutes, rather, an *integral* part of the very process of acquiring new abstract ideas and influences both the nature and the product of the cognitive processes involved in generating new concepts and abstract propositions. One of the important influences of language on concept development has been carefully studied by Whorf, particularly in contrasting native American Indian languages with European or English languages. Whorf (1956, p. 158) asserts: "concepts of 'time' and 'matter' are not given in substantially the same form by experience to all men but depend upon the nature of the language or languages through the use of which they have been developed."

The actual act of giving an arbitrary name to a newly generated abstraction is not, of course, an integral part of the abstraction process itself. At this point language *does* have merely a *labeling* function. But language is also involved in the *process* aspects of abstraction and thought in at least two other ways. First, the fact that abstractions have names—that their meanings can be represented by words—plays a very important role in the process of generating new concepts from their constituent abstractions. Looking backward, for example, to the abstraction process preceding the labeling of a given newly generated concept, it is evident that this process itself could never have taken place were it not for the representational power of words. In the abstracting, categorizing, differentiating, and generalizing aspects of combining and transforming known concepts into new abstractions, generic ideas are simply not sufficiently *manipulable* themselves to be handled in these designated ways. It is only because complex concept meanings can be represented by single words that these combinatorial and transformational operations become possible. Thus, by exploiting the unique manipulability of representational symbols, it is possible to generate new concepts and propositions that transcend by far—in inclusiveness, generality, clarity, and precision—the level of abstraction that could be achieved if concepts were unnamed. The naming of ideas is therefore a significant *prerequisite* for their later *use* in conceptualization and other forms of thinking, except, of course, in the case of generating new concepts and propositions at a very low level of abstraction.

Second, language plays an important role in verbalizing, or encoding into sentences, the new intuitive or subverbal product (concept or proposition) that emerges from the transformational operations involved in thinking. Verbalizing subverbal ideas (*expressing* them verbally in propositional form as opposed to the later act of *naming* them) is a refining process that results in their becoming much clearer, more explicit, more precise, and more sharply delineated. It is therefore a serious mistake to believe that the *entire* substance of an idea, as well as *all* of its transfer power, inheres in its subverbal form, as Hendrix asserts (1950). The old philosophical notion that verbalization "merely mirrors thought" or "clothes it in outer garments" is charmingly poetic but has little psychological utility or explanatory value today. By means of its significant refining functions, verbalization adds a great deal both to the meaning and transferability of the products of thought and thus must be considered an integral part of the process of thinking. "Piaget differentiates within cognition two aspects: *operative*, acting on and transforming a reality state, the basis of intelligent understanding; and *figurative*, referring to the static configuration. While symbolic functioning according to Piaget is indissociable from human cognition, a particular symbolic product (e.g., image, language) can be considered [only] a supportive but not a constitutive element of operality" (Furth, 1967).

In conclusion, it can be stated that language contributes in three important ways to concept formation and problem solving. First, the representational properties of words facilitate the transformational processes involved in thought. Second, verbalization of the emerging subverbal products of these operations, prior to naming them, refines and enhances their meanings and thereby increases their transfer power. In a larger sense, however, acquisition of language also enables developing human beings to acquire through reception learning, and to use in discovery learning, a vast repertoire of concepts and principles they could never discover by themselves in their own lifetimes. This is the case because the human capacity for representational symbolism and verbalization make possible both the *original* generation (discovery) of ideas at a uniquely high level of abstraction, generality, and precision, and the cumulation and transmission of these ideas during the course of cultural history. The scope and complexity of the ideas acquired through reception learning make possible and foster, in turn, a level of individual cognitive development that would be utterly inconceivable in the absence of language. Last, the kinds of concepts individuals learn in a particular culture are profoundly influenced, as Whorf has shown, by the vocabulary and structure ·of the language to which they are exposed in that culture. We have just shown that Piaget seriously denigrates the role of language in symbolic thought by denying that it plays a process (operative) role in the transformative and combinatorial aspects of thinking. The very emergence of complex logical operations ("internalizing *actions*," according to Piaget) would also be inconceivable in the absence of language. Thus preoperational (prelinguistic) thought is qualitatively discontinuous with operational (linguistic) thought (Ausubel, 1968a, 1968b).

# 3

# THE ACQUISITION AND USE OF CONCEPTS

Concepts constitute an important aspect of assimilation theory because comprehension and meaningful problem solving largely depend on the availability in the learner's cognitive structure of both superordinate concepts (in subsumptive concept acquisition) and subordinate concepts (in superordinate concept acquisition). It is also self-evident: (1) that human beings interpert "raw" perceptual experience in terms of particular concepts in their cognitive structures, and (2) that concepts constitute the building blocks both for the meaningful reception learning of propositions and for the generation of meaningful problem-solving propositions.

Concepts themselves consist of the abstracted criterial attributes that are common to a given category of objects, events, or phenomena, despite diversity along dimensions other than those characterizing the criterial attributes shared by all members of the category.

Because concepts have names, just like particular objects or events, they can be manipulated, understood, and transferred more readily than unnamed concepts. These concept names are acquired through meaningful representational learning after concept meanings are acquired. This latter process depends, of course, on the existence of a meaningful learning set and on relating the potentially meaningful criterial attributes to relevant ideas in the learner's cognitive structure in a nonarbitrary, substantive fashion.

During the preschool and early elementary-school years, concepts are primarily acquired by a process of meaningful, hypothesis-oriented concept formation. Most simple, perceptibly grounded, and everyday (primary) concepts are acquired by relating their discovered criterial attributes to cognitive structure after they are first related to the many particular exemplars from which they are derived. During the later elementary-school years, concrete-empirical props (tangible, perceptible, or verbal examples of the attributes) are necessary for concept assimilation. This latter process occurs when the criterial attributes of the concept are presented, by definition or context, and then related directly to the learner's cognitive structure (secondary concepts). Finally, beginning with the junior-high-school period, the learner can dispense with these props in directly relating presented criterial attributes to his or her cognitive structure.

With increasing age, concepts tend (*1*) to consist more of higher-order abstractions; (*2*) to exhibit more precision as well as differentiation; (*3*) to be acquired more through concept assimilation than through concept formation (except in creative persons, concept formation is a relatively rare phenomenon after the age of abstract logical operations); and (*4*) to be accompanied by awareness of the conceptualizing operations involved.

Other internal factors influencing concept formation and assimilation include relevant experience, intelligence, and sex. The important task factors affecting concept acquisition are (*1*) heterogeneity of instances after consolidation in a more homogeneous setting; (*2*) appropriate blending and sequencing of positive and negative instances; and (*3*) the relevance of the presented or available information to the concept in question.

The simplified categorical and schematic representation of reality achieved through concept formation or assimilation makes possible the invention of language with more or less uniform meanings (thereby facilitating communication). It also facilitates both acquisition of new meanings and propositional combinations of them. In turn, the properties of language in a given culture (the precision, availability, and differentiation of concepts; the prevailing value system; and the syntactical structure of the language) influence perception, concept acquisition (the Whorfian Hypothesis) and thought. Meanings acquire generic (categorical) properties when concept formation occurs in actuality or, in the case of concept assimilation, when definitions implicitly reflect the concept formation that occurred in the evolution of language.

During the more contemporaneous course of concept acquisition, concepts become increasingly less global and diffuse, focus more

on *salient criterial attributes, become more general and less idiosyncratic and subjective. Nevertheless, each individual has idiosyncratic denotative and connotative meanings for a given concept.*

*Concept names do not necessarily possess the same meanings for
individuals of different degrees of cognitive maturity. This is the
case because young children have no other choice but to use precise, culturally standardized concept names for concepts whose
meanings, for the child, are still vague, diffuse, overinclusive, or
underinclusive.*

## The Nature of Concepts

Anyone who pauses long enough to give the problem some serious
thought cannot escape the conclusion that we live in a world of concepts
rather than in a world of objects, events, and situations. The reality we
experience psychologically is related only indirectly to the physical properties of our environment and to our sensory correlates. Reality, figuratively
speaking, is experienced through a conceptual or categorical filter. That is,
the cognitive content a group of spoken or written words elicits in the
recipient of a message is a highly simplified, abstract, and generalized version both of the actual realities to which they refer in the physical world
and of the actual conscious experiences which these realities evoke in the
narrator. When someone, for example, tells us that he or she sees a "house,"
that person is not really communicating an *actual* experience, but a highly
simplified and generalized version of it—an interpretation that reflects the
cultural consensus regarding the essential (criterial, identifying) attributes
of "house." His or her *actual* conscious experience of the event is infinitely
more particularistic with respect to size, shape, style, hue, brightness, and
presumed cost than the message communicated by that individual's generic
use of the term "house." If the person actually tried to communicate his or
her detailed cognitive experience, it would not only take half a day, but he
or she would still be unable completely to express in words many of its
more subtle nuances.

Furthermore, even the narrator's *own* conscious experience of the event
—though more particularistic and idiosyncratic than the cognitive content
his or her verbal description elicits in others—is hardly a complete or faithful sensory representation of reality. It is rather a cognitive content per-
vasively molded by the nature of the existing concept of "house" in the
person's own cognitive structure. This latter concept influences him or her
to be differentially aware of certain properties of a house as a stimulus
object and to ignore others. This selective sensory experience, combined
with certain preconceived criterial attributes of "house" in the person's cog-

nitive structure may lead to an inference that this is the house of a poor family, or alternatively, of a wealthy family.

In short, because of the influence of concepts within their cognitive structures, humans experience a highly simplified, schematic, selective, and generalized conscious representation of reality, rather than a complete and faithful sensory representation of it. Nevertheless, this conscious experience is much more detailed, particularistic, and idiosyncratic in its denotative and connotative meanings than the culturally standardized meanings that the generic term "house" have. It is important to note that it is the idiosyncratic concept of "house" that one uses to mold one's experience, and not the more generic cultural concept. As we will see later, however, concept formation for an individual is both culturally determined and a product of a person's idiosyncratic experiences in acquiring the concept.

For our purposes we shall define concepts as objects, events, situations, or properties that *possess common criterial attributes* and are designated in any given culture by some accepted sign or symbol. *House, triangle, war,* and *truth* are a few of the culturally accepted concepts we use.

### Consequences of Conceptualization for Cognitive Functioning

The simplified and generalized representation of reality that is achieved through the existence and use of concepts makes possible the invention of a language with relatively uniform meanings for all members of a culture, thereby facilitating interpersonal communication (Vygotsky, 1962). Equally important, it also makes possible (1) the establishment in cognitive structure of inclusive and generic constructs (and of propositional combinations of them) in relation to which new correlative and derivative meanings can be acquired and retained more efficiently as part of an organized body of knowledge and (2) the manipulation, interrelation, and reorganization of ideas involved in the generation and testing of hypotheses, and hence in meaningful problem solving.

By setting up equivalences, that is, by grouping related items of experience into categories defined by the criterial attributes of their members, concepts therefore standardize and simplify the environment and hence facilitate reception learning, problem solving, and communication. Because it is cumbersome and cognitively inefficient to deal with continuously graded events, man resorts to categorization, responding to heterogeneous objects or events as a class or as members of a class.

Concepts free thought, learning, and communication from the domination of the physical environment. They make possible the acquisition of abstract ideas in the absence of concrete-empirical experience—ideas that can be used both to categorize new situations under existing rubrics and to serve as anchoring foci for the assimilation and discovery of new knowledge. Finally, the grouping of concepts into potentially meaningful combinations is responsible for the generation and understanding of propositions. Propositions, in turn, are the descriptions of reality that man invents, and these descriptions change over time as both his concepts and his propositions are altered or discarded.[1]

## Are Concepts Related to Physical Reality?

It would be fallacious to assert that conceptual reality bears no resemblance to the real world. A more supportable appraisal of the relationship between conceptual and phenomenological reality would be to characterize the former as a selectively schematic version of the latter. Out of the many possible and logically defensible ways of delineating categories into which objects and events, manifesting certain designated criterial attributes in common, can be sorted as members of generically more inclusive classes, a given culture chooses a *particular* set of alternatives. In this choice, distinctive values, attitudes toward life, social and economic institutions, and ways of institutionalizing interpersonal relationships—as well as sheer random decision, historical accident, and the patterning influence of earlier forms of the language itself—all play significant roles. But despite noteworthy intercultural differences in conceptual meanings, the impressive degree of cross-cultural uniformity in the denotative meanings and syntactic functions of analogous words in different languages clearly indicates the prepotent constraining influence exerted both by similar physical, functional, and relational properties of objects and events in the real world and by the inherent logic of classification. In short, conceptual reality is far from being either a capricious or illogical representation of the physical world.

Thus the extent to which a concept identifies salient and significant aspects of experience with objective reality is an important dimension of concept generation. In formulating new concepts one can choose to focus on criterial attributes that are more or less central, more or less subjective, more or less characteristic, or more or less idiosyncratic. The objective reality denoted by a concept determines in large measure its usefulness both in the structure of knowledge and for purposes of learning, problem solving, and communication.

## Are Concepts Themselves Real?

The notion implicit in classical Greek metaphysics that conceptual meanings or "essences" of things are axiomatic givens and exhibit a sepa-

---

[1] In Chapter 15 we shall discuss this idea at length in the section on the Epistemology of Discovery.

rate, concrete existence in their own right, apart from the physical objects from which they are selectively schematized, is both scientifically and philosophically unsupportable. As abstractions, concepts obviously represent only *one* of many possible ways of defining a class and enjoy no actual existence in the physical world. Psychologically speaking, however, concepts *are* real in the sense that: (1) they can be acquired, perceived, understood, and manipulated *as if* they enjoyed an independent existence of their own; and (2) they are perceived and understood, both denotatively and in terms of their syntactic functions, in much the same way both within a given culture and from one culture to another. For example, *culture* itself is an abstraction (concept) that has no independent existence of its own since it consists merely of *modal* attitudes, *typical* ways of thinking, and *characteristic* ways of institutionalizing interpersonal relationships in a particular society. Even though it is an abstraction that has no physical reality apart from the totality of the behaviors, attitudes, and values of its individual carriers, "culture" as an entity is psychologically real. The distinctive properties of a given culture (though only statistical abstractions in their own right) constitute reliably identifiable perceptual and cognizable conceptual entities about which there is much consensus of judgment.[2] The culture also influences the lives of its members in many predictable and uniform ways. Thus "culture" as a *generic idea* is a very useful tool both for acquiring and discovering new knowledge.

The concept meanings represented in a given language, therefore, may be thought of as both a product or reflection of culture and as a patterning or limiting factor in the cognitive development of the individual carriers of the culture. It reflects the idiosyncratic kinds of, and approaches to, categorization as well as the characteristic attitudes, values, and ways of thinking that prevail in a given culture. Once constituted, then, the structure of a language and the conceptual and syntactic categories it contains definitely influence, in turn, the perceptual and cognitive processes of developing individuals. They learn to perceive, think, and acquire new meanings selectively in terms of the classificatory schemes available to them in their mother tongue. If the latter fails to recognize certain conceptual distinctions, people are greatly handicapped in making these distinctions themselves. Thus characteristic patterns of thought in a particular culture affect the nature of the language that evolves; and the language reciprocally patterns and limits perceptual and cognitive experience and the types of thinking in which individual members of the culture engage (cf. Whorf, 1956).

---

[2] Undergraduate students, for example, can predict with almost uncanny accuracy the precise degree of orthodoxy or heterodoxy characterizing the mean beliefs of their classmates with regard to detailed issues relating to such controversial areas as theology and immortality (Ausubel & Schpoont, 1957).

Problems in the Acquisition and Use of Concepts

In considering the role of concepts or generic meanings in human cognitive functioning, it is evident that two quite different kinds of psychological problems require explanation. First, there is the problem of how concepts are acquired and the different kinds of psychological processes involved in such acquisition. Second, there is the equally important problem of how concepts, once acquired, influence:

1. The perceptual categorization of experience
2. The acquisition and retention, through reception learning, of new conceptual and propositional meanings
3. Meaningful problem solving (discovery learning)

Subsidiary issues requiring consideration include:

1. Alternative theories regarding the nature and acquisition of concepts
2. Developmental changes in acquiring concepts (changes from one age level to another)
3. Characteristic sequential changes occurring in the cognitive properties of a given concept from early to late stages in its acquisition *within* a particular age level
4. Reasons for discrepancies between the culturally standardized meaning of a conceptual term and the actual meanings it elicits in different individuals
5. Different ways of classifying concepts
6. The role of language in concept acquisition
7. The influence on concept acquisition of such factors as age, experience, IQ, sex, the availability of concrete-empirical experience, positive versus negative instances, relevant and irrelevant experience, contiguity and sequence of examplars, learning set, opportunities for application, and the homogeneity or heterogeneity of exemplars.

### Different Ways of Acquiring and Using Concepts

It is obviously one thing to acquire a concept and quite another to use it in categorizing naive sensory impressions, in learning related new meanings, and in solving problems. Let us consider, in general terms, some of the principal ways in which concepts are acquired and used, reserving for later sections more detailed discussion of underlying processes and developmental differences.

#### The Acquisition of Concepts

We need to distinguish at this point between two principal types of concept acquisition, namely, concept formation and concept assimilation. Most characteristically, concept formation takes place in preschool children, whereas concept assimilation is the dominant mode of concept acquisition for older children and adults.

*Concept formation* is characteristic of the preschool child's inductive[3] and spontaneous (untutored) acquisition of generic ideas (for instance, "house," "dog") from concrete-empirical experience. It is a type of discovery learning involving, at least in primitive form, such underlying psychological processes as discriminative analysis, abstraction, differentiation, hypothesis generation and testing, and generalization. Less typically, in real-life situations and in the laboratory, it is also exhibited by older individuals —but at a much higher level of sophistication with respect to the component psychological processes involved.

Most of our information about the nature of concept formation, both in young children and in individuals of school age and beyond, comes from laboratory-type situations. In these situations the learning task calls for the inductive identification of the common criterial attributes of a class of stimuli from a large array of instances that vary in regard to both criterial and noncriterial attributes (Vygotsky, 1962). The experimenter, for example, may present the subject with an array of squares, circles, and triangles, each of which is either red, blue, or yellow, and then say, "I have a particular idea in mind, either a particular form (square, circle, or triangle) or a particular color (red, blue, or yellow). Each of the cards in the display in front of you has one of these forms, which is red, yellow, or blue. You can point to any one of these cards, in any order you choose, and I will tell you whether it is or is not an example of the idea I have in mind. From the answers I give, you will eventually be able to determine which particular idea—one of the three forms or one of the three colors—I am thinking of. Your job is to discover this by using as few cards and asking as few questions as possible." Let us suppose that the experimenter had a "square" in mind. From the experimenter's response of "yes, this *is* an example" to red, yellow, and blue squares, and "no, this is *not* an example" to red, yellow, and blue triangles and circles, the subject finally discovers that "square" is the concept that the experimenter was thinking of.

Many other research designs have been used in the experimental investigation of concept formation. Only one additional method will be described here. This method involves a training session in which the subject first learns the nonsense-syllable names of different classes of stimuli by being presented with different exemplars of each class, each exemplar being appropriately labeled with its class name. The subject is then tested

---

[3] The use of the term "inductive" oversimplifies the actual process of concept formation. Few problem-solving or concept formation situations are approached from scratch —by generating new hypotheses solely from the data at hand. More typically the learner approaches new problems by generating hypotheses derived from existing concepts or propositions in his cognitive structure. These latter hypotheses may be influenced, initially or later on, by the distinctive features of the current problem situation.

for knowledge of the criterial attributes of each class by being asked to name correctly other exemplars of these same classes.

In real-life situations, of course, concept formation is both a more prolonged and less orderly process. For example, as a result of being exposed to many different sizes, shapes, and colors of both dogs and other animals, a preschool child eventually acquires a concept of "dog" that is both generic in nature and a reasonable facsimile of the cultural consensus regarding the nature of the concept in question. Both the component psychological processes underlying concept formation and developmental changes in the cognitive properties of concepts and in the processes involved will be discussed in subsequent sections.

Characteristically, however, older (school age) children, as well as adolescents and adults, acquire new concepts through a process of *concept assimilation.* That is, they learn new conceptual meanings by being presented with the criterial attributes of concepts and by relating these attributes to relevant established ideas in their cognitive structures. For young children the assimilation process requires the facilitating influence of concrete-empirical props, namely, exemplars of the criterial attributes which are related to cognitive structure in conjunction with the attributes they exemplify. Learning the names of concept meanings, on the other hand, involves a process of representational learning that typically follows concept assimilation itself. In other words, these children learn new generic terms either by being presented with their definitions or by encountering them in context, and then by representationally equating the meanings of new generic terms with the emergent new conceptual meanings in cognitive structure that are elicited by the combination of already meaningful words contained in the terms' definitions or contextual cues.

Since the necessary definitions and the appropriate context are presented rather than discovered, concept assimilation is typically a form of meaningful reception learning; but inasmuch as it still involves various active cognitive operations, it cannot be considered either a passive or simple perceptual phenomenon. In certain instances, however, where the meaning of a new word is *not* self-evident from its context, the learning process is not much different from that involved in concept formation. The learner must go through many of the same processes of abstracting, differentiating, hypothesis generating and testing, and generalizing before the new meaning emerges. The reader may wish to reflect on his own acquisition of the concept of "meaningful learning" to see how complex the process of concept assimilation can be.

### The Use of Concepts

Once acquired, concepts serve many purposes in cognitive functioning. At the simplest level of utilization, they are obviously implicated in the *perceptual* categorization of incoming sensory experience—for example, perceiving a particular house as an exemplar of the more general class. Simple forms of reception "learning" (where a particular, more or less obvious, and representational new member of a class is presented as illustrative or supportive of an existing concept in cognitive structure) are also reflective of perceptual categorization. Still another perceptual use of existing concepts in cognitive structure is exemplified by the immediate (perceptual) comprehension of the meanings of previously learned and already meaningful concepts and propositions when they are encountered on subsequent occasions.

*Cognitive* utilization of existing concepts is exemplified by that type of *reception* learning in which less self-evident representatives of a known generic class must be identified as such (cognitive categorization), and in which related new concepts, subconcepts, or propositions are acquired by being assimilated under more inclusive conceptual or propositional entities. Meaningful *discovery* learning represents another cognitive use of a learner's existing repertoire of concepts. It is exemplified by (1) simpler kinds of problem-solving operations, in which solution of the problem at hand merely requires that the learner be able to formulate it as a special case of an already meaningful and more general concept or proposition, and (2) the more complex kinds of problem solving, in which existing concepts and propositions must be extended, elaborated, qualified, or reorganized so as to satisfy the particular requirements of the means-end relationship that the learner is obliged to discover.

It is evident that the distinction between the acquisition and use of concepts is somewhat arbitrary, since one of the principal functions of existing concepts in cognitive structure is to facilitate the acquisition of new concepts, more so in the case of concept assimilation than in the case of concept formation. Nevertheless, this distinction is still useful inasmuch as it is consistent with the distinction that has been maintained throughout this volume between the original acquisition of a given item of knowledge and its subsequent use in the acquisition of further knowledge; it gets at the very essence of the transfer process and of the central role of cognitive structure variables in this process. Furthermore, existing concepts are utilized in many ways other than merely in facilitating the acquisition of new concepts, namely, in the perceptual categorization of experience, in problem solving, and in perceiving the meanings of previously learned concepts and propositions.

Problem solving, on the one hand, and concept formation and utilization, on the other, overlap in many ways. Simple concept formation—both the spontaneous, "inductive" variety in preschool children and those atypical instances of "concept assimilation" in which new generic meanings are acquired through a discovery-like process, after being encountered repeatedly in diverse verbal contexts—is actually one type of problem solving. Acquired concepts are also used in both simple and more complex varieties of meaningful problem solving to discover new concepts. When, for example, the learning of certain presented ideas requires drastic reorganization of existing concepts in cognitive structure (for instance, the formulation of a new concept that is sufficiently inclusive to subsume two or more otherwise irreconcilable presented ideas), the reorganization process constitutes a form of problem solving. This would be an instance of superordinate learning, which was discussed in Chapter 2.

Not all problem solving involves the acquisition and use of concepts; for example, maze learning, perceptual-motor learning, and simple discrimination learning typically do not involve the acquisition or use of concepts. On the other hand, perceptual categorization, simple derivative subsumption, perceptual apprehension of meanings of previously learned symbols, most instances of concept assimilation, and the use of newly assimilated concepts in the reception learning of related new ideas are instances of concept learning that do not involve problem solving.

Principles differ from concepts in that they involve meaningful relational combinations of concepts that are propositional in nature. In other words, a principle, by definition, is a composite idea. Although many concepts, especially those of a higher-order nature, involve one or more relationships between lower-order concepts, any given concept is only a unitary generic idea with a set of specifiable criterial attributes. "Velocity," for example, involves a relationship between time and distance, and "acceleration" is a concept in which force is related to mass.

## The Nature of Generic Meaning

A distinction has already been drawn between simple symbols referring to particular objects or events and generic symbols referring to classes of objects. Actually, most of the words used in ordinary language, except for proper nouns and such, are primarily generic symbols. Such words, therefore, represent clearly defined concepts with distinctive criterial attributes of their own. How then can we explain the generic meanings elicited by the conceptual use of terms in contradistinction to the characteristic kinds of meanings elicited by terms referring to particular objects? Obviously, since the meaning that emerges for any given individual depends on the cognitive content evoked by the eliciting symbol, the difference between the meanings elicited by particular conceptual terms must be sought in the type of cognitive content each category of term evokes in the individual.

Thus, paralleling the variety in the individual uses of the concept terms themselves, the recognized cognitive content corresponding to a conceptual term is generic rather than particularistic in nature. Instead of consisting of a concrete image of a particular object, it consists of either (1) a modal or idealized image of a first-order, relatively concrete concept such as "chair" or "dog," or (2) various combinations of first-order or higher-order conceptual meanings in ways that constitute the criterial attributes of more abstract and complex concepts, such as "chief of state or chief executive of a republic" in the case of "president."

The generic nature of the cognitive content of conceptual terms naturally reflects the prior occurrence and effects of the distinctive cognitive processes involved in concept formation. When a child, through hypothesis generation and testing, abstracts, for example, the criterial attributes of "dog" from diverse examples of dogs, differentiates them from those that are not criterial (or are criterial for other concepts), and then generalizes the criterial properties to all members of the class, the resulting cognitive content *has* to be generic in nature. The *train of experience* that leads to an individual's formation of a concept may be unique (idiosyncratic) but the *concept* acquired is *generic*, and frequently an individual cannot recall the specific instances that led to the formation of the concept.

The last step in concept formation is establishing representational equivalence between the generic symbol (the concept name) and the generic cognitive content it evokes. This is not actually part of the concept formation process itself, but is an example of *representational* learning that occurs *after* this process is completed.

### Concept Assimilation versus Concept Formation

In most instances of concept attainment after early childhood, particularly in the school environment, the criterial attributes of concepts are not discovered inductively through a process of concept formation, but are either presented to the learner as a matter of definition or are implicit in their context. Concept attainment therefore becomes largely a matter of concept assimilation.

Since the older learner of school age and beyond does not typically acquire a given concept through such processes as abstraction, differentiation and generalization, where does the potential generic meaning expressed in its presented criterial attributes come from? Evidently when an individual learns the meaning of a new concept as a consequence of didactic exposition, its corresponding generic cognitive content implicitly reflects the previous occurrence of these latter processes in the historical evolution of the language. That is, since the individual's cultural forebears did the abstracting, differentiating, and generalizing in evolving the concept (namely, in discovering its criterial attributes), its symbolic term subsequently elicits generic cognitive content after he or she currently assimilates the presented criterial attributes in question.[4]

---

[4] The process of evolution of concepts in the culture is well described by Toulmin (1972). See discussion in Chapter 15, Epistemology of Discovery.

Thus in concept assimilation, just as in concept formation, the learner's representational equation of a particular arbitrary term (the concept name) with its corresponding generic meaning to him or her is merely a form of representational learning that follows the concept attainment process. The more crucial preliminary operation, whereby the learner acquires the new conceptual meaning through reception learning, involves the acquisition of the new generic content itself. The most significant aspect of the concept assimilation process involves relating to relevant, established ideas in the learner's cognitive structure the potentially meaningful generic content contained in the term's definition or contextual cues (its criterial attributes). The phenomenological emergence of the new generic meaning in the learner is a product of this interaction. It reflects both the actual content of the new concept's criterial attributes and of the anchoring ideas to which they are related and the kind of relationship (derivative, elaborative, qualifying, or superordinate) established between them.

The acquisition of concepts by reception learning is not simply a process of passive absorption. It is true that there is not the same intensive discriminative analysis, abstraction, generalization, and differentiation as in concept formation; this is precluded by the direct presentation to the learner of the concepts' criterial attributes. Nevertheless, concept assimilation is typically characterized by an active process of relation to, differentiation from, and integration with existing relevant concepts. The more active this process is the more meaningful and useful assimilated concepts are.

As we shall see later, concepts acquired by assimilation undergo both contemporaneous and developmental change. The former change encompasses the modifications in meaning that occur over the relatively brief time span during which the concept is first acquired and then consolidated. The latter change, on the other hand, reflects the long-term effects on concept meaning wrought by developmental alterations in cognitive functioning and by increasing subject-matter sophistication. These effects, as Vygotsky (1962) notes, are reciprocal in nature; that is, systematic instruction in concepts influences as well as reflects developmental changes in cognitive functioning. Freyberg (1966) has shown that the level of concept development, expressed in Piagetian terms, correlates more highly with mental than with chronological age. When measures of this level are combined with mental age, the combined score accounts for a significantly larger portion of achievement test variance in spelling, arithmetical computation, and arithmetical problem solving than does mental age alone. Gubrud and Novak (1973) found that adequacy of prior learning of subordinate concepts was more important than age or IQ for subsequent concept learning.

Principles of concept formation based on laboratory studies are not necessarily relatable to principles of concept assimilation in mastering subject-matter material. In the first place, the variables influencing the processes involved in conceptualization, and thus underlying the *discovery* of the criterial attributes of concepts, are quite different from the variables influencing the meaningful *reception* learning of the same criterial attributes. Second, it should make some difference whether the learning task involves merely the short-term acquisition of single, somewhat contrived concepts in a laboratory setting or whether it involves the long-term acquisition of a complex network of interrelated concepts characterizing an organized body of knowledge. The *principles of concept assimilation* that are relevant to school learning are essentially the same principles of meaningful verbal reception learning discussed in the previous chapter and will be a central concern in other chapters. In learning a new concept, as much or more depends on existing properties of cognitive structure and on the general developmental status and intellectual ability of the learner as on the nature of the concept itself and the way in which it is presented. Because of this, Bruner's (1960) assertion that we can teach any concept to children of any age is obviously a gross overstatement.

### Sequential Stages in Concept Acquisition

Concept formation consists essentially of a process of abstracting the essential common features of a class of objects or events that vary contextually, in other noncriterial respects, or along dimensions other than the particular ones under scrutiny. Typically these "common features" are not discrete elements shared by a number of stimulus patterns, but are comparable configurations or sets of relationships. Component psychological processes involved in the most highly developed form of concept formation include the following, more or less, in the sequence given:

1. Discriminative analysis of different stimulus patterns
2. The formulation of hypotheses regarding abstracted common elements
3. Subsequent testing of these hypotheses in specific situations
4. Selective designation from among them of one general category or set of common attributes under which all of the variants can be successfully subsumed
5. Relation of this set of attributes to relevant anchoring ideas in cognitive structure
6. Differentiation of the new concept from related, previously learned concepts
7. Generalization of the criterial attributes of the new concept to all members of the class
8. Representation of the new categorical content by a language symbol that is congruent with conventional usage

The last-mentioned form of representational learning that follows conceptual learning has already been discussed; ordinarily it constitutes the final step in concept formation. In instances where the verbal symbol is simply learned by rote, in the absence of the preceding steps, it has no ideational referents and does not represent a genuine concept. For example, students in the social and behavioral sciences may learn early that Greek sigma designates "variance," but it may take years for them to acquire the *meaning* for the concept.

In concept formation the learner generates hypotheses or problem-solving propositions that aim at defining the abstracted criterial attributes of the concept to be learned. To be potentially meaningful a given hypothesis must embody a means-end relationship; that is, the hypothesized criterial attributes must be exemplifiable in the specific exemplars. The actual process of explicitly confirming or disconfirming that such is the case occurs during hypothesis testing. Finally, the confirmed criterial attributes are related to relevant ideas in cognitive structure and thereby become meaningful, that is, constitute the meaning of the concept after they have been internalized.

The anchoring ideas in cognitive structure to which the criterial attributes of new concepts are related naturally vary with the abstractness and complexity of the concept in question. When the referent of a concept is a perceptible object or event, its criterial attributes are related to a common perceptual core of the object or event. In the case of a relatively simple but superordinate concept, such as "vegetable," the anchoring ideas, at least initially, are probably mere exemplars of the class (carrots, peas, turnips), which are simple concepts in their own right. The criterial attributes of the same concept at a later stage of development (or of more abstract concepts with nonperceptible referents) are assimilated by those anchoring ideas to which the set of abstracted attributes ("something edible," "not tasty but good for you," in the case of "vegetable") is relatable.

The actual process of concept formation is facilitated by the child's acquisition of the general idea of categorization (Ausubel, 1968a; Edmonds, 1976). The development of this insight is similar in nature, and, in fact, is related to the acquisition of the insight that everything has a name. The latter insight, it will be remembered, is an outgrowth of the realization that: (1) all significates with approximately the same perceptual core have the same name; and (2) significates with basically different perceptual cores have different names. Simple "naming" itself therefore constitutes a primitive (perceptual) or precategorical type of concept formation. The more advanced idea of categorization conceivably arises from the gradually developing insight that adults also use words in a categorical sense, that is, to include exemplars that do not share a common perceptual core. As the child comes into contact with such categorical words as "vegetable," "fruit," "play," "work," "toy," and so forth, he acquires the insight that a given word can be used to represent a class of significates with a perceptually dissimilar core. This general insight motivates him, first, to identify some physically dissimilar exemplars of simple categorical concepts (for instance to discover that carrots, peas, and turnips are vegetables), and, later, to discover the abstracted criterial attributes both of such concepts and of even more abstract generic ideas that have no perceptible referents. Once several categorical ideas are actually acquired, they obviously serve as models for later instances of concept formation. The nature of the hypothesis testing needed to abstract criterial attributes from exemplars of concepts has sufficient commonality that positive transfer exists from learned concepts to new concept formation.

Contemporaneously, as a concept is acquired, certain characteristic changes gradually take place (Vygotsky, 1962). It becomes increasingly less global, less impressionistic, and less diffuse (Fisher, 1916); the learner focuses progressively on more salient criterial attributes. Generic conceptual content also tends to be emptied of particularistic attributes and to become more abstract and general in nature. The identification of relevant criterial attributes similarly becomes more precise and refined; noncriterial attributes are sloughed off and new criterial attributes are added. Distinctions from related concepts also tend to become sharper. Idiosyncratic and subjectivistic elements become less prominent as the learner's version of the concept comes increasingly to conform to a culturally standardized consensus (Rosch, 1973, 1976). Last, new contextual variants of the concept are acquired with the acquisition of greater sophistication in the same and related disciplines (Hibbard & Novak, 1975; Nussbaum & Novak, 1976; Rowell, 1976). Nevertheless, unique individual experience still tends to give an idiosyncratic denotative and connotative flavor to most concepts.

## Conceptual Terms and Cognitive Content

The use of the same conceptual terms by different members of a given culture does not necessarily imply uniformity of the underlying cognitive content. The most obvious reason for this variability inheres in the idiosyncratic nature of both experience and of the cognitive structures to which potentially meaningful concepts are related. A second reason is more reflective of developmental immaturity. Cognitively immature and intellectually unsophisticated individuals have no other choice but to use conventionally standardized conceptual terms with precise generic meanings to represent meanings of their own, which may be vague, diffuse, imprecise, under- or overinclusive, and often only semigeneric or preconceptual in nature. Studies by Hibbard & Novak (1975), McClelland (1970), Nussbaum & Novak (1976), Pines (1977), and Whitman (1975) show the range in variation in adequacy of children's science concepts.

The commonness of misconceptions during childhood may be attributed to several factors. First, children do not have the cognitive sophistication and the cumulative background of experience necessary for the complete development of many concepts. The pressure on children to mouth inadequately understood concepts, and at the same time to conceal their lack of understanding, further encourages the development and perpetuation of misconceptions. Some children who have inordinate "intolerance for ambiguity" are predisposed toward acquiring misconceptions since they are prone to reduce the threat and discomfort of tentativeness by resorting to premature conceptual closure (Levitt, 1953). Second, many of children's misconceptions are derived from erroneous and incomplete information, or from misinterpretation or uncritical acceptance of what they read or are told. This is especially true in a socially taboo area such as sex, which has both a rich folklore and a special mythology for children. Such misconceptions are highly resistive to extinction since they tend to be insulated from the corrective influences of social verification. Still another group of childhood misconceptions can be traced to confusion between words with different meanings that either look or sound alike.

Since there is often a time lag between the correction of misconceptions and the revision of language usage, it cannot be assumed that conceptual confusion necessarily exists in all instances where words are used inappropriately. On the other hand, some instances of incorrect diction that seem to be largely linguistic in origin may have a conceptual basis. The common tendency for children to use "tell" instead of "ask," for example, may indicate lack of cognitive appreciation of the distinction involved rather than a mistake in concept naming. It may also indicate that although some ego-expansive children appreciate the distinction, they conceive of themselves as "telling" in situations where others would be "asking."

## Concepts and the Structure of Disciplines

Although discussion of concepts and their relationship to the structure of disciplines will be considered more extensively in Chapters 10 and 15, it is necessary to recognize at this point that the idiosyncratic concepts acquired by a learner may be substantially different from these same concepts as they are perceived by scholars in a discipline.

> It should not be forgotten . . . that in addition to organized bodies of knowledge that represent the collective recorded wisdom of recognized scholars in particular fields of inquiry, there are corresponding psychological structures of knowledge as represented by the organization of internalized ideas and information in the minds of individual students of varying degrees of both cognitive maturity and subject-matter sophistication in these same disciplines. I am making a distinction, in other words, between

the formal organization of the subject-matter content of a given discipline, as set forth in authoritative statements in generally accepted textbooks and monographs, on the one hand, and the organized, internalized representation of this knowledge in the memory structures of particular individuals, especially students, on the other (Ausubel, 1964b, p. 222).

In recent years there has been an increased interest in methods for studying the cognitive organization of knowledge in individual students and comparisons with "expert" views of the organization of concepts in a discipline. Shavelson (1973) has shown, through word (concept) association tasks, that physics students who acquire concepts early in instruction consolidate more of the learning and achieve greater success in problem solving. Furthermore, as students gain new knowledge, their cognitive structures begin to show a hierarchy of relationships closer to those of experts in the discipline (Bogdin, 1977; Moriera, 1977; Rowell, 1975; Rudnitsky, 1976; Shavelson, 1972). The strategies employed by investigators of cognitive structure organization vary, but the conclusions are similar in that they show the idiosyncratic nature of cognitive structure development in learners and the disparity between cognitive organization of poor students and that of "experts" in the discipline, whereas good students show increasing similarities in their "cognitive maps" to those elicited from experts.

## Language and Concept Acquisition

The capacity for inventing and acquiring language is one of the most distinctive features of human development. It is both a prerequisite for the original development of culture and a necessary condition for the subsequent acquisition by the individual of the complex cognitive, social, and moral products of the culture in which he lives. Without language, the development and transmission of shared meanings, values, and traditions would be impossible. People would be unable to communicate with each other except in face-to-face situations, individual relatedness to and interaction between groups could not take place in the absence of physical proximity, and all of the countless intellectual, interpersonal, and institutional manifestations of cultural existence that depend on verbal conceptualization would be inconceivable (Ausubel, 1958; Johnson, 1962).

In many respects the speech behavior of infrahuman organisms resembles that of children in the early stages of language development. Thus untutored animals vocalize spontaneously, mimic sounds in their environment, and communicate effectively with each other. Many animals can also be trained to react differentially to different verbal cues, to mimic human words, and to make appropriate vocal responses to different situations.

True representational symbolism, however, in the sense that an arbitrary pattern of stimulation is used to signify the meaning of a totally unrelated and dissimilar referent that may also often be remote and abstract, is probably unknown at the infrahuman level; at most, sub-primate animals use symbols to represent relatively immediate, concrete, and physically similar referents. Verbal conceptualization and the use of symbols to represent ideas that transcend concrete experience are undoubtedly nonexistent at the infra-primate level. Furthermore, only humans can be said to possess a true (invented) language having symbolic meanings that are socially rather than genically determined and manifesting an organized syntactical structure.[5] It is highly questionable whether the recent demonstration of representational symbolism by chimpanzees on computers is qualitatively equivalent to its human counterpart.

Why only human beings have developed a true language is attributable to several factors. First, they possess an elaborate vocalizing mechanism capable of great versatility in sound production, tend to babble spontaneously as infants, and are relatively proficient at mimicry. Even more important is their immeasurably great capacity for representational symbolism, for verbal conceptualization, and for handling abstract ideas. Moreover, because they live in cultural aggregations, they are able to standardize and perpetuate shared meanings for the verbal symbols they invent.

It seems probable that both human infants and infrahuman primates develop rudimentary precategorical concepts that subsume significates with a common perceptual core. Because of the absence of language, however, the processes of abstraction, differentiation, and generalization are exceedingly primitive. Generic meanings largely consist of modal or generalized images abstracted from objects and events that are physically similar. Symbols are not used representationally either in the process of conceptualization, in the attainment of generic cognitive content, or in the labeling of concepts. It is largely because of their unique ability to acquire abstract concepts (which itself is so largely dependent on language) that human beings are singularly capable both of meaningful reception learning and of meaningfully solving complex relational problems without coming into direct contact with the objects and phenomena involved. The actual roles of (1) representational symbols, in facilitating the transformational operations involved in conceptualization, and (2) verbalization, in refining the product of these transformational operations, were discussed in another context. Evidence indicative of the facilitating effect of language on concept acquisition has already been cited.

Intuitive (semiabstract and often subverbal) concepts also exist—par-

---

[5] Recent studies of language acquisition by chimpanzees suggest that they can learn abstract symbolical representation but not syntactical structure (Gardner & Gardner, 1969).

ticularly in childhood, and afterwards in the early unsophisticated stage of acquiring a new discipline.[6] Such concepts are intuitive and relatively particularistic in nature because their acquisition is dependent on the availability of concrete-empirical props. They are functional for purposes of problem solving and further reception learning, but are not nearly as precise, transferable, or efficient for these latter purposes as are the truly abstract and verbal concept meanings that succeed them. However, when they precede the later developmental acquisition of their abstract-verbal equivalents, they often enhance meaningfulness and help prevent rote assimilation of new conceptual meanings.

In conclusion, therefore, language plays a central facilitating role[7] in the acquisition of concepts. In the first place, contrary to Piaget's (1964) view, language—by virtue of the crucial contributions that both the representational power of symbols and the refining aspects of verbalization make to the process of conceptualization—obviously determines as well as reflects the mental operations (level of cognitive functioning) involved in the acquisition of abstract and higher-order concepts. Second, as will be pointed out later, the very process of concept assimilation through definition and context would be utterly inconceivable without language. Third, language helps ensure a certain amount of cultural uniformity in the generic content of concepts, thereby facilitating interpersonal cognitive communication.

## Developmental Aspects of Concept Acquisition

General developmental changes in concept acquisition will be covered more definitively in Chapter 6 in considering the concrete-abstraction dimension of cognitive development. From the preoperational stage to the abstract operational stage there are progressive gains in the level of abstraction at which the process of concept acquisition occurs, in the level of abstraction of the concept meanings that emerge from this process, and in the abstractness and complexity of the kinds of concepts that lie within the child's grasp. These changes may be grouped under the three qualitatively distinct stages of cognitive development to be delineated further in Chapter 6.

[6] Prior to being verbalized, new concept meanings also typically exist for a short while on a subverbal level—even in sophisticated older learners. These subverbal concepts are less transferable than their verbal successors, except perhaps under conditions of premature verbalization when only rote representational learning has occurred.

[7] It should be appreciated, of course, that language is neither necessary nor sufficient for concept attainment. Nonverbal children as well as infrahuman mammals can acquire rudimentary concepts. It is also possible to attain a concept without realizing it or giving it a name. Even aphasics can utilize concepts in problem solving.

During the preoperational stage the child is limited to the acquisition of *primary* concepts—those concepts whose meanings he learns *first* by explicitly relating their criterial attributes to the exemplars from which they are derived *before* relating these same attributes to cognitive structure. Generally speaking the first of these two operations is performed during the hypothesis-testing aspect of concept formation. Sometimes, however, he is *presented* with the criterial attributes of a new concpet; but under these circumstances the latter attributes would not be relatable to his cognitive structure unless he were first able to test them explicitly against particular exemplars of the concept. In any case, since intimate contact with multiple particular exemplars of the concept is necessary for concept acquisition, both the conceptualization process itself and its products (the acquired new concept meanings) take place at a low level of abstraction.

The preoperational child's dependence on concrete-empirical experience also typically limits him or her to the acquisition of those primary concepts whose referents consist of perceptible and familiar objects and events (such as "dog," "house"). This is the case because only with respect to such concepts are there exemplars that are both sufficient available and at a sufficiently low level of abstraction for the child to handle at his or her level of cognitive maturity. Once the child advances in general cognitive development, he or she may discover new primary concepts whose exemplars are themselves highly esoteric abstractions, but at the preoperational stage the exemplars of such concepts are neither available nor usable for purposes of concept formation. This does not mean that the exemplars of concepts must necessarily be nonrepresentational in nature, that is, consist of actual objects or events. Exemplars may also be verbal (consist of concept names), as in the previously cited examples of such low-order superordinate concepts as "vegetable" and "work," provided that: (1) the concepts they represent are known and have perceptible referents themselves ("carrot," "bean," "housekeeping," "nursing"); and (2) the criterial attributes of the superordinate concept, whether discovered or presented, are explicitly related to the concrete exemplars.

Concrete-operational children's acquisition of concepts proceeds at a much higher level of abstraction and yields correspondingly more abstract concept meanings. These children are able to cope with *secondary* concepts whose meanings they learn without actually coming into contact with the concrete-empirical experience from which the concepts are derived. Since such concepts are acquired by assimilation (by reception learning), the children are presented merely with criterial attributes, either definitionally or by context. But they do *not* have to first relate these attributes to particular exemplars of the concept before the attributes become relatable to cognitive structure; they depend instead on the use of concrete-empirical props (exemplars of the *attributes*). It will be explained further in Chapter 6 why the use of such props implies a much higher level of conceptualizing operation than the corresponding use of exemplars of the concept itself. Nevertheless, the process of conceptualization is constrained by the particularity of the input data, and typically yields a semiabstract and subverbal type of concept meaning. Only the less complex kinds of secondary concepts, not too remotely removed from the learner's orbit of personal and vicarious experience, can be acquired at this time.

The highest level of abstraction in concept acquisition is reached during the stage of abstract logical operations. The criterial attributes of complex and higher-order secondary concepts can be related directly to cognitive structure without any concrete-empirical props whatsoever; and the emerging products of conceptualization are refined by verbalization to yield precise, explicit, and genuinely abstract generic ideas.

Concepts are generally attained more rapidly and efficiently with increasing age (Rossi, 1964; Yudin & Kates, 1963). In addition, several qualitative trends consistent with the stages delineated above have been adequately established.

### Increased Abstractness and Precision

One of the most significant developmental trends in concept acquisition consists of a gradual shift from a precategorical to a categorical basis of classifying experience, or from a relatively concrete to a truly abstract basis of categorizing and designating generic meanings. In the precategorical stage, conceptualization does not proceed beyond the step of discriminative analysis (Bruner & Olver, 1963; Goldman & Levine, 1963; Reichard, Schneider, & Rapaport, 1944; Russell & Saadeh, 1962; Sigel, 1953; Vygotsky, 1962; Wallon, 1952; Werner, 1948). Objects and events are grouped in terms of their immediately perceived properties rather than in terms of their class membership. Thus preschool children are likely to classify objects on the basis of nonessential, incidental features, spatial and temporal contiguity, or similarity of action and location. During the elementary-school years, similarity of structure and function becomes a more important classificatory criterion. With advancing age, however, as children approach adolescence and become verbal-directed and freed from dependence on concrete-empirical experience in their conceptualizing operations, *categorical* classification on the basis of abstract criterial attributes becomes the dominant mode of organizing experience.

At first, concrete images are employed to represent a general class of perceptible objects. But these are gradually replaced by more abstract representational symbols detached from the stimulus properties they signify (Malrieu, 1955; Piaget, 1950, 1954b; Werner, 1948). Various dimensional properties (for instance, size, form, color) also tend at first to be restricted to the particular objects in relation to which they are originally experienced. With increasing age they become conceptualized and attain independent status in their own right. They can then be applied to any relevant object or situation. Concomitantly, new and more inclusive higher-order abstractions tend to be formed out of existing first-order concepts (Bruner & Olver, 1963; Piaget, 1950; Welch, 1940b).

Thus concepts are cumulative precipitates of cognitive experience and "later meanings are not only built upon but absorb earlier and simpler ones" (Strauss, 1952). Conceptual development involves a continuous series of reorganizations in which existing concepts are modified as they interact with new perceptions, ideational processes, affective states, and value systems. Generally increasing cognitive sophistication also leaves its mark on specific conceptualization. Concepts become more elaborate, systematic and flexible (Schuessler & Strauss, 1950; Vinacke, 1951) and less diffuse, syncretistic, and subjectivistic (Spiegel, 1950; Vinacke, 1951). Older children, for example, are less disposed to regard conceptual opposites (for instance, ugliness and beauty) as reified entities than as opposite ends of a conceptual continuum. They not only generate concepts of much greater scope and inclusiveness but also make finer distinctions between closely related concepts (for example, "dog" and "wolf"). In the same way subconcepts develop within concepts ("terrier" and "beagle" within "dog").

It is important to appreciate that children's use of culturally standardized conceptual terms does not necessarily imply that these terms represent the same generic meanings that they do for adults in the culture. The difficulty arises from the fact that children have no other terms to represent their immature conceptualizations and hence are obliged (and are encouraged) to use prevailing linguistic terms. Thus "dog" to a toddler is typically a proper noun (rather than a concept) designating one particular dog; and "Daddy" does not refer to an adult male who is paternally related but rather to the most familiar adult male in his or her social environment. Later on, as children attempt to generalize their existing "concepts" to new experience, "dog" represents *any* quadruped and "Daddy" *any* adult male. Generalization or extension of use occurs on the basis of the objective, affective, or functional similarity of a new object or situation to the object or situation originally designated by the word in question (Lewis, 1951). Typically this extension is overinclusive and requires differentiation and restriction; to a much lesser extent it is also underinclusive and requires widening. After the true criterial attributes of a class are properly abstracted, overinclusive applications are appropriately restricted and underinclusive applications are appropriately extended. Developmentally speaking, therefore, this problem is one of fitting conventional symbols, which have culturally standardized generic meanings, to individual cognitive experience until symbol-concept relationships for the individual come to approximate corresponding relationships holding for the culture at large.

Brown (1958a) points out that the development of concepts does not necessarily proceed from the concrete (subordinate) to the abstract (superordinate). To the extent that part of the process of conceptual development consists of differentiating subconcepts out of more inclusive categories (for instance, "carp" and "perch" out of "fish"), this contention is undoubtedly valid. Nevertheless, it must be appreciated that "fish" to a toddler is not the same superordinate concept that it is to an adult. Actually, at first, it is not a concept at all, but, rather, a particularistic term referring to one or more exemplars of "fish"; and, later, before a categorical concept emerges, the basis of classification is a common perceptual core. Thus before subconcepts can be truly differentiated from a more inclusive concept, the latter itself must first be acquired by a conceptualizing process in which concrete (precategorical) criterial attributes are progressively replaced by attributes that are more abstract or categorical in nature.

### More Concept Assimilation and Less Concept Formation

Paralleling general trends in cognitive development, reception learning gradually becomes ascendant over discovery learning in the acquisition of concepts. After children enter school an increasing proportion of their concepts are acquired by definition or use in context. For most children it is only as they approach adolescence that such nonspontaneous concepts manifest true categorical and generalized meaning. Prior to this time the concepts of most children are still somewhat particularistic and intuitive in nature because of their dependence during acquisition on concrete-empirical props. There are wide ranges in the extent of concept differentiation, with some seven- to eight-year-old children manifesting concepts approaching or exceeding those held by adults. Chiappetta (1976) reviewed research studies with high-school and college students showing that only some 20 to 60 percent of these age groups demonstrate Piaget's "formal operations" even though they exceed the age norms typical for attainment of formal operations.

It is not difficult to understand why concept assimilation gradually becomes the predominant mode of concept acquisition once a child reaches school age, whereas concept formation, though possible at any age level, is generally most characteristic of the preoperational or preschool stage of cognitive development. Concept assimilation characterizes the acquisition of secondary concepts; it presupposes sufficient intellectual maturity to relate to cognitive structure the abstracted criterial attributes of a new generic idea even though the attributes are *not* first in intimate association with the multiple particular exemplars of the concept from which they are derived. Since this degree of maturity rarely exists before school age, and only does then when the child has the benefit of concrete-empirical props, the principal alternative open to preschoolers is to discover the criterial attributes of concepts by themselves, using the necessary conceptualizing operations of abstraction, differentiation, hypothesis-generation and testing, and generalization. In so doing, preschoolers are obviously limited to the more simple kinds of primary concepts whose referents are either perceptible and familiar objects or events, or known concept words that represent such referents. But the criterial attributes of a concept that are discovered through concept formation obviously meet the developmental conditions for relatability to cognitive structure, inasmuch as they have been abstracted from and tested against particular exemplars of the concept during the process of conceptualization. Hence there is no problem with respect to the potential meaningfulness of self-discovered criterial attributes.

However, once children can meaningfully relate to their cognitive structure the criterial attributes of a new concept without first relating them to multiple particular instances that exemplify it, these children can acquire concepts much more efficiently. By the time children reach this stage of development, they have also already acquired, for the most part, the available supply of primary concepts with familiar and perceptible referents. They would thus find it relatively difficult to discover by themselves (to acquire by concept formation) the more abstract and complex concepts attained relatively easily through concept assimilation. Hence after discovering the body of simple everyday concepts that are available to them before they enter school, most individuals *discover* very few concepts by themselves thereafter. Contributions to culture's store of more difficult concepts are made by its more gifted members over the course of generations and become readily available to all other adequately mature members through concept assimilation. Otherwise each child would have to regenerate the conceptual inventions achieved by geniuses over human history—clearly an impossible task and the *raison d'être* for schools.

During the elementary-school years, it thus appears that progressive development of the ability to *assimilate* concepts depends on the *same* three aspects of cognitive and language development that generally bring about the transition from concrete to abstract cognitive functioning: (1) gradual acquisition of an adequate working body of higher-order abstractions that provide the component properties and relational elements constituting the criterial attributes of more difficult concepts; (2) gradual acquisition of "transactional" terms, that is, of substantive words such as "state," "condition," "basis," "property," "quality," and "relationship," and of functional or syntactical terms, such as conditional conjunctives and qualifying expressions, that are necessary for bringing abstractions into relationship with each other in ways characteristic of the dictionary definition of new concepts; and (3) gradual acquisition of the cognitive capacity itself, which makes possible the relation of abstract ideas to cognitive structure without the benefit of concrete-empirical props. The first two principles are illustrated in the results of a study by Feldman and Klausmeier (1974), in which fourth-grade students performed better in concept acquisition when attributes were presented in a less than technically correct manner, whereas eighth-grade students performed best when given technically correct definitions. They concluded that if particular attributes of a concept cannot be stated in a way that is understandable to the learner it is better not to include them when defining the concept.

One should recognize the highly significant interaction that takes place between many assimilated concepts and their subverbal or intuitive precursors. As Vygotsky (1962) notes, the elementary-school child in acquiring assimilated concepts is greatly assisted by the existence in his cognitive structure of analogous spontaneous concepts at the preoperational level, which he uses nondeliberately and with relatively little cognitive awareness.[8] These provide a springboard for the acquisition of "scientific" concepts[9] and for their "downward" exemplification and everyday reference. But although these spontaneous concepts undoubtedly enhance the meaningfulness of their analogous assimilated counterparts, and probably discourage rote reception learning, they may also, because of their primacy and vividness, interfere with the learning of more precise and categorical criterial attributes.

In teaching scientific concepts, therefore, it is essential to take account of the nature of their spontaneous precursors, that is, explicitly to contrast the two sets of criterial attributes and to indicate why the adoption of the more abstract and precise set is preferable. Within the limits imposed by developmental readiness, systematic verbal instruction in abstract concepts at the elementary-school level, combined with appropriate use of concrete-empirical props, is pedagogically feasible and can greatly accelerate the acquisition of higher-order concepts (Arnsdorf, 1961; Davis, 1958). It is unnecessary and educationally wasteful to wait for such concepts to evolve spontaneously from direct experience. Further, many abstract concepts (for instance, "photosynthesis," "ionization") can only be acquired verbally since they are not susceptible to direct experience. Other, more concrete concepts ("house," "dog," "red," "hot"), on the other hand, are practically meaningless in the absence of actual experience with the objects or phenomena in question.

### Increased Awareness of Conceptualizing Operations

Both Piaget and Vygotsky agree that awareness of the cognitive operations involved in concept acquisition does not develop until the child approaches adolescence and has been exposed to considerable systematic instruction in scientific concepts.

---

[8] "Work," for example, is both a spontaneous concept acquired from direct experience and a more formal, abstract concept with precise *criterial attributes*.

[9] Vygotsky's term for assimilated concepts in contradistinction to concepts acquired by concept formation ("spontaneous concepts").

In operating with spontaneous concepts the child is not conscious of them because his attention is always centered on the object to which the concept refers, never on the act of thought itself. . . .

A concept can become subject to consciousness and deliberate control only when it is part of a system. . . . In the scientific concepts that the child acquires in school, the relationship to an object is mediated from the start by some other concept. . . . A superordinate concept implies the existence of a series of subordinate concepts, and it also presupposes a hierarchy of concepts at different levels of generality. . . . Thus the very notion of a scientific concept implies a certain position in relation to other concepts. . . . The rudiments of systematization first enter the child's mind by way of his contact with scientific concepts and are transferred to everyday concepts, changing their psychological structure from the top down (Vygotsky, 1962, pp. 92, 93).

Awareness of concept acquisition develops late, Vygotsky (1962) believes, because it requires awareness of similarity. This, in turn, presupposes "a more advanced structure of generalization and conceptualization than awareness of difference." Nevertheless, even though a child cannot use a word like "because" deliberately in a test situation, and does not really grasp causal relations except in a very primitive and intuitive sense, he or she is able to use "because" correctly in everyday conversation. The rules of syntax too can generally be employed correctly by young children despite complete lack of awareness of the nature of these rules. However, deliberate use of such words as "because" is possible in relation to scientific concepts because the "teacher, working with the pupil, has explained, supplied information, questioned, corrected, and made the pupil explain" (Vygotsky, 1962, p. 107). It is hardly surprising therefore that awareness of concept acquisition and deliberate use of concepts arise earlier in relation to scientific than to spontaneous concepts.

## Factors Influencing Concept Acquisition

### Experience, Intelligence, Sex

By virtue of the very way in which concepts are generally formed, it is inevitable that the acquisition of particular concepts is dependent on a rich background of relevant experience (Serra, 1953). Concepts in early and middle childhood, especially, reflect the cumulative impact of first-hand, concrete-empirical experience over extended periods of time. Hence there tends to be a higher relationship between degree of experience (as indicated by school grade and chronological age) and scores on concept tests than between the latter scores and IQ (Deutsche, 1937; Gubrud & Novak, 1973; Vinacke, 1951). For this reason also, genuine understanding of concepts involved in the appreciation of temporal and sociological relationships cannot be materially increased by exposing childen to brief special periods of essentially second-hand, verbal practice in school (Eaton, 1944; Pistor, 1940); at the very least, systematic didactic instruction using concrete-empirical props is necessary. When abstractions are introduced prematurely, some children become quite adept at mouthing them and, at the same time, concealing their lack of true understanding. This obviously becomes a fertile source for misconceptions and uncritical acceptance of ideas.

Although superior mental age, in the absence of corresponding life experience (chronological age), provides little advantage in comprehending abstractions, such comprehension is definitely related to IQ *within* a given grade level (Braun, 1963; Elkind, 1961b; Osler & Shapiro, 1964; Osler & Weiss, 1962; Serra, 1953). The correlation between concept scores and either vocabulary or verbal intelligence is higher than the correlation between these scores and nonverbal intelligence (Deutsche, 1937; Hoffman, 1955). Apart from conditions of actual cultural disadvantage, cultural or social class environment does not have much effect on ability to conceptualize (Deutsche, 1937), but it does sensitize the individual to particular areas of conceptual experience. Thus it is likely that conceptual learning ability is not a unitary trait; it varies with differential patterns of experience. Whatever sex differences appear in concept acquisition appear to conform to this explanation (Elkind, 1961a; Olson, 1963).

### Heterogeneity of Instances

Provided that sufficient redundancy or repetition is present to ensure adequate unit mastery (overlearning), the defining attributes of a concept are learned most readily when the concept is encountered in a large number of different contexts (Callantine & Warren, 1955; Duncan, 1958; Haygood & Bourne, 1964; Hull, 1920; Johnson & Zara, 1960; Lloyd, 1960; Morrisett & Hovland, 1959; Sassenrath, 1959; Shore & Sechrest, 1961; Stern, 1965; Wittrock & Twelker, 1964). By de-emphasizing the particularity of single or homogeneous instances, multicontextual learning facilitates the abstraction of commonality, strengthens the generality and transferability of the resulting concept, and endows it with greater stability. Small, barely discriminable differences among instances, on the other hand, increase the difficulty of concept attainment (Sechrest & Kaas, 1965). In practice, the proper balance between heterogeneity and consolidation can be achieved by promoting mastery within a given context or subcategory of exemplars before proceeding to another context.

### Positive versus Negative Instances

The weight of the evidence indicates that positive instances lead more effectively than negative instances to concept acquisition (Braley, 1963; Hovland, 1952; Hovland & Weiss, 1953; Olson, 1963). In part, this reflects the greater amount, and the more explicit nature, of the information conveyed by positive instances and the smaller burden they place on memory (Braley, 1963; Hovland & Weiss, 1953). More important perhaps is a disinclination on the part of most learners to make use of potentially useful information presented by negative instances and to adopt a strategy of exclusion (Bruner, Goodnow, & Austin, 1956). Houtz & Moore (1973) and Huttenlocher (1962) found that a negative followed by a positive instance was the most effective combination, and that older students are better adapted to cope with negative instances. With increasing practice the initial difference between the relative effectiveness of positive and negative instances tends to become progressively smaller (Freibergs & Tulving, 1961; Fryatt & Tulving, 1963). Harris (1973) and Nahinsky and Slaymaker (1970) found that positive instances of concepts appeared to carry the critical information best for generalizations, whereas negative instances carry it best for discrimination. This suggests that teachers should explicitly train pupils to make more effective use of negative instances in acquiring new concepts.

### Relevant versus Irrelevant Information

Increased salience of relevant dimensions of a concept tends to facilitate concept acquisition, whereas an increase in the amount or salience of irrelevant information has precisely the opposite effect (Haygood & Bourne, 1964; McConnell, 1964; Rasmussen & Archer, 1961; Thysell & Schulz, 1964; Walker & Bourne, 1961). Irrelevant information obviously complicates the task of concept acquisition by increasing the learner's task of identifying relevant criterial attributes. As might be readily predicted, relevant information is more effective when it is obvious rather than subtle (Archer, 1962; Olson, 1963).

### Contiguity and Set

When an entire array of instances is simultaneously available to the learner rather than being presented successively, concept acquisition is significantly facilitated (Bourne, Goldstein, & Link, 1964; Bourne & Jennings, 1963; Bourne & Parker, 1964; Kates & Yudin, 1964). This effect presumably reflects the avoidance of memory loss and the possibility of closer grouping during the process of abstracting the criterial attributes of a concept. A set or orientation to respond conceptually to stimuli also facilitates the acquisition of concepts (Della-Piana, 1957; Shaffer, 1961; Siegel & Siegel, 1965).

# 4

# MEANINGFUL RECEPTION
# LEARNING AND RETENTION

In preceding chapters we have explored the nature, conditions, and types of meaningful school learning with particular emphasis on concept learning. We have also examined, in some detail, three common examples of meaningful learning at different age levels: learning the syntax of one's native language (preschool); learning how to read (elementary school); and learning a second language (secondary school).

We now need to consider the psychological mechanisms whereby large quantities of subject-matter knowledge are retained in cognitive structure over extended periods of time. How is such knowledge assimilated and organized in cognitive structure and why is it subsequently forgotten? Is there more than one valid explanation for the discrepancy between learned and remembered content, that is, are there different kinds of forgetting? And last, how does meaningful learning differ as a process from rote learning, and why does it yield superior learning and retention outcomes?

Before turning to these problems, however, it will be useful to reexamine some of the more salient properties of meaningful reception learning, inasmuch as this type of learning underlies the acquisition of most subject-matter knowledge. In reviewing these issues, we shall provide examples to illustrate how the psychological principles presented are important in school learning. Our purpose is to move from the more theoretical issues discussed earlier to practical issues important in school learning.

115

Contrary to beliefs expressed in many educational quarters, meaningful reception learning need not necessarily be rote or passive (as it so often is in actual educational practice) provided that one uses expository teaching methods that are based on the nature, conditions, and development considerations characterizing meaningful reception learning. And, as we shall demonstrate in later chapters (Part Four), discovery learning can also be, and in most classrooms typically is, rote in nature because it does not conform to the conditions of meaningful learning.

Meaningful reception learning is an active process because it requires, at the very least (1) the kind of cognitive analysis necessary for ascertaining which aspects of existing cognitive structure are most relevant to the new potentially meaningful material; (2) some degree of reconciliation with existing ideas in cognitive structure—that is, apprehending similarities and differences, and resolving real or apparent contradictions, between new and already established concepts and propositions; and (3) reformulation of the learning material in terms of the idiosyncratic intellectual background and vocabulary of the particular learner.

The nature and conditions of active meaningful reception learning also demands a type of expository teaching that recognizes the principles of progressive differentiation and integrative reconciliation characterizing the learning, retention, and organization of subect-matter content in the learner's cognitive structure. The first principle acknowledges that most learning, and all retention and organization, of subject-matter is hierarchical in nature, proceeding from the top downwards in terms of level of abstraction, generality, and inclusiveness. Integrative reconciliation is facilitated in expository teaching if the teacher and/or instructional materials explicitly anticipate the confusable similarities and differences between new ideas and established relevant existing ideas already present in learners' cognitive structures.

An advance organizer (see Chapter 5) is a pedagogic device that helps implement these principles by bridging the gap between what the learner already knows and what he needs to know if he is to learn new material most actively and expeditiously.

As new learning material is assimilated into cognitive structure, it is related to, and interacts with, existing relevant content already present. The acquisition of new meanings is a product of such interaction. During the retention interval, the new meanings are stored (linked) and organized in relation to their anchoring ideas. Only for a certain limited period of time-(unless overlearned by repetition), are they dissociable as identifiable entities separate from their an--choring ideas. However, when dissociability strength falls below the

*threshold of a certain critical point (the threshold of availability),
forgetting or gradual reduction to the anchoring ideas (obliterative
subsumption) occurs. The variables that enhance or detract from the
initial acquisition of new meanings continue to operate similarly in
the retention period.*

*As will be explained later (Parts Three and Four), cognitive
variables, on the one hand, and motivational-personality-social
variables, on the other, affect meaningful learning and retention
through different mechnisms. Forgetting can also be influenced by
certain factors (such as initial "learning shock," "repression," the
elicitation of reproduction through recall versus recognition, hypnosis) that influence the threshold of availability without altering whatsoever the dissociability strength of the meanings in question.*

*Rote learning and forgetting depend on the acquisition of discrete
associative strength and its diminution through exposure to prior
and/or subsequent interference by similar but confusable discrete
elements already in storage or acquired subsequently (proactive
and retroactive interference). Meaningful learning and forgetting, on
the other hand, depend, first, on relating new, potentially meaningful material to relevant ideas in the learner's cognitive structure
and, second (in the absence of overlearning) on subsequent spontaneous and gradual loss of the dissociability of the new meanings
acquired through such interaction from their anchoring ideas (obliterative subsumption). In both rote and meaningful learning the actual
reproduction of retained material is affected by such factors as cultural or attitudinal bias and by the specific situational demands of
the reproduction setting itself. The differences between rote and
meaningful learning processes account in large measure for the
superiority of meaningful as opposed to rote learning and retention.*

## The Nature of Meaningful Reception Learning

We have already indicated that the acquisition of subject-matter knowledge in any culture is primarily a manifestation of reception learning. That
is, the principal content of what is to be learned is typically presented to
the learner in more or less final form. Under these circumstances the learner
is simply required to comprehend the material and to incorporate it into his
cognitive structure so that it is available for either reproduction, related
learning, or problem solving at some future date.

Yet few pedagogic devices in our time have been repudiated more
unequivocally by educational theorists than the method of expository verbal
instruction. It is fashionable in many quarters to characterize verbal learning as parrotlike recitation and rote memorization of isolated facts and to

dismiss it disdainfully as an archaic remnant of discredited educational tradition. Over the past five decades, activity programs, project and discussion methods, various ways of maximizing nonverbal and manipulative experience in the classroom, emphasis on "self-discovery" and on learning for and by *problem-solving, inquiry* approaches, or *process* methods were introduced largely in response to widespread dissatisfaction with techniques of verbal instruction. Quite apart from whatever their intrinsic values, these activities came into being primarily because of the general inadequacies of verbal instruction as practiced in schools. It has been commonly accepted, for example (at least in the realm of educational theory) that: (1) meaningful generalizations cannot be presented or "given" to the learner but can be acquired only as a product of problem-solving activity; and (2) all attempts to master verbal concepts and propositions are forms of empty verbalism unless the learner has recent prior experience with the realities to which these verbal constructs refer (Brownell & Hendrickson, 1950; Brownell & Sims, 1946; Romey, 1968; Rowe, 1973; Ryan & Ellis, 1974).

Adequate reasons, of course, exist for some of the disenchantment with expository teaching and reception learning. The most obvious of these is that potentially meaningful subject matter is frequently presented to pupils in such a way that they can only learn it *rotely*. Another less obvious but equally important reason why meaning is perceived as an exclusive product of problem-solving and discovery techniques of learning stems from two serious shortcomings of prevailing learning theory. First, psychologists have tended to subsume many qualitatively different kinds of learning processes under a single explanatory model. As a result, widespread confusion exists regarding basic distinctions between reception and discovery learning and between rote and meaningful learning. It has not always been sufficiently clear, for example, that such categorically different types of learning as problem solving and the understanding of presented verbal material have different objectives. Moreover, conditions and instructional techniques facilitating one of these learning processes are not necessarily relevant or maximally efficient for the other. Second, in the absence of an appropriate theory of meaningful verbal learning, many educational psychologists have tended to interpret long-term subject-matter learning and forgetting in terms of the same concepts (stimulus generalization, retroactive interference, and so on) used to explain laboratory forms of rote learning. It is hardly surprising, therefore, that reception learning has been widely perceived as a rote phenomenon.

Accordingly, one of the main goals of the present chapter will be to develop further the distinguishing attributes of reception learning and to *sharpen the distinction between rote and meaningful learning*. It should then be clear that verbal reception learning can be genuinely meaningful without prior discovery experience or problem-solving activity, and that the invariable rote outcomes attributed to the method of expository verbal instructions do not inhere in the method itself but are derived from various shortcomings in reception learning procedures as currently employed in schools.

### Is Reception Learning Meaningful?

How valid is the contention that abstract concepts and generalizations are forms of empty, meaningless verbalism unless the learner discovers them autonomously from his own concrete, empirical, problem-solving experience? Careful analysis of this proposition reveals that it rests on three logical fallacies:

1. The prevailing tendency to confuse the reception-discovery dimension of the learning process with the rote-meaningful dimension
2. Unwarranted generalization of the distinctive developmental conditions of learning and thinking during early childhood to adolescence and adult life
3. A straw-man representation of the method of reception learning

The first of these fallacies has already been considered in some detail in Figure 1.1 and Chapter 2. In Chapter 3 we distinguished between *concept formation* and *assimilation,* which are the primary modes of meaningful learning for younger children and adults respectively.

The use of the straw-man technique has been the simplest and most effective way of discrediting the method of verbal exposition. Instead of describing this pedagogic procedure in terms of its essential characteristics, it became fashionable to picture it in terms of its worst abuses. Examples of such abuses were naturally not difficult to find, since an appreciable number of teachers still rely on rote verbal learning in teaching potentially meaningful subject matter. Some of the more flagrantly inept practices include:

1. Premature use of pure verbal techniques with cognitively immature pupils
2. Arbitrary presentation of unrelated facts without any organizing or explanatory principles
3. Failure to integrate new learning tasks with previously presented materials
4. The use of evaluation procedures that merely measure ability to recognize discrete facts or to reproduce ideas in the same words or in the identical context as originally encountered

For the most part, courses in educational psychology and other courses for preparation of teachers have placed little stress on the important distinctions between rote and meaningful reception learning. In consequence, only those gifted teachers who had an intuitive grasp of the importance of prior learning in facilitating new learning and the role that concept formation and concept assimilation play in learning principles or propositions succeeded in using reception learning strategies of the kind described in this book. Since gifted teachers are uncommon in schools (as indeed gifted practitioners are uncommon in any field) and since most college courses for teachers are bad examples of expository teaching, it stands to reason that the potential existing for *meaningful* reception teaching is seldom realized in practice. We believe that a clear explication of the psychological principles underlying meaningful reception learning are easily within the grasp of any teacher and, when applied and combined with other kinds of teaching practices, can result in substantial improvement in school learning.

Contemporary representatives of the progressive education movement speak with disdain about the school's role of helping children learn by themselves. They assert that the former role is a paltry one and that it invariably results in the learning of glib and meaningless verbalisms. This is not necessarily true provided that the obvious abuses of expository instruction are avoided. Verbal exposition is actually the most efficient way of teaching subject matter and leads to sounder and *less trivial knowledge* than when pupils serve as their own pedagogues. We will show in a later chapter that empirical evidence indicates that success in problem solving is *primarily* dependent on the adequacy of specifically *relevant* concepts in cognitive structure and does not derive from training in generalized "problem-solving strategies." Thus, the art and science of presenting ideas and information effectively—so that clear, stable, and unambiguous meanings emerge and are retained over a long period of time as an organized body of knowledge—is really one of the principal functions of pedagogy. This is a demanding and creative, rather than a routine or mechanical, task. The job of selecting, organizing, presenting, and translating subject-matter content in a developmentally appropriate manner requires more than a rote listing of facts. If it is done properly, it is the work of a master teacher. It is hardly a task to be disdained.

Finally, we should recognize that various developmental considerations limiting the meaningfulness of reception learning during early childhood do not apply during later childhood, adolescence, and adult life. Learners who have not yet developed beyond the concrete operational stage are unable meaningfully to incorporate within their cognitive structures a relationship between two or more "secondary" abstractions unless they have the benefit of some current or recent concrete-empirical props (Inhelder & Piaget, 1958). Thus during the concrete operational stage, roughly covering the elementary-school period, many children are restricted by this degree of dependence on concrete-empirical experience to a semi-abstract, intuitive understanding of abstract propositions. Such learners cannot comprehend, or meaningfully manipulate in problem solving, verbally or symbolically expressed abstract propositions without the aid of concrete-empirical props. Even then their understanding tends to be intuitive and somewhat particularistic rather than precise, explicit, and truly abstract. Reception learning at this stage is also limited by the lack of higher-order abstract concepts in cognitive structure to which large amounts of information may be related and by the lack of transactional terms for relating ideas to each other. Many of these limitations derive from the general absence of emphasis on concept learning in elementary schools. A growing body of evidence indicates that better instructional practices can enhance the ability of both children and adults to engage in formal or abstract reasoning.

These limitations drastically curtail the scope of expository teaching and reception learning. Nevertheless, even during the elementary-school years, autonomous discovery is not indispensable for intuitive understanding and need not constitute a routine part of pedagogic technique. As every elementary-school teacher knows, meaningful verbal reception learning—without any problem-solving or discovery experience whatsoever—is perhaps the commonest form of classroom learning, provided that the necessary concrete-empirical props are available.

During the abstract stage of cognitive development, however, most students can acquire most new concepts and learn most new propositions by *directly* grasping higher-order relationships between abstractions (Inhelder & Piaget, 1958). To do so meaningfully, they need no longer depend on current or recent concrete-empirical props, and hence are able to bypass completely the intuitive type of understanding reflective of such dependence. In large measure this development reflects the availability of an adequate body of higher-order abstractions and transactional terms. Expository instruction thus becomes much more feasible. Through reception learning, students can proceed directly to a level of *abstract* understanding that is qualitatively superior to the intuitive level in terms of generality, clarity, precision and explicitness. At this stage of development, therefore, properly arranged verbal reception learning is highly meaningful. Hence it is unnecessary to introduce concrete-empirical props or time-consuming discovery techniques in order to make possible or to enhance *intuitive* understanding of abstract propositions.

This is the point at which some of the more zealous proponents of progressive education took a disastrously false turn. John Dewey had correctly recognized that understanding of abstract concepts and principles in childhood must be built on a foundation of direct, concrete, empirical experience, and for this reason he advocated the use of project and activity methods in the elementary school. But he also appreciated that once a firmly grounded first story of abstract understandings is established, it is possible to organize secondary and higher education along more abstract and verbal lines. Unfortunately, however, although Dewey himself never elaborated or implemented this latter conception, some of his disciples took precisely the opposite position. They blindly generalized childhood limiting conditions with respect to meaningful abstract reception learning broadly enough to encompass learning over the entire life-span. This unwarranted extrapolation, frequently but erroneously attributed to Dewey himself, provided an apparent rationale for, and thus helped perpetuate, the seemingly indestructible myth that—under any and all circumstances—abstractions cannot possibly be meaningful unless preceded by direct, empirical experience. In more recent years, proponents of alternate schools (Holt, 1964; Illich, 1970; Kozol, 1967) have repeated the errors of the progressive education movements of the 1930s and 1940s.

### Is Meaningful Reception Learning Passive?

The acquisition of meanings through meaningful reception learning is far from being a passive kind of cognitive process. Much activity is obviously involved, but not the kind of activity characterizing discovery. Activity and discovery are not synonymous in the realm of cognitive functioning. Merely because potential meanings are presented, we cannot assume that they are necessarily *acquired* and that all subsequent loss is reflective of forgetting.

Before meanings can be retained they must first be acquired, and the process of *acquisition is necessarily active*. Neither can we assume that reception learning is more passive and mechanical than independent data gathering and interpretation. The unmotivated student who gathers and interprets data manifests no greater intellectual activity than the unmotivated student who receives expository instruction. Collection of data and perfunctory compilation of charts, tables, or graphs and similar activities are among the strategies that students employ to "look busy," while in fact very little meaningful learning is occurring. Motivated students, on the other hand, reflectively consider, rework, and integrate new material into their cognitive structure irrespective of how they obtain it.

Thus meaningful reception learning involves more than the simple cataloging of ready-made concepts within existing cognitive structure. In the first place, at least an implicit judgment of relevance is usually required in deciding which established ideas in cognitive structure are most relatable to a new learning task. Second, some degree of reconciliation between them is necessary, particularly if there are discrepancies or conflicts. Third, new propositions are customarily reformulated to blend into a personal frame of reference consonant with the learner's experiential background, vocabulary, and structure of ideas. Finally, if the learner, in the course of meaningful reception learning, cannot find an acceptable basis for reconciling apparently or genuinely contradictory ideas, he or she is sometimes inspired to attempt a degree of synthesis or reorganization of his or her existing knowledge under more inclusive and broadly explanatory principles. The learner may either seek such propositions in more recent or sophisticated expositions of a given topic, or, under certain circumstances, may try to discover them independently.

All of this activity (except for the last-mentioned), however, stops short of actual discovery or problem solving. Since the substance of the learning task is essentially presented, the activity involved is limited to that required for effectively assimilating new meanings and integrating them into existing cognitive structure. This is naturally of a qualitatively different order than that involved in independently discovering solutions to new problems—in autonomously reorganizing new information and existing ideas in cognitive structure in such a way as to satisfy the requirements of a given problem situation.

The extent to which meaningful reception learning is active depends in part on one's need for integrative meaning and on the vigorousness of one's self-critical faculty. One may either attempt to integrate a new proposition with *all* of one's existing relevant knowledge or remain content with establishing its relatedness to a single idea. Similarly, one may endeavor to translate the new proposition into terminology consistent with one's own vocabulary and ideational background, or remain satisfied with incorporating it as presented. Finally, one may strive for the acquisition of precise and unambiguous meanings, or be completely satisfied with vague, diffuse notions.

The main danger in meaningful reception learning is not so much that learners will frankly adopt a rote approach, but rather that they will delude themselves into believing that they have grasped genuine meanings when they have *really* grasped only vague and confused sets of empty verbalisms. It is not so much that they do not want to understand, but that they lack the necessary self-critical ability and are unwilling to put forth the necessary active effort in struggling with the material, in looking at it from different angles, in reconciling and integrating it with related or contradictory knowledge, and in reformulating it from the standpoint of their own frame of reference. One may find it easy enough to manipulate words glibly so as to create a spurious impression of knowledgeability, and thereby delude oneself and others into thinking that the material is truly understood when it is not.

A central task of pedagogy, therefore, is to develop ways of facilitating an active variety of reception learning characterized by an independent and critical approach to the understanding of subject matter. This involves, in part, the encouragement of motivations for and self-critical attitudes toward acquiring precise and integrated meanings, as well as the use of other techniques directed toward the same end. Precise and integrated understandings are, presumably, more likely to develop if:

1. The central unifying ideas of a discipline are learned before more peripheral concepts and information are introduced.

2. The limiting conditions of general developmental readiness are observed.

3. Precise and accurate definition is stressed, and emphasis is placed on delineating similarities and differences between related concepts.

4. Learners are required to reformulate new propositions in their *own* words.

All of these devices come under the heading of pedagogic techniques that promote an active type of meaningful reception learning. Teachers can help foster the related objective of assimilating subject matter critically by encouraging students to recognize and challenge the assumptions underlying new propositions, and to distinguish between facts and hypotheses and between warranted and unwarranted inferences. Much good use can also be made of Socratic questioning in exposing pseudo-understanding, in transmitting precise meanings, in reconciling contradictions, and in encouraging a critical attitude toward knowledge.

### Progressive Differentiation and Integrative Reconciliation

During the course of meaningful learning, two important, related processes take place. As new information is subsumed under a given concept or proposition, new information is learned and the subsuming concept or proposition is modified (refer to Table 2.2). This process of subsumption, occurring one or more times, leads to *progressive* differentiation of the subsuming concept or proposition. In the assimilation theory of learning presented in this book, most of the meaningful learning that occurs could be characterized as involving progressive differentiation of concepts or propositions. For example, the new meanings that would be acquired over time for propositions such as Ohm's law or concepts like democracy or evolution would represent progressive differentiation of these propositions or concepts.

In superordinate or combinatorial learning (see Table 2.2), established ideas in cognitive structure may become recognized as related, in the course of new learning. Thus new information is acquired *and* existing elements of cognitive structure may take on new organization and hence new meaning. This recombination of existing elements of cognitive structure is referred to as *integrative reconciliation*. For example, students may know peas or tomatoes as vegetables, but these are classified as fruits in biology. The initial confusion a student may experience is resolved when new combinatorial meanings are learned and the student recognizes that the nutritional classification of foods is not the same as the botanical classification. Thus carrots, beets, and yams are vegetables and plant roots, but peas, cucumbers, and tomatoes are vegetables and plant fruits. After integrative reconciliation of new botanical information, previously learned concepts and propositions have been modified and new meanings have been added to cognitive structure. Integrative reconciliation proceeds best when possible sources of confusion are sorted out by the teacher or instructional materials. Hence students may be aided in resolving what may appear to be inconsistencies or conflicts between concepts or propositions.

All learning resulting in integrative reconciliation will also result in further differentiation of existing concepts or propositions. Integrative reconciliation is one form of progressive differentiation of cognitive structure that occurs in meaningful learning. One attribute of outstanding teachers is that they have sufficient breadth of knowledge and experience with learners in their field to enable them to aid students in explicit ways to form their individual integrative reconciliations. When students regard a course or textbook (rarely) as well organized, it is because the meanings of new concepts or propositions are clearly presented, possible conflicts in meanings are resolved, and new integrative reconciliations are facilitated.


## The Assimilation Process in the Acquisition, Retention, and Organization of Knowledge

To account more completely for the acquisition, retention, and organization of meanings in cognitive structure, it is necessary at this point to develop further the principle of *assimilation*.

When a new idea $a$ is meaningfully learned and linked to relevant established idea $A$, both ideas are modified and $a$ is *assimilated* into established idea $A$. This would be an instance of derivative or correlative subsumption and as indicated in Chapter 2, both the anchoring idea $A$ and the new idea $a$ become modified, forming the interaction product $A'a'$. For example if $A$ is a child's concept of sin, $a$ may be a new parental admonition that wasting food is a sin, thus modifying the child's concept of sin.

Stating the case more precisely, however, the *actual* or total interactional product of the new idea and the established idea is hypothesized as being greater and more complex than as originally described in Chapter 2. This is where the assimilation process enters the picture. We must examine more closely the new learning of $a$ and the recall or dissociability of $a'$ from $A'$, and the eventual loss of dissociability of $a'$ from $A'$. These processes are described in Table 4.1. As noted above, both the potentially meaningful idea $a$ and the established idea $A$ to which it is anchored are changed as well by the interactional process. This is indicated in Table 4.1 by use of the prime sign in each case. More important, both interactional products $a'$ and $A'$ remain in relationship to each other as linked comembers of a

TABLE 4.1 Stages in the Learning and Retention of a Subordinate Idea in Relation to its Dissociability Strength

| | New, Potentially Meaningful Idea $a'$ | related to and assimilated by | Established Idea $A$ in Cognitive Structure | Interactional Product $A'a'$ |
|---|---|---|---|---|
| I MEANINGFUL LEARNING OR ACQUISITION OF SUBORDINATE MEANING $a'$ | | | | |
| II POSTLEARNING AND EARLY RETENTION OF MEANING $a'$ | New meaning $a'$ is dissociable from $A'a'$ | $A'a' \leftrightarrow A' + a'$ (high dissociability strength) | | |
| III LATER RETENTION OF MEANING $a'$ | Gradual loss of dissociability of $a'$ from $A'a'$ | $A'a' \leftrightarrow A' + a'$ (low dissociability strength) | | |
| IV FORGETTING OF MEANING $a'$ | $a'$ is no longer effectively dissociable from $A'a'$ | | Dissociability of $a'$ from $A'a'$ is below the threshold of availability: $a'$ is reduced to $A'$ | |

composite unit or ideational complex, $A'a'$. In the more complete sense of the term, therefore, the actual interactional product of the meaningful learning process is not just the new meaning of $a'$ but includes the modification of the anchoring idea and is the composite meaning $A'a'$. Thus the subsumption process forms a new composite idea, which may undergo further change over time. Therefore, *assimilation* is not completed after meaningful learning but continues over a time course that may involve further new learning or eventual loss of retrievability of subordinate ideas.

Much of school learning involves the development and elaboration of meanings of *concepts*. Concepts were defined as objects, events, situations or properties that possess *common criterial attributes* and are designated in any given culture by some accepted sign or symbol. We distinguished between the process of *concept formation*, which occurs predominantly in preschool children, and *concept assimilation*, which is the dominant form of concept learning for schoolchildren and adults. Concept formation requires direct experience with objects, events, situations, or properties from which the child abstracts the criterial attributes through a form of discovery learning. Older children and adults can acquire new concepts through the process of concept assimilation when they are presented the criterial attributes of a new concept. Although direct experience may be beneficial for acquiring some concepts at any age level, most of the concepts humans acquire make use of the capabilities of language and concepts acquired earlier to assimilate new meanings and to form new concepts. *Representational* learning, which ordinarily follows concept formation, is the process by which a sign or symbol is recognized as the culturally designated form representing the meaning of the concept.

Most of the material taught in schools is in the form of *propositions*, which are comprised of concepts that in combination have some new composite meaning. To learn a proposition requires more than just learning the meanings of the component concepts, however. This might be illustrated by the proposition: green plants manufacture food. Nevertheless, the learning of new propositions usually requires learning of new concepts that are component parts of the proposition, as well as the special generic meaning of the proposition itself.

At the core of assimilation theory is the idea that new meanings are acquired by the *interaction* of new knowledge with previously learned concepts or propositions. This interaction process results in a modification of both the meaning of the new information and the meaning of the concept or proposition to which it is anchored. Thus a new ideational product with new meaning is created. This process of sequential assimilation of new meanings results in *progressive differentiation* of concepts or propositions with the consequent refinement of meanings and an enhanced potential for providing anchorage for further meaningful learning. When concepts or propositions are related through new superordinate or combinatorial learning, new meanings arise and conflicting meanings may be resolved through *integrative reconciliation*. In time, as the assimilation process continues, meanings of component concepts or propositions may no longer be dissociable from their anchoring ideas. The result is *obliterative* assimilation or meaningful forgetting.

### The Explanatory Value of Assimilation

The assimilation theory has explanatory value for both retention phenomena and learning phenomena because it helps account both for the memorial longevity of meaningfully learned ideas and for the way in which knowledge is organized in cognitive structure. Assimilation could conceivably enhance retention in three different ways. First, by becoming "anchored," so to speak, to a modified form of a highly stable existing idea in cognitive structure, the new meaning vicariously shares the stability of the latter.[1] Second, this type of anchorage, by *continuing* during storage the *original* nonarbitrary relationship between the new idea and the established idea, also protects the new meaning from the interference exerted by previously learned, concurrently experienced, and subsequently encountered similar ideas. This interference is what is so damaging when learning material is arbitrarily related to cognitive structure, as occurs in rote learning. Third, the fact that the new meaningful idea is stored in linked relationship to the *particular* idea(s) in cognitive structure to which it is most relevant (that is, to the idea(s) to which it was originally related in acquiring its meaning) presumably makes retrieval a less arbitrary and more systematic process.

The assimilation hypothesis can also help explain how knowledge is organized in cognitive structure. New ideas may be *stored* in linked relationship to correspondingly relevant existing ideas in cognitive structure. Moreover, assume that one member of the linked pair is typically super-

---

[1] It will be convenient henceforth to refer to the established relevant idea $A$ in cognitive structure to which the new potentially meaningful idea $a$ is related as the "anchoring idea." Strictly speaking, however, the actual anchoring idea (after subsumption) is $A'$—not $A$; but this distinction can be ignored for all practical purposes since $A'$ and $A$ are not very different from each other. It *is* important to bear in mind that it is not $a$ that is anchored to $A$, but rather $a'$ (the meaning of $a$).

It should also be noted that the term "assimilation" has been used here in the narrow sense of the term to apply to the linkage of the emergent new meaning with the anchoring idea for storage and to the later reduction process. It would also be legitimate to include the earlier aspects of the meaningful learning process (in which the new idea is related to and interacts with the established idea) as part of assimilation in the broader sense of the term. This broader usage not only is consistent with what is usually meant by assimilation, but also is consistent with the fact that the linkage of the new meaning with the anchoring idea necessarily implies that the potentially meaningful idea is *first* related to and interacts with the established idea.

ordinate to or more inclusive than the other and that the superordinate member (at least, once it is established) is the more stable member of the pair. It then necessarily follows that the cumulative residue of what is learned, retained, and forgotten (the psychological structure of knowledge or cognitive structure as a whole) conforms to the organizational principle of progressive differentiation. Thus, if assimilation were operative in the storage of meaningful ideas, it would then be quite understandable why an individual's mental organization of the content of a particular subject-matter discipline exemplifies a hierarchically ordered pyramid. The most inclusive and broadly explanatory ideas occupy a position at the apex of the pyramid and subsume progressively less inclusive, or more highly differentiated, ideas, each linked to the next higher step in the hierarchy through assimilative bonds.

As suggested above, the assimilation or anchoring process probably has a generally facilitating effect on retention. However, to explain how newly assimilated meanings actually become available during the retention period, we must assume that for a variable period of time they are *dissociable* from their anchoring ideas and hence are reproducible as individually identifiable entities. Thus, as shown in Table 4.1, the newly learned and assimilated meaning $a'$ is initially dissociable from its linked relationship to anchoring idea $A'$. The interactional product $A'a'$, in other words, dissociates into $A'$ and $a'$. Universal experience indicates that degree of dissociability, or dissociability strength, is at a maximum immediately after learning and therefore that new meanings, in the absence of direct or indirect practice, are maximally available at that time.

### Memorial Reduction; Obliterative Subsumption

The attractiveness of the assimilation process inheres in its ability to account for the superior retention of meaningfully learned ideas. The process also implies a plausible mechanism for the subsequent forgetting of these ideas, namely, the gradual "reduction" of their meanings to the meanings of the corresponding anchoring ideas to which they are linked. Thus, although the retention of newly learned meanings is generally enhanced by anchorage to relevant established ideas in the learner's cognitive structure, such knowledge is still subject to the erosive influence of the general reductionist trend in cognitive organization. It is more economical and less burdensome merely to retain the more stable and established anchoring concepts and propositions than to remember the new ideas that are assimilated in relation to them. Hence the meaning of the new ideas tends to be assimilated or reduced, over the course of time, to the more stable meanings of the established anchoring ideas. Immediately after learning, therefore, when this second, *obliterative* stage of assimilation is occurring, the new ideas become spontaneously and progressively less dissociable from their anchoring ideas as entities in their own right, until they are no longer available and are said to be forgotten. When the dissociability strength of $a'$ falls below a certain critical level (the threshold of availability), it is no longer retrievable. Eventually zero dissociability is reached, and $A'a'$ is further reduced to $A'$ itself, the original anchoring idea now modified.

Notice that in *meaningful* learning, the original new material $a$ may never be retrievable in precisely the same form it was presented. The very process of subsumption occurring in the assimilation of $a$ has already resulted in some alteration of $a$ to $a'$, and hence obliterative subsumption *begins* at the time meaningful learning occurs. For this reason evaluation practices that require *exact* repetition of information or ideas learned discourage meaningful learning.

The concept of a variable threshold of availability is useful. It can explain transitory fluctuations in availability that are attributable to general cognitive or motivational variables (attention, anxiety, change of set or context, release of repression) without any change in dissociability strength (the intrinsic strength of the item in memory) itself. By the same token it explains why items of low dissociability strength, which are ordinarily not available under typical conditions of consciousness, are available under hypnosis. It also explains why such items can be recognized but not recalled.

Forgetting is thus a continuation or later temporal phase of the same assimilative process underlying the availability of newly learned ideas. And the same nonarbitrary relatability to a relevant established idea in cognitive structure that is necessary for the meaningful learning of a new idea, and that leads to its enhanced retention through the process of anchoring the emergent meaning to that of the established idea, provides the mechanism for most later forgetting. We see in the principle of subsumption, therefore, an economy of thought (or parsimony). The same principle explains why there are individual variations in meaningful learning ability (depending in part on the availability and degree of differentiation of relevant subsumers) and why differential periods of retention should be expected (depending in part on factors influencing obliterative subsumption).

This process of memorial reduction to the least common denominator capable of representing cumulative prior ideational experience (to the relevant established ideas) is very similar to the reduction process characterizing concept formation. A single abstract concept is more manipulable for cognitive structure and is also more functional for future learning and problem-solving operations when stripped of the less stable meanings they have assimilated. Hence, barring repetition or some other special reason (for example, primacy, uniqueness, enhanced discriminability, or the availability of a specially relevant, clear, and stable anchoring idea) for the perpetuation of their dissociability, newly learned ideas that are related to established ideational systems tend gradually and spontaneously to become undissociable from their anchoring ideas. That is, they undergo obliterative assimilation and are forgotten. Forgetting thus represents a progressive loss in the dissociability of newly assimilated ideas from the ideational matrix in which they are embedded and in relation to which their meaning emerges.

Unfortunately, however, the advantages of obliterative assimilation for cognitive functioning are gained at the expense of losing the differentiated body of detailed propositions and specific information that constitutes the flesh, if not the skeleton, of any body of knowledge. The main problem of acquiring the content of an academic discipline, therefore, is counteracting the inevitable process of obliterative assimilation that characterizes all meaningful learning.

In the case of subordinate and combinatorial learning, the process of obliterative assimilation, as a reduction phenomenon, seems straightforward enough: The less stable (and more specific) meaning of a subordinate idea is gradually incorporated within or reduced to the more stable (and more inclusive) meaning of the specifically relevant idea in cognitive structure that assimilates it. And the less stable (and more specific) meaning of a combinatorial idea is similarly incorporated within or reduced to the more stable (and more generalized) meanings of the wider, less specifically relevant body of ideas in cognitive structure to which it is related.

But what about the forgetting of *superordinate* learnings, which, by definition, are more generalized and inclusive from the very beginning than the established subordinate ideas in cognitive structure that assimilate them? Here the process of obliterative assimilation must obviously conform to a somewhat different paradigm, since the more stable anchoring ideas in this case are *less* inclusive than the new superordinate meanings they assimilate. At least in the beginning, therefore, while a new superordinate meaning is relatively unstable, it is reduced to its less inclusive (subordinate) anchoring ideas during the process of obliterative assimilation. Later, however, if and when the new superordinate idea is further differentiated, it tends to become more stable than the subordinate ideas that originally assimilated it, inasmuch as the stability of an idea in memory tends to increase with its level of generality and inclusiveness. Thus, at this point, the direction of obliterative assimilation is reversed: the less inclusive, and now less stable, meanings of earlier-learned subordinate ideas tend to be incorporated within or reduced to the more generalized meaning of the later-learned and now more stable meanings of the superordinate idea. (See Table 4.2 and take time to integratively reconcile your understanding of this table with meanings in Table 2.1.)

The dynamics underlying the meaningful learning, retention, and forgetting of ideas can be appreciated more fully by considering certain detailed aspects of the interactional and assimilation processes that have not been mentioned as yet. Referring again to Table 4.1, consider, for example, the natural history of a potentially meaningful correlative concept or proposition *a* which a learner relates to (subsumes under) a specifically relevant

TABLE 4.2  Stages in the Learning and Retention of a Superordinate Idea in Relation to Dissociability

| | New, Potentially Meaningful Idea $A$ | related to and assimilated by | Established Ideas $a$ and $a$ | | Interactional Product $a'a'A'$ |
|---|---|---|---|---|---|
| I  MEANINGFUL LEARNING OR ACQUISITION OF SUPERORDINATE MEANING $A'$ | $A$ | related to and assimilated by | Established Ideas $a$ and $a$ | | Interactional Product $a'a'A'$ |
| II  POSTLEARNING AND EARLY RETENTION OF $A'$ | New meaning $A'$ is dissociable from $a'a'A'$ | | | $a'a'A' \leftrightarrow a' + a' + A'$ | |
| III  FORGETTING OF $A'$ | $A'$ is no longer effectively dissociable from $a'a'A'$ | | | $A'$ is reduced to $a' + a'$ | |
| IV  FURTHER DIFFERENTIATION OF $A'$ | $a'$ and $a'$ | subsumed under | More Stable and Established Idea $A'$ | | Interactional Product $A'a'a'$ |
| V  LATER RETENTION OF $a'$ and $a'$ | $a'$ and $a'$ are dissociable from $A'a'a'$ | | | $A'a'a' \leftrightarrow A' + a' + a'$ | |
| VI  FORGETTING OF $a'$ and $a'$ | $a'$ and $a'$ are no longer effectively dissociable from $A'a'a'$ | | | $a'$ and $a'$ are reduced to $A'$ | |

and more inclusive and stable established proposition $A$ in his or her cognitive structure. As a result of the subsumption process, an interaction product, $A'a'$, is formed in which both original components are modified as a consequence of the interaction.

It is obviously an oversimplification, however, to state that a new learning item, $a$, forms only a single interactional product with $A$. To a lesser extent, it forms additional interactional products with other ideas, which could be called $B, C, D, E$, and so forth. The amount of assimilation in each case is roughly proportional to the latter's place along a gradient of relevance. In this interaction, also, the subsuming idea is ordinarily modified considerably by particular new experience. Its defining attributes, for example, may be broadened to include new features that were formerly excluded, or they may be made less inclusive by excluding features that were originally included.

In this new interactional product, $A'a'$, $a'$ does not lose its identity completely, since a dissociation equilibrium, $A'a' \leftrightarrow A' + a'$, is set up in which $a'$, depending on prevailing conditions, has a given degree of dissociability as an identifiable entity. As will be explained in greater detail later (Chapter 5), the original degree of dissociability strength of $a'$, after meaningful learning occurs, varies with such factors as the relevance of the anchoring idea $A$, the stability and clarity of $A$, and the extent to which $A$ is discriminable from the learning material (that is, from $a$).

Actually, of course, assimilated items become unavailable (forgotten) long before the point of zero dissociability is reached, since they are no longer available when they are below the prevailing *threshold of availability* (the critical level of strength a given item must manifest in order to be retrievable). Much residual dissociability strength exists between this below-threshold level and the point of zero dissociability, but not enough to make the item available under ordinary conditions of recognition or recall. The existence of below-threshold dissociability may be demonstrated by the use of hypnosis (Nagge, 1935; Rosenthal, 1944), which greatly lowers the threshold of availability for all items with the result that many items that are below the level of availability become available under hypnosis. Relearning also demonstrates subthreshold dissociability strength (Burtt, 1941). The fact that forgotten materials can be *relearned* more effectively and in less time than that required for original learning is ample proof of the existence of subthreshold dissociability strength; because of its presence, less new learning is required to reach any given threshold level.

This concept of a dissociation equilibrium, in which an assimilated idea gradually and spontaneously becomes less dissociable from the established ideational system to which it is anchored and from which it derives its meaning, has considerable heuristic value. It accounts *both* for the original availability of the newly learned meaning and for the subsequent *gradual* decline in its availability during the retention interval until forgetting ensues. As will be pointed out shortly, assimilation theory differs markedly in principle from the Gestalt theory of forgetting in this respect. Gestalt theory holds that the assimilative process induced by interaction between traces is a matter of all-or-none replacement of a given trace by another stronger trace, on the basis of the similarity existing between them.

The familiar Gestalt phenomena of "leveling" and of "sharpening," in which forgetting is manifested by reduction to a familiar idea or by accentuation of a salient characteristic, can be easily reinterpreted in terms of assimilation theory. In the process of leveling (Allport & Postman, 1947; Wulf, 1922), for example, $a$, which is a specific derivative or illustration of $A$ or a slightly asymmetrical or incomplete variant of $A$, becomes $a'$ after it is learned and is simply reduced to $A'$ in the course of forgetting. In the process of sharpening, a more striking aspect of $a$ becomes its criterial feature and is remembered in accentuated form because it is subsumed under and eventually reduced to a preexisting representation of this feature in cognitive structure. Continuous and inverse principles and principles with qualifying conditions similarly tend to be remembered as discontinuous, direct, and unqualified in nature with the passage of time (Tomlinson, 1962).

### Learning versus Retention

In meaningful reception learning, the distinctive attribute of both learning and retention is a change in the availability or future reproducibility of the meanings derived from the assimilated learning material. Learning refers to the process of *acquiring meanings* from the potential meanings presented in the learning material and of *making them more available*. It represents an increment in the availability of new meanings. This situation prevails when they first emerge or are first established or when their dissociability strength is subsequently increased by repetition or by conditions enhancing their discriminability. Retention, on the other hand, refers to the process of *maintaining the availability* of a replica of the acquired new meanings. Thus, forgetting represents a decrement in availability. This situation prevails between the establishment of a meaning and its reproduction or between two presentations of the learning material.

Retention, as we have already noted, is largely a later temporal phase and diminished aspect of the same phenomenon or functional capacity involved in learning itself. Later availability is always, at least in part, a function of initial availability. In the absence of intervening practice, therefore, delayed retention cannot possibly surpass immediate retention. For example, the common phenomenon of *reminiscence* (the superiority of delayed over immediate retention) is not reflective of a later increase in the dissociability strength of newly learned material. It reflects, rather, the subsequent lowering, at a later retesting of retention, of temporarily elevated thresholds of availability.

Meaningful retention is not only a later attenuated manifestation of the same availability function established during learning but is also a later temporal phase of the *same interactional process* underlying this availability. During the learning phase the emergent meaning of new ideational material forms an interactional product with its anchoring idea and exhibits a given degree of dissociability from it. Continued spontaneous interaction between the meanings of the new and anchoring ideas during the retention interval results in a gradual decrease in the dissociability of the new meaning (that is, in forgetting) until the interactional product is reduced to the least common denominator capable of representing it, namely, to the anchoring idea itself. The *same* cognitive structure factors (the relevance, stability, clarity, and degree of differentiation of the anchoring idea) determining the original dissociability strength of the new meaning immediately after learning (initial interaction) also determine the rate at which dissociability is subsequently lost during retention (later interaction). In *rote* learning, on the other hand, the same interactional process is not involved in learning and retention. Hence, rote learning represents an increment in availability (associative strength) involving one discrete interactional process and set of variables, and rote forgetting represents a loss in this availability due to interference from *another* discrete process (and group of variables) set in motion shortly before or after learning.

Two reasons, therefore, probably account for the superiority of retention resulting from meaningful learning in contrast to retention after rote learning. First, since meaningful learning is more effective because of the advantages inherent in the substantive and nonarbitrary relatability of new ideas to relevant, established ideas in cognitive structure, a greater quantity of material is incorporated more easily and made more available immediately after learning (more learning occurs). Second, since the same relationship between new and established ideas is maintained by assimilation during the retention interval and since the same variables influence initial and later dissociability strength, this same relatability advantage *further* enhances the efficiency of the process whereby acquired meanings are subsequently *retained*. To put this another way, a new idea learned by assimilation to a well-established, relevant idea will tend to gain some of the inherent stability of the original idea and hence be retained longer. Similarly, when dealing with different conditions affecting meaningful learning itself, we would expect these same two sources of retention superiority to be operative whenever a cognitive variable—for instance, degree of differentiation—influences the learning-retention process. Johnson (1973) found that textual prose material with the highest level of meaningfulness was recalled three to eighteen times more often than material with the lowest level of meaningfulness. In the next chapter we will discuss some of the practical differences that accrue in school learning as a result of the differences between meaningful and rote retention processes.

Depending on the method used to measure meaningful retention, one may obtain either quantitative or qualitative indices of the assimilation process operative during the retention interval. If one merely counts the number of concepts or propositions in a learning passage whose meanings the learner can recognize or identify correctly, one ascertains what proportion of the learned material maintains sufficient dissociability strength to exceed the threshold of availability. If, on the other hand, one examines the *kind* of recognition or recall errors that are committed, one also obtains a picture of the *direction* of memorial changes induced by the assimilation process. These changes include both the end-products of obliterative assimilation (reduction to a more general or less qualified idea) and the various intermediate stages reflective of different degrees of dissociability strength. They must, of course, be differentiated from changes reflective of selective reconstruction of the memories that are available (see below).

This distinction between learning and forgetting is obviously much greater in discovery than in reception learning. In discovery learning, repeated encounters with the learning task give rise to successive stages in an autonomous problem-solving process. In reception learning, however, repetition (apart from some possible changes in degree and precision of meaning) primarily increases the future availability of the material. Thus the forgetting aspect of discovery learning hardly constitutes just a later continued phase of an original learning process that merely requires the learner to internalize and make presented material more available. Forgetting in this instance, therefore, has little in common with most of discovery learning, in which meaning must first be discovered by problem solving before it can be made available and retained.

### Forgetting versus Obliterative Assimilation

In Chapter 2 we distinguished between derivative and correlative subsumption. Derivative subsumption takes place when learning material is understood as a specific example of an established concept in cognitive structure or is supportive or illustrative of a previously learned general proposition. New learning may proceed easily in derivative subsumption, but forgetting may be more rapid also unless the new material is greatly overlearned. The reason for the rapid *obliterative subsumption* is simply that the meaning of the new material can be very adequately represented by the more general and inclusive meaning of the established subsumer, and that this latter process of memorial representation is more efficient and less burdensome than the actual retention of supportive or illustrative data. If such data are needed, they can be synthesized or reconstructed by appropriately manipulating specific elements of past and present experience so that they exemplify the desired concept or proposition. For example, in recounting a long-past incident, one ordinarily retains only the ideational substance of the experience and from this reconstructs or invents plausible details that are consistent with its general import and setting.

However, new subject matter is usually learned by a process of correlative subsumption. The new learning material in this case is incorporated by and interacts with relevant and more inclusive subsumers in cognitive structure. Even so, its meaning is not implicit in, and cannot be adequately represented by, these latter subsumers. Nevertheless, in the interests of economy of cognitive organization and of reducing the burden on memory, the same trend toward obliterative subsumption occurs. This trend is particularly evident if the subsumers are unstable, unclear, or insufficiently relevant or if the learning material is lacking in discriminability or is not overlearned. But in this instance the consequences of obliterative subsumption are not as innocuous as in the case of derivative subsumption. When correlative propositions lose their identifiability and can no longer be dissociated from their subsumers, a genuine loss of knowledge occurs. The subsumers cannot adequately represent the meaning of the new correlative propositions, and hence the mere availability of the subsumers in memory does not make possible a reconstruction of the substance of the forgotten material. The same situation exists when new superordinate and combinatorial meanings are forgotten. In the latter cases, we are not dealing with a subsumptive form of learning and hence it is more appropriate to speak of *obliterative assimilation*, although the basic forgetting process is similar following derivative or correlative subsumption, or superordinate or combinatorial learning.

The acquisition of a body of knowledge, therefore, is largely a matter of counteracting the trend toward obliterative assimilation in retaining correlative, superordinate, and combinatorial learnings. Thus Bruner's (1957, 1959, 1960) exclusive emphasis on "generic learning" or on acquiring "generic coding systems," as a means of facilitating school learning is unrealistic because it focuses on derivative aspects of subsumption that are atypical both of the assimilation process in general and of most instances of assimilating new subject matter. It is true, as he asserts, that most specific content aspects of subject matter can be forgotten with impunity as long as they are derivable, or can be reconstructed when needed, from those generic concepts or formulas that are remembered. But the analogous forgetting of correlative, superordinate, or combinatorial content results in a loss of knowledge that cannot be regenerated from residual generic concepts. The reductionist trend in memory (that is, obliterative assimilation), which is functional or, at the very worst, innocuous in the case of derivative material, constitutes the principal difficulty in acquiring a body of knowledge in the more typical context of learning correlative, superordinate, or combinatorial propositions.

Hence, the problem of meaningful learning and retention cannot ordinarily be solved by incorporating "a representation of the criterial characteristics of [a] situation [or] a contentless depiction of the ideal case" (Bruner, 1960) and then ignoring the loss of specific content that occurs. The main purpose of learning generic concepts and propositions is *not* so much to make possible the reconstruction of forgotten derivative instances as to provide stable anchorage for the learning of correlative, superordinate, or combinatorial material. And it is the inhibition of the rate of obliterative assimilation in relation to this material that is the major problem confronting teachers in transmitting subject matter.

There is an important difference between forgetting that occurs after rote learning and forgetting that occurs after meaningful learning. In both instances specifically learned materials fall below the threshold of recall. However, after obliterative assimilation has occurred following meaningful learning, the concept or proposition that provided anchorage for the learning remains and is normally *more* differentiated than it was previously. Thus although "meaningful forgetting" has occurred, there is a net gain in cognitive differentiation and an *added* potential for facilitation of learning for *any* new, relevant materials. No such residual cognitive enhancement exists following forgetting of rotely learned material. In fact, inhibition of new learning of similar material is likely.

### Assimilation of Abstract versus Factual Materials

The extent to which learning material is either abstract or factual in nature has an important bearing on its longevity or on the rate at which obliterative assimilation takes place. Comparison of the relative retention spans of substantive and verbatim items invariably shows that generally the longevity of different components of the learning material varies directly with degree of abstractness. The principal distinction between abstract and factual items, of course, is in terms of level of particularity or proximity to concrete-empirical experience. Typically, however, abstract material is also characterized by greater connectedness than factual material. Subordinate, as opposed to superordinate material, is less well retained (Kintsch, 1977).

All factual material, furthermore, is not of one piece. Some factual material can be learned meaningfully, whereas other factual data cannot be related to cognitive structure in nonarbitrary, nonverbatim fashion and hence must be rotely learned. But even if factual matter is potentially meaningful, it is more likely to be rotely learned than is abstract material because it is more difficult to relate to existing ideational systems in cognitive structure.

The previously made distinction between derivative and correlative subsumption is also important in accounting for the relative susceptibility to obliterative subsumption of different kinds of potentially meaningful factual material. Derivative facts undergo obliterative subsumption more rapidly because, unlike correlative matter, their meaning can be adequately represented by the ideational systems that subsume them. A degree of factual reconstruction that is satisfactory enough for most purposes of communication is thereby made possible.

The greater longevity of abstract than of factual material therefore can be partly accounted for in terms of the superiority of meaningful over rote learning and retention. Another credible explanation is that abstractions tend more often than factual material to be correlative rather than derivative in nature. Hence, because they are, from the very beginning, much less close than factual matter to the end-point of obliterative subsumption, they can be retained for longer periods of time.

### Assimilation: Inductive or Deductive Process?

At first glance, one might suppose that assimilation, in accordance with the principle of progressive differentiation, conforms to a deductive approach to cognitive organization and functioning. Actually, however, this supposition is correct only with respect to the relatively rare instance of derivative subsumption. Correlative, combinatorial, and superordinate materials quite obviously do not bear a deductive relationship to their established anchoring ideas in cognitive structure. Hence, simply because assimilation is not an inductive process, we cannot consider it to be necessarily deductive in nature. The inductive-deductive issue is mostly relevant in considering the order in which generalizations and supportive data are handled, either in presenting knowledge or in problem solving—not in characterizing the nature of the assimilation process.

Irrespective of whether new propositions are acquired inductively or deductively, however, their incorporation into cognitive structure still follows, if at all possible, the principle of progressive differentiation. At all age levels and at all levels of cognitive sophistication, new subordinate propositions—even when acquired inductively—are invariably subsumed under more inclusive, established ideational systems in cognitive structure; that is, they are hierarchically organized in cognitive structure. New superordinate propositions, in turn, subsume less inclusive existing ideational systems.[2] Moreover, it is questionable whether a pure inductive approach

---

[2] New combinatorial propositions, at the moment of incorporation, are neither subordinate nor superordinate to particular established ideas in cognitive structure. Almost inevitably, however, they either subsume or are subsumed by later learnings. Originally they are coordinate in level of abstraction and inclusiveness with existing higher-order concepts or propositions.

ever exists as such in problem solving. Human beings rarely start out from scratch in approaching new problems. They either employ explicit explanatory principles (hypotheses) on a provisional basis and try to fit the data to these hypotheses, or at the very least are implicitly guided from the outset by a set of general assumptions derived from past experience. In this sense, therefore, inductive problem solving itself may be considered a subsidiary phase within a generally deductive approach.

### Cognitive Organization in Children

Does the same hierarchical organization of knowledge based on the principle of progressive differentiation hold true for elementary-school children as for adolescents and adults, despite the fact that such children are dependent on concrete-empirical experience in learning unfamiliar new abstractions and relationships between abstractions? It would appear that an affirmative answer to this question is warranted. Even though the initial emergence of abstract meanings must be preceded by an adequate background of concrete-empirical experience, abstract concepts and propositions, once satisfactorily established, enjoy a very stable existence. They do not have to be reinforced by reference to concrete, particular experience in order to maintain their meaning. In addition, they serve as subsumers in the assimilative process, at or near the apex in the hierarchical organization of cognitive structure.

Thus the cognitive organization of children differs mainly from that of adults in containing fewer abstract concepts, fewer higher-order abstractions, and more intuitive-nonverbal than abstract-verbal understandings of many propositions. Children's learning of new verbal material can therefore proceed in much the same manner as in adults. However, proper allowance should be made for the smaller number of higher-order abstract concepts and truly abstract propositions in cognitive structure, and for the need for concrete-empirical experience in acquiring abstract concepts and propositions.

### The Threshold of Availability: Reminiscence

We have already observed that in order for assimilated materials to be reproducible at some future date, their dissociability strength must exceed a certain minimal value, namely, the threshold of availability. The most important cause of the unavailability of meaningfully learned materials is therefore a fall in dissociability strength below the level required to reach this threshold. Whether or not dissociability strength is sufficient to exceed threshold value, however, is partly a function of the method used in measuring retention. Recognition and recall, for example, make quite different demands on the availability of a given item. In the case of recognition, the originally learned material is presented with other alternatives, and the subject need only identify it. In the case of recall, the subject must *spontaneously* reproduce the substance of the original material. Obviously, therefore, recognition can be successful at a much lower level of dissociability strength than can recall. Items "on the tip of one's tongue" that cannot be recalled spontaneously can be recalled with the aid of a hint (such as providing the first letter of the correct answer) and recognized correctly on a multiple-choice test (Freedman & Landauer, 1966). Subjects can even predict recognition successes and failures for items they cannot recall (Hart, 1965). The threshold of availability, in other words, is higher for recall than for recognition, if dissociability strength is held constant.

Still another independent, though secondary, source of variability in the availability of subsumed materials inheres in fluctuations in the *threshold of availability itself*. Hence a particular item of knowledge may manifest more than sufficient dissociability strength to exceed the *typically* prevailing threshold value, but may still be unavailable because of some temporary elevation of the threshold of availability. The most common reasons for such an elevation of threshold value are "initial learning shock" (see below), the competition of alternative memories, and negative attitudinal bias or motivation *not* to remember (repression). Removal of these threshold-raising or memory-inhibiting factors (that is, disinhibition) results in an apparent facilitation of memory. The most extreme example of disinhibition occurs during hypnosis, when restriction of the learner's field of awareness reduces the competing effect of alternative memory systems to a bare minimum (Rosenthal, 1944).

Reminiscence (the Ballard-Williams phenomenon) refers to an apparent increment in the retention of meaningfully learned material over a period of two or more days without any intervening practice.[3] Since retention cannot possibly exceed original learning under these conditions, this phenomenon is probably reflective of spontaneous recovery from the threshold-elevating effects of initial learning shock. It is postulated, in other words, that (1) a certain amount of resistance and generalized cognitive confusion occurs when unfamiliar new ideas are first introduced into cognitive structure; (2) this confusion and resistance are gradually dissipated as the new ideas become more familiar and less threatening; and (3) the existence of the initial resistance and confusion and their gradual dissipation are parallelled, respectively, by a corresponding initial elevation and a subsequent lowering of the threshold of availability. This interpretation is strengthened by the fact that reminiscence occurs only when material is partially learned

---

[3] Short-term reminiscence manifested two to six minutes after learning (the Ward-Hovland phenomenon) will not be considered here since it is concerned with rote memorization.

or not overlearned and when practice trials are massed—that is, when opportunity for immediate confusion and later clarification exists.

The fact that reminiscence has been convincingly demonstrated only in elementary-school children (Sharpe, 1952; Stevenson & Langford, 1957; Williams, 1926) and declines (Sharpe, 1952) or is not manifested at all (Williams, 1926) in older subjects suggests that initial "learning shock" tends to decrease with increasing age as cognitive structure becomes more stable and better organized. Reminiscence also cannot be demonstrated for verbatim (Edwards & English, 1939; English, Welborn, & Kilian, 1934) and rotely learned (Ward, 1937) materials unless measured within minutes after learning, inasmuch as the retention span for such materials is exceedingly brief. Later increments in retention (increments other than a gain between an *immediate* and a subsequent test of memory) are, by definition, not indicative of reminiscence. They probably reflect the later removal of competing memories (or of negative motivational factors), temporarily raising the threshold of availability during the preceding retention test rather than the dissipation of initial learning shock.

The genuineness of reminiscence was originally in doubt because early studies (Ballard, 1913; Edwards & English, 1939; English, Welborn, & Kilian, 1934) used the *same* group of subjects in making both initial and subsequent tests of retention. It was possible, therefore, to explain reminiscence either in terms of the practice effect exerted by the immediate test of recall, or in terms of voluntary or involuntary rehearsal between immediate and later tests of retention. Since the reminiscence effect still shows up, however, when *separate* groups are used in determining immediate and later tests of availability (Sharpe, 1952; Stevenson & Langford, 1957), it is probably more than a mere artifact of method of measurement.

## Sources of Forgetting

Temporally, three distinct phases may be distinguished during meaningful reception learning and retention. Each phase, in turn, contributes in distinctive ways to measured discrepancies between presented learning material and reproduced memories of this material. During the first phase, *learning*, meanings are acquired. Potentially meaningful ideas and information are related to relevant ideational systems in cognitive structure, thereby giving rise to idiosyncratic phenomenological meanings with a given degree of dissociability strength. The second phase is concerned with the *retention* of acquired meanings or with the gradual loss of dissociability strength through a process of obliterative assimilation.

The third and final phase involves the *reproduction* of the retained material. It depends not only on the residual degree of availability (dissociability strength) in relation to the threshold of availability, but also on cognitive and motivational factors influencing both this threshold and the actual process of reconstructing or reformulating the retained meanings into a verbal statement.

These various temporal phases of meaningful reception learning and retention are significant in accounting for the various sources of error in memory. During the *learning* phase, vague, diffuse, ambiguous, or erroneous meanings may emerge from the very beginning of the learning process. Contributing factors are the unavailability of relevant anchoring ideas in cognitive structure, the instability or unclarity of these anchoring ideas, and the lack of discriminability between the learning material and the anchoring ideas. This unfavorable outcome is particularly likely if the learner's need for, and self-critical attitude about, acquiring adequate meanings is deficient.

Another source of discrepancy between presented and remembered content that is attributable to this first phase reflects the selective emphasis, omission, and distortion that takes place as a result of initial interpretation of the presented material. As will be pointed out shortly in the discussion of Bartlett's theory of forgetting, these phenomena are manifestations of the *selective* emergence of meaning (a *cognitive* process) rather than of selective perception. The emerging new meanings of learners are consonant with their cultural frames of reference (Bartlett, 1932), attitudinal biases (McKillop, 1952), and experimentally manipulated advance sets (Jones & de Charms, 1958), because each individual possesses an *idiosyncratic* array of established and relevant anchoring ideas (including biases) in his or her cognitive structure that assimilates the new material. The resulting meanings in each case are a function both of the *particular* assimilations that occur and of the selective distortion, discounting, dismissal, and reversal of intended meanings that are induced by the individual's particular set of biases.[4] In all of these instances, the relative weight of idiosyncratic cognitive structure in determining the content of meanings was greater than that of the learning material itself, because the investigators used prose material that was unfamiliar, ambiguous, cryptic, and interpretable in several alternative ways.

Contrary to common belief, fast learners remember more than the slow learners. This is so not because they forget at a slower rate, but because they learn more in a given unit of time and thus start out with a greater mass of knowledge. If initial level of mastery is held constant, there is no difference in retention between fast and slow learners (Underwood, 1954).

During the second phase, the *retention period itself*, newly learned meanings tend to be reduced to the established ideas in cognitive structure that assimilate them. That is, they tend to become more unqualified and

---

[4] For a more complete account of how attitudinal bias influences the learning of controversial material see Chapter 12.

similar in import to the anchoring ideas. The *same* cognitive structure, practice, and task variables that influence the *original* dissociability strength and truthfulness of the emerging meanings determine their *subsequent* dissociability strength and resistance to obliterative assimilation during the retention interval.

Finally, during the *reproductive* phase, factors raising the threshold of availability may inhibit the recall of ordinarily available meanings. Or available meanings may be altered in the very process of being reconstructed in accordance with the requirements of the current reproductive situation. This phase is more important in cultural settings where students are expected and trained to demonstrate retention by reconstructing their knowledge, as in essay tests, rather than by recognizing the correct alternative among multiple choices (Harari & McDavid, 1966).

## Meaningful Versus Rote Learning

Meaningfully and rotely learned materials are learned and retained in *qualitatively* different ways because potentially meaningful learning tasks are, by definition, relatable and anchorable to relevant established ideas in cognitive structure. They can be related to existing ideas in ways making possible the understanding of various kinds of significant (derivative, correlative, superordinate, combinatorial) relationships. Most new ideational materials that pupils encounter in a school setting are nonarbitrarily and substantively relatable to a previously learned background of meaningful ideas and information. In fact, the curriculum often is deliberately organized in this fashion to provide for the untraumatic introduction of new facts, concepts, and propositions. Rotely learned materials, on the other hand, are discrete and relatively isolated entities that are relatable to cognitive structure only in an arbitrary, verbatim fashion, not permitting the establishment of the above-mentioned relationships.

This crucial difference between rote and meaningful learning categories has important implications for the kind of learning and retention processes underlying each category. Since rotely learned materials do not interact with cognitive structure in a substantive, organic fashion, they are learned and retained in conformity with the laws of association. Their retention is influenced primarily by the interfering effects of *similar* rote materials learned *immediately* before or after the learning task. Learning and retention outcomes in the case of meaningful learning, on the other hand, are influenced primarily by the properties of those relevant and cumulatively established ideational systems with which the learning task interacts and that determine its dissociability strength. Compared to this kind of extended interaction, concurrent interfering effects have relatively little influence on and explanatory value for meaningful learning.

## Meaningful Learning Processes

Substantive and nonarbitrary incorporation of a potentially meaningful learning task into relevant portions of cognitive structure, so that a new meaning emerges, implies that the newly learned meaning becomes an integral part of a particular ideational system. The possibility of this type of relatability to and incorporability into cognitive structure has two principal consequences for learning and retention processes. First, learning and retention are no longer dependent on the rather frail human capacity for retaining arbitrary and verbatim associations as discrete and isolated entities in their own right. As a result, the temporal span of retention is greatly extended.

Second, the newly learned material becomes subject to the organizational principles governing the learning and retention of the system in which it is incorporated. To begin with, the very act of incorporation (assimilation) requires appropriate (relevant) placement within a hierarchically organized system of knowledge. Later, after incorporation occurs, the new material initially retains its substantive identity, by virtue of being dissociable from its anchoring ideas. It then gradually loses its identifiability as it becomes reduced to and undissociable from these ideas (obliterative assimilation).

In this type of learning-retention process, the formation and strengthening of arbitrary associative bonds between discrete, verbatim elements, isolated in an organizational sense from established ideational systems, play a small role, if any. Unfortunately, most of the research in psychology laboratories involves rote or verbatim learning, and unwarranted extrapolations are then made to school learning. Meaningful learning, dependent as it is on the idiosyncratic cognitive structure of individuals, does not lend itself to easy laboratory studies but it remains the predominant mode of human learning. The important mechanisms in this process are: (1) achievement of appropriate relational anchorage within a relevant ideational system, and (2) retention. The latter involves resistance to the progressively increasing inroads of obliterative assimilation or loss of dissociability and characterizes the organization and long-term memorial integrity of meaningfully learned materials in cognitive structure.

## Rote Learning Processes

It has already been pointed out that rote learning tasks *are* relatable to cognitive structure in an arbitrary, verbatim fashion, and that it is by virtue of this relatability that (1) already meaningful components of these tasks are perceived as such and thereby facilitate rote learning, and (2) concurrent interference with rote learning arises from within cognitive structure. However, the extreme arbitrariness of the learning task's relatability to ideational systems within cognitive structure (as well as the necessity for *verbatim* internalization and reproducibility) precludes the relational and substantive type of incorporation described above for meaningful learning. It thus makes for a basically different kind of learning-retention process. Rote learning tasks can be incorporated into cognitive structure only in the form of arbitrary associations. These associations are discrete, self-contained entities organizationally isolated, for all practical purposes, from the learner's established ideational systems. The requirement that these arbitrary associations be constituted on a verbatim rather than substantive basis (since anything less than complete verbatim fidelity is valueless in the case of purely arbitrary associations) further enhances the discreteness and isolated nature of rotely incorporated entities.

One important implication of the discrete and isolated incorporation of rote learning tasks within cognitive structure is that, quite unlike the situation in meaningful learning, anchorage to established ideational systems is not achieved. Hence, since the human mind is not efficiently designed for long-term, verbatim storage of arbitrary associations, the retention span for rote learnings is relatively brief. The much steeper gradient of forgetting in the case of rote compared to meaningful learning, requires that we examine the rote retention process and the factors that influence it within a highly abbreviated time span. Delay beyond this brief time span leaves us with nothing to study. The time span of retention is a matter of hours for nonsense syllables (Ebbinghaus, 1885/1913) and days for poetry (Boreas, 1930).

A second important implication of the arbitrary, verbatim incorporation of learning material within cognitive structure is that *association* necessarily constitutes the basic learning-retention mechanism. The laws of association constitute, by definition, the basic explanatory principles governing rote learning and retention. The major goals of rote learning and retention, therefore, are to increase and maintain associative strength—not to achieve appropriate anchorage and to preserve dissociability strength. Such variables as contiguity, frequency, and reinforcement are accordingly crucial for learning. Retention is influenced primarily by concurrent interference (of both internal and external origin), on the basis of intra- and intertask similarity, response competition, and stimulus and response generalization.

### Evidence of Meaningful Learning

It is not always easy to demonstrate that meaningful learning has occurred. Genuine understanding implies the possession of clear, precise, differentiated, and transferable meanings. But if one attempts to test for such knowledge by asking students to state the criterial attributes of a concept or the essential elements of a proposition, one may merely tap rotely memorized verbalizations. At the very least, therefore, tests of comprehension must be phrased in different language and must be presented in a somewhat different context than the originally encountered learning material. Perhaps the simplest way of doing this is to require students to differentiate between related (similar) but not identical ideas or to choose the identifying elements of a concept or proposition from a list containing those of related concepts and propositions as well.

Independent problem solving is often the only feasible way of testing whether students *really* comprehend meaningfully the ideas they are able to verbalize. But here we have to be careful not to fall into a trap. We may say that problem solving is a valid, practical method of measuring the meaningful comprehension of ideas. However, this is *not* the same as saying that the learner who is unable to solve a representative set of problems *necessarily* does not understand, but has merely rotely memorized, the principles exemplified by these problems. Successful problem solving demands many *other* abilities and qualities—such as reasoning power, perseverance, flexibility, improvisation, problem sensitivity, and tactical astuteness—in *addition* to comprehension of the underlying principles. Hence failure to solve the problems in question may reflect deficiencies in these latter factors rather than lack of genuine understanding. At the very worst it may reflect a lower order of understanding than that manifested in ability to apply successfully the principles to problem solving.

Another feasible method of testing the occurrence of meaningful learning does not involve this difficulty of interpretation. Here the learner is presented with a new, sequentially dependent learning passage that cannot possibly be mastered in the absence of genuine understanding of the prior learning task. This technique will be discussed in more detail later in Chapter 17.

In seeking evidence of meaningful learning, whether through verbal questioning or problem-solving tasks, the possibility of rote memorization should always be borne in mind. Long experience in taking examinations makes students adept at memorizing not only key propositions and formulas, but also causes, examples, reasons, explanations, and ways of recognizing and solving "type problems." The danger of rote simulation of meaningful comprehension may be best avoided by asking questions and posing problems that are both novel and unfamiliar in form and require maximal transformation of existing knowledge.

### The Superiority of Meaningful Learning and Retention

Several lines of evidence point to the conclusion that meaningful learning and retention are more effective than their rote counterparts. First, Briggs and Reed (1943) and Jones and English (1926) demonstrated that it is much easier to learn and remember the substance of potentially meaningful material than it is to memorize the same connected material in rote, verbatim fashion. Second, material that can be learned meaningfully (poetry, prose, and observations of pictorial matter) is learned much more rapidly than are arbitrary series of digits or nonsense syllables (Glaze, 1928; Lyon, 1914; Reed, 1938). The same difference holds true for gradations of meaningful learning. Simple narrative material is learned more quickly and remembered better than are more complex philosophical ideas that are difficult to understand (Reed, 1938). An increase in the amount of material to be learned also adds relatively less learning time to meaningful than to rote learning tasks (Cofer, 1941; Lyon, 1914). A third type of experimental evidence is derived from studies demonstrating that various problem-solving tasks (card tricks, matchstick problems) are retained longer and are more transferable when subjects learn underlying principles rather than rotely memorized solutions (Hilgard, Irvine, & Whipple, 1953; Katona, 1940).

A related line of evidence showing that "substance" items are learned (Cofer, 1941) and retained (Edwards & English, 1939; English, Welborn, & Kilian, 1934; Newman, 1939) more effectively than are "verbatim" items is more inferential than direct. Presumably, although verbatim items can be learned meaningfully, they are more likely to be memorized rotely than are concepts and generalizations. In this connection, an ingeniously designed study by Newman (1939) comparing retention during periods of sleep and waking throws light on the relative retention spans and respective forgetting processes of rotely and meaningfully learned materials. Unessential details of a narrative were remembered much better after a period of sleep than after a period of normal daily activity, whereas there was no corresponding difference in the case of substance items. A warranted inference here is that immediate retroactive interference, which is obviously greater during daily activity than during sleep, is an important factor in rote memory, but does not significantly affect the retention of meaningfully learned materials.

Many classroom studies support the findings of this last-mentioned experimental approach. In general, they show that principles, generalizations, and applications of principles studied in such courses as biology, chemistry, geometry, and physics are remembered much better over periods of months and even years than are more factual items such as symbols, formulas, and terminology (Eikenberry, 1923; Frutchey, 1937; Kastrinos, 1965; Kuhn, 1967; Tyler, 1930, 1934b; Ward & Davis, 1938). A second type of classroom evidence demonstrates that knowledge of number facts (addition, subtraction, multiplication, and division) learned with understanding is retained more effectively and is more transferable than when learned in mechanical, rote fashion (G. L. Anderson, 1949; Brownell & Moser, 1949; McConnell, 1934; Swenson, 1949; Thiele, 1938). Newson and Gaite (1971) found that students recalled more after one week from reading a short passage (300 words) than a long passage (2500 words) of science fiction. The short passage was written from information retained by students one week after reading the long passage, and thus represented information likely to be meaningfully learned by these students.

Both types of evidence lead one to believe that the discouraging picture of forgetting the vast majority of subject-matter learnings, which certainly characterizes most students today, is not necessarily inevitable. Much of this loss is reflective of rote learning, of poorly organized and programmed subject matter, of correctable ambiguity and confusion in the presentation of ideas, and of inadequate pacing and review of material (cramming). Subject matter can be adequately organized and programmed, relevant ideas can be identified in available cognitive structure, material can be presented lucidly, misconceptions can be corrected promptly, and suitably motivated students can learn meaningfully and pay attention to such considerations as optimal review and pacing. If this is done there is good reason to believe that students can retain over a lifetime most of the important ideas they learned in school. At the very least one would expect them to be able to relearn, in short order and with relatively little effort, most of what they had forgotten. In subsequent chapters we shall examine the important cognitive structure, practice, instructional material, and motivational variables that affect the longevity of meaningfully learned subject matter.

Many different kinds of explanations have been offered for the superiority of meaningful over rote learning and retention. One explanation identifies meaningful learning with the learning of meaningful material, and advances all of the arguments referred to above in explaining why meaningfulness facilitates rote verbal learning. Our definition of meaningful learning, however, implies that it is a characteristic *process* in which meaning is a *product* or outcome of learning rather than primarily an attribute of the content of what is to be learned. It is this process rather than the meaningfulness of the content[5] learned that characterizes meaningful learn-

---

[5] It was also pointed out earlier that in meaningful learning the materials are not *already* meaningful but only *potentially* meaningful. The very object of meaningful learning is to convert potential meaning into actual (psychological) meaning. *Both* rotely and meaningfully learned tasks contain already meaningful components, but in the first instance the task *as a whole* is not potentially meaningful, whereas in the second instances it is. The presence of the already meaningful components therefore is, at most, an *indirect* factor accounting for the superior learning (rote or meaningful) that occurs when such components are included in the task. It cannot possibly account for the superiority of meaningful over rote learning with respect to the task as a whole. The more important reason for the superiority of meaningful over rote learning obviously inheres in the fact that in meaningful learning the task as a whole is potentially meaningful and therefore can be nonarbitrarily and substantively related to cognitive structure.

That meaningful learning primarily refers to a distinctive *process* of learning, rather than to the meaningfulness of the content that is learned, is further highlighted by the fact that both the meaningful learning process and its outcome can be rote—even when the learning task as a whole is potentially meaningful—if the learner does not manifest a meaningful learning set.

ing. Thus the same reasons that explain why *more* meaningful materials are *rotely* learned and retained more readily than *less* meaningful materials are, do not necessarily explain why meaningful learning and retention outcomes are superior to their rote counterparts.

Gestalt theorists (Katona, 1940; Koffka, 1935), on the other hand, identify insight and the understanding of relationships with the establishment of stable "structural" traces, which are contrasted, in turn, with the relatively "rigid" and unstable discrete traces established by rotely memorized materials. This explanation, however, really begs the question, because it accounts for the superiority of meaningful learning processes simply by endowing the neural representation of these processes with superior potency. In effect, then, it is claimed that meaningful learning processes yield superior learning outcomes because they give rise to more stable traces. This obviously adds little to our understanding because the real problem is to understand why such processes result in more stable traces.

It should be noted, that although rote learning is more difficult than meaningful learning in most circumstances, it may actually be easier for the individual who lacks the necessary ideational background for a particular learning task. In addition, to the anxiety-ridden person who lacks confidence in his ability to understand difficult and unfamiliar new propositions, rote learning often *appears* easier than meaningful learning.

### Meaningful versus Rote Retention

Does the superiority of meaningful over rote retention reflect an actual difference in the efficacy of the respective *retention* processes, or does this superiority merely reflect the greater efficacy of meaningful *learning*? Obviously, if meaningfully learned material is mastered better to begin with, more incorporated meanings are available at any subsequent time when retention is tested. This is the case even if rote and meaningful retention processes themselves are equally efficacious. In the case of *rote* learning of materials varying in degree of meaningfulness, it has been demonstrated that *learning* is the only important variable. When more and less meaningful materials are learned to the same criterion of mastery (by allowing a greater number of trials for the less meaningful material), they do not differ in retention outcomes (Postman & Rau, 1957; Underwood & Richardson, 1956).

If, however, our theory regarding the existence of fundamental differences between rote and meaningful *retention* processes is correct, we would *not* expect that if rotely and meaningfully learned materials were mastered equally well, they would also be remembered ·with equal effectiveness. According to assimilation theory, the same variables influencing the outcome of meaningful learning, and the same factors accounting for the superiority of meaningful over rote learning processes, *continue* to operate during the retention interval and to affect retention outcomes. Hence, even if rotely and meaningfully learned materials were learned to the same criterion of mastery, the superiority of the meaningful retention process would be reflected in higher retention scores. Studies by Kastrinos (1965), Kuhn (1967), and Ring (1969) show that meaningfully learned concepts and propositions may be retained for a period of years and that they continue to function in the facilitation of new meaningful learning.

### Forgetting and Retroactive Interference

On the basis of assimilation theory of meaningful verbal learning, we hypothesized that retention and forgetting constitute later phases in cognitive functioning of the same interactional learning process between new learning materials and existing relevant ideas in the learner's structure of knowledge (Ausubel, 1958, 1960, 1963, 1968). By virtue of this interactional process, new concept or propositional meanings come into being. During retention, the newly emergent meanings remain functionally linked to the anchoring ideas but are dissociable from them. However, in the later period of forgetting, the dissociability strength of the newly learned meanings falls below the critical thresholds of recall or recognition, and these meanings are no longer available to the learner as separately identifiable entities. The same variables that influence meaningful learning in the first place thus continue to influence retention and forgetting in the same way afterwards. But there are other variables such as motivation, repression, and hypnosis that influence retention by affecting the threshold of availability without influencing in any way the dissociability strength of retained ideas in cognitive structure.

It is postulated that the functional incorporation of newly learned meanings into a network of relevant anchoring ideas in cognitive structure would protect these meanings from the proactive, concurrent, and retroactive interfering effects of similar but conflicting materials. Thus we predicted that the retroactive and proactive interference encountered in rote verbal learning would be largely inoperative in meaningful prose learning. This prediction was verified with respect to retroactive interference by Ausubel, Robbins, and Blake (1957). In fact, in one study (Ausubel, Stager, & Gaite, 1968) the interpolation of conflicting material actually *facilitated* the retention of the original material, presumably by increasing its clarity and discriminability and by prompting its rehearsal.

These latter studies were sharply criticized by neobehavioristically oriented learning theorists on three grounds. First, it was argued that the similarities and differences between original and interpolated learning passages were not objectively analyzed or measured but were selected on a purely subjective or impressionistic *a priori* basis (Anderson & Myrow, 1971; Cunningham, 1972; Myrow & Anderson, 1972).

Actually, of course, as clearly stated in the original articles (Ausubel,

Robbins & Blake, 1957; Ausubel, Stager & Gaite, 1968), the interpolated passages were not selected subjectively at all but by an objective process of overall logical content analysis in which a number of similarities and differences between original and interpolated passages were clearly identified. Thus, for example, anyone who knows about comparative religion would appreciate that there are many similarities, as well as many confusing and potentially conflicting differences, between the doctrines and rituals of Christianity on the one hand, and their counterparts in Buddhism, on the other (Ausubel, Robbins & Blake, 1957). The same holds true when Zen Buddhism and Buddhism are used as original and interpolated passages, respectively (Ausubel, Stager & Gaite, 1968). Hence judgments about potential interference were made in a practical, real-life manner, as they would be by a teacher in judging whether new material B interfered with previously taught material A. Admittedly, however, such judgments are difficult to verify objectively and replicate, and therefore an approach that uses perceived (scaled) similarity between original and interpolated passages appears to be preferable (Costa, 1975; Haveman, 1971; Slamecka, 1959).

Second, much was made of the fact that the specific relationships between the stems of the multiple-choice items in the criterion test on the one hand, and the material in the learning task, on the other, were not specified in these studies (Anderson & Myrow, 1971; Cunningham, 1972; Myrow & Anderson, 1972). When these relationships were made explicit by Anderson and Myrow (1971) and Myrow and Anderson (1972), retroactive interference was claimed to be found in much the same way as in rote verbal (for example, paired-associate) learning. Milonas (1976), however, failed to replicate these findings. Thus, largely on this basis, Anderson and Myrow (1971), Cunningham (1972), and Myrow and Anderson (1972), all conclude that we rejected interference theory prematurely in prose learning and that our failure to find retroactive interference in these studies was due to faulty research methodology and to our theoretical biases. Yet in the conclusion of the Myrow and Anderson (1972) study is the following startling but revealing admission about the true psychological significance of their research methodology (and findings):

> Observers of the classroom may wonder how frequently in "the real world," forgetting analogous to RI (retroactive interference) actually occurs. How often does it happen that the preconditions to RI—similar stimuli paired with different responses—coincidentially appear in ordinary classroom activity? We seldom teach students different answers to the same question. If RI is generated in prose only when the materials are so closely similar we must question the efficacy of the interference model as an inclusive explanation of forgetting in the classroom. The atomistic approach that was required to make good the analogy between paired-associate RI and prose RI seems at once necessary and potentially misleading (p. 308).

Finally, it was claimed that the failure to find retroactive interference in our studies did not in any way provide support for assimilation theory of forgetting (Cunningham, 1972).

> Ausubel also tends to draw conclusions that do not seem warranted on the basis of his data. He often takes as support for his theory of forgetting the failure to detect retroactive or proactive interference in his experiments. Failure to reject the null hypothesis is seldom accepted as support in scientific research however (p. 62).

This, in our opinion, is a completely pejorative straw-man argument since no claim was ever made that the demonstrated absence of retroactive interference supported an assimilation theory of forgetting. In our research articles on retroactive inhibition (Ausubel, Robbins, & Blake, 1957; Ausubel, Stager & Gaite, 1968) and in the concluding paragraph of the discussion of retroactive interference in the first edition of this text, the only claim was that "the assimilation theory of retention differs from the interference theory in defining retention in terms of the dissociability of an ideational element from its anchoring ideas, rather than in terms of the freedom of discrete and arbitrary associations from the interfering effects of concurrently active rote elements" (Ausubel, 1968, pp. 117–118). Actual support for the assimilation theory of forgetting was attributed to five well-documented strands of evidence indicating that meaningful retention is superior to and more stable over time than rote retention (Ausubel, 1963, 1968). In a recent study employing the same passages used by Anderson and Myrow (1971), but with evaluation that included more than rote recall, Milonas (1976) found no evidence of retroactive interference. His findings generally support the rationale discussed above.

### Gestalt Theory

According to Gestalt theory (Koffka, 1935), forgetting is brought about by two principal mechanisms, each of which has relatively little in common with the other. The first mechanism, *assimilation*, is conceptualized as a process whereby memory traces are obliterated or replaced by similar traces in cognitive structure that are relatively more stable. This phenomenon is superficially similar to the assimilative process described above in that it seems to imply *fusion* of or interaction between related ideas rather than the substitution of new stimulus or response members in a previously learned stimulus-response association. However, it is actually more congruent with the interference theory of forgetting. The behavioristic mechanisms of response competition and stimulus or response generalization could quite adequately account for the occurrence of Gestalt assimilation. The second, more distinctively Gestalt mechanism of forgetting is conceptualized as a process of *autonomous disintegration* within traces. In the case of unstructured or poorly organized material (for example, where figure and ground are poorly differentiated), unstable, "chaotic" traces are formed that rapidly undergo a type of spontaneous decay. In other instances, however, "dynamic stresses" derived from the original perception persist in the trace. These stresses are gradually resolved by such progressive changes as leveling and sharpening, in the direction of "closure," "symmetry," and "good form." Thus, both this aspect of Gestalt theory and our assimilation theory of forgetting differ from the interference theory in regarding the processes underlying forgetting as occurring continuously, rather than only during those times when the stimulus or response members of an association are exercised. The Gestalt theory however, is less parsimonious since it ignores the role of previously learned and more stable ideas both in the learning process and in determining the direction of forgetting. It postulates instead that: (1) new ideas do not interact with relevant established ideas in cognitive structure, but rather are incorporated as independent traces; and (2) these separate traces spontaneously undergo change in the direction of "more perfect" or "less stressful" form. Also, as pointed out above, the hypothesis that "poorly organized" materials are forgotten quickly because they form "chaotic traces" that undergo rapid "spontaneous decay" really begs the question.

Our assimilation theory differs from Gestalt theory in the following important ways:

1. It attributes *all* forgetting to interaction between the learning material and existing cognitive structure and denies that autonomous disintegration of traces occurs as a result of the resolution of perceptually derived intra-trace tensions. Asymmetrical figures, for example, would sometimes be remembered as more symmetrical than originally perceived ("leveling"), not because of any autonomous changes within the trace, but because they are subsumed by and eventually reduced to a memorial residue of familiar geometrical concepts in cognitive structure.

2. It conceives of assimilation (loss of identifiability or decreased dissociability of newly learned materials) as a *progressive* phenomenon rather than as an all-or-none type of replacement in which availability is lost completely and instantaneously. The obliterative or reductionistic aspect of assimilation is also regarded as only the *mechanism* accounting for forgetting; the net effect of the anchoring process itself *facilitates* retention.

3. Thus the forgetting attributable to assimilation is not conceived of as simple and abrupt *replacement* of one trace by another more stable trace (as in interference theory), but as the outcome of a gradual trend toward memorial reduction. As a result of this trend, a highly inclusive

and established ideational system comes to represent the import of less generalized ideas, the identifiability of which is correspondingly obliterated.

4. Learning material is believed to be assimilated by a more established ideational system, not because of *similarity between them* but because it is not sufficiently discriminable from that system. Hence its import can be adequately represented by the generality of the more established ideas. Similarity, of course, helps determine which potentially anchoring ideas in cognitive structure actually play principal and subsidiary anchoring roles. It is also one of the determinants of discriminability. A high degree of similarity, however, can facilitate initial anchorage without necessarily leading rapidly to obliterative assimilation, provided that differences are also clearly and explicitly understood.

5. Forgetting is regarded as a continuation of the *same interactional process* established at the moment of learning. According to Gestalt assimilation theory, on the other hand, a given trace is first established at the time of learning and then interacts with and is later replaced by *another* similar and separately established trace.

## Bartlett's Theory of Memory

Assimilation theory also has elements in common with Bartlett's (1932) views of cognitive functioning generally and of remembering in particular. He conceptualizes a *schema* as an organizing and orienting attitude or affect resulting from the abstraction and articulation of past experience. Although somewhat vague with respect to both nature and mode of operation, it is structurally and functionally comparable to that of an anchoring idea. In general, however, Bartlett's position on retention differs in two fundamental respects from assimilation theory. First, the schema itself is largely attitudinal and affective in nature rather than basically cognitive. In this sense it is similar to the connotative aspects of meaning. This difference probably reflects, in part, the fact that Bartlett's learning tasks consist of stories, pictures, and figures instead of the impersonal substance of subject-matter content. Second, Bartlett is primarily concerned with the interpretive and reproductive phases of meaningful learning and retention. He pays hardly any attention at all to the retention interval itself and its underlying processes.

Thus, in accounting for the discrepancy between presented and remembered content, he emphasizes both (1) the influence of idiosyncratic and culturally biased schemata on the original *perception* of the material and (2) a process of "imaginative reconstruction" at the time of recall, as a result of which particular content is selected and invented in accordance with the nature and requirements of the current situation. Assimilation theory, on the other hand, attributes most forgetting to an intervening interactional process involving anchoring ideas and assimilated content. The individual, in remembering, undoubtedly selects from what is available in memory and also invents some new material suitable for the occasion. On the other hand, he is actually *reproducing*, for the most part, materials that have undergone memorial reduction rather than *reconstructing* the retained residue of original meanings.

According to Bartlett, the first opportunity for schemata to influence memory occurs when they interact with incoming stimulus content. The subject attempts to make the content meaningful in terms of a relevant schema, as well as contextually consonant with it. Hence, schemata significantly determine the initial interpretation of the message, which, in turn, persistently influences the nature of what is retained. Contrary to Bartlett's contention, however, this interpretive process—which results in the emergence of meaning—is *cognitive* rather than perceptual in nature. Newly acquired meanings are not reflective of a perceptual process that yields an immediate content of awareness, but rather are products of a more complex cognitive process of assimilation. The idiosyncratic nature of meanings, therefore, does not lie in the fact that an attitudinal schema selectively influences the *perception* of learning material. Rather, it lies in the fact that such material is nonarbitrarily and substantively related to the idiosyncratic content of individual cognitive structures (a *learning* process) in selective fashion.

The importance of initial interpretation (acquisition of meaning) for the later reproductive content of memory has been demonstrated for both verbal (Jones & de Charms, 1958; Kay, 1955; McKillop, 1952) and pictorial (Carmichael, Hogan, & Walter, 1932) material. Subjects are prone to acquire meanings that are compatible with their own attitudinal biases in reading ambiguous controversial materials (McKillop, 1952). They also tend to interpret the hypothetical behaviors of people in accordance with the selective emphases embodied in experimentally manipulated advance sets (Jones & de Charms, 1958). Children are generally unable to remember a figure unless it reminds them of a familiar object (Granit, 1921); and in reproducing unfamiliar and meaningless figures, they alter them in ways that increase their familiarity and meaningfulness (Hildreth, 1944). The same tendency is also evident in problem solving. Learners consistently tend to reduce problems to a level of difficulty that they can understand and make meaningful (Hildreth, 1941). In studying qualitative changes in retention, therefore, it is important to use the immediate reproduction rather than the learning material itself as the baseline.

Bartlett largely ignores the next phase of the learning-retention sequence during which acquired meanings are retained. He states that the schema's principal impact on memory occurs during the *reproductive* phase. At this time the subject differentially selects those elements that are both most consistent with his or her own attitudes, interests, and cul-

tural milieu and most appropriate in terms of the requirements of the current situation. To this the subject adds some invented detail (to fill in gaps
and to enhance coherence, meaningfulness, and "fit") and combines and
reformulates both kinds of elements into a new, self-consistent whole. The
reconstructed product, therefore, when compared to the original learning
material, manifests such tendencies as simplification, condensation, ration-
alization, conventionalization, and importation. Dawes (1966), McKillop
(1952), Northway (1936), Paul (1959), Taft (1954), and Tresselt and
Spragg (1941) report similar findings in the recall of value-laden narrative
material. The weakness of Bartlett's position, therefore, does not inhere in
postulating the eixstence of imaginative reconstruction, but rather in the
fact that many of the memorial changes he attributes to such reconstruction actually reflect changes in availability due to assimilation.

### Psychoanalytic Theory

Psychoanalytic theory maintains that *all* forgetting is motivated, or in
other words, is a product of repression. Ideas or impulses that would generate anxiety if permitted to enter consciousness are said to be repressed
into the unconscious and thereby forgotten.

The chief difficulty with this theory, of course, is that it accounts at
best for a relatively rare type of forgetting. Only a very small percentage
of the ideas that are forgotten are in any sense productive of anxiety. In
these instances it is more parsimonious to hypothesize that their threshold
of availability is elevated, rather than that they are banished into a reified
topographical area of the mind. It is also true that many anxiety-producing
ideas remain painfully and obsessively at the forefront of consciousness.

### Computer Models of Cognitive Functioning

An increasingly popular theoretical position in recent years has been
a variant of the cybernetic or information-theory approach based on a computer model of cognitive organization and functioning. It combines various
postulated mechanisms of computer-based information processing and storage with the cybernetic principle of a control system. This control system
is regarded both as sensitive to feedback indicative of behavioral error (or
of discrepancy between existing and desired states of affairs) and as differentially responsive to such feedback in ways that correct the existing
error or discrepancy. The particular model of human thinking proposed by
Newell, Shaw, and Simon (1958), for example, assumes the existence of
receptors capable of interpreting coded information, a control system consisting of a store of memories, a variety of processes that operate on the
information contained in the memories, and a set of rules for combining
these latter processes into programs of processing. More recent varieties

of information processing models have been proposed by Gagné (1977), Lindsay and Norman (1977), Miller (1974), Norman (1965), Tulving (1972), and Waugh and Norman (1965). Some of these works take into account the biological memory process that includes (1) sensory or pattern recognition, (2) short-term memory, and (3) long-term memory.

> One aspect is primarily important for the proper operation of perceptual processing, including the mechanisms of pattern recognition. Thus, we appear to have a memory system that maintains a detailed image (for a few tenths of a second) of the sensory information that has arrived at a particular sense organ. This memory system is called *sensory information storage.* A second aspect of memory maintains information for a few seconds, perhaps a few minutes. This is the *short-term memory* system. But short-term memory is not like sensory information storage, for now the information is already encoded, already categorized by pattern recognition mechanisms. Short-term memory is also the stage where we maintain information that we need temporarily for a few minutes or that we are trying to organize and store permanently. The third aspect of memory is the *long-term memory* system. Here is where permanent records of our experiences are maintained. This memory has essentially unlimited capacity (Lindsay & Norman, 1977, p. 304).

The theoretical value of the computer model view depends, of course, on the tenability of the particular theories of information processing proposed by theorists of this persuasion to account for human cognitive functioning. Computer programs certainly seem capable of performing many of the same kinds of cognitive operations performed by humans—memorizing, generalizing, categorizing, problem solving, and logical decision making. The crucial question is whether human beings perform these operations by means of the *same underlying processes* imputed to computer models.

The processes underlying the operations involved in most computer models of cognitive functioning are incredibly simple when compared to the awesome complexities of the actual processes implied by relevant psychological considerations. Hence the postulated parllelism between the two sets of processes breaks down at innumerable points of comparison:

1. Computers are able to process and store vast quantities of discrete units of information that are simultaneously or sequentially presented. Human beings, on the other hand, can assimilate and remember only a few discrete items at a time. They compensate for this limitation by "chunking" (Miller, 1956), by processing larger units composed of sequentially dependent items, by learning generic codes that subsume specific derivative instances (derivative subsumption), and by cataloging new information under more inclusive subsumers (correlative subsumption).

2. Computers have no forgetting problem. There is no possibility of obliterative assimilation or of proactive or retroactive interference. Infor-

mation stored in a computer maintains its availability indefinitely. The entire notion of dissociability strength, of progressive loss of such strength, and of the dependence of rate of loss on such factors as discriminability and the clarity and stability of anchoring ideas makes little sense in the context of computer memory.

3. There is no problem of developmental change in connection with computers. They do not change with age in capacity for assimilating and storing information, or in the kinds of information-processing or problem-solving processes they employ.

4. As presently engineered, computers lack the human being's capacity for imaginative improvisation, for creative inspiration, and for independent thinking.

## Recapitulation of the Assimilation Theory of Meaningful Learning

We have now introduced all of the major ideas important to an understanding of the assimilation theory advanced in this book. Most of the remaining sections will constitute an elaboration and clarification of these ideas, correlation with other ideas important to school learning, and application to special issues commonly considered in educational psychology. It should be useful, therefore, to pause briefly to recapitulate and summarize the ideas presented.

Most of the discussion so far has dealt with *cognitive* learning. Although we recognize the importance of emotional or affective experience and will consider relevant aspects in later chapters, the predominant task of school learning to which the book is addressed is the acquisition of knowledge. We have already shown how some aspects of affective learning are influenced by cognitive learning, and vice versa, but our focus has been to elucidate processes involved in the acquisition of knowledge or cognitive learning.

In cognitive learning, we have described the continuum from *rote* learning to highly *meaningful* learning. In rote learning, new information is incorporated into cognitive structure in an arbitrary and verbatim manner. Few instances of pure rote learning occur, although much of school learning still unfortunately tends to occur toward the rote end of the continuum. Meaningful learning results when new information is acquired by deliberate effort on the part of the learner to link the new information with *relevant*, preexisting concepts or propositions in cognitive structure. The conditions necessary for meaningful learning of information are dependent upon (1) potentially meaningful learning material and (2) a meaningful learning set. Since the first factor is a function of the learner involved, we see that meaningful learning is always idiosyncratic. The substantive, nonverbatim, content-specific linkage between new knowledge and preexisting knowledge is dependent upon the previous experience and present disposition of the learner.

In contrast to stimulus–response (S–R) or associationist theories of learning, the assimilation theory postulates that new meaningful learning modifies both the nature of new information accepted into cognitive structure and the previously existing anchoring concepts or propositions. The interaction of potentially new knowledge with relevant aspects of preexisting cognitive structure results in an *interactional* product (meaning), and this is the core of the assimilation process.

We pointed out in Chapter 1 that meaningful learning and rote learning are cognitive learning processes and are distinct from learning strategies or procedures commonly labeled *reception* learning or *discovery* learning. In reception learning, the information to be learned is presented directly to the student, whereas in discovery learning, the student must determine what information is to be acquired. Both processes can be either rote or meaningful. The poor repute in which much reception learning in schools has been held derives from the common failure to understand and provide for meaningful reception learning. It is to this purpose that most of the remainder of this book is addressed.

# PART TWO

## COGNITIVE FACTORS IN LEARNING

# 5

# COGNITIVE STRUCTURE
# AND TRANSFER

*Having considered the nature of meaning and meaningful learning,
as well as the nature of reception learning and retention, we are now
in a position to discuss cognitive factors in classroom learning.
Among these factors, the existing structure of knowledge at the time
of learning (cognitive structure variables) is, perhaps, the most important consideration. Since this involves, by definition, the impact
of all prior learning experience on current learning processes, it is
coextensive with the problem of transfer.*

*How can the influence of this factor be distinguished from that of
developmental readiness, which will be discussed in Chapter 6?
What are the principal cognitive structure variables and how do
they affect meaningful learning and retention? What pedagogic
measures can the teacher take to maximize the influence of transfer
or the effect of cognitive structure variables on current classroom
learning? What about individual differences in cognitive functioning
("cognitive style")? What is the relationship between language and
transfer? In short, this chapter will attempt to explain in greater
detail the statement on the fly-leaf of this book:*

> *If we had to reduce all of educational psychology to just one principle, we
> would say this: The most important single factor influencing learning is what
> the learner already knows. Ascertain this and teach him accordingly.*

*It follows, from the very nature of increments to the psychological
structure of knowledge through the assimilation process, that existing cognitive structure itself—both the substantive content of an
individual's structure of knowledge and its major organizational
properties in a particular subject-matter field at any given time—is
the principal factor influencing meaningful learning and retention in
the same field. Logically meaningful material (subject-matter con-*

tent in the context of school learning) is always, and can only be, learned in relation to a previously learned background of relevant concepts, principles in a particular learner, and information that makes possible the emergence of new meanings and enhances their organization and retention. It is evident, therefore, that the substantive and organizational properties of this background crucially affect both the accuracy and the clarity of these emerging new meanings and their immediate and long-term retrievability.

If cognitive structure is clear, stable, and suitably organized, accurate and unambiguous meanings emerge and tend to retain their dissociability strength or availability. If, on the other hand, cognitive structure is unstable, ambiguous, disorganized, or chaotically organized, it tends to inhibit meaningful learning and retention. Thus it is largely by strengthening relevant aspects of cognitive structure that new learning and retention can be facilitated.

It is, therefore, a commonplace that the details of a given discipline are learned as rapidly as they can be fitted into a contextual framework consisting of a stable and appropriate body of general concepts and principles. When we deliberately attempt to influence cognitive structure so as to maximize meaningful learning and retention, we come to the heart of the educative process.

Thus, in any given discipline, the cognitive structure of the learner can be influenced (1) substantively, by the inclusiveness, explanatory power, and integrative properties of the particular unifying concepts and principles presented to the learner; and (2) programmatically, by appropriate methods of presenting, arranging, and testing for the meaningful acquisition of subject matter (Chapters 9 and 17), by using adequately programmed and pretested instructional materials (Chapter 10), and by suitably manipulating both the cognitive and motivational-personality-social variables discussed in this chapter and in the remaining chapters of Parts III and IV.

The most important cognitive structure variables considered in this chapter are (1) the availability in the learner's cognitive structure of specifically relevant anchoring ideas at an optimal level of inclusiveness, generality, and abstraction; (2) the extent to which such ideas are discriminable from both similar and different (but potentially confusable) concepts and principles in the learning material; and (3) the stability and clarity of the anchoring ideas.

The principal function of advance organizers was considered in the organizer preceding Chapter 4. They are introduced to the learner in advance of the learning material itself and enhance the effects of the first two variables mentioned above. Not only must they be more inclusive, abstract, and general than the learning *material they precede, but they must also take into account relevant existing ideas in the learner's cognitive structure (so that they themselves are learnable and can also explicitly mobilize all relevant content already available in that structure). Equivocal findings on the effects of advance organizers reflect in our opinion failure both to adhere to these operationally stated criteria and to methodological inadequacies in satisfactorily controlling other relevant variables. Stability and clarity of the relevant anchoring ideas (which also affect their discriminability) depend on overlearning (consolidation), initial mastery within a homogeneous context before turning to more heterogeneous settings, and the use of sequentially organized learning materials. ("Mastery learning" is consistent with these latter learning principles.)*

*In general, language facilitates the transferability of learned ideas—even in the case of mechanical principles.*

*Individual differences in cognitive-personality orientation to learning (cognitive style) have been identified that display self-consistency and generality over items within and between subject-matters as well as stability over time. The most important dimensions of cognitive style for meaningful school learning are: (1) differences along a generalizing-particularizing continuum; (2) the tendency to compartmentalize or integrate knowledge; (3) preference for cognitive simplicity or complexity and for broad or narrow categorization; (4) degree of openness to new information; (5) general personality aspects of dogmatism; and (6) degree of tolerance for ambiguity (avoidance of "premature closure").*

## Cognitive Structure and Transfer

We have just hypothesized that past experience influences, or has positive or negative effects on, new meaningful learning and retention by virtue of its impact on relevant properties of cognitive structure. If this is true, all meaningful learning necessarily involves transfer. It is impossible to conceive of any instance of such learning that is not affected in some way by existing cognitive structure. This learning experience, in turn, results in new transfer by modifying cognitive structure. In meaningful learning, therefore, cognitive structure is always a relevant and crucial variable, even if it is not deliberately influenced or manipulated so as to ascertain its effect on *new* learning. Let us examine, for example, those short-term learning situations where just a single unit of material is learned and transfer to new learning units is not measured. Here the effects of even a single practice trial both reflect the existing cognitive structure and induce modification of that structure, thereby influencing subsequent practice trials.

School learning requires, much more saliently than do laboratory types of learning situations, the incorporation of new concepts and information into an existing and established cognitive framework with particular organizational properties. The transfer paradigm still applies here, and transfer still refers to the impact of prior experience upon current learning. But prior experience in this case is conceptualized as a cumulatively acquired, hierarchically organized, and established body of knowledge that is organically relatable to the new learning task. It is not considered a recently experienced constellation of stimulus-response connections influencing the learning of another discrete set of such connections.

Furthermore, the relevant aspects of past experience in this type of transfer paradigm, which are inherent in the cognitive structure of the individual, are such organizational properties of the learner's subject-matter knowledge as clarity, stability, generalizability, inclusiveness, cohesiveness, and discriminability. They do not involve the degree of similarity between stimuli and responses in the two learning tasks. Recent experience is regarded as influencing current learning not by interacting *directly* with the stimulus-response components of the new learning task, but only insofar as it modifies significant relevant attributes of cognitive structure.

Because training and criterion tasks in laboratory studies of transfer have usually been separate and discrete, we have tended to think in terms of how prior task *A* influences performance on criterion task *B*. If performance has been facilitated in comparison with that of a control group that had not been exposed to task *A*, we say that positve transfer has occurred. Actually, however, in typical classroom situations, *A* and *B* are not discrete but continuous. *A* is a preparatory stage of *B* and a precursive aspect of the same learning process. *B* is not learned discretely but in relation to *A*. Hence, in school learning we deal not so much with transfer in the literal sense of the term as with the influence of prior knowledge on new learning in a continuous sequential context. This latter learning context also typically involves correlative, superordinate, or combinatorial assimilation. Thus, as pointed out above, the relevant transfer effect with which we are usually concerned is not the ability to reconstruct forgotten details from generic principles or to recognize new phenomena as specific variants of these principles (derivative subsumption). Rather it is the enhanced ability to learn and retain correlative, superordinate, or combinatorial material.

Moreover, unlike Bruner's (1960) "nonspecific transfer," the kind of transfer just described is not restricted to those instances in which "a general idea . . . can be used as a, basis for recognizing subsequent problems as special cases of the ideas originally mastered."[1] Actually, the principal effect of existing cognitive structure on new cognitive performance is on the learning and retention of newly *presented* materials in which potential meanings are *given*—not on the solution of problems requiring the application and reorganization of cognitive structure to new ends. Thus a transfer situation exists whenever existing cognitive structure influences new cognitive functioning, irrespective of whether it is in regard to reception learning or problem solving.

### Principal Cognitive Structure Variables

The learner's acquisition of a clear, stable, and organized body of knowledge constitutes more than just the major long-term objective of classroom learning activity or the principal *dependent* variable (or criterion) to be used in evaluating the impact of all factors impinging on learning and retention. This knowledge (cognitive structure), once acquired, is *also* in its own right the most significant *independent* variable influencing the learner's capacity for acquiring more new knowledge in the same field. The importance of cognitive structure variables, however, has been generally underestimated in the past. The main reason is that preoccupation with noncognitive, rote, and motor kinds of learning has tended to focus attention on such situational and intrapersonal factors as practice, drive, incentive, and reinforcement variables. But in searching for knowledge about the processes underlying meaningful reception learning and retention, it is not enough to stress the importance of relevant antecedent experience that is represented in existing cognitive structure. Before fruitful experimentation can be attempted, it is necessary to specify and conceptualize those properties (variables) of cognitive structure that influence new learning and retention.

Gagné puts it this way:

> The presence of [a] performance does not make it possible to conclude that learning has occurred. It is necessary to show that there has been a *change*

---

[1] Gagné (1962a) also views knowledge as the *capability* of performing different classes of problem-solving tasks once a subordinate set of capabilities in the hierarchy are mastered. In contrast, we have viewed knowledge as a *substantive* (ideational) phenomenon rather than as a problem-solving capability and have regarded the transfer functions of cognitive structure as applying more commonly to reception learning than to problem solving in the typical classroom situation. In more recent statements, Gagné (1968b, 1977) recognizes the importance of verbalizable knowledge but tends to discount its significance relative to subordinate intellectual skills. He also abandons his former modified neobehavioristic approach for a cybernetic information-processing model of learning.

*in performance.* The incapability for exhibiting the performance *before* learning must be taken into account as well as the capability that exists after learning. It is, in fact, the existence of prior capabilities that is slighted or even ignored by most of the traditional learning prototypes. And it is these prior capabilities that are of crucial importance . . . in determining the conditions required for subsequent learning (Gagné, 1965, pp. 20–21).

In the more general and long-term sense, cognitive structure variables refer to significant substantive and organizational properties of the learner's *total* knowledge in a given subject-matter field that influence his future general academic performance in the same area of knowledge. In the more specific and short-term sense, cognitive structure variables refer to the substantive and organizational properties of just the *immediately* or proximately relevant concepts and propositions within cognitive structure that affect the learning and retention of relatively small units of related new subject matter.

For two kinds of cognitive structure variables, Gagné (1965) makes a distinction between *lateral* and *vertical* transfer, which is partly analogous to the aforementioned general and long-term versus specific and short-term aspects. In the first instance, existing learning capabilities are applied somewhat indirectly, and in a general sense, to the solution of related problems or to the understanding of subject-matter material in other disciplines. This involves the generalizability of one set of existing learnings to the solution of tangentially related problems in a somewhat different area of knowledge. This, he says, is lateral transfer. Vertical transfer, on the other hand, applies to the situation where the mastery of a rather specific set of "subordinate capabilities" is prerequisite to the acquisition of higher-order capabilities within a rather limited subarea of knowledge.

One obviously important variable affecting the learning and retention of new, logically meaningful material is the *availability in cognitive structure of specifically relevant anchoring ideas* at a level of inclusiveness appropriate to provide optimal relatability and anchorage. Depending on the nature of the learning material and the learner's cognitive structure derivative or correlative subsumption, superordinate learning or combinatorial learning may occur.

Now what happens if such specifically relevant ideas are not available in cognitive structure when new, logically meaningful material is presented to a learner? If some existing, though not entirely or specifically relevant set of ideas cannot be utilized for assimilative purposes, the only alternative is rote learning. More typically, however, tangentially or less specifically relevant ideas are pressed into service. The outcome is thus either a form of combinatorial assimilation or less relevant correlative subsumption. In either case, less efficient anchorage of the new material to cognitive structure occurs, giving rise to relatively unstable or ambiguous meanings with little longevity. The same outcome may also result when appropriately or specifically relevant subsumers *are* available if their relevance is not recognized by the learner. For both reasons, therefore, in meaningful verbal learning situations, it is preferable to introduce suitable introductory materials at a higher level of generality and inclusiveness in advance of the learning material whose relevance to the learning task is made explicit. These more general, more inclusive learning materials serve as a kind of "cognitive bridge" to facilitate linkage of new learning material to available, relevant elements in the learner's cognitive structure. We shall discuss this process below as we explain the use of advance organizers for facilitation of learning.

A second important factor presumably affecting the learning-retention of a potentially meaningful learning task is the extent to which it is *discriminable* from the established ideational systems that assimilate it, and vice versa. A reasonable assumption here is that if the new ideas to be learned (for example, the tenets of Buddhism) are not clearly discriminable from established ideas in cognitive structure (in this case, the tenets of Christianity), the Buddhism meanings both manifest initially low dissociability strength and lose it rapidly because they can be adequately represented by the tenets of Christianity for memorial purposes. For both reasons they would tend *not* to persist as dissociable entities in their own right. In other words, only discriminable categorical variants or more inclusive established meanings have long-term retention potentialities.

Last, the learning and longevity in memory of new meaningful material are functions of the *stability and clarity* of its anchoring ideas. If they are ambiguous and unstable, they not only provide inadequate relatability and weak anchorage for potentially meaningful new materials, but also cannot be easily discriminated from them.

In later sections of this chapter we will present evidence from empirical studies supporting the relevance and importance of the above factors in school learning.

### Cognitive Structure Variables versus Readiness

Cognitive structure variables refer to the substantive and organizational properties of the learner's existing knowledge in a particular subject-matter field. "Readiness," as the term is generally understood, implies, on the other hand, that his *developmental level* of cognitive functioning is such as to make a given learning task possible with reasonable economy of time and effort. Thus, in contradistinction to cognitive structure variables, readiness, in the developmental sense of the term, is not determined by the existing *state* of the learner's subject-matter knowledge in a given field, but rather by his *cognitive maturity* or *level of intellectual functioning*. The latter factor will be considered in Chapter 6.

In both instances we are actually dealing with a type of *readiness* for new learning. But in one case the readiness is a function of previously acquired *subject-matter knowledge,* that is, of its organizational and substantive properties. In the other case, it is a function of the *maturity of his cognitive capacities* irrespective of his *particular* subject-matter background.

These two sets of factors are related, as we will show in Chapter 6. General cognitive maturation as well as specific subject matter mastery influence the acquisition of new knowledge.

## Learning and the Availability of Relevant Anchoring Ideas

Whether or not relevant anchoring ideas at an appropriate level of abstraction, generality, and inclusiveness are available in cognitive structure is an obviously important antecedent variable in meaningful learning and retention. In this section we propose to review various short-term studies of meaningful learning, retention, and problem solving in which this variable is implicated.

Studies such as these exemplify the transfer paradigm providing that the cognitive structure variable is manipulated during a preliminary or training period so that the effect of this manipulation on a *new* learning task can be ascertained. For example, a study indicating that the overlearning of a given passage results in increased retention would *not* constitute relevant evidence—from the standpoint of transfer—about the influence of cognitive structure on retention. It would merely reflect the influence of amount of practice on retention. In such studies, which usually require essentially rote recall, practice rather than altered cognitive structure is the only *measurable* independent variable that is relevant under these circumstances. On the other hand, evidence that the overlearning of passage *A* by an experimental group (as compared with a control group that does not overlearn passage *A*) leads to superior retention of meaningfully related passage *B* would be relevant evidence of the influence of cognitive structure on retention.

### The Nature and Use of Organizers

The principal strategy advocated in this book for deliberately manipulating cognitive structure so as to enhance proactive facilitation and to minimize proactive interference involves the use of appropriately relevant and inclusive introductory materials (organizers) that are maximally clear and stable. These organizers are normally introduced in advance of the learning material itself and are used to facilitate establishing a meaningful learning set. Advance organizers help the learner to recognize that elements of new learning materials can be meaningfully learned by relating them to specifically relevant aspects of existing cognitive structure.

In order to function for a variety of learners, each with somewhat idiosyncratic cognitive structure, and to furnish anchoring ideas at a superordinate level, *organizers are presented at a higher level of abstraction, generality, and inclusiveness than the new material to be learned.* Summaries and overviews, on the other hand, are ordinarily presented at the same level of abstraction, generality, and inclusiveness as the learning material itself. They simply emphasize the salient points of the materials by omitting less important information. They largely achieve their effect by repetition and simplification.[2]

The rationale for using organizers is based primarily on

1. The importance of having relevant and otherwise appropriate established ideas *already* available in cognitive structure to make logically meaningful new ideas potentially meaningful and to give them stable anchorage

2. The advantages of using the more general and inclusive ideas of a discipline as the anchoring ideas or subsumers (namely, the aptness and specificity of their relevance, their greater inherent stability, their greater explanatory power, and their integrative capacity)

3. The fact that they themselves attempt both to identify already existing relevant content in cognitive structure (and to be explicitly related to it) and to indicate explicitly both the relevance of the latter content and their own relevance for the new learning material

In short, *the principal function of the organizer* is to *bridge the gap*

---

[2] As noted in the Preface, we have started each chapter with an introductory statement (pseudo-organizer) that should facilitate meaningful learning of the ideas in the chapter by relating the material in each chapter to assimilation learning theory and to relevant other chapters in the book. However, *true* advance organizers are designed to facilitate the meaningful learning of unitary topics, or closely related sets of ideas. No research has yet been conducted on the effects of advance organizers on multiple heterogeneous topics. Thus it is not possible to write a single advance organizer for the breadth and heterogeneity of topics present in almost any textbook chapter that meets the operational criteria of a true organizer. Moreover, preparation of an advance organizer requires specific knowledge of potentially relevant anchoring concepts in the learner's cognitive structure. Although the authors have had many years of experience teaching students of educational psychology and with preparing organizers, the heterogeneity of cognitive structure of this group obviously, on logistical grounds alone, precludes the preparation of multiple advance organizers for all of the separate topics and degrees of subject-matter sophistication in this book. Therefore, while the introductory statements in each chapter have many of the attributes of advance organizers, the reader should consider them more as overviews or précis of the chapter rather than as models for writing genuine organizers as operationally defined in this chapter. Some chapters, of course, by virtue of having a single pervasive theme, lend themselves more than others to the preparation of true organizers.

between what the learner *already knows* and what he *needs to know* before he can meaningfully learn the task at hand.

The function of the organizer is to provide ideational scaffolding for the stable incorporation and retention of the more detailed and differentiated material that follows in the learning passage. Another function is to increase discriminability between the latter material and similar or ostensibly conflicting ideas in cognitive structure. In the case of relatively unfamiliar material, an "expository" organizer is used to provide relevant proximate subsumers. These subsumers, which bear a superordinate relationship to the new learning material, primarily furnish ideational anchorage in terms that are already familiar to the learner. In the case of relatively familiar learning material, a "comparative" organizer is used both to integrate new ideas with basically similar concepts in cognitive structure and to increase discriminability between new and existing ideas that are essentially different but confusably similar.

The advantage of deliberately constructing a special organizer for each new unit of material is that only in this way can the learner enjoy the advantages of a subsumer. The latter gives him a general overview of the more detailed material in *advance* of his actual confrontation with it and also provides organizing elements that are inclusive of and take into account the *particular content* contained in this material. Any existing subsumer in the learner's cognitive structure that he could independently employ for this purpose typically lacks *particularized* relevance and inclusiveness for the new material and would hardly be available in advance of initial contact with it. Students might possibly be able to improvise a suitable subsumer for future learning efforts *after* they became familiar with the material. It is unlikely, however, that they would be able to do so as efficiently as the skilled teacher, who is sophisticated in both subject-matter content and pedagogy.

Organizers also undoubtedly facilitate the learning of factual material more than they do the learning of abstract material, since abstractions, in a sense, contain their own built-in organizers—both for themselves and for related detailed items. Northrop (1952) showed that internal structuring enhances the learning of factual films but actually inhibits the learning of ideational films. It would, therefore, seem especially advisable to use organizers with learning material that embraces a substantial body of differentiated or factual content, for such materials offer maximum scope for the ideational scaffolding provided by abstract organizers.

The pedagogic value of advance organizers obviously depends, in part, upon how well-organized the learning material itself is. If it already contains built-in organizers and proceeds from regions of lesser to greater differentiation (higher to lower inclusiveness), rather than in the manner of the typical textbook or lecture presentation, much of the potential benefit derivable from advance organizers will not be actualized. Gubrud and

Novak (1973) and Schulz (1966) have noted this in their studies. Regardless of how well-organized learning material is, however, it seems reasonable to expect that learning and retention can still be facilitated for most learners by the use of advance organizers at an appropriate level of inclusiveness. Such organizers are available from the very beginning of the learning task. Their integrative properties are also much more salient than when introduced concurrently with the learning material. To be useful, however, *organizers themselves must obviously be learnable and must be stated in familiar terms.*

The relevance of the antecedent elements of cognitive structure for the new learning material is also an important factor in cognitive functioning. Concepts are more easily acquired if the specific instances from which they are abstracted are frequently rather than rarely associated with their defining (criterial) attributes, and if subjects have more rather than less relevant information about the nature of this attribute (Underwood & Richardson, 1956). Relevant and meaningful antecedent context similarly facilitates the perception of connected verbal material when subthreshold tachistoscopic exposure times are used (Haselrud, 1959). Saugstad (1955) has shown that the solution of problems, such as Maier's two-pendulum problem, is largely dependent on the availability of relevant concepts.

### Short-Term Studies

#### The Effect of Advance Organizers on Learning and Retention

Postman's (1954) study of the effect of learned rules of organization on rote learning and retention is an interesting precursor of the use of advance organizers in the meaningful learning of connected verbal discourse. This investigator found that explicit training in the derivation of figural patterns from code models facilitates the retention of the figural material and that the relative "effectiveness of such preliminary training increases with the retention interval." Further, the training reduces the susceptibility of the memory material to retroactive inhibition. In essence, then, this experiment involved the facilitation of rote retention by meaningful rules of organization. The learning task was relatively arbitrary, verbatim, and unrelatable to cognitive structure, but each component was relatable to an explicitly learned code, which in this instance was analogous to a subsuming principle. Reynolds (1966) similarly demonstrated that an organized perceptual structure can facilitate rote verbal learning.

In addition to their practical usefulness as a pedagogic device, organizers can also be used to study programmatically the effects of cognitive structure variables. By systematically manipulating the properties of organizers, one can influence various attributes of cognitive structure (the availability to the learner of relevant and proximately inclusive subsumers; the clarity, stability, discriminability, cohesiveness, and integrativeness of these subsumers). One can then ascertain the influence of this manipulation on new learning, retention, and problem solving. Such studies follow the transfer paradigm, provided that they employ control subjects who are exposed to similar but nonorganizing introductory materials.

The use of expository organizers to facilitate the learning and retention of meaningful verbal learning is based on the premise that logically meaningful material becomes incorporated most readily and stably in cognitive structure insofar as it is subsumable under specifically relevant existing ideas. It follows, therefore, that increasing the availability in cognitive structure of specifically relevant subsumers—by implanting suitable organizers—should enhance the meaningful learning of such material. Research evidence (Ausubel, 1960; Ausubel & Fitzgerald, 1961, 1962; Ausubel & Youssef, 1963; Kuhn & Novak, 1971; Merrill & Stolurow, 1966; Newton & Hickey, 1965; West & Fensham, 1976), in fact, confirms this supposition. The facilitating effect of purely expository organizers, however, typically seems to be limited to learners who have low verbal (Ausubel & Fitzgerald, 1962) and analytic (Schulz, 1966) ability, and hence presumably less ability to develop an adequate scheme of their own for organizing new material in relation to existing cognitive structure.[3] And the same availability of a relevant superordinate proposition in cognitive structure also enhances meaningful retention by decreasing the rate at which the original dissociability strength of the material declines (by decelerating the rate of obliterative assimilation) (Ausubel & Fitzgerald, 1961).

Advance organizers probably facilitate the incorporability and longevity of meaningfully learned material in three different ways. First, they explicitly draw upon and mobilize whatever relevant anchoring concepts are already established in the learner's cognitive structure and make them part of the subsuming entity. Thus, not only is the new material rendered more familiar and potentially meaningful, but the most relevant ideational antecedents in cognitive structure are also selected and utilized in integrated fashion. Second, advance organizers at an appropriate level of inclusiveness, by making subsumption under specifically relevant propositions possible (and drawing on other advantages of subsumptive learning), provide optimal anchorage. This promotes both initial learning and later resistance to obliterative subsumption. Third, the use of advance organizers renders unnecessary much of the rote memorization to which students often resort because they are required to learn the details of an unfamiliar discipline before having available a sufficient number of key anchoring ideas.

---

[3] When the learning task is particularly difficult, however, organizers may differentially benefit high-ability students (Grotelueschen, 1967) and those with more background knowledge (Ausubel & Fitzgerald, 1962) by making it possible for them to learn material that would in any case be beyond the capacity of less able and less sophisticated students (Barnes & Clawson, 1975; Grotelueschen & Sjogren, 1968.)

Because of the unavailability of such ideas in cognitive structure to which the details can be nonarbitrarily and substantively related, the material, though logically meaningful, lacks potential meaningfulness.

### In Defense of Organizers

The most pervasive cirticism of advance organizers is that their definition is vague, and thus different researchers have varying concepts of what an organizer is and can only rely on intuition in constructing one—since nowhere, it is alleged, is it specified how they are to be constructed. The critics apparently ignore the fact that approximately 23 pages were devoted in the first edition of this text (Ausubel, 1968a) to the nature and definition of an organizer and how it affects information processing, including a discussion of how to construct an organizer on the topic of biological evolution. The same material also appeared in briefer form in earlier studies (Ausubel, 1960; Ausubel & Fitzgerald, 1961, 1962; Ausubel & Youssef, 1963) on advance organizers. And apart from describing organizers in general terms with an appropriate example, one cannot be more specific; for the construction of a given organizer always depends on the nature of the learning material, the age of the learner, and his degree of prior familiarity with the learning passage.

From the exhaustive and explicit general discussion of the definition, nature, and effects of an organizer in various publications (Ausubel, 1960; Ausubel & Fitzgerald, 1961, 1962; Ausubel & Youssef, 1963), plus the description of how to construct an organizer for a particular topic (Ausubel, 1968a), there should be no difficulty in different researchers constructing comparable operationalized organizers for particular learning passages and in replicating each other's studies. Joyce and Weil (1972), for example, had no difficulty in operationalizing the distinction between expository and comparative organizers in relation to teaching concepts and facts in multiplication.

Somewhat equivocal findings have been reported for studies involving advance organizers (Hartley & Davies, 1976). This is due in part to failure to adhere to explicit criteria of what an organizer is (see above), and in part to various methodological deficiencies in research design. One of the commonest misconceptions about the organizer studies stems from R. C. Anderson's frequently quoted criticism in his well-known *Annual Review of Psychology* article (1967). He stated:

> Organizers are reported to contain nothing which could be directly helpful in answering post-test questions. Instead Ausubel believes that organizers facilitate retention in an indirect manner by providing "ideational scaffolding." The weak link in the argument is that none of the studies thus far have included controls to show that the organizer alone does not improve performance. Therefore the possibility remains that the organizers have a direct rather than an indirect effect.

Anderson apparently neglected to read the clear statement in the procedure of two of the organizer studies (Ausubel, 1960; Ausubel & Fitzgerald, 1961) that described the use of a special control group—in addition to the control group studying a nonorganizer introduction—that studied the organizer alone without the learning passage. The learning and retention scores earned by this special control group were not significantly greater than chance.

Still another criticism of organizers (Peeck, 1970) is that they are too time-consuming to be efficient adjunct aids and that, therefore, the time spent on them would be just as well or better spent studying the learning passage itself. To support this argument, Peeck simply understates by half the time actually spent by our subjects on the learning passage that is reported in the research paper he cites (Ausubel, 1962). He also ignores the relative amounts of time spent in studying learning and organizer passages, respectively, varying from 5- to 8-to-1 in favor of the former, that are reported in three other organizer studies (Ausubel, 1960; Ausubel & Fitzgerald, 1961; Ausubel & Youssef, 1963).

In our opinion, our understanding of the effects of organizers would advance much more rapidly (1) if the authors of the numerous critiques would first read the description and criteria of an organizer that has been set forth in numerous of our articles and books before castigating it as vague and intuitive in nature, and (2) if they would also consult the original primary sources on the research methodology used in the organizer studies, instead of quoting the same inaccurate and misleading secondary sources that bear little relation to the actual experimental procedures employed.

A recent study by Barnes (1972) indicates that organizers exert not only a statistically significant but also a *practically* important effect on school learning. Statistical analysis of her findings to assess "practical significance" showed that in 98 percent of the cases an advance organizer resulted in a 10 to 18 percent increase in mean learning score. Compared to groups not using an advance organizer, the percentage of increase in mean concept transfer score effected by an organizer varied from 16 to 50 percent depending on the type of learning task involved.

Finally, recent research on the use of adjunct questions in prose learning by Rickards (1976), Rickards and DiVesta (1974) and Rickards and Hatcher (1975) indicates that Rothkopf and Frase's rote learning methodological bias of requiring verbatim recall of single text phrases should be discarded in favor of demanding meaningful learning of entire paragraphs. Moreover, the vague and global "mathemagenic" variable should be replaced by differential variables, permitting the testing of more specific explanatory hypotheses regarding the facilitating effect of adjunct questions. When these requirements are met, superordinate concepts in the adjunct questions facilitate the learning of subordinate textual material in much the same way that advance organizers do. Also, consistent with the findings of the organizer studies, these latter workers found that conceptual *prequestions* yield higher recall and more highly structured memories than conceptual *post-questions*, that *conceptual* prequestions unlike *verbatim* postquestions increase delayed as well as *immediate* recall, and that meaningful postquestions, like advance organizers, tend differentially to facilitate the recall of *poor* as opposed to *good* comprehenders.

Working with 6- and 10-year-old children Lawton (1976) found an acceleration and facilitated effect from advance organizers on the learning of subject matter in that advance organizers significantly accelerated "a move from the level of pre-operations to that of concrete operations." In other cases it facilitated the more complete understanding of "concrete operations . . . at least within the context of a social studies unit" (Lawton & Wanska, 1976).

In addition to serious deficiencies in the preparation of advance organizers, many studies also fail to provide useful results due to serious methodological problems. Barnes and Clawson (1975) recently reviewed 32 studies on advance organizers and identified nine recommendations for improving research on advance organizers. Unfortunately, they failed to note two of the most serious problems. First, most studies do not attempt any systematic appraisal of the already available relevant concepts that might be employed through an appropriately constructed advanced organizer. Similarly, no effort was made to analyze the conceptual and propositional content of the passage to be learned to ascertain what kind of concepts are to be "bridged" to existing subsumers. In short, the analysis of both the learner's relevant subsumers and the concepts to be learned is missing. Hence it is very unlikely that an optimal advance organizer (or cognitive bridge) would be constructed. Lawton and Wanska (1977) have identified other deficiencies in the Barnes and Clawson (1975) report.

Second, most studies fail to consider carefully the proper level of item difficulty or item discrimination required for the questions raised. Many of the conflicting results as to whether advance organizers favor high-ability or low-ability students might be explained by the range of item difficulties on the criterion test(s). For example, we should expect a good advance organizer to facilitate learning only for high-ability students if most of the discriminating test items show a small percentage of students passing the items (technically, items with low difficulties). Similarly, we could not show benefit from advance organizers for high-ability students with criterion measures on which most better students obtain near-perfect scores on discriminating items.[4] We have already noted that advance organizers are designed to favor *meaningful* learning, and hence criterion tests

---

[4] For a good discussion of test item analysis see Henrysson (1971) and Tinkelman (1971). Kahle and Rostovac (1976) offer an example of item analysis used in an advance organizer study.

that require *verbatim* recall of material are inappropriate. Tests of application of concepts to novel problems, especially when administered six weeks or more after instruction, are much more likely to show the positive facilitation of meaningful learning that should result from appropriately designed advance organizers.

A complete discussion of research methodology issues important for the study of the value of advance organizers is obviously beyond the scope of this book. Moreover, advance organizers are only one of the strategies that can be employed to facilitate meaningful learning. We should like to see much more educational research in the future directed toward better understanding of the processes of subsumption, superordinate, and combinatorial learning, progressive differentiation of concepts over time, and the nature and methods of facilitation of learning through integrative reconciliation of concepts. Some suggestions for this kind of research are available (Novak, 1977).

### Transfer of General Principles in Problem Solving

Much positive transfer in problem solving and other kinds of learning is attributable to the carryover of general elements of strategy, orientation, and adaptation to the problem. Systematic instruction in approach to a given task has been shown to facilitate both motor learning (Duncan, 1953) and memorization (Woodrow, 1927).

More explicit facilitation of the learning of skills by deliberately making a transferable general principle (the nature of refraction) available, is seen in Judd's classical experiment on learning how to shoot submerged targets (Hendrickson & Schroeder, 1941; Judd, 1902; Overing & Travers, 1966). Prior learning of principles similarly enhances problem-solving ability in mathematics (Scandura, 1966a, 1966b). Ervin (1960b) also found that verbal instruction in the relevant physical principles underlying a given motor performance increases transfer to an analogous motor performance. However, this effect does not occur unless subjects are able to perceive both the similarity between the two motor tasks and the link between verbal principles and performance. In solving puzzle-type problems, both Katona (1940) and Hilgard and his co-workers (1953, 1954) have demonstrated that understanding of a general principle is more transferable to a given class of problems than is rote memorization of the solution. R. S. French (1954) obtained similar findings in a study that required subjects to learn sequentially dependent concepts. We will explore further the application of assimilation theory to problem solving and transfer in Chapter 16.

### Transfer and "Learning Set"

The "learning set" phenomenon, "learning to learn," "successive transfer," or progressive intraproblem improvement in performance (Harlow, 1949; Keppel & Postman, 1966), also illustrates the gradual acquisition of a general coding principle that facilitates the solution of a given class of problems. Duncan (1953) and Morrisett and Hovland (1959) have demonstrated that transfer in learning set problems is a function of mastery (practice) within a given type of problem, as well as of experience with a large number of specific variants of this problem type. These experiments, therefore, further substantiate the value of overlearning and multicontextual experience in learning generic coding systems.

Many complex learning tasks, particularly those that are sequential in nature, can be analyzed into a hierarchy of component learning sets or units. Gagné and Paradise (1961) define the latter as "a set of subordinate capabilities" consisting "of knowledge relevant to any given final task to be learned." The rate of learning these units and the extent to which they can be recalled are more highly related to final achievement on the learning task than are general learning ability or previous mathematics grades (Gagné, Mayor, Garstens, & Paradise, 1962; Gagné & Paradise, 1961). Serious breakdowns in learning can often be attributed to inadvertent omission of a logically essential component unit from the total task or to its inadequate integration with other components.

### Long-Term Studies

Despite their self-evident significance for school learning, long-term studies of cognitive structure variables involving subject-matter achievement are extremely sparse. Very little research in this area conforms to the minimally necessary research design (the transfer paradigm). This design requires that a single attribute of cognitive structure first be deliberately manipulated, using adequate experimental and/or statistical control procedures, and that this altered cognitive structure then be related to long-term achievement outcomes in an extended program of *new* studies in the same field.

#### Influence of Existing Degree of Knowledge on Academic Achievement

Studies in which degree of existing knowledge of subject matter at one level of educational attainment is related to performance at subsequent educational levels conform to the long-term transfer paradigm. Constancy of academic attainment is, of course, partly attributable to constancy of academic aptitude and motivation. But especially when these latter factors are controlled, it is reasonable to attribute some of the obtained relationship between earlier and later educational levels to the cumulative effects of cognitive structure variables (Garside, 1957; Ring & Novak, 1971; Swenson, 1957; West & Fensham, 1976). Swenson, for example, reported that, holding academic aptitude constant, students from the upper two-fifths of their graduating classes make significantly higher quality-point averages in college courses than do students from the lower three-fifths.[5] But Engle (1957) found that university grades in psychology for students who had psychology in high school were no higher than the grades of students who did not have psychology in high school. This lack of relationship reflected, in part, significant differences in content and emphasis between high school and college psychology courses.

From the standpoint of rational principles of curriculum development, however, introductory courses in a given field of knowledge might normally be expected to establish the type of cognitive structure that would facilitate the later assimilation of more advanced and highly differentiated material in the same field. Naegele (1974) found that learning time for sequential units in a physics course was more dependent on the adequacy of learning of earlier units than on pretest scores for physics, thus illustrating the importance of specifically relevant cognitive structure differentiation for facilitation of subsequent learning.

### Improvement of Instruction

Many of the curriculum reform movements attempt to enhance long-term learning and retention by influencing cognitive structure variables. The University of Illinois Committee on School Mathematics (Beberman, 1958), for example, stresses initial self-discovery of generalizations by students, followed by precise, consistent, and unambiguous verbalization of modern concepts. The Secondary School Physics Program of the Physical Science Study Committee (Finlay, 1959) places great emphasis on the more integrative and widely generalizable concepts in modern physics; on inquiry in depth rather than on broad, superficial coverage of the field; on careful, sequential programming of principles; and on conveying to the student something of the spirit and methods of physics as a developing experimental science. Implicit in each program is the assumption that whatever ultimate superiority in academic attainment is achieved by following these pedagogic principles is attributable to cumulative changes in the organizational and substantive properties of cognitive structure.

Achievement test data provided by evaluative studies of such programs offer presumptive evidence regarding the long-term effects of cognitive structure variables. Nevertheless, this type of research does not adequately conform to our transfer paradigm. The reason is that the learning of *new* material or later academic performance in the same subject-matter field is not studied as a function of earlier substantive or organizational changes in cognitive structure that can be plausibly attributed to *specifiable* characteristics of the curriculum. It tells us only that *cumulative* achievement at

[5] In a review of numerous studies, Novak, Ring, and Tamir (1971) found that achievement generally was predicted best by pretests or other indicators that are closely related to the specific learning tasks.

some designated point in time is presumably superior because of the *cumulative* effects of the program.

Furthermore, not only is it impossible in such programs to isolate the effects of the individual independent variables involved, but also only rarely is any effort made to obtain comparable achievement data from control groups or to control for the "Hawthorne effect."[6] Measurement is also a difficult problem because standardized achievement tests cover various traditional subject-matter units deliberately ignored by these new curricula. In addition, they fail to measure knowledge of the more modern content that the latter emphasize. All of these difficulties point up the feasibility of using curriculum development research as a source of rigorous experimental evidence bearing on a *single* cognitive structure variable.

### Improvement of Thinking

Attempts to enhance critical-thinking ability by influencing cognitive structure in particular subject-matter areas have been made by Abercrombie (1960), Novak (1958), and Smith (1960). Novak found that a six-week experience in problem solving in botany did not increase problem-solving ability as measured. Abercrombie tried to improve medical students' ability to reason more effectively by providing them with opportunities for "therapeutic" group discussion in an unstructured, nonauthoritarian atmosphere. Analysis of X rays was used as the criterion measure for assessing the effects of this training. Abercrombie's findings were generally in the predicted direction but are vulnerable on the grounds of failure to control for the so-called "Hawthorne effect."

Smith and Henderson developed instructional materials "designed to develop critical-thinking abilities, and . . . helped the teachers learn how to handle these materials in the classroom . . . [They] found wide differences among teachers with respect to improvement of their students in critical thinking" (Smith, 1960), but refrained from drawing definitive conclusions because they had not as yet devised a technique for describing and measuring what teachers were *actually* doing in this situation. Their next step, therefore, was to devise a method of categorizing the logical operations involved in teaching. The promise of this approach is twofold: First, the attempt to influence critical thinking is based on the simultaneous teaching of the logic of a particular subject-matter field along with its content, rather than on instruction in *general* principles of logic. Second, by quantifying crucially important but elusive teaching variables, this cate-

---

[6] The "Hawthorne effect" refers to the improvement in criterial task performance induced by some novel but superficial aspects of the treatment given the experimental group (or simply by the fact that this group is singled out for special treatment) rather than by the postulated experimental variable. It can be avoided by using a control group that is given an overtly similar but intrinsically different treatment than that given to the experimental group.

gory system can do much to place long-term classroom studies of cognitive structure variables on a sound experimental basis.

Aschner (1961) has developed another useful "category system for clarifying thought processes that are reflected in verbal behavior . . . [based] on Guilford's conception of the structure of intellect." We will discuss other related studies that bear on "improvement of thinking" in subsequent chapters.

## The Role of Discriminability in Meaningful Learning and Retention

The discriminability of new learning material from previously learned concepts in cognitive structure is a major variable in meaningful learning and retention. In the effort to simplify the task of apprehending the environment and representing it in cognitive structure, new learning material that resembles existing knowledge often tends to be interpreted as identical to the latter, despite the fact that objective identity does not exist. Existing knowledge, in other words, tends to preempt the cognitive field and to superimpose itself on similar potential meanings. Under these circumstances the resulting meanings obviously cannot conform to the objective content of the learning material. In other instances the learner may be cognizant of the fact that new propositions differ somehow from established principles in cognitive structure but is unable to specify wherein the difference lies. When this situation exists, ambiguous meanings emerge, permeated by doubt, confusion, and alternative or competing meanings. In either case, however, the newly learned meanings suffer from relatively little initial dissociability strength. In addition, if new meanings cannot be readily distinguished from established meanings, they can certainly be adequately represented by them for memorial purposes. Thus they tend to lose their initial dissociability strength, or become reduced more rapidly, than initially discriminable meanings. This is especially true for longer retention periods. Over short retention intervals, nondiscriminable material can be retained on a purely rote basis.

Lack of discriminability between new ideas and previously learned concepts or propositions in cognitive structure may account for some negative transfer (proactive interference) in school learning. This is particularly the case when the two sets of ideas are confusably similar, and when the previously learned ideas are neither clear nor well established. Under these conditions, the learner may possibly encounter greater difficulty in learning the new ideas than if he had not been previously exposed to a confusably similar set of propositions. Suppes and Ginsberg (1963), for example, found evidence of negative transfer when first-graders learned the concept of identity of ordered sets after previously learning the concept of identity of unordered sets.

The discriminability of a new learning task is in large measure a function of the clarity and stability of the existing ideas, to which it is relatable in the learner's cognitive structure. In learning an unfamiliar passage about Buddhism, for example, subjects with greater knowledge of Christianity make significantly higher scores on the Buddhism test than do subjects with less knowledge of Christianity (Ausubel & Blake, 1958; Ausubel & Fitzgerald, 1961; Ausubel & Youssef, 1963). This significantly positive relationship between Christianity and Buddhism test scores holds up even when the effect of verbal ability is statistically controlled (Ausubel & Fitzgerald, 1961). When an analogously organized passage about Zen Buddhism is introduced after the Buddhism passage, superior knowledge of the latter similarly facilitates the learning of the Zen Buddhism material when verbal ability is held constant (Ausubel & Youssef, 1963). Thus, much of the effect of overlearning—both on retaining a given unit of material and on learning related new material—is probably a reflection of the enhanced discriminability it induces; and this effect can be accomplished by overlearning either the learning material itself or its anchoring ideas.

When discriminability between new learning material and established ideas in cognitive structure is inadequate because of the instability or ambiguity of prior knowledge, comparative organizers that explicitly delineate similarities and differences between the two sets of ideas can significantly increase discriminability and hence facilitate learning and retention (Ausubel & Fitzgerald, 1961). This method of facilitating learning and retention is probably more effective than overlearning of the new material, since such overlearning does not in any way strengthen or clarify the established concepts that provide anchorage for long-term retention. When established ideas in cognitive structure are *already* clear and stable, however, organizers do not have a facilitating effect (Ausubel & Fitzgerald, 1961). Under these latter circumstances, overlearning of the new material is the only feasible way of further enhancing discriminability. In conceptual learning, presenting sequences of stimuli that provide successive contrasts between relevant and irrelevant criterial attributes tends to facilitate concept formation (Detambel & Stolurow, 1956).

Attempts to increase the discriminability of verbal learning materials through techniques other than overlearning of new material or the use of advance organizers have not been strikingly successful. Merely establishing a set to perceive differences between two related passages does not, in and of itself, enhance retention. However, the learning and retention of *differences* alone is enhanced "by the use of explicit directions to notice the differences" (Wittrock, 1963a). The inclusion of explicit comparisons within the learning passage itself produces somewhat equivocal results (Ausubel & Blake, 1958).

For several plausible reasons, advance comparative organizers are more effective than intramaterial comparisons. In the first place, they provide advance ideational scaffolding. Second, they provide the learner with a generalized overview of *all* of the major similarities and differences between the two bodies of ideas before he or she encounters the new concepts individually in more detailed and particularized form. Finally, they create an advance set in the learner to perceive similarities and differences, and, by avoiding overly explicit specification, encourage *active* differentiations in terms of the learner's own particular sources of confusion (Ausubel & Fitzgerald, 1961). Wittrock (1963b), for example, showed that part of the facilitating effect of a comparative organizer on learning and retention is attributable to the effects of a learning set. He demonstrated that merely a set to contrast or to compare and contrast Buddhism with Christianity, in the absence of a comparative organizer, enhances the immediate and delayed Buddhism retention scores of undergraduate students.

Sometimes in meaningful learning and retention, new learning material may be adequately discriminable from existing ideas in cognitive structure but may be in real or seeming contradiction to these ideas. When this happens, the learner may peremptorily dismiss the new propositions as invalid, may try to set them apart from previously learned knowledge (retain them on a rote basis), or, hopefully, may try to reconcile and integrate the two sets of ideas in relation to a more inclusive subsumer. The function of an advance organizer in this type of learning situation would be to provide just such a subsumer.

## Stability and Clarity of Anchoring Ideas

Little reliable evidence is available regarding the effect of overlearning on the relative stability of anchoring ideas in cognitive structure, and hence on their relative ability to enhance meaningful verbal learning and retention. Ausubel and Fitzgerald (1962) found that the degree of knowledge of antecedent learning material is positively related to the learning of a sequentially *dependent* passage. But the number of times that the first passage is read bears no relationship to the learning of an *otherwise* sequentially *dependent* passage if the latter includes all of the essential points of the first passage as introductory material (Ausubel & Youssef, 1966). In other words, the positive transfer effect of increased stability of previously learned material on the later *learning* of sequentially dependent material is no longer demonstrable if the essential elements of the antecedent material (the elements that make for the sequential dependence) are incorporated as introductory aspects of the second task. This, of course, does not imply that the stability of antecedent material in cognitive structure has no positive transfer effect on the *long-term retention* of otherwise sequentially dependent material when a summary of the antecedent material is included in the second task. Thus the two procedures—overlearning the antecedent material and incorporating a summary of it into the second task—are by no means mutually preclusive and can be used to complement each other in learning sequentially organized material. The previously cited work of Gagné, Mayor, Garstens, and Paradise (1962) and Gagné and Paradise (1961) is also relevant in this connection.

Presentation of heterogeneous stimulus material that does not provide sufficient repetition to allow for mastery is less effective than homogeneous presentation in learning a principle. Moreover, it does not facilitate the learning of a reversal principle during the transfer period (Sassenrath, 1959). According to Bruner, "learning often cannot be translated into a generic form until there has been enough mastery of the specifics of the situation to permit the discovery of lower-order regularities which can then be recombined into higher-order more generic coding systems" (Bruner, 1957, p. 60).

Reference has already been made to short-term research evidence on the relationship between existing degree of knowledge and the learning of unfamiliar material in the same subject-matter field. Students with an extensive knowledge of Christianity are better able to learn principles of Buddhism than are students of equal academic aptitude who have less knowledge of Christianity (Ausubel & Fitzgerald, 1961). Similarly, subjects who have more *general* background knowledge in endocrinology learn and retain more unfamiliar material about the endocrinology of pubescence than do those in a matched control group with less general background knowledge of endocrinology (Ausubel & Fitzgerald, 1962).

In the first instance, where the new learning material (Buddhism) is specifically relatable to existing knowledge (Christianity), the facilitating effect of increased knowledge about Christianity can be attributed both to the availability of more specifically relevant anchoring ideas and to greater discriminability between the two sets of analogous ideas. In the second instance, where the new learning material (endocrinology of pubescence) is not *specifically* relatable to previously learned principles, general background knowledge in endocrinology probably facilitates learning and retention. It provides at least a nonspecific background basis for relating the new material to cognitive structure (combinatorial learning). It also increases the familiarity of the pubescence material (and hence the learner's confidence in coping with it). The background knowledge here also seems to enhance the effect of an organizer. Similar results were obtained by Kuhn and Novak (1971) in a study involving instruction in "homeostasis" in an elementary biology course.

Perhaps the most important feature of automated teaching devices, insofar as the facilitation of meaningful learning and retention is concerned, is not the incentive and drive-reducing effects of immediate feedback.[7] Rather it is the extent to which these devices influence learning by enhancing the stability and clarity of cognitive structure. By deferring the introduction of new material until prior material in the learning sequence is consolidated, they maximize the effect of stability of cognitive structure on new learning. By supplying immediate feedback, these devices rule out and correct alternative wrong meanings, misinterpretations, ambiguities, and misconceptions before they have an opportunity to impair the clarity of cognitive structure and thereby inhibit the learning of new material. Because of the rigor with which such variables as degree of consolidation and amount and immediacy of feedback can be controlled, programmed instruction can be very useful in studying the effects of the stability and clarity of cognitive structure on sequential learning. With carefully programmed instruction, the facilitating effect of advance organizers may not be evidenced, since the entire instructional sequence can serve to augment learning (Gubrud & Novak, 1973; Kahle & Nordland, 1975; Koran & Koran, 1973; Mayer, 1976).

Many investigators have used automated teaching devices in short-term studies of learning and retention, but have generally restricted their attention to the relative effectiveness of these devices as compared to conventional classroom instruction. It has been reported, for example, that university students using simulated teaching machines (Coulson & Silberman, 1960b) and programmed textbooks (Evans, Glaser, & Homme, 1960b) are better able to learn small units of meaningful material than are control groups employing comparable conventional methods. These studies also isolated the effects of such variables as size of step and mode and overtness of response. But until the transfer paradigm is followed (that is, until the effect of prior exposure to such factors is related to the learning of *new* material), the rich potentialities of these devices for increasing our knowledge of cognitive structure variables will not be realized.

## Pedagogic Facilitation of Transfer

What are some of the pedagogic implications both of the foregoing model of the psychological structure of knowledge and of the factors that influence its accretion and organization? The major implication for teaching perhaps is that inasmuch as existing cognitive structure reflects the out-

---

[7] The reinforcement value of feedback, as conceived by Skinner, is discounted by the fact that subjects who make no spontaneous overt response that can be reinforced (who respond covertly or merely read the correct response), generally learn and retain programmed verbal material just as well as subjects who independently and overtly construct their own responses (Della-Piana, 1961; Evans, Glaser, & Homme, 1960a; Krumboltz, 1961).

come of *all* previous meaningful learning, control over the accuracy, clarity, longevity in memory, and transferability of a given body of knowledge can be most effectively exercised by attempting to influence the crucial variables of cognitive structure. This is particularly important in view of the geometrical increase in new knowledge.

In principle, deliberate manipulation of the relevant attributes of cognitive structure for pedagogic purposes should not meet with undue difficulty. As pointed out earlier, it can be accomplished: (1) *substantively,* by using for organizational and integrative purposes those unifying concepts and propositions in a given discipline that have the widest explanatory power, inclusiveness, generalizability, and relatability to the subject-matter content of that discipline; and (2) *programmatically,* by employing suitable programmatic principles of ordering the sequence of subject matter, constructing its internal logic and organization, and arranging practice trials. Hence transfer in school learning consists primarily of so shaping the learner's cognitive structure—by manipulating the content and arrangement of his antecedent learning experiences in a particular subject-matter area—that subsequent learning experiences are maximally facilitated.

### Substantive Factors Influencing Cognitive Structure

The task of identifying the particular organizing and explanatory principles in the various disciplines that manifest widest generality and integrative properties is obviously a formidable and long-range problem. However, experience with various curriculum reform movements indicates that it yields to sustained and resourceful inquiry, especially when it is possible to enlist the cooperative efforts of outstanding subject-matter specialists, talented teachers, and imaginative educational psychologists. "Correct and illuminating explanations are no more difficult and are often easier to grasp than ones that are partly correct and, therefore, too complicated and too restricted. . . . Making material interesting is in no way incompatible with presenting it soundly; indeed, a correct general explanation is often the most interesting of all" (Bruner, 1960, p. 23).

The substantive objectives underlying the choice of subject-matter content in the Physical Science Study Committee Secondary School Physics Program are relevant for most disciplines: "(1) to plan a course of study in which the major developments of physics up to the present time are presented in a logical and integrated whole; (2) to present physics as an intellectual pursuit which is part of present-day human activity and achievement" (Finlay, 1959, p. 574). The primary problem in implementing these objectives is:

> how to construct curricula that can be taught by ordinary teachers to ordinary students and that at the same time reflect clearly the basic or under-

lying principles of various fields of inquiry. The problem is two-fold: first, how to have the basic subjects rewritten and their teaching materials revamped in such a way that the pervading and powerful ideas and attitudes relating to them are given a central role; second, how to match the levels of these materials to the capacities of students of different abilities at different grades in school (Bruner, 1960, p. 18).

The rationale of the Physical Science Study Committee for its particular choice of subject matter is clearly defensible in terms of providing a stable and widely transferable basis for the assimilation and integration of knowledge:

> The Committee has chosen to select subject matter and organize it with the intent of providing as broad and powerful a base as possible for further learning—further learning both in and beyond the classroom. Through its materials the Committee seeks to convey those aspects of science which have the deepest meaning, the widest applicability. . . .
>
> The explanatory systems of physics and how they are made have much more forward thrust as educational tools than the individual application and the discrete, unconnected explanation. Thus the PSSC has chosen for its subject matter the big over-arching ideas of physics—those that contribute most to the contemporary physicist's views of the nature of the physical world. . . . The power of the big ideas is in their wide applicability, and in the unity they bring to an understanding of what may appear superficially to be unrelated phenomena. . . . Pedagogically this choice has virtues. . . . Principal among them is the acquisition of criteria by which subject matter can be selected and organized toward the coherence the subject itself strives for (Finlay, 1960).

According to Bruner:

> optimal structure refers to the set of propositions from which a larger body of knowledge can be generated, and it is characteristic that the formulation of such structure depends upon the state of advance in a particular field of knowledge. . . . Since the goodness of a structure depends upon its power for simplifying information, for generating new propositions, and for increasing the manipulability of a body of knowledge, structure must always be related to the status and gifts of the learner. Viewed in this way, the optimal structure of a body of knowledge is not absolute but relative. The major requirement is that no two sets of generating structures for the same field of knowledge be in contradiction (Bruner, 1964b, pp. 309–309).

Appropriate structure, of course, takes into account the developmental level of the pupil's cognitive functioning and his degree of subject-matter sophistication. Structure that is too elaborate in these terms constitutes more of a handicap than a facilitating device (Binter, 1963; Munro, 1959; Newman, 1957). Similarly, structure that is appropriate for the teacher is not always appropriate for the pupil. Premature acquisition of inappropriate structures may result in "closure" that inhibits the acquisition of more appropriate structures (Smedslund, 1961).

The great expansion in knowledge that is currently taking place demands special care in the selection of the "big ideas." As Ericksen puts it:

> teachers at all levels must begin to take more active measures to reduce the curricular lag between what is "nice to know" in contrast to what the present student generation "needs to know." The slow-to-change teacher might unknowingly actually hinder the student's educational efforts to protect himself from informational obsolescence. From the Medical School faculty, for example, I have heard expressions like: "Half of what we teach will be outdated ten years from now, and half of what the physician will need to know in ten years has not yet been discovered" (Ericksen, 1967, pp. 145–146).

Coordination and integration of subject matter at the different grade levels will also become more important.

> As the high school comes closer to doing the job professors imagine for it, professors will be forced to imagine an appropriate new job for the college. If so, we must first learn that the American educational system is sequential, that changes in one level of education require changes in others, that the task is shared by all teachers in all schools. We shall find ourselves engaged in re-examination and revision of our own programs, undergraduate and graduate. Starting late, the university must as usual scramble to catch up, to keep up, and finally to get far enough ahead to exercise its function of leadership by example as well as by precept (Diekhoff, 1964, p. 188).

Once the substantive organizational problem (identifying the basic organizing concepts in a given discipline) is solved, attention can be directed to the programmatic organizational problems involved in the presentation and sequential arrangement of component units. Here, it is hypothesized, various principles concerned with the efficient programming of content are applicable, irrespective of the subject-matter field. These principles naturally include and reflect the influence of the previously listed cognitive structure variables. These variables include the availability of a relevant anchoring idea, its stability and clarity, and its discriminability from the learning material.

### Progressive Differentiation

When subject matter is programmed in accordance with the principles of progressive differentiation, the most general and inclusive ideas of the discipline are presented first. Then they are progressively differentiated in terms of detail and specificity. This order of presentation presumably corresponds to the natural sequence of acquiring cognitive awareness and sophistication when human beings are spontaneously exposed either to an entirely unfamiliar field of knowledge or to an unfamiliar branch of a familiar body of knowledge. It also corresponds to the postulated way in which this knowledge is represented, organized, and stored in the human cognitive system. The two assumptions we are making here, in other words, are: (1) It is less difficult for human beings to grasp the differentiated aspects of a previously learned, more inclusive whole than to formulate the inclusive whole from its previously-learned differentiated parts.[8] (2) An individual's organization of the content of a particular subject-matter discipline in his own mind consists of a hierarchical structure. The most inclusive ideas occupy a position at the apex of this structure and subsume progressively less inclusive and more highly differentiated propositions, concepts, and factual data.

Let us assume that the human nervous system as a data processing and storing mechanism is so constructed that both the acquisition of new knowledge and its organization in cognitive structure conform *naturally* to the principle of progressive differentiation. If so, it seems reasonable to suppose that optimal learning and retention occur when teachers deliberately order the organization and sequential arrangement of subject matter along similar lines. A more explicit way of stating the same proposition is to say that new ideas and information are learned and retained most efficiently when more inclusive and specifically relevant ideas are already available in cognitive structure to serve a subsuming role or to furnish ideational anchorage. Organizers, of course, exemplify the principle of progressive differentiation and serve this function in relation to any given topic or subtopic where they are used. In addition, however, it is desirable that both the arrangement of the learning material itself within each topic or subtopic and the sequencing of the various subtopics and topics in a given course of study also generally conform to the same principle.

But even though this principle seems rather self-evident, it is rarely followed in actual teaching procedures or in the organization of most textbooks. The more typical practice is to segregate topically homogeneous materials into separate chapters and subchapters, and to order the arrangement of topics and subtopics (and the material within each) solely on the

---

[8] This proposition simply restates the principle that subsumptive learning is easier than superordinate learning. The argument for using organizers rests on the same principle. It is appreciated, however, that the learning of certain propositions requires the synthesis of previously acquired subordinate concepts or propositions (superordinate learning) (Gagné, 1962a). The need for periodic superordinate learnings, however, does not negate the proposition that both the psychological organization of knowledge and the optimal organization of subject matter *generally* exemplify the principle of progressive differentiation.

basis of topical relatedness without regard to their relative level of abstraction, generality, and inclusiveness. This practice is both incompatible with the actual structure of most disciplines and incongruous with the postulated process whereby meaningful learning occurs, with the hierarchical organization of cognitive structure in terms of progressive gradations of inclusiveness, and with the mechanism of accretion through a process of progressive differentiation of an undifferentiated field. Thus, in most instances, students are required to learn the details of new and unfamiliar disciplines before they have acquired an adequate body of relevant subsumers at an appropriate level of inclusiveness (Ausubel, 1960).

As a result of this latter practice, students and teachers are coerced into treating potentially meaningful materials as if they were rote in character. Consequently they experience unnecessary difficulty and little success in both learning and retention. The teaching of mathematics and science, for example, still relies heavily on rote learning of formulas and procedural steps, on rote recognition of stereotyped "type problems," and on mechanical manipulation of symbols. In the absence of clear and stable ideas that can serve as anchoring points and organizing foci for the incorporation of new logically meaningful material, students are trapped in a morass of confusion and have little choice but rotely to memorize learning tasks for examination purposes.

One outstanding example of a textbook that is organized in accordance with the principle of progressive differentiation is Boyd's (1961) famous *Textbook of Pathology*. In this book Boyd parts company with most traditional treatises on pathology, which typically consist of about twenty chapters, each devoted to describing serially the major kinds of pathological processes occurring within a particular organ or organ system. Boyd, in contrast, reserves serial consideration of the pathology of separate organ systems to the second half of his text, and devotes the entire first half to such general organizing and integrative topics as the different categories of pathological process (inflammation, allergy, degeneration, neoplasm), and their principal causes and characteristics; the various kinds of etiological agents in disease; types of humoral and tissue resistance to disease; the interaction between genic and environmental factors in the development of pathological processes; and general relationships between pathological lesions and clinical symptoms.

Progressive differentiation of cognitive structure through the programming of subject matter is accomplished by using a hierarchical series of organizers (in descending order of inclusiveness), each organizer preceding its corresponding unit of detailed, differentiated material, and by sequencing the material within each unit in *descending* order of inclusiveness. In this way an appropriately relevant and inclusive subsumer is made available to provide ideational scaffolding for each component unit of differentiated subject matter. Moreover, the ideas within each unit as well as the various units in relation to each other, are also progressively differentiated—organized in descending order of inclusiveness. The initial organizers, therefore, furnish anchorage at a global level before the learner is confronted with *any* of the new material. Thus, for example, a generalized model of class relationships is first provided as a general subsumer for *all* new classes, subclasses, and species before more limited subsumers are provided for the particular subclasses or species they encompass.

Hence, when undergraduates are first exposed to organizers presenting relevant and appropriately inclusive subsuming principles, they are better able to learn and retain completely unfamiliar ideational material (Ausubel, 1960). Differential analysis in another similar study showed that the facilitating effect of organizers is greatest for those individuals who have relatively poor verbal ability and who therefore tend spontaneously to structure such material less effectively (Ausubel & Fitzgerald, 1962). The greater retention by pro-Southern than by pro-Northern students of a controversial passage presenting the Southern point of view on the Civil War can also be explained in terms of the relative availability of appropriate subsuming ideas (Fitzgerald & Ausubel, 1963). The pro-Northern students lack relevant subsumers to which the pro-Southern passage can be functionally related. The material, therefore, cannot be clearly and securely anchored to cognitive structure, competes with existing meanings, and is consequently ambiguous and subject to rapid forgetting. The pro-Southern students, on the other hand, possess relevant subsuming concepts; thus the material can be readily anchored to cognitive structure and is less ambiguous and subject to forgetting.

### Integrative Reconciliation

The principle of integrative reconciliation of cognitive structure when achieved through programming instructional material can be best described as antithetical to the usual practice among textbook writers of compartmentalizing and segregating particular ideas or topics within their respective chapters or subchapters. Implicit in this latter practice is the assumption (perhaps logically valid, but certainly psychologically untenable) that pedagogic considerations are adequately served if overlapping topics are handled in self-contained fashion, so that each topic is presented in only *one* of the several possible places where treatment is relevant and warranted. It also assumes that all necessary cross-referencing of related ideas can be satisfactorialy performed, and customarily is, by students. Hence, little serious effort is made *explicitly* to explore relationships between these ideas, to point out significant similarities and differences, and to reconcile real or apparent inconsistencies. Some of the undesirable consequences of this approach are (1) that multiple terms are used to represent concepts that are intrinsically equivalent except for contextual reference, thereby generating incalculable cognitive strain and confusion, as well as encouraging rote learning; (2) that artificial barriers are erected between related topics, obscuring important common features, and thus rendering impossible the acquisition of insights dependent upon recognition of these commonalities; (3) that adequate use is not made of relevant, previously learned ideas as a basis for subsuming and incorporating related new information; and (4) that since significant differences between apparently similar concepts are not made clear and explicit, these concepts are often perceived and retained as identical.

The principle of integrative reconciliation also applies when subject matter is organized along parallel lines, that is, when related materials are presented in serial fashion but there is no *intrinsic* sequential dependence from one topic to the next. Unlike the case in sequentially dependent subject matter, successive learning tasks are inherently independent of each other in the sense that understanding of Part II material does not presuppose understanding of Part I material. Each set of material is logically self-contained and can be adequately learned by itself without any reference to the other; order of presentation is therefore immaterial. This situation, for example, prevails in presenting alternative theoretical positions in ethics, religion, and epistemology; opposing theories of biological evolution; and different systems of learning and personality theory.

Nevertheless, although successive learning tasks of material organized in a parallel fashion are not intrinsically dependent on each other, much cognitive interaction obviously occurs between them. Earlier learned elements of a parallel sequence serve an orienting and subsuming role in relation to later-presented elements. The latter are comprehended and interpreted in terms of existing understandings and paradigms provided by analogous, familiar, previously learned, and already established ideas in cognitive structure. Hence, for learning of the unfamiliar new ideas to take place, they must be adequately discriminable from the established familiar ideas. Otherwise the new meanings are so permeated with ambiguities, misconceptions, and confusions as to be partially or completely nonexistent in their own right. If, for example, the learner cannot discriminate between new idea $A'$ and old idea $A$, $A'$ does not really exist for him; it is phenomenologically the same as $A$. Furthermore, even if the learner can discriminate between $A$ and $A'$ at the moment of learning, the discrimination must be sharp and free from ambiguity and confusion. If not, there will be a tendency over time for $A'$ to be reduced to $A$ (as the two ideas interact during the retention interval) more rapidly than is usually the case.

In some instances of meaningful learning and retention, the principal difficulty is not one of discriminability but of apparent contradiction between established ideas in cognitive structure and new propositions in the learning material. Under these conditions the learner may summarily dismiss the new propositions as invalid, may try to compartmentalize them as isolated entities apart from previously learned knowledge, or hopefully may attempt integrative reconciliation under a more inclusive subsumer. Compartmentalization may be considered a common defense against forgetting in many school learning situations. By arbitrarily isolating concepts and information, one prevents confusion with, interaction with, and rapid obliterative assimilation by, more established contradictory ideas in cognitive structure. But this, of course, is merely a special case of rote learning. Through much overlearning, relatively stable incorporation may be achieved, at least for examination purposes. However, the fabric of knowledge learned in this fashion remains unintegrated and full of contradictions, and is therefore not very viable on a long-term basis.

Ward and Davis (1939) report a study of meaningful retention in which general science was taught to junior-high-school pupils by means of a textbook that made a special point of reconciling and integrating new ideas with previously learned content. Periodic examinations were also given that tested knowledge of earlier as well as of recently presented material. They found that students retained material as well after 16 weeks as on tests of immediate retention. Kastrinos (1965) found high retention of biology material for more than a year.

Organizers may also be expressly designed to further application of the principle of integrative reconciliation. They do this by explicitly pointing out in what ways previously learned, related ideas in cognitive structure are either basically similar to, or essentially different from, new ideas and information in the learning task. Hence, for one thing, organizers explicitly draw upon and mobilize all available concepts in cognitive structure that are relevant to and can play a subsuming role in relation to the new learning material. This maneuver effects great economy of learning effort, avoids the isolation of essentially similar concepts in separate, noncommunicable compartments and discourages the confusing proliferation of multiple terms to represent ostensibly different but essentially equivalent ideas. In addition, organizers increase the discriminability of genuine differences between the new learning materials and seemingly analogous but often conflicting ideas in the learner's cognitive structure. This second way in which organizers purportedly promote integrative reconciliation is predicated on the assumption that the distinguishing features of the new learning task are originally salient or readily discriminable from established ideas in cognitive structure. Otherwise they not only manifest initially low dissociability strength, but also lose it very rapidly because they can be adequately represented by the latter for memorial purposes. It is assumed, in other words, that only discriminable categorical variants of previously learned concepts have long-term retention potentialities.

Thus an organizer should first delineate clearly, precisely, and explicitly the principal similarities and differences between the new subsuming concepts and principles to be learned, on the one hand, and similar established ideas in cognitive structure, on the other. In that case it seems reasonable to postulate that the enhanced discriminability of the new anchoring ideas would enable the learner to grasp later the more detailed ideas and information in the learning passage itself with fewer ambiguities, fewer competing meanings, and fewer misconceptions suggested by the established ideas than would otherwise be possible. Moreover, as these clearer, more discriminable, and less confused differentiated new meanings interact with their subsumers and with analogous established meanings during the retention interval, they would also retain their identity longer. This is true because the new material is initially learned in a clearer, more stable, and more discriminable fashion by virtue of the greater discriminability of the new anchoring ideas under which it is subsumed. In addition, more differentiated subsumers are themselves more stable and hence better able to provide continuing secure anchorage. Comparative organizers, for example, have been successfully used in facilitating the meaningful learning and retention of an unfamiliar passage dealing with Buddhism (Ausubel & Fitzgerald, 1961; Ausubel & Youssef, 1963).

Organizers have also been used to facilitate the learning of controversial ideational material contrary to the established beliefs of the learner. The underlying hypothesis of this approach is that selective forgetting under these conditions is not so much a manifestation of selective perception and repression as an indication of the lack of adequate subsumers in cognitive structure for the stable incorporation of such conflicting material. In support of this hypothesis, an experimental group of Illinois high-school students, who studied a comparative ideational organizer prior to learning the Southern point of view about the Civil War, remembered more of this material than did a control group of students who studied a purely descriptive introductory passage (Fitzgerald & Ausubel, 1963).

### Sequential Organization

The availability of relevant anchoring ideas for use in meaningful verbal learning and retention may obviously be maximized by taking advantage of natural sequential dependencies among the component divisions of a discipline—of the fact that the understanding of a given topic often logically presupposes the prior understanding of some related topic. Typically the necessary antecedent knowledge is more inclusive and general than the sequentially dependent material, but this is not always true (as, for example, in superordinate learning). In any case, by arranging the order of topics in a given subject-matter field as far as possible in accordance with these sequential dependencies, the learning of each unit, in turn, becomes an achievement in its own right. It also constitutes specifically relevant ideational scaffolding for the next item in the sequence.

In sequential school learning, knowledge of earlier-appearing material in the sequence plays much the same role as an organizer in relation to later-appearing material in the sequence. It constitutes a relevant ideational foundation, and hence a crucial limiting condition, for learning the latter material when the influence of both verbal ability and general background knowledge is held constant (Ausubel & Fitzgerald, 1962; Gubrud & Novak, 1973; Royer & Cable, 1975; West & Fesham, 1976). For maximally effective learning, however, a separate organizer should be provided for each unit of material. Thus, sequential organization of subject matter can be very effective since each new increment of knowledge serves as an anchoring post for subsequent learning. This presupposes, of course, that the antecedent step is always thoroughly consolidated. Perhaps the chief pedagogic advantage of the teaching machine lies in its ability to control this crucial variable in sequential learning.

Another advantage of programmed instruction is its careful sequential arrangement and gradation of difficulty, which ensure that each attained increment in learning serves as an appropriate foundation and anchoring post for the learning and retention of subsequent items in the ordered sequence. Adequate programming of materials also presupposes maximum attention to such matters as lucidity, organization, and the explanatory and integrative power of substantive content. It should be noted, however, that the principles of progressive differentiation and integrative reconciliation are rarely applied in programmed instruction together with an emphasis on concept learning. This may account in part for the equivocal success of this method of teaching.

Sequential arrangement of learning tasks relies, in part, on the *general* facilitating effect of the availability of relevant anchoring ideas in cognitive structure on meaningful learning and retention. For any given topic, however, there is the problem of ascertaining what the *particular* most effective sequence is. This involves considerations of logical task analysis, progressive differentiation, developmental level of cognitive functioning, integrative reconciliation, and learning hierarchies. Further, in superordinate learning, it is essential to ensure that both subordinate concepts and propositions and the component conceptual elements of each proposition are previously mastered. Gagné states the problem very well by saying that:

> the planning that precedes effective design for learning is a matter of specifying with some care what may be called the *learning structure* of any subject to be acquired. In order to determine what comes before what, the subject must be analyzed in terms of learning involved in it. The acquisition of knowledge is a process in which every new capability builds on a foundation established by previously learned capabilities. . . . The importance of mapping the sequence of learnings is mainly just this: That it enables one to avoid the mistakes that arise from "skipping" essential steps in the acquisition of knowledge of a content area (Gagné, 1965, pp. 25, 173).

## Consolidation

By insisting on consolidation or mastery of ongoing lessons before new material is introduced, we make sure of continued subject-matter readiness and success in sequentially organized learning. This kind of learning presupposes, of course, that the preceding step is always clear, stable, and well-organized. If it is not, the learning of all subsequent steps is jeopardized. Thus, new material in the sequence should never be introduced until all previous steps are thoroughly mastered. This principle also applies to those kinds of intratask learning in which each component task (as well as entire bodies of subject matter) tends to be compound in content and to manifest an internal organization of its own. Consolidation, of course, is achieved through confirmation, correction, clarification, differential practice, and review in the course of repeated exposure, with feedback, to learning material.

Abundant experimental research (Duncan, 1959; Morrisett & Hovland, 1959) has confirmed the proposition that prior learnings are not transferable to new learning tasks until they are first overlearned. Overlearning, in turn, requires an adequate number of adequately spaced repetitions and reviews, sufficient intratask repetitiveness prior to intra- and intertask diversification, and opportunity for differential practice of the more difficult components of a task. Frequent testing and provision of feedback, especially with test items demanding fine discrimination among alternatives varying in degree of correctness, also enhance consolidation by confirming, clarifying, and correcting previous learnings.

In directly sequential tasks, where the learning of Part II materials presupposes understanding of Part I materials (where Part II is *sequentially dependent* on Part I) the stability and clarity of the antecedent material crucially affect the learning and retention of the later-appearing material (Ausubel & Fitzgerald, 1962; Gubrud & Novak, 1973; Kahle & Nordland, 1975).[9]

The stability and clarity of existing cognitive structure are important both for the depth of anchorage they provide for related new learning tasks and for their effects on the discriminability of these new tasks. The discriminability of new learning material, as shown by several of the experiments reported above, is in large measure a function of the clarity and stability of

[9] Consolidation (through correction and review) of each successive part of a hierarchically organized task does *not* facilitate the *learning* of later segments of the task when a summary and correction-review of the *entire* task are made part of the terminal test on the material (Merrill, 1965). The results of this experiment are therefore consistent with those of Ausubel and Youssef's (1966) study, in which a summary of Part I was presented as an introduction to Part II, thereby making Part II *no longer* sequentially dependent upon Part I.

existing concepts in the learner's cognitive structure. Even in the learning of controversial ideas contrary to prevailing belief (for instance, the learning by Illinois students of the Southern point of view about the Civil War), the more knowledgeable students—namely, those who know more about the Civil War period—are better able to learn and remember the "other side" arguments (Fitzgerald & Ausubel, 1963). Presumably they find them more discriminable from established ideas than do less knowledgeable subjects. Thus, much of the effect of overlearning—both on retaining a given unit of material and on learning related new material—is probably a reflection of the enhanced discriminability that can be induced by increasing the clarity and stability of either the learning material itself or of its subsumers.

Much additional research is needed to establish both the most economical degree of consolidation and the most efficient ways of effecting it. These methods (repetition, distribution of practice, feedback, use of organizers, internal logic of the material) will optimally facilitate the learning and retention of sequential and parallel subject matter. Such knowledge will obviously have greater pedagogic utility if the effects of these latter variables are tested together with consideration of the pupils' level of cognitive maturity, academic ability, and degree of relevant subject-matter sophistication.

## Mastery Learning and Learning Objectives

In the past decade, there has been an increasing concern for the importance of consolidation of learning prior to learning of new, related materials. This concern began to gain momentum with Bloom's (1968) paper, "Learning for Mastery." The concept of *mastery learning* rapidly gained wide popularity, and a variety of operational definitions emerged. Most commonly, mastery-learning approaches require a student to continue study of a learning segment until he can pass some criterion test to the level of 80 to 90 percent correct. The idea stemmed in part from Carroll's (1963) "A Model of School Learning," in which he suggested that most children could learn what we wish to teach in schools if varying amounts of learning time were made available and students were given the opportunity to "master" one segment of instruction before moving to a new segment. From the standpoint of consolidation, emerging "mastery-learning" strategies show promise. We will discuss this issue further in Chapter 10.

As mastery-learning instructional approaches gained in popularity, it became increasingly important to specify clearly what the criteria were for "mastery" of a segment of instruction. Mager's (1962) book on "behavioral objectives"[10] gained further popularity, even though critics such as Atkin (1968) and Eisner (1967) had already raised serious concerns over the use

---

[10] Behavioral objectives are described further in Chapter 10.

of behavioral objectives. It was natural, therefore, that research would be forthcoming to "test" the value of behavioral objectives. Duchastel and Merrill (1973) have reviewed some of these studies, and they concluded:

> Results obtained from the research which simply addressed the general issue [of the learning value of behavioral objectives] are, to say the least, inconsistent. Studies which have found no significant difference between experimental and control groups are as numerous as studies which have found such a difference. Furthermore, when we consider the total number of studies which have investigated effects on student achievement, an even smaller proportion of studies have found a significant main effect for this variable . . . (p. 63).

From our review of studies of the value of behavioral objectives we have noted the same instructional and research methodology problems cited earlier for the preparation and use of advance organizers. For the most part, we would expect that instructional objectives would facilitate meaningful learning (and hence long-term retention and transfer of learning) when the objectives can function as advance organizers. Of course, some instructional objectives also serve to define the scope of the program, procedural arrangements or protocols, and other nonpsychological functions. We must be careful in future research that we do not demonstrate an inability of the latter kind of objectives to facilitate *meaningful* learning. Moreover, when rehearsal or review after instruction is probable and/or practically necessary, long-term retention studies may also fail to show significant effects for advance organizers (Lesh & Johnson, 1976) unless study time is limited or carefully monitored (Kuhn, 1967).

## Other Pedagogic Means of Facilitating Transfer

We have presented above some of the principal pedagogic means of facilitating transfer through the manipulation of cognitive structure variables. According to this view, the incorporation of clear, stable, and integrative subsumers in cognitive structure is the efficacious way of promoting transfer. Although we have been primarily concerned with meaningful reception learning, the same general principle applies as well to meaningful discovery learning. Transferability, in other words, is largely a function of the relevance, meaningfulness, clarity, stability, integrativeness, and explanatory power of the originally learned subsumers. Rote learnings have little transfer value. But generalizations manifest transferability only when they are thoroughly grasped and overlearned (Mandler, 1954) and take into account the pupil's level of cognitive functioning. In elementary-school children, this usually requires the use of concrete-empirical props.

Even so, transfer does not take place automatically and without deliberate effort to appreciate and practice the opportunities that are present for transfer in a given learning situation. The learner must also perceive the relationship of the training to the criterial task (Ervin, 1960a). Geometry, for example, can increase ability to think logically in other subject-matter areas only if awareness of this applicability is *deliberately* induced (Fawcett, 1935; Hartung, 1942; Ulmer, 1939). The same is true of the teaching of genetics to reduce superstitious thinking and racial prejudice,[11] and of the transferability of Latin to English and second-language learning. In all probability, however, the same investment of time in *direct* study of the target languages, as opposed to prior study of Latin, would yield more satisfactory learning results. Merely telling learners that previous learnings might be useful in other situations increases transfer (Dorsey & Hopkins, 1930).

Transferability also depends upon the application of a principle, during original learning, to as many specific contexts as possible (Hull, 1920). Hull showed that familiarity with a concept in a large number of different specific contexts and illustrative forms is more efficacious for generalization than is intensive experience with a few illustrations—provided, of course, that mastery occurs within each context. Thus transfer can be facilitated by providing opportunity for learning principles in as wide a variety of situations as possible, by explicitly emphasizing the similarity between training and criterial tasks and by presenting the latter tasks continuously or in close succession. In the case of vocational learning, knowledge and skill become more transferable when they are learned originally in realistic and "real-life" situations that are similar to the settings in which final utilization of the training will take place.

Some tasks are so complex that they cannot be learned directly. The learner must be trained first on a simplified version of the task and then transfer this training to an attempt at mastering the task itself (Baker & Osgood, 1954). For example, in learning a complex tracking task (Lawrence & Goodwin, 1954) or oral comprehension of a foreign language, initial slowing of the learning task is desirable. In some instances the separate components of a very complex performance must be mastered separately before the task as a whole can be attempted with any hope of success (Eckstrand & Wickens, 1954).

---

[11] This does not necessarily imply that a grand heuristic strategy, which can be applied to all disciplines, is discoverable, or that critical-thinking ability can be enhanced by teaching general principles or logic apart from specific-matter content. It simply means that, in certain instances, specific models or analogies may have interdisciplinary heuristic value on a metaphorical basis and that certain substantive or methodological principles have applicability to more than one discipline, provided that their interdisciplinary relevance and implications are made explicit.

## Other Theories of Transfer

The cognitive structure theory of transfer we have presented in this chapter is most closely related to Judd's (1902) classical "generalization" theory. It differs from the latter mainly in being concerned with the reception learning of subject matter rather than with the application of generic principles to specific instances of problem solving. It also differs in being more specific about the nature and conditions of "generalization"—that is, in specifying various significant cognitive structure variables. It is somewhat related to the so-called "transposition" theory of Gestalt and field theorists, which emphasizes *perception of the relationship between principles and specific instances* in the training situation rather than the *process of generalization*. Two other theories of transfer, however, "formal discipline" and "identical elements," are markedly different and deserve special scrutiny.

### Formal Discipline

The "formal discipline" theory of transfer first emerged as a formalization of the belief widespread prior to 1930 that training in such abstract or difficult subjects as Latin, Greek, natural science, and mathematics improves *generally* such hypothetically distinct "mental faculties" as reasoning, memory, and concentration. Thorndike (1924) discredited this theory by demonstrating that these abstract subjects have no significantly greater facilitating effect than do shopwork or bookkeeping on tests of selective and relational thinking. Similar results were reported by Carroll (1940), Rapp (1945), Strom (1960), and Wesman (1945) in testing the effect of prior learning of one school subject on the learning of another.

The doctrine of formal discipline is still very much alive, as evidenced by the stubborn persistence of studies purporting to improve critical thinking ability or general academic performance by means of instruction in general principles of logic or the study of foreign languages. Hyram (1957), for example, concluded that upper-grade elementary-school pupils could be taught to "think critically, and therefore logically, through the use of instructional procedures" emphasizing principles of logic. His findings, however, provided no evidence of gain in critical-thinking ability *beyond* the actual area of training, since it was to be expected that pupils instructed in general principles of logic would make significantly higher scores than a matched control group on a test of reasoning based on these same principles. Skelton (1957) presented data showing that entering college freshman who had studied foreign languages in high school surpassed a comparable control group matched for IQ on English, mathematics, and history entrance examinations, as well as on first-year college grades. Although these differences between the two groups could not be attributed to the fact that the students electing foreign languages in high school were more intelligent to begin with, it does not necessarily follow that foreign-language study facilitates general academic achievement by improving ability to comprehend and use English more effectively. Much more would have to be known about the relative academic motivations of the two groups before this conclusion were warranted.

Although the theory of formal discipline was demonstrably fallacious in its major premise, it is, nevertheless, true that special training in efficient methods of memorization (Woodrow, 1927), in work-study habits (Leggitt, 1934), and in general techniques of efficient work (Cox, 1933) are transferable.

Furthermore, as Cronbach points out:

> there are many disciplines, each of them a way of coming to grips with certain types of problems. There is obvious sense in the contention that a mathematician is more competent to solve a new mathematical problem than a bright and educated nonmathematician, and not just because the mathematician knows more theorems. He has an ability to construct models, sense connections within the model and test the internal consistency among premises and conclusions. He has a wealth of apparatus at his command—notational systems, conceptual distinctions, operations. These are used not as the computer uses a formula but as an architect uses all that has been learned from past buildings. To solve a new problem he draws from his store this and that device that might work, juggles them in the air, begins to see a coherence, discards some misfit parts and designs some replacements, and finds more or less suddenly the shape of his mathematical system (Cronbach, 1965, p. 122).

### Identical Elements

Thorndike's (1913) view that transfer takes place to the extent that identical elements occur in both training and criterial situations is obviously much too narrow. In addition to transfer of identical elements, there is also transfer of principles; problem-solving techniques (Birch & Rabinowitz, 1951); work-study habits (Leggitt, 1934; Ruediger, 1908); affectively toned attitudes toward particular subjects, skills, and learning tasks; and such personality-related attitudes toward novel tasks as willingness to improvise, venturesomeness, self-confidence, level of aspiration, and rigidity.

### The Role of Transfer in Education

It is obviously impossible for classroom learning to prepare students to cope with every situation they will face in "real-life" contexts. Further, even if this were possible, the primary goal or function of education still would not be to provide students with knowledge that is applicable to the everyday problems of living. This "social utility" objective of education has long since been discarded as impracticable. In most instances of nonvocational classroom learning, the goal of transfer is considered accomplished if prior learning experience facilitates the learning of subsequent *classroom* learning tasks—even if the knowledge so acquired is neither applicable nor even applied to problems outside the classroom. Of course, if the knowledge *is* applicable to the problems of living, so much the better. However, this is not the primary objective of transfer in general education.

Another relevant issue here, as pointed out earlier, is that inability to apply knowledge in problem-solving situations is not necessarily proof of lack of understanding of the material in question. The ability to apply knowledge successfully in problem-solving situations depends also on many other variables completely unrelated to understanding.

In training students for particular professions, general theoretical principles are taught in the belief that they have considerable transfer value for the solution of practical professional problems. In addition, students are trained in specialized problem-solving skills and methods of inquiry. How well a particular trainee will be able to utilize his theoretical knowledge in practice, however, depends on his ability to apply this knowledge in problem-solving situations.

Informal, long observation of consistently good and poor problem solvers in the professions suggests that the "application" component of problem-solving ability is less trainable than the "knowledge" component. It may thus be more feasible to enhance problem-solving ability by improving the student's grasp and functional retention of theoretical knowledge than by training him directly in problem-solving skills.

## Cognitive Style

"Cognitive style" refers to self-consistent and enduring individual differences in cognitive organization and functioning. The term refers both to individual differences in general principles of cognitive organization (simplification and consistency trends) and to various self-consistent idiosyncratic tendencies (intolerance for ambiguity; memory for particular kinds of experience) that are not reflective of human cognitive functioning in general. It reflects differences in personality organization as well as in genically and experientially determined differences in cognitive capacity and functioning. In a very real sense it mediates between motivation and emotion, on the one hand, and cognition, on the other (Paul, 1959). The role of language here is crucial. However, a serious methodological weakness common to many of the studies in this area is the fact that the intra- or intertask generality of function of the measures that they use for cognitive style, its determinants, and its functional consequences has not been adequately established. It is questionable, therefore, whether these measures are actually indicative of stable and generalized cognitive traits.

The most significant dimension of cognitive style that has implications for subject-matter learning, in our opinion, is the tendency for individuals to be generalizers or particularizers or to be somewhere between these extremes on a continuum (Ausubel, 1968; Ausubel & Schwartz, 1972). The supposition of the existence of a generalizing-particularizing dimension of cognitive style assumes that there is a relative preference among individuals for focusing selectively on the general or particular aspects of ideas. A further assumption is that this preference has predictable implications for meaningful learning and retention by virtue of differential effects on information processing and storage. It grew out of the common observation that whereas some individuals in recounting their altercations with others characteristically give a circumstantial, word-for-word, blow-by-blow sequential account, other individuals characteristically give a highly succinct and telescoped synopsis of the main points at issue.

Ausubel and Schwartz (1972) devised a test to measure the proclivity to generalize or particularize that manifested a high degree of internal consistency over component items (that is, high split-half reliability). Schwartz (1972) further demonstrated that test scores on this instrument generalize to other subject-matter areas and are significantly related to *perceptual* style relative to detail and generalized features of ink-blot figures.

> The implications of the generalizing-particularizing cognitive style dimension for meaningful learning were established when the hypothesis was confirmed that generalizers would transform presented information, while particularizers would select presented informational elements verbatim in substantiating their conclusions in a decision-making task. It was concluded that generalizers tend to approach potentially meaningful material with a *meaningful* learning set to utilize information in supporting a decision while particularizers tend to approach potentially meaningful material with a *rote* learning set to utilize information in supporting a decision (Schwartz, 1972).

A complete discussion of the numerous proposed (but not adequately generalized) dimensions of cognitive style may be found in Ausubel (1968a).

# 6

# COGNITIVE DEVELOPMENT AND READINESS

The ability of the learner to process potentially meaningful ideas is in part a function of his general level of intellectual functioning or capacity. This developmental readiness or functional capacity naturally increases with age and experience (including school learning) and must be distinguished from the more specific subject-matter readiness discussed in Chapters 3, 4, and 5. The latter refers to the availability in cognitive structure of specific subject-matter ideas that are essential for the comprehension and manipulation of related new ideas in the same area or subarea.

Developmental readiness may be described in terms of qualitatively different levels or stages of cognitive maturity required for undertaking the learning task at hand with a reasonable degree of economy of effort and chance of success. Such readiness obviously fails to occur in the absence of appropriate environmental stimulation.

A given stage of cognitive maturity may be defined as qualitatively (discontinuously) different from adjacent stages. It typically occurs gradually at a certain critical point in continuous quantitative change. The sequence of stages is invariable; but the particular age at which a given stage appears within or between different cultures (and school systems), and in different subject-matter areas, varies depending on cultural, subcultural, and idiosyncratic experience (as well as on such factors as IQ and differential aptitude). Thus, in certain cultures or subcultures, and in retarded (or even in many intellectually normal) children, the most advanced stage may fail to emerge at all.

The most important dimension along which cognitive development proceeds in qualitatively discontinuous stages is the concrete–abstract dimension. The preschool child in our culture is generally unable to understand concepts unless he or she can spontaneously relate their abstracted criterial attributes to multiple specific but diverse examples of the concept before relating these same attributes to relevant ideas in his or her cognitive structure. Similarly, the child is unable to understand relationships between propositional higher-order abstractions in the absence of particular examples of the concepts involved. The elementary-school child, on the other hand, is typically capable of understanding the meaning of a concept by directly relating its presented criterial attributes to cognitive structure, provided he or she is furnished with concrete-empirical examples of these attributes. In most Western cultures and subcultures, however, beginning with the junior-high-school period, the learner can understand and manipulate abstract ideas (concepts and propositions) and the relationships between them directly, that is, without the benefit of any concrete-empirical props.

Although one may designate overall stages of cognitive maturity along the concrete–abstract dimension, it must be realized that in any particular learner the above maturational sequence in cognitive development occurs separately in each discipline. Hence, the older learner (high school or college) must undergo all three stages when first confronted with a new discipline. However, the factors that are responsible for maturational progress (the existence of a large body or "critical mass" of stable abstractions in cognitive structure and of sufficient transactional terms for relating them to each other, as well as considerable experience in comprehending and manipulating abstract ideas without the benefit of concrete props in other disciplines) are transferable to the new discipline. These factors, therefore, accelerate the transition from concrete to abstract comprehension and thought in the new subject-matter area. Thus, bearing the determinants of cognitive development in mind, it is possible, within limits, by providing appropriately constructed school experience shortly before the end of each stage, to accelerate the appearance of the next stage in the sequence.

We have had occasion to note previously that, unlike a computer, the information-processing and -storing capacities of the human being change as a function of age and experience. In this chapter we propose to consider cognitive development and developmental readiness as factors in meaningful learning and thinking. Emphasis will be placed on the changes in intellectual development that take place from kindergarten through high school and on their implications for school learning and pedagogy. Intellectual development during infancy and the preschool period is not germane to educational psychology except where it pertains to school learning issues. In Chapter 5, readiness, as a *developmental* mode of cognitive functioning, was differentiated from the readiness that reflects possession of particular *subject-matter* knowledge, or adequate subject-matter sophistication, for particular learning tasks. In this chapter the term "readiness" will be used only in a developmental sense.

Readiness is a cumulative developmental product reflecting the influence of all genic effects, all prior incidental experience, and all prior learning on cognitive patterning and the growth of cognitive capacities. Thus it reflects the effects of subject-matter learning as well, but only its *general* effects on *cognitive capacities* or *mode of cognitive functioning*, as distinguished from the acquisition of the *particular* learnings that constitute the basis of subject-matter readiness. In any particular instance of readiness, any one or all of these factors may be involved. Readiness may be general in the sense that an individual manifests a certain level of cognitive functioning required for a wide range of intellectual activities. On the other hand, it may be limited to the highly particularized cognitive capacities necessary for the learning of a narrow segment of new subject matter, and even to the particular teaching method employed in acquiring that knowledge.

## The Nature of Readiness

Cognitive readiness refers to the adequacy of existing cognitive processing equipment or capacity at a given level of development for coping with the demands of a specified cognitive learning task. Empirically, readiness is indicated by ability to profit from practice or learning experience. An individual manifests readiness when the outcomes of his or her learning actvity, in terms of increased knowledge or academic achievement, are *reasonably commensurate* with the amount of effort and practice involved. Readiness, in the developmental sense of the term, is a function of general cognitive maturity. General cognitive maturity, in turn, largely reflects age-level differences in intellectual capacity or stage of intellectual development. In any particular individual, of course, it also reflects individual differences in genic potentiality, incidental experience, intellectual stimulation, and educational background.

The particular kind of subject matter that an individual studies induces two main classes of effects: On the one hand, it determines *specific* readiness for *particular* other kinds of subject-matter learnings, that is, the type of subject-matter sophistication we considered in Chapter 5 under cognitive structure variables. On the other hand, it also contributes to *general* changes in cognitive readiness that are, at least in part, independent of the kind of subject matter studied. For example, the study of elementary-school science prepares pupils for high-school science, and the study of elementary-school grammar prepares pupils for high-school grammar. In addition, however, experience with each subject contributes to the pupils' *general* cognitive development and helps determine the *general* level of their cognitive functioning. In the present chapter we shall be concerned with these general developmental changes in readiness.

Thus, in appraising cognitive readiness, we would consider all relevant age-level changes in ability to cope with different kinds and levels of subject matter that are reflective of growth in cognitive capacity or mode of cognitive functioning. There are several examples of such changes in cognitive capacity that influence learning, retention, and thinking processes, and hence influence developmental readiness for learning different kinds and levels of subject matter. They include the following:

1. Increased widening and complexity of the cognitive field
2. Increased familiarity of the psychological world
3. Greater differentiation of cognitive structure
4. Greater precision and specificity of meanings
5. The possession of more abstract, higher-order concepts and transactional terms
6. Greater ability to comprehend and manipulate abstractions and relationships between abstractions without recent or current reference to concrete-empirical experience
7. Greater ability to deal with general propositions apart from particularized contexts
8. Decreased subjectivity in approach to experience
9. Increased attention span
10. Increased differentiation of intellectual ability

Some of these changes in cognitive sophistication (such as increased differentiation of cognitive content, structure, and intellectual ability; greater precision and specificity of meanings) have self-evident implications for general developmental readiness insofar as it bears on the breadth-depth issue in curriculum.

There is little disagreement about the fact that cognitive readiness always crucially influences the efficiency of the learning process. Moreover, it often determines whether a given intellectual skill or type of school material is learnable at all at a particular stage of development. Most educators also implicitly accept the proposition that an age of readiness exists for every kind of learning. Postponement of learning experience beyond this age of readiness wastes valuable and often unsuspected learning opportunities, thereby unnecessarily reducing the amount and complexity of subject-matter content that can be mastered in a designated period of schooling. On the other hand, when a pupil is prematurely exposed to a learning task before he is adequately ready for it, he not only fails to learn the task in question (or learns it with undue difficulty), but also learns from this experience to fear, dislike, and avoid the task.

Up to this point, the principle of readiness—the idea that attained developmental capacity limits and influences an individual's ability to profit from current experience or practice—is empirically demonstrable and conceptually unambiguous. Difficulty first arises when it is confused with the concept of *maturation*, and increases when the latter concept, in turn, is equated with a process of "internal ripening." The concept of readiness simply refers to the adequacy of existing cognitive *capacity* or level of cognitive functioning (not knowledge) in relation to the demands of a given learning task. No specification is made as to how this capacity is achieved—whether through prior learning activities, through incidental experience, through genically regulated changes, or through various combinations of these factors.

Maturation, on the other hand, has a different and much more restricted meaning. It encompasses those increments in capacity that take place in the demonstrable absence of specific educational experience, that is, those increments that are attributable to genic influences and/or incidental experience. Maturation, therefore, is not the same as readiness. It is merely *one* of the two principal factors (the other being learning) that contribute to or determine the organism's developmental readiness for coping with new learning tasks. Whether or not readiness exists, in other words, does not necessarily depend on maturation alone. In many instances it is solely a function of cumulative prior learning experience, and most typically it depends on varying proportions of maturation and learning.

To equate the principles of readiness and maturation not only muddies the conceptual waters, but also makes it difficult for the school to appreciate that insufficient readiness may often reflect cognitive immaturity on the part of pupils that is attributable to a generally unstimulating, inappropriate, or inefficient educational environment. "Lack of maturation" can thus become a conveniently available scapegoat whenever children manifest insufficient developmental readiness to learn. And the school, which is thereby automatically absolved of all responsibility in the matter, consequently fails to subject its instructional practices to the degree of self-critical scrutiny necessary for continued educational progress. In short, while it is important to appreciate that the current readiness of pupils determines the school's current choice of instructional methods and materials, it is equally important to bear in mind that this readiness itself is partly determined by the general appropriateness and efficiency of the previous instructional practices to which pupils have been subjected. The quality of education received, in other words, is a significant determinant of the pupil's *developmental* readiness, as well as of subject-matter readiness, for further learning.

The conceptual confusion is further compounded when maturation is interpreted as a process of "internal ripening" essentially independent of *all* environmental influences, that is, of *incidental experience* as well as of learning. Readiness then becomes a matter of simple genic regulation, unfolding in accordance with a predetermined and immutable timetable. In this case the school, by definition, becomes powerless to influence developmental readiness—even through a preschool or kindergarten program of providing incidental background experience preparatory to the introduction of more formal academic activities.

Actually, Gesell's (1954) "embryological" model of development, implicit in the "internal ripening" thesis, fits quite well when applied to the sensorimotor and neuromuscular sequences taking place during the prenatal period and early infancy. In the acquisition of simple behavioral functions (for instance, locomotion or prehension) that more or less uniformly characterize all members of the human species irrespective of cultural or other environmental differences, the evidence indicates that for all practical purposes genic factors largely determine the direction of development. Environmental factors influence developmental outcome only if they are extremely deviant, and then serve more to disrupt or arrest the ongoing course of development than to generate distinctive developmental progressions of their own. Thus the only truly objectionable aspect of the embryological model is its unwarranted extrapolation to those more complex and variable components of later cognitive and behavioral development where environmental factors make important contributions to the direction, patterning, and sequential order of all developmental changes.

It is hardly surprising, therefore, in view of the tremendous influence on professional and lay opinion wielded by Gesell and his colleagues, that many educators conceive of readiness in absolute and immutable terms, and thus fail to appreciate that, except for such traits as walking and grasping, the mean age of readiness can never be specified apart from relevant environmental conditions. Although the modal child in contemporary America may first be ready to read at the age of 6½ (Morphett & Washburne, 1931), the age of reading readiness is always influenced by cultural, subcultural, and individual differences in background and educational experience and in any case varies with the method of instruction employed and the child's IQ. Middle-class children, for example, are ready to read at an earlier age than lower-class children because of the greater availability of books in the home, and because they are "read to" and "taken places" more frequently (Milner, 1951). Exposure to television has undoubtedly decreased the age of readiness for reading in recent years, but even so, the typical child of average intelligence is not ready for formal instruction in reading prior to entering kindergarten (Kinsella, 1965).

*Pedagogic Applications of the Readiness Principle*

By virtue of his distinctive degree of cognitive sophistication at every age level, the child has a characteristic way of approaching learning material and "viewing the world" (Bruner, 1960). The pedagogic problem in readiness is to manipulate the learning situation in such a way that one takes account, and optimal advantage, of existing cognitive capacities and modes of assimilating ideas and information. This would include, for example, the learner's objectivity–subjectivity, his level of generality or particularity, and the abstractness and precision of his conceptualizations. "The task of teaching a subject to a child at any particular age is one of representing the structure of that subject in terms of the child's way of viewing things. The task can be thought of as one of translation" (Bruner, 1960).

The objection has been offered that we can have no *direct* knowledge of an individual's state of developmental readiness, and that we would therefore be better advised to ignore these factors and manipulate other learning variables about which we have more direct knowledge and over which we have more direct control. Among these are situational and interpersonal variables, reinforcement, attributes and organization of the learning task, and the conditions of practice. All of these latter variables can be manipulated independently of any reference to the existing cognitive capacities of the learner. But although it is true that we can have no *direct* knowledge of and control over the learner's state of readiness, we should not be unduly discouraged. We can still make some fairly shrewd and accurate inferences about existing cognitive readiness from detailed knowledge of the learner's family, cultural, social-class, and educational background, and from the use of diagnostic testing procedures such as pretesting and cognitive mapping. Furthermore, we can also exercise some control over the readiness factor by providing a pertinent background of incidental experience or special preparatory learning activities at the desired level of sophistication.

Much more significant in terms of pedagogic applications is the serious dearth of research on the cognitive aspects of readiness. We desperately need (1) studies indicating that certain kinds, components, and levels of subject matter that cannot be learned efficiently at one age level can be learned efficiently at another age level; (2) studies that achieve superior learning by taking general or particularized readiness factors into account; and (3) studies showing that more difficult kinds and levels of subject matter—ordinarily not learnable at younger ages—can be learned successfully and without inordinate effort if appropriate changes in teaching method are made. Until the principle of readiness is particularized in each academic discipline with respect to the various subareas, levels of difficulty, and methods of teaching that can be most advantageously employed at each level of development, this principle will have little pedagogic utility.

What light can the field of human growth and development throw on the issue of what the schools shall teach? We earnestly wish that it were possible to list and discuss a dozen or more instances in which developmental principles have been validly utilized in providing definitive answers to questions dealing with the content and organization of the curriculum. Unfortunately, however, at the present time this discipline can only offer a limited number of very crude generalizations and highly tentative suggestions bearing on that issue.

In a very general sense, of course, it is undeniable that concern with child development has had a salutary effect on the educational enterprise. It alerted school administrators to the fact that certain minimal levels of intellectual maturity are necessary before various subjects can be taught with a reasonable degree of efficiency and hope of success. It also encouraged teachers in presenting subject matter to make use of the existing interests of pupils, to consider their point of view, and to take into account prevailing limitations in command of language and grasp of concepts. On the other hand, premature and wholesale extrapolation of developmental principles to educational theory and practice has also caused incalculable harm. It will take at least a generation for teachers just to unlearn some of the more fallacious and dangerous of these overgeneralized and unwarranted applications.

Much of the aforementioned difficulty proceeds from failure to appreciate that human growth and development is a "pure" rather than an "applied" science. As a pure science it is concerned with the discovery of general laws about the nature and regulation of human development *as an end in itself*. Ultimately, of course, such laws have self-evident implications for the realization of practical goals in such fields as education, child rearing, and guidance. In a very *general* sense, for example, they indicate the effects of different interpersonal and social climates on personality development as well as the kinds of teaching methods and subject-matter content that are most compatible with developmental capacity and mode of cognitive functioning at a given stage of growth. Thus, because it offers important insights about the changing intellectual and emotional capacities of children as developing human beings, child development may legitimately be considered one of the basic sciences underlying education and guidance. It also may be considered a necessary part of the professional preparation of teachers—in much the same sense that anatomy and bacteriology are basic sciences for medicine and surgery.

Highly detrimental in their effects on pupils and teachers, however, have been the consequences of farfetched and uncritical extrapolation to educational practice of developmental generalizations that either have not been adequately validated or apply only to a very restricted age segment of the total span of children's development. Two illustrations of the latter category of unwarranted extrapolation of highly limited generalizations— the "internal ripening" theory of maturation and the principle of "self-selection"—have already been discussed. An example of a widely accepted but inadequately validated developmental principle frequently cited to justify general or overall ability grouping of pupils, is the proposition that a "child's growth and achievement show a going-togetheredness" (Olson & Hughes, 1943). Actually, except for a spuriously high correlation during infancy, the relationship between physical status and motor ability, on the one hand, and intelligence and intellectual achievement, on the other, is negligible and declines consistently with increasing age. Even among the different subtests of intelligence and among the different areas of intellectual achievement, the weight of the evidence indicates that as a child grows older his component rates of growth in these various functions increasingly tend to diverge from each other.

### Postponement and Premature Learning

Intellectual training should not be postponed merely on the theory that an older child can invariably learn anything more efficiently than a younger child. Instruction in typing (Wood & Freeman, 1932), for example, is more successful at age 7 than at age 5, but this is insufficient reason, in and of itself, to postpone this activity for two years. *Adequate* readiness rather than age by itself is the relevant crtierion. Waiting beyond the point of adequate readiness means that certain specific learnings (as well as the accompanying more general gains in capacity) that could easily have been acquired in the interim, if attempted, unnecessarily fail to take place.

The acquisition of many intellectual achievements that lie within the capability of children, but for which they are not adequately ready, can be accelerated by providing suitable contrived experience specially geared to their cognitive capacity and mode of functioning. The age at which children *can* learn a given intellectual task (like the age of adequate readiness itself) is, after all, not an absolute, but is always somewhat relative to the method of instruction employed (Gates, 1937). By taking advantage of the preschool child's curiosity and urge to explore, by placing extensive reliance on overt manipulative activity in understanding and using symbols, and by programming stimulation at appropriate rates and in suitable forms, Montessori (Rambusch, 1962), Moore (cited in Pines, 1963), and Fowler (1962) have been able to advance considerably the typical age of reading and writing.[1]

Similarly, by using an intuitive approach, it is possible successfully to teach the elementary-school child many ideas in science and mathematics (Arnsdorf, 1961; Brownell, 1960; Bruner, 1960; Davis, 1958; Dienes, 1964)

---

[1] That preschool children are able to learn to read is not so surprising when one considers that they do, after all, learn spontaneously to understand and use *representational auditory stimuli* (the denotative and syntactical meanings conveyed by words and sentences).

that were previously thought much too difficult. However, one must balance against the possible advantages of early intuitive learning the high risk of failure and excessive time and effort cost involved in many *premature* instances of such learning. Where genuine readiness is lacking, it is more feasible in the long run to postpone entirely the introduction of particular subject-matter fields until children are cognitively more mature. The decision regarding readiness must be based, in each case, upon the findings of particularized research. In one progressive school, for example, children who learned no formal arithmetic until the fifth grade equaled matched controls in computation by the seventh grade, and surpassed them in arithmetic reasoning (Sax & Ottina, 1958).

A good case can be made for the proposition that modern nursery schools and kindergartens fail to provide children with sufficient intellectual stimulation or that preschool children are *adequately ready* for more than they are taught (Pines, 1963; Wann, Dorn, & Liddle, 1962). Enrichment of the preschool curriculum so that it is more commensurate with existing levels of readiness is therefore quite defensible. But:

> even if it be demonstrated that young children *can* learn this or that "advanced" process, we should still need to decide whether it is desirable and appropriate for them to do so. Sociologically, we may ask whether this is the best way for children to spend their time and energy. Intellectually, we may ask whether this is the most suitable preparation for future intellectual activities. Emotionally, we may ask whether "early" systematic instruction in reading, mathematics, or what have you, will have a harmful effect upon motivation, or upon personal and social behavior. . . . The point we are trying to make here is simply this: Just the fact that children *can* learn this or that does not *by itself* mean that we, therefore, must *require* them to do so at some young age or in some early grade (Tyler, 1964, pp. 223, 224).

The crucial issues, in other words, are whether such early learning is reasonably economical in terms of the time and effort involved and whether it helps children *developmentally* in terms of their total educational careers. The concept of readiness does stipulate a "reasonable economy in learning time and effort" and warns against the risk and consequences of failure in instances of premature learning. As will be pointed out later, however, instruction in reading for culturally disadvantaged preschool children probably does *prevent* later retardation in reading.

### The Effects of Environmental Deprivation on Cognitive Development

What theoretical grounds and relevant evidence do we have for believing that prolonged environmental deprivation induces retardation in intellectual development? It is reasonable to assume, in the first place, that whatever the individual's genic potentialities are, cognitive development occurs largely in response to a variable range of stimulation requiring incorporation, accommodation, adjustment, and reconciliation. The more variable the environment to which individuals are exposed, the higher is the resulting level of effective stimulation. Hebb (1949) stresses the importance of early sensory and perceptual experience for later problem solving. Piaget (1952) similarly emphasizes the importance of such experience for the early stages of intellectual development. Characteristic of the culturally disadvantaged environment, however, is a restricted range and a less adequate and systematic ordering of stimulation sequences (Deutsch, 1963). The effects of this restricted environment include poor perceptual discrimination skills; inability to use adults as sources of information, correction, and reality testing and as instruments for satisfying curiosity; an impoverished language-symbolic system; and a paucity of information, concepts, and propositions (Deutsch, 1963). Sigel, Anderson, and Shapiro (1966) and Sigel and Olmstead (1970), for example, found that lower-class kindergarten children (particularly black children) were significantly inferior to their middle-class counterparts in categorization behavior.

Both the animal and human evidence indicates that early environmental deprivation stunts intellectual development. Cage-reared rats (Forgus, 1954; Gibson & Walk, 1956; Hebb, 1949) and dogs (Thompson & Heron, 1954) who are deprived of visual and exploratory experience are significantly inferior to pet-reared control animals in later problem-solving ability. When monkeys are deprived of stimulation during infancy, they tend to become inactive, to avoid exploration of the environment, and to "prefer visual and manipulatory stimuli of low complexity" (Sackett, 1965). When kittens are placed in a complex-free (simplified) environment, they exhibit inferior maze learning ability and less activity (Wilson, Warren, & Abbott, 1965). The longer children remain in substandard environmental conditions—in foundling homes (A. Freud & Burlingham, 1944; Spitz, 1945, 1949), in orphanages (Dennis & Najarian, 1957; Skeels & Fillmore, 1937; Skeels et al., 1938), or with mentally retarded mothers (Speer, 1940), the progressively lower their IQ scores become in comparison with those of control children placed in more favorable environments.

These findings are consistent (1) with the reports of progressive decline in the intelligence test scores of isolated mountain and canalboat children who also grow up in unstimulating and nondemanding intellectual environments (Asher, 1935; Gordon, 1923; Sherman & Key, 1932; Wheeler, 1942); (2) with the lower IQ scores of rural than of urban children (Asher, 1935; Ausubel, 1965d; Chapanis & Williams, 1945; Wheeler, 1942); (3) with the increasingly lower social-class differential in IQ scores (Bayley & Jones, 1937; Terman & Merrill, 1937); (4) with the upgrading effect of urban residence on black children's IQ scores (Klineberg, 1935); and (5) with the high correlation between the intrapair discrepancies in the IQ scores of separated monozygotic twins and the discrepancies in their educational advantages (Newman, Freeman, & Holzinger, 1937).

Evidence of depressed IQ, of special retardation in language skills and conceptualization, and of inability to concentrate is found as late as adolescence among children who spend varying periods of their early years in foundling homes (Goldfarb, 1945; Provence & Lipton, 1962).

It is one thing, however, to appreciate that lack of adequate intellectual stimulation in the preschool years may stunt later intellectual ability, and quite another to assert that "critical periods" exist for the learning of particular intellectual skills, that young children are invariably better able than adolescents or adults to learn *any* subject-matter material, or, according to Moore, that the human being is *extraordinarily* open and receptive to learning between the ages of 2 and 5 (cited in Pines, 1963).

### Language Retardation

It is in the area of language development, and particularly with respect to the abstract dimension of verbal functioning, that the culturally disadvantaged child manifests the greatest degree of intellectual retardation. Many factors contribute to this unfortunate developmental outcome. The culturally disadvantaged home, to begin with, lacks the large variety of objects, utensils, toys, pictures, and so forth, that require labeling and serve as referents for language acquisition in the middle-class home. The culturally disadvantaged child is also not spoken to or read to very much by adults.[2] Both for this reason and because of the high noise level of his home, his auditory discrimination tends to be poor. Unlike the middle-class child, he receives little corrective feedback regarding his enunciation, pronunciation, and grammar (Deutsch, 1963; John & Goldstein, 1964), and the vocabulary and syntactical model provided him by his parents is typically impoverished and faulty.

Various interpersonal aspects of adult-child communication and social control in the lower-class home also contribute to language retardation (Hess & Shipman, 1965). The lower-class mother's verbal behavior style in communicating with her offspring is typically "restricted"; that is, her speech tends to be abbreviated, lacking in precision and explicitness, and undifferentiated with respect to person, topic, and circumstances. This tendency toward constriction is further compounded by a style of social control in which parental decisions are arbitrary and are justified by an appeal to authority and status differences, rather than explained and justified by an appeal to reason and equity. In a social environment that offers

---

[2] In this connection it is interesting to note that Anastasi and de Jesus (1953) attribute the relative language superiority of Puerto Rican nursery-school children over comparable white and black children in New York City slum areas—in the face of more severe socioeconomic handicaps—to the fact that they enjoy more contact with adults in the home.

a very narrow range of alternatives of thought and action, there is little opportunity for learning precise and differentiated linguistic expression. But although the social use of language is constricted in lower-class families, it is at least more adequate than the virtually nonexistent *cognitive* use of language. Lower-class parents, unlike their middle-class counterparts, use language primarily as a means of expressing their feelings and controlling the behavior of their children, and not as a means of communicating ideas (naming, identifying, comparing, explaining, clarifying, differentiating) (Bereiter & Engelmann, 1966).

Later on, when new concepts and transactional terms are largely acquired verbally, by definition and context from speech and reading, rather than by abstraction from direct concrete experience, the culturally disadvantaged child suffers from the paucity of abstractions in the everyday vocabulary of his elders. He or she also suffers from the rarity of stimulating conversation in the home; from the relative absence of books, magazines, and newspapers; and from the lack of example of a reading adult in the family setting. The growth of syntactical knowledge in the elementary- and high-school years is also stunted by exposure to a poor model of syntax in home and peer group, and by lack of reading skills and practice.

It is small wonder, therefore, that the abstract vocabulary of culturally disadvantaged children is deficient in range and precision (Deutsch, 1963; McCarthy, 1930; Schulman & Havighurst, 1947; M. E. Smith, 1935) and that the representational functioning of these children is also deficient (Sigel & McBane, 1966). In addition, their grammar and language usage are shoddy, their attentivity and memory are poorly developed, and their impoverishment in such language-related knowledge as the number concepts, self-identity information, and understanding of the physical, geometric, and geographical environments is obvious (Sigel & McBane, 1966).[3] Social-class differences in language and conceptual measures also tend to increase with increasing age (Deutsch, 1963), thus demonstrating the cumulative effects of both continued environmental deprivation and early deficit in language development.

Culturally disadvantaged children's entire orientation to language is also different from that of the middle-class child. They respond more to the concrete, tangible, immediate, and particularized properties of objects and situations rather than to their abstract, categorical, and relational properties (Bernstein, 1958, 1960; Siller, 1957). Their speech is instigated more by objects and actions seen than by abstract ideas emanating from within, and they make more ancillary use of such nonverbal forms of communication as gestures and facial expressions (Bernstein, 1958; Riessman,

---

[3] These language deficiencies exist notwithstanding some compensatory features in the language equipment of lower-class and minority group children such as the richness in the interpersonal and social aspects of "street language" and "black English." (Labov, 1970).

1962). In short, the language of culturally disadvantaged children is more concrete, expressive, and informal than that of middle-class children, showing signs of impoverishment mainly in its formal, abstract, and syntactical aspects (Bernstein, 1960; Deutsch, 1963). Their sentences are short, staccato-like, and heavily interlaced with slang and clichés and are rarely compound or complex in structure (Bernstein, 1960; Deutsch, 1963). These children use few conjunctions, adjectives, adverbs, and qualifying phrases or clauses. In the case of black children, some writers have claimed that even the vocabulary and syntax are different (Baratz, 1970; Houston, 1970).

The most important consequence of culturally disadvantaged children's language retardation, however, is their slower and less complete transition from concrete to abstract modes of thought and understanding. This transition takes place more slowly and less completely for two reasons. First, culturally disadvantaged children lack the necessary repertoire of clear and stable abstractions and "transactional" terms (conditional conjunctives, qualifying adjectives) that is obviously prerequisite for the direct manipulation and understanding of *relationships* between abstractions. Second, for lack of adequate practice, they have not acquired sufficient facility in relating abstractions to each other *with* the benefit of concrete-empirical props, so that they can later dispense with these props at the same age as these children's environmentally more favored contemporaries. Because concrete thought operations are necessarily more time-consuming than their abstract-verbal counterparts, and also because of these children's distractibility, unfamiliarity with formal language, impaired self-confidence, and unresponsiveness to time pressure, culturally disadvantaged children typically work more slowly than middle-class children in an academic setting (Chapanis & Williams, 1945).

### Schooling and Intellectual Development

We still lack firm evidence concerning the influence of an optimal learning environment on the intellectual development of culturally deprived elementary-school and adolescent children, especially those who have been subjected for many years to the frustration and demoralization of inappropriate school experience.[4] This is an extremely urgent research problem that

[4] Some tangential evidence concerning the ameliorative effect of school experience on intellectual development comes from studies showing that the resumption of regular schooling in Holland after World War II raised the mean IQ scores of children (de Groot, 1948, 1951), and that long-term improvement in substandard school conditions raised the mean IQ scores among Hawaiian (Smith, 1935) and East Tennessee mountain (Wheeler, 1942) children. Current remedial programs for culturally disadvantaged children attending school, undertaken as part of the antipoverty movement, tend to be global action programs rather than controlled research studies that can yield valid evidence regarding the efficacy of any particular cognitive or motivational aspect of remediation.

should engage our immediate attention. We need to investigate the effects of an optimal learning environment on both IQ scores and on the acquisition of school knowledge, making special efforts to eliminate errors of measurement associated with test-content bias, test-taking skills, test rapport, and test motivation. Generalizing deductively, one might anticipate that school knowledge would be more ameliorable than intelligence level to the influence of environmental stimulation.

### Mechanisms Mediating Irreversibility

#### The Critical Periods Hypothesis

An increasingly more popular explanation that has been advanced in recent years to account for the apparent irreversibility of certain kinds of behavioral development in developmental retardation is the "critical periods" hypothesis. According to this hypothesis, irreversibility of behavioral development is a function of extreme susceptibility to particular types of stimulation during those brief periods in individual development when certain types of behavior are shaped and molded for life. By the same token, if the individual is deprived of the necessary stimulation during the critical period, when he or she is maximally susceptible to it in terms of actualizing particular potential capacities or developing in new directions, it is held that some degree of permanent retardation is inevitable. In other words, the child can never or only partly attain the capacities in question. Numerous examples of the existence of critical periods can be found in the perceptual, motor, and social development of infrahuman mammals. Infant chimpanzees isolated from normal tactual stimulation exhibit defective kinesthetic learning and cutaneous localization (Nissen, Chow, & Semmes, 1951). If reared in darkness, they fail to fixate or recognize familiar objects or to blink in response to a threatening object (Riesen, 1947). Newborn domestic lambs reared on a bottle and isolated from sheep for ten days experience difficulty later in adjusting to the flock and tend to graze by themselves (Scott, Fredericson, & Fuller, 1951). Similarly, puppies isolated for nine weeks or more are unable to adapt socially to other dogs. And if they are not removed from the litter by three months of age, they are extremely difficult to tame at a later date (Scott & Marston, 1950). "Imprinting" in animals is also a manifestation of the "critical periods" phenomenon. An isolated newborn duck, for example, will slavishly follow the first object or creature that moves (Hess, 1959). High susceptibility to stimulation during this period accounts both for the nonspecific nature of the imprinted response and for its "canalization" (its preemption of the response category in question). The latter feature, of course, also reflects the animal's isolation from competing stimuli.

An implicit form of the "critical periods" hypothesis was applied to intellectual development many years ago by Montessori and her followers to justify the particular graded series of learning tasks that children are set in Montessori schools (Rambusch, 1962). More recently it has been invoked by advocates of the proposition that young children can learn many intellectual skills and kinds of subject matter more efficiently than adults can. The argument in both instances is that since there are allegedly optimal (critical) periods of readiness for all kinds of cognitive acquisitions, children who fail to learn the age-appropriate skills at the appropriate times are forever handicapped in acquiring them later. Thus both Montessori (Rambusch, 1962) and Moore (cited in Pines, 1963) place particular emphasis in their preschool educational programs on the concept of "explosive" periods of intellectual growth when unique susceptibility to particular kinds of cognitive stimulation supposedly exists and when optimal readiness for particular kinds of intellectual acquisitions is allegedly present. Seize the opportunity for such learnings at these periods, they implore us, or be reconciled to the fact that they will be much more difficult, or even impossible, at some future date.

Serious difficulties, however, lie in the path of extrapolating the "critical periods" hypothesis to human cognitive development (Ausubel, 1965c). In the first place, it has been validated only for infant individuals in infrahuman species and in relation to those kinds of rapidly developing perceptual, motor, and social traits that are largely regulated by genic factors. In human individuals, especially beyond the prenatal period and first year of life, environmental determinants of development are more important and the rate of maturation is significantly slower. Second, it has never been empirically demonstrated that *optimal* readiness exists at particular age periods for specified kinds of *intellectual* activities, and that if adequate conditions for growth are not present during those periods, no future time is ever as advantageous, thereby causing irreparable developmental deficit.[5]

Hence, if specific intellectual skills or subject-matter content are not acquired at the earliest appearance of readiness, this does *not* mean that they cannot be acquired later just as well or even better. The same degree of cognitive capacity that establishes readiness at an earlier age would *still* be present at least in *equal* degree at some future date. The problem, therefore, is not that this degree of maturity disappears or *declines* in some mysterious fashion, but rather that it fails to *grow* at a normal rate in the interim because it is not appropriately exercised. The disadvantage of unnecessarily postponing such learning tasks thus inheres in the irreparable loss of precious years of opportunity when reasonably economical learning (and the concomitant growth in cognitive capacity) fail to occur simply because these kinds of tasks are not attempted. When this happens, the individual,

---

[5] Even older puppies learn just as well or better than those trained at an earlier age provided that they are not subjected to emotional distress at the time of learning (Scott, 1968).

in comparison with equally endowed peers, incurs a deficit in cognitive capacity that limits his or her current and future rate of intellectual development.

### The Cumulative Nature of Developmental Deficit

This brings us to a second, somewhat more credible, explanation of the possible irreversibility in cognitive development that results from pro-longed cultural disadvantage (Ausubel, 1965c). We refer to the tendency for existing developmental deficits to become cumulative in nature, since current and future rates of intellectual growth are always conditioned or limited by the attained level of development. The child who has an existing deficit in growth incurred from past deprivation is less able to profit devel-opmentally from new and more advanced levels of environmental stimula-tion. Thus, irrespective of the adequacy of all other factors—both internal and external—this deficit tends to increase cumulatively and to lead to permanent retardation.

New growth, in other words, always proceeds from the existing pheno-type (that is, from already actualized capacity) rather than from potential-ities inherent in the genotype (genic structure). It makes no difference in terms of this limiting influence whether the attained deficiency is attrib-utable to inferior genic endowment or to inadequate environment. If, as a result of a consistently deprived environment during the early formative years, potential intellectual endowment is not actualized, the attained de-ficit in functional capacity significantly limits the extent to which later environmental stimulation can increase the rate of cognitive growth. Hence, an individual's prior success or failure in developing his or her intellectual capacities tends to keep future rate of growth relatively constant. Initial failure to acquire adequate language, information-processing, and problem-solving abilities, for example, limits the later growth of cognitive capacities and of cognitive functioning.

#### Differentiation of Cognitive Functioning

In addition to the limiting condition of attained level of development or of existing degree of deficiency, we must consider the further limiting factor of the organism's degree of plasticity or freedom to respond developmen-tally in a given direction in response to appropriate environmental stimu-lation (Ausubel, 1965c).

Generally speaking, the plasticity of intelligence tends to decrease with increasing age. At first, intelligence is a relatively undifferentiated capacity that can develop in several different directions. But as children grow older, particularly during preadolescence and adolescence, it becomes increas-ingly more differentiated. This is shown by the decreasing intercorrelations among the subtests of a given intelligence scale (Garrett, Bryan, & Perl,

1935). Another indication of the trend toward the progressive differentiation of abilities is the fact that 10-year-old boys of high socioeconomic status make higher scores than 10-year-old boys of low socioeconomic status on tests of both verbal *and* mechanical ability, but at age 16 they are superior only on the verbal tests (Havighurst & Janke, 1944; Janke & Havighurst, 1945). Furthermore, the verbal ability scores of boys who drop out of school at the age of 17 tend to decline, whereas their scores on tests of mechanical aptitude continue to improve (Vernon, 1948). Thus, by the time an individual reaches adolescence, differential factors of interest, relative ability, specialization of training,[6] motivation, success and failure experience, and cultural expectation operate selectively to develop certain potential abilities and to leave others relatively undeveloped. Children with particular intellectual disabilities tend to avoid activities involving these disabilities, thereby increasing the original deficit (Kirk, 1958).

Once intelligence undergoes definite relative commitment in the various aforementioned channels, therefore, the individual manifests less potentiality for growing in areas of minimal development than was the case in the original undifferentiated state. Thus, for example, if because of inadequate stimulation during early and middle childhood, genic potentialities for verbal intelligence fail to be adequately actualized, other facets of intelligence (for example, quantitative), which are more satisfactorily stimulated, become differentially more highly developed. At this point, therefore, the development of individuals' verbal intelligence is limited not only by their existing deficiency in the verbal area, but also by the fact that much of their once undifferentiated potentiality for growth in intelligence has already been definitely committed in other directions. Hence it is no longer available to respond to an enriched verbal environment. Thus it is evident that the possibility for complete reversibility of environmentally induced retardation in verbal intelligence decreases as children advance in age. This is not to say, of course, that later enrichment is entirely to no avail. In our opinion, however, some of this failure in developmental actualization is irreversible and cannot be compensated for later, irrespective of the amount of hyperstimulation applied.

## General Stages of Intellectual Development

General theories of intellectual development, such as those advanced by Piaget and his collaborators (Inhelder & Piaget, 1958; Piaget, 1950, 1954a), include age-level changes in at least four major areas of cognitive function-

---

[6] Additional evidence of the effect of experience on the differentiation of intelligence comes from studies showing that the intelligence test scores of boys who continue longer in school tend to exceed, even twenty years later, the test scores of matched controls with less schooling (Lorge, 1945), and that gains in IQ scores are much more common in college than in noncollege populations (Thorndike, 1948).

ing: perception, objectivity-subjectivity, the structure of ideas or knowledge, and the nature of thinking or problem solving. The major focus of our concern in this chapter, however, will be on those developmental changes in cognitive capacities or cognitive-processing equipment that affect an individual's learning and retention of meaningful verbal material. For example, as children increase in age:

1. They tend to perceive the stimulus world more in general, abstract, and categorical terms and less in tangible, time-bound, and particularized contexts (Gollin, 1958; Piaget, 1950, 1954a; Serra, 1953).

2. They demonstrate increasing ability to comprehend and manipulate abstract verbal symbols and relationships, and to employ abstract classificatory schemata (Inhelder & Piaget, 1958; Piaget, 1950, 1954a; Wallon, 1952).

3. They are better able to understand ideational relationships without the benefit of direct, tangible experience, of concrete imagery, and of empirical exposure to numerous particular instances of a given concept or proposition (Goldman & Levine, 1963; Inhelder & Piaget, 1958; Szuman, 1951; Werner, 1948).

4. They tend more to infer the properties of objects from their class membership rather than from the direct experience of proximate, sensory data (Gollin, 1958; Reichard, Schneider, & Rapaport, 1944; Sigel, 1953; Wallon, 1952; Wohlwill, 1960b).

5. They are more disposed to use remote and abstract, rather than immediate and concrete criterial attributes, in classifying phenomena and to use abstract symbols rather than concrete imagery to represent emerging concepts (M. Annett, 1959; Inhelder & Piaget, 1958; Piaget, 1950, 1954a; Werner, 1948).

6. They acquire an ever-increasing repertoire of more inclusive and higher-order abstractions (Inhelder & Piaget, 1958; Serra, 1953; Welch, 1940; Werner, 1948).

In addition, with increasing age, the cognitive field of children tends to widen both spatially and temporally (Baker, 1942; Hill, 1930; Probst, 1931). Children become more capable of making both broader and more subtle inferences from empirical data (of "going beyond the information given") (Bruner, 1964a; Gollin, 1958; Kendler & Kendler, 1956). Their cognitive products tend to become both selectively more schematic (Gibson, 1953) and less subjective and egocentric in nature (Baker, 1942; Piaget, 1928, 1929). The older child is more capable of viewing situations from a hypothetical ("as if") basis or from the standpoint of others (Baker, 1942; Piaget, 1928, 1929). Finally, the child's attention span increases markedly (Gutteridge, 1935; Van Alstyne, 1932).

The most important of the aforementioned changes in intellectual development for educational practice is the gradual shift from concrete to abstract cognitive functioning. It defines the principal differences between the respective learning and thinking processes of elementary- and secondary-school pupils, as well as the corresponding differences in pedagogic strategy that they imply. This dimension of cognitive development will be considered in detail in a subsequent section and will be related to Piaget's designated stages of intellectual functioning. At this point it will be more profitable to consider in general terms both what is meant by a stage of cognitive development and whether the very concept of "stage" is tenable and useful in understanding age-level changes in cognitive capacity and their implications for education.

### The Meaning of Stages

Piaget's delineation of qualitatively distinct stages of intellectual development has been a powerful stimulus to research in this area, as well as a perennial source of theoretical controversy. Despite the general cogency and heuristic promise of his formulations, however, the issue of stages remains unresolved for a number of reasons. Some of these reasons, unfortunately, inhere in Piaget's unsystematic and faulty methods of conducting his research and reporting his findings.[7] In the first place, he is almost totally indifferent to problems of sampling, reliability, and statistical significance. He often fails to present adequate normative data on age level, sex, and IQ differences, to use uniform experimental procedures for all subjects, to designate unambiguous criteria for classifying the responses of his subjects, and to determine interrater reliability. In place of statistical analysis of data and customary tests of statistical significance, he often offers confirmatory illustrations selectively culled from his protocols. Second, he tends to ignore such obvious and crucial considerations as extent of intersituational generality and relative degree of intra- and interstage variability in delineating stages of development. Third, the cross-sectional observa-

---

[7] In the past 15 years the findings of other investigators (such as Braine, 1959; Case & Collinson, 1962; Goldstein & Scheerer, 1941; Jackson, 1965; Kohlberg, 1963; Laurendeau & Pinard, 1970, 1972; Lovell, 1959a, 1959b, 1961a; Lovell & Ogilvie, 1960; Lunzer, 1960; Mannix, 1960; Peel, 1959; Smedslund, 1960, 1961; Tanner & Inhelder, 1960; Trabasso, 1975; Werner, 1948; Wohlwill, 1960a, 1960b; Yudin & Kates, 1963), have, on the whole, been in general agreement with Piaget's more recent formulations regarding invariant general stages of cognitive development. They differ from Piaget's findings less in terms of the developmental sequences identified than in the specification of different age levels for particular stages and in the distinguishing properties of various stages, in exhibiting greater intrastage variability, and in manifesting less intersituational and intertask generality. Nevertheless, much more rigorous developmental data than have been presented to date, especially of a longitudinal nature, are required to substantiate Piaget's conclusions. (Ausubel, 1958; Wohlwill, 1973).

Among others who repudiate the invariant, qualitatively discontinuous stage theory of cognitive development are Bijou (1975); Brainerd (1974); Ezer (1962); J. McV. Hunt (1961); Mogar (1960); Novak (in press); and Strauss (1972). Flavell (1963, 1971) takes the position that the question of sequential invariability has not yet been definitely determined.

tions he uses to measure developmental change (observations on *different* age groups of children) are particularly ill adapted for his purposes. The transitional stages and qualitative discontinuities he purports to find can be convincingly demonstrated only by longitudinally extended studies of the *same* children. Logical inference is not an adequate substitute for empirical data in naturalistic investigation.[8] Finally, he refines, elaborates, and rationalizes the subdivision of his stages to a degree that goes far beyond his data. Hence, the psychological plausibility and freshness of the general outlines of his theory tend to become engulfed by a welter of logical gymnastics and abstruse, disorganized speculation.

## Criteria of Developmental Stages

The resolution of disagreement with respect to stages of intellectual development is prevented even more by the unwarranted and gratuitous assumptions made by his critics regarding the criteria that *any* designated stage of development must meet, than it is by Piaget's methodological shortcomings. Many American psychologists and educators, for example, have been sharply critical of Piaget's designation of stages for the concrete-abstract dimension of cognitive development. They argue that: (1) the transition between these stages occurs gradually rather than abruptly; (2) variability exists both between different cultures and within a given culture with respect to the age at which the transition takes place; (3) fluctuations occur over time in the level of cognitive functioning manifested by a given child; (4) the transition to the formal stage in a particular individual occurs at different ages both for different subject-matter fields and for component subareas within a particular field; and (5) environmental as well as endogenous factors have demonstrable influence on the rate of cognitive development. For all of these reasons, therefore, they deny the validity of Piaget's designated stages.

Actually, developmental stages imply nothing more than identifiable sequential phases in an orderly progression of development that are *qualitatively* discriminable from adjacent phases and generally characteristic of most members of a broadly defined age range. As long as a given stage occupies the same invariable *sequential position* in all individuals and cultures whenever and if it occurs, it is perfectly compatible with the existence of intraindividual, interindividual, and intercultural differences in age level of incidence and in subject-matter field. It reflects the influence of both genic and environmental determinants and can occur either gradually or abruptly. Hence all of the aforementioned arguments disputing the legiti-

---

[8] This is the case despite the fact that many ardent followers of Piaget infer sequential variability from purely cross-sectional research designs (for example, Elkind, 1961a; 1961b; Furth, 1970; Kooistra, 1963; Laurendeau & Pinard, 1970; Wohlwill, 1960a, 1960b).

macy of Piaget's stages of intellectual development seem quite irrelevant.

Although stages of development are qualitatively discontinuous in *process* from one to another, there is no reason why their *manner of achievement* must necessarily be abrupt or saltatory. This is particularly true when the factors that bring them into being are operative over many years and are cumulative in their impact. Unlike the situation in physical, emotional, and personality development, cognitive development is not marked by the sudden, dramatic appearance of discontinuously new determinants. Rather it appears more likely in cognitive development that *qualitatively* discontinuous change occurs when a certain critical degree of quantitative change is achieved.

It is also unreasonable to insist that a given stage must always occur at the *same* age in every culture. Since rate of development is, at least in part, a function of environmental stimulation, the age range in which a stage occurs tends to vary from one culture to another. Thus, considering the marked differences between the Swiss and U.S. school systems, it would be remarkable indeed if comparable stages of development took place at the same ages. Similarly, within a given culture, a particular stage cannot be expected to occur at the same age for all individuals. When a particular age level is designated for a given stage, it obviously refers to a *mean* value and implies that a normal range of variability prevails around the mean. This variability (Case & Collinson, 1962; Goldman, 1965; Jackson, 1965; Lovell, 1959a) reflects differences in intellectual endowment, experiential background, education, and personality. It is hardly surprising therefore that (1) about half of one population of African Bush children never acquired conservation of volume (Dasen, 1972; Greenfield, 1966); (2) bright and middle-class children exhibit conservation and combinatorial reasoning earlier than dull (Goodnow & Bethon, 1966) or culturally disadvantaged (Sigel & Olmstead, 1970) children; (3) bright adolescents enter the stage of abstract logical relations earlier than do dull adolescents; (4) many retarded as well as many ostensibly normal children never reach the formal stage of logical operations (Jackson, 1965; Lawson & Renner, 1974); (5) mental age correlates more highly than does chronological age with attained stage of cognitive development (Goldman, 1965); and (6) characteristic sex differences (for instance, in mathematical thinking), reflective of differences in cultural expectations and experiential background, are found in degree of cognitive development in different subject-matter areas (Elkind, 1962).

Thus a certain amount of overlapping among age groups is inevitable. A particular stage may be generally characteristic of 5- and 6-year-olds, but also typically includes some 4- and 7-year-olds and even some 3- and 8-year-olds. Piaget's age levels, like Gesell's, are nothing more than *average* approximations set for purposes of convenience. Hence, to attack the concept of developmental stages on the grounds that a given stage includes children of varying ages, instead of taking place at the precise age designated by Piaget, is simply to demolish a straw man.

One also cannot expect *complete* consistency and generality of stage behavior within an individual from one week or month to another, and from one subject matter or level of difficulty to another. Some overlapping and specificity are inevitable whenever development is determined by multiple, variable factors. A particular 12-year-old may use formal logical operations in a science course in October, but may revert for no apparent reason to a concrete level of cognitive functioning in November, or even several years later when confronted with an extremely difficult and unfamiliar problem in the same field. Furthermore, the child may characteristically continue to function at a concrete level for another year or two in social studies and literature.

Since transitions to new stages do not occur instantaneously but over a period of time, fluctuations between stages are common until the newly emerging stage is consolidated. In addition, because of intrinsic differences in level of subject-matter difficulty, and because of intra- and interindividual differences in ability profiles and experiential background, it is hardly surprising that transitions from one stage to another do not occur simultaneously in all subject-matter areas and subareas.[9] Abstract thinking, for example, generally emerges earlier in science than in social studies because children have more experience manipulating ideas about mass, time, and space than about government, social institutions, and historical events. However, in some children, depending on their special abilities and experience, the reverse may be true. In any developmental process where experiential factors are crucial, age by itself or degree of brightness is generally less important than degree of relevant experience (Deutsche, 1937; Dodwell, 1960, 1961; Elkind, 1961a; Vinacke, 1951). Finally, stages of development are always referable to a given range of difficulty and familiarity of the problem area. Beyond this range, individuals commonly revert (regress) to a former stage of development (Case & Collinson, 1962).

Neither is the concept of developmental stages invalidated by the demonstration that they are susceptible to environmental influence. It is erroneous to believe that stages of intellectual development are exclusively the products of "internal ripening" and hence that they primarily reflect the influence of endogenous factors. Gesell's embryological model of development has little applicability to human development beyond the first year of life when environmental factors become increasingly more important determinants of variability in developmental outcomes. In fact, as the educa-

---

[9] Stone & Ausubel (1969) found that with increasing age the intersituational generality of ability to comprehend abstract ideas increases (that is, intercorrelations between different subject-matter scores on such measures increases with advancing age.

tional system improves, we can confidently look forward to the earlier mean emergence of the various stages of cognitive development. This much is clearly evident from data indicating that schooled African Bush children acquire conservation of volume earlier and give fewer perceptual (as opposed to conceptual) reasons for conservation or nonconservation than do their unschooled counterparts (Greenfield, 1966). Urban living seems to have some of the same effect as schooling in this regard inasmuch as unschooled Hong Kong children do as well as schooled Hong Kong children on conservation tasks but not as well on a task of combinatorial reasoning (Goodnow & Bethon, 1966). And Swiss school children reach the stage of abstract logical operations at an earlier age and in greater proportions than American school children.

## Quantitative and Qualitative Changes in Intellectual Development

Still another reason for confusion and conflict about the problem of stages in intellectual development is the tendency to adopt an all-or-none position regarding the existence of such stages. Actually, the evidence suggests that some aspects or dimensions of intellectual development are characterized by quantitative or continuous change, whereas others are characterized by qualitative or discontinuous change. Hence if the issue is no longer approached from the standpoint of an all-or-none proposition, much truth can be found on both sides.

*Some* types of logical operations (equivalence, eliminative) and approaches to problem solving (trial-and-error versus insightful) appear to differ in degree rather than in kind from one age level to another.[10] The evidence indicates that these kinds of logical operations and problem-solving approaches are employed at all age levels, and differ principally in degree or complexity at different ages (Burt, 1919; Long & Welch, 1941a; Welch & Long, 1943). As Munn (1954) points out, the age differences are partly attributable to disparity in previous experience, motivation, and neuromuscular coordination. Perhaps an even more important source of

[10] It is important not to confuse *quantitative* changes in these *simple* logical operations with those reflective of *qualitatively* different stages along the concrete-abstract dimension of cognitive development. Thus the more significant logical operations (for instance, "reversibility") imply a capability to understand and meaningfully manipulate relationships between secondary abstractions—a capability that is not present in the preoperational (logically "nonoperational") child. Similarly, whether or not a given individual is dependent on concrete-empirical props in performing logical operations determines whether he or she is in the concrete or abstract stage of logical operations.

these age level differences, however, is the child's growing ability to generalize and use abstract symbols. Both trial-and-error and insightful problem solving, for example, are found in preschool children, elementary-school children, adolescents, and adults. The choice between these two approaches at all ages depends on the inherent difficulty of the problem, on the individual's prior background of experience, and on the problem's amenability to logical analysis. It is true that insightful approaches tend to increase with age, but only because increasing ability to generalize and use abstract symbols permits a more hypothesis-oriented approach.

Two dimensions of intellectual development characterized by gradually occurring *qualitative* change, on the other hand, are the transition from subjective to objective thought and the transition from concrete to abstract cognitive operations. Acquisition of the ability to separate objective reality from subjective needs and preferences results in the gradual disappearance of autistic, animistic, anthropomorphic, magical, absolutistic, and nominalistic thinking (Piaget, 1928, 1929, 1932). Reference has already been made to studies supporting Piaget's findings (Inhelder & Piaget, 1958; Piaget, 1950, 1954b, 1957b) regarding the transition from concrete to abstract thought. These findings will be discussed in greater detail below and in Chapter 16.

### General Implications of Developmental Stages for Education

Knowledge of the timetable of intellectual development should theoretically make possible, for the first time, the scientific, as opposed to the arbitrary or traditional, grade placement of subject matter. Detailed knowledge of the development, for example, of number and spatial concepts, of ideas regarding causality, and of appreciation of scientific method should be helpful in the grade placement of such subjects as mathematics and science. Even more specifically, Lovell (1961b) suggests a parallelism between basic principles of number theory (associativity, commutativity) and the particular cognitive operations ("groupings") elementary-school children use in intellectual functioning. Such parallelisms, as we shall see later, reflect Piaget's equation of thought with logic.

Insight into the course of intellectual development, according to Aebli (1951), could also enable teachers both (1) to guard against (and hence discourage) certain kinds of cognitive immaturity (subjectivity, egocentricity, animism, anthropomorphism, nominalism, teleological reasoning, ideas of "single causality," focusing on just a single aspect of a problem) and (2) to provide experience facilitating the transition from lower to higher stages of intellectual functioning (concrete to abstract logical operations). Actually, however, such knowledge is so general, nonspecific, and inexplicit in nature that it is more misleading than helpful as an aid in structuring and sequencing subject matter in a curriculum (Kohnstamm, 1970; Sullivan, 1967).

Reference has already been made to the possibility of the earlier, *intuitive* introduction into the curriculum of more "advanced" subject matter such as algebra, geometry, "set theory," quadratic equations, physics, and so forth. In certain selected instances, where *genuine readiness* actually exists, it may be desirable for children to acquire prior intuitive understanding of such material. This understanding reduces the unfamiliarity of the ideas in question when they are introduced later and discourages the possibility of rote verbal learning in high school and college. Such intuitively learned content may serve as anchoring ideas or as general background for the later learning of the same content at a higher level of abstraction, thereby increasing its potential meaningfulness. Bruner (1960) and Finlay (1960) refer to this philosophy of curriculum organization as the "spiral curriculum." Karplus (1962a) argues that unless children are taught scientific principles and methodology on an intuitive basis in elementary school, they spontaneously acquire, and later must unlearn, various misconceptions derived from spontaneous or folklore models of physical and biological causality. In any case, many considerations are involved in deciding which *particular* kinds of intuitively oriented subject matter lying within elementary-school children's scope of adequate readiness are suitable for such a curriculum.

### Piaget & Education

The tremendous vogue of Piaget among American educators has led to the largely unfounded belief that Piaget's work has significant implications for educational practice. Many educators, in fact, conceive of Piaget as a learning theorist as well as a developmental theorist. Actually, as we have seen, only the most general kinds of inferences may be drawn from Piaget's work with respect to developmental readiness for particular levels of abstraction that are appropriate at various grade levels: drawing more particular inferences regarding the grade placement of specific subject matter cannot be warranted. And even the more general inferences have very limited value both because of Piaget's tendency to underestimate the abstract thinking ability of young children and because such a high percentage of American high school and college students fail to reach this abstract level of cognitive logical operations.

With respect to learning theory, Piaget has little or nothing to say, since he is concerned completely with cognitive developmental sequences and not with the nature of *contemporaneous* acts of learning. Some readers may note a general similarity between his so-called "assimilation" process and our assimilation theory of learning and retention. The similarity lies in the fact that Piaget's notion of assimilation provides for the absorption of new into existing schema. In this sense it is analogous in a general way to the principle of subsumption. However, not only does Piaget fail to go beyond this general statement of assimilation and describe explicitly how assimilation occurs, he also conceives of assimilation solely in terms of developmental progressions rather than in terms of a contemporaneous learning phenomenon.

Many other features of Piaget's system also tend to give it an anti-educational flavor. First, Piaget is concerned solely with the development of thought as opposed to comprehension. Thus what he has to say about development lacks relevance for much of the learning that occurs in the classroom. Second, he tends to identify the operations of thought with the operations of logic, thereby confusing a special instrument or tool of thought for the derivation of valid inferences from data with the actual operations of thought in ordinary problem-solving situations. For example, his characteristics of concrete logical operations are equated with certain formal logical structures on a purely a priori basis. Third, Piaget adopts a wholly neobehavioristic view of thought, attributing to it the quality of implicit action. In fact he states that "operations are nothing but interiorized actions whose efferent impulses do not develop into external movements (1954b, p. 141). This conception is at variance with the generally accepted view of thinking as a reorganization of relevant educational elements in cognitive structure to meet the requirements of a new means–end relationship. Fourth, Piaget places sole emphasis on endogenous motivation, thus ignoring completely one important objective of education, which is to stimulate the development of new motivations from existing potentialities. It is this element of Piaget's position that has prompted educators illogically to count him as a supporter of discovery as against reception learning, which involves an entirely different issue. Fifth, Piaget, unlike Vygotsky, discounts completely the role of education in promoting cognitive development and places exclusive emphasis on spontaneous or incidental experience. Sixth, Piaget denies the role of education in accelerating cognitive development or in facilitating the transition from one cognitive stage to another. Last, Piaget insists that language has only a communicative role and that it has no operative or process role in thought (for example, in permitting greater manipulability or juxtaposition of ideas, and in refining subverbal thought).

The belief of Inhelder (Bruner, 1960) that it is feasible to teach general cognitive operations isolated from actual subject-matter content not only makes excessive cognitive demands on children, but is also artificial in terms of the particularized contents which such skills necessarily assume in each discipline. For a critique of this position, see Ausubel (1968a).

The Concrete-Abstract Dimension of Cognitive Development[11]

The concrete-abstract dimension of intellectual development has been divided by Piaget into three qualitatively distinct developmental stages: the preoperational stage, the stage of concrete logical operations, and the stage of abstract logical operations. These cover stages, respectively, the preschool, elementary-school, and adolescent-adult periods of development.

### Preoperational Stage

During the preoperational stage, the child is capable of acquiring *primary* abstractions (concepts) and of understanding, using, and meaningfully manipulating for problem-solving purposes both primary abstractions and the relations between them. *Primary concepts* are those concepts whose meanings a given individual originally learns in relation to genuine concrete-empirical experience. They include those concepts whose criterial attributes, whether discovered or presented, yield generic meanings during learning only when *first* explicitly related to the multiple and diverse exemplars from which they are derived, *before* being related alone to the individual's cognitive structure.[12] Once concept meanings are acquired, of course, the preoperational child can understand and use them apart from their particular exemplars. The child can also understand, and manipulate in problem-solving operations, relationships between these primary abstractions, namely, propositions composed of such abstractions.

But the child is limited to the acquisition of primary abstractions and to the understanding and manipulation of such abstractions and the relationship between them. He or she cannot similarly handle *secondary* abstractions and relationships between secondary abstractions. Obviously these considerations impose severe constraints on the level of abstraction at which the child operates. *Secondary concepts* are those whose meanings a given individual does *not* learn in relation to genuine concrete-empirical experience, that is, those concepts whose criterial attributes yield generic meanings during learning when these attributes are related to the individual's cognitive structure *without* being first explicitly related to the particular exemplars from which they are derived. The preoperational child's understanding and manipulation of abstract concepts and propositions take place at a level of abstraction that is only slightly removed from the inti-

---

[11] The following description of this aspect of cognitive development uses the same stage names but is really quite different from the account given by Piaget and Inhelder (Inhelder & Piaget, 1958; Piaget, 1950, 1954b, 1957b). (The term "abstract" is used synonymously with Piaget's term "formal.") The differences inhere both in the basic characteristics of the various stages and in their various determinants.

[12] The acquisition of primary concepts corresponds to concept formation and the acquisition of secondary concepts to concept assimilation (see Chapter 2).

mate participation of concrete-empirical experience in the acquisition of his or her primary concepts themselves.

One important manifestation of this constraint is that many significant logical operations (in fact, all those, such as "reversibility," that really make a child "logically operational") imply a capability to understand and manipulate relationships between secondary abstractions. Thus, because the child cannot perform the logical operation of "reversibility," he or she cannot (unlike the concrete- or abstract-operational child) grasp the idea of "conservation." For example, the child does not "conserve" mass; that is, he or she does not appreciate that mass remains constant even though its shape changes, because of a failure to realize that deformations of shape are reversible or that a loss in one dimension is compensated for by a gain in another.[13] Another consequence of his or her inability to perform true logical operations—and of the related fact that the meanings of many of the child's primary concepts are little more than idealized images embodying appropriate criterial attributes—is that problem solving at this stage involves much overt manipulation of objects and internal manipulation of near-images.

### Concrete-Operational Stage

During the concrete-operational stage, the child is capable of acquiring secondary abstractions and of understanding, using, and meaningfully manipulating both *secondary* abstractions and the relations between them. But both in acquiring secondary abstractions and in understanding and manipulating relations between them, he or she differs from the abstract-operational individual in using *concrete-empirical props*. In conformity with the definition of a secondary concept given above, the child does *not* learn the meaning of a concept by *first* relating its criterial attributes to the particular exemplars from which they are derived, *before* relating them to cognitive structure. Rather, he or she learns its meaning by relating the criterial attributes *directly* to cognitive structure, but typically with the benefit of concrete-empirical props, namely, exemplars of the various *attributes*. The use of such props in concept acquisition implies a more abstract process of learning than the actual use of "genuine" concrete-empirical experience itself for three reasons:

1. The exemplars of attributes are examples of the *abstracted* properties of a concept—not particular instances of the concept.
2. A *single* example of an attribute suffices as a prop as opposed to the

---

[13] Piaget's explanation of conservation is not that logical operations, such as reversibility, imply a capability to understand or manipulate relationships between secondary abstractions (a capability whose existence he denies at the stage of concrete logical operations), but rather that logical operations (which he defines as "internalized actions") first exist, by definition, at the concrete operational stage.

multiple exemplars of the concept that are given in concrete-empirical experience.

3. The prop serves mainly as a "crutch" in relating the criterial attribute to cognitive structure rather than as the concrete-empirical matrix from which either the criterial attribute itself is derived or in relation to which it derives its potential meaningfulness.

For example, while the concept of "work" is being learned as a primary concept, the preoperational child may eventually hypothesize such attributes as "activity," "necessary," and "useful" as criterial, by abstracting them from farming, fixing cars, keeping house, nursing, and so forth, or the child may be given these attributes. In either case, however, the individual tests each of the attributes against each of the multiple exemplars before relating it to cognitive structure. If, in elementary school, the child learns the concept of "work" as a secondary concept, its attributes are presented in definitional form, and he or she may use an exemplar for one or more of the attributes in relating them to cognitive structure. Finally, as a high-school student, in the abstract operational stage, the individual relates the criterial attributes directly to cognitive structure without props, and if he or she does not know the meaning of a given attribute, it too need only be defined.

Once secondary concepts are acquired, the concrete-operational child is no longer dependent on props in understanding or using their meanings. Understanding *relationships between secondary abstractions* (or meaningfully manipulating these relationships for problem-solving purposes), however, is quite another matter. This kind of learning task depends upon recent or concurrent concrete-empirical props consisting of a particular exemplar for each of the abstractions in the relationship. When such props are not available, the child finds abstract propositions unrelatable to cognitive structure and hence devoid of meaning. This dependence upon concrete-empirical props self-evidently limits the generality and abstractness of attempts to grasp and manipulate relationships between abstractions meaningfully. The individual can acquire only those relational understandings and perform only those relational problem-solving operations that do not go beyond the somewhat particularized representation of reality implicit in his or her use of these props. Thus, where complex propositions are involved, the individual is largely restricted to an intuitive or semiabstract level of cognitive functioning, a level that falls far short of the clarity, precision, explicitness, and generality associated with the more advanced abstract stage of intellectual development.

During the elementary-school years, therefore, abstract verbal propositions (propositions consisting of relationships between secondary abstractions) that are presented on a purely expository basis are too remotely removed from concrete-empirical experience to be relatable to cognitive structure. This does not mean, however, that autonomous discovery is required before such propositions can be meaningfully learned. As long as concrete-empirical props are made an integral part of the learning situation, the propositions are eminently learnable. Concrete-empirical props also need not necessarily be nonverbal or tangible (objects, pictures). "Concrete" and "nonrepresentational" are not synonymous; words that represent particular exemplars or attributes of a concept are very adequate concrete-empirical props in learning abstract propositions and secondary concepts respectively.

With the advent of logical operations, and particularly of the operation of reversibility, conservation is exhibited (Eifermann & Etzion, 1964; Piaget, 1950, 1952; Smedslund, 1962) in the concrete-operational child's thinking and understanding. This phenomenon, however, does not emerge in unitary fashion over all kinds of problem-solving tasks and materials. In order of emergence, conservation of mass, weight, number, and volume are acquired (Piaget, 1950; Uzgaris, 1964). Because the child can perform these operations, and because meanings of concepts are more abstract in nature, problem solving involves less overt manipulation of objects and internal manipulation of images.

It is important to realize that just because the concrete-operational child uses concrete-empirical props in understanding and thinking about relationships between abstractions, this stage of intellectual development is not really concrete in the sense that objects or *concrete images* of objects are relationally manipulated in meaningful reception or discovery learning. Piaget contends that the child at this stage conducts logical operations on concrete objects and that his or her thought processes are closely tied to concrete experience. However, the evidence suggests that the child essentially understands and manipulates relations between the verbal representations of secondary abstractions. The concreteness of this stage inheres rather in the fact that secondary abstractions and the relationships between them can be understood and meaningfully manipulated *only* with the aid of current or recent concrete-empirical props. Logical operations are therefore constrained in the generality and abstractness of their implications by the particularity of the props in question. Unlike the situation in the later stage of abstract logical operations, they do not involve logical transformations of all possible and hypothetical relationships between general abstract variables.[14] Nevertheless they are more closely related in level of abstraction

[14] Brown (1958b) argues that the cognitive processes of adults are more abstract than those of children only in the sense that they manifest more discriminative generalization —that children actually exhibit more simple stimulus generalization than do adults (that is, generalization not requiring prior discriminative analysis). Hence he claims that adults do not really use a wider range of abstract concepts in their thinking, but merely employ a more highly differentiated repertoire of subcategories within existing categories. Simple stimulus generalization, however, can hardly be considered a form of abstract thinking that reflects the use of abstract concepts. Thus it seems more plausible to believe that adults also characteristically use more *generic categories* and more differentiated subcategories than children do.

to the following than to the preceding stage of cognitive development, and represent a very significant advance over the latter. It also appears that Piaget overstates his case and gives children too little credit when he does not differentiate between primary and secondary abstractions in asserting that only in the final stage can children understand and manipulate relationships between abstractions. As far as relationships between primary abstractions are concerned, this capability is evident without props in the concrete operational and even in the preoperational stage. With respect to secondary abstractions, this capability is present with props in the concrete operational stage.

### Abstract Logical Stage

Beginning in the junior-high-school period, the pupil becomes increasingly less dependent upon the availability of concrete-empirical props in meaningfully relating abstract relationships to cognitive structure. Eventually he or she no longer needs them at all in understanding and meaningfully manipulating relationships between abstractions. The pupil can then assimilate abstract propositions and solve abstract problems in terms of all-inclusive hypothetical possibilities rather than in terms of these possibilities as constrained by their reference to "the here and now." In other words, he or she attains full conceptual and propositional generality. "Instead of just coordinating facts about the actual world, hypothetico-deductive reasoning draws out the implications of all possible statements and thus gives use to a unique synthesis of the possible and the necessary" (Piaget, 1957a, p. 19).

Inhelder and Piaget (1958) present considerable evidence indicating that "formal" (abstract) operations appear slightly before the onset of adolescence. On the whole their findings are corroborated by other investigators (Goldman, 1965; Jackson, 1965; Lovell, 1961a; Yudin, 1966; Yudin & Kates, 1963). Lovell's subjects attained this stage of development somewhat later than Inhelder and Piaget's, and Case and Collinson's (1962) somewhat earlier.[15] Both Goldman and Jackson reported greater age variability, and Jackson less intertask generality, than did Inhelder and Piaget in the development of formal thinking. None of these findings, however, detract from the essential validity of Piaget's conclusion that for the first time the child entering this stage of cognitive development thinks in terms of all-inclusive hypothetical possibilities (instead of the "here and now").

Eventually, after sufficient gradual change in this direction, a qualitatively new capacity emerges. The intellectually mature individual becomes capable of understanding and manipulating relationships between abstrac-

---

[15] As pointed out later (see p. 238) several studies indicate that a sizable percentage of American junior and senior high-school (as well as college) youth never reach the abstract stage.

tions without any reference whatsoever to concrete-empirical reality. Instead of reasoning directly from a particular set of data, the individual uses indirect, second-order logical operations for structuring the data. Instead of merely grouping data into classes or arranging them serially in terms of a given variable, he or she formulates and tests hypotheses based on all *possible* combinations of variables (see also Grodskaya, 1962). Since logical operations are performed without props on abstract verbal propositions, these individuals can go beyond the operations that follow immediately from concrete-empirical reality and deal with all possible or hypothetical relations between ideas. They can now transcend the previously achieved level of intuitive thought and understanding and formulate general laws relating to each other, general variables that are divorced from the concrete-empirical data at hand. Their concepts and generalizations, therefore, tend increasingly to be second-order constructs derived from relationships between previously established verbal abstractions that are already one step removed from the original data. And, since these people are freed from dependence on nonabstract contact with empirical data in independently *discovering* meaningful new concepts and generalizations, they are obviously also liberated from this same dependence in the much less rigorous task of merely *apprehending* these constructs meaningfully when verbally presented to them.

Careful analysis of the experiments performed by Inhelder and Piaget and by the other investigators cited above, as well as Lunzer's (1965), does not substantiate their view that the *distinctive* feature of formal or abstract (as opposed to concrete) operations is that the older child is able to deal internally with ideas about ideas or to perform "second-order operations." The younger ("concrete-operational") child can *also* do these things, as shown by the studies of Case & Collinson (1962), S. A. Hill (1961), and Ennis (1969). Hill demonstrated, for example, that most children aged 6 to 8 can easily draw correct inferences from hypothetical premises involving abstract relationships. Ennis reported that children in the same age range can master conditional logic. It is rather the preadolescent's and adolescent's ability verbally to manipulate relationships between ideas *in the absence of recently prior or concurrently available concrete-empirical* props that is the distinctive attribute of formal operations. (Hill's subjects, after all, were given logical problems that were invariably stated in terms of *particular* instances.) This new capability emerging at about age 11 and beyond invests propositional thought with a genuinely abstract and nonintuitive quality. Ideas about ideas now achieve a truly general status that is freed from any dependence whatsoever on particular instances and concrete experience. It is for this reason that thinking becomes hypothetic-deductive in nature; that is, it refers to all *possible* relationships between variables rather than to relationships constrained by reference to particular instances.

Under the specific conditions of the U.S. educational system, however, it appears that achievement of the abstract logical stage of cognitive development is retarded and is not even manifested by the majority of college students. Representative studies have indicated that only 15.6 percent of junior-high-school students (Nordland, Lawson, & Kahle, 1974), 13.2 percent of high-school students (Norland et al., 1974), and 22 percent of college students (Lawson & Renner, 1974) were at this stage of development. Although these findings are at variance with Piaget's age norms for Swiss children and may possibly have implications for current teaching methods in U.S. schools, they obviously do not invalidate the place of this stage in the sequence of cognitive development.

### Determinants of Change

It is evident from the foregoing account of developmental stages along the concrete-abstract dimension of cognitive functioning that there is a developmental aspect to meaningful learning. At successive stages along this dimension, the individual is able meaningfully to relate increasingly more abstract materials to cognitive structure. In part, this is attributable to developmental changes in the content of cognitive structure itself. These changes either make the same logically meaningful material, which is not potentially meaningful at an earlier stage, potentially meaningful at a later stage, or else enable the individual to generate more abstract and complex problem-solving propositions. In part, also, this is attributable to growth in whatever cognitive processes are involved in nonarbitrarily and substantively relating learning tasks to established ideas in cognitive structure and in generating new problem-solving propositions.

Thus it is hypothesized that the combined influence of three concomitant and mutually supportive developmental trends accounts for the transition from concrete to abstract cognitive functioning. In the first place, the developing individual gradually acquires a working vocabulary of "transactional" or mediating terms (for example, conditional conjunctions, qualifying adjectives). The use of these terms makes possible the more efficient juxtaposition and combination of different relatable abstractions into potentially meaningful propositions and their subsequent relationship to established ideas in cognitive structure.

Second, the individual can relate these latter propositions more readily to cognitive structure, and hence render them more meaningful, because of the growing fund of stable, higher-order concepts and principles encompassed by, and made available within, that structure. Russell and Saadeh (1962), for example, found that between the sixth and ninth grades children's use of concrete definitions decreases, and their use of abstract and functional definitions correspondingly increases. A sufficient body of abstract concepts that are clear and stable is obviously necessary before one can hope efficiently to manipulate relationships between them so as to generate meaningful general propositions. The possession of a working body of inclusive concepts also makes possible the formulation of more general statements of relationship, greater integration of related ideas and different aspects of the same problem, the elaboration of more precise distinctions and finer differentiations, and less dependence on complete concrete-empirical data in reaching warranted inferences.

Finally, it seems reasonable to suppose that after many years of practice in understanding, and meaningfully manipulating relationships between, abstractions *with* the aid of concrete-empirical props, the older child gradually develops greater facility in performing these operations. Eventually (after acquiring the necessary transactional and higher-order concepts) the child is able to perform the same operations just as effectively *without* relying on these props. The same sequence of events is seen in acquiring many other neuromuscular and cognitive skills—walking without "holding on," bicycling "without hands," speaking a foreign language without internal translation from one's mother tongue, transmitting Morse code in sentences rather than in word or letter units.

Piaget and Inhelder (Inhelder & Piaget, 1958; Piaget, 1950, 1953, 1957b) largely embrace a maturational position in explaining how developmental transition is effected during the various stages of intellectual development. Their view of maturation, however, which they call "equilibration," is inclusive of both internal (genic) factors and *incidental* learning (including idiosyncratic, intracultural, and intercultural). It is therefore closer to the empirical concept of maturation than it is to Gesell's notion of maturation as a process of internal ripening. Nevertheless, Piaget places greatest weight on the factor of equilibration. According to Smedslund,

> conservation of weight is acquired by a process of internal equilibration, independently of external reinforcement. By equilibration is meant a change in the direction of increasing stability, consistency, and completeness of behavioral structures. Conflicts are eliminated and gaps are closed. . . . [Equilibration] is heavily dependent on activity and experience, [but such experience] is not assumed to act through external reinforcements, but by a process of mutual influence of the child's activities on each other (Smedslund, 1961).

Thus, according to Piaget, maturation (genic factors and general aspects of incidental experience) accounts for the universality of the sequential stages and the order in which they occur. However, variability in the kinds of incidental learning experience accounts for interindividual, intraindividual, and intercultural differences in the age at which stages occur and in the content area in which they are manifested. Piaget and his followers (for instance, Smedslund, 1961) deny that specific learning experience or training (practice)—particularly of a verbal nature—or, for that matter, education in general has any significant influence on the emergence of stages of intellectual development. We shall return to this problem later in another context in considering whether training and education can accelerate stages in cognitive development.

Both general and specific motivational explanations (Inhelder & Piaget, 1958) have been advanced to account for the transition from the concrete-operational to the abstract-operational stage. Desire to obtain greater meaning out of experience is not a convincing explanation, since this desire does not arise suddenly or uniquely at adolescence. Furthermore, although motivation may energize and facilitate cognitive change, it cannot convincingly explain either its occurrence or direction. Desire to identify with and participate in the adult world has more specific relevance for this age period. Again, however, no amount of motivation would suffice to effect the change in question in the absence of the necessary genic potentialities and supportive experience.

### General and Specific Aspects of the Transition

We have already rejected complete generality over subject-matter areas and levels of difficulty as a legitimate criterion of a developmental stage.[16] Too much unevenness exists in any individual's experiential background and pattern of abilities for the transition from concrete to abstract functioning to occur *simultaneously* in all areas. A stage of development, also, is always referable to a typical range of difficulty and familiarity of the problem at hand. Beyond this range, regression to an earlier stage of development commonly occurs. It is apparent, therefore, that the transition from concrete to abstract cognitive functioning takes place *specifically* in each subject-matter area and presupposes a certain necessary amount of sophistication in each of the areas involved.

This specificity, however, does not invalidate the existence of qualitatively distinct stages of development. It is still possible to designate an individual's *overall* developmental status as concrete or abstract on the basis of an estimate of his *characteristic or predominant* mode of cognitive functioning. Stone and Ausubel (1969) found that, beginning with junior-high-school age, the generality of abstract cognitive functioning increases with age (that is, gradually encompasses more subject-matter fields in older pupils). This trend was evidenced by successively higher intercorrelations with increasing age among learning scores on tests of ability to learn abstract verbal material in different disciplines.

This distinction between specific and general aspects of developmental status is important for two reasons: First, the individual necessarily continues to undergo the same transition from concrete to abstract cognitive

---

[16] Piaget refers to this phenomenon as horizontal *décolage* (Flavell, 1963).

functioning in each *new* subject-matter area encountered—even *after* he or she reaches the abstract stage of development on an overall basis. Second, once the individual attains this latter general stage, however, the transition to abstract cognitive functioning in unfamiliar new subject-matter fields takes place much more readily than is the case at earlier phases of the transition. For example, a cognitively mature adult who has never studied astronomy is not completely in the same developmental position as an 11- or 12-year-old with respect to the concrete-abstract dimension when both begin an introductory course in astronomy.

Thus, even though an adolescent or adult characteristically functions at the abstract level of cognitive development, he or she tends *initially* to function at a concrete, intuitive level when first introduced to a wholly unfamiliar subject-matter field. But this individual is able to draw on various transferable elements of his or her more *general* ability to function abstractly. Hence the individual passes through the concrete stage of functioning in this particular subject-matter area much more rapidly than would be the case were he or she first emerging from the stage of concrete logical operations. These facilitating transferable elements presumably include transactional terms, higher-order concepts, and ability *directly* to understand and manipulate relationships between abstractions (without the benefit of concrete-empirical props). These abstractions, though acquired in other specific subject-matter contexts, are generally applicable to new learning situations (see below).

In other words, growth in cognitive development always proceeds at two levels concomitantly—specific and general. Experience in learning *any* subject matter produces general as well as specific *developmental* changes in cognitive capacity in addition to specific changes in subject-matter readiness. As a result of experience in studying a given discipline, pupils not only learn *particular* ideas that facilitate the later learning of other particular ideas, but also acquire greater *capacity* meaningfully to process more abstract material of *any* nature in *that* particular discipline and *other* disciplines as well. General cognitive development, in any given dimension, therefore occurs with increasing age and education and is independent of particular kinds of subject-matter experience.

It is these general and transferable aspects of changed cognitive capacity occurring in the transition from concrete to abstract intellectual functioning in any particular discipline that facilitate the same transition in *any* new subject-matter area. Thus the cognitively mature adolescent, confronted with a learning or problem-solving task in an unfamiliar discipline, does not have the benefit of *specific* cognitive changes along the concrete-abstract dimension resulting from past experience with that subject-matter area. In this sense the adolescent is no better off than the immature child who has not undergone the overall transition from the concrete to the abstract stage; this transition must be made anew in the unfamiliar area. But he or she makes the transition more readily because of the *general* cognitive changes that have occurred along this dimension and are transferable to the particular new subject-matter field.

Hence, in contrast to the cognitively immature child who continues to use concrete-empirical props in relating abstractions to each other during the concrete stage, the adolescent uses the props only initially—to develop the necessary higher-order abstractions and transactional terms in the new discipline—and then proceeds to dispense with props entirely in acquiring additional abstractions. The adolescent's dependence on concrete-empirical props, in other words, is temporary and reflective of circumscribed cognitive immaturity in *particular* subject-matter fields rather than reflective of an overall concrete level of cognitive functioning.

## Educational Implications of the Concrete, Intuitive Level of Cognitive Functioning

### Dependence on Concrete-Empirical Props

Elementary-school children are completely dependent upon current or recent concrete-empirical props in understanding or meaningfully manipulating *relational* propositions consisting of secondary abstractions. They tend to appreciate relationships between such abstractions intuitively—as rather immediate logical extensions of their own personal experience—rather than in the truly abstract sense of relationships between general variables. Hence, general laws and methodological canons of science, in their own right, have little meaning and intellectual appeal for these children. These laws make sense only insofar as they are relatable to more tangible types of experience. "Utility" is a major example of this type of experience, but it is certainly not the only possible example.

As far as elementary-school children are concerned, therefore, one cannot hope to reduce science to "first principles" and basic abstract laws.[17] At the very best one can strive for a semiabstract, intuitive grasp of these laws on a descriptive or perhaps semianalytic level that is somewhat tied to particularized experience. On the methodological side, abstract principles of scientific inquiry and strategy also have much less meaning for children than a purely concrete-empirical explanation of how it is possible for humanity to know the facts and generalizations under discussion.[18]

---

[17] Both Karplus (1962) and Shamos (1961) deplore the emphasis in elementary-science education upon the practical utilitarian aspects of science and the attempt "to relate science primarily to everyday experience." They advocate, instead, stress upon the concepts and methods of science.

[18] Atkin and Wyatt (1961) emphasize the "how we know" aspects of astronomy, using didactic exposition and simple exercises and demonstrations.

The developmental characteristics of the elementary-school child's cognitive functioning do not require, however, that we restrict the pedagogic use of these years to teaching the fundamental intellectual skills. His or her cognitive equipment is certainly adequate enough for acquiring an intuitive grasp of many concepts in the basic disciplines. Thus, for example, the psychological argument for teaching science in the elementary school is extremely convincing (Karplus, 1962).

First, it is well known that young children spontaneously acquire many animistic and subjectivistic conceptions about the physical and biological universe (Piaget, 1932). These notions also tend to persist and often compete with more mature conceptions, especially when not counteracted by early scientific training. Second, without early and satisfactory instruction in science it is difficult for children both to assimilate positive interests in and attitudes toward the scientific enterprise and to avoid being negatively conditioned to scientific subject matter. Third, since elementary-school pupils can easily acquire an intuitive grasp of many scientific concepts, failure to provide suitable opportunities to do so wastes available readiness for such learning. It also wastes valuable time in junior and senior high school that could be used for more advanced instruction in science. Finally, as pointed out above, these intuitive ideas constitute a foundation for the later assimilation of more abstract, general, and precise versions of the same content, thereby increasing their potential meaningfulness and preventing rote learning.

Thus the concept of a "spiral curriculum," mentioned earlier, is eminently sound provided that an attempt is *not* made to teach at an intuitive level "reduced" versions of *anything* or *everything* that is presented later at a more abstract level. The use of concrete-empirical props, after all, does not make *every* secondary abstraction, and *every* proposition composed of secondary abstractions, intuitively understandable irrespective of the learner's antecedent subject-matter experience. The content of an appropriate intuitively oriented curriculum should, therefore, include only such intuitively based materials for which the elementary-school pupil exhibits adequate developmental and subject-matter readiness. Even with respect to these materials, much selectivity is required in choosing the *particular* intuitive content that will be most useful for later subject-matter learning.

In any case, the suggestion that sciences be studied in the order of their phenomenological complexity—that one start with "the basic concepts of physics and chemistry before tackling the complex phenomena of biology and geology" (Shamos, 1961)—though logically sound, is psychologically unfeasible. More important pedagogically than the logical structure of knowledge is the pupil's intellectual readiness to handle different kinds of subject matter. From the standpoint of relevant experience and readiness, the phenomenologically "simple" laws of physics are far more abstract and difficult than the phenomenologically "complex" laws of biology and geology, which are so much closer to everyday experience. This is not to deny the possibility that some aspects of physics might be profitably introduced in the elementary-school curriculum. However, before this could be done in the "rigorous fashion [physics] deserves," the teaching of elementary-school mathematics would first have to be sufficiently improved to make possible a more functional intuitive understanding of the quantitative relationships that figure so prominently in the physical sciences (Shamos, 1961).

The teacher's task of translating ideas into language that is compatible with the elementary-school child's cognitive capacities and level of cognitive functioning is difficult indeed. First, in teaching others, the natural tendency is to adopt the same level of discourse he or she characteristically uses in learning new ideas. Second, once the teacher has acquired difficult concepts, he or she tends to regard them as self-evident and to forget both the limiting developmental factors involved in the learning process and the numerous misconceptions and ambiguities to be overcome in the course of learning. After mastering a particular discipline, the teacher tends to think of its structure only in terms of the logical relationships between component ideas, forgetting the psychological process of progressive differentiation involved in acquiring any new body of knowledge. Finally, because of his or her more sophisticated and highly differentiated cognitive structure, the teacher is very aware of the various subtleties, connotations, ramifications, and qualifications connected with even simple ideas, and often fails to realize that the introduction of such complications only confuses pupils.

Although the *preschool* child is restricted to relatively nonabstract (primary) concepts in the learning of most propositions, it is not necessary that all relational learning during this period take place on a nonverbal, problem-solving, or completely autonomous self-discovery basis in order to be meaningful. Simple derivative propositions involving primary concepts can certainly be directly apprehended without the use of particular exemplars. Simple correlative, superordinate, and combinatorial propositions can also be learned on a reception basis, particularly if specific verbal exemplars of the concepts involved or an opportunity for manipulation of objects or concrete images is provided. Autonomous self-discovery of the proposition to be learned might conceivably enhance current learning and provide additional motivation for future learning. However, it is certainly not indispensable for meaningful learning.

Neither does the *elementary-school* child's dependence on concrete-empirical props for the understanding of more abstract propositions require that all, or even most, teaching be conducted on an inductive, problem-solving (discovery), and nonverbal basis. The only essential condition during this period for the reception learning of propositions embodying secondary concepts is the availability of specific exemplars of the concepts in question. Such exemplars may be purely verbal in nature. Didactic exposition with such verbal props can easily be combined with other concrete-empirical props in the form of demonstrations. This combination usually suffices for the presentation of most subject matter that is neither excessively complex nor excessively unfamiliar. In these latter instances it may be desirable to enhance the understanding achieved through verbal expression by subjecting the pupil to Socratic questioning—or by providing a semiautonomous type of problem-solving experience (guided discovery) in which discovery itself is accelerated by the arrangement of materials and by the use of prompts, hints, and Socratic questioning.

It is a serious mistake, therefore, to believe that meaningful intuitive learning during the stage of concrete logical operations must necessarily be restricted to nonverbal problem solving. Verbally expressed relationships between abstract ideas can be adequately comprehended when presented didactically—though in a somewhat particularized sense—as long as concrete-empirical props (verbal or nonverbal) are available. Hence, concurrently with providing elementary-school children with "particularly informative and suggestive experience as a base for their [more difficult] abstractions," one must provide them "with a conceptual framework that permits them to perceive the phenomena in a meaningful way and to integrate their inferences into generalizations of lasting value" (Karplus, 1962a, pp. 243–244).

## Can Any Subject Be Taught Intuitively at Any Age Level?

By suitably adapting methods of teaching to the child's level of cognitive functioning, Bruner believes that it is possible to teach preschool and elementary-school children any subject that can be taught to adolescent and adult students.

> At each stage of development the child has a characteristic way of viewing the world and explaining it to himself. The task of teaching a subject to a child at any particular age is one of representing the structure of that subject in terms of the child's way of viewing things. The task can be thought of as one of translation (p. 33). . . . If one respects the ways of thought of the growing child, if one is courteous enough to translate material into his logical forms, and challenging enough to tempt him to advance, then it is possible to introduce him at any early age to the ideas and styles that in later years make an educated man (p. 54). . . . Any idea can be represented honestly and usefully in the thought forms of children of school age and . . . these first representations can later be made more powerful and precise the more easily by virtue of this early learning (p. 33). . . . [Actually] any subject can be taught effectively in some intellectually honest form to any child at any stage of development (Bruner, 1960, pp. 33, 54).

It is quite possible, of course, that prior intuitive understanding of certain concepts and principles during childhood can facilitate their learning and stabilize their retention when they are taught at a more formal, abstract level during adolescence—even if the child's readiness for the earlier learnings is not adequate. However, confirmatory empirical evidence is still unavailable. Further, as pointed out above, one must consider the greater risk of failure and the excessive time and effort cost involved in premature instances of intuitive learning. Hence it may be more feasible to postpone entirely the introduction of certain subject-matter fields until children are cognitively more mature (adequately ready for them). In general, therefore, it is preferable to restrict the intuitively oriented content of the elementary-school curriculum to materials for which the child exhibits adequate developmental readiness even if the child *can* intuitively learn more difficult, ingeniously presented material beyond his or her intrinsic level of readiness.

In addition, it undoubtedly overstates the case to claim that *any* subject can be taught to children in the preoperational stage, or in the stage of concrete logical operations, provided that the material is presented in an informal, intuitive fashion with the aid of overt manipulation or concrete-empirical props. It is readily conceivable that some topics, such as set theory, algebra, and quadratic equations in mathematics, can be successfully learned by fourth-grade pupils when recast in accordance with their characteristic ways of thinking and conceptualizing experience (Dienes, 1959, 1964). Through such kinds of teaching, many more abstract and "difficult" concepts can undoubtedly be made intuitively comprehensible to elementary-school children than was believed possible in the past. Moreover, these concepts can be brought within the category of learnings for which they *are* adequately ready. This hardly rules out the possibility, however, that:

1. The comprehension of many *other* ideas presupposes certain specific antecedent learnings in a given subject-matter area or a certain minimal level of general subject-matter sophistication.

2. Some abstractions are so inherently difficult or complex that they cannot be made intuitively understandable to children below a certain level of cognitive maturity, even with the aid of suitable concrete-empirical props.

3. Certain abstractions become relatively useless when restructured on an intuitive basis.

4. It is virtually impossible in the case of certain highly abstract concepts to find particular exemplars that are meaningful to cognitively immature children. These latter kinds of ideas would be *intrinsically* too difficult for preschool or elementary-school children irrespective of the method of presentation.

Thus, even assuming that all abstract concepts could be restructured on an intuitive basis, it would still be unreasonable to expect that they could *all* be made comprehensible to children at *any* grade level. Although the intuitive comprehensibility of any given intuitively restructured idea is best determined empirically, it would surely be plausible deductively to expect that a certain proportion of these ideas could not be rendered comprehensible to typical pupils in some of the preschool and elementary grades.

As Tyler points out:

> It is . . . difficult to understand how [Bruner] can maintain "that any subject can be taught effectively in some intellectually honest form to any child at any stage of development," and at the same time say, first, that the "preoperational" child cannot grasp the idea of "reversibility," and second, "because of this fundamental lack the child cannot understand certain fundamental ideas that lie at the basis of mathematics and physics." . . . It goes without saying that teachers are severely limited in transmitting concepts to a child at this age even in a highly intuitive manner. . . . Grasping the idea of invariance is beset with difficulties for the child often unsuspected by teachers. . . . Do common experience and observation not convince us of the impossibility of teaching such a class of responses as "solving linear equations" to a neonate? (Tyler, 1964, pp. 220, 223)

### Accelerating Stages of Intellectual Development

Is it possible to accelerate children's progress through the preoperational stage or the stage of concrete logical operations by taking account of their characteristic cognitive limitations, and by providing suitably contrived experience geared to their cognitive capacity and mode of functioning? Can we, for example, train them, as Inhelder (cited in Bruner, 1960, pp. 43–45) suggests, to focus on more than one aspect of a problem at a time or to acquire genuine appreciation of the concept of conservation of mass? If stages of development have any true meaning, the answer to this question can only be (as Piaget, cited by Flavell [1963] indicates) that although some acceleration is certainly possible, it is necessarily limited in extent.

Developmental considerations inevitably impose a limit on the extent of acceleration that is possible. The reason is that transition to the next higher stage is invariably an organic outgrowth of, and hence presupposes, the attainment of a certain level of consolidation or proficiency at the preceding stage. Such consolidation, in turn, implies gradual and cumulative change over an extended period of time. In accounting for the transition from the preoperational stage to the stage of concrete logical operations, Piaget (1957b), for example, emphasizes such mechanisms as successive and contrasting "decentration" (less exclusive preoccupation with a particular aspect of a phenomenon) and gradual appreciation of the theory of probability.

In our opinion, however, Piaget unwarrantedly excludes the role of training and education, particularly the role of verbal instruction, in bringing about transition from one stage of intellectual development to another.

As Vygotsky (1962) points out, the relationship between intellectual development and education is reciprocal. On theoretical grounds there is no reason why *only* incidental (spontaneous, undirected, unexplained) experience (despite Piaget's insistence to the contrary) must effect the gradual, cumulative change in intellectual capacity that makes transition to a higher stage possible. Since guided practice is demonstrably more efficient than incidental learning, it should be quite possible for suitable training to accelerate the rate at which the various stages of intellectual development succeed each other. In fact, evidence was presented earlier which indicates that schooling and urban living accelerate the acquisition of conservation and of combinatorial reasoning. But it was also pointed out above that the mere fact that a given type of learning task *can* be mastered before the age of readiness, or that the age of readiness itself *can* be accelerated, does not necessarily mean that stages of development *should* be accelerated or that maximum acceleration is desirable.

Generally speaking, simple drill or training, in which the preoperational child is exposed to contrived conservation experience and given reinforcement for correct responses, does not suffice to bring about stable acquisition of conservation concepts. Such training merely leads to the acquisition of an "empirical rule," which, unlike the stable and organized concept in the "natural conserver," cannot withstand (is easily extinguished by) the influence of such spurious disconfirmation experience as countersuggestion and perceptually deceptive appearances (Smedslund, 1961). Similarly, in another area of intellectual functioning, kindergarten children who receive laboratory training in learning the principle of a teeter-totter (that the longer side of the fulcrum falls when both sides are equally weighted) fail to exhibit resistance to the later learning of a spurious causal relationship about the operation of a teeter-totter (that the color of the blocks placed at either end of the teeter-totter is the determining factor) (Ausubel & Schiff, 1954). Beilin and Franklin (1962) also report that "no first-grader achieves operational area measurement even with training." Wohlwill and Lowe (1962) found improvement in conservation behavior on a nonverbal posttest after three kinds of training, but no transfer of this conservation learning to a verbal postest. Piagetians (for example, Bovet, 1974; Inhelder, Sinclair, & Murray, 1972; Silverman & Geiringer, 1973; Silverman & Stone, 1972) prefer to accelerate conservation by inducing nonverbal conflict (either by contrasting the child's conflicting perceptions, his perceptions and verbalizations, or his perceptions and those of his peers). Other investigators (for example, Brainerd, 1974; Brison, 1966; Rosenthal & Zimmerman, 1972; Sullivan, 1960; Zimmerman & Rosenthal, 1974) place greater weight on language and didactic exposition.

Considerable evidence, however, indicates that the use of various verbal *didactic* procedures (prior verbalization of principles, the use of verbal rules, filmed verbal explanations, the use of arranged instances of reversibility, confronting the child verbally with his own contradictions), in conjunction with concrete-empirical props, *can* accelerate the acquisition of conservation and probability theory (Bearison, 1969; Brison, 1966; Frank in Bruner, 1964b; Gelman, 1969; Kohnstamm, 1966; Miller & Dyer, 1975; Ojemann, Maxey, & Snider, 1966; Ojemann & Pritchett, 1963; Pufall, 1972; Sheppard, 1973; Sullivan, 1966; Wallach & Sprott, 1964; Wallach, Wall, & Anderson, 1967; Winer, 1968). Such didactic teaching, combined with the use of concrete-empirical props, also induces generalization of conservation responses to other materials (Kohnstamm, 1966; Sullivan, 1966). It also promotes retention of these responses over periods as long as six months (Kohnstamm, 1966), and makes them resistant to extinction after an interval of seven days (Sullivan, 1966).

All of these findings strongly suggest that short-term verbal training can bring about a limited degree of stable, sustained, and somewhat generalized transitional change from the preoperational stage to the stage of concrete logical operations. Long-term training along similar lines should, therefore, be even more effective.

Nevertheless, it appears that the diversity and long-term nature of experience constitutes the essential difference between learning and development. Englemann (1967), for example, taught formal operations to young children through a training procedure and concluded therefrom that "the ability to handle formal operations is a function of specific instruction and not of development." This position is very close to that of Gagné (1968) and Novak (in press) who contend that children's readiness to learn proceeds from specific training operations and specifically relevant ideas in cognitive structure rather than from more general experience in mode of cognitive functioning during the course of development. In our view, however, the more general nonexplicit instances of intellectual capability (for example, the ability to reason abstractly without using concrete-empirical props) are general long-term resultants of diverse, nonspecific experience. They bear little relation to the short-term acquisition of specific intellectual skills or ideas that affect the development of the former only in the aggregate. New learning is influenced *both* by specific prior learning and by more general developmental variables.

Thus it appears that after a certain degree of consolidation of the preoperational stage occurs, one can anticipate, and thereby accelerate, the attainment of the next higher (concrete operational) stage. This can be done by training the child under the learning conditions that apply to the latter stage, by requiring him or her to relate secondary abstractions and abstract verbal propositions to cognitive structure with the aid of concrete-empirical props. In a similar way the transition from concrete to abstract logical operations can be facilitated by gradually withdrawing concrete-empirical props as the prior stage becomes consolidated—that is, by withdrawing the props well in advance of the actual attainment of abstract cognitive functioning.[19] Thus in Vygotsky's (1962) terms, didactic instruction can, and *normally* does, play a role in facilitating (accelerating) transition from one stage of cognitive development to another. The technique provides suitable contrived, directed, and explained learning experience by making intellectual demands on pupils that go beyond their current capabilities—that is, demands that anticipate or are pointed toward the conditions of cognitive functioning at the next higher stage.

### Can Children Learn Anything More Efficiently than Adults?

Related to the proposition that children can learn anything that adults can—provided that it is suitably presented—is the contention that they can also do so more efficiently. David Page, for example, makes the following assertion:

> In teaching from kindergarten to graduate school, I have been amazed at the intellectual similarity of human beings at all ages, although children are perhaps more spontaneous, creative, and energetic than adults. As far as I am concerned, young children can learn almost anything faster than adults do if it can be given to them in terms they understand (cited in Bruner, 1960, pp. 39–40).

In our opinion, although this proposition is generally untrue and unsupportable, it is nevertheless valid in a very limited sense of the term. Even more important, however, it is, in many instances, partially true for reasons that are very different from those offered by its advocates.

Many reasons exist for believing that under *certain* conditions young children *can* learn more efficiently than older and intellectually more mature persons. In the first place, older individuals, particularly if miseducated, must often unlearn what they have previously been taught before they are ready for new learning. This is frequently the case when a student's knowledge is unclear, unstable, or disorganized because of a prior history of rote or nonmeaningful learning. Second, older individuals are more likely to have "emotional blocks" with respect to particular subject-matter areas. Third, their intellectual abilities tend to be more highly differentiated. Finally, there is a marked falling off of intellectual enthusiasm, venturesomeness, and flexibility as children move up the academic ladder.

Generally speaking, however, adolescents and adults have a tremendous advantage in learning any new subject matter—even if they are just as

---

[19] Galperin (1957) describes a method of teaching arithmetic to slow-learning pupils in which concrete-empirical props are eliminated very gradually and are replaced by abstract verbal representations.

unsophisticated as young children in that particular discipline. This advantage inheres in the fact that they are able to draw on various transferable elements of their *overall* ability to function at the abstract level of logical operations. Hence, in their initial contact with a new discipline, they are able to move through the concrete-intuitive phase of intellectual functioning very rapidly. Unlike comparably unsophisticated children, who function *generally* at the level of concrete logical operations, they are soon able to dispense entirely with concrete-empirical props and with intuitive understandings. These facilitating transferable elements, as indicated above, include the possession of transactional terms and higher-order concepts, as well as successful past experience in *directly* manipulating relationships between abstractions (without the benefit of concrete-empirical props).

The advocates of the child-superiority proposition maintain, however, that this shift on the part of older learners from a concrete-intuitive to truly abstract and verbal level of intellectual functioning in the unfamiliar new subject-matter area results in *less* efficient learning processes and outcomes. Research findings, nevertheless, suggest precisely the opposite conclusion, namely, that genuinely abstract and verbal learning is both more efficient and yields a more precise, general, and transferable form of knowledge than its concrete-intuitive and nonverbal counterparts. To argue that a more primitive type of learning is more "natural" because it occurs before a more advanced type of learning, and that it is also more efficient because it is more "natural" is a circular type of reasoning that overlooks the obvious facts that: (1) The earlier learning process is used first not because it is more efficient, but because it is the *only* mode of learning possible at the lower level of development, and hence is more "natural" only for this reason. (2) When a more advanced learning process is available at a later stage of development, it is both less "natural" and less efficient to use its more primitive precursor.

A final argument sometimes advanced for the child-superiority proposition is that since there are allegedly optimal ("critical") periods of readiness for all kinds of developmental acquisitions, many intellectual skills can be acquired more easily by younger than by older pupils. But although this argument is supported by some aspects of motor, physical, and perceptual development, it has still to be validated in the field of intellectual development.

## Educational Implications of the Transition from Concrete to Abstract Cognitive Functioning

From the standpoint of the secondary-school teacher, the most significant development in cognitive functioning that occurs during the preadolescent and early adolescent years is the gradual transition from a predominantly concrete to a predominantly abstract mode of understanding and manipulating complex abstract propositions. This developmental shift has far-reaching implications for teaching methods and curricular practices in the secondary school.

Once developing individuals reach the abstract stage of cognitive functioning, they become in large measure abstract verbal learners. They now acquire most new concepts and learn most new propositions by *directly* (without the mediating and constraining influence of concrete-empirical props) apprehending verbally or symbolically stated relationships between previously learned abstractions. To do so meaningfully, these individuals need no longer refer to first-hand, concrete, or nonrepresentational experience, nor actually perform any of the abstracting or generalizing operations on the underlying empirical data. With developmental dependence on concrete-empirical props removed, the only condition necessary for the understanding and meaningful manipulation of higher-order concepts and abstract propositions is that their substantive import be nonarbitrarily relatable to cognitive structure. Of course, the individuals must also adopt a set to learn these concepts and propositions in this fashion. Hence, on developmental grounds, these individuals are ready at the secondary-school level for a new type of verbal expository teaching that uses particular examples primarily for *illustrative* purposes—that is, to *clarify or dramatize truly abstract meanings rather than to make possible the emergence of intuitive meanings.*

It would be very misleading, however, to assert that secondary-school, and even older, students can *never* profit either from the use of concrete-empirical props to generate intuitive meanings or from the use of inductive discovery and deductive problem-solving techniques to enhance such meanings. As previously suggested, generally mature students tend to function at a relatively concrete or intuitive level when confronted with a particularly *new* subject-matter area in which they are as yet totally unsophisticated. But since abstract cognitive functioning in this new area is rapidly achieved with the attainment of a minimal degree of subject-matter sophistication, concrete-empirical props and discovery methods should be employed to generate and enhance intuitive learnings only during the *early* stages of instruction. However, continued use of discovery techniques for other purposes (to improve problem-solving skills, to foster appreciation of scientific method, or to test verbal understanding) is thoroughly defensible. And once students function abstractly in a given discipline, it is one thing for teachers to use examples and analogies *occasionally* to clarify the *abstract* meanings of particularly difficult or unfamiliar new concepts or principles. It is quite another for teachers to use them *routinely*, either as invariably necessary props for transmitting *all* abstract meanings or in the mistaken belief that students are *still* functioning or would be *better off* still functioning on an intuitive level.

A largely abstract and verbal type of expository teaching is both more economical in terms of time-cost and also leads to abstract verbal understandings that are qualitatively superior to and more transferable than intuitive understandings. Therefore one might reasonably ask why the secondary school has not placed greater emphasis on more abstract and verbal techniques of effecting meaningful verbal learning. In the first place, by unwarrantedly extrapolating childhood learning conditions to adolescence and adult life, the progressive education movement fostered widespread acceptance of the proposition that all verbal concepts and generalizations are *necessarily* nothing more than rotely memorized glib verbalisms unless they both reflect current or recent concrete experience and are products of independent problem solving or discovery. This belief led, in turn, to the summary rejection of verbal exposition. It also led to the paradoxical acceptance of such inherently rote problem-solving and discovery practices as the teaching of "type problems," the wholly mechanical manipulation of mathematical symbols, and the performance of cookbook laboratory experiments.

Second, there was the tendency among educational psychologists to extrapolate findings uncritically from laboratory studies of nonverbal or rote verbal learnings to meaningful verbal learning in the classroom. This practice reinforced educators' perception of verbal learning as necessarily rote in character, and further encouraged them to repudiate expository verbal teaching.

Third, the failure of educational psychologists to investigate the nature and conditions of meaningful verbal learning and retention delayed the discovery of more effective techniques of verbal exposition. Moreover, it helped perpetuate the use of traditional rote techniques. Only within the past two decades have curriculum specialists and educational psychologists concerned themselves with substantive and programmatic aspects of the problem of facilitating the meaningful acquisition and retention of viable bodies of knoweldge.

The fact that children become less "empirical" and more "hypothetical" in their approach to scientific problems with increasing age does not necessarily mean that they accordingly rely more blindly on authority and show less appreciation of scientific method. Piaget (1928, 1932) has shown that quite the opposite holds true. The decreased emphasis on an empirical approach with increasing age is simply a function of cognitive maturation, that is, of greater ability to grasp concepts and generalizations on a purely abstract basis without prior need for experience with multiple particular instances of a concrete nature.

# 7

# INTELLECTUAL ABILITY

In the two previous chapters we have considered specific subject-matter readiness and more general developmental aspects of cognitive functioning. An important internal factor influencing meaningful learning yet to be considered is the quantitative level of intellectual functioning at a given age. This factor may be best defined as intellectual ability or intelligence. It is a measurement construct that attempts to quantify such intellectual abilities as reasoning, problem solving, verbal comprehension, and functional grasp of concepts, and to express the composite score in terms of general scholastic aptitude or intelligence.

Much unnecessary controversy has arisen regarding the use of IQ tests. Most of the controversy would be completely irrelevant (1) if an IQ score were regarded merely as a current, fallible, functional, and phenotypic measure of ability to understand and manipulate abstract symbols for problem-solving purposes rather than as an expression of a fixed and innate (wholly genically determined) capacity; and (2) if it is appreciated that an IQ score purports to measure only the kinds of cognitive abilities that are involved in school learning and not all kinds of intelligence (such as mechanical or social).

Hence, intelligence is influenced (1) by genic factors determining various intellectual abilities, (2) by such other internal factors as motivation, and (3) by such external factors as degree of environmental stimulation, culture, and social class. Although it manifests with increasing age a considerable and increasing degree of stability over time (especially during the school years) it is by no means completely stable, immutable, or impervious to environmental factors. It is most useful for predicting academic performance. But because of the large variety of factors involved in such performance (motivation, social class membership, degree of intellectual stimulation, and so on), it is predictive of only approximately 25 percent of the variance in such achievement.

Although intelligence tests are so constructed as to favor middle-class children, this measurement bias accounts for very little of the measured social-class differences in IQ scores. Intelligence tests are not inherently unfair to lower-class children, provided that these social-class differences are regarded as at least in part a reflection of environmental and motivational factors rather than as completely a function of relative genic endowment. They purport to measure rather than to account for functional expressions of intellectual ability.

With increasing age, intelligence becomes increasingly more highly differentiated as well as more stable. Modifiability is possible but limited by the factor of cumulative intellectual deficit and by increasing degree of differentiation. In general, compensatory intellectual intervention is more successful the earlier it is introduced (in the preschool period), particularly if continued during the early elementary-school years. Typically, IQ scores are normally distributed. Most authorities agree that a disproportionate share of intellectual growth occurs during the preschool period.

Because of the increasing differentiation of intelligence with increasing age, composite measures such as Stanford-Binet IQs become increasingly less useful for predicting scholastic performance than tests measuring factorially pure, differential intellectual abilities. Sex differences, for example, are much greater for particular cognitive abilities than for composite IQ scores.

Because the relative influence of genic and environmental factors varies in every culture, subculture, and individual, it is futile to make even an average quantitative estimate of their relative influence on intelligence. The weight of the evidence, however, is predominantly in favor of more genic than environmental determination. In any case, the nature–nurture problem must be decided by empirical evidence rather than political philosophy. Although, for example, the possibility of innate racial differences in intellectual endowment cannot be dismissed out of hand, it is not supported either by theoretical considerations in behavioral genetics or by the weight of the empirical evidence available. Practical implications for education based on such tenuous evidence are both scientifically and ethically questionable.

In this chapter we propose to discuss the nature and growth of intelligence considered as a *measurement construct designating general level of cognitive functioning*. Developmental changes in the actual psychological capacities and processes involved in cognitive functioning—symbolization, language use, concept formation, and problem solving—are considered in Chapters 2, 3, 6, and 16.

When level of ability in performing these functions is measured by a graded series of tasks and regarded as representative of a *general* capacity for processing information and for utilizing abstract symbols in the solution of abstract problems, the construct designating this measured capacity may be referred to as intelligence. An intellectual ability, in other words, is really nothing more or less than a *functional* manifestation of a distinct and identifiable cognitive process as expressed in a range of individual performance or capacity differences. Since the nature of cognitive processes varies in accordance with stage of development, tests of intellectual ability should take account of and try to reflect stage-related, qualitative changes in cognitive functioning (Décarie, 1965; Flavell, 1963; Laurendeau & Pinard, 1962; Smedslund, 1964; Stott & Ball, 1965).

## The Nature of Intelligence

In the sense that the construct of intelligence is derived from a particular set of measurement operations, it is obviously an abstraction that has no real existence apart from these constituent operations. It is also an abstraction in the sense that a *general* level of cognitive functioning has no actual reality apart from the *particular* kinds of cognitive functioning represented in an intelligence test. Nevertheless, insofar as the construct is logically tenable, related to naturalistic data, and derived from relevant and technically appropriate operations, it is by no means merely an arbitrary and fictitious invention of psychologists. It is definitely related to an existing state of affairs in the real world (cognitive capacity). It has much theoretical and practical value both in explaining cognitive and other aspects of behavioral development and in predicting the cognitive level at which individuals function.

The concept of intelligence, by definition, clearly excludes level of functioning in all *noncognitive* areas of behavior. This definition renders largely irrelevant the commonly voiced criticism that the IQ is misleading because it does not indicate an individual's capacity for coping with nonrepresentational, concrete, mechanical, or interpersonal problems. The IQ is not intended to represent these latter capacities, and no claim is made that it does. In fact, if the intelligence test were modified so that it *could* perform these functions, it would automatically lose whatever effectiveness it possesses as a measure of cognitive ability. The argument here is not that indices of maturity level in other noncognitive areas are theoretically or practically unimportant, but rather that it is utterly naive to expect a single instrument adequately to measure several largely unrelated kinds of abilities.

Also irrelevant in much the same sense is the criticism that the IQ does not indicate *particular* cognitive strengths and failings or *typical ways* of attacking problems. No single *summary* score could possibly do so. If such information is desired, it is available in the detailed test protocol from which the IQ is derived and in the qualitative observations of the examiner. Quite beside the point, also, is the frequently voiced complaint that the intelligence test fails to identify *creativity*. As will be pointed out in Chapter 16, creativity refers to a unique degree of originality in some *substantive* area of human endeavor. It does not refer to the possession of a high degree either of general intelligence or of one of its component abilities.

Much futile controversy rages over the issue of whether or not the intelligence test measures *native* (genically determined) *cognitive endowment*. Although an effort is made to maximize the influence of *genic* factors by using test items that presuppose only very *generally available* kinds of experience, it is obviously impossible to rule out the differential effects of exposure to different types of cognitive experience, to different levels of cognitive stimulation, and to different personality and motivational variables. Hence, intelligence can be regarded only as a *multiply determined functional capacity*, the level of which in a given individual reflects the relative potency of these various factors as they exist and interact in his or her particular case.

Most general intelligence tests, for instance the Binet type, explicitly attempt to avoid the impact of *particular* kinds of past experience by presenting the subject with relatively *novel* tasks. Even so, however, many of the component subtests, such as vocabulary, obviously reflect the influence of environmental factors, such as socioeconomic background. Special aptitude tests, such as language usage, are even more dependent on the nature of prior experience and socioeconomic background.

Another equally pointless controversy is the argument over whether the intelligence test score is a measure of performance or capacity. Obviously, capacity cannot be measured directly and must therefore be *inferred* from performance. But if the IQ score were only an index of how adequately an individual's cognitive capacity is utilized rather than an index of existing capacity *itself*, its theoretical and practical usefulness would be seriously limited. Hence, the more meaningful and relevant question here is whether capacity can be validly *inferred* from performance or whether test performance provides a *fair* sample of capacity. An affirmative answer to this question is indicated if: (1) the test includes a representative sample of cognitive functions; (2) the specific items on the test are related to equally available experience; and (3) the individual is motivated to perform as well as possible. If the latter two conditions are not met, performance is an un-derestimate of capacity. Any subsequent improvement in score that is attributable to correction of test disadvantage or inadequate test motivation reflects a gain in performance rather than a gain in capacity. All increments in IQ, however, do not necessarily fall in this category of more efficient utilization or fairer opportunity of displaying unchanged capacity. If the change is brought about through significant alterations in level of cognitive stimulation or in personality structure, it is reflective of a *genuine* change in capacity, since cognitive capacity (according to the definition of intelligence adopted above) refers to a multiply determined phenotype (actualized genic endowment) rather than to genic potentiality.

If we are primarily interested in using IQ scores as predictors of an individual's actual academic achievement, we would, perhaps, be better advised to obtain them under *typical* motivational conditions. In this case, they would be more reflective of performance than of capacity.

In this chapter we shall be concerned with such *general* issues as the nature of intelligence, what IQ tests purport to measure, the organization of intelligence in terms of its component abilities, and the distribution of IQ scores. We shall also discuss various *developmental* issues bearing on intelligence, when intelligence is considered either in absolute terms (as a developmental or mental age) or relative to group norms (as a developmental quotient—IQ or brightness level). These issues include: (1) quantitative and qualitative changes in intelligence with increasing age; (2) the constancy of individual rates of growth; and (3) the nature–nurture problem—that is, the relative contributions of heredity and environment to the development of intelligence and the extent to which intelligence is modifiable.

### Intelligence Tests and Culturally Disadvantaged Children

The term "culturally disadvantaged" implies a lack of opportunity to learn. It generally refers to children with low socioeconomic backgrounds, who live in poverty conditions. "Liberal" educators often unwarrantedly castigate the intelligence test as being "unfair" to the culturally disadvantaged child, both because it emphasizes verbal ability, rather than the mechanical and social kinds of abilities in which children of low socioeconomic background excel, and because the middle-class environment is more propitious than the lower-class environment for the development of verbal intelligence.

Reasoning such as this, for example, led to the decision (1964) to ban group intelligence tests from the New York City public schools. Actually, however, the intelligence test is not really unfair to the disadvantaged child on either count. In the first place, it purports primarily to measure verbal ability and to predict school performance—not ability or performance in the mechanical and social areas. Second, any intelligence test can hope only to measure functional or operating capacity at a given point of development (degree of actualized genic potentiality) rather than innate potentiality itself. Adequacy of environmental stimulation is always a significant determinant of functional capacity and hence affects performance on an intelligence test. If the environment is inadequately stimulating, then functional capacity is naturally impaired. But this does not mean that our measuring instrument, the intelligence test, is unfair, since its function is merely to identify and measure impaired operating capacity irrespective of the origin of the impairment. The intelligence test, in other words, purports to measure functional capacity rather than to account for it. If the disadvantaged child scores low on an intelligence test because of the inadequacy of his or her environment, it is not the test, but rather the social order that permits him to develop under such conditions, that is unfair.

Traditional verbal intelligence tests are unfair to disadvantaged children in the sense that such children, in comparison with their middle-class agemates, have fewer test-taking skills, are less responsive to speed pressure, are less highly motivated in taking tests, have less rapport with the examiner, and are less familiar with the specific vocabulary and tasks that make up the content of the test (Haggard, 1954; Riessman, 1962). In a study of nonstandard English spoken by blacks (Labov, 1970), it was found that young blacks who would be assessed as retarded by standard test procedures could converse and present logical arguments. The results indicated a difference in language rather than a deficit. Golden and Birns (1968) tested young black children from different levels of social disadvantage and found that when given more time to complete the tests there was no significant difference between the groups. The tests or test administration are, therefore, unfair in that they do not give the lower-class child a fair opportunity to demonstrate his true attained level of cognitive capacity. When some of these errors of measurement are eliminated, however, substantial social-class differences in IQ still remain (Coleman & Ward, 1955; Haggard, 1954). These may reflect both hereditary and environmental influences. Cattell (1963) postulates that "culture-free" tests, emphasizing "crystallized" as opposed to "fluid" abilities, are fairer to disadvantaged children.

Even if "culture-free" tests are devised that minimize the effects of a culturally disadvantaged environment and give a theoretically truer picture both of the disadvantaged child's genic endowment and of his attained level of cognitive capacity, it is likely:

> that these tests, in comparison with tests reflecting experiences within the culture, will predict less well those behaviors dependent upon cultural differences. Furthermore, one can argue that since the growth of intelligence does not occur in a vacuum but is nourished by the cultural milieu, the impact of the culture on tests should not be ignored (Millman & Glock, 1965, p. 21).

### The Organization of Intelligence

How are intellectual abilities and scholastic aptitudes organized? The answer to this question is both complex and technical. For purposes of this textbook, suffice it to say that the organization of intelligence depends in large measure on the age of the pupil in question.

The weight of the evidence indicates that intelligence consists of both a *general* or unitary ability and a constellation of discrete and separately measurable abilities or aptitudes. The relative importance of these two characteristics varies as a function of age. Typically, the various subabilities measured by an IQ test intercorrelate about .40; that is, they show a moderate degree of generality. This reflects both the general and specialized nature of the intellectual abilities comprising intelligence or general scholastic aptitude. Thus the significance and predictive value of a composite score on a general intelligence test depend both on the age of the subject and on the purpose for which predictions are made. The tendency in recent years, at least for older students, has been to place greater reliance on the measurement of diverse and relatively separate abilities. This approach, however, has undoubtedly been carried to an extreme by factor analysts such as Guilford (1959). The latter suggests that there are 120 separately identifiable mental abilities comprising the structure of intellect. These consist of the various combinations relating to five classes of operations, four kinds of content, and six types of product.[1] Actually, only about a half-dozen factors—such as vocabulary, spatial relations, number ability, numerical reasoning, and language usage—have been well established and shown to have predictive value for related aspects of academic achievement.

---

[1] Guilford's factors are derived from a purely hypothetical three-dimensional model comparable to the periodic table of chemical elements, except for the fact that it is wholly speculative rather than based on a projection from known empirical data. Not only has the existence of many of these factors never been empirically demonstrated, but also most of the demonstrated factors have not been shown to have any predictive significance for academic achievement, vocational accomplishment, or anything else. The low intercorrelations among Guilford's tests purporting to measure the same factorially pure ability (Guilford, 1964) suggest, in addition, that scores on these tests are reflective of highly specific situation-bound abilities, rather than of the true intellectual subabilities that manifest generality of function and hence psychological reality and significance.

It should also be pointed out that factor analysis is merely a statistical method of reducing the number of abilities measured by a given test(s) to the smallest number of common denominators capable of accounting for most of the variance in a particular population. The number of factors that emerge from a given analysis therefore depends in large measure on the particular tests used, at what point the investigator chooses to stop the reduction process, and how the investigator chooses to conceptualize, interpret, and name the least common denominators that emerge.

*The Distribution of IQ Scores*

The distribution of IQ scores typically shows a characteristically wide and continuous range of variability. This distribution is consistent with the interpretation that intelligence (like most human traits) is *polygenically* determined; that is, it is determined in large part (but not exclusively) by the cumulative and additive effects of a large number of genes, each of which exerts a small positive or negative effect on the development of the trait. Approximately 64 percent of all IQ scores fall between the range of 85 and 114 (Terman & Merrill, 1937). A somewhat smaller range of variability prevails with respect to achievement test scores, inasmuch as the uneducable mentally handicapped do not attend school.

Intelligence tests continue to yield normal distribution during the course of adolescence (Cornell, 1936; Thorndike et al., 1926). Variability in test scores at any age or grade level is considerable. The distribution of mental ability, for example, among 14-year-old students in New York State is represented by a range of mental ages from 10 to 18 with the mode at 14 (Cornell, 1936).

## Developmental Changes in Intelligence

We must consider *quantitative* developmental changes, such as the growth curve of intelligence and the constancy of individual rates of growth. In addition, we must consider such *qualitative* developmental changes as age-level changes in (1) ability to process large bodies of organized and potentially meaningful bodies of information, (2) the organization of intellectual abilities, and (3) the breadth and depth of subject-matter knowledge ("horizontal growth").

### Growth Curve of Intelligence

Most investigators agree that intelligence increases most rapidly in infancy and early childhood and tends to increase thereafter at a progressively decreasing rate. This conclusion is in accord with everyday experience and with the fact that overlapping between score distributions of adjacent age groups increases with advancing age (Bayley, 1933). A linear growth curve of intelligence is simply an artifactual outcome of plotting mental age in terms of units that are deliberately calibrated so that one year of intellectual growth is, on the average, achieved during the course of a calendar year. In general, the growth curve of general intelligence is negatively accelerated (shows a progressively decreasing rate of growth) when based either on raw scores (Terman & Merrill, 1937), on absolutely scaled[2] scores, or on scaled scores transformed into percentages of adult attainment. Some investigators report a slight reversal in the rate of negative acceleration during the preadolescent period (Freeman & Flory, 1937; Terman & Merrill, 1937; Wechsler, 1950). On the basis of scaled intelligence test scores, Thorndike et al. (1926) postulated a parabolic growth curve according to which about half of mature intellectual status is attained by the age of 3. A similar conclusion was reached by Bloom (1964a), placing the mid-point of attainment of adult intelligence at age 4. Growth begins to taper off in middle adolescence and continues very slowly thereafter until ultimate capacity is achieved (Bayley, 1949; Freeman & Flory, 1937; Garrett, Bryan, & Perl, 1935).

Since the tapering-off process is so gradual, it is difficult to tell when growth actually ceases. The widely accepted finding of Terman and Merrill (1937) that mental age does not increase after the age of 15 is now attributed to the limited ceiling of the 1937 revision of the Stanford-Binet test. The best estimates, based on testing a wide age sample of a relatively homogeneous population (Jones & Conrad, 1944; Wechsler, 1944), or on retesting the same population at suitable intervals (Bayley, 1955, 1966; Freeman & Flory, 1937; Jones & Conrad, 1944; E. L. Thorndike, 1926, 1928), place the age of terminal growth at 18 or 20 and even beyond. Bayley (1966, 1968a, 1968b), by extending the Berkeley Growth Study curves through 36 years, found that Wechsler scores increased through age 26, after which they leveled off and remained unchanged through 36 years. Gains in intelligence test scores have been reported at age 50 on the Army Alpha (Owens, 1953) and Concept Maturity tests (Bayley & Oden, 1955). The age of terminal growth obviously varies for different individuals and for different kinds of cognitive processes (Jones & Conrad, 1944).

The growth of intelligence—considered as a measurement construct—is the least typical aspect of adolescent development. In all other components of growth—hormonal, skeletal, motor, personality, moral, and social—there is an accelerated period of transitional development or a growth spurt.[3] Quantitative aspects of intellectual growth, on the other hand, follow a pattern very similar to the development of fine mechanical abilities. Of all the major tissues of the body and segments of personality, it seems

---

[2] The purpose of scaling is to make raw scores from different tests and from different age groups comparable by expressing them in such a way that at any point of the scale, the distances between units of measurement are equal in difficulty value.

[3] Ljung (1965) has described an "adolescent growth spurt" in mental development that is more marked in girls than in boys. But the tests he used were more comparable to academic achievement tests than to conventional intelligence tests; and, as we know from our description of cognitive development, there is a definite spurt at adolescence in ability to master academic subject matter. This ability, however, is hardly synonymous with the construct of intelligence as defined above.

that only the small muscles and intelligence remain unaffected by the cata-lytic impetus to growth supplied by pubescence. Their development con-tinues to respond to the hereditary and environmental influences impinging upon them, just as if pubescence were not taking place. Their growth curves proceed smoothly, unmarked by any discontinuity, to assume the adolescent form that could be projected for them from developmental data of earlier years.

Growth of this kind is not unimportant. In such growth, new capacities are attained by the gradual accumulation of small increments of progress rather than by abrupt and discontinuous spurts of development. In terms of *degree of cognitive ability*, the adolescent is a different and more mature person than the preadolescent, but not discontinuously so.[4] And the acqui-sition of these increased cognitive abilities plays an important role in personality, moral, and religious development.

The termination of growth in "vertical" capacity also does not mean that all intellectual development ceases. Although beyond this point the individual may be unable to solve more difficult *novel* problems, he or she continues to grow "in a 'horizontal' direction—in the sense of increased information, knowledge, ability to draw upon past experience, increased ability to make decisions, to form judgments, to exercise common sense, and so forth" (Jersild, Chayer, Fehlman, Hildreth, & Young, 1946). Also, because of the shift from concrete to abstract modes of cognitive function-ing, the capacity both to learn large bodies of subject matter and to reason in terms of abstract, general hypotheses (to use propositional logic) shows a discontinuous rate of increase. And since the majority of problems an individual encounters can hardly be classified as novel, the continuing horizontal growth may be of much greater practical significance than the level of vertical growth already attained.

### Growth Curve of Separate Intellectual Abilities

Subtest analysis of various tests of intellectual ability shows that sev-eral important differences exist in the rate of growth, age of terminal growth, and rate of decline among the component subabilities. Simple rote memory (memory span) reaches an earlier peak of development than either general intelligence (Conrad, Freeman, & Jones, 1944), vocabulary, or arith-metical ability (Garrett et al., 1935); but this is not the case with respect to more meaningful and analytical types of memory (Jones & Conrad, 1933). During the preadolescent and adolescent periods, vocabulary and ability to dissect sentences grow at a more rapid rate than does reasoning ability despite identical rates of growth during early and middle childhood (Conrad et al., 1944). Growth of ability terminates earlier on the analogies test than

---

[4] In terms of *mode* of cognitive functioning, however, discontinuity in development probably does occur at adolescence (see Chapter 6).

on either the completions or opposites tests. On the other hand, decline in ability sets in earlier for such functions as analogies and completions than for vocabulary and general information (Jones & Conrad, 1933). In conclusion, it appears that the more complex intellectual abilities have a more gradual rate of growth, reach maturity at a later age (Bradway & Thompson, 1962), and then show evidence of decline earlier in life.

Cattell (1963, 1967) has isolated "fluid" and "crystallized" components of intelligence. The "crystallized" factor consists largely of "process" functions, presumably not much influenced by learning or educational experience, and reaches maturity at a relatively early age. The "fluid" factor, in contrast, consists more of "product" functions. These are appreciably affected by education and experience and therefore reach maturity later in life and continue to show increases in adults to 30 years of age or older (Bayley, 1970). In looking at a wider age range from 14 to 61 years Horn and Cattell (1967) found differences in intellectual functioning associating with aging in adults. "Fluid" intelligence was higher for younger adults, whereas "crystallized" intelligence was higher for older adults. The culturally disadvantaged are much more deficient in the fluid than in the crystallized component of intelligence (Cattell, 1963).

### Growth Curves of Bright and Dull Individuals

Available evidence indicates that bright, dull, and average children grow intellectually at different rates and differ with respect to organization and qualitative pattern of cognitive abilities. Although the terminal age of intellectual growth is the same for all three groups, dull children attain a disproportionately large percentage of their ultimate intellectual status during the early years (Bayley, 1956) and tend to grow stepwise in spurts and pauses (Cornell & Armstrong, 1955). Normal children exhibit a more constant rate of growth (Freeman & Flory, 1937), whereas bright children "show an accelerated rate of growth in later childhood" that slows down somewhat in middle and late adolescence (Cornell & Armstrong, 1955; Freeman & Flory, 1937). The net effect of these differences is that the bright tend to "grow away" from the dull (Conrad et al., 1944; Thurstone & Ackerson, 1929). Duller individuals (as might reasonably be anticipated from their greater chronological age) also show greater differentiation of intelligence than do brighter younger children of the same mental age (Thompson & Margaret, 1949).

There are also good reasons—from analysis of intelligence test scores alone—for believing that normal (average) cognitive functioning at a given maturity level is *qualitatively* different from the performance of accelerated younger or retarded older individuals of the same mental age.

1. Subscale analysis of the Stanford-Binet test shows significant differences between old-dull and young-bright individuals of comparable mental age in the types of items handled successfully (Jones, 1931; Laycock & Clark, 1942; Merrill, 1924).

2. Bright and dull children tend to exhibit more "scatter" (spread of successes and failures on component subtests over a wider range of difficulty) on this test than do average children (Merrill, 1924).

3. Bright and dull children of equivalent mental age excel in different kinds of cognitive abilities. The bright are generally superior in tests demanding comprehension, imagination, use of language, reasoning, abstraction, and generalization (Aldrich & Doll, 1931; Cunningham, 1927; Gallagher & Lucito, 1961; Purvis, 1938; Ramaseshan, 1950; Witkin, Paterson, Goodenough, & Birnbaum, 1966). Dull children, on the other hand, are superior in spatial ability (Ramaseshan, 1950), word fluency (Ramaseshan, 1950) and manipulation of concrete materials (Aldrich & Doll, 1931).

4. Normal children do better than mentally retarded children of the same mental age in such school skills as arithmetic reasoning (Dunn, 1954), spelling (Dunn, 1954), reading comprehension (Bliesmer, 1954; Dunn, 1954; Merrill, 1924), ability to profit from contextual cues (Dunn, 1954), memory for factual details (Bliesmer, 1954), and understanding of ideational relationships (Bliesmer, 1954). No significant differences were found in the simpler and more mechanical reading skills (Bliesmer, 1954) and in arithmetic fundamentals (Dunn, 1954).

5. Bright and dull children of the same mental age show characteristic differences in approach to problem solving.

There is evidence also that some kinds of intelligence increase well into middle age, in the dull as well as the bright. In the Berkeley Growth Study, Bayley (1968a) found continued increases in scores through 36 years for the lowest-scoring half of the sample. McCulloch (1957) found evidence of increased scores on verbal tests through 30 years or longer on mentally retarded institutionalized adults.

In view of the fact that they continue to grow in intelligence just as long as their brighter peers, dull students need not drop out of high school at the tenth grade, as they frequently do at present. Rather, they could profit from continued schooling or work training programs. To maximize the benefit that such students can derive from continued instruction, the more difficult subjects could be placed at the end of the high-school curriculum, and abstract materials could be concretized and made more meaningful in terms of life situations (Segel, 1948). And "in order to recognize their peculiar capacities and help them achieve success rather than failure, the school needs to provide for them a wide variety of learning activities" (Segel, 1948).

### Developmental Changes in Organization

Since there is much disagreement regarding the way in which intelligence is organized, it is obviously impossible to make any definitive statement about developmental changes in its organization. The weight of the evidence, however, points to: (1) an initial stage (infancy and the early preschool period), in which the abilities measured by intelligence tests are predominantly perceptual and sensorimotor in nature and are largely unrelated both to each other and to later manifestations of abstract intelligence; (2) an intermediate stage (from approximately the late preschool period to preadolescence), in which abstract intelligence is highly general in nature, cognitive abilities are highly intercorrelated; and (3) a later stage (preadolescence and beyond), marked by increasing differentiation of intellectual abilities.

At the age of 5, abstract abilities are much in evidence and are so highly intercorrelated that it is relatively difficult to isolate independent factors. In contrast to the eight "primary abilities" that he was able to identify in a population of adolescents and young adults, Thurstone was able to isolate only five comparable abilities among 5- and 6-year-olds (Thurstone, 1938; Thurstone & Thurstone, 1946). As children grow older, particularly during the preadolescent period and beyond, there is evidence from factor analysis[5] of increasing differentiation of intellectual ability (Garrett, 1946; Garrett et al., 1935; Green & Berkowitz, 1964; Guilford, 1966; Heinonen, 1963; Ljung, 1965; Meyer, 1960). Increased integration also occurs *within* the various component subabilities (Ljung, 1965).

By the time an individual reaches adolescence, differential factors of interest, relative ability, specialization of training, motivation, success and failure experience, and cultural expectation operate selectively to develop certain original abilities and to leave others relatively undeveloped. Children with highly "differentiated" mothers (Dyk & Witkin, 1965) tend to undergo most differentiation. Original aptitude and experience seem to reinforce each other in circular fashion since children who are gifted in a particular area benefit differentially from instruction in that area (Lesser, 1962). However, inasmuch as considerable interrelatedness among different cognitive functions still remains (Schulman & Havighurst, 1947), evidence of increasing differentiation at the older age levels does *not* render the concept of general intelligence completely untenable. Furthermore, there are relatively high correlations between intelligence test scores obtained in the primary grades and retest scores obtained during adolescence. These correlations indicate a high degree of overlapping between the factors determining early

---

[5] Using other kinds of tests, Cohen (1959), Hagen (1952), and Vernon (1950) failed to obtain consistent evidence of increasing differentiation.

level of general cognitive ability and later level of differentiated cognitive ability.

For practical purposes an intelligence test score has less utility after preadolescence than during the early elementary-school years. The older child's relative standing in one ability has relatively little predictive value for his relative standing in another ability. In addition, *composite* scores on intelligence tests are not very useful for predicting performance in a *particular* school subject. Much more meaningful than a total score is a profile showing the relative standing of an individual on a wide variety of basic intellectual abilities. Thurstone's tests of "primary mental abilities," for example, provides such a profile. This profile expresses intelligence in terms of the smallest number of relatively "pure" and independent factors. Thus it gives a much more definitive, convenient, and quantifiable qualitative analysis of cognitive ability than could be obtained from examination of the protocol of the more traditional Binet-type scale composed of heterogeneous subtests.

In conclusion, therefore, it can be stated that when differential aptitude batteries, purporting to measure only the relatively few and well-established "primary mental abilities" are used, they probably have more predictive value for the particular kinds of subject-matter achievement for which they are relevant than do composite scores on tests of general intelligence or of general scholastic aptitude. However, the latter tests, as McNemar (1964) points out, are not completely without psychological significance or predictive value. In fact, they are more useful for predicting complex criteria of academic achievement, involving the interaction among several abilities, than are even the well-established differential aptitude batteries. They are incomparably more useful than are differential batteries consisting of unvalidated factors or of factors manifesting little generality of function.

The increased differentiation of intellectual ability during adolescence is a *general* phenomenon, but it also varies in relation to many differential factors. Segel's evidence (1948) shows that differentiation among intellectual traits is greater for bright than for dull adolescents. Intellectual abilities are also differentiated along social-class and sex lines and as a result of prolonged or specialized education. Especially interesting are data indicating that superiority in a given function, reflecting higher *general* ability at a younger age level, may undergo reversal during adolescence as a result of differentiation. For example, girls have higher language *and* arithmetical ability than boys at the beginning of adolescence, but boys eventually surpass them in arithmetical ability before the close of adolescence (Kuhlen, 1952; Maccoby & Jacklin, 1974). Children from upper socioeconomic groups are superior to lower-class children on tests of both verbal *and* mechanical ability at age 10, but at age 16 retain their superiority only on the verbal tests (Havighurst & Janke, 1944; Janke & Havighurst, 1945).

This progressive differentiation of mental ability requires a correspondingly increasing differentiation of curricular offerings. As Segel points out, a "core curriculum" is better suited to the intellectual organization of junior- than of senior-high-school students. Another consequence of this increasing differentiation that is apparent from studies of dropouts from school is:

> that between the ages of 10 and 14, maladjustment through lack of general mental ability is an item of importance among the factors causing youth to leave school. However, between the ages of 15 and 18 such maladjustment does not result in large numbers of youth leaving school (Segel, 1948).

### Constancy of Individual Rates of Growth

Quite apart from normative fluctuations in the rate of intellectual development, it is important to ascertain whether children tend to retain the same *relative* status in their age group as they grow older. To the extent that this type of constancy prevails, the child's developmental quotient (IQ) will fluctuate little from one age level to another. The child's score at an earlier stage of development will not only be indicative of his or her relative status at that age level, but will also have predictive value for relative status at later stages of development. The constancy of the IQ may be expressed either in terms of its probable error, or in terms of the coefficient of correlation between the intelligence test scores of a group of children that are determined on two separate occasions (the coefficient of stability).

Generally speaking, once the IQ approaches stability it tends to remain relatively constant, and existing degrees of inconstancy tend to be normally distributed. At the age of 9, for example, the probable error of an IQ (Terman & Merrill, 1937) is about 5 points[6] (varying with brightness level), and the coefficient of stability (with an interval of three years between tests) is approximately .85 (Honzik, Macfarlane, & Allen, 1948). The predictive value of the IQ is greatly influenced both by the age of the child at the time of initial testing and by the length of the interval between test and retest. The older the child when first tested and the shorter the interval between tests, the greater will be the predictive accuracy of the initial test (J. E. Anderson, 1939; L. D. Anderson, 1939; Bayley, 1940; Bradway & Thompson, 1962; Honzik et al., 1948; W. J. Meyer, 1960). Intelligence test scores gradually become more stable with advancing age. They first acquire sufficient stability to be practically useful for predictive purposes when the child reaches school age (Bayley, 1949). Stability in *component* mental abilities, however, is not impressive until the fourth grade, and first be-

---

[6] This means that one-half of the IQ-tested persons do not deviate more than 5 points on immediate retesting. Over an interval of 6 to 8 years, approximately 10 percent of all IQ scores change at least one standard deviation (16 points).

comes high enough for boys during the eighth grade to forecast adult aptitudes (Bennett & Doppelt, 1951; W. J. Meyer, 1960). Among girls, the
findings are more equivocal (Meyer & Bendig, 1961). In this section we
shall consider age-level changes in the stability of the IQ, as well as various
measurement, genic, and environmental factors that account for both consistency and fluctuations in individual rates of growth.

Preschool intelligence tests measure a larger portion of abstract intellectual ability than do infant scales and hence have greater predictive value.
After the age of 2, scores on preschool tests show a moderate (.46 to .66)
and progressively increasing correlation with scores determined at the age
of 7 (J. E. Anderson, 1939; Honzik et al., 1948). But it is not until the age
of school entrance that scores on intelligence tests are reasonably well correlated with terminal intellectual status (Bayley, 1949; Honzik et al., 1948).
If preschool tests are administered accurately and on more than one occasion, school-age status can be predicted with a degree of error that rarely
exceeds one category on a 5-point scale. During the later elementary-school
years, IQ remains relatively stable, both on a year-to-year basis and over
a period of three or more years (Bayley, 1949; Honzik et al., 1948). Although some fluctuations in test scores do occur, most children tend to
retain the same *relative* position in their age group.

When the child is at the age of adolescence, test scores of general intelligence acquire a fair amount of stability. The correlation between scores
on intelligence tests given at the onset of adolescence with those given at
the close of adolescence is in the neighborhood of .80 (J. E. Anderson, 1940).
From year to year this correspondence is even greater (Thorndike, 1926).
Thus, while some fluctuation in test score occurs in individual growth
curves, most individuals tend to retain the same relative position in the
group throughout the adolescent period (Freeman & Flory, 1937). In extreme instances, of course, there are large fluctuations in test scores. But
these fluctuations tend to be associated with such unusual disorganizing
factors in life history as, for example, serious illness (Honzik et al., 1948)
rather than with intrinsic irregularity of the growth pattern or unreliability
of the measuring instrument. For purposes of *individual* guidance, however, a reliability coefficient of .80 is not too reassuring. In dealing with a
*particular* individual it does not suffice to know that a *majority* of individuals at age 18 will occupy the same relative position in the group with
respect to IQ as they did at age 13. There is sufficient variability in individual growth patterns to warrant frequent and periodic testing of intelligence
if test scores are to be used at all for guidance purposes.

### Causes of Constancy and Fluctuation

Much of the constancy of the IQ can undoubtedly be attributed to
genic factors. To the extent that the development of intelligence is determined by polygenic influences, some degree of constancy is inherent in

the fact that the genotype of an individual remains invariable throughout his or her lifetime. A second factor, the environment, also accounts for some constancy, since for any particular individual it tends, within limits, to remain relatively stable. The relative contributions of heredity and environment to the constancy of the IQ are, of course, proportionate to their relative weights in determining cognitive development. A third factor making for constancy is the phenomenon of *developmental irreversibility*—that is, the limiting influence of current developmental status on potentialities for future growth. New growth always proceeds from the existing phenotype rather than from potentialities inherent in the genotype. Often, as a result of a consistently poor environment during the early formative years, existing genic endowment is not actualized. Then the *attained* level of functional capacity (although incommensurate with genic potentiality) significantly limits the extent to which *later* environmental improvement can increase the rate of cognitive growth. One's prior success in developing one's intellectual potentialities, in other words, tends to keep future rate of growth relatively constant despite fluctuations in relevant environmental variables. Finally, constancy is, in part, a reflection of the overlap that prevails in the intellectual abilities measured by intelligence tests at different age levels (J. E. Anderson, 1939).

Fluctuations in IQ are caused by measurement, genic, and environmental factors. Included under the first heading are:

1. Errors of measurement inherent in the selection and placement of test items and in the use of items that are not equally representative of generally available experience—thereby leading to variable amounts of test disadvantage at different points in the life cycle and for different groups of children

2. Errors of test administration and scoring, especially during infancy and early childhood when difficulties of communication are maximal

3. Situational variability in such factors affecting test performance as personality of the test administrator, rapport (Pasamanick & Knobloch, 1955), fatigue, physical well-being, general attitude, motivation (Haggard, 1954; Zigler & Butterfield, 1968), attention span, frustration tolerance, self-confidence, level of aspiration, emotional stability, level of anxiety, reaction to failure, venturesomeness, and negativism (Hill & Sarason, 1966; Rust, 1931)

4. Variation in the standardization sample over the age range

5. Variation among age groups in test ceiling and in degree of variability of test scores

6. Variable exposure to practice and coaching on intelligence tests (Wiseman, 1954) and to test experience generally

The most important measurement factor making for instability of the

IQ are age-level changes in the composition of intelligence tests and in the degree of overlap of test content between adjacent age groups (J. E. Anderson, 1939; Bayley, 1955). Infant intelligence scales measure a largely unrelated type of sensorimotor ability, instead of the cognitive ability tested at later age levels. Thus a child with high genic endowment for abstract intelligence tends to score much closer to the mean on earlier than on later tests. The child makes a spuriously low score on the initial test and registers a spurious gain on the second test; the reverse holds true for the child deficient in abstract intelligence (J. E. Anderson, 1939). Dissimilarity in test content, on the other hand, is necessary and desirable in instances where genuine developmental change occurs in the organization of intelligence. For example, intelligence tests should be more highly differentiated at age 15 than at age 5.

Just because the genotype remains constant, we cannot *assume* that its effects on development necessarily lead to individual constancy in relative rate of growth. Since genic factors also determine *normative* fluctuations in rate of cognitive development over the life-span, they may also conceivably give rise to *intraindividual variability* in rate of growth. Longitudinal analyses of individual growth curves of intelligence by Bayley (1940) and Cornell and Armstrong (1955) are consistent with this interpretation. The latter investigators were able to classify most growth curves under three main patterns: a continuous growth curve from age 5 to 18, a steplike curve consisting of alternate spurts and pauses, and a discontinuous curve breaking at puberty and showing either a steeper or more gradual slope thereafter.

Environmental factors contribute in two ways to fluctuations in the IQ. First, physical and emotional vicissitudes of a transitory nature (illness, emotional trauma, separation from parents, rejection by peers) may impair a child's intelligence test *performance* without basically affecting cognitive *capacity*. Second, radical and sustained changes in cognitive stimulation or motivation may modify actual capacity for intellectual functioning. However, significant alterations in IQ of such origin can be anticipated only in young children who are removed from a markedly impoverished to a normally adequate or enriched environment.

Personality traits associated with parent attitudes influence the constancy of the IQ. "Democratic" homes, encouraging the development of children's independence, tend to be associated with a rising IQ (Baldwin, Kalhorn, & Breese, 1945; Grant, 1939). Gains in IQ are correlated with independence (Sontag, Baker, & Nelsen, 1955) and high achievement motivation (Kagan, Sontag, Baker, & Nelsen, 1958). Losses in IQ, especially in girls, are correlated with dependence (Sontag et al., 1955). The greatest changes in IQ tend to occur in intellectually gifted children (Lindholm, 1964).

Sex Differences

The issue of sex differences in intelligence has become of greater concern in recent years as a result of the feminist movement which questions the conventional roles for women. The results of studies to determine whether or not the sexes differ in general intelligence have not been consistent.

Sex differences in general intelligence tend to be negligible in magnitude and inconsistent in direction (Terman & Tyler, 1954). In a recent review of the research, Maccoby and Jacklin (1974) found that the sexes do not differ consistently on tests of total intellectual abilities. The most widely used individual tests of general intelligence—the Revised Stanford-Binet Scale and the Wechsler Intelligence Scale for Children—after all, have been constructed so as to eliminate sex differences. Most of the obtained differences can be attributed to the fact that the particular tests used are differentially weighted with respect to the various component aspects of intelligence in which boys and girls differ in opposite directions—vocabulary, verbal fluency, rote memory, spatial and numerical abilities (Terman & Tyler, 1954).

Recent research generally supports the finding that girls and women obtain higher scores on tasks measuring verbal abilities (Maccoby & Jacklin, 1974). At the preschool level, most sex differences in cognitive abilities are not evident with the exception of verbal fluency (Terman & Tyler, 1954). Girls learn to talk, use sentences, and read earlier, but it is possible that such differences are, for the most part, culturally determined (Kagan, 1964). Girls are superior to boys in categorizing ability in the first grade, but by the sixth grade this difference is no longer evident (Bruner & Olver, 1963). Although girls generally receive higher grades than boys do in school, achievement test differences tend to disappear beginning in junior high school. Girls also show a slight superiority over boys in general intelligence during early adolescence (Conrad et al., 1944; Freeman & Flory, 1937) which is related to their more precocious sexual maturation.

Differences between the sexes in particular cognitive abilities tend to be larger and more significant than in tests of general intelligence and to increase with increasing age (Terman & Tyler, 1954). Differences, however, in most areas are equivocal. A summary of 26 studies in sex differences (Oetzel, 1962) showed that the most consistent differences are in language development, verbal fluency, and spatial abilities. In language development and verbal fluency, girls showed higher scores in 23 studies; boys showed higher scores in 1; and 2 studies failed to mark a difference between the sexes. In spatial abilities, boys came out higher in 14 studies; there were no differences between the sexes in 5 studies; and in no studies did the girls show any superiority over boys. The situation with respect to vocabulary is more confusing: 16 studies showed no difference between the sexes; 4 studies indicated higher scores for boys; and 8 studies showed higher scores for girls. In reasoning and numerical reasoning, boys' superiority appeared in 13 studies; girls obtained higher scores in 4 studies; and 8 studies showed no difference between the sexes (Gallagher, 1964). Maccoby and Jacklin (1974) found no sex differences for quantitative ability up to adolescence, but after this age boys move ahead.

Evidence regarding differences in variability in general intelligence also tends to be inconsistent and equivocal. Boys exhibit greater variability in IQ than girls, achieving a larger proportion of extreme scores at either end of the distribution (McNemar & Terman, 1936). Interpretation of this finding is difficult because many variables other than genic factors are influential.

Terman's 25-year, longitudinal study of intellectually gifted children showed that boys more frequently than girls retained their high intellectual status as they advanced in age (Terman & Oden, 1949). Differential factors of motivation, cultural expectation, and opportunity can perhaps explain part of the sex difference at the upper extreme of intelligence, but it cannot very well account for differences at the lower extreme.

Other complicating factors raise questions of interpretation at the lower extreme of intelligence. For example, there is a preponderance of boys in classes for the learning disabled and in institutions for the mentally retarded. In addition, paranatal brain injury occurs more frequently among male infants (Lillienfeld & Pasamanick, 1956; Pasamanick & Knobloch, 1955), and mental deficiency is a socially more conspicuous disabling handicap in the case of boys. Furthermore, parents are less reluctant to commit sons than daughters to institutions. We must conclude, therefore, that, until more definitive evidence is available, it is impossible to decide to what extent obtained sex differences in variability are attributable to such genuine determinants as genic and relevant environmental factors, on the one hand, and to purely extraneous considerations, on the other.

## Nature and Nurture

Various methods have been used in attempting to arrive at a *quantitative* estimate of the relative influences of heredity and of environment on the development of a given trait. Applying these methods to the study of twins (Newman, Freeman, & Holzinger, 1937), foster children (Burks, 1928; Leahy, 1935), and relationships between intelligence, schooling, and reasoning ability (Burt, 1955, 1966), different investigators have reached quite different conclusions regarding the proportionate contributions of nature and nurture to measured differences in expressed intelligence. However, both because of the many uncontrollable sources of error involved in making precise quantitative estimates, and because of the questionable validity of the assumptions underlying the statistical procedures employed (Loevinger, 1943), it seems preferable in the present state of our knowledge merely to examine the various kinds of evidence bearing on the heredity-environment issue and to assay only *roughly* their relative effects on inter- and intragroup variability in intelligence test scores.

In any case, any estimate of the relative influence of heredity and environment in determining the development of intelligence necessarily varies both from one culture to another as well as within a given culture. An equally important issue is how the respective effects of heredity and environment are mediated.

*Heredity* imposes *absolute* limits on level of cognitive attainment in an individual. It influences the rate and patterning of one's intellectual growth, and affects the differentiation of one's intellectual abilities. Except for such relatively rare conditions as phenyl-pyruvic amentia, cerebral agenesis, and cretinism, the mechanisms mediating genic influences on intellectual development are not presently understood. As in the determination of any trait that varies among individuals, *environment* also plays a limiting and patterning role in the development of intelligence.

Even if it could be held *constant* over individuals, it would still play this *active* regulatory role, rather than merely constituting a passive field for the unfolding of a trait completely determined by genic factors. Its effects under such conditions would simply operate in a uniform way for all individuals. However, since it varies in important ways that affect the development of intelligence, it also contributes to inter- and intracultural variability, both in the patterning of intelligence and in the realization of genic potentialities for developing intelligence. It determines the extent to which existing genic endowment can be converted into overt functional capacity. Moreover, it helps determine which *particular* components will be selectively emphasized as the latter capacity undergoes differentiation with advancing age.

Culture, social class, and family have many ways of influencing attained level of cognitive development. Through operation of these factors, more or less opportunity for training and experience can be provided, more or less encouragement and stimulation can be offered, and intellectual attainment can be selectively valued and rewarded. Thus substantial differences in ultimate outcome may exist among individuals with comparable genic potentiality. Personality variables of temperamental and environmental origin play a similar role. Especially important in this connection are:

1. Such determinants of *task-oriented* motivation as intellectual curiosity, activity level, and venturesomeness
2. Intensity and area of ego involvement
3. Such correlates of ego enhancement motivation as need for achievement, competitiveness, responsiveness to prestige incentives, level of ego aspiration, goal tenacity, frustration tolerance, and anxiety level

4. Need for volitional and executive independence[7]

Intellectually gifted children tend to excel in most of these traits (Light-foot, 1951; Terman & Oden, 1949). Some of the positive relationship between motivational and intellectual superiority can be attributed to their common association with high socioeconomic status or to the better ability of more intelligent children to perceive the characterological ingredients of success. However, it is entirely conceivable that level of motivation directly influences extent of actualization of genic potentialities for developing intelligence (Zigler & Butterfield, 1968). Independent and competitive children, for example, tend to show large increases in IQ in the period from 6 to 10 years of age (Sontag & Kagan, 1963).

### The Problem of Modifiability

Once we grant that the IQ represents a *multiply determined functional capacity*, in the development of which experiential and motivational factors play an important regulatory role, it is superfluous to inquire whether it can be modified by significant changes in such factors. The more relevant questions at this point are the extent of modification that is possible and the conditions under which it occurs. The most important limiting factors are: (1) irreversible loss in attainable capacity following prolonged failure to actualize genic potentiality; (2) diminished plasticity with increasing age; and (3) the crucial role of genic influences in setting absolute as well as relative restrictions on the amount of change that can occur. From these considerations it is apparent that significant environmental modification is optimum in early childhood and after correction of serious deprivation. It is hardly likely that discriminable changes in IQ will be found following improvement in an environment that is already reasonably adequate from the standpoint of intellectual stimulation and motivation.

Before changes in IQ can be validly interpreted as evidence of environmental modification of cognitive capacity, it should be obvious that such changes must be reliably greater than fluctuations attributable to *measurement* factors alone. Failure to take this consideration into account has led to many unwarranted and exaggerated claims regarding the modifiability of the IQ. Hence, before we review studies of the effects of such factors as foster-home placement, continued institutionalization, or preschool attendance on level of intellectual functioning, we would do well to consider various nonenvironmental sources of change.

[7] When overprotecting parents try to keep their children emotionally dependent or when the latter attempt to retain an infantile, dependent status, failure to develop intellectual competence admirably serves both purposes (Stover, 1953). See also Sontag et al., (1955). Children from homes characterized by warmth, freedom of exploration, and "acceleratory pressure" make the largest gains in IQ (Baldwin et al., 1945).

First, because of very large errors of measurement in infancy and early childhood, infant and preschool scales are not even very reliable measures of current "intellectual" status. Many of these errors of measurement lead to underestimation of a given child's actual intelligence; in other instances intelligence is overestimated. In either case there is a tendency toward regression to the mean upon subsequent testing (statistical regression). Relatively large changes in measured IQ, reflective of test unreliability, therefore occur irrespective of any concomitant alteration in environment. Instability of such origin should certainly not be confused with evidence of genuine plasticity (J. E. Anderson, 1939).

Second, because of their emphasis on neuromuscular and sensorimotor functions, infant scales do not really measure abstract verbal ability. Thus they have very little predictive value for later intellectual status. Scores on infant scales therefore constitute neither an adequate baseline from which to measure subsequent gains or losses in relative intellectual standing nor an adequate criterion in terms of which infant or preschool subjects may be matched for relative intellectual ability (J. E. Anderson, 1939; McCall, Hogarty, & Hurlburt, 1972).

Simply on the basis of actual genotypic capacity for abstract cognitive functioning that is *not* measured by the initial test, large *spurious* increments and decrements in intelligence are registered in later years. For example, quite apart from any environmental influence, progressive decline in IQ may be anticipated from poorly endowed orphanage children simply because of their spuriously high scores on infant scales. Contrariwise, progressive increases in IQ may be anticipated from well-endowed orphanage children simply because their genic potentialities for developing abstract intelligence are underestimated by the infant scales. Selective factors that operate in the adoption of orphanage children (greater likelihood of placing brighter, better-endowed children) may thus account, in part, for the retention or even improvement of the initial IQ status of adopted children. In evaluating the gains associated with a "good" foster-home or nursery-school environment, it is also important to realize that test disadvantage (relative unfamiliarity with specific test material or indifferent test motivation) is more likely to occur in an impoverished than in a reasonably adequate environment.

In appraising studies of attempted modification of the IQ, attention should also be paid to the principle of filial regression[8] and to the possibility of genically oriented *intraindividual variation* in rate of growth. Thus, quite independently of any errors of measurement or of any change in the environment, the children of intellectually dull individuals tend to score

---

[8] The tendency for children of parents manifesting deviant traits to score closer to the mean than their parents with respect to these traits.

higher than their parents on intelligence tests. Many children also show considerable spontaneous fluctuation in relative status during their growth careers.

## Deprivation and Enrichment

Because of the great practical importance of the possibility of modifying intellectual capacity, a voluminous and highly controversial literature dealing with the effects of environmental deprivation and enrichment has arisen during the past four decades. Interpretation of this literature is extremely difficult since very few studies have been sufficiently well controlled to exclude many nonenvironmental sources of measured change in IQ. In general, the weight of the evidence suggests two tentative conclusions. First, serious and prolonged deprivation, especially during late infancy and the preschool years, seems capable of inflicting *permanent* damage on intellectual growth. Second, enrichment of the existing environment can effect substantial improvement of intellectual status in young children with a prior history of serious deprivation.

### Effects of Deprivation

We have already considered evidence of the immediate and long-term detrimental effects of early cognitive deprivation on sensorimotor, language, and intellectual development. Such studies are obviously vulnerable to criticism on the grounds of the unreliability of the infant scales employed and on the basis of inadequate matching of control and experimental groups (Pinneau, 1955). Unqualified dismissal of these findings, on the other hand, is unwarranted when they are considered in the larger context of related evidence. In the first place, the very grossness of the findings, and their consistent replication by many independent investigators in different parts of the world, compensate in part for their methodological weaknesses. Second, they are consistent with observational and clinical data on the children concerned, with studies of animal deprivation, and with studies of older children growing up in orphanages and in depressed areas.

It seems highly probable, as stated previously, that the longer children remain in substandard environmental conditions, for example, orphanages (Skeels & Fillmore, 1937; Skeels et al., 1938) or with mentally retarded mothers (Speer, 1940), the progressively lower their IQs become in comparison with the IQs of children reared in more favorable environments. Providing greater credibility for these findings are reports of progressive decline in the intelligence test scores of isolated mountain and canalboat children who also grow up in intellectually nonstimulating and unchallenging environments (Asher, 1935; Gordon, 1923; Sherman & Key, 1932).

The facilitating effect of migration to and prolonged residence in the North on the IQs of southern black children has already been considered.

In general, prolonged exposure to extremely disadvantaged environments depresses the IQ about 20 points—more during the preschool years than in older children (Bloom, 1964a). However, some of the loss registered by children who remain in the less favorable environments is attributable (1) to relatively poor genic endowment and (2) to progressively greater test disadvantage as intelligence tests place increasing emphasis on verbal abilities. Further, despite the so-called "leveling effect" of the institutional environment variability in intelligence scores does not decline with advancing age (J. E. Anderson, 1939), thereby demonstrating the prepotent influence of original differences in genic endowment.

When orphanage children from relatively poor hereditary and social backgrounds are placed at an early age in superior foster homes, there is evidence of either improvement in IQ (Freeman, Holzinger, & Mitchell, 1928) or of maintenance of an above-average rate of intellectual growth that is sustained over many years (Skodak, 1939; Skodak & Skeels, 1949). Part of these changes may reflect the influence of an improved environment. But any complete explanation must also take into account the effects of filial regression and selective adoption as well as the greater probability of test disadvantage and unfavorable test conditions at the time of initial testing.

The provision of an enriched (experimental) nursery-school environment to orphanage children has much the same effect as placement in a good foster home; it raises intelligence level only in the very young among those who have been seriously disadvantaged (Reymert & Hinton, 1940). In comparison with corresponding groups of control children, experimental children who initially test relatively high do not lose ground after a period of one-half to two and one-half years; and experimental children who initially test relatively low make larger gains (Skeels et al., 1938). Kirk (1958) and Sayegh and Dennis (1965) have also demonstrated the value of systematic intellectual stimulation in raising the IQ scores of mentally retarded preschool children.

During the past decade, numerous enriched training programs, such as Project Headstart, have been started with the purpose of enriching the background of the culturally disadvantaged urban child. This movement was encouraged by the Johnson Administration "War on Poverty." The primary focus was for early intervention with younger children, although some attention was given to high-school students entering college. Many of these programs have experienced success, whereas others have not shown long-term gains. Deutsch and Brown (1964) found that preschool and later training increased the IQ scores of disadvantaged urban children. The effect is cumulative, being greater at grade 5 than at grade 1. The investigators of the early training project at Peabody College (Gray & Klaus, 1965) reported that the preschool program resulted in average IQ gains, but three years later IQs declined in the children who did not receive special training. Other investigation on the effects of a preschool experience with disadvantaged children shows that children given the early school experience made gains in IQ (Beller, 1973).

An extensive evaluation of Head Start programs (Westinghouse & Ohio University, 1970) indicated that school readiness for Head Start youngsters at grade 1 approached the national norm. However, by the end of third grade their academic achievement was one year below the national norm. More recently, Larson and Dittman (1975) in analyzing state-level data revealed that even the most effective compensatory programs at the primary grades do not show cumulative gains. Although it is too soon to establish definitive conclusions on the value of compensatory education, there is indication for a need to give continued help in basic cognitive skills to disadvantaged students at all levels including the intermediate and secondary grades (Hanesian & Regan, 1976; Larson & Dittmann, 1975).

### Effects of Enrichment

Quite unlike its effects on children reared under substandard home or school conditions, a program of school enrichment cannot be expected to increase intelligence test scores when provided to children who *already* enjoy reasonably adequate educational opportunities. Although children attending preschool tend to have a slightly higher mean IQ than non–preschool children (Wellman, 1945), the difference is small enough to be accounted for on the basis of dissimilarity in parental IQ, errors of measurement, and the advantage of superior test rapport.[9] In support of this interpretation is the fact that children who initially test high tend to make lower scores on retesting, despite the intervening nursery-school experience (Goodenough, 1940). Moreover, no significant differences are found when experimental and control groups are carefully matched with respect to home background (Goodenough, 1940; Olson & Hughes, 1940). Kindergarten children who receive an intensive program of training in activities related to the Primary Mental Abilities Tests make larger gains than control children on these latter tests but not on a different and more general test of intelligence (Holloway, 1954). This suggests that the improvement in mental test scores following such training is largely a specific practice effect rather than a genuine gain in intellectual status.

Prolonged schooling (H. E. Jones, 1954) also probably does not appreciably modify an individual's basic cognitive capacity. It is true that follow-up studies of children matched for IQ in the eighth grade indicate that even 20 years later reliable differences in intelligence test scores appear in favor of those who completed more grades in school (Lorge, 1945). Nevertheless,

---

[9] The same general conclusion applies to studies of curriculum enrichment at the elementary school level (Goodenough, 1940).

gains are proportional to initial status and are rarely great enough to alter the relative positions of individuals in the original ranking of IQ. Improvement in IQ accompanying college attendance is largely a function of test advantage accruing from continued academic pursuits and of selective factors (high academic aptitude) associated with admission to and success in college (H. E. Jones, 1954). Continued schooling, in turn, further enhances the differentiation of general intellectual ability along those abstract verbal lines making for high scores on intelligence tests. In a number of subtests involving reasoning and abstract ability, improvement continues until the end of the college period (Hartson, 1936; Rogers, 1930; Shuey, 1948; R. L. Thorndike, 1948). Furthermore, the particular areas in which greatest improvement occurs (for example, verbal or numerical ability) seem to depend on the area of specialization in college (Hartson, 1936). It is therefore difficult to avoid the implication that schooling differentially influences the growth of the more complex components of verbal intelligence.

Conrad, Freeman, and Jones stress two further implications of these data:

> In order to secure the full development of intelligence, either to fit the individual for his highest vocational attainment, or for discharging the responsibilities of citizenship, or for realizing the fullest development of personality, it is essential to continue general education beyond the teens. This does not imply full-time schooling for all. For many, it means participation in adult education. Many persons can better carry forward the later stages of this intellectual development in association with the prosecution of a vocation rather than as a full-time enterprise.
>
> One of the aims of [mental measurement] . . . has been to find means of measuring *inherent* capacity and growth. So far as the later stages of development of the higher intellectual powers are concerned, this aim seems incapable of realization. Without training, the later stages are not evidenced. . . . It is desirable to free our tests so far as possible from the effects of *specific* variations in training, but to free them from the *general* effects of education is probably impossible. To seek to do so is to restrict the tests to the measurement of narrow and perhaps unimportant functions (Conrad et al., 1944, pp. 178, 179).

### Parent–Child Resemblance

Correlations between parent and child IQ are initially about zero (H. E. Jones, 1954; Skodak, 1939) but increase gradually with advancing age as amount of overlap between the abilities measured by intelligence tests at successive age levels increases. By school age, parent–child correlations are in the neighborhood of .50 (Burks, 1928; Conrad & Jones, 1940; Leahy, 1935). However, since the existing degree of relationship could reflect the influence of either heredity or environment, these data shed little light on the nature–nurture problem. Nevertheless, two clues point to the greater weight of heredity. If environment were a highly significant factor, we would expect that: (1) since mothers bear the major burden of child rearing in our society, the IQ of children would be more highly correlated with mothers' than with fathers' IQ; and (2) since siblings share a more uniform developmental environment with each other than with their parents, intersibling resemblance would be greater than parent–child resemblance. Since available data (Conrad & Jones, 1940) confirm neither hypothesis, the environmentalist position is accordingly weakened.

More crucial evidence on the nature–nurture problem is provided by comparison of foster-parent–foster-child and true-parent–true-child resemblances in IQ. Foster children share only their foster parents' environment, whereas true children share both heredity and environment with their parents. In the foster-home situation, where the genic basis of resemblance is removed, parent–child correlations (Burke, 1928; Leahy, 1935) are considerably lower[10] (approximately .20) than in the natural-home situation (approximately .50). Similarly, intrapair differences between children whose *own* fathers are at opposite extremes of the occupational hierarchy are markedly higher than intrapair differences between children whose *foster* fathers are in comparable positions (Burks, 1938). It seems, therefore, that the greater part of the variance in children's IQs is attributable to genic rather than to environmental factors (Honzik, 1957). This conclusion is consistent with findings (Skodak, 1939; Skodak & Skeels, 1949) that whereas the IQ of foster children is only negligibly related to their foster parents' educational status, it is moderately correlated at school age with true mothers' educational status (.35) and IQ (.40). The latter correlation is almost as high as that between children and true parents who are domiciled together.

### Sibling and Twin Resemblance

We have already noted that the absence of significant differences between the parent-child and intersibling correlations in IQ lends support to the hereditarian position. Other related findings point in the same direction:

1. The resemblance between true siblings reared in the same home is substantially greater than the resemblance between foster siblings (Freeman, Holzinger, & Mitchell, 1928).

2. Similarity with respect to age and sex does not increase intersibling resemblance in IQ, as one might expect if environmental factors exercised considerable weight (H. E. Jones, 1954).

---

[10] Some of the resemblance between children and foster parents may also reflect the influence of selective adoption—the tendency to match foster and true parents in terms of IQ and occupational background (Conrad & Jones, 1940; Leahy, 1935).

3. Resemblances between foster siblings are no greater than foster-parent–foster-child resemblances despite greater similarity in environment (Burks, 1928; Freeman et al., 1928; Leahy, 1935).

4. Separation of siblings does not lower intersibling correlations (Burt, 1966; H. E. Jones, 1954).

5. When *interfamilial* environmental variability is eliminated, as in the orphanage situation, neither the resemblance between sibling pairs nor the degree of variability in IQ scores is correspondingly reduced (H. E. Jones, 1954).

Comparative studies of identical and fraternal twins shed more light on the nature–nurture problem, inasmuch as identical twins have approximately identical genotypes, whereas fraternal twins are genically no more similar than ordinary siblings. Here, too, the findings give little comfort to environmentalists. Identical twins are markedly more similar in IQ than fraternal twins (correlations of .80 to .90 as against .50 to .60); and even when identical twins are separated, differences in IQ are generally smaller than among fraternal twins reared together (Burt, 1958, 1966; Newman, Freeman, & Holzinger, 1937; Woodworth, 1941). Sizable differences in the IQs of separated identical twins are only found when their educational backgrounds are highly dissimilar. On the basis of these small differences in IQ when heredity is held constant, while the usual degree of environmental variability prevails, Woodworth (1941) concludes that "the differences found among the children of an ordinary community are not accounted for, except in small measure, by differences in home and schooling."

## Socioeconomic Differences

The influence of environmental stimulation on the development of general intelligence is fairly well established. Prior to 18 months of age, zero or low negative correlations are found between scores on infant intelligence scales and various socioeconomic factors (Bayley & Jones, 1937). Thereafter the magnitude of correlational indices increases rapidly, and at school age varies between .30 and .50 for different educational, occupational, and economic criteria of social-class status (Bayley & Jones, 1937). The early absence of relationship simply indicates that intelligence tests cannot possibly measure the same cognitive abilities during infancy as in later years. The increasing correspondence between IQ and socioeconomic variables as degree of test overlap increases, may reflect either the cumulative impact of environmental influences or "an increasing manifestation of hereditary potentialities" (Bayley & Jones, 1937; Jensen, 1968).

Beginning with the preschool period, a range of about 20 points separates children of the highest and lowest socioeconomic groups (Deutsch & Brown, 1964; Terman & Merrill, 1937). The relationship between children's relative intellectual status and father's position in the occupational hierarchy is practically linear (Deutsch & Brown, 1964; Terman & Merrill, 1937), and in correlational terms varies between .20 and .43 for different tests of intelligence (Eells & Davis, 1951).

Upper socioeconomic groups also contribute a disproportionately large number of intellectually gifted and a disproportionately small number of mentally retarded children to the total population (McGeehee & Lewis, 1942). These relationships refer, of course, to group averages, since differences within an occupational group are actually much larger than differences between the means of various groups. Although social class differences are greatest in the area of verbal abilities (Eells & Davis, 1951), significant differences have also been found for all of Thurstone's primary mental abilities (Havighurst & Breese, 1947) as well as for other nonverbal tests.

The interpretation of these social class differences in intelligence has led to much heated controversy between hereditarians and environmentalists. Actually, three different kinds of explanations based respectively on measurement, environmental, and genic factors seem equally plausible, but the evidence currently available is not sufficiently definitive to establish their relative weight. The measurement argument stems from a certain amount of middle-class bias in the construction of most intelligence tests. This creates test disadvantage for the lower-class child and results in an underestimate of his true level of cognitive functioning. In order to derive a valid and fair estimate of intellectual capacity from test performance, it is necessary that: (1) specific test items be based on experiences and symbols that are equally available and familiar to individuals from all social class strata; and (2) test materials arouse comparable degrees of interest and motivation in persons of different social-class origin (Davis, 1948; Eells & Davis, 1951).

Most present-day tests are heavily weighted with specific items that are more familiar and appealing to middle- than lower-class children, and with the kinds of *cognitive functions* (vocabulary, linguistic skills) that are particularly emphasized in middle-class environments.[11] The tests are thus "unfair" in the sense that their specific item content does not give the lower-class child a fair opportunity to demonstrate his *attained* level of cognitive capacity. Intelligence tests do not purport to measure either genic potentialities in themselves or noncognitive abilities. Thus they should not be considered unfair simply because they fail to measure level of functioning in those noncognitive abilities in which lower-class children excel or because the middle-class environment is experientially or motivationally more propitious for the development of native cognitive endowment. The

[11] As noted above, however, large socioeconomic differences also prevail for other nonverbal tests.

very fact that these tests favor middle-class children demonstrates that the environment *can* operate selectively to develop certain aspects of intellectual endowment. This conclusion is compatible with the findings that intelligence becomes more and more differentiated with increasing age (Garrett et al., 1935; Segel, 1948), and that sex differences in many specific intellectual functions increase or reverse themselves as children grow older (Kuhlen, 1952).

Acceptance of the test-bias explanation of social-class differences by no means rules out the genic or environmental interpretations.[12] Insofar as environmental factors contribute to some of the variance in intelligence test scores, it would not be unreasonable to expect that differential social-class levels of stimulation and motivation affect extent of *actualization* of genic endowment. Evidence for this type of mediation of environmental influence comes from the finding that children's IQs are more highly correlated with parents' education than with the economic status of their homes (Loevinger, 1940; Bayley, 1970). Social-class environment also *selectively* influences the differentiation of intellectual and other abilities. This is shown by the fact that middle-class children are superior to their lower-class contemporaries in both verbal *and* mechanical abilities at age 10, but are superior only in the former ability at age 16. The environmentalist position is weakened, however, by the existence of large social-class differences in the *preschool* period (Terman & Merrill, 1937), by the failure of social-class differentials to increase with advancing age (Shuttleworth, 1940), and by the significantly greater correlation of foster children's IQ's with *true* mothers' than with *foster* parents' educational status (Skodak, 1939; Skodak & Skeels, 1949).

The hereditarian position rests on the assumption that (1) since there is indisputable evidence of substantial genic contribution to individual differences in IQ and (2) since more intelligent persons, on the average, choose and are selectively successful in the intellectually more demanding occupations, it is reasonable to ascribe at least part of the consistently obtained social-class differences in IQ to genic variability in cognitive potential. The tendency for more highly endowed individuals to reach the higher rungs of the occupational ladder is especially evident in a society characterized by a fair degree of social mobility. Since such persons also tend to marry at their own intellectual level (H. E. Jones, 1954), their offspring acquire a genic advantage from both parents. Although logically tenable, it is understandably difficult to put this hypothesis to empirical test. It is supported, in part, by the applicability of principle of filial regression to social-class

---

[12] The finding that approximately the same social class differentials appear on the Davis-Eells "culture fair" test as on the Kuhlmann-Finch test (Coleman & Ward, 1955) casts doubt on the claim that the Davis-Eells test is culturally more fair, but does not necessarily invalidate the test-bias hypothesis of social-class differences.

differences. That is, children of professional parents tend to have a lower IQ than their parents, whereas the reverse holds true for children of unskilled laborers (Outhit, 1933).

## Racial Differences

The data on differences in IQ between racial groups are consistent. A survey of 382 studies on this issue (Shuey, 1966) indicated that, on the average, blacks score from 10 to 20 IQ points below whites. These findings were based on a wide range of age groups, from varied geographic locations, using approximately 80 different tests. Shuey (1966) pointed to a hereditarian conclusion on the native differences between whites and blacks in intelligence. In 1969, Jensen marshaled evidence to support the view that genetic factors are more important than environmental influences in determining racial differences in IQ. His article (Jensen, 1969) stimulated strong rebuttals by those who believe that it is the interaction between heredity and environment that determines intelligence and that the totality of the evidence does not exclude the role of environmental factors in accounting for these differences. For example, Lesser, Fifer, and Clark (1965) have reported some relevant racial and ethnic differences in school-age children for different mental abilities. On verbal ability Jewish children scored highest, blacks second, Chinese third and Puerto Ricans fourth. On reasoning ability, the rank order was Chinese, Jews, blacks, and Puerto Ricans. On number ability, the ranks were: Jews, Chinese, Puerto Ricans, blacks. On space, the order was Chinese, Jews, Puerto Ricans, blacks. These findings raise the question of the extent to which the ethnic differences result from innate potentials or from differences between the groups of cultural value systems and hence of differential rewards for skills in mental abilities tested (Bayley, 1970).

The difference in average intelligence test scores between racial groups is not questioned, but at the present time there is no unequivocal or definitive evidence regarding the causes for lower average scores. Birch and Gussow (1970) maintain that many biological and health factors of non-genic origin affect intelligence. Low intelligence, for example, can be caused by prenatal conditions such as malnutrition in the mother during and before pregnancy, insufficient oxygen to the fetus, disease or the use of drugs. During the child's life, measured intelligence as amply documented above is affected not only by genic variables but also by home environment, school, society, and by the measuring instrument employed. All of these factors negatively affect the phenotypic intelligence of black children who come from poverty backgrounds. The hereditarian point of view, however, should not be ruled out on purely a priori grounds or because it is considered "politically reactionary." Just as genes determine certain physical traits in a racial group, they could conceivably in part determine certain intellectual traits. The only relevant arguments bearing on this issue must be based on empirical evidence that attempts to minimize environmental and test-bias differences between racial groups. Unfortunately in most studies there has been no attempt to control adequately for such variables. In addition, there is no evidence that would warrant differential educational treatment of racial subgroups.. Finally, in studying racial differences in intelligence and in considering their educational implications, it is important to note there are greater differences in IQ within than between racial groups.

### Urban–Rural Differences

The mean IQ of rural children is consistently lower than that of urban children and also tends to diminish with increasing age (Asher, 1935; Chapanis & Williams, 1945; Wheeler, 1942). As in the case of lower-class children, this inferiority is most marked on verbal and speed items and is undoubtedly attributable, in part, to test bias (H. E. Jones, 1954). Intelligence scales are typically devised by urban-reared psychologists and are validated on urban schoolchildren. However, since rural children also do more poorly on items presenting no special experiential or motivational handicap, it is unwarranted to ascribe all urban–rural differences to test disadvantage. Equally plausible are explanations based either on the cumulative impact of a low level of intellectual stimulation or on the selective migration of more highly endowed individuals to urban areas.

### Intelligence and Family Size

In most investigations of the relationship between IQ and number of siblings in the family, a negative correlation of .20 to .30 is reported (Anastasi, 1956). Since there is no evidence whatsoever of any intrinsic relationship between IQ and procreative ability, only two other explanations seem plausible. First, the presence of a large number of children in the family may reduce the amount of cognitive stimulation available for each child. The per capita expenditure on education, recreation, housing, medical care, and so forth is ordinarily lower when there are many siblings in the family. Even more important, in terms of language development, the extent of parent–child contact is restricted (Nisbet, 1953). Second, IQ and size of family are indirectly related by virtue of a common relationship to social-class status; that is, persons in the upper economic strata tend to have both a higher IQ and to raise relatively small families.

To the extent that the intellectual superiority of their children is a function of either measurement or environmental factors, the inverse relationship between parents' fertility and social-class status obviously has no implications for eugenics. However, insofar as persons in the upper occupational strata may be presumed to possess a superior genic endowment with respect to cognitive capacity, their relatively low fertility rate may be expected, over the course of many generations (in the absence of compensatory genic factors), to contribute to a national decline in the genotypic basis of intelligence.

## Intelligence as a Predictor of Academic Achievement

Academic achievement or success in various subject-matter fields generally correlates about .50 with intelligence or academic aptitude test scores. Some components of academic aptitude tests such as vocabulary (Locke, 1963), reasoning, and information (French, 1964) have more predictive value than others for scholastic achievement. Intelligence test scores are also negatively correlated with dropout rate from high school (Dillon, 1949). Specific aptitude tests such as quantitative ability or numerical reasoning naturally correlate much more highly than IQ with such related subject-matter fields as mathematics. In any case, the predictive value of academic aptitude scores varies greatly with such factors as sex (Locke, 1963; McGuire, 1961) and type of community (McGuire, 1961).

Low intelligence can apparently be compensated for, in part at least, by grading learning tasks to pupils' current achievement levels. When this is done for arithmetic materials, no significant differences are found among children of low, average, and high IQ in learning, retention, and transfer (Klausmeier & Check, 1962; Klausmeier & Feldhusen, 1959). Longer exposure times can similarly compensate for the effects of low intelligence on level of perceptual organization (Allen, Tyrrel, Schulz, & Koons, 1958). Considerable evidence generally supports the proposition that instructional aides, organizing devices, and superior textual materials differentially benefit the duller and initially less knowledgeable as opposed to the brighter and initially more knowledgeable student. Correlations between scholastic aptitude and subject-matter achievement tests tend to decline consistently from the beginning to the end of the course in question. However, this same trend toward progressively decreasing discrepancies between the achievement levels of the bright and dull does not necessarily prevail when pupils are permitted to learn at their own rate of speed.

Intelligence level also influences *qualitative* aspects of achievement. It affects the rate of acquiring learning sets (Ellis, 1958; House & Zeaman, 1959; Kaufman & Peterson, 1958; Stevenson & Swartz, 1958), performance on structured categorization tasks (Stephens, 1964), and the strategy of problem solving (Battig, 1957; Klausmeier & Loughlin, 1961). High-IQ subjects are more likely to correct mistakes independently, to verify solutions, to use a logical approach, to employ a more efficient method, and to be persistent.

It has been argued, with some validity, that since achievement tests take into account both motivation in past learning tasks and scholastic aptitude, they are more highly predictive of future achievement than are intelligence tests. Thus grades in Algebra I correlate more highly with success in Algebra II than does either general scholastic aptitude or fresh-man grade-point average (Sommerfeld & Tracy, 1961); and high-school grade-point average predicts academic achievement at the university level better than do scholastic aptitude scores (Endler & Steinberg, 1963). Some studies (Getzels & Jackson, 1962; Torrance, 1963) suggest that so-called tests of creativity correlate just as highly with academic achievement as do intelligence tests. A methodologically more definitive study by Flescher (1963), however, failed to confirm this finding and did not demonstrate the existence of any significant generality of function among various tests of creativity.

Why is the relationship between scholastic aptitude and academic achievement only moderate in degree? For one thing, measures of neither variable are completely reliable or valid. More important, however, is the operation of other relevant factors, such as motivation, interests, person-ality traits, adjustment, and family, peer-group, social-class, and cultural influences, that affect the degree to which existing scholastic aptitude is actualized in the form of academic achievement. Comparison of education-ally successful and unsuccessful gifted children reveals that the successful have better study habits, exhibit more self-control and "compensatory" as contrasted to "protective" ego mechanisms, have more realistic levels of aspiration, and excel in such personality traits as dependability, self-reli-ance, ambition, investigativeness, and persistence (W. D. Lewis, 1941; Locke, 1963; Regensburg, 1931; Sears, 1940; Terman & Oden, 1949). Dif-ferences between students who complete one curriculum in college and those who complete another are also greater in interests than in abilities (J. W. French, 1961; King, 1958). Parental attitudes, aspirations, and financial resources, as well as students' degree of insight into their own abilities, are highly related to whether or not high-school graduates will attend and remain in college (Kahl, 1953; Parsons, 1959). Scholastic apti-tude scores and rank in high-school graduating class have more predictive value for boys than for girls with respect to entrance into and graduation from college (Kahl, 1953). This fact confirms the greater value our culture places on male vocational achievement. McClelland (1973) further reported evidence that school achievement in itself is not a valid predictor of suc-cess in the world of work. He points out that even when IQ does correlate significantly with job success, the relationship may be reflecting the values and habits influenced by social class.

As a group, intellectually superior individuals tend to gravitate toward professional occupations, to be more successful vocationally, and to experi-ence less unemployment (Terman & Oden, 1949). *Within* a group of gifted children (IQs over 140), however, the adults successful 25 years later were as children more integrated in goal structure, more self-confident, and more persevering than the unsuccessful adults, even though the two groups were quite evenly matched in intelligence. We can conclude, therefore, that better-than-average intelligence is undoubtedly a vocational asset, but given this degree of intellectual ability, unusual success in a vocation is more a function of special talent or creativity and of various personality traits than of extremely high general intelligence. There is no evidence to indicate that creativity and general intelligence are positively related beyond this critical minimal point.

*Under- and Overachievement*

Considering the methodological hazards involved in the identification of under- and overachievers (students who achieve less or more than could be anticipated by their scholastic aptitude scores) and the only moderate degree of relationship between academic aptitude and school achievement, it is somewhat questionable what practical utility these widely used concepts have for educational practice (Thorndike, 1961, 1963). In any case, underachievers, as contrasted to achievers, tend to be characterized by more withdrawal behavior and by less "social, work-oriented interaction with peers" (Perkins, 1965); by more negative self-concepts (Shaw, Edson, & Bell, 1960); by higher mechanical and artistic interests and by lower verbal and mathematical aptitude (Frankel, 1960); and by membership in lower-status occupational groups (Frankel, 1960).

The underachievement syndrome starts as early as the third grade in the case of boys, but not until the ninth grade in the case of girls (Shaw & McCuen, 1960). Bright underachievers in college have lower and less clearly defined "real-life" (academic and vocational) goals than bright normal achievers (Todd, Terrell, & Frank, 1962). But the reverse paradoxically appears to be true when the achievement needs of overachieving and normally achieving college students are assessed by thematically induced achievement imagery (Cole, Jacobs, Zubok, Fagot, & Hunter, 1962). In both studies these differential findings apply only to males. Differentially high thematically induced achievement imagery is elicited for achieving versus underachieving adolescent girls only in achievement-oriented conditions and in relation to female (as opposed to male) figures (Lesser, Krawitz, & Packard, 1963). The authors suggest that achieving girls tend to accept academic achievement as appropriate for females whereas the underachieving girls do not.

# 8

# PROVIDING FOR INDIVIDUAL DIFFERENCES IN INTELLECTUAL ABILITY

We have already seen how intellectual ability influences school learning in a general way. How are we to make appropriate pedagogic allowances for the individual differences in intellectual ability that are found in the average classroom? Are any special provisions indicated for gifted, mentally retarded, and culturally disadvantaged children, or for children with learning disabilities?

In general—and for many reasons—individualization of instruction within a heterogeneous classroom is more feasible than grouping by IQ scores. If grouping is to make any pedagogic sense at all it should be differential in nature (in accordance with subject-matter aptitude or achievement). Although nonpromotion may have a more deleterious effect on scholastic achievement than "social promotion," the latter results in the production of functionally illiterate high-school "graduates" or dropouts who have a distorted conception of the relationship between achievement and reward in the real world.

With respect to intellectually gifted (high-IQ) children, "acceleration" appears to be preferable to "enrichment." In handling the mentally retarded, the principal issue is whether to assign them to regular or special-education classes. This issue, in turn, depends upon the pupil's ability level and adaptive capacity and upon the *possibilities for appropriate individualization of instruction within regular classrooms. The learning-disabled child, although normal in intelligence, exhibits difficulties in particular intellectual skills, along with hyperactivity, distractabiltiy, and emotional lability. These children can benefit from expert tutoring in the area of their disabilities and from counseling for their secondary adjustment problems.*

*The culturally disadvantaged child usually comes from a lower-class home that is generally demoralized socially and provides markedly inadequate intellectual stimulation (particularly in language-related skills). Preventively, the culturally disadvantaged can benefit from preschool training in reading and in language and other intellectual skills. To have lasting effects, however, this special training should be extended into the early elementary-school years. In any case, the culturally disadvantaged child should not be presented with advanced subject-matter material until the basic intellectual skills are mastered and consolidated, and until adequate cognitive and developmental readiness is present. Current educational practices in most inner-city schools do not take these considerations into account. Thus they both compound the original cultural disadvantage stemming from the home situation and lead to further demoralization and ego-disinvolvement from scholastic achievement.*

Previous discussion of both developmental and particularized (subject-matter background) readiness for learning, as well as of general intelligence and particular scholastic aptitudes, has made it abundantly clear that a wide range of individual differences exists at any given age level of pupils. These differences are expressed in general (overall) mode of cognitive functioning, in approach to problem solving, in subject-matter sophistication, in general level of intelligence, in specific academic aptitudes, in motivation for learning, in intellectual curiosity, in self-critical ability, in need for precise meanings and integrated knowledge, and in ability to think independently, critically, and creatively. Obviously, therefore, no realistic system of teaching can afford to overlook such differences. Hence individualization of teaching must necessarily constitute one of the primary goals of instruction. As far as possible, the individual student, rather than the class as a whole, must become the working unit in the instructional process. Each child must be challenged at a level appropriate to his or her potentialities, and encouraged to learn at a commensurate pace.

The need for individualization of instruction is also implicit in the school's responsibility to develop problem-solving ability, to encourage intellectual curiosity and initiative, to promote independent, original, and critical thinking, and to stimulate pupils' desire and ability to learn on their own. As pointed out above, these educational objectives are neither incompatible with meaningful reception learning nor inconsistent with the primary responsibility of the school for organizing and directing the curriculum. Nor do they constitute the primary goals of education or the principal means of transmitting subject-matter knowledge.

In general, two principal approaches have been taken to the problem of individual differences in pupils: ability grouping and individualized instruction. These approaches are by no means mutually exclusive. Obviously, some form of group instruction is inevitable because *completely* individualized instruction is not economically feasible. Neither is it necessary, desirable, or efficient for many educational purposes. Furthermore, learning in a group context has many *positive* advantages of its own—both from the standpoint of cognitive development and from the standpoint of the child's emotional and social needs. Evidently, then, some form of compromise must be found between grouping and individualization.

## Advantages and Disadvantages of Grouping

Ability grouping purportedly takes account of individual differences in two ways. First, by bringing together children of similar ability, it permits the teacher to gear the level and method of instruction to the *particular* level of ability prevailing in the group. The teacher no longer has to accommodate to the hypothetical ability level of the *average* child as the fairest approximation of the group's ability. Thus the teacher can avoid a pace and level of instruction that is too difficult for the dull pupil and too easy for the bright pupil.

Second, when pupils of comparable ability interact in the learning process, "social facilitation" of learning presumably occurs by making it possible for bright children to be stimulated by their intellectual peers. This latter advantage, however, has never been unequivocally demonstrated. Gurnee (1962), for example, found group learning to be superior to individual learning not because of social facilitation but because it provides an opportunity for less successful group members to imitate their more successful classmates. If this is the case, it is evident that the possibilities for such imitation would be even greater in a heterogeneous group. Klausmeier, Wiersma, and Harris (1963) also discovered that although pupils working in small groups learn better initially, they do less well than individual pupils on tests of transfer. The research evidence (Drews, 1959; Fleming, 1959; Herrick, 1960; Spitzer, 1954) generally shows that grouping in small homogeneous units does not itself lead to superior learning outcomes.

On the other hand, there are many disadvantages to grouping.

1. Whichever criterion is chosen as the basis of grouping (chronological age, mental age, social maturity, specific scholastic aptitude, or subject-matter sophistication in a particular discipline), group heterogeneity with respect to most *other* factors is almost inevitably bound to increase.

2. Grouping on the basis of a composite intelligence test score becomes progressively less efficient for purposes of individualization as children's cognitive and scholastic aptitudes become increasingly more differentiated, or less highly intercorrelated, with increasing age.

3. Heterogeneity itself has positive values. It enables children better to adjust to the wide variety of ability levels they meet outside the school environment. It provides intellectual stimulation and models for imitation for dull children, and also gives brighter pupils an opportunity to clarify and consolidate their understanding of concepts by explaining them to less precocious classmates.

4. Ability grouping tends to stigmatize the dull and to generate arrogance and conceit in the bright. This disadvantage, however, has undoubtedly been overemphasized. Children who do not measure up to their contemporaries almost inevitably appreciate their inferiority and suffer self-depreciation with or without ability grouping. It can be argued further that more explicit realization by a child of his relative profile of abilities promotes a more realistic self-concept and level of aspiration.

5. Perhaps most important is the fact that individualization is accomplished more effectively (while simultaneously preserving the advantages of group instruction) by bringing together children of *diverse* ability levels in one class, and by arranging for each pupil to progress at his or her *own* pace by means of varying the amount, nature, and difficulty level of the material learned. In this way, differences in motivation, interest, and curiosity, as well as ability, are taken into account.

Montessori (Rambusch, 1962) discovered long ago that when preschool children are confronted with learning tasks that both interest them and are commensurate with their developmental level of readiness, their attention span is greatly increased, and they manifest much more intellectual curiosity and persistence than is commonly realized.

### Differential Ability Groupng

If ability grouping is practiced at all, it should undoubtedly be based on the results of differential aptitude tests or on particularized measures of subject-matter achievement (for instance, mathematics, science, language arts). In accordance with this point of view, a given pupil is placed in those particular sections of various school subjects that correspond to his relative aptitude or achievement standing in the disciplines in question. One may set up separate sections of a given course or several subgroups within a given section. This procedure is more suitable from grade 7 on than at the elementary-school level.

Other kinds of administrative arrangements are compatible with the principle of grouping. The organization pattern used in more recent years, primarily at the elementary-school level, has been nongrading. The concept of the "nongraded school" (Goodlad, 1971) combines both an extreme emphasis on individualization and acceptance of learning in a group context. First proposed by Montessori (Rambusch, 1962), it permits each child to master the curriculum at his or her own individual rate of speed in a social environment consisting of children of varying ages. It presupposes the availability of a wide range of programmed materials and of a high teacher–pupil ratio. It also envisages the use of older children as emulatory and learning models for their less advanced peers and avoids the stigmatization of nonpromotion.

Also related to the practice of grouping are the approaches of independent study and team teaching. The assigning of independent study or seat work to a portion of the class is a common method that allows the teacher to work in small groups. Similarly, in team teaching, certain activities are conducted by one teacher while other team members are free to work with smaller groups (Bolvin & Glaser, 1971). In any case, whatever the administrative pattern, differential ability grouping implies specialist teachers in the various specialty subjects. It also implies teaching methods and instructional demands that are appropriate for the existing developmental readiness and subject-matter sophistication of the groups in question.

### Individualization

Complementary to differential ability grouping is the provision of individualized instruction (differential assignments) within each group. On theoretical grounds it seems rather self-evident that individualized instruction should be incomparably more efficient than instruction in groups for most aspects of subject-matter learning. Here instruction is geared to the individual pupil's (1) general level of sophistication in a particular discipline, (2) mastery of relevant antecedent concepts and principles, (3) particular preconceptions and misconceptions, (4) general and specific intellectual aptitudes, (5) operating level of abstraction, (6) idiosyncratic cognitive style and relevant personality attributes, (7) progress in mastering a current learning task (for example, consolidation, precision and clarity of new meanings), and (8) most comfortable pace of learning. Thus it necessarily follows that learning outcomes should be superior to those that eventuate when instruction is geared to a hypothetical set of characteristics and requirements reflective of the mean pupil in a group. Surprisingly enough, however, empirical testing and confirmation of this proposition has only recently received attention by educators and educational psychologists.

One of the difficulties here lies in the very narrow conception of what is meant by the individualization of instruction.[1] Until relatively recently the only variables taken into account were scores on a general or differential test of intellectual ability. Similarly when programmed instruction enthusiasts entered the field of individualized instruction, they focused their attention myopically on practice and reinforcement aspects of the current learning task. Ericksen (1967) has stated the case very well in demonstrating that, for the most part, instructional aids have contributed very little thus far to the goal of individualized instruction.

Another important research consideration in this context is the need for testing the separate effects of particular dimensions of individualization and the interactions among them, as opposed to performing global studies in which the separate contributions of different variables are not conceptualized, identified, or measured. This, of course, does not preclude but rather highlights the desirability of multivariate research designs.

Cronbach (1967) discusses adapting education to meet individual differences by presenting various patterns of instruction. One of the approaches favored by most educators is to alter instructional methods to accommodate for strengths and weaknesses in individual pupils. This method of aptitude-treatment interaction matches the pupil's aptitude to the suitable method of teaching. For example, a student who is high in auditory abilities will learn to read more readily if taught by a phonics method. It is evident that in order to match students to treatments, teachers must have some training in diagnostic skills. Further research is needed to provide us with more information about aptitude-treatment interactions and its practical implications for educational programs. Until then, teachers must be aware of individual differences and know that these characteristics call for differential treatment.

Individualization can be implemented better by specialist teachers who are more conversant with subject-matter content, with different methods of presentation, and with diagnostic skills. To be effective, individualization also presupposes continuity between the different levels of instruction to

---

[1] It should be noted here that individualized instruction is not synonymous with self-instruction. Individualized instruction is sometimes best accomplished in a group setting, as, for example, in the learning of those kinds of subject matter calling for group discussion (see below). It may also be teacher- as well as self-directed. Ungraded classes imply both self-instruction and individualized instruction in a group context.

which a child is successively exposed (elementary school, junior and senior high school, and university). The benefits of individualization in elementary school, for example, are largely wasted if a bright pupil who has already mastered most seventh-grade work as a sixth-grader is placed in an undifferentiated and nonindividualized seventh-grade junior-high-school class.

### Programmed Instruction

The highly complex logistical task of individualizing instruction for each pupil in terms of the pupil's differential abilities and aptitudes, cognitive style, personality traits, existing preconceptions, and current performance is rendered much more manageable with the assistance of programmed materials. During the past decade instructional materials have flooded the market. These programmed materials, such as workbooks and tests, are called "software." The machines, such as the computer, are called "hardware."

When using programmed materials, each student works independently at his own optimal pace with sequentially organized materials for self-testing. The careful sequential arrangement and gradation of difficulty that is characteristic of programmed instruction maintains subject-matter readiness by ensuring that each attained increment in learning serves as an appropriate foundation or anchoring post for the learning and retention of subsequent items in the ordered sequence. This is accomplished by optimal self-pacing, by frequent testing and the provision of feedback, and by furnishing adequately spaced reviews and opportunity for differential practice of the more difficult components of a task. Properly programmed materials also take into account the principles of progressive differentiation and integrative reconciliation as implemented in the use of appropriate advance organizers.

Similar to programmed materials, the computer can be used to select the appropriate content and sequence of material and is also invaluable for record keeping, monitoring, pacing, simulation of problem-solving and laboratory situations, and the generation of instructional material. It is questionable, however, whether the advantages the computer offers with respect to the individualization of instruction are that much greater than those inherent in the use of appropriate textbooks, enrichment materials, frequent testing and feedback, and teacher-directed self-instruction as to warrant the tremendous expense involved. Recent technological development, however, promises to make computer-assisted instruction more economically feasible for use in schools.

In any case, the use of programmed and computer-assisted instruction cannot constitute a complete and self-contained program of individualization since it does not provide for pupil-pupil and pupil-teacher interaction. In addition, those aspects of instruction in which knowledge is less well defined and in which the acquisition of independent and critical thinking ability is a major goal obviously require more class discussion and direct teacher participation. But teachers have more time to devote to these latter objectives, to cultivate a questioning attitude toward established knowledge, and to focus on the discovery aspects of acquiring new knowledge if the more stable and substantive aspects of a discipline are learned individually by means of programmed instruction. Lindvall and Bolvin (1967) have indicated effective use of programmed instruction through basic texts, enrichment work, remedial work, and outside assignments.

## Nonpromotion

Nonpromotion constitutes an attempt at homogeneous grouping by withholding progression to the next higher grade from the extremely low achiever. Theoretically it provides a necessary and desirable second opportunity for mastering the same material that the pupil was not able to learn the first time it was presented during the course of a given year or semester. In practice, however, the repeater makes less academic progress than the promoted child of comparable ability and achievement (Goodlad, 1952). Recently, Jackson (1975) reviewed 44 studies on the effects of grade retention. He reports that there is no reliable evidence to indicate that nonpromotion is beneficial for students with scholastic and adjustment difficulties. Although some low achievers do profit from repetition, more of them actually do worse on achievement tests a year later than immediately after failing the grade in question. It is not repetition *itself* that has these damaging effects, but rather the stigma of nonpromotion, the impairment of morale, and the exposure to the same inappropriate methods that previously led to failure. It is true that promoted nonachievers are maladjusted and cannot "keep up" in the new grade. However, they actually do worse by remaining a second time in the same grade—in terms of their schoolwork, their self-confidence, and their acceptance by peers (Gilmore, 1968; Goodlad, 1952; Segel, 1951). The student who is not promoted is more likely to drop out of school and show negative behavior while in school (Thomas & Knudsen, 1965). On the other hand, unearned promotions tend to generate unrealistic attitudes toward, and expectations about, the general relationship between achievement and reward found in adult life.

All of this argues less for a policy of "social promotion" than it does for more imaginative ways of teaching subject matter to pupils who are unable to learn adequately when taught by more conventional methods. Most nonpromoted children come from disadvantaged homes (Hall & Demarest, 1958).

## The Academically Gifted: Enrichment or Acceleration

Individualization in the case of pupils with high intelligence or scholastic aptitude scores generally takes one of two forms. Advocates of *enrichment*—the provision of more advanced, difficult, or supplementary schoolwork to such pupils while keeping them with their chronological and social peers—argue that this procedure avoids social maladjustment among the gifted, equips them better to adapt to persons of all ability levels in later life, and enables them to stimulate their duller agemates. Enrichment is typically accomplished by means of ability grouping, by individualizing instruction within a given class, or by segregating gifted children in special schools.

Proponents of *acceleration*, on the other hand, point out that under present educational conditions it is very difficult for a busy teacher to enrich instruction adequately for gifted pupils (Gallagher & Lucito, 1961). They claim that enrichment usually involves drawing upon subject-matter materials from the next higher level of instruction, thereby creating problems of boredom and loss of interest when the pupil reaches that level. Moreover, special schools often generate unwholesome attitudes of conceit and superiority, as well as isolate the gifted from average children (thereby depriving the latter of necessary social experience and the former of desirable intellectual stimulation). Most important, the proponents of acceleration believe that acceleration *itself* has many positive advantages for pupils planning on professional careers.

Acceleration can be implemented in many different ways: by early admission to school and college; by double promotion; by admission to college with advanced standing; and by such means of concentrating instruction as lengthening the school year, completing two years of work in one, and more rapid self-pacing in ungraded classes. The latter procedures avoid the hazard of possibly missing certain important learnings that are essential in sequentially organized curriculums.

In general, reviews of acceleration procedures (Shannon, 1957) indicate that they do not handicap the gifted child either socially, emotionally, or in terms of academic accomplishment. Children who are admitted at an early age to kindergarten (Worcester, 1956), or who are accelerated from second to fourth grade after a five-week summer session (Klausmeier, 1963; Klausmeier, Goodwin, & Ronda, 1968) do as well or better academically in the later grades than other pupils. In addition, they are just as well-adjusted emotionally and socially, are accepted just as readily by their classmates, and are most likely to go on to college and advanced professional training (Pressey, 1965, 1967). Similarly, students who enter college at an early age tend to make better grades, are more likely to graduate and go on to advanced study, manifest fewer disciplinary problems, and tend to be more successful in their careers (Fund for the Advancement of

Education, 1957; Pressey, 1962c; Terman & Oden, 1949). Meister (1956) found that high-school students who enter college with advanced standing or who pass advanced placement examinations do as well as regular students in their freshmen years.

## The Mentally Retarded

The proper educational handling and teaching of mentally retarded children are highly technical subjects and ordinarily require special training. The major educational decision affecting such children is whether to place them in special classes or to admit them to regular ability-grouped classes. The latter procedure probably provides them with greater intellectual stimulation and broader social experience, but it neither gives them the benefit of specially trained teachers nor protects them from social rejection by their peers (Johnson & Kirk, 1950; Miller, 1956). The decision hinges upon such factors as the type of curriculum and methods of instruction available in the regular classes, the retardate's ability level and adaptive capacity, and the attitudes and resourcefulness of the teachers in question (Dunn, 1960).

In recent years, court decisions and state regulations have led to the development of mainstreaming for all handicapped children, including the mentally retarded. The concept of mainstreaming implies moving children from special education classes and integrating them with the children in regular classrooms. This does not mean that all special education classes will be eliminated, but rather that those disabled students who would benefit from learning in regular classes will be assigned to these classes. In some cases the placement will be only part time for subjects such as art and physical education. In other cases it can mean regular class placement with additional help in special education such as intensive language development. In order for mainstreaming to provide a favorable learning experience for all students concerned, class size must be small enough to enable individualized instruction, and the classroom teacher must have the strong backing and support of special education personnel (Ryor, 1976). Although this current movement is strong, the typical classroom teacher is more likely to have greater contact with learning disabled and culturally disadvantaged children than with mentally retarded children.

## The Learning Disabled

Learning disabled children differ from mentally retarded children in that they are not retarded generally. The child with a learning disability usually has average intelligence and is able to learn in most areas with a specific learning difficulty in one area. These differences within the individual learner are often manifested in fluctuation in school performance related to various subjects and on different tests or parts of tests (Kirk & Kirk, 1971).

The field of learning disabilities is relatively new and multidisciplinary in approach. The major disciplines include medicine, psychology, education, and other professions. Medical specialists such as neurologists, psychiatrists, ophthalmologists, and pediatricians are concerned with the etiology of the condition. They view learning disability as a pathological health problem often related to damage of the central nervous system. They use descriptive terms such as brain damage, minimal brain dysfunction, dyslexia, aphasia, and dysgraphia. Psychologists observe and evaluate the outward behavior and functioning of the child and show concern for manifestations of perceptual handicaps, impulsivity, perseveration, and concrete versus abstract thinking. Educators focus on the learning behavior of the child in relation to acquisition of subject matter through suitable presentation of methods and materials. Other professionals such as optometrists, audiologists and language specialists view the learning difficulty from the point of view of their own disciplines.

Because so many professions are involved, there is diversity and confusion in both terminology and discussion of learning disabilities. The definition that is most widely accepted as clarifying was developed by the National Advisory Committee on Handicapped Children (1968):

> Children with special learning disabilities exhibit a disorder in one or more of the basic psychological processes involved in understanding or using spoken or written languages. These may be manifested in disorders of listening, thinking, talking, reading, writing, spelling or arithmetic. They include conditions which have been referred to as perceptual handicaps, brain injury, minimal brain dysfunction, dyslexia, developmental aphasia, etc. They do not include learning problems which are due primarily to visual, hearing, or motor handicaps, to mental retardation, emotional disturbance, or to environmental disadvantage (p. 4).

The possibility must be considered that learning disabilities in many cases may represent an extreme degree of intellectual "scatter" in a child's component abilities rather than a reflection of "minimal brain dysfunction." That is, there is typically a certain amount of variability in a given child's component cognitive and perceptual abilities as measured by the subtests of an intelligence test. And thus in the population at large such variability tends to be normally distributed; only in relatively few cases is it extreme.

Both genic and environmental influences could account for such extreme cases. For example, genic and cultural factors may result in abnormally discrepant spatial, symbolic, and computational abilities, despite an overall normal IQ. In such instances we would say that the child is suffering from a learning disability. Often, however, some children who are unable to read or compute may develop such secondary behavioral reactions to their disability as inattentiveness, emotional lability, distractability, and hyperactivity. What we are suggesting, in other words, is that *all* cases of learning disability are not necessarily caused by minimal brain damage and that treatment with drugs such as Ritalin® is not necessarily indicated.

The vast majority of cases in the author's experience exhibit neither electroencephalographic nor neurological signs of brain damage.[2] Stimulants such as the amphetamines, Ritalin®, and Cylert® are effective in about 80 percent of the cases in decreasing hyperactivity and distractability, thus indirectly causing improvement in learning and behavior. Contrary to general belief, such conditions often persist into adolescence and adult life and give rise to acting-out behavior (Wender, 1975; Zambelli et al, 1977).

An indeterminate number of cases are simply "statistical artifacts"—children with extreme "scatter" in the component intellectual abilities comprising achievement or scholastic aptitude tests. That is, they are, for genically determined reasons, extremely poor in one or more components while average or above average in all others.

Lerner (1971) cites studies that estimate the prevalence of the learning disabled child in the school population as ranging from 1 percent to 30 percent. She further compares these estimates with those of other exceptional children and concludes that the number of children with learning disabilities is greater than the number of children with other handicaps such as mental retardation, deafness, blindness, and physical disability. Thus in the typical classroom situation there will be several children who can be described as learning disabled. The identification of the specific problem and the approach to correct the difficulties is the major concern of educators. McCarthy and McCarthy (1969) discuss several educational approaches with specific emphasis on such areas as perceptual-motor, visual perception, neurophysiological, linguistic, and diagnostic-remedial. In reviewing the methods and research they state that the findings are inconclusive. The results suggest that each child with a learning difficulty has a unique set of problems, and no single method of instruction can apply to all cases. The most beneficial educational approach would be to find those methods that would be successful with each particular child. Secondary emotional reactions to the learning disability may, in part, give rise to the characteristic emotional lability and instability, or to particular behavior problems involved. In such cases counseling (as well as special tutoring by trained personnel) is indicated.

---

[2] Occasionally "soft" neurological signs are observed.

## The Culturally Disadvantaged

The hypothesis of cumulative developmental deficit, which was invoked earlier to explain the irreversible effects of cultural disadvantage, implicitly assumes the *continued* operation of a learning environment whose stimulating value remains average or below average during the crucial formative years of childhood. Hence, despite the twin limiting effects in disadvantaged pupils of (1) attained deficit in intellectual development and (2) increasing differentiation of intelligence on subsequent responsiveness to cognitive stimulation, it is still consistent with the above theoretical analysis to hypothesize that an *optimal* learning environment could arrest, or even *partially* reverse the existing degree of retardation. Such an environment must obviously be adequately stimulating and must be specially geared to the disadvantaged individual's particular level of readiness in each subject-matter area and intellectual skill as well as to his overall level of cognitive maturity. It presupposes much individualized attention and guided remedial effort.

This, of course, is a far cry from the kind of school learning environment that culturally disadvantaged children typically enjoy. In actual practice their existing intellectual deficit is usually compounded by the fact that they are not only less able than their peers to profit from appropriate new learning experiences, but they are also usually overwhelmed by exposure to learning tasks that exceed by far their prevailing level of cognitive readiness. They do not function at the required level of cognitive maturity and do not possess the necessary background of knowledge required for efficient learning. Hence they typically fail, lose self-confidence in their ability to learn, become thoroughly demoralized in the school situation, and disinvolve themselves from it. Much of the lower-class child's alienation from the school, therefore, is not so much a reflection of discriminatory or rejecting attitudes on the part of teachers and other school personnel—although the importance of this factor should not be underestimated. Rather, it is in greater measure a reflection of the cumulative effects of a curriculum that is not suitable for the child and of the resulting load of frustration, confusion, demoralization, resentment, and impaired self-confidence that he or she must bear, superimposed on the handicaps wrought by a culturally disadvantaged home that he or she brings with him to school. The plain fact of the matter is that

> the children of this group are *not* doing as well in school or in the world of juvenile work as did the children of 50 or 100 years ago. . . . [Unlike] most ethnic groups in the past—the Irish, Germans, Swedes, Italians, etc.—[they will not] become assimilated into the general society [as the others] have done in the past. Furthermore, there is a growing conviction that the proof of the existence of economic and educational *opportunity* is the achievement

of economic and educational *equality* by the previously disadvantaged groups within a reasonable period of time measured by decades and not by centuries or even by generations (Havighurst, 1970, p. 313).

Despite recent progress in this regard in the last two decades and the adoption of so-called "affirmative action" and "reverse discrimination," blacks, Puerto Ricans, American Indians, and Mexican Americans are still vastly under-represented in the managerial and professional occupations, in politics and government at the higher-echelon levels, and in the white middle-class segment of the population. Only a veritable, though growing, handful of these people have been "able to make it" out of the "bombed-out" inner-city ghettos or the urban slums and reservations where the majority of their fellow ethnics have subsisted on welfare or unskilled labor for three or more generations.

The tragedy of it is that *all other* ethnic Americans have "made it" out of the original "culture of poverty" in which they first lived a generation ago. One difference, perhaps, is that other ethnic groups, like Jews, Chinese, and Japanese, brought with them to America a veneration of learning and academic competence and were not handicapped by insurmountable barriers of caste (skin color). Havighurst (1970) contends, however, that the really important reason that these children do not learn is that teachers have not applied to classroom learning Thorndike's "law of effect" (which is a discredited and simplistic theory of learning widely used by Skinner and others in the now-defunct teaching machine movement). The real reason, in our opinion (apart from the motivation factors discussed in Chapter 13) is that the schools still follow, with the blessing of most educational psychologists, the obsolete learning theory of classical and operant conditioning, which may be applied to pigeons and rats but has no applicability whatsoever to children's learning of potentially meaningful subject matter, as described in Chapters 1 through 5.

In this section we shall consider only the cognitive aspects of an appropriate teaching strategy for culturally disadvantaged children. The basic principles underlying this strategy are essentially little different than those applying to the instruction of *any* pupil. As Bruner (1960) points out, however, it is the less able student who suffers most from poor teaching. In another chapter we shall discuss motivational, social, and interpersonal considerations applicable to the culturally disadvantaged.

An optimal cognitive environment for culturally disadvantaged pupils focuses on the two complementary aspects of cognitive readiness for learning—readiness in terms of general level of intellectual functioning and readiness in terms of specific subject-matter background. It emphasizes, therefore, these four considerations:

1. *Prevention* during the preschool years of the intellectual and lan-

guage retardation characteristic of children growing up under culturally disadvantaged circumstances

2. The selection of learning tasks at all stages of the curriculum that are consonant with the learner's *existing* state of readiness

3. Mastery and consolidation of all ongoing learning tasks before new tasks are introduced, so as to provide the necessary foundation for successful sequential learning and to prevent unreadiness for future learning tasks

4. The use of structured and self-paceable learning materials optimally organized to facilitate efficient sequential learning

Attention to these four factors can go a long way toward ensuring effective learning for the first time and toward restoring the culturally disadvantaged child's educational morale and confidence in his ability to learn. Later possible consequences are partial restoration of both intrinsic and extrinsic motivation for academic achievement, diminution of antiintellectualism, and decreased alienation from the school to the point where the child's studies make sense and he or she sees some purpose in learning.

### Preschool Enrichment

Much of the discouraging picture of language retardation in the culturally disadvantaged child and of its grim consequences for school learning could undoubtedly be prevented by an enriched program of preschool education that would emphasize perceptual discrimination and language acquisition. In addition to the usual preschool activities, much time would be spent in reading and talking to children; in furnishing an acceptable model of speech; in supplying corrective feedback with respect to grammar and pronunciation; in developing listening, memory, and attentivity skills; and in providing appropriate reading readiness, reading, and writing instruction. Concomitantly, of course, an attempt would be made to raise the cultural and intellectual level of the home through a long-range program of involvement in adult education.

Several systems of early childhood instruction have been developed to provide an enriched curriculum for culturally disadvantaged children. Many of the programs represent different philosophies of education such as traditional, child-centered and programs with emphasis on cognitive development, perceptual development and academic development. The Early Training Project (Klaus & Gray, 1968) provided a general enrichment approach through small group instruction and home visitation for work with the family. The gains tended to be maintained after a four-year period (Gray & Klaus, 1970).

More academically oriented programs (Bereiter & Engelmann, 1966; Blank, 1970; Fowler, 1971; Sigel & Olmstead, 1970) emphasize cognitive, logical, semantic, and information processing skills. Although one program has been questioned (Spicker, 1974), primarily because it seems to foster rote learning rather than learning of general language and thought processes, it attempts to meet the needs of disadvantaged preschool students and reports gains in IQ and scholastic readiness (Bereiter, 1972). Two other longitudinal studies claim effectiveness for the Ypsilanti Perry Preschool Project, a cognitively oriented program based mainly on Piagetian Theory (Kamü, 1972; Weikart, 1972). Beller (1973) reports on other important preschool projects that support the conclusion that when researchers regulate the project through curriculum implementation and research design the results have importance for the emotional, intellectual and academic growth of disadvantaged preschool children (Horowitz & Paden, 1970). Lavatelli (1970) has extended the Piagetian-type curriculum into elementary school.

### Readiness

General unreadiness for school learning among culturally disadvantaged children largely reflects their slower and less complete transition from concrete to abstract modes of thought during the junior- and senior-high-school years. Thus, in the presentation of abstract ideas and propositions, it is important for instructional materials and audiovisual aids to provide more concrete-empirical props and opportunities for direct physical manipulation of objects and situations than would be considered desirable in a more typical classroom.[3] Such props, for example, might include generous use of such techniques as Cuisenaire rods, the abacus, schematic models and diagrams, and role-playing activities. In the teaching of mathematics and science, much reliance would be placed on the applicability of principles to common problems in the immediate environment and on supportive illustrations and analogies drawn from everyday experience.

It should be appreciated, however, that these techniques are merely ways of facilitating the transition to a more abstract level of cognitive functioning. We do not want to induce permanent dependence on concrete-empirical props or to be satisfied with this state of affairs as our ultimate objective.

Specific subject-matter unreadiness among culturally disadvantaged children is a consequence of their failure to master the basic intellectual skills and to acquire an adequate foundation of integrative concepts and principles in the hierarchically organized disciplines. It is essential, therefore, that the initial selection of learning materials take account of pupils' existing state of knowledge and sophistication in the various subject-matter areas, irrespective of how primitive this happens to be. Once the appropriate starting point is ascertained, continued subject-matter readiness can

---

[3] In addition to promoting the understanding of abstractions, such overt, manipulative activity is also consistent with the disadvantaged child's more physical or "motoric" mode of learning (Riessman, 1962). The same consolidation would apply to overt versus passive responding in programmed learning and to discussion versus lecture modes of presentation.

then be assured by using structured, sequentially organized materials and by insisting on mastery of all ongoing lessons before new learning tasks are introduced. These latter teaching strategies can, in turn, be most effectively implemented through the kind of programmed instruction described above.

A curriculum that takes the readiness of the culturally disadvantaged child into account always takes as its starting point the child's existing knowledge and sophistication in the various subject-matter areas and intellectual skills, no matter how far down the scale this happens to be. This policy demands uncompromising elimination of all subject matter that cannot be economically assimilated on the basis of the child's current level of cognitive sophistication. It presupposes emphasis on the acquisition of the basic intellectual skills before any attempt is made to teach such subjects as algebra, literature, science, and foreign languages. However, in many urban high schools and junior high schools today, pupils who cannot read at a third grade level and who cannot speak or write grammatically or perform simple arithmetical computations are subjected to irregular French verbs, Shakespearean drama, and geometrical theorems (Ausubel, 1963b). Nothing more educationally futile or better calculated to destroy educational morale could be imagined!

In terms of readiness for a given level of schoolwork, a child is no less ready because of a history of cultural disadvantage, chronic academic failure, and exposure to an unsuitable curriculum than because of deficient intellectual endowment. Hence realistic recognition of this fact is not undemocratic, reactionary, or evidence of social-class bias, of intellectual snobbery, of a "soft" patronizing approach, or of a belief in the inherent uneducability of lower-class children. Neither is it indicative of a desire to surrender to the culturally disadvantaged child's current intellectual level, to perpetuate the status quo, or to institute a double, class-oriented standard of education. It is merely a necessary first step in preparing the child to cope with more advanced subject matter, and hence in eventually reducing existing social-class differentials in academic achievement. To set the same initial standards and expectations for the academically retarded culturally disadvantaged child as for the nonretarded middle- or lower-class child is automatically to ensure the former's failure and to widen prevailing discrepancies between social-class groups.

With respect to the culturally disadvantaged child's language retardation, a sorely needed change within the classroom setting is the long overdue introduction of more imaginative and effective ways of teaching the language arts. More emphasis, for example, needs to be placed on the mastery of the principal syntactical forms in spoken and written discourse, through repetitive practice with feedback, than on the pedantic labeling and classifying of different varieties of grammatical structure. The culturally disadvantaged child with his pragmatic and nonabstract approach to knowledge couldn't care less, after all, about the different parts of speech and the various esoteric names attached to the different uses of each. And, for the most part, he is correct insofar as the value or functional utility of much of such knowledge is concerned.

The study of the culturally disadvantaged child's language development has led to the deficit versus different theory. Researchers such as Bernstein (1960) and Hess and Shipman (1968) maintain that children from culturally disadvantaged homes suffer from inadequate verbal stimulation and show deficiencies in language and cognition. The deficit hypothesis has been challenged on the grounds that the disadvantaged environment fosters language development that is different rather than deficient (Cole & Bruner, 1971; Labov, 1970). Strickland (1974) further suggests the use of black dialect to teach beginning reading while standard English is taught as a second language.

It seems clear that both in preschool and school programs for the culturally disadvantaged, exclusive emphasis on either verbal or concrete-empirical aspects of instruction represents a pseudo-dichotomy. Culturally disadvantaged pupils must obviously be helped to overcome their language retardation. If they are ever to function competently as abstract, verbal learners, they must acquire a basic repertoire of verbal concepts and transactional terms as well as a basic mastery of syntax. But the very fact of their language retardation also requires simultaneous compensatory remediation along concrete-empirical lines. In the preschool and kindergarten (preoperational) period, like all children at this stage of development, they are highly dependent on concrete-empirical experience and on the manipulation of objects or images in relational learning, concept formation, and problem solving. They are unable to relate abstract relationships to cognitive structure in correlative, superordinate, or combinatorial fashion. And since they must also achieve a certain critical level of proficiency at the stage of concrete logical operations before they can move on to the stage of abstract logical operations, and since existing language retardation delays this transition, they are dependent longer than are their nondisadvantaged peers on concrete-empirical props in various forms of relational learning before attaining the abstract stage of cognitive development.

## Teaching and Administrative Arrangements

The success of this type of teaching strategy naturally depends a great deal on the availability of dedicated teachers who have been specially trained and are desirous of working with culturally disadvantaged children. They must *really* be concerned that materials are genuinely understood and mastered. They must be able to convey the impression that they are confident of and expect successful learning from their pupils. This obviously assumes much more personal involvement in the teaching function and in the intellectual development of culturally disadvantaged children than merely going through the motions of presenting subject-matter while being essentially indifferent about learning outcomes.[4] For purposes of restoring intrinsic motivation for learning (cognitive drive) it is also important that teachers be able to communicate a sense of excitement about the subjects they teach and that they be the kinds of mature, stable, and self-confident persons with whom children can identify. This latter objective can also be furthered by the assignment of more male teachers to schools in culturally disadvantaged neighborhoods, by lowering the pupil-teacher ratio, by using multiple-period classes, and by keeping teachers with the same elementary-school classes over a period of several years. Ungraded and ungrouped elementary-school classes facilitate the process of enabling each child to progress at his or her own pace without being subjected to the discouraging and stigmatizing effects of nonpromotion and placement in slow-learning groups.

Other types of compensatory educational arrangements that have been suggested for the culturally disadvantaged child include particularly intensive remedial work in reading, academic coaching, an extended school day and school week, free summer school, the postponement of formal instruction in the first grade for pupils who have not had preschool and kindergarten training, and a five-year high-school and college program for the academically slow-developing individual. For high-school students whose school orientation is definitely vocational, realistic prevocational courses should be provided in the eleventh and twelfth grades, integrated in some instances with work experience and apprenticeship programs.

---

[4] This does not necessarily imply a permissive or "child-oriented" as opposed to a "task-oriented" approach to teaching. The family background of culturally disadvantaged, and of lower-social-class children generally, does not make them very responsive to a permissive environment characterized by either laissez-faire attitudes or unstructured techniques of instruction (Riessman, 1962).

# 9

# PRACTICE

The significance of practice and drill in meaningful learning and retention has, in our opinion, been unwarrantedly downgraded. In many educational circles drill is viewed as the hallmark of rote learning. Practice is obviously less important in meaningful than in rote learning, because in the latter the learning task cannot be related nonarbitrarily to any ideas in the learner's cognitive structure, and can only be retained for long periods of time by dint of much effortful repetition. Nevertheless, repetition is still a very significant variable that must be reckoned with if we are concerned with long-term meaningful learning and retention, and with transfer to related sequentially dependent aspects of subject matter.

Although a single presentation of relatively simple new ideas to a sophisticated learner often suffices to result in long-term retention, more complex ideas generally require a sufficient number of appropriately spaced reviews (overlearning) in order to be retained over long periods of time and in order to be sufficiently clear and stable to have transfer value for related new ideas. Also, because meaningful learning is both intrinsically less difficult than rote learning, and less vulnerable to rapid forgetting, longer intervals between practice sessions (review rather than practice) are possible.

Repetition enhances learning in essentially two different ways: (1) Shortly after initial learning, before much forgetting occurs, it is able to consolidate the learned material most effectively and to bring about the learning of more subtle nuances and implications that are missed on the first presentation. (2) Later, after considerable forgetting occurs, it gives the learner an opportunity to profit from (and thus avoid in later presentations) his awareness of negative factors (such as ambiguity or confusion with similar ideas) responsible for such forgetting. It also enables him or her to focus attention and effort on those components of the learning task that are idiosyncratically most difficult. Short and progressively more widely spaced reviews are generally more effective than massed practice for the second of these two reasons. Recitation (as opposed to study sessions) is similarly less important for meaningful than for rote learning, because the learner can largely anticipate and rehearse later-occurring portions of meaningfully learned material on the basis of logic or plausibility in the absence of overt recitation.

Guided discovery has been found to be more efficacious than either pure discovery or pure reception learning in meaningful but contrived and relatively isolated and novel laboratory tasks. This does not mean, however, that guided discovery is necessarily more efficient than meaningful reception learning in acquiring the larger bodies of interrelated concepts and propositions involved in subject-matter learning. We shall return to this topic in greater detail in Chapter 15.

Consistent with the idiosyncratic and active nature of meaningful reception learning discussed in Chapters 3 and 4, recall is more effective for long-term retention when reformulated in the learner's own words than when verbatim recall is practiced. Review is also more effective when differential practice schedules are used—that is, when more time and effort are devoted to correcting and clarifying initial errors in comprehension—than when a fixed and uniform amount of time is devoted to all components of a learning task.

Drill (reviews congruent with the above principles) is more efficacious in meaningful learning (1) when it occurs in structured rather than in incidental, haphazard, or naturally occurring settings; and (2) when learning tasks are first consolidated in homogeneous contexts before they are applied to more heterogeneous contexts.

Feedback (knowledge of results) facilitates meaningful learning cognitively (primarily through clarification and correction) rather than by "reinforcing" correct responses. In any case, feedback is less important for meaningful than for rote learning because the internal logic of meaningfully learned material allows for more self-provided feedback than do inherently arbitrary associations.

Meaningful learning refers to the acquisition of meanings and to the non-transitory organizational changes in cognitive structure accompanying this process as the learner responds to initial and successive presentations of the learning task. Although much significant meaningful learning obviously occurs during initial presentation of the instructional material, both overlearning and most long-term retention presuppose multiple presentations or trials (practice). Both learning process and outcome customarily encompass various qualitative and quantitative changes that take place during these several trials. Learning and retention, therefore, ordinarily imply practice. Such practice, furthermore, is typically specific (restricted to the learning task) and deliberate (intentional).

Long-term organizational changes in cognitive structure that occur in the demonstrable absence of specific and deliberate practice experience (that is, incidental learning) may be more properly considered manifestations of maturation. Short-term fluctuations in the availability of learned material, on the other hand, are reflective of changes in the threshold of availability.

As previously suggested, the effects of practice both reflect the influence of existing cognitive structure and also modify that structure. Thus the cognitive impact of initial presentation of potentially meaningful new learning material (the emergence of new meanings) is largely determined by the organizational attributes of the established ideas in cognitive structure to which the learning task is related. By establishing these new meanings in cognitive structure, such presentation influences in turn both the learner's response to subsequent trials of the same learning task and his or her learning of related new materials. Practice therefore affects learning and retention by modifying cognitive structure. Generally speaking, it increases the stability and clarity of newly learned meanings in cognitive structure. Hence it enhances their dissociability strength and retention.

Practice is not a cognitive structure variable itself but is one of the principal factors (along with instructional material variables) influencing cognitive structure. The most immediate effect of practice is to increase the stability and clarity, and hence the dissociability strength, of the emergent new meanings in cognitive structure. In turn, the increments and decrements in the stability and clarity of the new meanings (and the correlated changes in their dissociability strength) accompanying their initial learning, intertrial forgetting, and later learning, facilitate the learner's assimilation of the instructional material during subsequent trials. As will be postulated later, the changes in cognitive structure wrought by the first trial (namely, the establishment of the new meanings), "sensitize" the learner to the potential meanings inherent in the material. The forgetting that occurs between successive trials or reviews "immunizes" the learner (enables him or her to take preventive steps) against further forgetting on additional trials. In addition, the consolidation of this new material, as a result of practice, makes available in cognitive structure stable new anchoring ideas for other related learning tasks introduced at a later date. Practice, therefore, influences cognitive structure in at least four different ways:

1. It increases the dissociability strength of the newly learned meanings for a given trial and thereby facilitates their retention.
2. It enhances the learner's responsiveness to subsequent presentations of the same material.
3. It enables the learner to profit from intertrial forgetting.
4. It facilitates the learning and retention of related new learning tasks.

But even if each learning trial influences subsequent learning trials by virtue of its "sensitizing" and "immunizing" effects on cognitive structure, the mediating influence of these effects on the next practice trial are not experimentally measurable. The transfer paradigm (comparing learning outcomes of the two groups after the experimental group receives two trials and the control group receives only one trial) is inapplicable under these circumstances. As long as training and criterion tasks are identical (consist of two presentations of the *same* material), it is impossible in accounting for the superiority of the experimental group on the second learning trial to distinguish between (1) the practice effect *itself* (the direct effect of an additional presentation upon learning or dissociability strength) and (2) the *indirect* mediating (sensitizing or immunizing) influence of previously altered cognitive structure.

In classical transfer situations, on the other hand, inasmuch as criterion and training tasks differ, the superiority of the experimental group on the criterion task can be unequivocally attributed to the modification of cognitive structure induced by the training task. However, simply because the influence of a cognitive structure variable is not demonstrable under certain conditions, we cannot warrantedly infer that it does not affect learning-retention outcomes. The reality of a variable's effect on a phenomenon cannot be denied just because the variable itself currently defies reliable and valid measurement or because methodological and/or statistical procedures are not yet available to isolate this effect from that of other variables.

In this chapter we shall *not* be concerned with the problem of how different dimensions of the practice variable (overlearning, multicontextual exposure) affect transfer, that is, influence the meaningful learning and retention of *new* material by altering cognitive structure. We will consider instead the effects of repeated presentations of the *same* learning task (practice) on the learning and retention of that task.

Relevant dimensions of the practice variable to be considered include the number, type, and distribution of practice trials; the method and general conditions of practice; and the learner's awareness of the effect of practice on learning-retention outcomes (feedback). It should be appreciated, however, that only a slight alteration in experimental design would be necessary to make the relevant studies in this area conform to the transfer paradigm.

Thus they could shed light on the pedagogically more significant issue of how different aspects of practice influence the meaningful learning and retention of related new material.

Unfortunately, most of our knowledge about the effects of practice variables pertains to rote and motor learning and to single rather than sequentially organized tasks. The research void, with respect to the role of repetition in meaningful verbal learning, is especially glaring despite the time-honored place of practice and review in pedagogic technique. Practically all of the research conducted to date has dealt either with the frankly rote-type learning of nonsense syllables and paired adjectives or with the verbatim learning of such potentially meaningful material as poetry and short prose passages.

## Frequency

In terms of historical significance, theoretical importance, and relevance for current educational practice, few issues in educational psychology are more crucial than the role of frequency in learning and retention. Yet, ever since Thorndike (1931, 1932) "repudiated" the "law of frequency," the theoretical stance of educational psychology on this issue has tended to be confused, contradictory, and somewhat "schizophrenic." On the one hand, in accordance with Thorndike's pronouncement, it is held that frequency in itself is unnecessary for and really makes little difference in learning outcomes. This position finds much favor with progressivist educators who are hostile to drill of any kind, with Gestalt theorists who conceive of all learning as insightful, and with "discontinuity" ("nonincremental") learning theorists who maintain that learning invariably takes place in a single trial. Thus, we frequently tend to minimize the role of drill in educational theory, regarding it as rote, mechanical, passive, and old-fashioned, as psychologically unnecessary for the learning process, and as actually harmful for active, meaningful learning.

The progressivists, of course, did not entirely deny the value of practice. As a matter of fact, their espousal of "naturalism," incidental learning, and of project and activity programs, as well as their battle cry of "learning by doing," carried an implied endorsement of the importance of appropriate practice. But by appropriate practice they meant direct (concrete, manipulative), nondeliberate (unintentional), and autonomous (unguided) learning encounters with different (diversified) examples of the same concept or principle in uncontrived "real-life" situations. Their mistake lay in assuming that all structured practice (drill) is necessarily rote; that unstructured, unguided, and unintentional (incidental) practice is maximally effective for school learning tasks; and that "doing" necessarily leads to learning simply because it involves direct experience and occurs repeatedly in natural problem-solving situations.

Actually, for practice to result in meaningful mastery of material the only really essential conditions are that: (1) the learning task be logically meaningful; (2) the learner exhibit a meaningful learning set and possess the necessary anchoring ideas; and (3) the number, distribution, sequence, and organization of practice trials conform to empirically established principles of efficient learning and retention. The uncontrived or unstructured quality of practice is an unessential condition of meaningful, effective learning. Moreover, it often leads to no meaningful mastery whatsoever. This is so because incidental practice is typically haphazard in terms of frequency and distribution of trials. In addition, the spontaneous, unstructured organization of learning experiences is more frequently than not inconsistent with established criteria of effective programming.

Problem solving and laboratory exercises may similarly lead to little or no meaningful learning if the student's learning set is simply rotely to memorize "type" problems or techniques of manipulating symbols. This is particularly true if the student has an inadequate background in, or appreciation of, the methodological principles illustrated by specific laboratory procedures. It should also be realized, finally, that just as "doing" does not necessarily lead to understanding, understanding does not necessarily imply ability successfully to solve problems involving meaningful appreciation of the principles in question. Factors other than understanding are also implicated in the outcome of problem-solving activities.

On the other hand, educational psychologists implicitly accept the concept of a "learning curve," in which they plot gradual increments in learning against successive trials. They place great stress on the importance of overlearning for long-term retention and transfer. This latter position is actually adopted by the vast majority of teachers, coaches, parents, and students who follow the maxim that "practice makes perfect." Quite obviously, both positions cannot be simultaneously valid.

The upshot of this conflict in our beliefs is that we still place considerable reliance on drill in actual classroom teaching, but do so halfheartedly, apologetically, and in ways that detract from its effectiveness. Actually, on theoretical grounds, there are many reasons for believing that repetition is typically required for the long-term retention of adequately clear, stable, and valid meanings (and often for their acquisition as well). It is also required for that degree of consolidation of antecedent portions of sequentially organized subject matter that is necessary for efficient learning of subsequent portions.

### Meaningful versus Rote Learning and Retention

The role and significance of frequency are different for meaningful than for rote learning and retention precisely because rote and meaningful learning processes themselves are so different from one another. Repeated encounters with the same array of stimulation presumably enhance rote learning and retention by increasing the strength of discrete, arbitrary, and verbatim associative linkages, that is, their resistance to the short-term interfering effects of prior and subsequent stimulation. The same repetition presumably enhances meaningful learning and retention by increasing the dissociability strength of instructional materials that have been nonarbitrarily and substantively incorporated in relation to an existing concept or principle in cognitive structure. In other words, it enhances the emergence of clear and stable meanings and their resistance to forgetting (Ausubel, 1963a).

Thus it is reasonable to assume that sheer repetition would play a more significant role in the learning and short-term retention of discrete and arbitrary associations, largely isolated from cognitive structure, than it would in the learning and longer-term retention of materials that can be meaningfully incorporated within that structure. In meaningful learning situations, such other factors as the availability of clear and stable anchoring ideas, the discriminability between these anchoring ideas and the learning task, and the internal logic and lucidity (logical meaningfulness) of the learning task undoubtedly detract somewhat from the role played by repetition. Nevertheless, the influence of repetition is still considerable in the establishment and consolidation of meanings and in the enhancement of their resistance to decremental processes. In any case, it cannot be dismissed as basically extrinsic to the process whereby increments in availability are effected.

From the standpoint of frequency, the chief practical implication of the differences between rote and meaningful learning for classroom teaching is that review can, and largely should, take the place of practice. Since meaningful learning occurs relatively quickly, and since the forgetting of meaningfully learned materials takes place relatively slowly, much of the potentially facilitating effects of frequency can be used more profitably for review than for original learning purposes. In terms of what is actually learned and retained, the relatively long interval between the initial learning and the review sessions in meaningful learning is comparable to the short intertrial practice interval in advanced stages of rote learning. Thus in teaching the meanings of a series of programmed scientific terms and in meaningful prose learning Reynolds and Glaser (1964) and Ausubel and Youssef (1965) respectively found that "repetition has only a transitory effect upon retention," whereas "spaced reviews produce significant facilitation in retention of the reviewed material."

### Frequency and Learning

Until relatively recently, most of the empirical research bearing on the frequency issue in rote learning had been conducted by Thorndike (1931,

1932). In amassing experimental evidence against the role of frequency, however, he chose highly atypical learning tasks that could not possibly be mastered in the absence of either explicit intention or knowledge of results, and then deliberately failed to provide these conditions. Hence, since the minimally necessary conditions for learning were lacking in his particular experiments, he did not find it very difficult to demonstrate that numerous repetitions of the task, under the same impossible conditions he set, were just as ineffective for learning as was the provision of a single trial. Needless to say, such evidence is almost universally cited in educational psychology textbooks as definitively proving the negligible influence of frequency by itself on learning. However, it merely demonstrates that certain atypical kinds of learning cannot take place in the absence of explicit intention or feedback, no matter how frequently the learning task is repeated.

In one series of experiments, for example, Thorndike endeavored to prove that frequency has no effect in the absence of belongingness (in the sense that two items are perceived as belonging together). By eliminating this latter condition he successfully demonstrated that frequency was, in fact, ineffective. This result was hardly surprising because, although contiguity is an essential condition of associative learning, not all contiguous events are necessarily associated: some selectivity based on belongingness is always involved in the particular items that are associated.

In the case of meaningful learning material, belongingness is a reflection of functional or logical relatedness. In rote learning tasks, however, where the association to be formed is purely arbitrary, belongingness is established either by explicit instructions (and the formation of corresponding explicit sets or intentions) or by habitual expectancies based on previous experience. Hence much "incidental learning" (learning in the absence of explicit instruction and intention) can occur either if the learning material is potentially meaningful or if the rote learning task is constituted in accordance with habitual expectancies.[1] But if a particular rote learning task is unrelated to or inconsistent with habitual expectancies (for instance, associating the second member of one paired associate with the first member of the next paired associate in the series), it is understandable that little or no learning will occur in the absence of explicit intention, despite numerous contiguous repetitions (Thorndike, 1931, 1932).

Similarly, in another widely cited series of experiments, Thorndike (1931, 1932) showed that in the absence of knowledge of results, fre-

---

[1] Children, for example, acquire much specific information about objects irrelevant to the solution of particular incentive-motivated problems (Stevenson, 1954); and, without any obvious motivation for so doing, they effectively retain, over long periods of time, information presented in motion pictures (Holaday & Stoddard, 1933). Experimenters who administer lists of nonsense syllables to subjects incidentally learn many of these syllables themselves (Jenkins, 1933).

quency of repeating certain tasks (for instance, drawing a line of specified length, estimating the length of paper strips) bears no relation to learning (improvement). In instances where a constant-stimulus situation is repeated but the response is variable or indeterminate, it is obvious that some knowledge of results is essential for learning. Feedback, however, is not indispensable for learning in situations where *both* stimulus and response are specified or where the learner's task is simply to reproduce the material presented. Furthermore, not only is frequency effective in these latter instances where feedback is *not* required for learning, but it also enhances learning in those situations where feedback *is* essential and is provided.

In many military and industrial training situations involving perceptual-motor skills (for instance, gunnery) and the learning of sequential procedures, practice of the task itself apparently has no facilitating effect (Gagné, 1962b). Thus in learning a patterned alternation maze, for example, it is more efficacious for a subject to observe another's performance long enough to grasp the pattern than to start in directly with trial-and-error learning (Bruner, Wallach, & Galanter, 1959). This is so because the *real* learning task under these circumstances does not involve the acquisition of appropriate responses or stimulus-response connections (which, in fact, are already highly familiar or overlearned). Rather it involves appreciation of underlying principles or memorization of a correct sequence of activities. In the one instance, therefore, instruction and guidance in the relevant principles are more effective than practice in bringing about improvement. In the other instance, memorization of a sequential list and use of it in conjunction with practice are similarly more effective than mere practice of the task (Gagné, 1962b). This does not mean, of course, that the principle of practice or frequency does not apply to these types of learning, as Gagné (1962b) asserts. It simply means that for frequency to be effective, the learner must practice *the actual task that needs learning*—not overt responses that are already thoroughly mastered.

Despite its immense practical significance for pedagogy and classroom learning, amazingly little experimental research has been conducted on the relationship between frequency and *meaningful* learning-retention. As far as the effect of repetition on meaningful learning is concerned, most educational psychologists seem content to cite the relevant rote learning studies and to suggest on theoretical grounds that less practice is required for learning if the subject can acquire clear, unambiguous, and discriminable meanings from the learning task.[2]

Paralleling Thorndike's research on the effect of repetition on the estimation of length of lines, it has been demonstrated that frequency of writ-

---

[2] Maier and Hoffman (1960) have shown that a group's second solution of a human relations problem in industry tends to be superior to its first solution in terms of speed, integrativeness, and acceptability to group members.

ing themes, in the absence of feedback, has little effect on the acquisition of composition skills (Dressel, Schmid, & Kincaid, 1952; Schrom, 1953). Although the provision of suitable feedback does result in improvement of these skills (Buxton, 1958; Page, 1958), the role of frequency under these latter conditions has yet to be empirically determined. The experiments of Ausubel and Youssef (1965), Reynolds and Glaser (1964), and Crewe (1969) showed that spaced review facilitates the learning and retention of meaningfully learned material. Crewe (1969) found that review (particularly cramming) markedly facilitated retention just before testing. The latter finding, however, is contaminated by rote learning effects as shown by the universal experience of most students—almost total forgetting shortly after the examination.

### Frequency and Retention

More is known about the effect of overlearning on meaningful retention than about its effect on meaningful learning. The degree of delayed retention of poetry (Ebbinghaus, 1913) and connected discourse (Slamecka, 1959) is directly related to the number of repetitions of the learning materials,[3] but diminishing returns may set in more rapidly than in the case of rote retention. McTavish (1949), for example, showed that the first repetition of a film on general science substantially increases retention, but that second and third repetitions add little or nothing to the effect of the first. Yoakam (1924) obtained similar results. Peterson et al. (1935) and Gilbert (1957), on the other hand, failed to find diminishing returns with increasing degrees of practice or review.

As is also true of rote retention, the *slope* of the retention curve for meaningful materials is not altered by degree of overlearning (Gilbert, 1957). Review (delayed practice) enhances meaningful retention, particularly when an attempt is made to integrate old and new materials (Ward & Davis, 1939), but is generally less necessary for meaningful than for rote memory. Bruning (1968) found that both criterion-test relevance on a review and testing basis independently enhance learning in additive fashion.

### Timing of Reviews

For purposes of meaningful learning and retention, should review be introduced shortly after original learning, when the material is still fresh in mind and relatively little has been forgotten? Or would it be more effective to introduce review after an appreciable amount of material has been forgotten? This issue has significant implications for student study prac-

---

[3] In these studies there was actually a combination of meaningful and rote retention of potentially meaningful material, inasmuch as verbatim recall of the material was demanded.

tices and for the programming of potentially meaningful instructional materials. It also has important theoretical implications for the psychology of meaningful learning and retention. Credible arguments can be adduced in support of each alternative, but the issue can obviously be decided only by empirical test.

The findings of two early studies are particularly relevant for the problem at issue. Peterson et al. (1935) reported no difference between the effects of a rereading review introduced one or nine days after original learning. Sones and Stroud (1940) found that there was a slight, but nonsignificant, tendency for a delayed rereading review to be more effective than an early rereading review. In both instances, however, these findings are somewhat equivocal because the criterion retention test was given an equal number of days after the original learning. Hence, there was a greater time interval between the early review and the retention test, thereby tending to bias the results in favor of the latter condition.

Ausubel's (1966) study was designed to eliminate this methodological difficulty. The review session was administered on the same day for both early and delayed review groups and was followed by the retention test after an equal time interval for both groups. The same relearning of the material constituted early or delayed review for the two groups as a result of varying the interval between original learning and review. Even under these experimental conditions, the earlier findings were confirmed.

The results of this latter experiment can best be explained by supposing that the respective advantages of early and delayed review counterbalance each other. The theoretical advantages of *delayed* review are perhaps more self-evident than those of early review. In the first place, after a longer retention interval, when more material is forgotten, the learner is more highly motivated to profit from the opportunity for review. He or she is less likely to regard this opportunity as unnecessary and superfluous, and is therefore more disposed to take good advantage of it in terms of effort and attention.

Second, and even more important, *prior forgetting* conceivably has a facilitating ("immunizing") effect on meaningful learning and retention. As a result of both trying and failing to remember material, the learner tends to become aware of negative factors in the learning and retention situations that promote forgetting—that is, of areas of instability, ambiguity, confusion, and lack of discriminability (Ausubel & Youssef, 1965). Thus forearmed, he or she can take the necessary steps during the relearning session to strengthen particularly weak components of the learning task, to resolve existing confusion and ambiguity, and to increase discriminability between previously learned ideas and related new propositions. Furthermore, it would seem that greater potential benefit could presumably be anticipated from repetition when a larger proportion of the learning task is forgotten, inasmuch as more remains to be relearned under these circumstances.

In what ways can *early* review conceivably counterbalance these evident advantages of delayed review? The most likely possibility is that repetition (review) has a specially potent consolidating effect on recently learned material while it is still appreciably above the threshold of availability. This consolidating effect probably decreases as the material becomes progressively less available. Obviously, another trial provides additional opportunity for the learner to interact cognitively with the learning material and to relate the potential meanings it embodies to his or her existing structure of knowledge. New actual or experienced meanings are acquired and previously acquired meanings are consolidated. The learner has another opportunity to acquire more subtle potential meanings in the material that were partially or completely missed on the first trial, as well as to consolidate meanings initially established at that time. To be optimally effective, however, the opportunity for such consolidation may very well presuppose a certain minimal level of residual availability.

Another study trial also provides the learner with informational feedback, in the form of textual reference, for testing the correctness of the knowledge retained from the first trial. This testing confirms correct meanings, clarifies ambiguities, corrects misconceptions, and indicates areas of weakness requiring differential concentrated study. The net effect is consolidation of learning. When the learning task is largely forgotten, however, as in delayed review, the "feedback" role of repetition is minimal.

In what other ways may early review be more advantageous than delayed review? It will be remembered that in addition to enhancing meaningful learning and retention in the two aforementioned direct ways, repetition also influences these processes in another indirect way through modification in cognitive structure wrought by earlier trials. Not only do repeated presentations of the learning task strengthen the newly acquired cognitive content, but the latter cognitive content itself also *reciprocally* induces changes in the *perceived* learning task that make it more learnable. That is, initial acquisition of the meanings of the learning material and their presence in cognitive structure *sensitize* the learner to the potential meanings it contains when encountering it again. The learner had previously derived meanings from the learning material on the first trial by incorporating potential meanings into cognitive structure. Now the new ideas as a whole, not merely the component words, immediately (that is, perceptually) convey *actual* rather than merely *potential* meaning on second reading.

Hence, on the second trial, actual rather than potential meanings interact on a perceptual basis with the residue of those recently acquired meanings in cognitive structure that were established as a consequence of the learner's first encounter with the material. This type of interaction particularly enhances consolidation of the previously established meanings because this time the learner does not have to *grasp* meanings and can concentrate solely on trying to *remember* them. Moreover, establishment of gross meanings on the first trial sensitizes the learner to more refined meanings and subtle distinctions on the second trial. It stands to reason, therefore, that both the consolidation and "sensitizing effects" of repetition are greater earlier than later during the retention interval, when more of the learned meanings are still available to exert sensitizing effects or to be consolidated.

In summary, then, the principal advantage of *early* review would appear to be its superior consolidating, "feedback," and "sensitizing" effects in relation to more highly available material. On the other hand, the principal advantage of *delayed* review probably inheres in the superior relearning of partially forgotten material, both on motivational and cognitive grounds. Thus, since each kind of review has its own distinctive function and advantage, the two varieties are presumably complementary rather than redundant or mutually exclusive, and can thus be profitably combined.

### How the Influence of Frequency Is Mediated

The role and importance of frequency (number of trials or presentations) in learning and retention have received varying emphasis over the years in psychology and education. For the most part, in the history of psychological thought, frequency has been regarded as one of the cardinal laws of associative learning and, more recently, of classical conditioning as well. In the early Thirties, however, "the law of frequency" received a severe setback at the hands of E. L. Thorndike (1931, 1932) who concluded, after much experimentation, that frequency *in itself* has little or no impact on the learning process, and that its supposed influence must really be attributed to reinforcement (satisfying effect), knowledge of results, belongingness, or intention.

The authority of Thorndike's pronouncement was subsequently bolstered by the influence of such nonfrequency conceptions of learning as the Guthrian "contiguity-single-trial" model of learning (Estes, 1960; Estes, Hopkins, & Crother, 1960; Guthrie, 1952; Rock, 1957), the Hullian emphasis on drive reduction as the principal variable determining habit strength (Hull, 1943), the Skinnerian preoccupation with reinforcement in operant conditioning (Skinner, 1938), Tolman's (1932) view of learning as the gradual acquisition of cognitive sophistication, and the Gestalt formulation of learning as the abrupt emergence of "insight" (Köhler, 1925).

The combined influence of these theoretical developments in the psychology of learning and of the prevailing progressivist and child-centered trends in the philosophy of education led to a widespread de-emphasis of the value of practice or drill in the teaching-learning process. Drill was unwarrantedly stigmatized as necessarily rote in nature, and a fetish was made of uncontrived, unstructured, and incidental learning experience.

It is apparent, therefore, that two principal issues must be considered in evaluating the role of frequency in learning and retention. First, is repetition typically required both in gradually establishing associative or dissociability strength at or above threshold level in rote and meaningful learning respectively and in sufficiently enhancing such strength so that the span of retention is extended, or is all effective learning and retention actually accomplished in a single trial? Is frequency, in other words, *intrinsically* related to the learning-retention process, or is gradual improvement with repetition merely an artifactual consequence of various factors involved in the investigation, measurement, and representation of learning-retention outcomes? Second, does frequency affect learning and retention in any *distinctive* way apart from affording repeated opportunities for other variables such as contiguity, drive reduction, and confirmation-clarification to operate in cumulative fashion?

Our position regarding both the role and mediation of frequency in meaningful verbal learning and retention has already been made clear in discussing the effect of temporal position on review. Evidently, frequency is neither a necessary nor a sufficient condition for meaningful learning to occur. The substance of much relatively easy, potentially meaningful material can be grasped after one reading. Typically, however, several rereadings are required for more difficult learning, for overlearning, for delayed retention, and for transfer. *Frequency, in other words, usually makes a difference* in meaningful learning and retention.

On the other hand, let us assume the absence of a meaningful learning set, of potentially meaningful material, of sufficient effort and attention, of active attempts to understand, of intention to integrate knowledge and to reformulate it in idiosyncratic terms, and of belongingness, feedback, and intention (where these are necessary for learning). Under these conditions no amount of frequency *by itself* can eventuate in substantial amounts of meaningful learning. In addition, we have insisted that practice *alone* does more than just provide opportunity for such variables as contiguity, reinforcement, feedback, belongingness, and intention to influence learning. Subsequent opportunities to encounter learning material are facilitated by the cognitive changes (increased dissociability strength) that they themselves induce.

Thus we hold that frequency has a distinctive effect of its own on learning and retention that operates in addition to (and cannot simply be reduced to) the opportunity that subsequent trials provide for other effective variables to influence, in cumulative fashion, the process and outcome of learning and retention. That is, we propose that frequency does more than merely make possible a summation of the repeated effects of some other variables such as contiguity, reinforcement through drive reduction, or cognitive confirmation and clarification. Frequency does admittedly provide opportunity for the recurrent operation of these variables, but it also serves as more than just a vehicle for the cumulation of their repeated effects.[4]

Frequency is obviously insufficient for learning under conditions that lead either to extinction (lack of reinforcement) or to motivation *not* to learn (for instance, punishment). The same holds true for conditions that either presuppose prior knowledge that is absent in a particular learner, or call for discovery or difficult reception learning that may or may not take place. Some learners, for example, may never acquire the necessary insight for certain kinds of insightful problem solving. In other instances, frequency may gradually engender the necessary understanding or insight. Although this insight may appear to arise very abruptly, it may actually reflect the testing of many prior hypotheses and their reformulation following negative results.

### Transfer versus Direct Practice in Sequential Learning

Repetition is important not only for the mastery of the current or ongoing learning task but also for the learning of new, sequentially dependent tasks that presuppose such mastery or consolidation of the current task. This, of course, is an example of positive transfer. The relative value of transfer and direct practice has already been considered in another context (see fn. 9, p. 197). One might anticipate in the case of sequentially dependent learning material that the learning of such material would be significantly influenced by the extent of retention of relevant antecedent material. The availability of such relevant material—particularly if it were clear and stable—would provide a more secure basis for new learning than if this material were not available at all or were not clear and stable. Since repetition of the earlier background material tends to increase its stability and clarity, it should enhance the learning and retention of sequentially dependent material.

---

[4] Some of the effect of repetition on learning and retention probably has a neurophysiological basis related to the theory that repeated excitation of a given neural connection lowers the synaptic resistances involved in conduction of neural impulses. This theory is in accord with the well-established facts that: (1) everything else being equal, the older of two memory traces is stronger and is strengthened more by practice (Jost's laws); and (2) memories in storage tend to increase in strength over time. It is also consistent with the pattern of memory loss and recovery in amnesia, cranial trauma, electroshock therapy, and senile dementia—with the fact that older memories are lost last and recovered first (Wooldridge, 1963). Not only does repeated reexcitation apparently lower synaptic resistances, but so also do randomly and spontaneously generated electric brain currents. The latter phenomenon would account, in part, both for Jost's laws and for the superiority of distributed practice.

The facilitating effect of repetition (consolidation) of background material on the learning of subsequently presented material apparently seems to operate only when the latter material is sequentially dependent on the prior background material. Thus, in classroom learning tasks it is important to distinguish between (1) sequentially related materials that are sequentially *dependent* on prior learnings and (2) sequentially related materials that are sequentially *independent* of such learnings. When we say that materials are sequentially related, we merely imply that, in terms of the logic of subject-matter organization, it is more reasonable for one set of materials to precede another than vice versa.

Sequential *dependence*, however, also implies that the learning of the later material actually presupposes knowledge of the earlier material and is impossible without it. In sequentially *independent* situations, on the other hand, knowledge of the earlier material is not required for learning the later material. The latter set of material is self-contained and can be learned adequately by itself without any reference to the previous set. Such sequential independence is frequently brought about in sequentially related lessons by including in the second lesson a synopsis or review of all of the material from the first lesson that is absolutely essential for the understanding of the second.

The effect of consolidating knowledge of the first of two sequentially related but sequentially *independent* passages on ability to learn the second was investigated by Ausubel and Youssef (1966). The first passage was concerned with the normal physiology of pubescence and the second with clinical (pathological) aspects of pubescence. It was found that greater knowledge of the passage dealing with the normal physiology of pubescence did not facilitate the learning of the sequentially related but sequentially independent (self-contained) passage dealing with clinical conditions of pubescence. Degree of knowledge of the normal physiology passage was manipulated by permitting subjects zero, one, or two readings of this passage prior to studying the clinical passage. This finding was attributed to the current availability in the clinical passage of the minimum background material of normal physiology necessary for understanding the clinical material. Under these conditions, the stability and clarity of both the directly relevant and of the collateral background material apparently became nondeterminative factors in learning the new material.[5] Merrill (1965), Merrill and Stolurow (1965), and Merrill, Wood, and Starr (1969), obtained substantially equivalent results using programmed materials.

One can best interpret these findings, perhaps, by comparing them to

---

[5] As previously suggested, however, prior consolidation would probably enhance the long-term *retention* of the new material under these conditions.

the results one might have anticipated with sequentially dependent passages and the presumed reasons for same. In a sequentially dependent situation, one would expect the degree of retained knowledge of early background material crucially to affect the learning of later material by providing relevant ideational scaffolding for it. If such relevant ideational scaffolding were available and were clear and stable, it would provide a better foundation for new learning and retention than if it were not available, or, if available, were not clear and stable. Repetition of the early background material is one of the factors that enhances its stability and clarity, and hence should facilitate the learning of sequentially dependent later material.

However, when the directly relevant ideational scaffolding from the first passage is *included* in the first part of the second passage, and is thus *currently* available for the learning of that second passage, the fact that the learner has been exposed to the same relevant material in another context (and that his knowledge of it had thereby become consolidated) apparently becomes a nondeterminative factor in learning the second passage. The collateral background material is, in any case, of too tangential a nature to constitute relevant ideational scaffolding and hence to affect significantly the learning and *immediate* retention of the second passage. It is quite possible, of course, that consolidation of the first passage would result in superior *delayed* retention of the second passage.

These findings have some obvious implications for professional education that would, of course, have to be validated by direct research evidence. They suggest that much preprofessional education does not enhance professional competence as such. We might be able to produce physicians, engineers, teachers, and so forth who are just as competent professionally without giving them an elaborate series of preprofessional courses, provided that the basic minimum of relevant preprofessional material necessary for understanding professional content were included within and made part of professional instruction. These preprofessional courses can naturally be defended on other grounds—the broadening of the individual's intellectual horizons and general culture. But if this latter function rather than the enhancement of professional competence were actually their main justification, it might be important for educators to revise their concept of professional education, particularly today when so many persons must be retrained quickly for new professional fields.

## Distribution of Practice: Effect on Learning and Retention

The distribution of practice has long been a favorite topic of research and theoretical inquiry in the psychology of learning. In fact, more empirical evidence is available regarding the effects of distributed practice on learning and retention than regarding the comparable effects of simple frequency of practice. Generally speaking, the evidence supports the conclusion that distributed practice is more effective than massed practice for both learning and retention. The relative efficacy of distributed practice, however, depends on such factors as the age and ability of the learner, and the nature, quantity, and difficulty of the learning task. The advantages of distributed over massed practice, for example, are greater for younger and less able learners, or for long, rote, and difficult tasks, than they are for older and more able learners, or for short, meaningful, and easy tasks. For tasks requiring a prolonged warm-up period or considerable concentrated effort, distributed practice is demonstrably *less* effective than when it is massed.

Distribution of practice facilitates meaningful as well as rote learning. For reasons that will be specified later, however, it has less effect on meaningful than on rote learning[6] (Ash, 1950; Bumstead, 1940, 1943). Massed practice is more effective for the *immediate* retention of meaningfully learned materials (probably because of reminiscence), but distributed practice is superior when *delayed* tests of retention are administered (Fishman, Keller, & Atkinson, 1968; Gordon, 1925). An outstanding practical implication of this fact is the efficacy of cramming for immediate examination purposes but not for long-term retention.

Review of meaningfully learned material by rereading facilitates retention equally well when it is  delayed for about two weeks or when it is given soon after original learning (Peterson et al., 1935; Skaggs et al., 1930; Sones & Stroud, 1940). When the review is conducted by *testing*, however, it is most advantageously given shortly after original learning (Sones & Stroud, 1940; Spitzer, 1939; Tiedeman, 1948). The reason for this latter difference is quite self-evident: If the material to be reviewed must be supplied from the learner's memory, he or she must be able to recall enough of it to make review profitable. Hence, review by testing must be undertaken soon after learning, before very much is forgotten. But if the learner is not dependent on memory for his review material, he or she can wait for the most advantageous moment, which, as we have seen, occurs either shortly after original learning or after the original learning has been appreciably but not completely forgotten. The longer a memory trace is in storage, other things being equal, the stronger it tends to be. Learning and retention are thus positive functions of the intertrial interval (Bumstead, 1964).

---

[6] Meaningfulness reduces the facilitating effect of distributed practice on rote learning, but not significantly (Ellis, 1960; Underwood & Schulz, 1960).

## Mechanism of Action

The facilitating effect of distributed practice has been explained in terms of perseveration, work decrement, motivational, and forgetting theories. According to perseveration theorists, massed trials provide no opportunity for the necessary "fixation" of the neural activity accompanying and following practice. However, in addition to being vague and relying on empirically unvalidated and metaphorical neural phenomena, this theory fails to account for the differential effectiveness of distributed practice in relation to length, difficulty, and meaningfulness of the learning task, to prior relevant learning, and to length of the retention interval.

*Rehearsal*, a psychological variant of perseveration involving implicit practice, does not require any unparsimonious neurological assumptions, and may very well explain part of the effect of distributed practice in certain instances. But it definitely does not offer a complete explanation of the value of distributed practice, because the provision of intertrial rests has also been shown to facilitate learning in animals, in motor activities where rehearsal is improbable, and in practice schedules where rest intervals are filled with sleep (Spight, 1928) or other activities precluding rehearsal (Hovland, 1938, 1939, 1940a, 1940b, 1949).

Fatigue or boredom (manifestations and causes of work decrement) do not provide very satisfactory explanations of the effects of distributed practice because few learning tasks in the laboratory are long or strenuous enough to give rise to either phenomenon. Neither aspect of work decrement, furthermore, can account for the differential learning task and temporal position findings associated with distributed practice.

A somewhat more sophisticated work decrement explanation, couched in terms of "reactive inhibition" (the postulated self-inhibitory potential produced by a given response following its elicitation, which supposedly dissipates with rest), is hardly more enlightening. Inasmuch as the postulated mechanism of reactive inhibition invokes a purely hypothetical behavioral or neurophysiological process that has not been independently validated and is merely metaphorically descriptive of the empirical facts it purports to explain (the facilitation of learning when practice trials are distributed), the theory tends to be circular. Motivational theories stress the decline in interest and drive accompanying fatigue or boredom. These are vulnerable, of course, to the same criticisms that have been applied to the other theories.

Forgetting theories are both theoretically most cogent and most in accord with experimental evidence. They specify the following ways in which intertrial rests can facilitate later learning and/or retention trials:

1. If it is true that on any given trial, repetition primarily strengthens

those components of the learning task that are yet unlearned, the forgetting of previously learned components that occurs between trials in distributed practice schedules makes it possible for these latter components, as well as for the yet unlearned components, to profit from the strengthening effect of later trials.

2. Rest provides an opportunity both for the dissipation of the initial confusion and resistance characterizing initial learning shock, and for the forgetting of interfering (wrong, alternative, competing) responses or meanings (Underwood, 1961). The dissipation of initial learning shock here is comparable to that underlying the reminiscence effect in retention, except that it occurs in relation to numerous rest intervals rather than to a single rest interval. On the other hand, the dissipation of the inhibition caused by incorrect competing alternatives reflects the differentially faster rate of forgetting for these latter relatively weak elements than for their stronger counterparts (Easley, 1937).

3. Finally, and probably most important, the forgetting that takes place during intertrial rests enhances the facilitating influence of later trials. As a result of experiencing and becoming aware of the interfering processes that underlie the loss of associative and dissociability strength and bring about forgetting, the learner is better able to cope with and resist the decremental effects of these processes when he or she encounters them again during and after subsequent learning trials. Previous obliterative experience with interfering processes, in other words, appears to confer some degree of "immunity" to the recurrence of their detrimental effects on learning. Hence it tends to promote a higher residual level of associative or dissociability strength.

The "immunizing" effect of prior forgetting on later relearning and retention can also be inferred from Jost's laws, which state that the older of two associations of equal strength both profits more from additional repetition and is retained longer (Jost, 1897; Youtz, 1941). These laws are obviously implicated in the advantages conferred by distributed practice. For any given trial, intertrial rest intervals render the component associations or meanings of a learning task older than corresponding associations or meanings learned by means of massed practice.

Prior forgetting has this "immunizing" effect because the experience of learning and trying to remember makes the learner aware of relevant related concepts in cognitive structure and indicates areas of weakness, ambiguity, confusion, and lack of discriminability. Thus forearmed, he or she can take the necessary steps to strengthen appropriate related concepts in cognitive structure and particularly weak components of the learning task, as well as to increase discriminability between established ideas and related new propositions.

The forgetting theory of distributed practice effects is supported by research evidence (mostly in rote learning, however) showing that the relative effectiveness of distribution increases under conditions producing maximum interference or obliterative assimilation. Experimental studies already cited indicate that distributed practice is relatively more effective for longer than for shorter lists of nonsense syllables; for centrally placed than for end-of-list items in serial learning; and for rote learning tasks preceded by similar tasks in the laboratory than for completely novel rote tasks. Youtz (1941) has also demonstrated that subjects make fewer errors in central portions of older series of nonsense syllables than they do in central portions of more recently learned series. The principal reason why the facilitating effect of distributed practice is less striking for meaningful than for rotely learned material is probably the fact that less intertrial forgetting occurs when material is meaningfully learned. Fatigue, boredom, and motivational factors are also presumably less relevant for meaningful than for rote learning, and rehearsal is obviously less beneficial when less intertrial forgetting takes place.

In conclusion, it appears that short and widely spaced practice (or review) sessions that are introduced progressively further apart are best for meaningful learning and retention. One must be careful, however, not to space these sessions so far apart that total practice time is excessively reduced, that too much forgetting occurs, that a long warm-up period is required, or that the learning task is fragmented.

## Method of Practice

Method of practice refers to those factors concerned with the arrangement or ordering of practice trials, apart from the distribution of trials and rest intervals. It includes the following variables:

1. The relative proportions of study trials (presentation of the material) and test trials (recitation or recall)
2. The nature of the response—overt or covert, constructed or multiple-choice, verbatim recall or reformulated, prompted or unprompted
3. Whether the number of repetitions and the rate of presenting new material is or is not related to the success of prior performance

### Recitation versus Recapitulation

In reception learning, where the learning task is to internalize presented materials (facts, principles, arbitrary associations) so that they are available for later reproduction, the learner may either be presented with numerous study trials or repetitions of the task or may elect or be required to spend varying proportions of the total practice time in attempting to recall (recite) the material in test trials, with or without the benefit of prompting. The relevant research findings support the conclusion that whereas increasing proportions of recitation tend to facilitate *rote* learning and retention (Forlano, 1936; Gates, 1917; Hovland, Lumsdaine, & Sheffield, 1949) (retention more than learning), the facilitating effect of recitation on *meaningful* learning and retention is both less striking and more equivocal (Gates, 1917; Michael & Maccoby, 1953; H. A. Peterson, 1944).

The effectiveness of recitation, particularly for rote material, may be attributed to several factors. First, since the attempt to recall presented material actually tests whether and to what extent internalization (learning) has taken place, the "feedback" that is provided in the next trial is therefore a much more significant factor after recitation than after recapitulation. It indicates explicitly and systematically what the correct associations or meanings are in relation to the internalized learning that has already taken place. Under these circumstances, all of the effects of feedback—as an incentive condition; as cognitive confirmation, correction, clarification, and evaluation of the adequacy of learning; and as reinforcement following reduction of cognitive and ego-enhancing drives—are considerably intensified.

A closely related immediate consequence of feedback in this context is that as a result of discovering which parts of the learning task have not yet been sufficiently mastered, one is better able to focus one's attention and effort selectively on these latter aspects.

Second, the kind of participation involved in recitation, which is more active than rereading, implies greater learning effort. In addition to exerting a general facilitating influence on learning, this participation differentially salvages items at or near threshold strength and leads to more active and meaningful organization of the learned material (use of rhythm, mnemonic devices, and conceptual organizers).

Third, the conditions of recitation more nearly resemble the conditions under which the learning will eventually be exercised than do those of recapitulation.

For rote learning, where prompting is used, recitation is most effective if it is introduced after only a few study trials (Skaggs et al., 1930). Without the benefit of prompting, however, recitation is more advantageously introduced at a later stage of practice (L. O. Krueger, 1930; W. C. F. Krueger, 1930). Recitation apparently cannot prove helpful until enough material is learned so that a test trial can provide almost as much practice as a study trial. But if prompts are furnished to fill in gaps of knowledge, recitation obviously becomes feasible at an earlier point in a series of practice trials. Thus the principle governing the optimal temporal position for introducing recitation is similar to the principle determining the optimal spacing of reviews: If, on any given trial, the learner has to provide, from what has been previously learned, the stimulus material to be used for that trial, the temporal arrangements must ensure the existence of sufficient learning or retention, respectively, to make practice or review profitable. If, on the other hand, the learning task is presented to the learner, in whole or in part, sufficiency of learning or retention is a less important consideration than Jost's laws.

The markedly reduced effectiveness of recitation with respect to *meaningful* learning and retention is not difficult to understand. To begin with, the logical sequential structure of connected meaningful discourse makes *implicit* recitation possible during the same trial; that is, in the course of rereading, subjects typically tend to anticipate the remembered facts and propositions that follow logically from the material they are currently perusing. In the case of meaningful material, also, where the achievement of understanding is both a reward and an incentive in its own right, less effort is required for learning, and the incentive and ego-enhancement values of feedback are less important. Explicit testing is similarly less necessary for the confirmation, correction, clarification, and evaluation effects of feedback in view of the fact that the internal logic of the material partly provides its own feedback. It enables subjects to appreciate whether they have grasped meanings correctly and, in any case, implicitly to test their understandings against the next presentation of the material. Finally, meaningful learning tasks benefit less from the organizing effects of recitation since they possess an inherent organization of their own. Nevertheless, recitation can still facilitate meaningful learning—even when conducted early in the course of learning and without the use of prompts. Random recitation is superior to predictable recitation in enhancing both immediate and delayed retention because it compels the learner to remain attentive (Hudgins & Gore, 1966).

### Nature of the Response

#### Overtness

Closely related to, but not completely co-extensive with, the recitation-recapitulation issue is the problem of whether the subject's mode of response during practice is overt or covert. Overtness of response does not necessarily imply recall or construction, as does recitation, but merely some measure of activity and externality (observability). Hence either reading, listening to, or "mentally composing" answers to questions can be regarded as "covert" responses, whereas both the construction of an appropriate answer and the selection of a suitable multiple-choice alternative must be categorized as "overt." Admittedly, however, constructed responses rank higher on a scale of overtness than do selected responses.

The overt-covert dimension of practice has been explored principally in relation to a limited variety of automated instruction contexts—those involving meaningful learning, using programs of short duration, and for the most part requiring short-term retention. The research findings under these conditions indicate that subjects who respond covertly not only learn and retain verbal material as well as or better than subjects who construct their responses, but also do so more efficiently in terms of learning time[7] (Anderson, Faust, & Roderick, 1968; Della-Piana, 1961; Evans, Glaser, & Homme, 1960c; Goldbeck & Briggs, 1960; Goldbeck, Campbell, & Llewellyn, 1960; Krumboltz, 1961; Lambert et al., 1962; Pressey, 1962a; Roe, 1962; Silberman, 1962; Silverman & Alter, 1960; Stolurow & Walker, 1962; Wittrock, 1963d; Yarmey, 1964). Overt selection of multiple-choice answers, for instance, by pushing a button, is similarly no more effective than listening to or reading the correct underlined answers (Kaess & Zeaman, 1960; Keislar & McNeil, 1961; McNeil & Keislar, 1961). Under certain circumstances, however, overtness of response may facilitate learning and retention.

In trying to understand these findings and to reconcile them with the research on recitation, it is necessary to consider the various ways in which overtness of response influences, or allegedly influences, learning and retention. In the first place, it is self-evident that overtness of response facilitates perceptual-motor learning in instances where the overtly practiced response itself is one of the objects of learning (that is, part of the learning task). But in most instances the overt response (for example, writing, pressing a lever) is already a well-established component of the learner's response repertory and constitutes merely a nonspecific means of responding to test questions. Here the response-acquisition advantage of overtness is irrelevant and overt responses are more time-consuming and less efficient than their covert counterparts (Gagné, 1962b; Walker & Stolurow, 1962).

Second, it is widely asserted that behavior must be "emitted" in order to be properly reinforced through drive reduction (Holland, 1960; Skinner, 1958). Nevertheless, although this notion is a key assumption of the more orthodox brands of behaviorism, there is little theoretical justification for believing that associations and response dispositions (sets) cannot be similarly reinforced.

Third, overtness of response plainly makes more explicit testing of knowledge possible, which in turn enhances the cognitive, drive-reduction, and motivational effects of feedback. This consideration is probably very

---

[7] Krumboltz and Weisman (1962a) found the overt response mode more effective in delayed (two-week) retention, but Wittrock (1963d), using a one-year retention criterion, failed to confirm their findings. Hillix and Marx (1960) reported that subjects who actively made their own trial-and-error responses in learning light circuits learned less efficiently than subjects who observed others making the very same responses. Goldbeck and Campbell (1962), on the other hand, found the *covert* response mode differentially more effective in delayed versus immediate retention.

important for rote learning, and undoubtedly accounts for much of the value of recitation when rote materials are used. However, for reasons already specified, it has little applicability to meaningful learning. Thus, since practically all of the research in this area has been conducted with potentially meaningful programmed materials, it is not surprising that the findings have been almost uniformly negative.

The facilitating effect of overtness of response on meaningful learning is further reduced in an automated instruction context, inasmuch as the provision of feedback tends to make relatively little difference when the error rate is low (Evans, Glaser, & Homme, 1960a). If because of small step size (slow rate of introducing new material), the subject's responses are almost invariably correct in any case, he or she obviously does not stand to profit very much from the potentially facilitating cognitive effects of feedback. In support of this interpretation is the fact that overtness of response is differentially more effective for difficult than for easy programmed material (Goldbeck, 1960; Goldbeck & Campbell, 1962) and for intellectually less able than for intellectually more able students (Wittrock, 1963d). Suppes and Ginsberg (1962b) report that overt correction of error facilitates mathematical concept learning in 6-year-old children. But from their data it is not clear whether the overtness of the correction or merely the correction procedure itself is the determinative variable.

Meaningfulness of material, as previously explained, also negates a fourth possible reason for the effectiveness of overt responses: the fact that the latter imply greater activity and hence greater effort and more efficient organization of learning.[8] It is interesting to note in this connection that when overtly and covertly responding subjects do not differ in motivation, they also do not differ in learning outcomes (McNeil & Keislar, 1961). This suggests but does not confirm the possibility that the facilitating effects of overtness, when they do occur, are partly mediated by motivational variables.

Finally, overt response during practice could conceivably facilitate learning by resembling more closely than covert response the response mode that is typically required in the criterial situation. In an empirical test of this hypothesis, however, response mode had no more effect on learning outcomes when the overt response was directly relevant to the behavior sampled on the posttest (Wittrock, 1963d) than when such relevance was lacking (Keislar & McNeil, 1962). Finally, constructed response modes yield superior learning outcomes when used with technical as opposed to familiar material (Tobias, 1969), probably because it demands greater effort and concentration.

---

[8] According to Holland (1960), automated instruction even leads to a more active type of covert learning, inasmuch as the material "stands still" instead of moving past the learner (as in a book or lecture) when his attention wanders.

### Constructed or Multiple-Choice

The rationale for constructing rather than selecting answers during practice trials is precisely the same as that already specified for overtness of response. In addition, exposing subjects to wrong answers presumably engenders and strengthens undesired competing responses (Skinner, 1958). These considerations, of course, apply primarily to the learning of rote materials, both because overtness of response is not particularly advantageous in meaningful learning (see above) and because the presence of competing responses affects meaningful learning differently than it does rote learning. In the case of arbitrary, verbatim learning, the increased availability of competing responses is self-evidently harmful. The reason is that the desired arbitrary response is correct by definition and only has to be discriminated from similar rote responses that *actually* occur in recent proximity (rather than from all other logically plausible alternatives). In these circumstances, furthermore, one response is inherently just as plausible as another. In the case of meaningful learning, however, the new learning task largely consists of discriminating the correct meaning from other relevant alternatives, and built-in criteria exist in cognitive structure and in the learning material itself for assessing relative degrees of plausibility. Therefore the identification of the relevant alternatives constitutes the first step in enhancing the discriminability of the newly presented ideas.

The clarification of meaningful new ideas, in other words, is largely a process of differentiating the propositions in question from related established propositions in cognitive structure and from other plausible alternatives in the learning material (Pressey, 1962a, 1962b). But before the comparative and evaluative aspects of such differentiation can be successfully undertaken, it is first necessary to identify as precisely as possible the nature and source of the confusion, that is, to make explicit the various relevant alternatives.[9] Pressey's "adjunctive auto-instruction" (1960) uses multiple-choice items to sharpen meanings *after* initial presentation and learning of the material. Crowder (1960), on the other hand, employs the multiple-choice format as part of the programming procedure itself ("intrinsic programming"). The subject chooses one of several presented alternatives for a given test item and, depending on the particular wrong alternative he or she chooses, is then given a differential set of corrective materials that both explain the nature of the error and retest the subject for evidence of clarification.

Research on the relative efficacy of constructed and selected responses (Briggs, 1958; Coulson & Silberman, 1960a; Evans, Glaser, & Homme,

---

[9] That learners can profit from the exposure to and mistaken choice of wrong alternatives is shown by the fact that the percentage of correct answers increased on retest one month later for subjects in an experimental group who were given automated instruction (auto-instruction) with multiple-choice items after studying the learning task (R. S. Jones, 1950). This increase did not occur in the case of control subjects who did not receive any auto-instruction.

1960b; Roe, 1962) generally indicates that the two response modes are not significantly different in terms of learning and retention outcomes, but that the constructed mode is less efficient (requires more time). Since all of the above-cited studies used meaningful programmed materials to which the advantages of the constructed response are least applicable, it is not surprising that the latter response mode was not shown to be superior. In the one study reporting a significant difference in favor of constructed responses (Fry, 1960) the learning task (Spanish vocabulary) was both more rotelike and relatively difficult (high error rate). In two other studies the constructed response mode proved superior only in relation to technical versus general items (Tobias, 1969; Williams, 1966). On the other hand, the hypothesized superiority of the multiple-choice format for the learning and retention of meaningful materials also failed to be empirically substantiated by these studies. It is conceivable, however, that the discriminability advantage inherent in the multiple-choice response mode was counteracted by the greater learning time and effort involved in constructing responses.

### Prompting and Guidance

The learner's responses during the course of practice may be completely unaided, on the one hand, or receive the benefit of varying degrees of external assistance, on the other. The nature and significance of such assistance obviously differ greatly depending on whether reception or discovery learning is involved. In a discovery learning situation, assistance takes the form of guidance—providing cues that detract from the learner's opportunity for autonomous discovery. Hence guidance refers to and affects the reception-discovery dimension of learning. The provision of complete guidance is tantamount to presenting the learner with the essential content of the learning task (reception learning), whereas the absence of any guidance whatsoever requires completely autonomous discovery. The degree of guidance furnished in most instances of discovery learning typically falls between these two extremes. Guided discovery, for example, often consists of:

1. Socratic or rhetorical questioning (Larson, 1963)

2. The arrangement of a hierarchical series of examples of problems for the learner, graded in difficulty, which, when completed, leads almost inevitably to the correct principle or generalization (Beberman, 1958)

3. The provision of a general rule without examples or the provision of worked examples without a rule (Wittrock, 1963c)

4. Furnishing verbal directions that guide discovery (Gagné & Brown, 1961; Gagné, Mayor, Garstens, & Paradise, 1962)

5. Providing a demonstration, special exercises, or didactic instruction that highlight underlying substantive principles, correct form, critical cues, or efficient strategies of attack (T. Anderson, 1942; Cox, 1933; Davies, 1945; Goodenough & Brian, 1929; May & Lumsdaine, 1958; Vander Meer, 1945).

All of the foregoing methods have proved more effective than either *complete* discovery or reception learning, particularly in the retention and transfer of problem-solving skills.

In a reception learning situation, external assistance takes the form of *prompting* during the test trials. This assistance does not affect the autonomy of discovery, since the content of the learning task is wholly presented in any case. It does influence the autonomy of reproduction, however. The learner is assisted, in whole or in part, to reproduce previously presented material that as yet has not been internalized above the threshold of availability. If the entire and explicit substance of the information demanded by the test item is furnished, the stimulus support can be regarded as a *prompt*. If the stimulus support is less complete and explicit during the test trial, it can be considered a *cue*.

Prompting is more necessary and effective in the earlier stages of reception learning because at this time the learner has not yet internalized sufficient material to receive much practice benefit from unaided recitation (Briggs, 1961; Della-Piana, 1961). Furthermore, the provision of prompts at this early point of practice can prevent guesswork and the learning of errors (incorrect competing responses) and thus obviate the necessity for costly unlearning. For such reasons, prompting is more efficacious than confirmation (feedback) for relatively short periods of practice in reception learning (Briggs, 1958, 1961; Cook & Spitzer, 1960; Hovland, Lumsdaine, & Sheffield, 1949; Kaess & Zeaman, 1960; Merrill, Wood, & Starr, 1969; Silberman, Melaragno, & Coulson, 1961a, 1961b; L. M. Smith, 1962).

During the later stages of practice, however, these considerations are obviously less relevant. In addition, it is important that the conditions of practice gradually begin to approximate the desired (unprompted) end-point of the learning product. Hence, as the amount of correct learning increases, both reduction of the completeness and explicitness of the prompts (Holland, 1960; Israel, 1960; Lumsdaine, 1961; Popp & Porter, 1960) and their replacement by confirmation (Angell & Lumsdaine, 1960; Lumsdaine, 1961; Stolurow, 1961) are advantageous for further learning. On theoretical grounds it also seems plausible that prompting could be profitably dispensed with earlier in the case of meaningful than of rote reception learning because of the more rapid rate of acquisition and the different role played by competing responses.

A review of short-term studies of the role of guidance in meaningful discovery learning leads to the conclusion that guided or semiautonomous discovery[10] is more efficacious for learning, retention, and transfer than is

---

[10] Either providing the learner with a verbal explanation of the underlying principles and permitting him or her to apply them autonomously to specific examples, or encouraging self-discovery of the principles after working a carefully graded series of relevant problems.

either completely autonomous discovery or the provision of complete guidance. Wittrock (1963c) and Wittrock and Twelker (1964) further substantiated this conclusion recently in well-controlled studies in which college students were taught to decipher transposition codes. Although more retention and transfer[11] occurred when the rule was provided than when it was not provided, an "intermediate" type of guidance (furnishing either the rule itself or a worked example of it) was more effective than furnishing both rule and worked example or furnishing neither rule nor example. The provision of rules was more effective in all instances than the provision of worked examples. Guidance under these circumstances apparently sensitizes the learner to the salient aspects of the problem, orients him or her to the goal, and promotes economy of learning by preventing misdirected effort.[12]

Some opportunity for autonomous discovery is obviously necessary in those instances where the object of learning is not merely the acquisition of knowledge but also the development of skill in formulating general principles and in applying them to particular problem situations. Verbally presented principles, it is true, are transferable to such situations even if they are not self-discovered. However, the ability to solve a particular class of problems efficiently also presupposes experience in coping with the distinctive features of that class of problems, in hypothesis formulation and testing, in the strategy of application, in identifying fruitful approaches that minimize costly risk and unnecessary cognitive strain, in using systematic and economic methods of inquiry, and in maintaining a flexible and meaningful learning set.

Actual discovery experience is even more important in trial-and-error learning and in the learning of perceptual-motor skills. Adequate learning

[11] This superiority of guided discovery over reception learning is partly reflective of an experimental artifact. Since criterial tests in this experimental design invariably involve discovery learning, the guided discovery group enjoys the advantage of transferable discovery experience (problem-solving, strategy of attack) in the learning trials. This interpretation is especially pertinent to Larson's (1963) study in which a guided discovery group obtained higher scores on a transfer test than did either a complete discovery or a "no discovery" group. These results were evident despite the fact that all three groups performed almost identically on an immediately preceding delayed retention test.

[12] Even though subjects who learn by the complete or guided discovery methods enjoy the advantage of transferable discovery experience from learning to criterial trials, they are, in another sense, at a disadvantage compared to the reception learning group with respect to opportunity for acquisition, retention, and transfer. Insofar as they fail in many instances to discover the principles that are simply presented to the latter group, they necessarily manifest less ability to demonstrate acquisition, retention, and transfer. Larson (1963) controlled this variable by presenting the discovery groups a summary of the correct principles *after* an initial period of autonomous or guided learning. Nevertheless, he found that the guided discovery group was still inferior on the acquisition trials since the "experimenter's verbalization of the principles interfered with the consolidation of intuitive principles emerging during the training."

in these circumstances also requires that the individual learn what *not* to do. This requires first-hand experience in making mistakes and correcting them. Thus, although appropriate guidance helps the learner avoid unnecessary error in the early stages of practice, its value tends to diminish as it increases in amount or extends into the later stages of practice (Carr, 1930; Gates & Taylor, 1926). Since he or she must eventually perform the learning task unaided, the learner must also avoid becoming overdependent on guidance.

In conclusion, the unquestioning faith that advocates of incidental learning have in autonomous unguided discovery is justified neither by logic nor by research evidence. In the first place, laboratory and problem-solving exercises are not inherently or necessarily meaningful. They may lead to little or no meaningful learning if a student's learning set is simply rotely to memorize "type" problems or techniques of manipulating reagents and symbols and if the student has inadequate background in or appreciation of the substantive and methodological principles underlying specific problem-solving or laboratory procedures.

Second, what is typically called the "discovery method" is really a contrived type of discovery that is a far cry from the truly autonomous discovery activities of the research scholar or scientist. Pure discovery techniques could lead only to utter chaos and a waste of time in the classroom, inasmuch as immature students generally lack sufficient subject-matter sophistication both to formulate workable problems and to devise appropriate and relevant research methods. Before students can "discover" generalizations reasonably efficiently, problems must be structured for them in such a way as to make ultimate discovery almost inevitable.

Third, numerous short-term studies have demonstrated that guided discovery is more efficacious for learning, retention, and transfer than is either completely autonomous discovery or the provision of complete guidance. However, these findings do not necessarily indicate that guided discovery is more effective for teaching *subject-matter content* than is simple didactic exposition. For one thing, the solving by a naive subject of a few novel problems in a laboratory setting is hardly comparable to the learning of a large body of sequentially organized material by learners with varying degrees of subject-matter sophistication. The problems used in laboratory studies are deliberately chosen on the basis of their relative unrelatedness to previously acquired knowledge. For another, even contrived discovery techniques are typically more time-consuming than expository teaching.

Much also depends on the relative time-cost of the two approaches, on the learner's cognitive maturity and degree of subject-matter sophistication, on the nature of the learning task (descriptive information, representational equivalents, or principles that are discoverable by stating and testing hypotheses), and on whether the objective of the learning experience is to acquire knowledge, enhance problem-solving ability, or obtain insight into scientific method.

Fourth, guidance in the form of prompting has been shown to be very helpful during the early stages of learning. At this point in the learning process the learner has not yet mastered sufficient material to receive much practice benefit from unaided recitation. Further, the provision of prompts can prevent the learning of errors and thus obviate the necessity for costly unlearning.

### Verbatim Recall Versus Reformulated Response

In measuring comprehension and retention of meaningful verbal content, test items can be appropriately constructed either to encourage verbatim recall of the presented material, or to lead the learner to reformulate understanding of the material in terms of his or her own vocabulary and ideational background. Although explicit empirical evidence is lacking on this issue, the reformulation approach has at least three theoretical arguments in its favor:

1. It constitutes a valid measure of genuine understanding.
2. It requires active participation of the learner in the testing situation.
3. It tends to discourage the adoption of a rote learning set in future learning efforts.

Other ways of accomplishing the same purposes in a formal testing context include the use of a multiple-choice format, employing application or problem-solving items, and measuring ability to learn a new set of propositions presupposing mastery of the content being tested. In a less formal testing context, the substitution of appropriate recitation trials for study trials tends to encourage reformulation rather than verbatim reproduction.

### *Differential Practice Schedules*

Should all learners complete uniform practice schedules irrespective of the quality of prior performance, or should the content and step size of subsequent practice trials be differentially adjusted in terms of the individual learner's success or failure and type of error on preceding learning tasks or test items? Three types of differential adjustment are possible. First, in a constructed response program the unsuccessful learner is repeatedly confronted with the same item and is not permitted to advance further in the program until the correct answer is obtained. Second, in a multiple-choice type program the successful learner merely proceeds to the next set of items, and the unsuccessful learner is given another easier series of items or a differential set of corrective materials related to the nature of his or her errors. Third, in either type of program the size of step may be increased on subsequent items for the successful individual and decreased for the unsuccessful individual.

The nondifferential program, in which all learners proceed through the same sequence of steps, is conventionally referred to as "linear," in contrast to the "branching" or "multiple-track" type of differential program. Available research evidence regarding this issue is far from definitive. The weight of the evidence suggests that branching programs, requiring either simple repetition of incorrectly answered items or more differential corrective exercises, are more efficient in terms of learning time (Briggs, 1958; Coulson & Silberman, 1960a). Branching programs also result in learning outcomes that are either equal to (Beane, 1962; Briggs, 1958; Coulson & Silberman, 1960a; S. R. Meyer, 1960a; Silberman, Melaragno, & Coulson, 1961b) or better than (Coulson et al., 1962; Holland & Porter, 1961; Irion & Briggs, 1957; Melaragno, 1967) those of linear programs.

On purely theoretical grounds the branching procedure should be superior to the linear procedure because it ensures mastery (consolidation) of a prior item of knowledge in a sequentially organized program before the learner can proceed to the next step in the sequence. It accomplishes this objective by adapting both to *intraindividual* differences with respect to the relative difficulty level of different portions of the program and to *interindividual* differences in general intellectual ability and in particular subject-matter sophistication. The branching program, in other words, requires both that *all* learners devote selectively greater learning effort to those items they find more difficult and that generally less able learners, on the average, take more practice trials than generally more able learners in mastering a given unit of material. It also takes into account the particular reasons or misconceptions underlying errors in each individual and endeavors to correct rather than ignore them. Thus quite apart from, and in addition to, the effect of consolidation on sequentially dependent learning, differential practice and feedback result in greater original learning of each component item in a related series of learning tasks.

Skinner (1958) argues, on the other hand, that consolidation can be assured, without requiring repetition of incorrectly answered items, by using a linear program with small task and step size and correspondingly low error rate. Under these circumstances differential programs are allegedly unnecessary for different ability levels, since even low-ability students do not make an appreciable number of errors, and high-ability students can simply move through the program more rapidly. Shay's (1961) study provides some support for this position by indicating that differential adjustment of step size to ability level does not significantly enhance learning outcomes. His findings, however, have no bearing whatsoever on the repetition or correction issue.

In this latter connection, previously cited evidence suggests that learning outcomes are adversely affected by lack of opportunity to correct errors.

This is particularly true for low-ability students who, despite an ostensibly low error rate, actually learn considerably less than high-ability students after completing the same linear program (Beane, 1962; Keislar & McNeil, 1961; Shay, 1961; Silberman, Melaragno, & Coulson, 1961b; Wittrock, 1963d). It is, therefore, unsafe to assume that dull students necessarily learn as much as bright students from the linear programs that they both complete and that the only difference between them lies in the number of programs each group is able to master in a given unit of time.

## General Conditions of Practice

In addition to frequency, distribution, and various specific aspects of method of practice (recitation versus recapitulation, nature of the response, linear versus branching programs), many *general* conditions of practice undoubtedly influence learning and retention outcomes. These conditions include learning set, naturalness of the practice setting, and degree of task homogeneity. Unfortunately, however, relatively little research evidence is available regardng the effects of these important variables.

### Natural versus Structured Settings (Drill)

One of the strongest legacies of the progressive education movement and of Thorndikian educational psychology that still remains on the pedagogic scene is a confused and contradictory attitude toward structured practice or drill. As a result, we often tend to minimize the value of drill—but more in educational theory than in actual practice. The very term *drill* still evokes unsavory connotations in educational circles. Actually, of course, drill is a necessary and indispensable aspect of classroom learning. In a generic sense, it refers to those aspects of the practice variable that affect learning outcomes. Stroud puts the matter very well:

> In our anxiety over the abuses, alleged and real, we have a tendency to forget the fact that there are intelligent, constructive uses of drill. . . . Drill is currently purported, and by some who have been identified with education long enough to know better, to be the handiwork of stimulus-response psychology.
>
> In appraising drill as a teaching procedure, it is well to remember that it is not mere repetition but repetition of the conditions of learning that is effective. Drill can be effective, ineffective, or positively detrimental; spirited or spiritless. Pupils do not necessarily learn just because they engage in drill. . . . In the best educational practice, pupils are engaged in drill after the need of it has been demonstrated.
>
> Drill should be recognized for what it is worth and no more. Perhaps no one has ever maintained seriously that drill in spelling will teach a pupil

to think, cultivate his character, improve his social adjustment, or make him more democratic. Other provisions are made for these aspects of his education. By drill in spelling he does learn to spell. The cultivation of his rational abilities or of his personality, be it ever so well done, is not sufficient to teach him to spell.

Undoubtedly, there are many undesirable features of drill work in our schools. It should not be allowed to become monotonous. Excessive and unessential written work should be avoided. Because of its repetitive character, pupils are likely to lose interest in it more quickly than in most other kinds of activity. For this reason, the length of such practice periods should be relatively short (Stroud, 1942, pp. 362, 364).

The fetish of naturalism and incidental learning embodied in the activity program movement emphasizes these five points:

1. Unstructured and uncontrived learning situations
2. Direct kinds of experience, in a concrete, manipulative sense
3. Unintentional or nondeliberate learning effort
4. Learning by autonomous, unguided discovery
5. Exposure to diversified rather than repetitive experience

The issue of intentional learning will be considered in Chapter 11. Some attention has already been given to the problem of guided learning, and the matter will be considered at greater length in the discussion on learning by discovery in Chapter 15. The issue of task homogeneity will be considered in the next section.

How desirable is it that practice takes place in natural (real-life, uncontrived) settings? Enthusiastic supporters of project and activity methods, as we have already seen, take a rather extreme position on this issue, rejecting all kinds of highly structured practice (drill) and advocating, in effect, an incidental type of learning. It is true, of course (providing that all factors are equal), that learning is enhanced when the conditions of practice closely resemble the conditions under which the skill or knowledge in question will eventually be used. Such learning is also less likely to be monotonous and enjoys the benefit of higher levels of interest and motivation. Wholly natural settings, however, rarely provide the practice conditions that are either necessary or optimal for efficient learning.

Generally, it is only during the latter stages of learning, *after* component aspects of the learning task have already been identified and mastered in structured practice sessions, that naturalistic "dress rehearsals" become feasible. In the first place, uncontrived learning experiences typically fail to include a sufficient number of properly spaced practice trials as well as adequate opportunity for differential repetition of particularly difficult components. Second, unstructured practice does not receive the benefit of skilled pedagogic selection, presentation, and organization of material; of careful sequencing, pacing, and gradation of difficulty; and of optimal balancing of intratask repetition, intratask variability, and intertask variability. Third, most learning effort is enhanced by deliberate intention to learn.

The important teaching principle of initial simplification of difficult learning tasks for unsophisticated pupils runs counter to the doctrine of natural or unstructured learning. Exposing unsophisticated learners to all of the complexities of natural, "unarranged" data in the laboratory or of subtle distinctions and qualifications in expository teaching is the surest way of confusing and overwhelming them. The use of artificial "crutches," gradation of difficulty, and slowing down the rate of presentation (Baker & Osgood, 1954; Lawrence & Goodwin, 1954; von Wright, 1957) are common forms of simplification in classroom learning.

In an introductory course, simplification of content—*without* teaching wrong ideas that have to be unlearned later—is always justifiable and indicated. This can be accomplished by simply presenting more general and less complete versions of much of the same material that can be presented subsequently in greater depth and at high levels of sophistication. In an introductory course in biology, for example, it is less damaging to present inadequate historical detail and experimental evidence than to obscure the major concepts by providing excessive historical and experimental data.

It is possible, for example, to present ideas relatively simply—yet correctly—in an introductory course in high-school biology (1) by deleting a great deal of the dispensable terminological, methodological, and historical detail, as well as many of the intermediate steps in argumentation; (2) by telescoping or condensing material; (3) by eliminating tangential "asides" and less important qualifications; (4) by limiting the scope of coverage; (5) by omitting formulas, equations, and structural diagrams of complex molecules that are actually meaningless to unsophisticated students; (6) by keeping the level of discourse general and simple; (7) by writing lucidly, using terms precisely and consistently, and giving concise and familiar examples; (8) by using schematically simplified models and diagrams; (9) by removing as many irrelevant cues as possible[13] (Amster, 1966); and (10) by bearing in mind that a satiation point exists for any student. An atypically high level of sophistication may sometimes be employed simply to illustrate the complexity of a given topic, but in these instances students should be explicitly instructed not to master the details.

Many features of the "activity" program were based on the self-evident proposition that the elementary-school child perceives the world in relatively concrete and intuitive terms. The child requires considerable direct

---

[13] Amster (1966) found that such cues inhibited learning and diminished the effects of practice. Irrelevant information when presented irregularly together with relevant information, however, enables learners to better pace rehearsal of the current learning situation (Monty, Karsh, & Taub, 1963).

experience with many concrete instances of a given set of relationships before he or she can acquire genuinely meaningful concepts and generalizations. Thus, an attempt was made to teach factual information and intellectual skills through the medium of direct, manipulative experience in natural settings rather than through verbal exposition and drill.

In older pupils, however, once a sufficient number of basic abstract concepts is acquired, new concepts are primarily derived from other verbal abstractions rather than from direct experience, and new propositions are comprehended without any direct reference to or manipulation of concrete props. In the secondary school, therefore, it may be desirable to reverse both the sequential relationship and relative proportion between abstract concepts and concrete data. Thus there is good reason for believing that much of the time presently spent in busywork laboratory exercises in the sciences could be more advantageously employed in formulating more precise definitions, differentiating explicitly between related concepts, generalizing from hypothetical situations, and so forth.

### Task Homogeneity

Proponents of "activity" programs tended to favor task heterogeneity in practice. That is, they sought, in part, to escape the opprobrium associated with drill by stressing diversity both in the types of learning tasks and in the examples of each type that are presented to the learner.

Relative degree of task homogeneity is often an important practical consideration in the learning of skills and inductively acquired concepts and principles. The issue is whether such learnings can be acquired most efficiently as a result of intensive practice with just a few exemplars or as a result of less intensive practice with a large variety of exemplars. We have already concluded in an earlier chapter that, other factors being equal, the defining attributes of a given concept are learned most readily when the concept is encountered in many diverse contexts. Such experience obviously lessens the particularity and enhances the generality of abstract knowledge and transferable skills.

It is important to quality this conclusion, however, by pointing out that if this multicontextual experience is acquired at the expense of attaining adequate mastery of the particular component tasks that comprise it, its overall effect on learning is detrimental. In learning general concepts, principles, and skills inductively, experience with a particular exemplar has a positive transfer effect on other exemplars *only* if it is adequately consolidated. Similarly, it is only by mastering several exemplars in the same fashion that the total experience can be successfully utilized in formulating a transferable generalization. Thus, transfer in "learning set" problems requires mastery *within* a given type of problem as well as experience with many variants of this problem type. "When compared with giving only one class (with eight problems), two classes (with four problems per class) may be enough of a variety to enhance transfer to new [problem-solving] instances" (Wittrock & Twelker, 1964). Also, if the supportive empirical instances of a concept (Kurtz & Hovland, 1956) or a proposition are too heterogeneous in content or sequence of presentation, learning is impeded.

It seems therefore that efficient learning of transferable skills and knowledge demands a proper balance between the overlearning of particular intratask instances, on the one hand, and adequate exposure to intra- and intertask diversity, on the other. These two conditions of practice are complementary and mutually supportive rather than antithetical or mutually preclusive. It is quite probable, however, that their optimal proportions vary in different learning tasks. Many cases of disability in particular academic skills can undoubtedly be attributed to overemphasis on the importance of diversified experience in unstructured learning situations, with consequent insufficiency of practice and failure to attain mastery of the component habit exemplars from which the skill in question is derived. Hence we should not lose sight of the fact that the acquisition of general skills is dependent upon the prior consolidation of more particular habit exemplars[14] and that these skills are therefore not efficiently or satisfactorily established unless learners practice the underlying exemplars sufficiently to master them thoroughly. Generally speaking, educators have tended to stress the importance of extensity as opposed to intensity in learning. Actually, if a choice must be made, it is preferable to know a few things well than to have a passing acquaintance with many. A small quantity of consolidated knowledge is both useful and transferable; a large quantity of diffuse and unstable knowledge is utterly useless.

Another obvious advantage of multicontextual learning, if it does not interfere with intratask mastery, is that it prevents boredom and enhances the exploratory drive. This is particularly true in the case of more intelligent learners; less intertask variability is required to sustain the interest of duller pupils (Armistead, 1961). Learning set considerations bearing on desirable degree of intertask variability in practice will be considered in the next section.

### Learning Set

The term "learning set" refers to current disposition to learn or perform in a particular way. Hence in its broader meaning it also includes the learner's disposition to learn in a rote or meaningful fashion. Meaningful

[14] Skills are generally differentiated from habits (1) in being executed more deliberately and less mechanically, and (2) in embodying a general capacity to perform a whole class of operations rather than mere facility in executing a particular exemplar of that class. When a person becomes highly proficient at a given skill, however, the psychological distinction between skill and habit tends to vanish. The entire class of operations then acquires nearly as much particularity as the former habit and becomes almost as mechanical in its execution.

learning set, as one of the major prerequisites for meaningful learning, is obviously an important general condition of practice, but it has already been fully discussed in another context.

In the present context, therefore, we shall consider learning set only insofar as it reflects the influence of *recently prior* learning experience or activity. This aspect of learning set reflects both general methodological sophistication in approaching a given learning task or attacking a particular type of problem ("learning to learn") and an appropriate performance attitude or momentary state of readiness for engaging in a particular kind of activity ("warm-up" effect). Both of these components of learning set obviously contribute to positive transfer.

Irrespective of the kind of learning involved (nonsense syllables, mazes, poetry, paired adjectives), practice on one task tends to facilitate the learning of another similar task, provided that there is no conflictful overlapping of content between them (Thune, 1950a; Ward, 1937). Harlow's (1949) "learning set" phenomenon largely reflects the cumulative influence of "learning to learn" as a result of successive intra- and intertask experience with a particular type of discrimination problem. Learning set is therefore a significant general condition of practice to bear in mind in ordering the distribution and sequencing of practice as well as the optimal degree of intertrial task homogeneity.

It is important on theoretical grounds not to confound the learning-to-learn and warm-up aspects of learning set. The former consists of relatively stable *cognitive* acquisitions, concerned with the strategy of learning, that are derived from past learning experience. These acquisitions influence the actual content and direction of ongoing learning activity. The latter consists of transitory readiness factors involved in the momentary focusing of attention, mobilization of effort, and overcoming of initial inertia that are associated with "being appropriately set" to perform a given task. Warm-up effects, naturally, are rather rapidly dissipated (Hamilton, 1950), accounting at most for part of the intertask improvement in learning that occurs during the course of a single day's practice. Longer-term improvement (from one day to another) must be accounted for solely in terms of learning-to-learn effects (Thune, 1950b). Irion (1949) has shown that much rote forgetting is caused by the loss of set to recall that takes place during the retention interval. By using a "warming-up" (color-naming) task during the "rest" interval he was able greatly to facilitate the retention of paired associates.[15] In the case of meaningful retention, warm-up effects are also presumably

---

[15] In the familiar retroactive inhibition paradigm, the net decrement in retention that results from the interpolation of a similar task occurs despite the facilitating warm-up effect of the interpolated task. Evidently the general retroactive facilitation attributable to warm-up is not great enough to overcome the specific interfering influence of similar conflicting content in rote learning.

operative, but probably less conspicuously so than in rote retention.

In programming potentially meaningful material, it is obviously important to preserve sufficient commonality between successive learning tasks to take advantage of both the learning-to-learn and warm-up components of learning set. At the same time, however, enough heterogeneity of inter-task content should be introduced to prevent the mechanical perseveration of a given learning set and to discourage rigidity of approach and the development of a rote learning attitude. The need for multiple warm-up periods is one of the chief disadvantages of distributed practice. It renders such distribution unfeasible in certain tasks requiring considerable sustained effort.

### Knowledge of Results (Feedback)

On theoretical grounds, knowledge of results (or feedback) would appear to be an extremely important practice variable. Nevertheless, because of serious gaps and inadequacies in the available research evidence, we possess very little unequivocal information either about its actual effects on learning or about its mechanism of action.

As previously indicated, some knowledge of results is apparently essential for learning in those perceptual-motor tasks where a variable or indeterminate response must be given to a constantly presented stimulus. If, for example, the task is repeatedly to draw a 3-inch line, the learner obviously cannot manifest any improvement unless he or she knows to what extent previous efforts approximate the desired standard (E. L. Thorndike, 1931, 1932). In other instances, however, where *both* stimulus and response are provided (for instance, paired-associate learning), or where the learner must simply comprehend and internalize the material presented, feedback facilitates learning and retention (Hershberger, 1964). However, it is certainly not indispensable for either outcome. Feedback, furthermore, is not even indispensable for all types of perceptual-motor learning. In tasks such as gunnery, where appropriate responses or stimulus-response connections are already well established, enhancing knowledge of results (for example, by sounding a buzzer whenever the learner is exactly on target) improves current performance but does not result in any transferable gain in learning (Gagné, 1962b).

### Mechanism of Action

An equally important issue, assuming that feedback is indispensable for some kinds of learning and has a facilitating influence on others, concerns the mechanism whereby this facilitation is effected. Behavioristically oriented theorists (Holland, 1960; Hull, 1943; McGeoch & Irion, 1952;

Skinner, 1938, 1958; E. L. Thorndike, 1931; Trowbridge & Cason, 1932) tend to attribute the effects of feedback largely to reinforcement or to the direct strengthening effect of drive reduction on the responses that are instrumental in obtaining the reward and gratifying the drive. Informing the learner that a given emitted or covert response[16] is correct presumably gratifies the cognitive, affiliative, and ego-enhancing drives motivating the response. Hence it allegedly increases the probability of its recurrence ("reinforces" the response[17]—"law of effect"). In addition, however, it retroactively increases these same motivations for further learning. Locke and his associates (Locke, 1967; Locke, Cartledge, & Koeppel, 1968) attribute the main effect of knowledge of results to its enhancement of the learner's goals for improvement in learning. On the other hand, Flook and Saggar (1968) credit the effects of feedback to improved self-evaluation resulting from social comparison. Explicit awareness that the results of learning will be made available also constitutes an incentive condition, thereby enhancing the strength of the underlying drives.

But the facilitating effects of feedback are hardly exhausted by these reinforcement and motivational mechanisms. Knowledge of results also has other purely cognitive effects on learning. It confirms appropriate meanings and associations, corrects errors, clarifies misconceptions, and indicates the relative adequacy with which different portions of the learning task have been mastered. Thus, as a result of the feedback received, the subject's confidence in the validity of his or her learning products is increased and his or her learnings are consolidated. The learner is also better able selectively to concentrate on those aspects of the task requiring further refinement.

### Rote versus Meaningful Learning

On both motivational and cognitive grounds, feedback probably has less facilitating effect on meaningful than on rote learning. Since the achievement of understanding is a reward in its own right and requires less brute effort than rote learning, it is less necessary in meaningful learning to invoke the energizing assistance of extrinsic motives and incentives. Selective reinforcement of successful responses through drive reduction (gratification) is similarly less necessary for learning, even if it were possible, when logical considerations are applicable to the content of the learning task than when a purely arbitrary and verbatim connection must be established. The internal logic of the learning material also makes possible some implicit confirmation, correction, clarification, and evaluation of

---

[16] The significance of the distinction between emitted and covert responses insofar as the reinforcing effect of feedback is concerned was discussed earlier in this chapter.

[17] As will be indicated later, however, reinforcement probably occurs only in simple instrumental learning and in *rote* verbal learning—*not in meaningful learning*. Where it does occur, it is more likely attributable to lowering of thresholds of elicitation than to strengthening of response tendencies.

the learning product, even in the absence of any explicit provision of feedback.

## Completeness, Immediacy, and Frequency

Some research has also been conducted on the completeness, immediacy, and relative frequency of feedback. Provision of the entire correct answer facilitates concept learning more than does simply indicating "right" or "wrong" (Bourne & Pendleton, 1958; Chansky, 1960), since it enables the learner who does not adequately know the answer to clarify and consolidate his knowledge. Trowbridge and Cason (1932) also found that furnishing the subject with precise information about the magnitude and direction of his error is more effective than telling him "right" or "wrong" when he is learning to draw a line of specified length. Explanation of the logic of the correct answer is still another dimension of the completeness of feedback that influences learning. Subjects who are told *why* their answers are right or wrong learn more effectively than subjects who merely continue responding and receiving feedback until they obtain the correct answer (Bryan & Rigney, 1956).

Sassenrath and Garverick (1965) found that discussion of midsemester examination questions has a greater beneficial effect on final examination results than does either checking wrong answers from a list of correct answers placed on the blackboard or looking up in the textbook the correct answers to incorrectly answered questions. The use of specific relevant comments in grading themes is also much more effective in improving the quality of later writing than is the use of perfunctory encouraging comments (Page, 1958).

Crowder's "intrinsic programming" includes explanation of the nature of the error as an integral part of the branching procedure. In certain kinds of concept learning situations where many irrelevant cues are available, informing the subjects when they are wrong facilitates learning more than does informing them when they are right (Curry, 1960; W. J. Meyer & Offenbach, 1961; W. J. Meyer & Seidman, 1960, 1961). "Right" apparently gives less information than "wrong" under these circumstances because it also rewards irrelevant cues.

Research findings regarding the immediacy and frequency of feedback are more equivocal. Some investigators have reported that feedback given immediately has a significantly greater facilitating effect on learning than does delayed feedback (Angell, 1949; S. R. Meyer, 1960b; Sax, 1960). However, Evans, Glaser, and Homme (1960a) and Sax (1960) found no significant difference between the two kinds of feedback on learning and retention, respectively. Other investigators (Brackbill, Wagner, & Wilson, 1964; Brackbill, Adam, & Reaney, 1967; More, 1969; Sassenrath & Yonge, 1968; Sturges, 1969) have even reported a positive relationship between delay of feedback and retention. These findings are quite credible considering the role of feedback in meaningful verbal learning. In any case, the evidence that errors made initially tend to persist despite repeated correction (Kaess & Zeaman, 1960; Merrill, Wood, & Starr, 1969)—and that prompting is superior to confirmation (at least in the early stages of practice)—suggests that it is preferable to avoid errors in the first place than to correct them immediately.

Except for two studies (Auble & Mech, 1953; Sax, 1960) reporting no significant differences, continuously as opposed to intermittently administered feedback has been shown to be more effective in concept learning (Bourne & Haygood, 1960; Bourne & Pendleton, 1958; Chansky, 1960). In more sequential types of programmed instruction, however, the relative frequency of feedback does not appear to influence learning outcomes (Krumboltz & Weisman, 1962b; Lambert, 1962). Chansky (1964) obtained best results with an intermittent type of information feedback and with a continuous grading procedure. Whatever procedure is used, however, it is obviously advantageous to employ indicators of success that the learner can use autonomously for purposes of feedback and self-evaluation, that is, indicators that are available outside the training situation (J. Annett, 1959). In this way the learner is not dependent for feedback on an external source such as the teacher.

To summarize, feedback is not generally indispensable for learning, but on both motivational-reinforcement and cognitive grounds it should facilitate the learning process, more so in the case of rote than of meaningful learning. However, the research evidence tends to be equivocal, particularly in relation to programmed instruction, because of the failure to control other relevant variables. Further compounding the difficulty of interpreting the effect of feedback on automated meaningful learning is the fact that both low error rate and the possibility of implicit feedback reduce the facilitating potential of explicitly provided feedback.

# 10

# INSTRUCTIONAL MATERIALS

Atlhough teachers play an important and in many ways crucial role in guiding learning, the problems associated with the preservice and inservice education of teachers are enormous. Therefore, we believe that one of the more promising avenues for the improvement of school learning is through the improvement of instructional materials. The most significant factors influencing the learning value of instructional materials are the extent to which these materials facilitate meaningful learning.

It is important to recognize at the outset that curriculum planning is distinct from instructional planning. The former centers attention on the conceptual and methodological structure of disciplines, whereas the latter centers attention on the selection of learning activities that best link to the existing cognitive structure of the learner and embody the concepts and skills identified in curriculum planning.

Learning objectives should be specified in such a way that they make evident to the student concepts or principles to be learned in language that facilitates recognition by them of linkages between what they already know and the new concepts or principles to be learned. Advance organizers, properly constructed, can play an important role in facilitation of the learning specified by behavioral objectives or other forms of learning objectives.

For longer instructional sequences, such as a semester course, or a major portion of a course, a series of advance organizers should be constructed proceeding from the most general, most inclusive ideas to be learned to more specific ideas, with occasional reference back to the major organizing ideas of the instructional program.

Instructional aids, such as models, slides, films, and television, can be helpful when they serve to clarify concepts or principles by extending the range of examples, or when some skill or performance that involves motion is to be demonstrated. However, their value inheres primarily as supplements to a well-planned instructional program, including extensive printed materials, rather than as a principal means of instruction.

Computer Assisted Instruction (CAI) shows promise where the learner plays a major role in determining the rate of new learning. Errors are corrected as they occur, and linkages between subordinate concepts (or tasks) are made explicitly with more general, more inclusive concepts or tasks when correlated printed and/or tutorial support is available.

Mastery learning strategies, which require some reasonable criterion of mastery of each study unit before proceeding to new units, are consistent with assimilation learning theory and are more effective when planned for progressive differentiation and integrative reconciliation of concepts and principles.

In designing a new curriculum or planning a segment of an instructional program, it is important to keep constantly in mind that "the most important thing influencing learning is what the learner. already knows." This means that instructional planning requires careful assessment of the concepts and skills the learners possess that are relevant to the new learning tasks. Rate of learning will be strongly influenced by the adequacy of relevant background. The best instructional strategies therefore allow for varying rates of learning time. Since subsumption of new information is generally much easier than acquisition of new superordinate concepts, curricula should be planned to introduce the major concepts or propositions early in the course to serve as a cognitive anchorage for subsequent learning. It is important to remember that constant reference to the major organizing ideas is necessary if progressive differentiation of these ideas is to occur and if integrative reconciliation of subordinate, as well as superordinate, ideas is to be achieved.

Problems associated with motivation, personality factors, group and social factors, and teacher characteristics that influence learning will be discussed more extensively in subsequent chapters. Although the design of instructional materials must take cognizance of all of the factors, the principal emphasis in this chapter is on how to maximize meaningful learning through proper design of instructional materials.

Up to this point we have discussed principally the nature of cognitive learning and factors that influence an individual's success in cognitive learning. The next four chapters will deal with affective and social factors in learning; the present chapter will serve to synthesize the meaning of earlier chapters as they relate to school learning and as a general advance organizer for the remaining chapters. We will consider here the distinction between curriculum planning and instructional planning, the role of advance organizers, alternative instructional strategies, methods of accommodating for individual differences in ability and experience, and the role of laboratory work where skill development, investigatory procedures, and concrete experience are important instructional objectives.

To make rational decisions in selecting content and instructional methods requires that we employ methods whereby the recommendations arrived at by one individual (or group) are not based solely on private information available only to that person (or group) but show a logical correspondence between assumptions and recommendations that can be recognized by another individual (or group). We seek a process whereby some consensus can be reached as to what evidence or assumptions are valid and relevant to the selection of what is to be taught and to how we are to teach.

It has been popular in education groups to refer to "curriculum and instruction" simultaneously and in one breath, as though this were a single entity. More recently, M. Johnson (1967, 1977) and others have emphasized that we have been careless in referring to curriculum and have not distinguished between curriculum (content) issues and instructional (teaching approach) issues. We will show that some of the difficulties encountered by the curriculum reform movements of the 1950s and 1960s resulted from poor delineation of curriculum and/or instructional issues and from a lack of understanding of the differences between the rote $\rightarrow$ meaningful continuum and the reception $\rightarrow$ discovery continuum.

Curriculum *theory* building is a relatively recent phenomenon. Although descriptive studies of curriculum can be found in the literature of the early 1900s, such as Bobbitt (1918), the first organized effort to clarify curriculum *theory* took place in 1947 and appeared as a published monograph in 1950 (Herrick & Tyler). Beauchamp published a book on curriculum theory in 1961; other books proposing models for curriculum building were published by Tyler in 1949 and Taba in 1962. None of these books emphasized a close relationship between learning theory and curriculum or instruction, which will be an important emphasis in this chapter. Unlike Johnson's work, the "theory" books mentioned do not clearly distinguish curriculum from instruction, and therefore we will draw on Johnson's (1967, 1977) writing as a primary source for some of the ideas presented in this chapter. Joyce and Weil (1972) have proposed sixteen models of teaching, but this eclectic approach in combining learning theory and instruction cannot be directive, for almost all teaching options appear to have feasibility.

## Johnson's Model for Curriculum and Instruction

Figure 10.1 shows a simplified version of Johnson's model. Here we see that the curriculum (a structured series of intended learning outcomes) is a *product* of a curriculum development system in which selection criteria and ordering criteria are used to select knowledge from the available culture and organize this knowledge into a "curriculum." The product of the curriculum development system is used in turn for the process of instructional design. Drawing specific activities and examples from the available culture, an instructional program is developed. As students are involved in the instructional program, learning hopefully occurs and "actual learning outcomes" can be evaluated. The actual learning outcomes are a product of the instructional system as manifested by the learners. Information obtained from evaluation can in turn be used to redesign the curriculum and/or instructional components.

The value of Johnson's model to instructional planning is that it helps to clarify issues that are primarily concerned with the status of knowledge in the disciplines and society's goals for schools (curriculum issues) from those issues that place the focus of attention on learners and methods for optimizing learning (instructional issues) (Posner, 1974). It is the latter

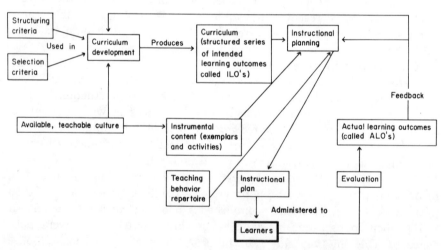

FIGURE 10.1   A simplified version of Johnson's (1967) model for curriculum and instruction. The curriculum development system (far left) is distinguished from the instructional system. Evaluation provides feedback on the extent to which "intended learning outcomes" (ILOs) are achieved by the learners as "actual learning outcomes" (ALOs). The curriculum and/or instructional program can be modified accordingly. (Figures 10.1–10.5 and 10.7–10.9 are reproduced from J. Novak, *A theory of education*. Ithaca, N.Y.: Cornell University Press, 1977. Reproduced by permission.)

issues to which educational psychology has most to contribute. Thus instructional issues will be the major area of concern in this chapter.

Our cultural heritage provides not only the knowledge that is to be transmitted but also strategies for teaching, or what Johnson calls the teaching behavior repertoire. Technological advances have made it possible substantially to enhance the repertoire of teaching approaches, but all too commonly we see little use of anything more than the lecture method, where the teacher serves as the primary source of information from the discipline. In Figures 10.2 through 10.4 we have shown a schema for viewing the process of education with alternative ways for transmitting our cultural heritage.

Returning to the relevance of Johnson's model, we can redraw Figure 10.1 to illustrate correspondence between this scheme for teaching and Johnson's model. Figure 10.5 shows that we draw from the discipline to form our curriculum and to select specific instructional activities. We also draw from the discipline of education to plan instruction, and hopefully our

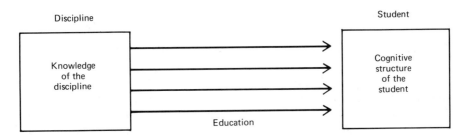

FIGURE 10.2    A representation of the process of education when viewed as the transfer of knowledge as it exists in the discipline to the student's cognitive structure.

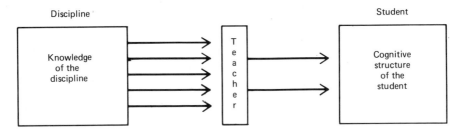

FIGURE 10.3    The process of education where the teacher serves as the principal source of information for learning, as in "traditional" instruction.

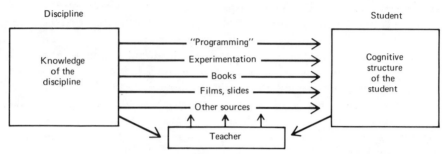

FIGURE 10.4    The process of education where the teacher's role is primarily in planning for appropriate learning resource material and playing a supporting, tutorial role. Newer instructional approaches more closely approximate this scheme.

instructional program will result in positive growth in the cognitive structure (conceptual structure) of our students and in positive affective growth as well.

## The Role of Learning Theory in Curriculum and Instruction

It has been noted that none of the curriculum theorists in the past have shown the relevance of learning theory in curriculum design. Although Taba (1962) devotes considerable space to the discussion of learning theories, subsequent application of learning theories to curriculum design is, at best, ambiguous. With respect to instructional theory, the situation has been only slightly better. Most papers and books on the subject give hardly more than passing acknowledgment that there should be some connection between learning theory and the theory of instruction. Bruner, in his book *Toward a Theory of Instruction* (1966), actually puts the cart before the horse and says, ". . . a theory of instruction, which must be at the heart of educational psychology, is principally concerned with how to arrange environments to optimize learning according to various criteria—to optimize transfer or retrievability of information, for example" (pp. 37–38). But it is specifically to the issue of "how to arrange environments to optimize learning" that useful educational psychological theory (and not instructional theory) should apply (Glaser, 1976). It is educational psychology that should be at the heart of instructional theory, and not vice versa. Before we can design a learning environment to optimize learning of some specific element of knowledge, we must know how students learn in general.

After reviewing briefly some of the more common learning theories Taba makes the following observation:

As was pointed out earlier, these theories suggest diverse ideas about learning but have not yet produced a science of learning—a coherent set of explanations, laws, and principles to guide education. The more "scientific" behavioristic observations in experimentally confined situations cannot be used to understand or to guide learning of a more complex nature, such as the development of cognitive processes or the formation of attitudes. On the other hand, field theories of learning present too great a complexity of variable factors, with the result that it is difficult to examine adequately their regularities to translate them into appropriate principles and laws. If the possibility of drawing educational applications were limited only to what the experimental psychologists consider precise laws and explanations, one would have to conclude that there can be little correspondence between 'the studies of learning and the practice of education. One reason for this is the fact that although there are wide varieties of learning, experimental psychology, which is primarily concerned with developing a theory of learning, deals with only a limited range (Taba, 1962, p. 85).

We concur with her statement as regards the situation in 1962. However, a major contention in this book is that the assimilation theory of human learning presented here not only has value for explaining learning mechanisms as they operate in the classroom but also for guiding school curriculum development, instructional design and evaluation practices.

Carlow (1976) has attempted to apply assimilation theory to a curriculum development project, but his work lacked the support of complementary curriculum and instructional theory. In this chapter we will use Johnson's model for curriculum and instruction together with assimilation theory as

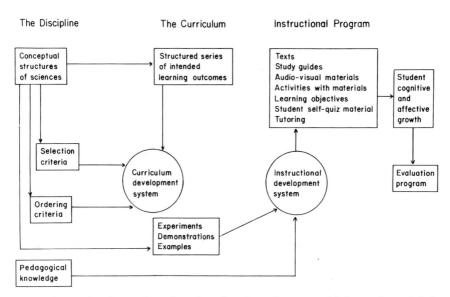

FIGURE 10.5   A schema for education showing elements of Johnson's model for curriculum and instruction.

a basis for describing better instructional materials. Glaser (1976) describes four components of a psychology of instruction. Since his description is wedded to a behaviorist view of learning, it is difficult to see how it can be used to guide the wide array of activities involved in planning instruction for meaningful learning.

The principal focus in assimilation theory is on the role of relevant elements in cognitive structure (subsumers) for effecting *meaningful* learning. Additional consideration of progressive differentiation of subsumers, superordinate learning, and integrative reconciliation further lends relevance to curriculum planning and instructional planning. If learning is to be meaningful, then the new knowledge to be learned must have *relevant* anchoring concepts available in the learner's cognitive structure.

Since there is an enormous array of information to be learned in any discipline, only the most general, most inclusive concepts are likely to provide anchorage in a wide variety of learning situations. Therefore, Johnson's stress on selection criteria for curriculum planning can be related to stress on subsumption in assimilation theory, which indicates that we must begin early with the most general, most inclusive concepts and propositions. And Johnson's equal emphasis on ordering criteria can be linked to a description of *progressive differentiation* of concepts in cognitive structure. The correspondence between elements in Johnson's model and assimilation theory is shown in Table 10.1. We must structure our curriculum in such a way that major concepts and propositions are introduced early, thus serving to facilitate meaningful learning of a wide array of information and also serving to facilitate learning of subordinate concepts.

We have already discussed the problem of *readiness* and the fact that early learning in any discipline must proceed from development of primary abstractions based on experience with concrete-empirical props prior to instruction. This experience leads to development of secondary abstractions. Moreover, assimilation theory stresses that there is no age at which all learners can handle secondary abstractions in *any* subject matter area, in contrast to Piaget's views that this ability (which he calls formal operations) is not available until the age of 12 to 14 and presumably from then on in any situation. Our stress has been that *meaningful* learning is *content-specific*, which means that curriculum planning cannot ignore either the learner's general level of cognitive development or *specific* fund of primary and secondary abstractions in the discipline to be learned.

Assimilation theory gives both more freedom and more constraints to the curriculum planner. In principle, any disciplinary subject matter can be meaningfully learned by any student. However, and this is a big qualifier, we must organize our curriculum to assure that all the necessary motor skills and primary and secondary abstraction needed at any stage of the learning sequence are available. This can be prohibitively time-consuming, costly, and/or inefficient. For example, we tried to design some audio-tape guided lessons to teach first-grade children elementary concepts of electrostatics. The children's motor proficiency was so poor that most of them could not get a good electrostatic charge on a plastic rod except with extended instruction (three or four 20-minute lessons) showing them how to charge the rod and hold it close to (but not touching) a pith ball. We could see that in time (perhaps with fifty or so 20-minute lessons) we may have been successful in teaching some concepts of electrostatic charge, but our patience ran out. We decided to work with third-grade children instead. Their much better motor coordination meant that they could easily charge a glass or plastic rod, test its effect on a suspended pith ball, and follow other instructions on the audiotape. We experienced a situation where motor skills were at least as limiting as available cognitive structure for these first-grade youngsters.

Since it is well known that training in many simple motor skills is a waste of time (all children eventually learn to walk), we made a curriculum decision (that is, not to teach concepts of electrostatics to first-graders) on the basis of our experience and not on a priori grounds. We see in this example an interplay between instructional planning and curriculum planning. Some concepts we may wish to teach to students are best placed later in a curriculum plan to avoid undue difficulties in executing instruction in these concepts. We must avoid, however, the common practice of making arbitrary decisions on the placement of concepts to be learned without reference to theoretical learning issues or empirically tested instructional alternatives. Unnecessary postponement of instruction in basic concepts and propositions that can operate to effect meaningful learning of a wide array of knowledge may lead to the common school practice of rote learning where meaningful learning could have been achieved. The design of instruction for teaching fundamental concepts in science, mathematics, social sciences and other fields is no easy matter. Subsequent sections of this chapter will deal selectively with important issues in this regard.

In order to plan curriculum and design instruction consistent with assimilation theory, as suggested in Table 10.1, a primary—and exceedingly difficult—task is to identify *concepts* in any given discipline and to organize these concepts into some hierarchical or relational scheme. This task requires the best available talent with respect to knowledge of the discipline and also skillful guidance by curriculum "experts" in the process of "unpacking" knowledge from a discipline.

If we cannot succeed in identifying salient concepts in a field of study, distinguishing among concepts and isolating relatively trivial or subordinate concepts, the result is likely to be that curriculum planning will proceed from an array of topics. The simplest definition we can give for topics is that this is what you find in the table of contents of most books. Sometimes topics are also concepts (for example, "Cells—Structure and Function" or "Mercantilism"), but more often they represent a conglomeration of con-

**TABLE 10.1   Corresponding Elements in Johnson's Model and Assimilation Theory of Learning**

| Johnson's Model Component | Relevant Elements in Assimilation Theory |
| --- | --- |
| Selection criteria for knowledge in our culture. | Stress on concepts—implies need to identify major and minor *concepts* in a field of study. |
| Ordering criteria for knowledge selected. | Meaningful learning and progressive differentiation require that the most general, most inclusive concepts and propositions be presented early, and that subsequent information be provided to clarify meaning and show connections to subordinate concepts. (Recall distinction between logical order and psychological order in Chapter 2.) |
|  | Superordinate learning and integrative reconciliation require that subordinate concepts be presented in a manner that allows linkage with more-inclusive concepts, and that meanings of apparently disparate concepts will be clarified to show distinctions and relationships between subordinate concepts (integrative reconciliation). Properly designed advance organizers can contribute to integrative reconciliation. |
|  | For young learners, care must be taken to assure that primary abstractions are available in the learners' cognitive structures prior to instruction in concepts which require secondary abstractions. |
| Curriculum intended learning outcomes (ILOs) | Although Johnson does not specify the form of ILOs, assimilation theory would indicate that these should be *concepts or propositions* to be learned, for it is these that are involved in effecting *meaningful* learning. In other words, Johnson's "curriculum matrix" produced by the curriculum development system should be a matrix of *concepts and propositions*. To the extent possible, this matrix should suggest hierarchical and subordinate relationships between concepts, although this feature is in part confounded with the *sequence* in which concepts are taught and the specific exemplars used in instruction. Skills, attitudes, and values should be considered especially as they bear on learning of the concepts specified. |
| Instructional planning system selection of exemplars (instrumental content) | Assimilation theory requires that examples used meet the following conditions: (1) necessary motor skills are available or practiced, (2) relevant primary abstractions are available or taught, (3) secondary abstractions presented do not ignore (1) and (2) above, and (4) explicit linkage between new learning and existing cognitive structure is provided (use of advance organizers). |

| Johnson's Model Component | Relevant Elements in Assimilation Theory |
|---|---|
| Selection of teaching approaches | Concrete props, when needed, require teaching approaches that introduce these props in proper order. Development of primary and secondary abstractions will be somewhat idiosyncratic, hence teaching approach must allow for *varying rates of learning*, for alternative exemplars, variation in exposure to concrete props, and adjustment to motivation patterns of students. |
| Actual learning outcomes | Achievement will be a function of the general cognitive maturation (degree of overall cognitive structure differentiation) but primarily dependent on initial or developed *relevant* subsumers in the learner's cognitive structure. Presence of a meaningful learning *set* will lead to growth in relevant subsumers, in contrast to rote learning, and should facilitate problem-solving capabilities to the extent that progressive differentiation and integrative reconciliations of relevant concepts and propositions has occurred. |
| Evaluation | *Rate* of new learning will be a function of quality of existing or developed relevant subsumers, and motivation for learning. Transfer of learning to new problem-solving situations will be a function of the degree of concept differentiation, superordinate subsumption, and integrative reconciliation achieved. Genic variation in learners will be confounded with achievement of the above. |
| Feedback to curriculum planning | Concepts selected may require: (1) more general cognitive structure development than typically present in the learners, (2) alternative sequences of *concept* presentation, (3) better clarification of relationships between concepts in the matrix and/or better description of salient aspects of the concept(s). |
| Feedback to instruction | Failure to achieve mastery (as evidenced by lack of transfer to novel, relevant problems) may indicate a curriculum problem as above, or (1) poor selection of exemplars (not easily or extensively linked to existing cognitive structures of learners); (2) inappropriate pacing leading to rote learning or failure to learn (too fast) or boredom and decline in motivation (too slow); (3) necessity for provision for more motor-skill development, greater use of concrete props for primary concept development, more extensive development of secondary abstractions and/or relationships between the latter; (4) better advance organizers to link new concepts to existing cognitive structures; (5) selection of alternative instructional strategies better to achieve above items such as tutorial assistance where existing relevant cognitive development of learners is highly variable or unusually idiosyncratic. |

cepts, perhaps with some *logical* coherence but without psychological organization. In other words, it is not possible to show how early instruction on a topic leads to progressively better differentiated concepts—wherein superordinate learning occurs as less inclusive concepts are related through higher-order concepts, and integrative reconciliation occurs wherein apparently disparate meanings of a concept are recognized as aspects of the same concept or as essentially different and associated with another concept.

### The Organization of Knowledge

Gagné (1970, 1977) has argued that not only is knowledge *structured*, but also the sequence for learning must be tightly structured. Therefore, he sees curriculum planning for successful learning as a process that requires explicit *hierarchies of learning*, such as that shown in Figure 10.6. Moreover, Gagné's model specifies that we must begin with the simplest learning tasks—that is, those shown at the bottom of his hierarchy, and then proceed sequentially to more complex learning tasks (see Gagné & Briggs, 1974).

However, we see elucidation of the physical concept of "work" as proceeding in essentially the reverse direction. Children first form intuitive concepts of "work" from their experience with carrying toys "up to their room," recognizing in time that carrying more weight to higher levels takes more "work." As children gradually recognize the scalar values for weight and height and learn how to perform simple arithmetic operations on scalar quantities, their concept of "work" can *subsume* new meanings and become differentiated to include the mathematical characterization that forces (or weights) and distances combine to define the physical quantity "work." Gagné's model derives from behaviorist views that see learning primarily as a sequence of stimulus–response (S–R) chains, with the first S–R connections formed between simple elements. Although this procedure is effective with infrahumans and rote learning of nonsense materials, it is not supportable as an approach for meaningful learning. We have already discussed (Chapter 4) the important differences that exist in learning and retention of meaningful as contrasted to nonsense or rote learning material.

Assimilation theory stresses the importance of superordinate concepts for facilitation of new learning through subsumption of new, relevant information or concepts. When this does not occur, students of physics may learn to perform the algebraic manipulation necessary for "solving" problems using the algorithm $W = f \cdot d$ and still not recognize that it takes more work to move a Cadillac up a mountain than it does to move a Toyota. It is more important to assess the available concepts students have for meaningful learning in any area than to attempt instructional adherence to some relatively arbitrary "learning hierarchy" (Case, 1975). The research

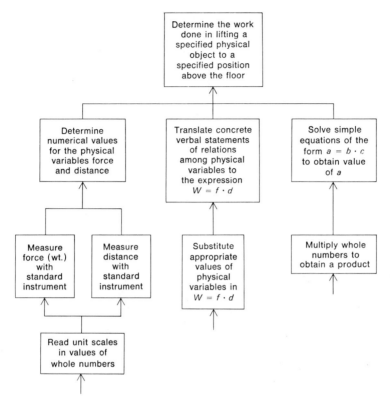

FIGURE 10.6  Solving physical work problems; a learning hierarchy pertaining to a science topic. (From R. M. Gagné, *The conditions of learning* (2nd ed.). New York: Holt, Rinehart and Winston. Copyright 1970. Reprinted by permission.)

results from studies of the validity of learning hierarchies are equivocal (White, 1973), although better research designs might lend support to the validity of learning hierarchies at least in narrow disciplinary areas (White, 1974a, 1974b).

Our own view is that, although it is useful to identify and organize concepts and propositions in any discipline as an aspect of curriculum planning, the relationships between these ideas need not be expressed in a strict, unidirectional hierarchy. Figure 10.7 shows one scheme for organizing ideas in the field of economics. Senesh (1960) has stressed the importance of the relationship between fundamental ideas in economics and the fact that this relationship must underlie what he calls the "organic curriculum" for the subject. However, we can see that Senesh's scheme does not indicate a specific *sequence* for organizing course content and that this would be left largely to the instructional planner.

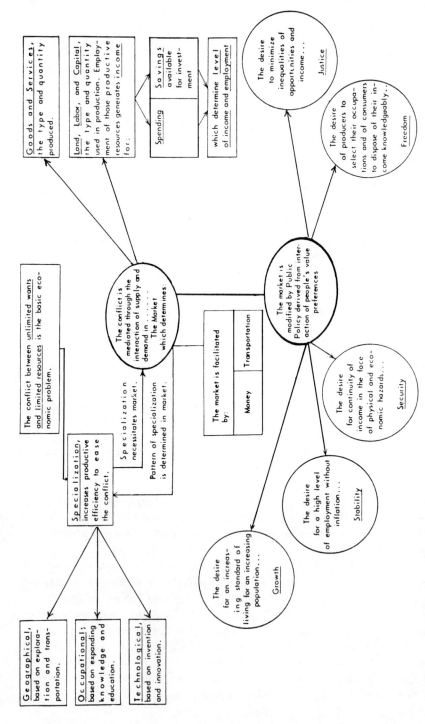

FIGURE 10.7    The fundamental idea relationships of economic knowledge.

From what we have indicated earlier, it is evident that the selection of *examples* to illustrate each of the fundamental ideas of economics would depend on the age and prior experience of our students (Senesh uses the same basic scheme in programs designed for students from grade 1 to college). We see here that the *curriculum* plan places primary emphasis on the organization of knowledge in the discipline, whereas the instructional plan places primary emphasis on the learner and the kind of entering subsumers the learners have to serve as anchorage for new learning. Furthermore, even in grade 1, Senesh would begin with the most general, most inclusive ideas. These not only would link more easily with the existing concepts of the children but also would serve subsequently as powerful subsumers for anchorage of a wide array of specific new knowledge. The important element from assimilation theory that enters into curriculum planning is that optimal meaningful learning requires progressive differentiation of concepts or propositions in cognitive structure. Therefore these concepts must be the basic elements of our curriculum plan.

There is often confusion among educators as to the value of concept hierarchies or "idea relationships" as a tool for *curriculum* planning as distinct from the problems involved in *instructional* planning. For example, "conceptual schemes of science" (NSTA, 1964) devised by a committee of the National Science Teachers Association have been criticized as too general and too abstract for most practicing teachers and especially for students. However, the "conceptual schemes" were never intended to be used by teachers for daily lesson planning or to be learned directly by students. Rather they were designed to provide a basis for coherent curriculum planning for science programs extending from grade 1 to college. Furthermore, it was specifically recommended that the conceptual schemes be used as a basis for instructional planning only by science teaching experts and in consultation with practicing scientists.

Detailed consideration of issues involved in curriculum planning is beyond the scope of this book. It is important to note at this point that rarely in the design of a new instructional program have the epistemological issues underlying instructional planning or the psychological issues underlying instructional planning been given careful attention. Even the multimillion-dollar, federally funded projects of the 1950s and 1960s relied primarily on the intuitions of the scientists, mathematicians, and teachers involved, and not on theory-based careful analysis of epistemological and psychological issues. This may account in part for the dubious success of these teaching innovation efforts. Further discussion of these issues appears elsewhere (Novak, 1976).

## Planning for Instruction

The interdependence of the elements shown in Johnson's model (Figure 10.1) becomes evident as soon as we begin to plan a specific piece of instructional material. Since we cannot consider simultaneously every possible contingency, the first question is: where do we begin in instructional planning? Our experience has been that the best program is made when we begin considering one or two major concepts to be illustrated, as well as motivational issues. For example, we might decide to begin a science course with field study, since the early fall is a nice time to have outdoor classes in most sections of the United States. If our student audience is sixth-graders, we may begin to consider one or two major concepts of science that can best be illustrated through field work to students with the general maturation of sixth-graders.

We can see that at least initial choices of concepts to be taught (a curriculum decision) can be very much a function of what kind of instructional material may be most meaningful to a given group of students at a certain time of the year (instructional planning decisions). However, we cannot ignore the fact that substantial development of one major concept (such as, the concept of diversity of living things) cannot be realized until some progress has been made in the development of other major concepts (such as the hierarchical organization of living things). Any arbitrary decisions that would be made in curriculum planning with respect to the *sequencing* of concepts to be presented might result in undesirable or unmotivating instructional consequences. Conversely, arbitrary decisions on topics or activities in instructional planning might obviate any chance for concept differentiation or integrative reconciliation. We can schematize this starting dilemma in curriculum and instructional planning as shown in Figure 10.8.

We have shown earlier (Table 10.1) that one set of instructional exemplars may illustrate two or more concepts. A consideration in choosing activities or examples for instruction is the extent to which maximum pay-off can be achieved for the development of one or more significant concepts. Some exemplars are rejected even though they work well with a student group when other successful exemplars can be found from which a greater range of conceptual differentiation is possible. On the other hand, some exemplars may relate to a dozen or more concepts in our curriculum plan, but the learning experience with these may result in conceptual confusion. For example, one of the difficulties with educational games is not in their success in engaging students in active involvement. Rather, the problem lies in the discrepancy that often exists between learning the strategies of the game and learning the concepts or relationships between concepts that are supposed to be illustrated in the game. Busch (1973) found that students playing a game one time showed some gain in understanding sociology concepts, but the students who worked with her to design the games showed a better understanding of the concepts and relationships between the concepts. In most reports on the use of instructional games, however, no results are reported as to the extent of concept growth, although some reports do show positive, if not superior, learning outcomes (Seidner, 1976).

Curriculum Problems                    Instructional Problems

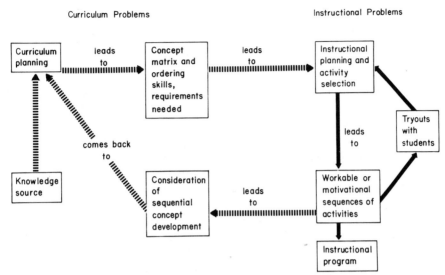

FIGURE 10.8   Curriculum design and instructional design decisions are interrelated, and successful planning requires "cycling" back and forth
through the instructional (right) side and curriculum (left) side
design systems.

### Amount of Material: Task Size

The amount of material contained in a given learning task—that is, the
relative size of the task—is an important consideration in planning instruction and in arranging practice schedules. Task size influences the structure
of the material and its difficulty, as well as the learner's motivation.

The relative efficacy of different task sizes is closely related to the
traditional part-whole problem in rote practice tasks both because the total
magnitude of the task confronting the learner is a significant factor determining his or her choice of approach, and because the part method obviously involves working with a smaller task size than does the whole method.
Nevertheless, the two issues are hardly coextensive. Task size is a much
more inclusive issue than the choice of a whole-or-part strategy of practice.
In choosing between different task sizes in programming subject matter only
relatively rarely is one faced with a decision that is comparable to the choice
between memorizing a poem as a whole or memorizing it by stanzas. Although component task units of a subject-matter program are sequentially
related to each other, they are more typically related in a derivative or
correlative sense rather than as successive links of a chain that would have
to be welded together if first learned separately.

## Organization of Material

Throughout this volume it has been repeatedly stressed that the conditions of learning primarily influence the meaningful acquisition and retention of ideas and information by modifying *existing* cognitive structure. The effect of such modification on learning and retention cannot be empirically demonstrated except by using the transfer paradigm (by measuring its effect on the learning and retention of related new tasks). However, the changes in cognitive structure wrought by practice or by exposure to successive aspects of the task obviously have an important impact on intratask mastery itself. This is particularly true in the case of those kinds of learning in which each component task (as well as entire bodies of subject matter) tends to be compound in content and to manifest an internal organization of its own.

Thus, in school learning, conditions influencing and altering cognitive structure are typically crucial both for the acquisition of a particular task as well as for transfer purposes (the learning of related new tasks). Of all the possible conditions of learning that affect cognitive structure, it is self-evident that none can be more significant than organization of the material. In previous chapters we have already considered in great detail how learning material can be most effectively written and organized so as deliberately to induce those changes in cognitive structure that are most advantageous for the learning and retention of meaningful school material. Hence in the present context it will be necessary only to summarize briefly the more salient of these considerations.

### Organizers versus Overviews

The principles of progressive differentiation and integrative reconciliation have been represented throughout as being of central importance in the programming of meaningful subject matter. Optimal utilization of these principles presupposes not only their consistent use in the sequential presentation of subject matter material but also the supplementary availability of a hierarchical series of advance "organizers." These latter organizers provide relevant ideational scaffolding, enhance the discriminability of the new learning material from previously learned related ideas, and otherwise effect integrative reconciliation, generality, and inclusiveness that is much higher than that of the learning material itself. To be maximally effective they must be formulated in terms of language and concepts already *familiar* to the learner and use appropriate illustrations and analogies if developmentally necessary.

True organizers, thus defined, should not be confused with ordinary introductory overviews. The latter are typically written at the same level of abstraction, generality, and inclusiveness as the learning material and achieve their effect largely through repetition, condensation, selective emphasis on central concepts, and prefamiliarization of the learner with certain key words. Grotelueschen and Sjogren (1968) have shown that there are significant differences in achievement when differing introductory materials are used.

Summaries are comparable to overviews in construction, but are probably less effective because their influence on cognitive structure is retroactive rather than proactive relative to the learning task. They are probably more useful, in place of the material itself, for purposes of rapid review than for original learning. However, insofar as they may imply to some learners that the material they do *not* include is relatively superfluous, they may promote neglect of and failure to study or review much significant subject matter. Lathrop and Norford (1949) found that neither overviews nor summaries appreciably improve the learning of instructional films.

### Organizers versus Intramaterial Organization

Organizers also have certain inherent advantages both over various kinds of intramaterial organization (organizing aids within the body of the material) and over any existing subsumers within cognitive structure that could be used for organizational purposes. Intramaterial organization (executed in accordance with the principles of progressive differentiation and integrative reconciliation) successively provides necessary anchorage for and differentiation of new ideas at a particularized level just before each new idea is encountered. In contrast, organizers perform the same functions in advance at a much more global level before the learner is confronted with any of the new material. Hence, for example, a generalized model of class relationships is first provided as a general subsumer for *all* new classes, subclasses, and species before more limited subsumers (classes or subclasses) are provided for the particular subclasses or species they encompass. And the various kinds of forests are first distinguished from each other before the component subforests and trees are similarly differentiated. Spontaneously existing subsumers in cognitive structure, on the other hand, lack both particularized relevance for the new material (since the learner cannot possibly anticipate its precise nature) as well as the benefit of the sophisticated knowledge of subject matter and pedagogy available to expert programmers.

### Perceptual Organizers

Perceptual organizers, in contrast to the integrative organizational devices just described, merely provide built-in mechanical aids that make the material perceptually more salient and apprehensible or otherwise facilitate practice. These include rhythmic aids, vocal emphasis, the isolation[1] and familiarization effects of underlining, and the "fractionation" effect (breaking of wholes into parts) of providing headings and subheadings. Under certain circumstances, however, some perceptual organizers can be said to have true integrative effects (for instance, underlining that helps make ideational distinctions or emphasizes central concepts; headings that reveal the organizational structure of the material more clearly).

Perceptual or mechanical organizers generally facilitate meaningful learning—more so in the case of factual than of abstract material.[2] The learning of meaningful material, for example, is enhanced by appropriate vocal emphasis (Dearborn, Johnson, & Carmichael, 1949), by underlining (Klare, Mabry, & Gustafson, 1955), and by breaking instructional film content into parts by means of inserted questions (Kurtz, Walter, & Brenner, 1950). Typographical highlighting of the more important material to be learned reduces the amount of learning of less important content but does not facilitate the learning of the more important core content (Hershberger, 1964). The failure of informational learning to increase proportionately with increase in the density of facts in film (Vincent, Ash, & Greehill, 1949) may be partly ascribed to the loss of the patterning or isolation effect as "filler" material is removed.

Northrop (1952) found that the use of headings facilitates the learning of factual films but either has no significant effect on or inhibits the learning of more abstract films. The abstract material in this study was evidently more highly organized than the factual, simply because the abstract concepts themselves served an organizing function. Hence the learners not only benefited less from the presence of extrinsic mechanical organizers, but also seemed in some instances to be distracted by them.

Apparently, integrative organizers are required for material that is more abstract than informational in character. In none of the above studies, however, is it possible to distinguish clearly between the perceptual and the integrative effects of the organizers in question. Conflicting results have also been reported regarding the relative effects of such organizers on bright and dull students (Barnes & Clawson, 1975).

---

[1] In several adequately controlled laboratory studies, "isolation" effected by introducing patterned heterogeneity of content or color, has been shown to facilitate rote learning of segregated and immediately adjacent items (Saul & Osgood, 1950; Shay, 1961; Smith & Stearns, 1949). Retention, however, was not facilitated.

[2] Christensen and Stordahl (1955) obtained uniformly negative results in studying the effects on comprehension and retention of various combinations of such organizational aids as underlining, headings, outlines, and summaries. However, the possibility of obtaining significant differences between experimental and control groups was seriously prejudiced by the leveling effects of using familiar learning material, using the same test as both a pretest and measure of retention, and testing the same subjects for both immediate and delayed retention.

*Organizers in Textual Material*

Generally speaking, therefore, it makes good organizational sense if the presentation of more detailed or specific information is preceded by a more general or inclusive principle to which it can be related or under which it can be subsumed. This not only makes the new information more meaningful and enables the student to anchor more easily forgotten specifics to more easily remembered generalizations but also integrates related facts in terms of a common principle under which they can all be subsumed.

In a physics, engineering, or biology course, for example, the general characteristics of *all* regulatory or cybernetic systems should be presented before considering any *particular* regulatory or cybernetic system. The latter, in turn, should be explicitly related to the more general principles, showing how they exemplify them (Moriera, 1977). This makes for some redundancy; but such redundancy, in turn, greatly reinforces the general principles. Of course, the general principles themselves must be stated in terms and concepts that are already familiar to the learner. Many teachers and textbooks are guilty of introducing complex and detailed information for which no adequate foundation has been laid in terms of organizing, unifying, or explanatory principles.

Thus a substantive introductory statement of the principal new ideas to be considered in the chapter, stated at a high level of generality and inclusiveness, to which the more detailed information in the chapter can be related, could be very helpful in learning the latter information. For example, a brief overview of the chief propositions underlying homeostasis was shown to facilitate learning more than an historical overview of early work in this area (Kuhn & Novak, 1971).

It is desirable not only for the material in each chapter to become progressively more differentiated (to proceed from ideas of greater to lesser inclusiveness), but for textbooks as a whole (from one chapter to another) to follow the same organizational plan. The *spiral* kind of organization, in which the same topics are treated at progressively higher levels of sophistication in successive sections, is an extension of the same principle. Textbook series in a given field that are intended for use at different instructional levels (elementary school, high school, undergraduate, and graduate) can also follow this organizational plan. In this instance there is a progressive increase in scope, depth, complexity, level of abstraction, and level of sophistication at successively higher grade levels, with the earlier acquired knowledge serving as a foundation for the more abstract and complex material introduced later. In addition, however, some entirely new topics are introduced at the higher levels, since many advanced topics are too complex and abstract to be taught successfully on an intuitive basis.

In certain instances new concepts are introduced that are similar or related to—but not identical to and hence confusable with—previously learned concepts (for instance, instinct and imprinting; fermentation and respiration; spontaneous generation and performationism; elimination and excretion; behavioral versus physiological or morphological adaptation; variation as both a cause and product of evolution). In these cases it is advisable to point out explicitly the similarities and differences between them and to make this connection in both contexts. This practice integrates knowledge by making relationships between concepts explicit; by preventing artificial compartmentalization and the proliferation of separate terms for concepts that are basically the same except for contextual usage; and by differentiating between ostensibly similar but actually different concepts. Ignoring such relationships between later-appearing and previously learned content assumes, rather unrealistically, that students will independently perform the necessary cross-referencing by themselves.

Organizers that are intended for elementary-school pupils should be presented at a lower level of abstraction and should also make more extensive use of concrete-empirical props. They should take into account rather than ignore preexisting organizing principles (preconceptions) in the learner's cognitive structure. Often these preconceptions are based on widely accepted elements of cultural folklore that are very tenacious unless explicitly undermined.

### Pervasive Themes

Good organizational advantage can be taken of pervasive or recurrent themes that can integrate or interrelate many different topics or general ideas. This book uses the theme that what the learner already knows (his or her relevant cognitive structure) is most important in subsequent learning. It is obviously necessary for pervasive themes to be introduced early in a book if they are to serve an integrative function, but frequently such general themes are not presented until late in the book or program.

### Preconceptions and the Individualization of Instruction

The role of preconceptions in determining the longevity and qualitative content of what is learned and remembered is crucial. It may very well be the most important manipulable factor in the individualization of instruction. This problem will be discussed further in the section on individualized instruction. Unfortunately, however, very little research has been conducted on this crucial problem, despite the fact that the unlearning of preconceptions might very well prove to be the most determinative single factor in the acquisition and retention of subject-matter knowledge.

In any case, anyone who has attempted to teach science to children, or to adults for that matter, is painfully aware of the potent role of preconceptions in inhibiting the learning and retention of scientific concepts and principles. These preconceptions are amazingly tenacious and resistant to extinction because of the influence of such factors as primacy and frequency and because they are typically anchored to highly stable, related, and antecedent preconceptions of an inclusive nature. They are inherently stable (for example, general; unqualified; expressive of a positive rather than inverse relationship; predicated on single rather than multiple causality or on dichotomous rather than continuous variability). Moreover, resistance to the acceptance of new ideas contrary to prevailing beliefs seems to be characteristic of human learning. Some of the reasons for individual differences in the tenacity of preconceptions probably include those that are related to cognitive style, to such personality traits as closed-mindedness, and to self-consistent individual differences in generalized aspects of reductionism in cognitive functioning. Pines (1977) has shown that when misconceptions are not uprooted, they may become more elaborated and stable as a result of instruction.

General findings regarding the role of cognitive organizers would appear to have significant implications for those aspects of individualization of instruction that are related to the problem of preconceptions. Let us assume that advance organizers can be used in nonindividualized fashion generally to bridge the gap between what learners already know and what they have to learn at any given moment in their educational careers. Then individualized organizers, specially tailored to the particular preconceptions of a particular learner, will have an even more facilitating effect on meaningful learning and retention. Unless proposed organizers take explicit account of—and attempt explicitly to extinguish—existing preconceptions, it seems likely that these preconceptions will both inhibit related new learning of more valid scientific concepts and principles and eventually assimilate, through memorial reduction, the proposed new ideas designed to replace them.

A very common preconception, for example, among elementary-school children is that the outer integument constitutes a kind of sack filled with blood. Prick it at any point and it bleeds. Actually this is not an implausible hypothesis. It is conceivable therefore that one can effectively instruct such children about the circulatory system without taking into account and trying to undermine the relative credibility and explanatory value of this preconception as compared with that of a closed system of vessels. Oakes (1945, 1947) has shown that misconceptions exist at all age levels.

Thus a seemingly important precondition for constructing individualized organizers for instructional units in science is to ascertain what the more common preconceptions of learners are by means of appropriate pretests and then to match suitably tailored organizers with pupils exhibiting corresponding preconceptions. If we had to reduce all of educational psychology to just a single principle, we would say this: "Find out what the learner already knows and teach him or her accordingly."

### Instructional Aids[3]

With the growth of our psychological and pedagogic knowledge about, and technological capacity for, presenting instructional materials efficiently to learners at each stage of cognitive and subject-matter sophistication, the role of instructional aids in education is gradually changing. No longer do these aids serve merely enrichment or evaluative functions in transmitting subject-matter content to students, but do, and largely should, carry the routine burden of such transmission. Thus, ideally, after the primary grades, curriculum materials should be produced for students rather than for teachers.

When the content of a curriculum program is appropriately prepared and pretested for learnability and lucidity and contains adjunctive feedback devices, there is little value in using the teacher as a filter through which the content of subject matter reaches pupils (Novak, 1966). Perhaps 0.1 percent of teachers can present subject matter as lucidly and efficiently as properly programmed materials; and the use of "programmed" material does *not* necessarily imply teaching-machine programs or "scrambled textbooks" that granulate material into such small segments that its logical structure and interrelationships are no longer perceptible.[4]

When programmed subject-matter material is transmitted to pupils directly, it not only reaches them more clearly and effectively but also can be delivered on an individualized, self-paceable basis, thereby circumventing the ideational and pedagogic limitations of many teachers. The teacher's role is not eliminated, but is channeled more into the stimulation of interest; the planning and direction of learning activities; the provision of more complete and individualized feedback in instances that are idiosyncratic to particular learners; the evaluation of achievement; the guidance of independent study, thinking, and problem solving; and the direction of discussion about issues that are too controversial or speculative to be programmed efficiently. Teachers are far too valuable to spend their time giving routine lectures about relatively stable and fixed areas of knowledge (Ericksen, 1967).

Typically, programmed materials would consist of texts that are written

---

[3] This term is used in the generic sense and includes all media that the teacher uses for instructional purposes apart from oral communication: textbooks, workbooks, schematic models and diagrams, demonstrations, laboratory work, motion pictures, television, teaching machines.

[4] Unless otherwise noted, "programmed textbook" in this volume does *not* refer to the typical "scrambled textbook" currently on the market, but rather to conventional-format textbooks that are written in accordance with the instructional strategy advocated in this and preceding chapters. Such books are typically supplemented by the "adjunctive" type of automated instruction advocated by Pressey (1960, 1962a, 1962b) for purposes of feedback and evaluation.

by teams of subject-matter and learning theory specialists in accordance with established psychological principles of presentation and organization. These materials would be empirically pretested and suitably revised to guarantee the maximal lucidity of each idea. They would either present adjunctive tests of genuine understanding plus appropriate feedback after each self-contained subsection or call upon the teacher to do so. They would provide for consolidation (confirmation, correction, and differential practice) before new material is presented and also provide for adequate review after progressively increasing intervals of time.

For the most part, instructional aids have contributed very little thus far to the goal of individualized instruction.

> Elementary schools, high schools, and colleges throughout the country are engaging in a variety of programs to "improve" instruction. More often than not, however, these modifications and innovations do not come to grips, in a direct and systematic way, with the primary event—the acquisition of knowledge by the individual student. One basic goal for educational change must be to recognize the individual student rather than the class as the functional unit in the instructional process. . . . The widely publicized claims that teaching machines and programmed instruction have established the educational breakthrough for adapting to individual differences, is a gross overstatement. Adapting to the *rate* of learning is only one dimension, and any tutor, live or automated, must be able to respond to the other differences that mark the idiosyncratic learning progress of each student (Ericksen, 1967, p. 176).

We will consider further the role of instructional aids in a later section on individualized instruction.

### Printed Materials

For the routine transmission of subject-matter content, printed materials are undoubtedly the method of choice. Not only can a much greater quantity of material be presented in a given unit of time, but rate of presentation is also under the control of the learner. Thus, one can pace oneself in accordance with one's intelligence, reading skill, and subject-matter sophistication. One can also take as much time as one wishes to savor the language, to reflect on the material, and to relate it to other relevant ideas. The objective of increasing speed of reading to the point that precludes these latter activities is educationally unsound. Contrary to general belief among teachers and students, James (1962) found that the use of a preferred method of learning meaningful material (for instance, reading versus lecture) makes no difference whatsoever in learning outcomes.

The deficiencies frequently ascribed to textbooks are not really inherent in the medium itself but reflect, rather, deficiencies that are common to all inadequately prepared instructional materials, such as lack of lucidity, ineffective communication, inappropriate level of sophistication, and absence of explanatory and integrative ideas. Relatively few textbooks have ever been written that take into account considerations such as progressive differentiation, integrative reconciliation, sequentiality of subject-matter content, and use of organizers.

Although textbooks can contain some built-in adjunctive feedback and evaluative devices, and can, to a limited extent, stimulate and guide the student's independent study, thinking, and problem-solving activities, further provisions along these lines must be made by the teacher. The latter is also responsible for such matters as differential practice, review, recitation, and prompting, and for coordinating the textbook with lectures, discussion, laboratory work, other audiovisual aids, supplementary reading, and independent student projects (such as essays, reports). It should be remembered that beyond the junior-high-school period concrete-empirical props should not ordinarily be used to foster an intuitive type of meaningful learning— except in the early stages of introducing students to an unfamiliar new discipline. At other times, their function is to facilitate and clarify the *abstract* learning of concepts and propositions.

## Laboratory

The laboratory as a medium of instruction implies more than *direct* contact with and observation of objects and events. As differentiated from demonstration and observational exercise, it also involves discovery experience and concern with such aspects of the process of science as hypothesis formation and testing, designing and conducting experiments, controlling and manipulating variables, and making inferences from data. Thus in science education one can hardly disagree with the proposition that:

> . . . a heavy emphasis should be placed on the nature of science or the *process* by which new knowledge is obtained. Instruction should be planned to develop understanding of the basic ideas of science concomitant with the appreciation of the methods of science; these two aspects should not be treated independently (NSTA Curriculum Committee, 1964, pp. 17–18).

The trouble with this statement, in our opinion, is that it is not sufficiently explicit. It emphasizes the role of the laboratory in teaching the process of science, and the importance of coordinating laboratory and expository instruction; they certainly should not be treated independently. But primary responsibility for transmitting the content of science should be delegated to teacher and textbook, whereas primary responsibility for transmitting appreciation of scientific method should be delegated to the laboratory. This does not imply that laboratory and classroom should not be coordinated or that related substantive and methodological principles should not be considered together whenever relevant.

Yet science courses at all academic levels are traditionally organized so that students waste many valuable hours in the laboratory collecting and manipulating empirical data that, at the very best, help students to rediscover or exemplify principles that the instructor could present verbally and demonstrate visually in a matter of minutes. Hence, although laboratory work can easily be justified on the grounds of giving students some appreciation of the spirit and methods of scientific inquiry and of promoting problem-solving, analytic, and generalizing ability, it is a very time-consuming and inefficient practice for routine purposes of teaching subject-matter content or illustrating principles, where didactic exposition or simple demonstration are perfectly adequate. Knowledge of the methods whereby data and principles in a particular discipline are acquired also need not be gained always through self-discovery in the laboratory. In many instances, this purpose can be accomplished much more efficiently through didactic exposition in conjunction with demonstrations and exercises.

Laboratory work in this context refers to inductive or hypothetico-deductive discovery experience and should not be confused with demonstrations and simple exercises. Nevertheless, it involves a contrived type of discovery that is very different from the truly autonomous discovery activities of the research scholar and scientist. Immature or unsophisticated students are only confused by the natural complexities of raw, unselected, and unsystematized data. Before these students can discover generalizations efficiently, the problem must be structured for them, and the available procedures and methods of handling data must be skillfully "arranged" by others, that is, simplified, selectively schematized, and sequentially organized in such a way as to make ultimate discovery almost inevitable. Occasional independent design of experiments may have a salutary effect in conveying the actual spirit of scientific inquiry, but should hardly be a routine procedure.

Most students below the graduate level of instruction lack both sufficient sophistication in science and sufficient ingenuity and originality autonomously to devise all of the experiments that are necessary for learning the process of science. Even if they could, the procedure would be much too time-consuming to warrant the modest advantages in understanding and appreciating scientific method that such an approach would confer over "arranged" laboratory work (Novak, 1958). It is no more necessary autonomously to discover methods of discovering scientific knowledge in order genuinely to understand and appreciate the process of science than it is necessary autonomously to discover the products of scientific investigation in order meaningfully to learn scientific concepts and principles.

In short, personal laboratory experience is both useful and necessary for the understanding of science, but "truly independent laboratory research" in the schools is useful only occasionally (rather than as a routine practice) to give students the flavor of autonomous scientific inquiry. The latter kind of experience, in other words, can hardly be equated with individualized laboratory work. Individualization of instruction in the laboratory conforms to the same principles of individualized instruction in expository teaching that were discussed above. It does not necessarily or typically presuppose independent design of experiments or wholly autonomous discovery learning.

Thus, in dividing the labor of science instruction, the laboratory typically carries the burden of conveying the method and spirit of science, whereas the textbook and teacher assume the burden of transmitting subject-matter content. The laboratory, however, should be carefully integrated with the textbook; that is, it should deal with methodology related to the subject matter of the course and not with experiments chosen solely because of their suitability for illustrating various strategies of discovery. It goes without saying, of course, that laboratory methods can be used only where the underlying methodology and substantive principles are thoroughly understood rather than followed mechanically in cookbook fashion (Ausubel, 1963).

### Educational Television and Motion Pictures

As self-contained instructional media, educational television and motion pictures have undoubted advantages over conventional lectures. In the first place, the expository aspect of instruction is typically handled by a pedagogically more highly skilled and substantively better-informed individual than the classroom teacher. Second, these media can provide much vicarious experience that would otherwise be either totally unavailable or available only with great expense and difficulty, for instance, close-ups of surgical operations, demonstrations of counseling and classroom teaching, descriptions of remote regions and complex events, historical pageants, and demonstrations involving expensive equipment and special personnel. Third, through such techniques as animation, schematic diagrams and flowcharts can be presented more effectively. Fourth, by means of videotape recordings, one can preserve a complete record of student teacher or student physician performance for later feedback, critical analysis, and guidance where otherwise such records would be irretrievably lost. The absence of direct, "live" contact between instructor and students is not necessarily a handicap, since all of the feedback, guidance, discussion, and evaluative aspects of instruction can be carried out by teachers in small groups preceding and following the audiovisual presentation.

A more serious limitation is the fact that educational television and motion pictures are typically intended for mass presentation. But this deficiency is not necessarily inherent in the media; most of the dimensions of instructional materials that can be geared to individual differences in learners can be suitably manipulated in educational television. This becomes possible by producing multiple versions of the same material and by providing for individual projectors that enable students both to adjust the speed of presentation and to repeat portions of the material.

On balance, therefore, it is hardly surprising that typical studies of the efficacy of these instructional media show that they are approximately as effective as conventional teaching methods in high school and college with respect to such criterial objectives as long-term retention, problem solving, ability to synthesize information, interest, and motivation (Siegel & Macomber, 1957). This is the case even though students generally prefer conventional media of instruction. As primary, self-contained sources of subject-matter material, however, they are undoubtedly less efficient than appropriately programmed textbooks. They are most useful as adjunctive devices for making available to students vicarious concrete-empirical experience that they could not otherwise obtain.

There is a considerable body of research on the educational value of television. Unfortunately, most of these studies have contrasted learning outcomes when television is used in contrast to learning outcomes with some other instructional procedure. In summarizing a review of the literature on the effectiveness of television and film, Leifer (1976, p. 334) states:

> Television and film are most likely to be successful teachers when educators participate in careful planning of the material, select material that conforms to our present knowledge about more successful ways of presenting content, and actively work to integrate television or film into the entire educational experience of the student. The most useful strategies for increasing learning, either with a program or through classroom activities, are active participation by students, feedback of student responses, and repetition.

We are in agreement with Leifer's statement but would add far more detail to the meaning of the last sentence. The preceding eight chapters of this book were devoted to elucidation of what is necessary in "active participation" and "feedback."

### Instructional Objectives

One of the crusades in education in the 1960s called for specific statement of *instructional objectives*. This movement was powered to a considerable extent by Mager's *Preparing Objectives for Programmed Learning* (1962). The ideas in the book evolved from Mager's experience with vocational training programs and with programmed instruction which, together with educational television, were popular in the 1950s. Mager and his supporters believed that instruction was most likely to be effective if learning goals were carefully specified so that the student understood the criteria for successful achievement.

To facilitate clarity in instructional objectives, Mager recommended that they be stated in *behavioral* form—that is, the *activity* to be displayed by the learner should be manifest and comparable to a criterion behavior against which it is evaluated. Learning objectives so stated are characterized by action verbs, such as to identify, to diagram, to list. Objectives written with these kinds of action verbs are much less subject to ambiguous meanings than objectives written with phrases such as to fully understand or to show concern for. Mager's work does not call for stating objectives that aim at specific concept differentiation or at integrative reconciliation of concepts. Under Mager's guidelines, learning objectives become statements of the type illustrated below:

After the instruction the learner shall be able to:

1. *list* ten capital cities of the world
2. *construct* a bird house for wrens
3. *differentiate* between angiosperm and gymnosperm
4. *identify* six attributes of Australian aborigines

Mager was correct, of course, in saying that this type of learning objective can be unambiguous to the learner and that evaluation based on these objectives is much less subject to varying interpretations. The primary difficulty, however, is that an entire instructional program can be planned using Mager-type objectives without giving any consideration to concepts to be learned or to hierarchical relationships between concepts. It is possible, in fact, to plan an instructional program in *rote* learning which will be most expedient for attainment of the objectives, and where meaningful learning will be discouraged and/or result in lower achievement. Atkin (1968), Ebel (1970), and Eisner (1967) have identified some of the problems associated with indiscriminate use of behavioral objectives. Although there is research support for the use of behavioral objectives (Duchastel & Merrill, 1973), some studies (Olsen, 1973) used no form of alternative objectives with comparison groups. Undoubtedly, well-written objectives, behavioral or not, could serve as advance organizers in appropriately planned instruction. As noted in Chapter 5, there is substantial evidence to support the value of strategies that can augment meaningful learning.

To look at the problem in terms of Johnson's model, we see that use of behaviorally stated learning objectives can be useful in instructional planning and in evaluation. The important consideration is that we *begin* with a matrix of *concepts* (and/or propositions and skills) to be learned and then develop our behavioral objectives. Too many workshops for teachers have emphasized the action-verb form of behaviorally stated learning objectives and have ignored completely the problem of unbundling knowledge from a discipline and developing an appropriate curriculum matrix. In so doing, the emphasis has been on a kind of pedagogical mechanics that ignores the central intellectual issues involved in instructional planning for meaningful learning.

Furthermore, it is undoubtedly premature at this point of development and degree of conceptual consensus in educational psychology to specify detailed and specific behavioral objectives in the cognitive and affective domains when general agreement does not exist even regarding the nature of such general processes as learning, memory, discovery, problem solving, or creativity. This is comparable to using a micrometer in instances where a yardstick would be much more applicable.

The research evidence on the value of behavioral objectives is far from conclusive. In a review of studies, Duchastel and Merrill (1973) found inconsistencies in results but concluded that behavioral "objectives sometimes help and are almost never harmful." When we take into account the kind of concerns expressed by critics of behavioral objectives, however, there is more reason to be pessimistic regarding the use of behavioral objectives, especially where the result may be an over emphasis on minute details or isolated concepts.

On theoretical grounds, learning objectives should be effective when they serve as advance organizers, as we indicated in Chapter 5, but such objectives need not be in "behavioral" form. Mager's (1962) insistence on behaviorally stated learning objectives derives from his behaviorist psychology of learning and it is not surprising to see limited empirical support from classroom research. Better research studies are needed that focus on the value of learning objectives to induce a meaningful learning set and to serve as advance organizers for subsequent meaningful learning evaluated by appropriate delayed retention tests of transfer of knowledge.

## Individualized Instruction

Perhaps the most popular educational bandwagon of the 1970s will be *individualized instruction*. The number of species of individualized instruction are almost as numerous as the books and articles on the subject; the generic meanings, however, all place focus on one or more of the following aspects:

1. Students proceed at their own speed through segments of the program.

2. Students can select alternative lessons or activities to meet a given set of instructional objectives.

3. Students are instructed as individuals or in small groups for all or a major portion of "class time."

4. Students can select when they wish to study a given subject and how long they want to spend in a given study session.

5. Students select or design their own learning activities.

6. A much broader range of learning material is provided.

7. Technology is used to permit or augment individual study of materials.

8. Instructional materials are organized into distinct segments, blocks, or modules.

9. Didactic and direct experience activities are integrated into learning blocks or modules.

10. Instructional objectives and criteria for assessment or achievement are made clear to the students.

11. Student-student associations are encouraged.

12. The teacher's role is primarily counseling and advising rather than presenting information.

13. Emphasis on the "methods of knowing" in a discipline is at least as important as acquisition of knowledge.

14. Efforts to encourage individual creative expression are more common than in group instructional programs.

Some of the forms of individualized instruction have been labeled in ways that suggest their nature. "Learning Activity Packages," for example, as used at Nova High School (Bethune, 1966), consist of printed study guides and associated materials that allow for varying rates of student progress (some students complete a year's "course" in several weeks). Optional study units provide for variety in students' programs. The principal instructional tool is the printed study guide, but teachers are available for tutorial help, technicians provide "laboratory packs" or the like, and a testing center staffed by clerical persons is used for evaluation.

A variation of Learning Packs has been developed for use in college courses under the label of Keller Plan instruction (Keller, 1968). With Keller Plan programs, students are guided primarily by printed materials, although some programs also employ work with computers. The primary characteristic of Keller Plan programs is that they usually permit students to move at their own rate of speed in progressing through a course. The programs contain explicit guidance as to the objectives of study together with student evaluation checks to assess attainment of these objectives. In general, Keller Plan courses show superiority over other forms of instruction (Taneggia, 1976).

In recent years various forms of *modular* courses have appeared. A useful publication describing modules was prepared by the Commission on Undergraduate Instruction in the Biological Sciences (Creager & Murray, 1971), but much of this book would be useful to teachers of any subject, at any grade level. It is suggested (page 5) that a "module" should consist of the following components:

1. Statement of Purpose
2. Desirable Prerequisite Skills
3. Instructional Objectives
4. Diagnostic Pre-Test
5. Implementers for the Modules (needed equipment, supplies, etc.)
6. The Modular Program (printed material, A-V material, etc.)
7. Related Experiences
8. Evaluative Post-Test
9. Assessment of the Module (by students and staff)

The centuries-old practice of dividing textbooks into chapters is a kind of effort to "modularize" a course of instruction, but textbooks seldom contain all of the above elements. However, an easy way to conceive of modular courses would be to consider a textbook torn into separate chapters, and then pages added to provide all of the above elements. Now if the chapters were rewritten carefully to elucidate each learning objective, integrated together with laboratory, studio, or field experience and provided with appropriate evaluation material, we would have a good beginning for a *modular* individualized course. Courses using Learning Packs and Keller Plan materials are two kinds of modular programs.

### Audio-Tutorial Instruction

One form of modular instruction was developed by Professor Postlethwait at Purdue University in 1961. He used a tape recorder to provide audio guidance to students as they proceeded in study of botanical materials. A description of his method was first published in 1962, and subsequently audio-tutorial instruction (or A-T, as it is known) has become probably the most widely used instructional innovation on college campuses since the advent of 16mm educational films. One of the reasons for the success of A-T instruction has been that it employs simple technology to augment individualization of instruction.

The A-T approach used by Postlethwait provided for individualization of instruction through tutorial aid and in flexibility of study time. The approach has been shown to be more effective than conventional lecture-laboratory instruction (Fisher, 1976; Rowsey & Mason, 1975; Sparks & Unbehaun, 1971). Each week a new "study unit" was available in the laboratory and students could choose how long and how often they wished to work on the material during days and evenings of the week. More recently Postlethwait, together with Robert Hurst, developed a biology program consisting of some eighty *minicourses*. Students can select from a variety of "optional" minicourses which, together with a required "core," accommodates their varying interests or vocational objectives. Minicourses are essentially A-T units that contain all of the components listed above for instructional modules.

### Tutorial Instruction

From the standpoint of assimilation theory, tutorial instruction could be the most effective method of teaching. In tutorial instruction with a single learner, it is theoretically possible to maximize the probability that new concepts or propositions will be provided with examples that very obviously link to previous relevant concepts held by the learner, and that the pace of presentation of new information will be most appropriate for the learner. In practice, however, graduate students or ordinary teachers seldom possess the broad fund of examples or understanding of concepts necessary to present the most meaningful information for each tutee, at least not on the spur of the moment. Moreover, the cost of tutorial instruction if used as the only method of teaching is out of the range that society can afford, although it may be cost-effective under some circumstances (Ellson, 1976).

We have all experienced successful learning in group settings or from readings and hence it is obvious that tutorial instruction is not necessary in spite of the idiosyncratic nature of learning. However, judiciously employed as an adjunct to group instructional strategies, especially when tutorial aid is available immediately at critical points, this individualization of instruction can substantially enhance learning and may account for much of the positive experience with audio-tutorial strategies. Fisher (1976), Postlethwait (1972), and others have shown that audio-tutorial programs are also cost-effective.

### Programmed Instruction

In the generic sense of the term, programmed instruction is an individualized form of self-instruction in which emphasis is placed on sequentiality, lucidity, and graded difficulty in the presentation of learning tasks, on confirmatory and corrective feedback, and on consolidation and subject-matter readiness. An attempt is made in programmed instruction to manipulate as optimally as possible all practice, task, and transfer variables that are relevant for the acquisition and retention of subject-matter content.

Our conclusion with regard to programmed instruction has been that it is potentially the most effective method for transmitting the established content of most subject-matter fields. Although programmed instruction can include some guided discovery and vicarious concrete-empirical experience, it is obviously less effective than laboratory and demonstration for learning scientific method and for acquiring observational and discrimination skills. It is also less suitable than discussion and project methods for considering more controversial aspects of subject matter, for expressing originality and independence of thought, and for learning how to adopt and defend a debatable position.

As pointed out above, the most efficient form of programmed instruction can be effected within a conventional textbook format, provided that the material has been pretested for sequentiality and lucidity, contains adequate provision for the testing of knowledge and for feedback, and takes into account established substantive and programmatic principles of facilitating the acquisition and retention of subject-matter content.

The weight of the evidence regarding the effectiveness of programmed instruction indicates that it leads to learning outcomes that are either equally as good as or slightly better than those of conventional methods (Glaser, 1965; Hughes & McNamara, 1961; Poppleton & Austwick, 1964; Schramm, 1964; Whitlock, Copeland, & Craig, 1963). Most students tend to react favorably to the programmed learning format (Eigen, 1963), at least in the beginning; loss of enthusiasm sets in earlier at the university level (Roth, 1963) than in elementary school (Porter, 1959). This latter finding suggests that some of its demonstrated effectiveness may be attributable either to novelty or to the Hawthorne effect.

It cannot be stressed too strongly that most of the available evidence about this mode of instruction is *not* derived from programmed instruction in the generic sense defined above, but rather from research on "teaching machines" and "scrambled textbooks" that employ a relatively small-frame and small-step-size approach. Various other special features of the Skinnerian linear programming technique such as emphasis on overt, constructed responses, on a low error rate (on invariably inducing success and avoiding uncertainty), and on the direct reinforcing effect of rewarding every correct response, have already been shown to be either empirically unsupportable or theoretically untenable.

Whatever effectiveness automated instruction has been found to possess can be attributed to such factors as consolidation, lucidity, individualization, prompting, and confirmatory and corrective feedback. The important programming principle of sequentiality has not really been tested yet on a long-term basis. Most programs (at least insofar as subunits within a given learning task are concerned) do not presuppose a logical sequence of items such that each subunit is sequentially dependent on the preceding intratask subunit. Hence it apparently makes little difference whether the frames are carefully sequenced or presented in random order (Hamilton, 1964; Levin & Baker, 1963, Roe, Case, & Roe, 1962).

Also, apart from several short-term studies, the effects of both substantive aspects of programming and of such programmatic principles as progressive differentiation, integrative reconciliation, the use of organizers, spaced review, and attention to the internal logic of the instructional material, have not been investigated. Pressey's (1962a, 1962b) adjunctive use of self-scoring devices makes possible only those beneficial effects on learning that follow from evaluation and feedback. It does not deal with the optimal organization and presentation of subject matter.

### Computer-Assisted Instruction

Much of the excitement that existed in the late 1950s regarding the promise of computer-assisted instruction (CAI) faded away as teachers and computer technicians became aware of the inadequacies of "second-generation" computers for instruction. These computers had more information storage capacity, faster response, and easier programming characteristics than early vacuum tube computers. But they were still too limited in information handling capacity and reliability to function satisfactorily in teaching. Some improvement was achieved with third-generation "printed circuit" computers of the 1960s; more recently we are beginning to see fourth-generation computers employing new advances in solid-state circuitry with capabilities that begin to match the needs for instruction.

In less than two decades we have seen an enormous advance in computer technology. It is possible that this rate of progress may continue; however, present-day computers will probably suffice to have a useful role in schools partly as a result of their high reliability and partly because they do have extraordinary data processing capability, relative to present needs. Bunderson and Faust (1976), after reviewing recent developments in CAI, express optimism for future development.

The application of computers in education now includes small or medium-sized models that can be used for calculations, control of video displays, generation of test questions, maintenance of performance records for individual students, and direct instruction to individual students. As staff members acquire more experience with the small or medium-size computers and as more are purchased for use, we should expect to see an increasing percentage of courses using some CAI programs and also an increasing percentage of instruction conducted in this mode.

The most "spectacular" CAI development is the continuing work at the University of Illinois on the PLATO system. This program is now in its second decade of development (Smith & Sherwood, 1976). The PLATO (Programmed Logic for Automatic Teaching Operations) system has advanced as new computers and new programming techniques became available.The newest version, called PLATO IV, shows immense promise for CAI instruction. This system employs a special large computer developed by Control Data Corporation to which up to 4000 student terminals can be connected via telephone wires. The enormous storage capacity and data processing capacity of the PLATO IV system provides not only access to standard reference items, such as boiling points of materials, but can allow one teacher access to any or all portions of other courses already in storage.

The result is that new course materials are comparatively easy to write. The immense capacity of the system means that when fully operational, CAI instruction can be available for about 50 cents per student hour. Considering the efficiency of learning that has been demonstrated with good CAI programs as compared to conventional teaching, the cost-effectiveness of the PLATO IV system is *now* attractive to schools. The state of Illinois is contributing to the cost of development for this program and plans are moving forward to use the PLATO IV system in all Illinois colleges.

The most important advantage of CAI, however, is that only computers are logistically capable of simultaneously manipulating *all* of the variables influencing individualized instruction. To be truly effective, however, we need not only sophisticated hardware at a cost within the means of educational budgets but also sophisticated principles of instruction based on an empirically validated theory of meaningful reception and discovery learning. Moreover, we should not labor under the misapprehension that CAI can be a complete self-contained means of instructions. No computer can ever be programmed with answers to *all* of the questions that students will raise. And in the less well established areas of knowledge, discussion and pupil–pupil and pupil–teacher interaction are essential for learning.

### Mastery Learning

The practice of *mastery learning* (Block, 1971; Bloom, 1976) is a natural corollary to individualized instruction. A basic assumption in most individualized study programs is that a student will "master" the content of each block or module he or she attempts. Commonly, this means that the student must successfully complete 80 to 90 percent of the evaluation items for a given study unit. Students achieving this level have presumably mastered the content of the unit and can now proceed to other study units. If their performance is less than the mastery level specified, the students restudy all or part of the unit and are then retested. The assumption is that most students can master any study unit or module, given adequate time. In practice, 60 to 75 percent of the students will show mastery on the evaluation schedule after one pass through a well-designed module. Most of the remaining students will succeed after restudy of all or selected parts of the module. A small percentage of students may find it necessary to bypass a given module, perhaps to return to it later, or to study an alternative lesson package that uses different examples or activities to achieve similar conceptual growth.

With mastery learning practices, achievement is based on successful completion of study units, not on comparative standing on a group test. Differences in student achievement exist, but they are differences in the number of study units mastered and/or the amount of time needed successfully to complete the units.[5] Successful completion of evaluation items for each study unit forms the basis for each student's evaluation rather than group testing that ranks each student in some position in the class. There is still competition among students; this takes the form of striving to be the first to complete a set of units, or competing to see who has time to complete the most "optional" units. However, realistic standards for passing a course may permit the majority of students to receive A or B grades without extraordinary effort. This results in part from the fact that *mastery* of early units of instruction, although this may take more time for some students than others, can lead to significant facilitation of learning in later units and a minimization of initial student differences in background knowledge.

In our work with college physics students, we found some of the students who required the most study time for early units *in a related sequence* were among those using the least study time to master later units of the sequence. In accordance with assimilation theory, the principle of facilitation of learning through early development of relevant subsumers was evident in Naegele's (1974) results. Similar results were found in a study with junior-high-school students (Gubrud & Novak, 1973).

Mastery learning practices employ *criterion-referenced* evaluation whereas traditional instruction usually employs *norm-referenced* evaluation. In norm-referenced evaluation students strive for a "position on a curve," whereas in criterion-referenced evaluation students are essentially in competition with themselves. The important difference in evaluation practice is that in one case students know explicitly what they are expected to master, whereas in the other case they see themselves in a kind of intellectual horse race with their peers. It is difficult to foster warm relationships between students when they view themselves in competition with one another. It is also difficult for staff members to play the role of sympathetic facilitators of learning when they are identified with ranking of students on tests that label one-fourth or more as failures.

It should be recognized that norm-referenced evaluation and criterion-referenced evaluation are not mutually exclusive. Instructional programs that use criterion-referenced evaluation to evidence satisfactory completion

---

[5] This principle differs radically from Skinnerian linear programming, which assumes that if learning material is sufficiently fragmented, and thus yields a "low error rate," differential practice schedules are unnecessary and simple reinforcement is adequate to ensure learning. Theoretical arguments and empirical evidence presented in Chapter 8 prove conclusively that this approach is simplistic, theoretically implausible, and empirically untenable. The fragmentation of potentially meaningful material into discrete and logically unrelated "facts" bearing no relation to superordinate explanatory principles is an unsound relic of reductionism and extrapolation carried to the point of absurdity.

of a study unit or module may also employ norm-referenced evaluation to rank students on midsemester or final course achievement. Some instructors have found that a combination of unit criterion-referenced exams and norm-referenced exams stressing integration of concepts presented in units not only enhances group achievement but provides added incentives for better students to achieve beyond the minimums required to pass unit exams. Such evaluation programs obviously encourage rehearsal of knowledge presented in individual study units. They also augment the potential for integrative reconciliation and consequent further differentiation of concepts and propositions of individual units.

Many instructors employing individualized instructional strategies now use a combination of criterion-referenced and norm-referenced evaluation strategies. A common practice is to specify the performance required to complete "basic" materials in the course; mastery-learning and criterion-referenced evaluation are used for this "basic" material. Successful completion of the "basic" program results in a grade of C or B or some other less-than-perfect indicator. Higher rankings are obtained through (1) high performance on norm-referenced, comprehensive exams, (2) special papers or written reports, (3) extra projects or special assignments, (4) completion of additional study units to a mastery level, (5) some combination of (1) through (4).

Most instructors who have used individualized approaches for a number of years now recommend a "mixed" approach with both norm-referenced and criterion-referenced evaluation. This recognizes in part the important role that competition plays in personality development and recognition of developing adult personality traits necessary for living in a competitive society. Norm-referenced evaluation may provide the individual with a more realistic evaluation of his or her intellectual abilities vis-à-vis others in the peer group. The student's comparative standing may help him or her to form a more realistic self-concept and more realistic academic and vocational aspirations. These factors will be discussed further in later chapters.

With the use of mastery learning strategies, course performance tends to be more a function of the quality of instructional materials and the student's motivation to succeed than a function of individual differences in initial background knowledge. The result is that grade distribution can shift from the typical "bell-shaped" curve obtained in nonmastery instructional approaches with norm-referenced grading to highly skewed "curves" with the majority of students receiving A's or B's. In our work with college physics students we observed this change in grade distribution as shown in Figure 10.9. An obvious question is whether A students under criterion-referenced evaluation and mastery learning strategy *actually* know as much physics as A students under traditional approaches. We do not have a definitive answer to this question now, but we do know that tests used under the mastery learning schedule were at least as difficult in substance

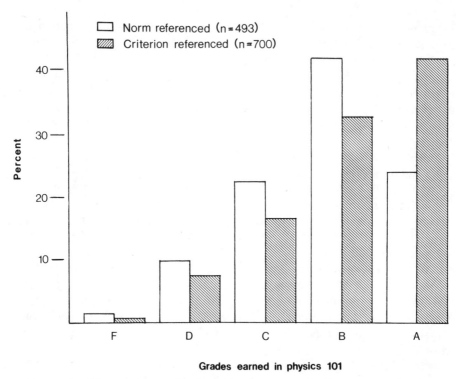

FIGURE 10.9    Norm-referenced achievement versus criterion-referenced achievement.

as exams used in former norm-referenced evaluation, based on the judgment of physics professors involved in both types of instruction and some item statistics comparisons.

We may raise the question as to how we can judge "excellence" if most students get A's in a course. Clearly, other criteria than course grade are needed. We need to consider providing some kind of indication of the *rate* at which mastery (an A grade) was achieved for those who insist on classifying students in some "ability" rank system. Recall, however, that meaningful learning is sometimes *slower* than rote learning since the individual is involved in reorganization of cognitive structures and differentiation of subordinate and superordinate concepts. A physics student who may be "slow" in introductory physics may later demonstrate the best capability for problem solving or new learning requiring physics concepts long after rotely learned information is forgotten. Although genic differences in learning ability will be functional in rates of mastery of subject matter, the relative adequacy of prerequisite concepts may be more important in achievement of any specific segment of instruction.

Variables associated with the relative adequacy of cognitive structure variables for any given learning task need much more careful attention in the design of instruction and in future educational research studies.

## The Leveling Effect of Instructional Aids on Degree of Existing Knowledge

It seems reasonable to suppose that in a nonindividualized learning environment organizational aids and other improved methods of teaching tend to benefit the average and dull student more than the bright student. In other words, they tend to exert a leveling influence on the relationship between degree of existing knowledge and aptitude, on the one hand, and new learning in the same subject-matter area, on the other. Bright students, after all, could be expected to structure and organize unfamiliar learning materials more successfully by themselves. The research evidence in this area, however, tends to be equivocal.

The lucid, integrative teaching in the PSSC high-school physics program not only brings it well within the ability of most high-school physics students (Ferris, 1960), but also tends to produce progressively decreasing correlations between academic aptitude and physics achievement as the course progresses. Brighter students are evidently able to do for themselves part of what improved methods of teaching do for mediocre students. Conventional methods of teaching, on the other hand, tend to maintain and perpetuate the existing learning and achievement advantages inherent in superior verbal ability. When students are thrown back on their own devices, the superior student has a better chance of learning.

Porter (1959) and Detambel and Stolurow (1956) obtained almost zero correlations between general ability measures and achievement on programmed learning tasks, and Joos (1961) showed that automated teaching programs in arithmetic differentially benefit low-IQ children. Boblick (1972) found that over 90 percent of chemistry students achieved success in writing chemical formulas, and they did so with substantially less study time using CAI than with conventional instruction. Naegele (1974) found that correlation with achievement in college physics and physics pretest scores was near zero ($r = .003$) in a student-paced program using a mastery mode of instruction. When the same course was offered previously using norm-referenced evaluation a significant correlation ($r = .40$) between physics scores and final achievement was obtained. The correlation between achievement in physics and math pretest scores dropped from $r = .53$ to $r = .25$ when instruction went from the traditional to the mastery mode, showing some opportunity for students to compensate for weakness in mathematics under mastery mode.

Northrop (1952) similarly found that whatever increased learning results from emphasizing the outline of an instructional film comes primarily from the low-ability group. The use of organizers is suggestively more beneficial for low-ability students in the learning of completely unfamiliar material (Ausubel & Fitzgerald, 1962), but is unrelated to academic aptitude when the learning material is substantively related to existing knowledge (Ausubel & Fitzgerald, 1961). Dull individuals are more apt to profit from advance organizers than bright individuals are. The former are both less likely to possess and choose existing relevant subsumers in cognitive structure for the new material and are also less able to improvise appropriate new organizers by themselves.

Teaching-machine programs that gear the difficulty of the material to the ability level of the lowest-ability group quite naturally tend to reduce the relationship between general ability and ultimate learning outcomes. In addition to lowering difficulty level by such devices as prompting and the use of small task and step size (Smith, 1962), such programs benefit slow learners more than fast learners by compensating for the former's relatively greater inability both to organize the material sequentially by themselves and to keep pace with a rate of instruction aimed at pupils of average ability. Stolurow (1961, pp. 124, 126, 136–138) has summarized considerable research evidence showing increased homogeneity of performance following teaching machine training, as well as practically zero correlations between general ability scores and gain scores resulting from automated instruction. Meyer (1960a) obtained a moderate negative correlation between pretest scores on knowledge of English prefixes and gain in such knowledge after ten days of self-instruction with a programmed workbook.

Programmed instruction in electrocardiography differentially benefits academically poorer students (Owen et al., 1965). Little (1960) similarly found that drill machines giving immediate knowledge of results of practice tests in an educational psychology course, as well as opportunity to correct mistakes by drill, benefits those students most who usually score in the lower half of the distribution. As a result of such teaching, both the more and the less knowledgeable students move upward in attainment, but the terminal achievement of the two groups converges.

Keislar (1959), on the other hand, found that programmed instruction in elementary arithmetic was more successful for brighter pupils. Klare et al. (1955) showed that patterning, in the form of outlining, inhibited learning in the low-ability group but facilitated learning in the upper-ability group.

When teaching machine programs are more demanding, low-ability students make lower scores than high-ability students on tests covering material completed by each group (Beane, 1962; Keislar & McNeil, 1961; Shay, 1961; Silberman, Melaragno, & Coulson, 1961a; Wittrock, 1963c). If the abler students are also permitted to learn at their own pace and to complete as many programs as rapidly as they can, individual differences in achievement between the bright and the dull obviously tend to increase rather than to decrease during the course of sequentially organized instruction (Beberman, 1958). This phenomenon apparently reflects both the increased learning opportunities given the more able pupils, as well as the reciprocal circular relationship between relative success and failure, on the one hand, and interest and motivation, on the other. Despite this divergence, however, dull pupils who are permitted to learn at their own rate of speed obviously acquire a sounder foundation of knowledge, and also maintain higher educational morale than when forced to proceed and flounder at a rate exceeding their ability level.

The complex interactions between instructional program, teacher, and students bring into play a wide range of motivational factors other than those inherent in the instructional program alone. Each learner is moving through some form of ego development and personality development, and these factors can profoundly influence motivation for learning. We will review some of the salient psychological aspects influencing motivation and learning climate in the following four chapters.

# PART THREE

# AFFECTIVE AND SOCIAL FACTORS IN LEARNING

# 11

# MOTIVATIONAL FACTORS
# IN LEARNING

*Thus far we have examined the nature and conditions of meaning-
ful learning and retention and the cognitive factors that influence it.
We have also shown how such variables can be manipulated in
various practical ways to facilitate classroom learning. Further differentiation of these pedagogic principles lies within the realm of
teaching theory and methodology.*

*We turn now to the affective and social domain of factors influ-
encing classroom learning. Our previously stated belief is that they
are less crucial in their impact on subject-matter learning than are
cognitive structure, developmental readiness, intellectual ability,
practice, and instructional material variables. Nevertheless this estimate of relative importance is only an expression of difference in
degree. Motivational, personality, group, social, and teacher characteristics are sufficiently important in school learning to engage our
most serious consideration if we wish to maximize the influence of
educational psychology on classroom learning.*

*Motivation, although not indispensable for limited and short-term
learning, is absolutely necessary for the sustained type of learning
involved in mastering a given subject-matter discipline. Its effects
are largely mediated through such intervening variables as the
focusing of attention, persistence, and increased frustration tolerance.*

*Cognitive variables directly and specifically enhance the assimi-*

lation of meanings by influencing the cognitive interactional process (as a result of which new meanings emerge) and by increasing their dissociability strength. Motivational variables, however, influence the meaningful learning process only catalytically and nonspecifically by energizing it. They also (unlike cognitive variables) cannot influence meaningful retention per se once the learning phase of assimilation is completed. They affect retention only by raising thresholds of availability (such as "repression" due to guilt feelings or feelings of hostility that would generate anxiety if experienced at a conscious level). In addition, as Bartlett suggests, they influence the process of reproduction or reconstruction through which retained material is expressed.

Achievement motivation, contrary to much current thinking in the area, is not a unitary variable. It consists (depending on normative personality factors; individual differences in personality development; differential interaction with parents, peers, teachers, and the wider culture; genically determined temperamental traits; and social class, racial, ethnic and sex membership) of varying proportions of (1) cognitive drive, (2) affiliative drive, and (3) ego-enhancement motivation.

Cognitive drive is potentially the most important and stable of the three components because it is largely inherent in the task itself. It is solely task-oriented in the sense that successful learning per se is its own reward, apart from any extrinsic considerations of reward or approval.

Affiliative drive is expressive of a pupil's need to do well in school in order to retain the approval (and the continued derived status this signifies) of the superordinate figure (parent, teacher) with whom he identifies in an emotionally dependent sense (satellization). It becomes decreasingly important as the child approaches adolescence.

Ego-enhancement motivation reflects the need for the earned status achieved by one's own competence or performance ability. It becomes increasingly important beginning with school age and is the major component of achievement motivation in our culture. It need not necessarily have an ego-aggrandizing flavor. In many primitive cultures it is "group-oriented."

Punishment (nonreward or fear of failure), as expressed in "aversive" motivation, has been unwarrantedly denigrated by American educators and educational psychologists. Within reasonable limits, it exerts a demonstrably necessary influence on sustained long-term education, particularly on university and professional education, because of the all-too-human proclivity for procrastination.

Positive attitudes toward a particular controversial issue enhance *learning and retention on both cognitive and motivational grounds. As explained above, however, negative attitudinal bias influences retention only on cognitive grounds. No channel for communication exists for such bias to influence retention per se (except in those rare instances of ego-threatening situations in the classroom where the attitudinal bias might generate high levels of anxiety).*

After sixty years or more of research on motivation, perhaps the most striking conclusion that emerges from consideration of the staggering mass of research data and theory in this area is how little we really know about it and how much is still a matter of conjecture and speculative preference. Fortunately, however, since the focus of our concern is only on the role of motivation in learning, particularly on long-term, meaningful reception learning, we shall not have to grapple with such general issues as the nature and classification of drives. Only the following kinds of issues need engage our attention: Is motivation necessary for learning? How do motivational variables differ from cognitive variables? What are the respective roles of intrinsic and extrinsic motivation in subject-matter learning and how do they change with the age of the learner? In what ways does reward (the satisfaction of drives) influence learning and retention? Can meaningful learning be reinforced? How do intention, ego involvement, and attitude influence learning? Are punishment and aversive drives effective in motivating learning?

One of the theoretical biases that should be made explicit at the very outset is the assumption that both the role and relative importance of different kinds of motivations (for example, cognitive, homeostatic, material, ego-enhancing, aversive, and affiliative) vary depending on the type of learning involved and on the species membership and developmental status of the learner. Hence, it could be anticipated that the role and relative importance of these various kinds of motivations in classroom learning would be quite different than in short-term and fragmentary varieties of rote, instrumental, motor, and discovery learning.

## Is Motivation Necessary for Learning?

Few theoretical issues in psychology provoke more heated controversy than the role of motivation in learning. Positions vary all the way from the assertion that no learning whatsoever takes place without motivation to a complete denial that motivation is a significant variable in the learning process. The weight of the evidence indicates that although motivation is a highly significant factor in and greatly facilitates learning, it is by no means an indispensable condition.[1]

Considerable research suggests that much learning is apparently neither energized by motivation nor reinforced by drive satisfaction (reduction). Classical or Pavlovian conditioning, for example, merely depends on temporal contiguity of the conditioned and unconditioned stimuli. A good deal of learning, as pointed out above, occurs incidentally without any explicit intention to learn. Appreciation of a means-end relationship is frequently acquired and selectively retained, either through insight or trial-and-error variation of responses, even if unaccompanied by the original existence and later reduction of a drive state.

Apart from classical conditioning, however, motivation is probably more dispensable for meaningful reception learning (particularly on an unorganized, short-term basis) than it is for any other kind of learning. Because such learning requires relatively little effort, less reliance need be placed on existing drives and motives within the learner, on incentive conditions, and on extrinsic rewards than is the case, for example, in rote learning or problem solving. But to assert that meaningful learning (particularly of a fragmentary and short-term nature) can occur in the absence of motivation, does not, of course, deny the fact that motivation can significantly facilitate learning whenever it is present and operative.

Even where motivation is clearly operative in human learning, it is misleading to extrapolate the familiar paradigm of homeostatic drive reduction that is characteristically used to explain animal learning (Harlow, 1953). Such drives are quickly satiated and, when accompanied by intense affect, disrupt learning (Harlow, 1953). Hence hunger, thirst, pain, and the like, rarely motivate human learning. And although material rewards are often effective, intrinsic (task-oriented) and ego-enhancing motives increasingly tend to dominate the motivational picture with advancing age. Material rewards also tend to become less ends in themselves than symbols of earned or attributed status and sources of self-esteem.

The trend in recent research and thinking has been to place greater emphasis on the motivational power of such intrinsic and positive motives as curiosity (Berlyne, 1960), exploration (Montgomery, 1954), activity (W. F. Hill, 1956), manipulation (Harlow, 1950; Terrell, 1959), mastery or competence (Ausubel, 1956a; White, 1959), and the need for stimulation (Butler, 1954). In addition, these latter drives have been elevated to the status of

---

[1] On theoretical grounds it may be hypothesized that motivation becomes a progressively less important factor in learning as children advance in age. As learning becomes easier and less effortful due to the growth of cognitive capacity, attention span, and ability to concentrate, less energization of the learning process is necessary. In addition, cognitive structure variables become increasingly more important as determinants of learning. Finally, since the child is motivated more by cognitive, affiliative, and ego-enhancement drives, material reward and punishment become less salient factors.

primary drives in their own right. Unlike other drives, they are, further-more, gratified (reduced) merely by the very fact of successful learning itself. It is hardly surprising, therefore, that in many human learning situa-tions the provision of explicit rewards makes relatively little (Abel, 1936) or no (Auble & Mech, 1953) difference in speed of learning or in perform-ance level. Because so much learning attributable to task-oriented or ego-enhancing motives has already occurred, the later introduction of homeo-static or material rewards into the learning situation does not dramatically accelerate the rate of learning as it does in comparable animal ("latent learning") experiments.

At the human level, cognitive drive (the desire for knowledge as an end in itself) is more important in meaningful than in rote or instrumental learning. It is, at least potentially, the most important kind of motivation in classroom learning. This is so because of its inherent potency and because meaningful learning, unlike these other kinds of human learning, auto-matically provides its own reward. That is, as in the case of all intrinsic motives, the reward that satisfies the drive inheres in the task itself. In addi-tion, as Tolman (1932) points out, motivation may facilitate learning in ways other than by energizing behavior and by reinforcing the successful variant through drive reduction. It also exerts a purely cognitive effect by highlighting or emphasizing what is to be learned, and by providing con-firmatory and corrective feedback. This is evident both in meaningful dis-covery learning and in meaningful reception learning, where the choice of correct alternatives is rewarded and the choice of incorrect alternatives is not.

The causal relationship between motivation and learning is typically reciprocal rather than unidirectional. Both for this reason and because motivation is not an indispensable condition of learning, it is unnecessary to postpone learning activities until appropriate interests and motivations have been developed. Frequently, the best way of teaching unmotivated students is to ignore their motivational state for the time being and to concentrate on teaching them as effectively as possible.

Some degree of learning will ensue in any case, despite the lack of motivation. And from the initial satisfaction of learning, these students develop retroactively the motivation to learn more. In some circumstances, therefore, the most appropriate way of arousing motivation to learn is to focus on the cognitive rather than on the motivational aspects of learning and to rely on the motivation that is developed from successful educational achievement to energize further learning.

Even though *particular* instances of learning may be largely unmoti-vated, it is undoubtedly true that the subject matter in question must be related to felt needs if significant, *long-term* meaningful learning is to occur. Inability to see any need for a subject is the reason students mention most frequently for losing interest in high-school studies (Young, 1932). Doing something without being interested in what one is doing results in relatively little permanent learning (Cantor, 1953). It is reasonable to suppose that only subject-matter material that is relevant to areas of concern in the psychological field of the individual can be meaningfully and efficiently incorporated and integrated into cognitive structure on a long-term basis.

Learners who have little need to know and understand, quite naturally, expend relatively little learning effort. They manifest an insufficiently meaningful learning set. They fail to develop precise meanings, to reconcile new material with existing concepts, and to reformulate new propositions in terms of their own idiosyncratic background and vocabulary. Moreover they do not devote enough time and effort to practice and review. Knowledge is, therefore, never sufficiently consolidated to form an adequate foundation for sequential learning. Hence, it is unrealistic to expect that school subjects can be effectively learned and retained until pupils develop a felt need to acquire knowledge as an end in itself—since much school knowledge can never be rationalized as necessary for meeting the demands of daily living.

Once such a need is developed, learning naturally becomes both a more meaningful and a more satisfying experience. But it is difficult to stimulate the development of such needs until subject matter is presented meaningfully in the first place.

Since meaningfulness is largely a personal phenomenon, it can be achieved only if one is willing to expend the *active* effort required to integrate new conceptual material into one's unique frame of reference. This means translating and rephrasing new ideas into one's own terms and relating them to one's own experience, personal history, and systems of ideas (H. D. Carter, 1935).

If learning is to be active, greater responsibility for its accomplishment must lie with the pupil. Pupils, not teachers, need to ask more of the questions and to be more concerned with formulating perceived problems than with learning answers to questions where problems are not perceived (Cantor, 1953). The teacher cannot learn, or navigate intellectually, for the pupil. The teacher can only present ideas as meaningfully as possible. The actual job of articulating new ideas into a personal frame of reference can be performed only by the learner. It follows that ideas that are forcibly imposed upon pupils, or passively and uncritically accepted by them, cannot possibly be meaningful in the true sense of the term.

## Cognitive Drive

Because meaningful learning provides its own reward, cognitive drive (the desire to know and understand, to master knowledge, to formulate and solve problems) is more important than in rote or instrumental learning.

And it is potentially the most important kind of motivation in meaningful learning. It is probably derived, in a very general way, from curiosity tendencies and from related predispositions to explore, manipulate,[2] understand, and cope with the environment (Ausubel, 1956a, 1963; White, 1959).

These latter predispositions, however, originally manifest *potential* rather than actual motivational properties, and are obviously nonspecific in content and direction. Their potential motivating power is actualized in expression, and particularized in direction, by the developing individual, both (1) as a result of successful exercise and the anticipation of future satisfying consequences from further exercise, and (2) as a result of internalization of the values of those significant persons in the familial and cultural environments with whom the individual identifies. Far from being largely endogenous[3] in origin, therefore, specific cognitive drives or interests are primarily acquired and dependent upon particular learning experience. Hence we observe again that the relationship between cognitive drive and learning, like the relationship between motivation and learning generally, is reciprocal from a cause-effect standpoint.

Despite the potential centrality of cognitive drive for classroom learning, it is nevertheless true that in our utilitarian, competitive, and achievement-oriented culture, such extrinsic considerations as ego-enhancement, anxiety-reduction, and career advancement become, with increasing age, progressively more significant sources of motivation for school learning. Beginning with the first four years of school life, ratings of achievement and recognition-seeking behavior tend to remain quite stable. They are reasonably

---

[2] The desire to explore, manipulate, and be stimulated does not, in and of itself, lead to disciplined learning effort. In its untutored expression it is directed more toward immediate gratification.

[3] We have already referred to the mistaken notion in some educational circles of regarding endogenous or spontaneously expressed needs as the only possible basis on which to organize a curriculum and as axiomatically reflective of what is "truly best" for the individual (see p. 36). The choices that individuals make themselves are not invariably as appropriate as teleological theorists would have us believe. In fact, one of the primary functions of education is to stimulate the development of potentially worthwhile needs and interests. Recognition of the role of needs in learning means that teachers should try to develop needs in pupils for mastering the subject matter they present as well as take cognizance of existing concerns. It does not mean that the curriculum should be restricted to the specific interests that happen to be present in a group of children growing up under particular conditions of intellectual and social-class stimulation.

Some theorists (for example, Mischel, 1971; Piaget, 1970, 1973) maintain that all motivation is endogenous and inseparable from cognition. That is, they perceive motivation to be an inextricable aspect of cognitive functioning or totally task-oriented. Piaget (1973), while maintaining that all true motives are endogenous, speaks of the "energizing" aspects of drive. For a critique of this position, see Ausubel (1971). Piaget's position has been interpreted as an endorsement of "discovery learning" and is, in part, responsible for his current vogue among American educators. He equates understanding with independent discovery (Piaget, 1974).

predictive of analogous behavior during adolescence and early adult life (Moss & Kagan, 1961). Even material rewards tend to become less ends in themselves than symbols of academic status, achievement, and competitive advantage. Their effects are mediated through the specific needs of the learner.

Eventually, of course, the viability of the cognitive drive as an intrinsic, task-oriented type of motivation is impaired as a consequence of the increasing, almost exclusive, association of intellectual interests and activities with ego-enhancing and anxiety-reduction motives. If the desire to learn and understand is almost invariably exercised in the context of competing for grades, obtaining degrees, preparing for a vocation, striving for advancement, and reducing the fear of academic and occupational failure, there is little warrant for believing that much of it survives as a goal in its own right. This trend is reflected in the progressive decline in school interests and intellectual enthusiasm as children move up the academic ladder (Jersild & Tasch, 1949). Theoretically, of course, it is true that some cognitive drive may be developed as a functionally autonomous by-product of successful learning, even though the intellectual activity in question is originally motivated by extrinsic considerations.

Hence if we wish to develop the cognitive drive so that it remains viable during the school years and in adult life, it is necessary to move still further away from the educational doctrine of gearing the curriculum to the current concerns and life-adjustment problems of pupils. It is undoubtedly unrealistic and even undesirable in our culture to eschew entirely the utilitarian, ego-enhancement, and anxiety-reduction motivations for learning. However, we must place increasingly greater emphasis upon the value of knowing and understanding as goals in their own right, quite apart from any practical benefits they may confer.

We should avoid denigrating subject-matter knowledge, as so many allegedly progressive educators have done over the past fifty years. Instead we must discover more efficient methods of fostering the long-term acquisition of meaningful and usable bodies of knowledge, and of developing appropriate intrinsic motivations for such learning.

## The Mediation of Motivational Influences

How do motivational factors actually influence meaningful learning and retention, and how does this influence differ from that of the cognitive variables we have considered in previous chapters? In the first place, *cognitive variables influence directly the very conditions (parameters) determining the interaction between new learning material and existing cognitive structure.* Hence they influence the emergence of new meanings and the maintenance of their separate identity and availability during the retention interval (their dissociability strength). Such variables, for example, include:

1. The availability in cognitive structure of relevant anchoring ideas, the stability and clarity of such ideas, and their discriminability from the learning material

2. Additional opportunity to relate the new learning material to a cognitive structure already sensitized to its meaning by virtue of prior exposure (spaced review)

3. The confirmation and correction of newly acquired meanings through recitation, implicit testing against original or subsequent presentations of the material, or explicit testing with feedback

4. Opportunity to profit during review from awareness of specific factors promoting forgetting

5. The amount, difficulty, pacing, and internal logic of the instructional material

Second, *the effects of cognitive variables are also mediated through the same mechanisms in both learning and retention.* That is, these variables determine the accuracy, clarity, and discriminability of emerging new meanings during learning (their dissociability strength) by influencing the cognitive interactional process in the particular aforementioned ways. This same influence of cognitive variables on dissociability strength both: (1) can be exerted during the retention period as well as during learning, and (2) continues to operate cumulatively during the retention interval, thereby determining the relative degree of availability of newly learned meanings.

Typically, however, *motivational and attitudinal variables are not directly involved in the cognitive interactional process.* They energize and expedite this process during learning by enhancing effort, attention, and immediate readiness for learning. Thus they facilitate dissociability strength catalytically and nonspecifically (rather than through direct involvement in the parameters of the interactional process involved in the acquisition of meanings). Furthermore, *the effects of motivational variables on learning and retention, respectively, unlike their cognitive counterparts, are not mediated through the same mechanisms.* After learning is completed, these variables cannot independently affect dissociability strength (that is, apart from their effects on learning itself). Therefore they can only influence retention during the reproductive phase of memory by elevating thresholds of availability and by shaping the qualitative aspects of imaginative reconstruction.

Thus motivational and attitudinal factors affect meaningful learning and retention in ways that are *qualitatively* different from the comparable effects of relevant cognitive variables. These latter variables (for example, the availability of relevant anchoring ideas and their relative discriminability, stability, and clarity) directly and specifically influence the parameters of the cognitive interactional process underlying meaningful reception learning and retention. Hence they are intrinsically involved in the determination of dissociability strength.

Motivational and attitudinal variables, on the other hand, are not intrinsically involved in the cognitive interactional process or in the determination of dissociability strength. For the most part they merely impinge indirectly on this process and influence dissociability strength in a nonspecific facilitating or energizing fashion. For example, through such motivational effects as mobilization of effort and concentration of attention, more repetitions of the material can be completed within the stipulated learning time, and each repetition is conducted more efficiently. The net result is an indirect, nonspecific, overall increase in dissociability strength for the learning process so energized.

It is also reasonable to assume that the effects of cognitive variables on meaningful learning continue along similar lines during retention and are mediated by the same mechanisms. Whatever these effects on the interactional process are, they are simply extended temporally from learning to retention. Thus the rate at which disssociability strength declines during retention reflects the continuing influence of these same *cognitive* variables on the interactional process during the retention interval. However, once the learning sessions have been completed and the cognitive interactional products have been formed, a channel of communication no longer remains open for the energizing and expediting aspects of *motivation* to influence dissociability strength, even in a catalytic or nonspecific sense. Hence if motivational factors are to affect retention independently of learning, a new mechanism is required to mediate this influence—a mechanism that does not operate during the retention interval but during the reproductive stage of memory.

### Learning

During meaningful reception learning, motivational and attitudinal variables may energize all or selected aspects of the learning field. They impinge catalytically and nonspecifically on the cognitive interactional process, resulting in the emergence of meanings by enhancing effort, attention, and immediate readiness. And they do this without affecting any of its basic parameters (for instance, the availability of relevant appropriate subsumers; the latter's stability, clarity, and discriminability from the learning task). Hence they neither determine any of its qualitative attributes nor differentially influence dissociability strength apart from a nonspecific facilitating or energizing effect on learning.[4]

---

[4] Apparent exceptions to this generalization include the effects of meaningful learning set, integrative drive, self-critical attitudes, and cognitive style, which influence the emergence, precision, integrativeness, and other qualitative aspects of meanings. But despite the terms used, these factors must, by definition, be considered cognitive, or at most quasi-motivational variables. They impinge directly on the dissociability strength of new meanings, but their influence, unlike that of true cognitive variables, is not carried over into the retention interval.

Illustrative of the energizing effect of motivation on learning is the fact that subjects who have high needs for achievement are more persistent (Feather, 1961), learn more effectively (Costello, 1968; Kight & Sassenrath, 1966; Nickel, 1968; Robinson, 1965) and tend to reach solutions in problem-solving tasks more often than do subjects with low achievement needs (French & Thomas, 1958). Persistence in task performance is also related to strength of cognitive drive (Kohn, 1965), to strength of drive and task involvement (Farley, 1968), and to the relative incentive value of the task (Nakamura & Boroczi, 1965). On a long-term basis, high achievement motivation tends to be associated with greater academic achievement (Costello, 1968; Entwistle, 1968; Krug, 1959; Uhlinger & Stephens, 1960).

Measures of such motivation, when used in conjunction with measures of academic aptitude, are excellent predictors of college performance (Weiss, Wertheimer, & Groesbeck, 1959). Training in achievement motivation enhances the long-term academic performance of underachieving high school boys, particularly those of higher socioeconomic status and greater achievement motivation (Kolb, 1965). Positiveness of the self-concept and of ego functions have much the same effect on academic performance as does achievement motivation (Bhatnagar, 1966).

Much of the facilitating effect of motivation on learning is mediated by an increase in attention.[5] Merely directing students' attention to certain aspects of subject matter, irrespective of how this is done, promotes learning (Entwistle, 1961). Academically achieving male college students are less susceptible to distraction than their underachieving peers (R. W. Baker & Madell, 1965). Learners high in achievement motivation covertly rehearse and think more about missed problems than learners with low achievement motivation (Werner, Johnson, & Merabian, 1968).

Many properties of the learning situation that foster cognitive drive facilitate learning by attracting and sustaining attention. These include novelty, incongruity, surprise, change, and conceptual conflict or "cognitive dissonance" (Berlyne, 1960; Cottrell & Wack, 1967; Festinger, 1958).[6] A moderate amount of discrepancy, incongruity, or gap between existing knowledge and a new learning task is most effective in mobilizing attention, particularly when the learner is dissatisfied with what he knows. In Piaget's terms, a child is most attentive to new learning tasks when they require some degree of accommodation on his or her part before they can be

---

[5] Attention, of course, also depends on factors other than motivation (for instance, ego involvement, relevant experience and training). One of the principal reasons why culturally disadvantaged and learning-disability children fail to learn is that (1) they have not been adequately trained at home in paying attention (M. Deutsch, 1963) and (2) distractibility is part of the minimal brain dysfunction syndrome. In part, however, their low attention span is reflective of insufficiently developed intrinsic and extrinsic motivation to learn.

[6] Cottrell and Wack (1967) consider "cognitive dissonance" as a direct motivational variable that operates selectively on "habit strength."

assimilated—when existing schemata are not wholly adequate for understanding or problem solving and require some, but not much, modification.

In addition to its energizing effects on meaningful reception learning (by enhancing effort, attention, and persistence), motivation also mobilizes nonspecifically the individual's immediate readiness for such learning by lowering the thresholds of those *general* kinds of perceptions and responses that are customarily implicated in the learning process. Exemplifying this latter mechanism is the lowering of reaction times that occurs in response to instructions to "work faster" (Owens, 1959) (as opposed to task-oriented instructions or instructions to relax). It is important, however, not to confuse this nonspecific motivational facilitation with the more direct and specific influence on dissociability strength that is exerted by such variables as meaningful learning set, integrative drive, and self-critical attitudes.

As a result of the operation of these latter, more specific quasi-motivational mechanisms during learning, clearer and more stable meanings are acquired and retained. In turn, the sequential type of learning involved in the mastery of subject matter is facilitated. For example, both Festinger (1958) and Berlyne (1960) speak of the need to reduce dissonance, incongruity, or conflict between two cognitions. This may lead to change in one of the beliefs, to integrative reconciliation, or, as pointed out above, to summary dismissal or compartmentalization of the contradictory cognition.

An optimal level of motivation or ego involvement (neither too high nor too low) apparently exists for complex kinds of learning (Iverson & Reuter, 1956). According to Bruner (1957), impelling drive states may conceivably disrupt meaningful generic learning—both by overemphasizing the particularity of newly learned concepts and by limiting the learner's ability to apply previously learned principles to newly learned tasks. Hence the learner's ability "to go appropriately beyond the information given" becomes limited. In support of this proposition he cites an experiment he conducted with Postman, in which subjects under stress made less improvement than a nonstress group in lowering their perceptual thresholds while learning to recognize tachistoscopically presented three-word sentences. Stated in terms of an hypothesized physiological basis of motivation, a moderate amount of activation or arousal seems to have an optimal effect on learning (Malmo, 1959). Motivational arousal enhances simple problem solving without affecting complex problem solving, apparently by increasing utilization of cues (Suedfeld & Goeller, 1967).

*Retention*

Once the learning sessions have been completed and the cognitive interactional products (meanings) have emerged, a channel of influence no longer remains open for the energizing and expediting aspects of motivation to affect dissociability strength, even in a catalytic or nonspecific sense.[7] At this point, therefore, it is more parsimonious to postulate that motivational and attitudinal variables continue to affect retention outcomes —that is, independently of their prior effects on learning—only insofar as they impinge on the threshold of availability and on the *reproductive* aspects of memory.

Both theoretical considerations and the weight of the available evidence suggest that motivational factors influence *meaningful* retention selectively by inhibiting (raising) rather than facilitating (lowering) particular thresholds of recognition and recall.[8] Positive ego involvement and favorable attitudinal bias, in other words, do not increase retention by lowering thresholds of memorial elicitation. Rather, strong motivation to forget and certain kinds of attitudinal bias (for example, in ego-threatening or anxiety-producing situations) may selectively promote forgetting by raising thresholds of availability (repression).

Thus, unlike the situation in learning, the selective influence of motivational variables on meaningful retention is inhibitory rather than facilitating (catalytic). Moreover, the influence of these variables is also mediated solely through a change in thresholds of memorial elicitation, without any change whatsoever in dissociability strength itself. Although the latter remains constant, recall or recognition is nevertheless rendered momentarily

---

[7] As will be pointed out below in the discussion of selective retention of those controversial materials toward which learners have a positive as opposed to a negative attitudinal bias, positive ego involvement (in this instance, positive attitudinal bias) *can* facilitate retention by increasing dissociability strength. However, this is not a genuine motivational effect on retention. Rather, it is attributable to *cognitive* or nonaffective components of attitude structure, which, in the case of positive attitudinal bias, tend to provide a highly clear and stable set of subsuming concepts for the learning and retention of the controversial material.

[8] There is suggestive evidence that thresholds of availability of *rotely* (but not meaningfully) learned items can be *lowered* after learning: (1) Motivational and affective factors (ego involvement, ego-enhancement considerations, a need to remember, and so forth) have been shown to enhance rotely learned memories. (See Ausubel [1963a, p. 231] for a summary of relevant studies.) (2) Drive states, such as hunger, both generally lower all response thresholds and selectively lower the thresholds of elicitation of simple responses (for instance, sucking) and perceptions that are particularly relevant for satisfying the underlying needs (Ausubel, 1958, p. 207). The fact that this selectivity is manifested at birth implies that the thresholds of elicitation of these relevant responses are differentially sensitive, on an unlearned or genically determined basis, to the general threshold-lowering effects of drive states. It is conceivable, therefore, that when this same relevance is acquired on the basis of prior successful learning experience, the affectively satisfying effects of drive reduction selectively sensitize the thresholds of elicitation of the drive-reducing responses to the later, general threshold-lowering effects of the drive. The only comparable evidence for meaningful learning outcomes suggests that negative affective and motivational states (for instance, anxiety) *raise* but do not lower thresholds of availability.

more difficult because of the selective elevation of particular thresholds of availability.[9]

It appears likely, therefore, that motivational factors influence retention —by raising thresholds of availability—only in those relatively rare instances where retrieval of particular information would be ego-threatening or productive of anxiety. One example is the repression of memories that would, if recalled, give rise to feelings of guilt, hostility, or self-disparagement. These kinds of forgetting, however, would not occur very frequently in typical classroom learning situations.

How, then, would one explain the more common facilitating effect of positive attitudinal bias on retention? Why, for example, would a Democrat tend to remember more pro–New Deal material than a Republican? The most parsimonious explanation is not that pro–New Deal sentiments lower and anti–New Deal sentiments raise thresholds of availability, but rather that attitudes have a cognitive as well as an affective component. That is, along with his pro–New Deal sentiments a New Dealer tends to possess a stable set of abstract and inclusive propositions in his cognitive structure reflective of New Deal ideology that more easily enable him to learn and retain differentiated information and evaluative implications favorable to New Deal ideology.

The primary and direct effect of motivational variables on meaningful retention, when they do operate, is to elevate thresholds of availability (or to make the memories in question less available in relation to their intrinsic dissociability strength). It is theoretically conceivable, however, that motivation (a strong incentive to recall) could also indirectly lower thresholds of availability. It would do this by counteracting or disinhibiting certain inhibitory factors (distraction, inattention, inertia, disinclination toward effort) that temporarily raise such thresholds.

We have already observed how various inhibitory conditions such as initial "learning shock" and the competition of alternative memories tend to dissipate spontaneously and how hypnosis can reduce the inhibitory effect both of competing memories and of motives and attitudes promoting repression—as, for example, in the case of anxiety-producing material. It still has to be empirically determined whether strong motivation or positive ego-involvement could similarly facilitate retention by disinhibiting temporarily elevated thresholds of availability.

Finally, as Bartlett (1932) points out, motivational variables are probably also involved in the reconstructive aspects of the reproductive phase of memory—in making a selection from among the available remembered

---

[9] As previously indicated, motivational and attitudinal factors not only help determine, by raising thresholds of availability, whether or not material of near-threshold dissociability strength is available in the reproductive phase, but also influence *qualitatively* the content of what is reconstructed.

items and in organizing them into a coherent verbal response to meet the demands of a current situation. Strictly speaking, however, the framing of a response in which memories are reported is not part of the retention process per se.

## Ego-Enhancement and Affiliative Components of Achievement Motivation

What is generally regarded as achievement motivation in school settings is by no means the reflection of a unitary or homogeneous drive. It has at least three components. One of these, which we have already encountered, is cognitive drive—the need for acquiring knowledge and solving academic problems as ends in themselves. This drive certainly underlies the need for academic achievement to the extent that such achievement represents to the learner the attainment of the knowledge he seeks to acquire. It is completely *task-oriented* in the sense that the motive for becoming involved in the task in question (acquiring a particular segment of knowledge) is intrinsic to the task itself; it is simply the need to know. Hence the reward (the actual attainment of this knowledge) also inheres completely in the task itself since it is capable of wholly satisfying the underlying motive.

A second component of achievement motivation, on the other hand, is not task-oriented at all. It may be termed *ego-enhancing* because it is concerned with achievement as a source of earned status, namely, the kind of status that an individual earns in proportion to his or her achievement or competence level. It is ego-enhancing inasmuch as the degree of achievement determining the individual's earned status simultaneously determines how adequate he or she feels (level of self-esteem), feelings of adequacy in this case always being a direct reflection of relative earned status.

The ego-enhancement component of achievement motivation is therefore directed both toward the attainment of current scholastic achievement or prestige, and toward the future academic and career goals (later sources of earned status) that depend on this achievement. One of its central ingredients, as we shall see later, is anxiety—fear in response to any anticipated threat to the loss of earned status and self-esteem that results from threatened academic failure. Approval from teachers satisfies the ego-enhancement component of achievement motivation by constituting confirmation of achievement or a source of earned status rather than (as in the cast of affiliative drive) constituting confirmation of the derived status acquired from the superordinate person(s) with whom the learner identifies.[10]

---

[10] High need achievement, coupled with low test anxiety, increases achievement in college courses perceived as instrumentally related to success in career goals (Raynor,

The final or *affiliative* component of achievement motivation is neither task-oriented nor primarily ego-enhancing. It is not oriented toward academic achievement as a source of earned status, but rather toward such achievement insofar as it assures approval by a superordinate person or group with whom the individual identifies in a dependent sense, and from whose acceptance he or she acquires vicarious or derived status. The latter kind of status is determined not by the individual's own achievement level but by the continuing intrinsic acceptance by the person(s) with whom he or she identifies. And one who enjoys derived status is motivated to obtain and retain the approval of the superordinate person—by meeting the latter's standards and expectations, including those for academic achievement— since such approval tends to confirm one's derived status.[11]

Varying proportions of the cognitive, ego-enhancement, and affiliative components are normally represented in achievement motivation, depending on such factors as age, sex, culture, social-class membership, ethnic origin, and personality structure. Affiliative drive is most prominent during early childhood. At this time children largely seek and enjoy a derived status based on dependent identification with, and intrinsic acceptance by, their parents. During this period they strive for academic achievement as one way of meeting their parents' expectations and, hence, of retaining the approval they desire. Actual or threatened withdrawal of approval for poor performance therefore motivates them to work harder to retain or regain this approval. Since teachers are largely regarded as parent surrogates, they are related to in similar fashion.

Affiliative drive is thus an important source of motivation for academic achievement during childhood. As we shall see in the following chapter, however, children who are not accepted and intrinsically valued by their

---

1970). Students with higher motives to achieve than to avoid failure set higher levels of aspiration that tend to persist despite repeated failure experiences (Feather, 1967).

Generally, hard, as opposed to easy or "Do your best" goals, increase task performance. The same applies in relation to enhancing task interest. Overall task liking and satisfaction is a positive linear function of number of prior successes. Objective test difficulty and telling children it is difficult for others, results in greater persistence after failure than under opposite conditions of task description (Wyer & Bednar, 1967). Similarly, when tasks are both objectively and apparently easy for others, previously successful subjects persevere longer than subjects who had previously failed (Wyer & Bednar, 1967).

Feather (1967) found that initial success after initial failure led to completion of a greater number of anagrams. Subjects characterized by greater "external controls" ("outer-directedness") exhibited less changes in self-confidence. Large changes in confidence (up or down) after uniform failure experience are associated with better performance than when subjects exhibit less change in confidence.

[11] Men with high affiliative drive make better grades in classes with a high level of affiliative cues and vice versa (McKeachie et al., 1966). Compare this finding with differential effect of teacher "warmth" on satellizing and nonsatellizing pupils (see Chapter 14).

parents, and who therefore cannot enjoy any derived status, are compensatorily motivated to seek an inordinate and often unrealistic amount of earned status through academic achievement. Thus high levels of achievement motivation typically represent low affiliative drive that is more than compensated for by high ego-enhancement drive.

During late childhood and adolescence, affiliative drive both diminishes in intensity and is redirected from parents toward agemates. Thus academic competition against the opposite-sex group or other age-grade classes constitutes a powerful motivating factor (Maller, 1929; Sims, 1928). Desire for peer approval, however, may also depress academic achievement when such achievement is negatively valued by the peer group. This is a more common occurrence among lower-class and certain culturally disadvantaged minority groups (Ausubel, 1965d). Middle-class peer groups, as pointed out later (Chapter 12), place a high value on academic achievement and expect it from their members.

In most cultures, and particularly in Western civilization, ego-enhancement drive is the dominant component of achievement motivation in adolescence and adult life.[12] This is especially true among males and middle-class groups in our culture.

For about a decade and a half after World War II, however, cognitive drive and need for earned status gave ground in the United States to the affiliative drive as epitomized by the character structure of the "organization man." Affability, social poise, and ability to "get along," "play it safe," equivocate, conform, and "swim with the tide" displaced initiative, competence, individualism, forthrightness, and moral courage as the dominant values in United States society. Then, partly in response to the challenge emanating from spectacular Soviet achievements in science and technology, traditional American values staged a remarkable but far from complete comeback during the Sixties. A new and emergent feature of this latter shift in cultural values is an almost cultlike veneration of intellectual achievement and creativity.

### Efficacy of Ego-Enhancement Motivation

The effectiveness of ego-enhancement drive for academic achievement is borne out empirically by many kinds of evidence. Achievement motivation leads to greater persistence and a higher rate of success in problem-solving situations (Feather, 1961; French & Thomas, 1958) and to higher

[12] Thus, with increasing age, material rewards are sought less as ends in themselves than as symbols of earned status, prestige, and ego enhancement. Remote goals also become more salient as long-term ambitions displace the need for immediate hedonistic gratification, as the temporal dimensions of children's psychological world expand, and as their frustration tolerance increases.

short-term (Kight & Sassenrath, 1966) and long-term (Krug, 1959; Uhlinger & Stephens, 1960; Weiss, Wertheimer, & Groesbeck, 1959) academic performance. Relative need for academic achievement discriminates significantly between normally achieving and underachieving men (Todd, Terrell, & Frank, 1962).

In ego-oriented laboratory situations, as when successful completion of a task is represented to subjects as being reflective of intelligence, both level of motivation and performance level are enhanced (Alper, 1946; Kausler, 1951). Under achievement conditions, high need for achievement in high-school boys is associated with greater meaningful learning of academic materials[13] (Caron, 1963).

Subjects who are given bogus low scores on IQ tests tend to regard themselves less highly and believe that significant other persons feel the same way about them. They are also unhappy about "being different" and exhibit less intellectual productivity (Gibby & Gibby, 1967). Perseverance on an objectively easy task is greater following failure rather than success; the converse is also true. These findings, however, are greatly weakened when approval is concomitantly administered.

Finally, Maller (1929) and Sims (1928) found that individual rivalry stimulates academic performance more than group rivalry does. And Ausubel (1951) found that gifted elementary-school children work much harder at an academic task in response to a prestige incentive than when merely "trying their best" but believing their work products are anonymous.[14]

Achievement motivation, however, is not linearly related to achievement level. As is the case with potent motivational status generally, very strong achievement motivation may lower the level of performance and achievement, probably because of its frequent association with disruptive neurotic anxiety.

### Advantages and Disadvantages of Ego-Enhancement Motivation

The emphasis that has been placed on intrinsic motivation for learning should not be interpreted as a denigration of the importance of developing extrinsic motivations. The need for ego enhancement, status, and recognition through achievement and the internalization of long-term vocational aspirations are, after all, traditional hallmarks of personality maturation in

[13] Data from studies using thematic (fantasy) measures of achievement motivation tend to be equivocal because of the tendency in many instances for an inverse relationship to prevail between "real-life" and fantasy indices of ego-enhancement drive.

[14] When group concerns are more important, pupils work harder for such goals than for individual goals (Wyer, 1968). This suggests that group-oriented achievement motivation is more common than generally believed, especially in primitive cultures characterized by strong kinship ties and negative valuation of "being better than others" (Ausubel, 1965d; Leighton & Kluckhohn, 1947).

our culture. Educational aspirations and achievement are both necessary prerequisites for, and steppingstones to, their vocational counterparts. Hence in addition to encouraging intrinsic motivation for learning, it is also necessary, from the standpoint of personality maturation, to foster ego-enhancement and career advancement motivations for academic achievement. Furthermore, few individuals ever develop enough cognitive drive to master large bodies of subject matter as an end in itself. Long-term ego-enhancement motivation is also necessary.

One might legitimately even go a step further and assert the unfashionable view that aversive motivation—namely, the threat of those penalties associated with academic failure—is as necessary as the positive motivation stemming from anticipated rewards for sustaining the long-term academic achievement required for reaching long-term academic and professional goals. Although educators theoretically decry the use of aversive motivation, they implicitly rely on it to keep students studying regularly for their credits, degrees, and diplomas. They do this because they know that cognitive drive and anticipated reward for hard work are not sufficient to overcome both inertia and the typical human proclivity toward procrastination and aversion to sustained, regular, and disciplined work.

Teachers who imagine that the majority of their students would continue at their studies in the absence of structured programs, assigned work, deadlines, and examinations are living in a world of fantasy. The motivational force of an examination lies more in the threat of failure than in the hope of success. Thus, within reason, the threat of failure is a pedagogically legitimate form of motivation. Students study not only to avoid the actual consequences of failure but also to reduce both the anxiety that this threat generates and the guilt feelings that accompany lack of attention to academic duty.

On the average, ego-enhancement motivation is undoubtedly the strongest motivation available during the active portion of an individual's academic and vocational career. More than any other factor, it accounts for the persistence of high levels of aspiration (Ausubel & Schiff, 1955; Ausubel, Schiff, & Goldman, 1953; Ausubel, Schiff, & Zeleny, 1953; Sears, 1940) and task attractiveness (Schpoont, 1955) both in laboratory and "real-life" settings, despite exposure to repeated failure experience.

Carried to an extreme, of course, this type of motivation may generate sufficient anxiety to disrupt learning (Ausubel, Schiff, and Goldman, 1953). It may also lead to highly unrealistic academic and vocational aspirations that are later followed either by catastrophic failure and collapse of self-esteem (Ausubel, 1956) or by disinvolvement from academic tasks as manifested by unrealistically low levels of aspiration (Sears, 1940). A related possibility is that excessively high needs for academic achievement may impair students' capacity for perceiving their limitations, may predispose them to rationalize their failures, and may discourage them from acknowledging that their views are logically or empirically untenable.

Still another disadvantage of exaggerated ego-enhancement motivation is that its utilitarian orientation limits its longevity. Thus, students whose academic motivation is principally extrinsic tend to perceive little value in a subject after they pass a course, or in continuing to learn after they receive their degrees—if such knowledge is unrelated either to future course work or to vocational success. In other words, they no longer evince a desire to learn when they do not have to.

Finally, overemphasis on academic achievement (assignments, examinations, grades) in such countries as France and Switzerland suggests that individuals normally manifest an upper limit of tolerance for academic stress and pressure, and that when this limit is reached relatively early in life it leads to disinclination for further academic striving in adult life. A comparable phenomenon in the United States, attributable to the "publish or perish" climate in the early stages of a university career, is the premature "burning out" of academic motivation once the initial hazards of perishing are overcome.

## Reward and Punishment

Rewards influence learning in three general ways. First, by serving as incentives they help set a meaningful problem by relating a specific sequence or organization of component learning activities to a specified goal outcome. Without such goal-relatedness, learning would often tend to be amorphous and undirected. Concomitantly, by providing significant information about the success or failure of responses, rewards give selective emphasis at critical choice points to desired or correct meanings, thereby facilitating discrimination between relevant and irrelevant cues.

Second, the actual receipt of rewards tends to augment, on a long-term basis, whatever motivations (drives) are originally operative in energizing and directing behavior toward them (the rewards). By satisfying certain drives at a given time, rewards strengthen, on a more permanent basis, those drives that they satisfy at the moment (or temporarily "reduce").

Finally, rewards may increase the relative probability of response recurrence by selectively "sensitizing" to later lowering the thresholds of elicitation of the particular learnings that lead to obtaining the reward and thereby satisfy (or temporarily reduce) the drive in question. This last property of rewards will be considered in greater detail in the discussion of reinforcement in the next section, where the position will be taken that reinforcement occurs only in relation to rotely learned associations and instrumental responses and does not characterize meaningful learning outcomes.

Punishment (in the sense of nonreward or failure to obtain the reward) acts as the reverse of reward in the following ways. First, it also helps structure a problem meaningfully, furnishing direction to activity—and information about progress toward goal—in terms of what is to be avoided. Thus, the unsatisfying consequences of an act tend to elicit avoidance, withdrawal, or variation rather than repetition. The individual learns which responses lead to nonreward and hence should be avoided. Second, punishment tends to weaken, on a long-term basis, the motivations energizing the behavior that is punished. Finally, punishment may decrease the relative probability of response recurrence, by failing to sensitize to later lowering the thresholds of elicitation of the particular responses that lead to nonreward.

It should be borne in mind, however, that the informational aspect of nonreward is less explicit than that of reward. Although it does aid discrimination between correct and incorrect cues through the information it gives as to the consequences of an act, it is less directive and provides less guidance than reward. It tells individuals only that something else must be done, but does not tell them *what* to do. Reward, on the other hand, clearly indicates that the same response is to be repeated.

It should be noted at this point, however, that "punishment" was considered above only in the sense of nonreward and not in the more *active* sense of the term. In the animal learning literature, for example, it is customary to distinguish between nonreward and *true punishment* on the grounds that nonreward, unlike "true punishment," does not necessarily imply noxious or painful stimulation. It is therefore both not necessarily threatening and not necessarily productive of anticipated fear and of the need to avoid painful, threatening stimulation. This distinction is actually quite defensible in many animal learning situations where nonreward for learning merely frustrates an appetitive drive. Nonreward is also not equivalent to punishment in relation to the purely cognitive drive component of human achievement motivation, since mere failure to acquire knowledge, when knowledge is sought as an end in itself, is not particularly threatening.

In practice, however, because of the affiliative and ego-enhancement components of achievement motivation, failure to learn in the school environment almost invariably implies either the threat of disapproval or the threat of current and/or future loss of earned status and self-esteem. Thus, for all practical purposes, nonachievement or academic failure has all of the aversive properties of "true punishment." To the effects of punishment considered as nonreward that are listed above we must therefore add the drive to avoid the threatening implications of failure.

Reward and punishment are positive and negative sides of the same motivational coin in school learning. Both are typically involved, in varying degrees, in motivating such learning. It is admittedly more enlightened from the standpoint of mental hygiene for the school to focus on reward rather than on punishment and to minimize rather than emphasize explicit threats of failure. On the other hand, it is both unrealistic to deny the existence and effectiveness of punishment as a motivational variable in school learning and unwarranted to deplore it as either immoral or pedagogically unsound.

It has already been asserted that effective extrinsic motivation implies both reward and punishment. Over the past four decades, however, the role of punishment in learning has been unwarrantedly denigrated by both psychologists and educators. Confusion about the legitimacy and effectiveness of punishment as a motivational factor in learning may be attributed to five principal sources.

First, the progressive education movement fostered various child-centered and permissivist views about the philosophical and mental hygiene impropriety of punishment. Sentimentalists associated with this movement regarded punishment as unnecessary, authoritarian, and reactionary. Education was supposed to be an exclusively happy and non-anxiety-producing experience. In accordance with this gratuitous assumption, proper motivation for learning could be only intrinsic in nature or be instilled by positive incentives (reward). In support of this assertion, numerous straw-man arguments were adduced (see below).

A second source of confusion is more semantic, emanating from failure to distinguish between the more restricted meaning of punishment in psychology as the opposite of reward (as nonreward or as the threatening consequences of failure to learn or perform successfully) and its more general meaning as a penalty for moral infraction (blame, rebuke, reproof, chastisement, censure, reprimand). Thus the suggestion that punishment, in the more restricted sense of the term, be used for motivational purposes tends to arouse a storm of protest simply because of confusion with its more general meaning as retribution for moral wrongdoing. Illustrative of such confusion is the use of the term "reproof" as synonymous with "disapproval" in describing various classroom experiments comparing the relative effects of approval and disapproval on learning.

Actually, moral censure is never seriously advocated today for honest mistakes or failure to learn, but only for irresponsibility, laziness, culpable neglect, or inexcusable failure to display reasonable effort.[15] It is obviously

---

[15] On the basis of two frequently cited experiments (Chase, 1932; Hurlock, 1924), it is generally held that praise is more efficacious than "reproof" (disapproval) for classroom learning. Other studies, however, either report equivocal findings (for example, Schmidt, 1941) or suggest that the relative effectiveness of the two practices depends on the personality of the child (Grace, 1948; Thompson & Hunnicutt, 1944) or of the administrator (Schmidt, 1941). Frase (1963) reported that negative social reinforcement (implied disapproval) has a greater facilitating effect than positive social reinforcement (approval) on the learning of logic. Spear (1970) indicates that approval and disapproval affect learners' motivational level rather than their learnings per se. Its effects (W. F. White, 1967) on school learning are also more positive and generalized than those of disapproval. The latter investigator also found that no marked personality differences resulted from either practice, although such differences generally influence over- and underachievement.

even wider of the mark to equate reproof with such punishments as objective criticism of performance or report of learning failure, which are less explicitly threatening than disapproval. The latter kinds of punishment also constitute an informational form of feedback that is quite essential for meaningful learning—even if it has threatening implications over and above its purely informational value. Thus, on purely cognitive grounds, awareness of learning failure is necessary and unavoidable in school learning. And the dreaded anticipation of such awareness is also inevitably threatening and productive of aversive motivation.

Third, critics of aversive motivation in the school environment apparently fail to appreciate that its objective is the facilitation of learning through the anticipated *threat* of failure (thereby overcoming inattention, procrastination, laziness, and lack of effort) rather than through the actual application of the punishment itself. Its aim, in other words, is to make the student *avoid* punishment by learning rather than to *experience* punishment by failing to learn. Thus, in the vast majority of instances, serious punishment is never actually experienced because it is circumvented by the learning that is motivated by the fear of the threatened consequences of not learning.

Fourth, no distinction is frequently drawn between the long-term effects of failure itself in weakening the motivations energizing unsuccessful behavior and in reducing the attractiveness of failed tasks, on the one hand, and the corresponding effects of anticipated threat of failure to self-esteem (i.e., of anxiety), on the other. Actually the evidence indicates that a high level of anxiety and/or ego involvement is associated with intense motivation, a high and sustained level of aspiration despite failure experience, and high task attractiveness, both for short-term learning tasks and for academic achievement generally.[16]

Similarly, it is frequently not appreciated that although failure has a disruptive effect on the quality of performance that follows immediately (Sears, 1937; Waterhouse & Child, 1953), anxiety does not typically have a negative effect on learning unless the task is extremely unfamiliar or the level of anxiety is extremely high (see Chapter 12).

Finally, next to progressive education, Skinner has provided the chief ideological ammunition against the motivational use of punishment in learning. According to Skinner (1948), positive reinforcement is the utopian key to all learning. Hence suitable programming should make learning tasks so easy that almost every response can be correct and thus be rewarded and

---

[16] These findings are not incompatible, as one might think at first glance, with the fact that generally speaking, overall task attractiveness and satisfaction are linearly related to the number of prior successes in the task in question (Locke & Bryan, 1967). They apply generally to success and failure as *external* variables affecting self-esteem, etc. The variables considered above, however, reflect *interpersonal* differences in ego involvment, anxiety level, and tenacity of level of aspiration.

positively reinforced (Skinner, 1958). Under these circumstances, there is little need for even nonreward to extinguish incorrect responses.[17]

The actual doctrine regarding the ineffectiveness of punishment is generalized from two operant conditioning experiments (Estes, 1944; Skinner, 1938) in which punishment (as contrasted to nonreward) was shown to lead to temporary suppression (rather than to extinction) of a simple, previously reinforced learned response (lever pressing) requiring no discrimination whatsoever. The difficulty with this line of reasoning, of course, lies in the fact that the extinction paradigm in this type of operant conditioning is hardly comparable to the typical situation in which threat of punishment is used to motivate classroom or laboratory learning.[18]

Contrary to Skinner's and Estes' findings, punishment, conditioned fear, and anxiety have been remarkably effective in a wide variety of avoidance-training (Solomon & Brush, 1956), instrumental-conditioning, and discrimination-learning (Penney & Lipton, 1961) experiments. The object of threatened punishment in these experiments (as is also the case in classroom learning) was not to extinguish or induce *unlearning* of a simple and non-discriminating type of previously reinforced response. Rather, the object was to motivate a more complex and discriminating variety of *original* learning by training the learner to avoid either a painfully cued choice or the pain associated with failure to learn or respond.

It is quite probable, therefore, that punishment is more effective than nonreward in complex and discriminating instances of original learning, both because it generates aversive motivation (motivation to avoid the punished response) and because it gives more information emphasis to the alternatives that are to be avoided.

As pointed out above, caution is indicated in the application of aversive motivation. Used excessively, it may generate a level of anxiety out of all proportion to the actual risk of failure involved in a particular learning task. This may not only disrupt learning but also generalize to other areas. It could induce a negative self-concept (an "emotional block") about entire fields of knowledge, such as mathematics. It can also lead either to ego disinvolvement from a task or to unrealistically high levels of aspiration.

---

[17] Meaningful learning, as previously indicated, is sufficiently complex, and involves sufficient discrimination, that successful outcomes *cannot* be guaranteed by the cognitively undesirable practice of fragmenting the learning task into discrete bits. It is also greatly facilitated by the purely cognitive or informational effects of nonreward or report of learning failure, particularly if such report is differential in nature.

[18] Even using an extinction paradigm, Weingold and Webster (1964) were able to extinguish previously reinforced cooperative behavior by punishment but not by nonreinforcement. High-intensity punishment is more effective than low-intensity punishment when cognitive (subject-matter) readiness is low. Early rather than late punishment is similarly more effective in response inhibition. Such inhibition is mediated by emotional arousal under some conditions and by prohibitive rules in others (Cheyne & Walters, 1969).

The solution, however, is not to outlaw aversive motivation, but to keep it within reasonable bounds, to balance it with cognitive and positive ego-enhancement drives, to make learning more successful for most pupils, and to provide particularly anxious children with counseling.

## Drive Reduction and Reinforcement

Whether drive reduction (temporary satisfaction of a need) has a selective reinforcing effect on drive-reducing learning outcomes (thereby increasing their later availability or the probability of their recurrence) and how this effect is mediated are exceedingly complex and controversial topics, full discussion of which is obviously beyond the scope of this chapter. It will suffice to state, and briefly to justify, the following position: (1) Drive reduction selectively reinforces drive-reducing learning outcomes only in the *rote* learning of discrete, arbitrary, and verbatim associations or of instrumental and stimulus-response connections. (2) It does so not by retroactively and selectively increasing associative strength between stimuli or between stimuli and responses but by retroactively and selectively sensitizing to later lowering the thresholds of elicitation or availability of such associative units.

In rote, as in meaningful learning, drives also merely energize and direct behavior nonspecifically and catalytically. The actual strength of association that actually develops in the course of learning is determined by such factors as contiguity, frequency, primacy, and the informational effects of reward. It has also been found that the affectively satisfying effects of drive reduction (e.g., as in "social reinforcement" [Stein, 1969]) may retroactively and selectively make more susceptible to later lowering the thresholds of availability of those particular associative units whose acquisition was instrumental in obtaining the reward.[19]

The likelihood of this possibility is enhanced by evidence suggesting that: (1) Affective and motivational factors can retroactively increase memory (lower thresholds of availability) for rotely learned items; and (2) a generalized drive state (for instance, hunger and sex) can selectively lower the thresholds of elicitation of those responses and perceptions that are particularly relevant for their satisfaction by virtue of their prior reduction of the drives during learning. This effect of drives (in selectively lowering such thresholds of elicitation) can be explained most parsimoniously, in turn, by assuming that the retroactive satisfying effects of drive reduction on drive-satisfying learning outcomes makes them differentially more sensitive to the general threshold-lowering effects of drive states.

---

[19] Contrary to her hypothesis, this same investigator found that fourth-grade girls are not more responsive to external approval for achievement (that is, are not more "outer-directed") than fourth-grade boys.

It is understandable, therefore that when particular responses frequently satisfy a given drive, their thresholds of elicitation become preemptively sensitized to lowering whenever the drive in question is operative. And what applies generally in relation to a given drive also presumably applies to the satisfaction of the same drive in a particular learning task.

In the case of *meaningful* learning, on the other hand, no mechanisms exist through which the satisfying effects of reducing the cognitive, affiliative, and ego-enhancing components of achievement motivation can reinforce successful (drive-reducing) learning outcomes. Unlike the informational (cognitive) consequences of feedback (confirmation, correction, and dissociability strength of *previously learned* meanings), the affectively satisfying effects of drive reduction are not *intrinsically* related to the factors determining dissociability strength. Hence they cannot increase it retroactively; they can increase it only *indirectly during* the course of learning by nonspecifically and catalytically enhancing learning itself.

The possibility remains, of course, that the effects of drive reduction could be mediated retroactively through their influence on the thresholds of availability of meaningful learning outcomes—just as in the case of rotely learned items. However, there is no comparable evidence suggesting that motivational and affective factors can directly *lower* the thresholds of availability of meaningfully learned items. Apparently thresholds of availability, in relation to dissociability strength, differ in this crucial respect from corresponding thresholds of availability in relation to associative strength.

This does not mean, however, that reward and punishment do not facilitate meaningful learning in other ways. Reinforcement, after all, is only one consequence of reward—the aspect that directly increases the elicitability of *rotely* learned responses by sensitizing their thresholds of availability to later lowering when drive states are operative. In the case of meaningful learning, reward and punishment have two other more indirect kinds of facilitating effects. In the first place, from a motivational standpoint, awareness of successful learning (satisfaction of cognitive, affiliative, and ego-enhancing drives for acquiring new knowledge) energizes subsequent learning efforts by enhancing the learners' self-confidence, by encouraging them to persevere, and by increasing the subjective attractiveness of the learning task. At the same time it motivates individuals to make further use of, that is, to practice, rehearse, and perform what they have already learned. It also encourages them to continue developing and exercising the motives that were satisfied or rewarded, namely, the desire for knowledge both as an end in itself and as a means of enhancing status and self-esteem.

The experience and threat of punishment (nonreward or failure to learn successfully), on the other hand, generate considerable aversive motivation. The learner is thus generally motivated to avoid learning failure by paying attention, by displaying suitable effort and perseverance, by delaying the gratification of hedonistic needs, and so forth. In addition, when the learner is informed that a particular, previously learned understanding is incorrect, the threatening implications of this report motivate him or her, to some extent, to avoid or reject it, thereby presumably raising its threshold of availability.[20]

These facilitating effects of aversive motivation undoubtedly more than counterbalance the negative impact of failure experience on the long-term strength of the underlying motivation and on task attractiveness. However, when experience of failure predominates, or when aversive motivation is unsuccessful in averting failure, this is obviously not the case.

Second, reward (awareness of successful learning outcomes) and punishment (awareness of unsuccessful learning outcomes), whether in relation to the intrinsic or extrinsic components of achievement motivation, also have all of the cognitive or *informational* effects of feedback. These latter effects are probably just as important for meaningful learning and retention as are the motivational effects of reward and punishment. By confirming correctly understood meanings and, at the same time, indicating areas of confusion, correcting errors, and clarifying ambiguities and misconceptions, the cognitive aspects of feedback increase the stability, clarity, and discriminability of meaningfully learned ideas (enhance their dissociability strength). They also increase the subject's confidence in the correctness of what is understood, and enable him or her to focus learning efforts selectively on inadequately learned portions of the material. They not only have informational value for subsequent trials of the same learning task, but also have transfer value for related new tasks (Keislar, 1960).

## The Effects of Intention on Meaningful Learning and Retention

Although individuals can acquire much miscellaneous information and some skills incidentally, deliberate effort is required for the efficient learning of most types of academic material. Deliberate intention to learn (in response to explicit instructions) is not essential for learning as long as belongingness is present. Such belongingness prevails, even in the absence

[20] Since the threat implied by any *particular* wrong learning is obviously not very formidable, the elevation of its threshold of availability is only a very minor factor in forgetting misconceptions. Many misconceptions are amazingly tenacious because of the influence of such factors as primacy and frequency. Also because they are anchored to highly stable subsumers, because they are inherently more stable (more general; less qualified; expressive of a positive rather than an inverse relationship; indicative of single rather than multiple causality) than their "correct" counterparts, they are highly resistive to extinction. This is why they must always be *explicitly* undermined by the teacher or by instructional materials (including advance organizers).

of explicit instructions, either when the learning material is potentially meaningful or when habitual expectancies are applicable to rote learning tasks. In the latter instances, of course, a certain amount of implicit or self-instruction may be operative.

Nevertheless, many experiments show that deliberate learning in response to explicit instructions is both more effective (Bromer, 1942; Huang, 1944; Myers, 1913; Reed, 1946) and more precise and specific (Postman & Senders, 1946) than is unintentional or implicitly instructed learning. To explain these findings it is necessary only to invoke the typical energizing and expediting effects of motivation on learning. We have already considered why incidental practice, in the sense of being unstructured and uncontrived, rather than unintentional, does not lead to efficient learning outcomes.

Somewhat more important for long-term school learning is the widespread belief that intention to *remember* facilitates the retention of meaningfully learned verbal materials. Actually, however, the experimental evidence bearing on this issue is quite equivocal because the experimental arrangements have been such as: (1) to induce intentions to *learn* rather than to remember, or (2) to make impossible the isolation of the effects of intention on learning from its effects on retention.

Numerous studies, for example, have shown that intention to remember enhances the longevity of retention. When subjects learn material with the expectation of recalling it for a designated period of time, recall is superior for the expected interval than it is for either a longer or shorter interval (Aall, 1913; Biel & Force, 1943; Geyer, 1930; Thisted & Remmers, 1932). Lester (1932) demonstrated that retention is facilitated by expectation of recall and by foreknowledge of the occurrence and possible interfering effect of interpolated materials.

Unfortunately, however, since these experiments introduced differential intentions to remember at the time of original learning, they did not isolate the effects of the intention on what was learned in the first place from its effects on retention alone. Under the circumstances, therefore, all of the superior retention could be plausibly attributed to the energizing effects of the intention on learning, without assuming that it had any independent influence on retention.

To test this latter interpretation, Ausubel, Schpoont, and Cukier (1957) conducted an experiment in which undergraduate students learned an extended historical passage and were then tested on it immediately afterward. After this test, an explicit intention to remember was induced by announcing that an equivalent form of the test would be given two weeks later. The same procedure was followed with a control group, except that an unannounced retest was administered. The two groups were not significantly different in mean learning scores or in the percentage of material retained from test to retest. It was concluded, therefore, that intention to remember in the previously reported studies primarily facilitated retention by enhancing learning rather than by virtue of any effect on the retention process itself.

The reason why positive ego-involvements, such as intention to remember, presumably do not facilitate retention is because motivational variables, as postulated above, can neither influence dissociability strength *after* the material is already learned nor *lower* thresholds of availability for meaningfully learned material.

In another group of studies, it was shown that retention is superior (Maso, 1929; J. Peterson, 1916; Prentice, 1943), and retroactive inhibition less marked (Prentice, 1943) when practice is accompanied by "intent to learn" than when learning takes place incidentally. That this difference is largely attributable to superior original learning, however, is demonstrated by the fact that it no longer prevails when experimental and control subjects are equated for original mastery of the learning task (Biel & Force, 1943). In any event, the evidence yielded by such studies is at best indirect because in each instance an explicit experimental set was induced to *learn* material for immediate reproduction rather than to *retain* it for an extended period of time.

## Values and Attitudes

In addition to teaching subject matter, schools also have an obligation to transmit to pupils the major values of our culture, including those (such as the social equality of persons irrespective of race, religion, and ethnic origin) that unfortunately are honored more in theory than in practice. It is unnecessary either to pretend that this does not constitute indoctrination or to apologize for it, as long as the teaching aims at rational persuasion rather than at uncritical acceptance based primarily on emotional grounds. The assimilation of values will, of course, tend to follow the developmental trends outlined above for motivation generally.

Younger children are naturally influenced by considerations of personal loyalty and prestige suggestion. With increasing age, however, considerations of intrinsic ideational merit and ego enhancement become more important. For example, college students who prepare statements of position contrary to their currently held beliefs tend to maintain these positions if they are rewarded for doing so (Bostrom, Vlandis, & Rosenbaum, 1961; Scott, 1957).

### Changing Attitudes

It is admittedly difficult through mere presentation of facts to change attitudes that are firmly established both on a cognitive and on an emotional basis. However, this goal can still be accomplished if it is attempted systematically and if the implications of the facts for the attitudes in question are drawn *explicitly*. Bond (1940) demonstrated this to be the case in modifying racially prejudiced ideas through a special instructional unit on genetics.

Greater lasting change in attitudes can be effected if a two-sided presentation of the issues is made (Lumsdaine & Janis, 1953). This approach not only discounts the counterarguments in advance but also is less likely to give the impression of constituting biased propaganda. The evidence is equivocal whether discussion leads to more lasting change of attitude than does mere presentation of a controversial position in lecture form. But it does appear that a greater change in opinion occurs if an individual plays the role of a sincere advocate of a given point of view (Janis & King, 1954).

Teachers, of course, are particularly concerned with pupils' attitudes toward school. As pointed out previously, there is, unfortunately, progressive disenchantment with school as children climb the educational ladder. Although part of this trend can undoubtedly be attributed to the progressive alienation of children from the adult world, much of it also reflects the school's failure to stimulate and satisfy the child's interest in knowledge as an end in itself. It is noteworthy in this connection that high-school students who are satisfied with school generally outperform on achievement tests those who are dissatisfied with school[21] (Brodie, 1964). This relationship between favorable attitude and achievement also holds true in such individual subject-matter fields as biology (Garverick, 1964). In this same connection it may be noted that interests are better predictors of the completion of a given college curriculum than is ability (J. W. French, 1961). Surprisingly, need for academic achievement is distinct from vocational achievement values (Scanzoni, 1967).

## The Effects of Attitudes on Meaningful Learning and Retention

Only relatively recently has it been recognized that cognitive, as well as affective, factors account for the differential effects of positive and negative attitudinal bias on the learning of controversial material. This recognition was largely an outgrowth of Peak's (1955) theoretical formulation of attitude structure as consisting of an interrelated group of ideas organized around a conceptual nucleus and manifesting affective properties.

Little doubt exists that the learner's prevailing attitude structure differentially enhances or inhibits the *learning* of controversial materials that are congruous and incongruous, respectively, with it. Both motivational

---

[21] This effect is not mediated by greater attentiveness in class although attention does increase achievement and IQ scores (Gilmore, 1968).

and cognitive variables are probably involved in such differential learning outcomes. When their attitudes toward the controversial material are favorable, subjects are highly motivated to learn. They put forth more intense and concentrated effort, and relevant general perceptual and cognitive thresholds are generally lowered. Furthermore, since the cognitive component of the attitudes in question is well established, the subjects possess clear, stable, and relevant anchoring ideas for incorporating the new material. When, however, their attitudes toward the controversial material are unfavorable, all of these factors operate in precisely the opposite direction.

However, a strong need to reduce cognitive dissonance or incongruity— operating either as a generalized trait or aspect of cognitive style, or more specifically in relation to a particular set of strongly held beliefs—may lead to a closed-minded attitude that obviously impairs ability to learn new ideas contrary to existing beliefs. People who summarily dismiss such new ideas on this basis fail to learn them adequately because they may not even be willing to read or listen to them, because they make little or no effort to understand or reconcile these ideas with existiing beliefs, or because they selectively misunderstand, distort, discount, or reverse the implications of such ideas in accordance with their biases. But although these motivational, quasi-motivational, and affective components of negative attitudinal bias selectively inhibit, both specifically and nonspecifically, the learning of controversial ideas contrary to belief (account for the low dissociability strength of these ideas), they probably affect retention only insofar as they adversely affect learning itself. No channel exists for the purely affective-motivational components of such bias to exert a direct influence on retention unless it arouses sufficient anxiety to elevate thresholds of availability.

Several studies (Edwards, 1941; Levine & Murphy, 1943; Zillig, 1928) have demonstrated that controversial materials are learned most readily when they are consistent rather than inconsistent with the subject's evaluative framework. But in none of the aforementioned studies, despite the fact that selective learning was attributed solely to affective mechanisms, was any attempt made to differentiate between the respective effects on learning of the cognitive and affective components of attitude structure.

Fitzgerald and Ausubel (1963), however, conducted a classroom experiment, involving the ability of central Illinois high-school students to learn the Southern point of view about the Civil War, in which the effect of the cognitive factor (knowledge about the Civil War period) was statistically controlled. The learning difference attributable to *affective* factors, or to attitudinal bias under these conditions, was in the predicted direction (in favor of the relatively pro-Southern or positively biased group), but it was not statistically significant. In this same study, two additional findings pointed to the influence of cognitive variables on learning outcomes. Not only did advance organizers facilitate the learning of the controversial material, but the more knowledgeable subjects, irrespective of attitudinal bias, were also better able to learn the material, presumably because they found it more discriminable from previously learned related ideas than did the less knowledgeable subjects.

Further evidence concerning the role of cognitive factors in the effects of attitude structure on learning, comes from E. E. Jones and Kohler's (1958) study of the interaction between attitudinal bias and plausibility in their effects on learning. These investigators found that prosegregation subjects learned plausible prosegregation and implausible antisegregation statements better than they learned implausible prosegregation and plausible anti-segregation statements. The reverse was true of the antisegregation subjects. Evidently, plausibility enhanced the learning of the position favored by a particular subject and inhibited the learning of the position he opposed. This suggests that controversial material is learned least well when it is least relatable to the prevailing ideational component of attitude structure—when favorable material is implausible and unfavorable material is plausible.

Gustafson (1957) found that members of three different American ethnic groups selectively learned best those facts about American history and culture that pertained to their own ethnic group. This finding held up even when general knowledge of American history and culture was held constant. But since the effects of *specific* knowledge of *own*-group culture (in relation to which the differential learning was manifested) were not controlled, the influence of ideational factors on learning outcomes was not eliminated. The results of this study are, therefore, consistent with the hypothesis that both cognitive and motivational mechanisms account for the effects of positive ego involvement in learning.

### Retention

In many studies (Alper & Korchin, 1952; Clark, 1940; Watson & Hartmann, 1939) of the effects of attitude structure on retention, no measure of initial learning was obtained. Hence there was no certain way of ruling out the possibility that selective differences in retention (in favor of the group positively biased toward the material) were wholly attributable to attitudinal effects on learning. In some studies (Edwards, 1941; Levine & Murphy, 1943; Taft, 1954), however, retention was measured both immediately after learning and at subsequent intervals thereafter. Original differences in learning between positively and negatively biased groups were found to widen progressively during the course of the retention interval. These latter findings suggest that attitude structure exerts an additional facilitating influence on retention that is independent of its cognitive and motivational effect on learning.

But although attitudinal variables undoubtedly facilitate the learning of controversial material through both cognitive and motivational mechanisms, it is likely that cognitive factors alone mediate most of the effects of attitude structure on *retention*. In the first place, as pointed out earlier, motivational variables cannot independently affect the cognitive interactional process or dissociability strength during the retention period (once the learning phase of the process is completed). Second, even though it is theoretically possible for negative attitudinal bias directly to raise (but not to lower) thresholds of availability for controversial material, this mechanism applies only in those relatively rare instances where anxiety-producing material is repressed. Yet, despite the fact that the "repression" explanation is almost universally invoked to explain selective forgetting of controversial materials, it hardly seems likely that such materials are capable of instigating significant amounts of anxiety. In none of these studies, furthermore, was the influence of cognitive factors controlled.

The cognitive mechanism that purportedly mediates the effects of attitude on retention is the complex of ideas that, together with various affective components (attitudinal bias), characterizes the structure of all attitudes. Controversial materials that instigate positive affect or attitudinal bias are relatable to a set of subsuming ideas that are clearer, more stable, more relevant, and more discriminable from the learning task than are the general run of subsumers in the learner's cognitive structure. The reverse holds true for controversial materials instigating negative affect or attitudinal bias. Although these ideational factors are part of attitude structure, they influence retention in the same manner as cognitive variables generally, resulting in the progressive divergence of retention scores for subjects whose attitudinal bias toward the controversial material is positive and negative, respectively.

Fitzgerald's and Ausubel's (1963) previously described experiment was primarily designed to test this latter hypothesis by measuring and controlling the effects of cognitive factors (knowledge of the Civil War period) on retention. As in the Edwards (1941), Taft (1954), and Levine and Murphy (1943) studies, they also found a suggestive tendency toward differential forgetting on the basis of the degree of congruence of the Civil War passage with the subject's attitudinal framework. However, when the influence of the cognitive dimension of attitude structure was statistically controlled, the residual affective dimension of attitude structure (attitudinal bias) had no differential effect on retention.[22] Thus it appears that in nonanxiety-producing situations, selective retention can be more parsimoniously attributed to the cognitive rather than to the affective dimension of attitudes.

---

[22] In Gustafson's (1957) experiment selective retention of own-ethnic-group material occurred even after general knowledge of American culture was held constant. But, as already explained, since the effects of *specific* knowledgeability were not eliminated, the influence of cognitive factors was not completely controlled. The "repression" hypothesis is also particularly inapplicable here, inasmuch as all of the material was favorable to the ethnic group under discussion.

In learning "other-side" arguments, the conceptual schemata constituting the cognitive dimension of attitudes is usually devoid of relevant anchoring ideas to which the new material can be functionally related. The material, therefore, cannot be readily anchored to cognitive structure, competes with existing meanings, and is consequently ambiguous and subject to rapid forgetting. In the case of positive attitudinal bias, on the other hand, it seems reasonable to suppose that the cognitive dimension of attitude structure contains more relevant and appropriate subsuming concepts than in the case of negative bias. Hence, the material can be readily anchored to cognitive structure, need not compete with existing meanings, and is therefore less ambiguous and less subject to forgetting (Fitzgerald & Ausubel, 1963, pp. 73, 74).

Further substantiating the cognitive interpretation of the findings in the latter experiment is the fact that organizers facilitated the retention of the controversial material.

In support of the above findings, Garverick (1964) also found that the facilitating effect of positive attitude toward biology on a *delayed* test of retention was no longer present when end-of-course achievement in biology was held constant.[23]

## Increasing Classroom Motivation

The following practical implications for increasing classroom motivation may be drawn from the foregoing discussion.

1. Motivation is as much an *effect* as a cause of learning. Thus, it is not necessary to wait for motivation to develop before engaging a student in learning activities.

2. The objective in a given learning task should always be made as explicit and specific as possible. In the case of nonpractical and remote objectives, the relationship of learning tasks to other kinds of knowledge and intellectual capabilities should be pointed out.

3. Make full use of, but do not be limited by, existing interests and motivations.

4. Maximize cognitive drive by arousing intellectual curiosity, by using attention-attracting materials, and by arranging lessons so as to ensure ultimate success in learning.

5. Set tasks that are appropriate to each learner's ability level. Nothing

---

[23] In Hagen's (1967) experiment, distraction had a very significant effect on retention of task-relevant material without affecting recall of task-irrelevant (incidental) retention. The investigator attributed this difference to "selective attention." It is obvious from the evidence considered above, however, that this factor influenced retention only *indirectly* by enhancing original learning.

dampens motivation as much as an unrelieved diet of failure and frustration.

6. Help pupils to set realistic goals[24] and to evaluate their progress toward these goals by providing tasks that test the limits of their ability and by providing generously informative feedback about the degree of goal attainment.

7. Take account of developmental changes and individual differences in motivational patterns.

8. Make judicious use of extrinsic and aversive motivation, avoiding excessively high levels of each.

---

[24] Often merely providing highly specific attainable goals enables a low-motivation group to equal a high-motivation group in performance (Bryan & Locke, 1967).

# 12

# PERSONALITY FACTORS IN LEARNING

Like motivation, personality factors influence meaningful learning largely through the same type of mechanisms specified in the preceding chapter. In fact, motivational orientation to learning is itself the principal mediating variable through which many personality variables affect learning. Unlike motivation, however, personality variables help account more for individual differences in learning outcomes.

In the preceding chapter we described three differential motivational orientations to learning—cognitive drive, affiliative drive, and ego-enhancement motivation. What are the personality antecedents of the latter two orientations? If parents intrinsically accept and value a child (love him for himself), he tends to satellize in relation to them, that is, he acquires a derived or vicarious status that reflects such intrinsic acceptance. He is not dependent on his relative competence or performance ability for his feelings of self-esteem; and he desires to do well in school largely because he accepts his parents' values uncritically (out of personal loyalty to them), including their value that he achieve satisfactorily in school. Thus he is motivated scholastically in order to retain the approval that signifies parental acceptance and guarantees his derived status; and he feels guilty and disloyal if he accepts values contrary to those persons in relation to whom he satellizes.

The nonsatellizing child, on the other hand, is typically either rejected or extrinsically valued (valued not for himself but for the vicarious ego-enhancement his parents can obtain from his achievements). Since he enjoys no derived status, he must strive compensatorily, and often unrealistically, for a higher degree of earned status. Hence, his motivation for school achievement is ego-enhancement (through superior standing in his class). Ego-enhancement motivation is typically stronger than the affiliative drive of the satellizer. The nonsatellizer is also predisposed to accept values on the basis of their relevance for ego-enhancement rather than on the basis of personal loyalty to parents or teachers. However, his higher level of scholastic aspiration does not always lead to superior achievement: (1) because he may fear failure more than he desires success; (2) because he lacks the personality traits or intellectual ability to implement his aspirations; or (3) because he is predisposed to a disabling level of anxiety that impairs learning more than increased (anxiety—reductive) motivation enhances it.

Nonsatellizers are more predisposed to neurotic anxiety than satellizers because they have no intrinsic feelings of self-esteem, and because their compensatorily, and often unrealistically, high needs for earned status are frequently frustrated. This situation leads to catastrophic impairment of self-esteem. The impairment of self-esteem, in turn, causes them to overreact with anxiety to any learning situation that threatens to impair self-esteem further, especially a novel one for which they have no ready-made solution in cognitive structure. Because they lack the self-confidence necessary for improvising in novel learning situations, their performance is impaired initially. Once the task becomes more familiar, however, neurotic anxiety no longer inhibits learning. For the latter reason (as school learning situations become more familiar), and because anxiety also increases motivation to learn, anxiety has little or no negative effect on later school achievement, particularly in secondary school and beyond.

Dogmatism impairs the learning of controversial material that is contrary to the learner's belief or value systems. Three factors must be considered here: (1) dogmatism as a general personality trait that leads to closed-mindedness; (2) negative attitudinal bias; and (3) negative informational bias. The influence of the latter two factors is issue-specific, and explains why a generally dogmatic individual may be surprisingly open-minded in learning particular controversial materials contrary to his or her beliefs, and vice versa.

Generally, poor personality adjustment tends to be associated with inferior school achievement. This is so because most serious personality problems tend to interfere with school learning. Much of this relationship, however, is probably spurious, (1) because low *school achievement is a cause as well as an effect of poor personality adjustment, and (2) because of the "halo effect" of each variable on the others in teachers' ratings.*

*Although the school obviously bears some responsibility for the personality development of pupils (because it provides so important an opportunity for pupils to interact with each other and with adult authority figures), it shares this responsibility with many other agencies (home, peer group, church, youth organizations, and so forth). However, since it is the only organized social institution responsible for guiding the child's intellectual development, we cannot endorse the frequently stated proposition that the primary responsibility of the school lies in the area of furthering the personality development of pupils.*

How do personality factors enter into the learning process, and how are their effects similar to and different from motivational and cognitive factors? In the first place, like motivational variables, personality factors deal with subjective and affective-social rather than with objective and intellectual aspects of learning. This means that they typically affect meaningful learning *nonspecifically* and *catalytically* rather than being directly and specifically involved (like readiness, cognitive structure variables, intellectual ability, and cognitive style) in the parameters of the cognitive interactional process. Second, like measures of intellectual ability and cognitive style (and unlike motivational variables), personality factors deal with stable and self-consistent *individual differences* in learners, but in the affective-social rather than in the cognitive domain.

In other words, it is not sufficient for the educational psychologist to be able to make generalizations and *actuarial* predictions about the *average* effects on classroom learning of either cognitive or motivational variables in a *group* of individuals. In addition that he or she must endeavor to determine the impact on learning of stable individual differences, both cognitive and affective-social. It is also important for the educational psychologist to try to ascertain whether general cognitive and affective-social variables affect learning processes and outcomes differently for individuals who are bright rather than dull, who tend to be particularizers rather than generalizers, who are primarily motivated by ego-enhancing rather than by cognitive and affiliative drives, who manifest a high rather than a low level of anxiety, or who tend to be open rather than closed to new ideas.

In this chapter we cannot consider all kinds of personality traits (generalized, stable, and self-consistent behavioral tendencies in the affective-social domain). Rather, we will concentrate on those selected personality variables that have been shown significantly to influence learning effort, value assimilation, and problem-solving style. The most important of these variables are motivational orientation to learning, anxiety level, dogmatism, authoritarianism, tendency to conform, and personality adjustment.

## Motivational Orientation to Learning

In the preceding chapter we distinguished between two essentially different extrinsic components of achievement motivation. One component, termed *affiliative drive*, is oriented toward vicarious or derived status. It is concerned with achievement as a source of earned status only insofar as it secures the approval of, and hence signifies continued intrinsic acceptance by, superordinate persons (parents, teachers) or groups with whom the learner identifies. The other component, termed *ego-enhancement drive*, is concerned with achievement as a source of earned status.

It was pointed out that affiliative drive is typically predominant during the preschool and elementary-school periods and is then gradually superseded by ego-enhancing drive, particularly during adolescence. Although this is the typical developmental state of affairs and cognitive, affiliative, and ego-enhancing components are invariably present in the achievement motivation of all learners, their relative proportions tend to vary depending on both individual interpersonal experience with parents and cultural and social-class factors.[1] In this section we shall examine the developmental basis for individual differences in the relative strength of affiliative and ego-enhancement drives and the consequences of these differences for degree of achievement motivation, for mode of assimilating values, and for academic achievement.

### Satellization versus Nonsatellization

Interpersonal and group life is typically characterized by differences in roles and status and by dependence of one person on another or on the group as a whole. One of the more basic kinds of human interaction that arises under such conditions is identification of the dependent party with the superordinate party. This type of relationship includes, in varying proportions, the elements of "dominance–subordination," "leadership–followership," and "care–dependency" described by Scott (1953) for different infrahuman vertebrates. Much confusion, however, results from the failure

---

[1] Not infrequently, also as a result of continued successful experience, motivations that are originally absent in a given learning activity are developed afterwards during the course of that activity. A rejected child, for example, may seek originally to achieve competence in some academic field solely for compensatory ego enhancement. Eventually, however, he or she may develop genuine task-oriented interests that are functionally autonomous of the original motivation.

to distinguish between two essentially *different* kinds of identification, each of which involves a reciprocal relationship between a relatively dependent and subordinate individual, on the one hand, and a relatively independent or dominant individual (or group), on the other (Ausubel, 1949, 1952).

One type of identification, which is characteristic of the early parent-child relationship in humans, may be called *satellization* (Ausubel, 1952). In a satellizing relationship the subordinate party (child) renounces his or her independent, earned status and primarily accepts a status dependent on that of the superordinate party (parent). The child identifies in a dependent sense with the parent's status; and the superordinate party, in turn, accepts the child as an intrinsically valuable entity in the parent's personal orbit. The satellizer thereby acquires a vicarious or derived biosocial status. This is wholly a function of the dependent relationship and independent of his or her own competence or performance ability. This status is bestowed upon the child by the fiat of simple unqualified acceptance by a superordinate individual or group whose authority and power to do so are regarded as unchallengeable.

On the other hand, the two parties to the same "transaction" could relate to each other in quite a different way. The subordinate party—in this case a *nonsatellizer*—could acknowledge his or her dependency simply as a temporary, regrettable, and much-to-be-remedied fact of life requiring, as a matter of expediency, various acts of conformity and deference, but without really accepting a dependent and subordinate status as a person (Ausubel, 1952). In turn, the child either could be rejected outright or could be accorded acceptance—not unqualifiedly as an individual—but in terms of his or her current or potential competence and usefulness to the superordinate party. The act of identification, if it occurs at all, consists solely in the child using the parent as an emulatory model so that he or she can learn the latter's skills and methods of operation and thus eventually succeed to the parent's enviable status. And, accordingly, the only type of biosocial status the child can hope to enjoy in this type of relationship is an earned status that reflects his or her own degree of functional competence or performance ability.

The nonsatellizing type of identification occurs primarily for one or both of two reasons. Either the superordinate party does not extend unqualified intrinsic acceptance (the parent who either rejects the child or values the child basically for extrinsic, ulterior self-enhancing purposes) or the subordinate party is reluctant to, or incapable of, accepting a dependent role.

Illustrating the latter possibility is the typical cat, who condescendingly does the "master" a favor by drinking the "master's" saucer of milk, in contrast to the typical dog, who simply oozes devotion, slavishness, and self-effacement. It would also be reasonable to expect that children who are temperamentally more assertive, self-sufficient, independent, and "thick-skinned" would be less disposed to satellize than children with the opposite set of characteristics.

Differences related to culturally determined social sex role might also be anticipated. For example, an experimental population of 10-year-olds in Champaign, Illinois (Ausubel et al., 1954), rated 36 items of parent attitude and behavior reflective of acceptance-rejection and intrinsic-extrinsic valuation. Analysis of the ratings confirmed the hypothesis that girls are (or perceive themselves to be) more highly accepted and intrinsically valued than are boys. Due to the more militant stance of the feminist movement since 1954, this sex difference is probably less than it was then.

### Effects on Achievement Motivation

From the standpoint of school learning, the wider significance of satellization versus nonsatellization in early personality development is that each of these outcomes is associated both with a distinctive pattern of achievement motivation and with a distinctive mode of assimilating norms and values (Ausubel, 1952, 1954; Ausubel & Kirk, 1977). Generally speaking, the nonsatellizer, especially during childhood, exhibits a much higher level of achievement motivation in which the ego-enhancement component is predominant. The satellizer, on the other hand, exhibits both a lower level of achievement motivation and one in which the affiliative component tends to predominate prior to adolescence. Level of ego aspiration (according to McCleland et al., 1953, and Atkinson and Feather, 1966)[2] is a multi-

---

[2] Thus these latter authors predict that the tendency to strive for success (rather than avoid failure) is strongest when the difficulty of the task is intermediate in degree, and the research findings today confirm this prediction. They do not regard the related incentive values of success and avoidance of failure as independent of subjectively estimated probabilities of success and failure. However, they concede that this issue of independence is at least in part dependent upon situational factors and idiosyncratic life experience. In addition, although their structured thematic (projective) measure of achievement motivation possesses much interrater reliability, its concurrent and construct validity is highly questionable.

Atkinson and Feather also focus almost exclusively on the ego-enhancement component of achievement motivation. They seem to ignore entirely the well-established clinical and experimental finding that the cognitive-drive and affiliative components are concomitantly operative with the ego-enhancement component in most persons and are also inversely related in strength to the latter component rather than orthogonally or nonselectively related to it (Ausubel, Schiff, & Zeleny, 1953; Hartogs, 1950). Thus, individual differences in strength of achievement motivation tend to be obfuscated in terms of pathogenesis rather than clarified because of their persistent blind-spot that predisposes them to regard achievement motivation as a unitary trait.

Cross-cultural evidence (for example, Ausubel, 1965d) generally disputes the validity of their formulation of the unidimensional nature of the need to achieve. In most Western, as well as primitive cultures, achievement motivation not only manifests the three components we specify above but the ego-enhancement component also has either a predominantly ego-aggrandizing or group orientation (Ausubel, 1965d; Benedict, 1938; Leighton & Kluckhorn, 1947; Mead, 1939). Other important distinctions they

factorial resultant of the strength of the motive involved, the subjective probability of success, and the relative values of anticipated success and fear of failure.

Satellizers identify with their parents in an emotionally dependent sense and are accepted by their parents for themselves. They enjoy, by the fiat of this acceptance, both an assured derived status and the accompanying feelings of intrinsic adequacy or self-esteem that are relatively immune to the vicissitudes of achievement and competitive position (Ausubel, 1952; Ausubel & Kirk, 1977). Thus they have relatively little need to seek the kind of status that they would have to earn through their own competence —the kind of status that would generate feelings of extrinsic adequacy commensurate with their degree of achievement. They do not, in other words, view academic achievement as the basis of their status or as the measure of their worth as people. It is merely a means of meeting the expectations of their parents and of retaining thereby the approval that confirms their "good standing" and thus their derived status (Ausubel, 1949, 1952; Ausubel & Kirk, 1977) in their parents' eyes.

Nonsatellizers, on the other hand, are either rejected or are accepted on an extrinsic basis by their parents (Ausubel, 1949, 1952, 1954, 1958; Ausubel & Kirk, 1977). Enjoying no derived status or intrinsic self-esteem, nonsatellizers have no choice but to aspire to a status that they earn through their own accomplishments. Since any feelings of adequacy are almost entirely a reflection of the degree of achievement they can attain, they necessarily exhibit a high level of aspiration for academic achievement and prestige—a level that is much higher, and more tenacious in the face of failure experience, than that of satellizers. This is obviously a compensatory reaction that reflects these children's lack of derived status and intrinsic self-esteem.

Consistent with their higher aspirations for achievement, they manifest more volitional and executive independence than do satellizers. Nonsatellizers are better able to defer the immediate gratification of hedonistic

---

apparently ignore are those between positive (motivational) and disruptive ("behavioral disorganization") effects of anxiety (Alpert & Haber, 1960) and between the different kinds of motivational and behavioral effects attributable to the test (situational) and neurotic (general chronic personality trait) anxiety, respectively (Ausubel, Schiff, & Goldman, 1953).

Tobias and Abramson (1970), for example, have shown that there are interactional effects between facilitating or debilitating anxiety, induced stress, and level of difficulty or familiarity of the learning material. Facilitating anxiety only interacts with the stress and response mode for difficult technical material. Debilitating anxiety, on the other hand, interacts with stress and response mode for easier, more familiar learning material. (By "response mode" these investigators mean relative tendency to use overt rather than covert responses.) O'Neill, Spielberger, and Hansen (1969) found that anxiety inhibited learning more in the case of *difficult* than of easy learning tasks.

needs in order to strive for more long-term goals (Ausubel et al., 1954). Similar personality differences between individuals manifesting ego-enhancement and affiliative drive orientations to learning, respectively, were reported by Atkinson and Litwin (1960) and by McClelland et al. (1953). As will be pointed out shortly, however, higher achievement motivation does not necessarily lead to higher academic achievement. In any case, this relationship is complicated by age and sex factors.

Other aspects of the parent-child relationship are also implicated in the development of achievement motivation. Achievement motivation tends to be higher in those children whose parents have high intellectual achievement aspirations both for themselves (Katkovsky, Preston, & Crandall, 1964a, 1964b) and for their offspring (Rosen & D'Andrade, 1959); whose parents stress independence training and high standards of excellence (McClelland et al., 1953; Winterbottom, 1958); and whose parents, when present in problem-solving situations with their offspring, exhibit greater participation, instigation, encouragement, and disapproval (Katkovsky et al., 1964b; Rosen & D'Andrade, 1959). It is also apparently stronger in instances where an achievement-oriented mother is dominant in the home; a dominant, demanding, and successful father, on the other hand, is perceived by his sons as providing a competitive standard that is too overwhelmingly superlative to be challenged successfully (Strodtbeck, 1958).

Significant normative fluctuations (as well as individual differences) in the balance between earned and derived status occur throughout the course of ego development. But, as already indicated, initial ways of relating to others tend to persist, especially if they occur at critical periods of ego development and socialization (Ausubel, 1952, 1954; Ausubel & Kirk, 1977). It is true that as satellizing children grow older, they increasingly strive for *earned* status. However, even as adults, they continue to enjoy the *residual* sense of intrinsic worth that their parents conferred on them earlier. Moreover, they will continue to satellize in some aspects of their current interpersonal relationships (in relation to spouse, supervisor, and so on).

### Effects On Value Assimilation

In addition to their effects on achievement motivation, the satellizing and nonsatellizing modes of identification have important implications for the mechanisms by which norms and values are assimilated from elders and from membership and reference groups (Ausubel, 1949, 1952, 1954; Sherif & Sherif, 1964). The essential motivation directing satellizers' organization of their value systems is the need to retain the acceptance and approval of the persons or group that provide their derived status. Hence they develop a generalized set to perceive the world in the light of the values and expectations they attribute to the latter individuals. Value assimilation is thus an act of personal loyalty in which the actual content of what is internalized is largely irrelevant (that is, from a motivational standpoint).

Nonsatellizers, on the other hand, are primarily motivated in their orientation to values by considerations of expediency and attainment of earned status. Hence their motivational set is *not* to accept values blindly and uncritically from considerations of personal loyalty but in accordance with these general aims. The prestige suggestion of authority figures, in this instance, is not derived from the learners' need to agree with them, but from their acknowledgement of the authority figures' suitability as emulatory models and stepping stones to power and prestige (Ausubel, 1949, 1952, 1954; Ausubel & Kirk, 1977). Nonsatellizing elementary-school children are more disposed than satellizing children to disagree with the perceived opinions of their parents (Ausubel et al., 1954).

When ideas are accepted on a satellizing basis, resistance to new learning stems largely from conflicting ideological trends in the new set of values, which can be accepted only at the cost of repudiating prior loyalties and assuming the associated burden of guilt (Ausubel, 1949, 1952). Nevertheless, this must take place before new values can be assimilated. Satellizers feel secure in their derived status only as long as approval is forthcoming. They find disapproval threatening and (when incurred through disloyalty) productive of guilt feelings (Ausubel, 1949, 1952).

In the case of nonsatellizers, on the other hand, new ideas are resisted because they constitute a potential threat to self-esteem by challenging (1) the existing system of values organized on an ego-prestige basis, and (2) various presumptions of independence, originality, infallibility, and omniscience (Ausubel, 1949, 1952; Ausubel & Kirk, 1977).

Because they lack intrinsic feelings of worth and are therefore more vulnerable to the ego-deflating implications of failure, they are more reluctant than satellizers to venture into new areas of learning where their capabilities still remain to be demonstrated (Ausubel, 1949, 1952, 1954; Ausubel & Kirk, 1977). Such learning activities, in any case, are highly threatening until success is assured. Resistence to new learnings, as well as to new values, is usually overcome when the nonsatellizer can perceive their usefulness for future ego enhancement.

The different motivational orientations toward learning characterizing satellizers and nonsatellizers, respectively, suggest differential interpersonal handling on the part of teachers (Ausubel, 1949). On theoretical grounds, satellizers should learn best in a warm and supportive interpersonal environment in which they can relate to teachers as parent surrogates. It has been shown, for example, that they achieve best when teaching methods are "indirect" rather than direct (Amidon & Flanders, 1961). Teachers, however, must always guard against the tendency of satellizers to overconform to their directions and expectations (Kagan & Mussen, 1956; Livson &

Mussen, 1957). Both their resistance to and acceptance of new values stem largely from considerations of personal identification and loyalty that are reinforced by approval.

Nonsatellizers, on the other hand, require teacher approval as objective evidence of achievement rather than as confirmation of personal acceptance. They resist accepting new values not because of loyalty to parents or teachers but because they tend to feel threatened by unfamiliar ideas. By the same token, novel learning tasks and methods of instruction should be presented to them gradually, with as much prefamiliarization as possible (Ausubel, Schiff, & Goldman, 1953). Overcritical, deprecatory, demanding, and authoritarian teacher behavior appears to raise the anxiety level of anxious nonsatellizers, precipitating hostility, aggressiveness, and withdrawal. Accepting and supporting treatment, on the other hand, lowers their anxiety level and promotes more task-oriented and integrative behavior (Flanders, 1951).

### Effect on School Achievement

It is self-evident that an excess of the ego-enhancement component of achievement motivation can have long-term effects on school achievement only if it is a highly stable and somewhat generalized personality trait. Research data clearly indicate that both of these conditions actually prevail. The impressive evidence of stability characterizing achievement motivation from age 6 to adult life (Moss & Kagan, 1961) undoubtedly reflects, in large measure, the strongly enduring properties of ego-enhancement or affiliative drive derived from the nonsatellizing type of parent–child relationship. It is also a reasonably generalized trait, as can be inferred from the moderately high intercorrelations both between (1) level of aspiration and goal-tenacity scores over a wide variety of laboratory tasks and "real-life" achievement situations and (2) goal-tenacity scores over a broad range of hypothetical vocational situations (Ausubel & Schiff, 1955; Ausubel, Schiff, & Zeleny, 1953).

Furthermore, adolescent boys who have strong needs for vocational prestige tend to make high vocational-tenacity scores and to be unrealistic, from the standpoint of their basic interest patterns, in their choice of vocations (Ausubel, Schiff, & Zeleny, 1953). Interestingly enough, these findings do not hold true for adolescent girls, at least in the early 1950s. Evidently girls in this age group who by interest or ability are attracted to high-prestige occupations are not similarly driven by the culture to actualize their ambitions.[3] Hence they need not be so unrealistic and tenacious in their vocational behavior. Finally, high levels of aspiration in both academic and laboratory situations tend to be associated with a high level of anxiety and

---

[3]Because of the influence of the current, more militant stance of the feminist movement these sex differences would probably be less pronounced today.

with poor personality adjustment (Ausubel, Schiff, & Goldman, 1953; Ausubel, Schiff, & Zeleny, 1953; Eysenck, 1947; Hartogs, 1950).

The actual effect of motivational orientation to learning on school achievement depends on many factors, including age, sex, anxiety level, and other personality traits. It is empirically demonstrable that high ego-enhancing drive (reflective of parental rejection or extrinsic acceptance) *generally* leads to higher levels of aspiration (Ausubel, Schiff, & Goldman, 1953). However, the school performance of these individuals is not necessarily superior to that of intrinsically accepted pupils of comparable academic ability. In some individuals the corollary need for avoiding failure is so much stronger than the need for success that the level of striving is grossly lowered to prevent even the remotest possibility of failure experience (Atkinson & Feather, 1966; P. S. Sears, 1940).

Other individuals with high achievement motivation lack the personality traits (persistence, self-denial, high frustration tolerance, ability to defer hedonistic gratification) necessary for implementing high aspirations (Ausubel, 1952, 1954; Ausubel & Kirk, 1977). Merely aspiring high, without ever intending to implement the aspirations in question, yields a certain compensatory measure of ego enhancement.

Another factor interfering with the facilitating effect of high ego-enhancement drive on academic achievement is a disablingly high level of anxiety, particularly the kind that leads to withdrawal from competitive situations or to paralysis of adaptive behavior (Alpert & Haber, 1960). In addition, cultural influences mediated through age and sex role expectations are important determining factors. Thus low-nurturant and unaffectionate mothers tend to have daughters (but not sons) with superior school achievement in elementary school (Crandall et al., 1964). This is a culturally sanctioned form of compensatory ego enhancement for girls at the elementary-school level. At the late adolescent and young adult level, on the other hand, the much greater cultural stress on male vocational achievement is apparently responsible for the association of parental rejection with high anxiety and academic achievement in male but not in female prospective teachers (Gnagey, 1966).

### Anxiety and School Learning

Anxiety must be differentiated from other kinds of fearlike states. Generically, it refers to an actual fearlike response or to a tendency to respond with fear to any current or anticipated situation that is perceived as a potential threat to self-esteem. It differs from ordinary fear in that the threat is directed against self-esteem rather than against physical well-being, and may be anticipated or current in nature (Ausubel, 1952, 1958). One is fearful when a mad dog lunges for one's throat; one is anxious when experiencing or contemplating the loss in self-esteem that results from academic or vocational failure.

Anxiety differs, likewise, from feelings of insecurity, which are similar to fear but arise only in response to *anticipated* threat, in the fact that the threat eliciting anxiety is specifically directed against one's self-esteem and not against one's physical safety or well-being (Ausubel, 1952, 1958; Ausubel, Sullivan, & Ives, in press). In many situations, however, insecurity and anxiety are aroused concomitantly. The threat of possible vocational failure, for example, is not only damaging to one's self-regard but also generates genuine apprehension regarding one's chances for a reasonably adequate standard of living.

### Normal versus Neurotic Anxiety

Within the generic meaning of the term, as defined here, one can conceive of several qualitatively different varieties of anxiety arising under basically different conditions of instigation. Situationally, for example, anxiety is generated in medical students when they are confronted with important examinations that threaten the achievement of a life goal closely identified with their sense of adequacy. One can induce a similar type of situational anxiety experimentally by giving subjects bogus examination reports that reflect adversely on their competence or personality integration.

Anxiety is aroused during transitional periods of personality development, such as adolescence, when individuals have to achieve a new biosocial status and are kept in a prolonged state of uncertainty regarding the outcome. Feelings of hostility can generate anxiety by threatening an individual with loss of status, as a result of antagonizing persons on whom he or she is dependent (Horney, 1937, 1939). Similarly, feelings of guilt can generate anxiety by exposing individuals to sullied, reprehensible portraits of themselves, at odds with the moral values they have internalized.

These different varieties of normal anxiety have one property in common that distinguishes them from neurotic anxiety: In each situation described, anxiety is instigated by an *objectively* adequate threat to self-esteem. In some instances this threat may be external in origin—as, for example, the crucial examination in the case of medical students or the need to acquire adult status under conditions of uncertainty in the case of adolescents. In other instances the source of the threat is within the person. It may come from aggressive impulses or from the individual's awareness that he or she has violated certain of his moral scruples.

The important differential factor in all of these cases—regardless of whether the source of the threat is internal or external—is that the threat is *objectively* capable of impairing self-esteem in normal persons. In all cases the threat comes from a source distinct from the entity that is being threatened; in no case does the threat to self-esteem arise from impaired self-esteem itself. In all cases the response to the threat is appropriate and proportionate to the objective degree of jeopardy confronting the individual's self-esteem.

In *neurotic* anxiety, on the other hand, the essential source of the threat to self-esteem does not lie outside self-esteem but is to be found in catastrophic impairment of self-esteem itself. Hence, a person suffering from neurotic anxiety apparently overreacts with fear to an anticipated further threat to his self-esteem. But this overreaction is an overreaction only when considered in relation to the ostensible source of the threat to self-esteem—the threat lying ·outside self-esteem that precipitates the anxiety. It is not an overreaction when it is considered subjectively in relation to the major source of threat to self-esteem that lies *within* impaired self-esteem itself. Highly anxious children tend to manifest more self-dissatisfaction and self-disparagement than less-anxious children (Lipsitt, 1958; Phillips, Hindsman, & Jennings, 1960).

The distinction between normal and neurotic anxiety can be clarified by an analogy from heart physiology. When a person has a normal, undamaged heart, how can he or she develop heart failure? It is not very easy. The person has to be subjected to tremendous exertion without rest, prolonged and severe exposure to heat, severe pulmonary disease, and so forth. The threat to cardiac adequacy when one has a normal heart, therefore, lies in an objectively punishing situation. Less rigorous threats to cardiac adequacy are easily compensated for because of the great reserve power of the heart. If the heart actually shows signs of beginning to fail when the external pressure increases, the outcome is hardly disproportionate to the degree of strain involved.

But a person with a damaged heart has already exhausted most of his or her power to compensate for increased external demands. If this person is required to run up a flight of stairs quickly, such symptoms of heart failure as labored breathing will likely occur. In his case, the source of the threat to cardiac adequacy lies in the damaged heart muscle, just as the source of the threat to self-esteem in a person with neurotic anxiety lies in his or her own damaged self-esteem. Certainly the heart patient is overreacting with signs of cardiac insufficiency to the mild degree of exertion posed by climbing a flight of stairs, just as the anxiety neurotic is overreacting to a novel adjustive situation with signs of fear and further impairment of self-esteem. But in neither case is the reaction disproportionate to the actual degree of jeopardy confronting the heart or self-esteem.

### The Origin of Neurotic Anxiety

How do anxiety neurotics develop catastrophic impairment of self-esteem so that they overreact with fear to anticipated threats to self-esteem? A definitive answer to this question cannot be given at this time because there is as yet no definitive evidence. But considerations of normal personality development, as well as clinical study, suggest that individuals can never develop neurotic anxiety as long as they enjoy intrinsic feelings of self-esteem. This means that they have a deep inner conviction that they are important and worthwhile for themselves—apart from what they can do or accomplish, and apart from the position they hold in life (Ausubel, 1952, 1956). As long as they possess this intrinsic self-esteem, failure in achieving superior competence or status is intense, deeply felt, discouraging—but always peripheral to the basic core of self-esteem, and hence never catastrophic.

However, if they must rely on success in school performance or vocation for whatever self-esteem they enjoy, catastrophic impairment following some very traumatic failure experience is much more probable. If such failure occurs, it is not peripheral but central—since there is now no basis whatsoever (intrinsic or extrinsic) for a feeling of worth as human beings. These individuals' sense of adequacy being purely a function of their competence or reputation, little self-regard can remain if these are seriously undermined.

Feelings of intrinsic self-esteem, as we have already seen, can develop only in one way—from a young child identifying in a dependent sense with his parents. He can do this if he perceives that he is accepted and valued for himself. His all-powerful, omniscient parents can endow all objects, including him, with intrinsic value if they so desire. If they respond to him as a person who is worthwhile and important in his own right—just because they accept him as such—he tends to react to himself in the same way, since he has no other standards of value but theirs. He thus acquires an intrinsic sense of adequacy, a vicarious status that is derived from his dependent relationship to his parents and is independent of his actual competencies. As he becomes older, he will increasingly strive for more earned status based upon his own accomplishments, and will develop feelings of self-esteem related to them. But there will always remain a residual sense of worth that his parents conferred on him by fiat—when as a child he perceived this to lie within their power.

As pointed out above, however, not all children are fortunate enough to be accepted and intrinsically valued by their parents. Some are rejected outright, and others are accepted but extrinsically valued, that is, accepted only in terms of their potential capacity for enhancing their parents' egos by becoming important and successful individuals. Such children do not undergo dependent identification with their parents, since they cannot acquire any vicarious status or intrinsic feelings of self-esteem from such a relationship. From the very beginning, their self-esteem becomes a function of what they are able to do and accomplish, and hence it becomes very vulnerable to catastrophic impairment.

Of course, vulnerability to catastrophic impairment of self-esteem does not, in itself, guarantee that such impairment must inevitably occur. However, this catastrophic impairment frequently occurs for another related reason. It has already been pointed out that when individuals lack intrinsic feelings of self-esteem, they are compensatorily motivated to aspire to higher goals and ambitions than the general run of mankind. This is hardly surprising when one considers that the less adequate an individual feels intrinsically, the more need there is to prove the individual's adequacy to himself or herself and others by superior accomplishments. In a learning experiment with anxious subjects, for example, it was found that their levels of aspiration, in relation to previous performance and to prior feelings of failure, were significantly higher and more tenacious than those of non-anxious subjects (Ausubel, Schiff, & Goldman, 1953). This means that their aspirations were more unrealistic. Their goals were not only too high but were also extremely resistive to lowering in the face of realistic indications for so doing. S. B. Sarason et al. (1958) also found that highly anxious children were less task-oriented and had higher achievement motivation than less-anxious children.

Thus, it seems reasonable to expect that rejected and extrinsically valued children, who have no intrinsic feelings of self-esteem, will tend to set their academic and vocational goals high—often unrealistically high. If they happen to be extremely able individuals, all may go well, and they may achieve in accordance with their aspirations. However, there is no reason to believe that such rejected and extrinsically valued individuals tend to be more than usually gifted; and there are limits to what motivation alone can accomplish. Hence the chances for large-scale collapse of their grandiose and unrealistic aspirations are rather high. And since they have no intrinsic self-esteem to fall back upon, a defeat is centrally traumatic to self-esteem and commonly precipitates acute anxiety. Recovery from this condition, furthermore, tends to leave a permanently damaged self-esteem or, in other words, a chronic anxiety neurosis, which may flare up at any time and become acute when the environment becomes too threatening.

### Effect of Anxiety on Learning

We have postulated that "personality" (neurotic) anxiety is the fear-like overreaction of an individual with impaired self-esteem to the threat antici-pated in adjusting to novel learning situations. The threatening implications of the latter are derived from their capacity to further impair self-esteem in the face of an inner feeling of inadequacy to cope with them. Normal anxiety, on the other hand, is the fear evoked by anticipation of objectively hazardous threats to self-esteem (Ausubel, 1956). Normal subjects do not display anxiety when confronted with ordinary adjustive situations because they do not lack confidence in their ultimate capacity to acquire the neces-sary adaptive responses.

The relationship between anxiety and learning is complicated by the fact that although high-anxiety individuals exhibit more than average *motivation* (that is, although they tend originally to manifest an excess of ego-enhancement drive (that tends to be facilitating) and are further driven to achieve (as the only practicable means of reducing anxiety), their high level of anxiety also tends to have a disruptive effect on *novel* problem solving. Thus it has been generally found that anxiety facilitates rote and less difficult kinds of meaningful reception and discovery learning. However, it has an inhibitory effect on more complex types of learning tasks that are either highly unfamiliar or are more dependent on improvising skill than on persistence (Ausubel, Schiff, & Goldman, 1953; Caron, 1963; Castenada, Palermo, & McCandless, 1956; Lantz, 1945; Marks & Vestre, 1961; McGuigan, Calvin, & Richardson, 1959; Palermo, Castenada, & McCandless, 1956; Pickrel, 1958; Russell & Sarason, 1965; Sarason et al., 1960; Stevenson & Odom, 1965; Tomkins, 1943; Zander, 1944).[4] The latter kinds of learning situations are obviously highly threatening to anxious individuals and tend to induce a disabling level of anxiety.

It does appear, however, that anxiety may *enhance* the learning of complex tasks when they do not seriously threaten self-esteem—when they are not inordinately novel or significant (Van Buskirk, 1961; Wittrock & Husek, 1962); when the anxiety is only moderate in degree; or when the learner possesses effective anxiety-coping mechanisms (Suinn, 1965). The learning of complex verbal materials in a typical school setting, for example, seems to be a relatively familiar and nonthreatening task as compared to novel problem-solving situations. Thus Degnan (1967) found that achievers in mathematics not only were more anxious than nonachievers but also had a more positive attitude toward the subject.

These findings make sense when one considers that it is precisely with respect to the need for improvising solutions to *novel* problems that individuals with neurotic (generalized personality) anxiety experience feelings of inadequacy. Such problems pose an exaggerated threat to their self-esteem (and sensitize them to overrespond with fear when obliged to cope with these problems). It follows that these individuals can mitigate their anxiety most easily by removing, as best as possible, the element of improvisation from the problem-solving process. The "response set" of neurotically anxious individuals, therefore, is to avoid putting their improvising ability to the test, and frantically to search their *available* problem-solving repertory for an appropriate solution that would not involve any reorganization of existing problem solutions in cognitive structure. However, if it so happens that the problem is one that requires improvisation for solution, this inflexible response set to avoid improvisation will

---

[4] One way in which anxiety inhibits problem solving is by disrupting short-term memory processes (Sieber, Kameya, & Paulson, 1970).

not only inhibit learning but will also render learning impossible until the set is eventually abandoned.

Thus, to the panic that results from anticipatory overreaction to any new situation is added the panic resulting from initial failure to make any progress toward problem solution. The cumulative impact of this disorganization may be disabling enough to induce blocking of response (Hartogs, 1950), which in turn may stimulate a "face-saving" attempt to produce *any* kind of response regardless of how inappropriate or unadaptive. Later, with increasing exposure to the problem—provided that the panic is not too disruptive—the individuals may become sufficiently desensitized to its unfamiliarity and fear-instigating properties to recover from their disorganization and adopt a more efficacious (improvising) response set.

In one experimental study of the effects of anxiety on learning (Ausubel, Schiff, & Goldman, 1953), university undergraduates who showed either low or high levels of neurotic anxiety were required to solve a stylus maze blindfolded. This situation constituted a mild form of threat to self-esteem. If the subject was not able to solve the problem, he demonstrated to the experimenter and to himself that he was not very good at a certain type of learning. (Even rats are reputed to learn to solve mazes.) For all of the subjects in this study, the maze represented a novel learning task for which past experience with vision was not only of no help but was actually a hindrance. Successful solution of the problem could not be accomplished without improvisation.

The low-anxiety subjects with normal self-esteem tended to assume that they could learn to improvise successfully with a little practice. And if they failed, so what? So they weren't good at solving mazes blindfolded. The high-anxiety subjects had a different orientation. Lacking normal degrees of intrinsic self-esteem, they lacked confidence in their ability to cope with new adjustive situations. They were frightened when their habitual visual learning cues were removed and they had to improvise. And lacking any intrinsic feelings of adequacy, they were naturally very dependent on the self-esteem they could achieve through successful performance. Thus, they could less afford to say, "So what?" to failure.

What were the results? The high-anxiety subjects *apparently* overreacted to the threat to self-esteem emanating from the maze situation. The real threat, however, came from their own impaired self-esteem. And in terms of *that* threat they certainly did *not* overreact. On the first trial of the maze they became panicky and flustered, making a significantly greater number of errors than the low-anxiety subjects. But after the first trial the maze was no longer a new learning task requiring improvisation. It became more and more familiar and "old hat." By the end of ten trials, there was no longer a significant difference between the two anxiety groups.

In investigating anxiety in neurotically anxious subjects, the role of novel adjustive situations that demand improvisation was demonstrated in a corollary experiment (Ausubel, Schiff, & Goldman, 1953). When high-anxiety subjects were allowed to practice on an easier maze, first with and then without vision, they benefited significantly more from this advance preparation than did low-anxiety subjects. Consistent with these findings, highly anxious subjects show less reactive curiosity than nonanxious subjects (Penney, 1965), exhibit more rigidity and earlier perceptual closure (Cohen, 1961; Smock, 1958), and evince less preference for novel toys (Mendel, 1965).

These experiments could defensibly illustrate the following facts about the nature of neurotic anxiety and its effect on learning: (1) that an actual threat to individuals apart from their own impaired self-esteem is the *precipitating* factor;[5] (2) that the most effective threat is a novel adjustive situation requiring improvisation, since it hits at the very core of impaired self-esteem (when adjustive situations become routine and familiar they are no longer threatening); (3) that the anxiety response is disproportionate to the objective danger of the threat but not to the *actual* degree of threat experienced; and (4) that the major source of threat in neurotic anxiety lies in impaired self-esteem itself.

Test anxiety, on the other hand, emanates from the test situation and is not a generalized personality trait. It also lacks all of the correlates of chronicity (such as rigidity and perseveration). Motivation does not influence performance in high-test-anxiety subjects. However, highly motivated subjects with low test anxiety make more correct responses than subjects who are not highly motivated (Matsuda & Matsuda, 1968). Thus, though test anxiety adversely affects learning performance, aptitude test scores, and study habits (Sassenrath, 1967), it does so differently from neurotic anxiety. Disruption of learning is attributable less to rigidity, perseveration, and avoidance of improvisation than to contemporaneous situational factors and to high levels of anxiety induced in such specific contexts. It can be counteracted by desensitizing students to testing, by accustoming them to be tested frequently (so that a single final test has less threatening implications). Unlike the case in neurotic anxiety, there seems to be little or no negative effect on intelligence or curiosity (Penney, 1965).

There is considerable evidence (for example, Evans, 1969) demonstrating that moderate levels of anxiety (like moderate levels of motivation) facilitate learning, while both low and high levels are associated with diminished learning (the "U-shaped curve"). Achievement anxiety is positively correlated with cheating when subjects are aware of their reference group's performance levels (Skelton & Hill, 1969). As might be anticipated, high

---

[5] Of course, objectively threatening situations will also elicit proportionally greater anxiety from an individual with catastrophically impaired self-esteem than would be the case in a person not afflicted with neurotic anxiety.

anxiety combined with high aptitude tends to facilitate learning, but when it is combined with low or average aptitude, high anxiety tends to inhibit learning (Katahn, 1966; Weiner & Rosenbaum, 1965). Overachieving students (high achievement relative to ability level) exhibit more anxiety and other neuroticism than high-achieving students who have higher academic ability (Robinson, 1966).

### Effect of Anxiety on School Achievement

Regardless of whatever effects anxiety has on school achievement, it is apparent that academic achievement, particularly in low-ability students, is often a reflection of neurotic anxiety. Nevertheless, as could be reasonably anticipated, the effect of anxiety on school achievement is comparable to its effect on learning, except that on a long-term basis its disruptive influence is much less intense. School achievement tasks, after all, tend to lose their threatening implications as students gain experience in coping with them.

At the elementary-school level, anxiety generally depresses scholastic achievement (Cowen et al., 1965; Feldhusen & Klausmeier, 1962; Lunneborg, 1964; Reese, 1961; S. B. Sarason, Hill, & Zimbardo, 1964). In high school, as the motivational effects of anxiety become stronger relative to its disruptive effects, the negative correlation between anxiety and academic achievement decreases, particularly in boys. It is either weaker or entirely absent when grades are used as an index of achievement (I. G. Sarason, 1961, 1963; Walter, Denzler, & I. G. Sarason, 1964). This weak negative or zero correlation also prevails at the college level (Alpert & Haber, 1960; Grooms & Endler, 1960; Spielberger & Katzenmeyer, 1959), or is replaced by a positive relationship between anxiety and academic achievement (Lundin & Sawyer, 1965), especially among academically superior students (Spielberger, 1962).

In highly structured learning tasks such as programmed instruction, a positive relationship has been reported between anxiety and achievement (Kight & Sassenrath, 1966; Traweek, 1964). This finding is consistent with the fact that anxious pupils, particularly when compulsive, do much better in highly structured learning situations where novelty and the need for improvisation are minimal.

### Anxiety and Intelligence

Research evidence indicates almost uniformly that there is a low but significant negative correlation between anxiety and intelligence (Cowen et al., 1965; Feldhusen & Klausmeier, 1962; Feldhusen, Denny, & Condon, 1965; Hafner & Kaplan, 1959; S. B. Sarason, Hill, & Zimbardo, 1964; Spencer, 1957; Spielberger & Katzenmeyer, 1959; Wrightsman, 1962). The findings are consistent with the previously discussed inverse relationship between anxiety and novel problem solving. They suggest that in a threatening test situation, the negative effects of anxiety on relatively novel complex learning (problem-solving) tasks overshadow its positive motivational effects on test performance.

Another equally plausible explanation of this relationship is that low-IQ individuals may feel generally anxious as a result of their inferior school achievement. A less likely interpretation is that anxiety may actually depress the development of intellectual ability rather than merely depress performance on an intelligence test.

### Dogmatism and Authoritarianism

Dogmatism, as pointed out above, is both an aspect of cognitive style and an affective-social personality trait. It is self-evidently related to the formation of beliefs and value judgments, inhibits problem solving and synthetic thinking, and is positively correlated with anxiety (Fillenbaum & Jackman, 1961; Rokeach, 1960). An inverse relationship prevails between (1) dogmatism and (2) academic achievement (Linton, 1968), "initial adaptation to concept-learning tasks" (Ladd, 1967), and recall of information inconsistent with own opinion (Kleck & Wheaton, 1967). Dogmatic individuals, however, tend to evaluate more positively information that is congruent with their own belief systems. Both latter tendencies were not statistically significant although in the anticipated direction (Kleck & Wheaton, 1967). As in other studies, these investigators found marked preference among persons high in dogmatism for opinion-consistent information.

According to Mouw (1969), open-minded subjects exhibited a tendency to increase their scores on measures of cognitive processes as the latter became more complex and autonomous, whereas the reverse was true among subjects who made high scores on the Rokeach Dogmatism Scale. From this he concluded that closed-minded individuals are more dependent on authority for direction and support than are more open-minded persons. Torcivia and Laughlin (1968) concluded from the comparative functioning of open- and closed-minded subjects on a concept-attainment task that the latter are less able to organize new beliefs and to reconcile them with existing beliefs in problem-solving situations. Greenwald (1969) found that dogmatic subjects "tended strongly to accept arguments supporting their own position and to reject opposing ones when expecting to defend their own position, but accepted nearly equal numbers of arguments on both sides when expecting to advocate the opposing position." Finally, Smith's (1968) data suggest that "low dogmatics, when highly interested [in a particular issue] place their cognitive items in logical juxtaposition and change their opinions to fit the knowledge they know and believe, while high dogmatics successfully compartmentalize the cognitive items, thereby retaining and believing information which is actually contradictory to the opinion they hold on the issue."

Research findings in conflict with the above conclusions (Miller & Lobe, 1967) have indicated that when a highly credible source is used, opinionated language has more of an effect than nonopinionated language, irrespective of the learner's open- or closed-mindedness. Opinionated language merely "provides cues" concerning one alternative set of reinforcing contingencies correlated with acceptance of a given point of view.

In Rokeach's (1960) pioneering conceptualization of closed-mindedness, both the structure of the trait and the relationship between closed-mindedness and dogmatism are left unresolved. Our view of the dogmatism–closed-mindedness relationship is that dogmatism is only one aspect of closed-mindedness—the aspect that is reflective of a *generalized* personality trait or characteristic of cognitive style that an individual brings into *any* learning situation when confronted by controversial views contrary to his or her belief system, irrespective of the topic or issue in question.

Rokeach, in our opinion, neglects two other crucial aspects of closed-mindedness, both of which are *specific* to a particular issue, namely, an affective component (attitudinal bias) and a cognitive component (informational bias). To understand adequately how any given individual will respond to a controversial learning task contrary to his or her beliefs, one must consider all three components of closed-mindedness. Bearing these three components in mind, one can readily appreciate why persons who are generally very closed-minded about most controversial issues may be surprisingly open-minded about one or more particular issues, and vice versa.

The attributes of dogmatism as a generalized personality trait are well defined (Rokeach, 1960). They include the following characteristics:

1. Unwillingness to examine new evidence after an opinion is formed
2. Resistance to suspending judgment until sufficient evidence is available
3. A tendency summarily to dismiss evidence or arguments in conflict with one's beliefs
4. A tendency to view controversial issues in terms of blacks and whites
5. A tendency to form strong beliefs, highly resistant to change, on the basis of equivocal evidence
6. A tendency to reject other persons because of their beliefs
7. A tendency to isolate contradictory beliefs in logic-tight compartments
8. Intolerance for ambiguity (a need for early, typically premature, closure in reaching conclusions about complex issues)

It is not difficult to understand why these tendencies can impair ability to learn new ideas contrary to existing beliefs. People who manifest them fail to learn such ideas adequately because they may not even be willing to read or listen to these ideas carefully and attentively, because they make little or no effort to understand or reconcile them with existing beliefs, or because they selectively misunderstand, distort, discount, or reverse their implications in accordance with their biases.

The measurement of dogmatism is a much more difficult problem. Most of the items on Rokeach's Dogmatism Scale (1960) bear little if any discernible relationship to the above-designated attributes of dogmatism. But since they have been validated against presumably dogmatic individuals and also exhibit reasonably high coefficients of stability and internal consistency, they apparently measure, on some purely empirical basis, a stable and generalized facet of dogmatism. Nevertheless, because we believe that the external validating criteria of dogmatism are, at best, highly tenuous, we have preferred to rely on fact (content) validity in constructing our own scale, despite the self-evident disadvantage of greater transparency of the items (Ausubel & Tenzer, 1970).

Several nonexperimental studies have demonstrated a negative relationship between dogmatism and the learning and retention of controversial material. Dogmatism, as measured by the Rokeach Dogmatism Scale, was found to be inversely related to the learning of sociological material in the classroom (Ehrlich, 1961) and positively related to the retention of specific misconceptions about human behavior (Costin, 1968). However, it was not significantly related to course achievement in the more objective and less controversial course content of psychology (Christensen, 1963; Costin, 1965). On a more experimental basis, Kleck and Wheaton (1967) found that dogmatic subjects showed less recall of information inconsistent with their own opinions, and a greater tendency to evaluate opinion-consistent information more positively than did less dogmatic subjects.

Research on the effects of issue-specific bias on the learning of controversial material tends to be somewhat equivocal because not until relatively recently was Peak's (1955) distinction between the affective and cognitive components of attitude structure taken into account in the design of such studies. More recent studies in this area have differentiated between the respective effects on learning of the cognitive and affective components of attitude structure (Fitzgerald & Ausubel, 1963; Gustafson, 1957; E. E. Jones & Kohler, 1958). Their findings are consonant with the interpretation that both cognitive and affective-motivational mechanisms account for the superior learning that occurs when controversial materials are consistent rather than inconsistent with the learner's attitudinal framework.

The affective-motivational mechanisms involved in specific attitudinal bias per se are presumably similar to those described above for the effects of dogmatism on learning. Insofar as cognitive mechanisms are concerned in the operation of the informational bias components of attitude structure, it may be plausibly assumed that learners more frequently possess clear, stable, and relevant anchoring ideas for the incorporation of controversial new material when their attitudes toward such material are favorable than when this is not the case.

Authoritarianism is a related personality trait that is characterized by orthodoxy, veneration of traditional beliefs, and a tendency to overconform uncritically to the views of authority figures (Adorno, Frenkel-Brunswick, Levenson, & Sanford, 1950). The authoritarian personality tends to be ethnocentric, prejudiced against minority groups, and intolerant of ambiguity (Adorno et al., 1950). This type of personality is found more commonly in lower-class and low-status occupational groups (Adorno et al., 1950; Livson & Nichols, 1957). Students making high scores on scales of authoritarianism are more likely to structure novel stimuli in rigid fashion, to reach closure more quickly, to change their attitudes in response to prestige suggestion (Duncan, Signori, & Rempel, 1964; Harvey, 1963; Wright & Harvey, 1965) and to be high conformers (Vaughan & White, 1966). The last cited researchers feel that rigidity and narrow-mindedness characterize both the authoritarian personality and the personality of the high conformer. Undergraduates with high self-esteem and low commitment were found to be less persuasible than any of the other three combinations of these traits (Stimpson, 1970). Subjects with high self-esteem in this same study tended to "use selective perception as a dissonance-reducing technique." Similar findings were obtained by Stimpson (1970) using self-esteem combined with "attitude-discrepant" behavior.

### Miscellaneous Personality Variables

Cole, Miller, and Dean (1967) have made the significant inference from their research data that the *value* placed on academic achievement (as well as the influence of intellectual ability per se) contributes in an important way to the prediction of the grade point average of university men and women. Among the male freshmen, however, the value placed on the university was predominantly negative. Positive *attitudes* toward mathematics, with mathematical ability statistically controlled, tends to be positively related to such traits as intellectual and social maturity, self-control, and greater valuation of theoretical matters, as well as to a wider variety of personality traits indicative of good adjustment and level of interest in intellectual pursuits (Aiken, 1963). Finally, the British educational researcher, Robinson (1965), contends that the influence of intelligence and achievement motivation on academic achievement in secondary school is largely exerted by the common association of both factors with success in primary school. This view is consistent with our own view that cognitive-structure variables are the most potent determinants of subject-matter learning and retention.

The pupil's perception of "locus of control" has received increasing attention in recent years as a personality variable affecting school performance. In general the research findings are consistent with the notion that pupils who perceive reinforcement as contingent upon their own behavior (for example, degree of learning) tend to be more actively involved in information-seeking than those pupils who perceive such reinforcement as dependent upon external controls or on chance (Davis & Phares, 1967). Warm, supportive, and praising parent behaviors also enhanced children's beliefs in internal control; the converse was also true (Katkowsky, Crandell, & Good, 1967).

British educational research has shown that girls have more favorable attitudes toward school than boys despite the fact that the latter tend to have a more flattering academic self-image, to be better adjusted socially, and to be less anxious in the classroom. Brighter and middle-class children have more favorable school attitudes than duller and working-class pupils. Favorableness of school attitude is in part a function of academic performance (Lunn, 1972).

### Personality Adjustment and School Achievement

Several lines of evidence indicate that poor personality adjustment is associated with inferior academic achievement. Both teachers' ratings of adjustment (Ausubel et al., 1954; Ullman, 1957) and scores on the California Psychological Inventory (Gough, 1964) are moderately correlated with such criteria of success in school as grade-point average, completion of high school, and graduation with honors.

High achievers in school indicate fewer problems on the Mooney Check List (Frankel, 1960), and are characterized by such traits as high ego integration, independence, maturity, and responsiveness to cultural pressures (d'Heurle, Mellinger, & Haggard, 1959). Negative self-concept in kindergarten is predictive of poor progress in reading[6] (Wattenberg & Clifford, 1964). Brookover, Thomas, and Patterson (1964) found that a positive self-concept is associated with higher achievement in four subject-matter areas. Academic success is correlated with realistic goalsetting (Byers, 1962) and with self-confidence and clear vocational goals (Todd, Terrell, & Frank, 1962).

It is hardly surprising, of course, that personality maladjustment is negatively related to school achievement, inasmuch as all of the symptoms of such maladjustment self-evidently interfere in one way or another with the motivational factors promoting effective long-term learning (Phillips, 1968):

---

[6] The identification of negative self-concept at *kindergarten age* in this study precludes the interpretation that all of the inverse relationship between personality adjustment and academic achievement can be attributed to the negative effects of school failure on the self-concepts of pupils.

1. A common complex of symptoms accompanying learning disabilities and associated with diffuse brain damage—namely, hyperactivity, hyper-irritability, distractability, and emotional lability—impedes effort, attention, and persistence.

2. In elementary school, school achievement correlates negatively with anxiety despite the high achievement motivation characterizing this condition.

3. Severe withdrawal reactions obviously render any kind of long-term learning impossible.

4. Exaggerated aggressiveness leads to hostility toward the teacher, uncooperativeness, and a negativistic attitude toward learning.[7]

5. Lack of self-confidence is associated with failure to try, low frustration tolerance, "learning blocks," and a tendency to withdraw from difficult situations.

6. School achievement depends, in large measure, on such attributes of personality maturity as responsibility, executive independence, long-term goals, impulse control, persistence, and ability to defer gratification of hedonistic needs.

7. Both personality maladjustment and inferior school achievement are correlated with lower social class status and cultural disadvantage, and hence with each other.

The more common signs of personality maladjustment associated with these conditions are low attention span, hyperactivity, aggressive reactions, low level of academic aspiration, and personality immaturity.

Two other factors also help account for the inverse relationship between personality maladjustment and school achievement. In the first place, the cause-and-effect aspect of the relationship obviously works in both directions; that is, school achievement is a determinant as well as a consequent of personality adjustment. Second, it is almost impossible to eliminate the halo effect of each variable on the other; teachers tend both to downgrade the academic achievement of poorly adjusted children, particularly if they are aggressive, inattentive, or hyperactive, and to give poor adjustment ratings to nonachieving pupils. Halo effects are minimized if objective measures of achievement and adjustment are used.

The type and frequency of various behavior disorders in the school naturally vary with race, ethnicity, and social class and with their respective relationships to achievement motivation and school performance (Phillips, 1968). According to an American educational researcher, however, the gradual erosion of children's positive attitudes during the school year is not a function of IQ, social class, or the proportion of low or high grades

---

[7] Aggressive, acting-out high-school boys tend to perceive their parents as less loving than do well-adjusted boys, and also identify less with their parents (Longstreth & Rice, 1964).

awarded by particular teachers (Flanders, Morrison, & Brode, 1968). It depends rather on the "internality" or "externality" of pupils and on teachers' verbal classroom behavior.

## The Personality Development and Mental Health Responsibilities of the School

Most reasonable persons would agree today that the legitimate functions of the school extend beyond the development of intellectual skills and the transmission of subject-matter knowledge. The school also has undeniable responsibilities with respect to mental health and personality development, simply because it is a place where children spend a good part of their waking hours, perform much of their purposeful activity, obtain a large share of their status, and interact significantly with adults, agemates, and the demands of society. By virtue of their interaction with teachers and peers and of their participation in curricular and extracurricular school activities, adolescents, for example, make significant strides toward emancipation from parents and the acquisition of adult personality status.

Particularly during adolescence, current problems of adjustment—vocational choice, emancipation from parents, somatic deviations, relationships with peers, adults, and members of the opposite sex—are very real and important to pupils. Psychologically, these developmental tasks are too urgent to be ignored. Hence, education must perforce be concerned with problems youth consider to be important. If young people perceive the school as unconcerned with these problems, they react either by losing interest in the academic areas the school values or by feeling guilty for being preoccupied with supposedly trivial matters. If current concerns are not relieved, they inevitably serve as distractions from academic responsibilities.

Hence as long as the organizational, administrative, disciplinary, and interpersonal aspects of the school environment inevitably affect the mental health and personality development of its future citizens, it obviously behooves society to arrange these matters as appropriately and constructively as possible. Nevertheless, because the mental hygiene role of the school has been oversold and misrepresented so frequently by educational theorists, it will be worth our while to consider some of the more serious misconceptions about the mental health functions of the school.

### The Primary Responsibility of the School

To begin with, we need to recognize that the primary and distinctive function of the school in our society is not to promote mental health and personality development but to foster intellectual growth and the assimilation of knowledge. The school admittedly has important responsibilities with regard to the social, emotional, and moral aspects of the pupil's development. Nevertheless, these are only supplementary to those of other socializing agents such as the home, the church, the peer group, and the neighborhood.

The school's role in intellectual development, however, is incontrovertibly primary. Furthermore, much of the school's legitimate concern with interpersonal relations in the classroom does not stem merely from interest in enhancing healthful personality development as an end in itself, no matter how important this object may be. It also reflects appreciation of the negative effects that an unfavorable social and emotional school climate has on academic achievement, on motivation to learn, and on desirable attitudes toward intellectual inquiry. For example, if pupils feel unhappy and resentful about the discipline and social environment of the school, they will neither learn very much while they are in school nor remain much longer than they have to. And if they are goaded by fear to accept uncritically the views of their teachers and to memorize materials they do not really understand, they neither learn how to think for themselves nor build the foundations of a stable and usable body of knowledge.

### The Limits of Normality

As was long true in the area of physical hygiene, some educators also tend to exaggerate the seriousness and permanence of the effects on mental health of minor deviations from the norm of desirable hygienic practice. There is every reason to believe, however, that a wide margin of safety is the rule both in physical and mental health.

Within fairly broad limits, many different kinds of teacher personality structure and ways of relating to children are compatible with normal mental health and personality development in pupils. This principle applies when either mildly undesirable classroom practices prevail over an extended period of time, or when more serious deviations from optimal standards occur occasionally. In general, children are often resilient and do not develop permanent personality disabilities from temporary exposure to negative interpersonal practices. Furthermore, many pupils who manifest signs of behavior disturbance in school either do so only temporarily (Harris, 1960; MacFarlane, Allen, & Honzik, 1954) or fail to show any symptoms of maladjustment at home or in the peer group.

### The Cult of Extroversion

In education, as in many other vocational fields, professional leaders have unduly succumbed to the cult of the warm, outgoing, amiable, and extroverted personality and have tended to regard any deviation from this standard as axiomatically undesirable from a mental hygiene standpoint. Formerly, pupils would be referred to the school psychologist if they were boisterous, aggressive, and refractory to discipline. Now children who are reserved, contemplative, and unconcerned about the opinion of their peers arouse the clinical concern of the child guidance specialist. Similarly, many excellent teachers who happen to be shy and introverted are viewed with alarm by their psychologically oriented superiors. Yet there is absolutely no evidence that they impair their pupils' mental health, even though they may conceivably be less popular as individuals than their extroverted colleagues.

As far as pupil popularity is concerned, it has been definitely established that this characteristic may be a grossly misleading index of social adjustment. An ostensibly popular pupil may be little more than a "stranger in the group" in terms of the depth of his or her attachments or may be popular simply because he or she is docile, conforming, and willing to be directed and "used" by others (Wittenberg & Berg, 1952). Contrariwise, the pupil who is unpopular because of temperamental shyness or strong intellectual interests is not necessarily socially maladjusted or inevitably fated to become so (Morris, Soroker, & Buruss, 1954; Robins, 1966).

## The Teacher's Responsibility in Handling
## Personality Maladjustments

It is important for teachers to recognize that their responsibility in handling personality maladjustment in their pupils is, at most, extremely limited. In the first place, the origin of serious maladjustment does not typically lie in the school but rather in the home and neighborhood and sometimes in brain injury or genically determined temperamental traits. Hence, amelioration of the condition largely depends on factors outside the school environment and beyond the teacher's control. Second, valid diagnosis and appropriate treatment of personality maladjustment call for qualifications that obviously extend beyond the teacher's training and competence.

Available evidence indicates that teachers are not very successful in assessing the personality makeup and adjustment of their pupils. They cannot predict very accurately pupils' responses to questions on their hobbies, interests, problems, and personality characteristics (Amos & Washington, 1960; H. L. Baker, 1938), their motivations and academic strivings (Ausubel, 1951; Ausubel, Schiff, & Zeleny, 1953), their scores on objective and projective tests of adjustment (Ausubel, Schiff, & Zeleny, 1953), and the extent to which they are accepted by their classmates (Ausubel, Schiff, & Gasser, 1952; Bonney, 1947; Gronlund, 1950). These latter perceptions become increasingly more inaccurate as pupils progress through the grades (Ausubel, Schiff, & Gasser, 1952; Moreno, 1934).

It is not difficult to find explanations for this state of affairs. Teachers are simply not aware of the distinctive standards and values that operate in the lives of their pupils. By the age of adolescence, the estrangement between children and their elders has made considerable progress and is often compounded by the outright hostility and antiadult attitudes manifested by youth. Channels of communication break down and teachers are obliged to interpret pupils' behavior at face value or by their own standards and frames of reference. They fall back upon interpretive biases from recollections of their own adolescence and from norms of behavior that pertain exclusively to their own middle-class backgrounds.

In evaluating other aspects of the adolescent's personality or adjustment, they are also not unnaturally influenced by the pupil's conformity to the requirements of the school situation. As pointed out above, "halo effect" accounts for some of the moderately high correlation between high-school pupils' school achievement and teachers' ratings of personal adjustment. Teachers also tend to overvalue the popularity of children with whom they have satisfactory relationships (Bonney, 1947; Gronlund, 1950).

The implications of these findings are obvious. If teachers cannot accurately perceive the interests, attitudes, motivations, aspirations, and problems of their pupils, they will naturally be unable either to counsel them very intelligently or to adapt effectively the interpersonal climate of the school to the special personality needs of those who are maladjusted. Lacking adequate understanding of pupil behavior, they will be unable to interpret misbehavior, to respond adequately to it, or to institute appropriate preventive and disciplinary measures. And, unfortunately, although general knowledge of child development does facilitate the understanding of *particular* pupils, it is no substitute for adequate psychological perceptiveness or sufficient intimate contact with pupils.

Ability to empathize with pupils does not, of course, obligate teachers to adopt their values, nor does it guarantee effectiveness in dealing with them. Understanding is necessary but not sufficient for skilled interpersonal relationships or effectiveness in counseling, since many other abilities and personality traits that are probably uncorrelated with psychological sensitivity (such as poise, self-assurance, firmness, leadership qualities) are necessary for translating accurate perceptions into appropriate interpersonal behavior or skill in guidance. Thus the teacher's actual role in handling the behavior disorders lies in recognizing signs of serious maladjustment and in referring disturbed pupils to the appropriate mental health personnel such as counselors, school psychologists, and psychiatrists. It is important, however, that they view realistically what these "experts" can typically hope to accomplish. First, it is evident that counseling and psychotherapy have been greatly oversold. The analogy of mental disease to physical disease is still quite euphemistic, since incomparably less is known about the causes, nature, and treatment of the former than about corresponding aspects of the latter. Second, many of the so-called psychological "experts" in the schools have had little more clinical training and supervised clinical experience than teachers. Lastly, even the well-trained counselor, clinical psychologist and psychiatrist frequently lacks the psychological sensitivity, empathy, and perceptiveness necessary for valid personality assessment. This much is evident from the fact that when counselors use impressionistic interview and anecdotal data (in addition to grades and aptitude test scores) in predicting the academic success of pupils, their predictions become less (rather than more) accurate than predictions based on the objective measures alone (Meehl, 1954). This, of course, does not argue for the elimination of trained clinical judgment from the assessment of personality adjustment, but, rather, for the use of more sensitive criteria in selecting empathetic clinicians.

# 13

# GROUP AND SOCIAL FACTORS IN LEARNING

Social and group variables must be considered in school learning since they inevitably impinge both on subject-matter learning and on the learning of values and attitudes. Their influence on learning subject matter is largely mediated through motivational variables.

Although the weight of the evidence indicates that classroom climate (democratic, authoritarian, laissez faire) has little effect on academic achievement per se, it does affect attitudes toward the school, the learning of culturally approved values, and school behavior. A genuinely democratic school climate is most effective with respect to all three objectives but is frequently confused with a laissez faire or overly permissive classroom climate. Also, an authoritarian school climate is not necessarily detrimental (1) if the adult culture is similarly authoritarian and (2) if adults are consistent in demanding as much from themselves as from children.

Individualized instruction is much more effective than instruction in groups, except in learning situations where the material is more controversial and learners require cross-fertilization and exposure to other views. Group problem solving is not intrinsically superior to individual problem solving, except insofar as (1) the likelihood of at least one pupil finding a correct solution, (2) the avoidance of extreme judgments, and (3) the stimulation provided by more able pupils, are greater in a group setting. In the case of certain tasks, however, individuals solve problems more efficiently than do groups.

*Satellizers are individuals who tend to seek derived status in group settings by identifying in a dependent fashion with the group, whereas nonsatellizers perceive the group situation as an opportunity for obtaining earned status.*

*Unless extreme in degree, competition does not have detrimental effects on learning. It stimulates individual effort, raises the aspirations and standards of pupils, promotes self-realization, and prepares pupils for effective participation in a competitive culture. However, when competition is overly stressed, it arouses anxiety, encourages less able children to withdraw from the academic field, tends to weaken the relative strength of cognitive drive, and replaces the desire for knowledge by such spurious symbols of scholastic attainment as high marks. Nevertheless, competition and cooperation are by no means mutually exclusive.*

*The adolescent's exaggerated need to conform to peer group values is a function of his marginal and prolonged interim status in our culture. He is unduly dependent on his peers for much of the derived and earned status he enjoys, and for whatever opportunity he has to learn the skills of adult socialization. Although these pressures for conformity tend to wane spontaneously with the approach of adulthood, adolescents should be encouraged both to express their individuality and to adhere to their moral convictions, as well as to submit, at least minimally, to these conformity pressures for the sake of adequate socialization and adjustment during the adolescent period. Teachers should understand that the adolescent conformity and adult–youth alienation promoted by adolescent peer groups not only encourages desatellization, but also generates indifference to adult norms and sanctions aggressive, antiadult and "acting out" behavior.*

*Social-class stratification affects both the academic and the vocational aspirations of youth, and leads to victimization (unfair streaming, higher drop-out rate) of lower-class and minority-group pupils because of the discriminatory attitudes and the predominantly middle-class values of teachers. The social-class gap in aspirations, however, is being rapidly reduced while the difference in academic and vocational implementation of these aspirations progressively increases. This phenomenon is a reflection of differential social-class pressures for achievement in the home and peer group and of the general trend toward decreased social mobility.*

*Both the IQs and academic achievement of black pupils are depressed by factors of caste and cultural disadvantage, as well as by their predominantly lower-class membership. Recently, however, there has been an increase in militancy, racial pride and identification, and an improvement in self-concept among black pupils, attributable, in part, to the Civil Rights Movement. The academic motivation of blacks and other culturally disadvantaged pupils may be increased (1) by focusing on cognitive drive, (2) by developing motivation retroactively through successful learning, (3) by identifying with black counselors, and (4) by concentrating on mastery of basic intellectual skills before introducing them to more complex subject matter, instead of resorting to the ubiquitous practice of "social promotion" (which produces "functionally illiterate" high-school graduates).*

Since school learning takes place in a social context, teachers must obviously be concerned with group and social factors that impinge on the learning process. Since pupils are members of a classroom group, their motivation for learning, the kinds of motivations they exhibit, and their social behavior, personality development, and the values and attitudes they learn are affected by their interaction with the teacher and other pupils. How then is classroom learning influenced by such group variables as working with and in the presence of agemates, cooperation and competition, conformity to group norms, relative responsiveness to peer versus adult expectations, and the social-emotional climate of the classroom? We shall also want to consider how pupils' membership in a sex, social class, ethnic, and racial subgroup affects the motivational and attitudinal aspects of school learning. Apart from general classroom climate, the teacher's contribution to the social context in which learning occurs—his or her role, cognitive and personality characteristics, and teaching style—will be reserved for the following chapter.

It must be appreciated at this point that many group and social factors impinge on school learning—for example, authoritarianism in the classroom, cooperation and competition, conformity and its changes with age, individual differences in orientation to group experience, the alienation of pupils from adult society, social class stratification, racial and ethnic factors, motivational aspects of cultural deprivation, and so forth. These factors do so quite *indirectly* by affecting both the degree and kind of motivation of learners for acquiring subject-matter knowledge and their mode of assimilating cultural norms and values. The relevance of these factors for educational psychology is therefore less immediate and more tangential than that of cognitive factors, motivation, or such personality factors as anxiety and dogmatism. Nevertheless they must still be taken into account both by the teacher and by the educational psychologist in assessing all of the significant determinants of academic performance. To a certain extent, also, they must first be understood as phenomena in their own right before their impact on school learning can be evaluated.

Hence a *minimal* background of developmental and social psychological data and discussion is presented below to serve this purpose. It is not intended as complete coverage of the topics in question, or as a substitute for the more definitive treatment that these topics receive in courses in developmental and social psychology, where they are quite properly considered as ends in themselves and not merely in relation to their influence on learning and academic achievement.

## Classroom Climate

The weight of the evidence indicates that the choice between authoritarian and democratic classroom climates in the United States has little effect on subject-matter achievement (Stern, 1963). But there is good reason to believe that it has profound effects on attitudes toward school, on general social behavior in the school, and on the learning of adult values (Ausubel, 1965d; DeCecco, 1972; Stern, 1963). It seems reasonable to suppose that as children become older in a democratic society, particularly in adolescence and beyond, authoritarian controls should be progressively liberalized to meet increasing needs for self-determination and growing capacities for self-direction and self-discipline. This is generally the case in American secondary schools, but prevailing practice in schools which have minority group students still falls far behind desirable standards of appropriate democratic classroom practice.

In a study involving 6700 high-school students in greater New York and Philadelphia areas DeCecco (1972) reports that two-thirds of the students viewed themselves as helpless recipients of arbitrary orders that were autocratically enforced. They were more concerned with the lack of real choices in their school experiences than in racial or political issues. Fifty percent of the incidents involving institutional conflicts had to do with school governance and individual choice. Ninety-one percent of the students felt that tensions escalated because of the way school authorities handled conflict. Tensions were reduced, however, when principals and teachers negotiated from positions of equality.

In general, overt compliance is the most common response that preadolescents and adolescents make to excessive authoritarianism in the classroom, especially if they are girls and if they come from middle-class homes that place a great premium upon success in school. Adolescents from other backgrounds, however, may react with open aggression and hostility to teachers, with negativism, or with passive sabotage. Still others may drop out of school as soon as it is legal to do so. Yet even those adolescents who apparently become overtly reconciled to a continuation of an incongruously submissive childhood role probably do not really accept the authoritarianism to which they outwardly defer, but respond with suppressed resentment and various negatively toned emotional reactions.

Experimental studies of the impact of authoritarian leadership on children's groups also point to various undesirable effects on group morale and solidarity (Lippitt, 1940). In comparison with children in democratically governed groups, pupils who are subjected to autocratic control are more aggressive, direct their aggression against scapegoat group members rather than against the group leader, and adopt more submissive, placatory, and attention-demanding attitudes in dealing with the leader. They also manifest less "we-feeling," show less capacity for mobilizing constructive group effort in overcoming frustrating conditions, and are less capable of self-disciplined work and behavior when direct supervision is removed. H. H. Anderson (1943) obtained similar findings in studying the effects of "dominative" and "integrative" behavior by teachers.

There has been, however, a strong tendency on the part of educators to overgeneralize the significance of these findings. In the first place, the authoritarian leaders in the Lippitt study were hostile and unfriendly, and tended to give disruptive commands. Typically, authoritarian leadership tends to be more friendly, subtle, and benevolent, and thus has less damaging effects on social behavior and group morale. Second, the effects of autocratic and democratic classroom climate are relative, in part, to the personality structure of individual students. Students who have a strong need for direction and organization react favorably to a directive approach and very critically to a more permissive one (Wispé, 1951). Most important of all, it is undoubtedly ethnocentric to claim that only democratic teacher-pupil relationships are compatible with normal mental health and personality development.

Many examples of authoritarian Western cultures (for example, Germany, Italy, Switzerland), exist in which all of the indices of mental health and mature personality development compare very favorably with those prevailing in the United States. Hence, it is obviously not authoritarianism *itself* that has damaging mental health consequences, but rather the existence of authoritarian practices in home and school that are incongruous with the general pattern of interpersonal relations in the culture at large.

Children *are* able satisfactorily to internalize adult personality traits and mature attitudes toward authority, even in an authoritarian home and school environment, provided that (1) personal, social, and working relationships among adults are *similarly* authoritarian, and (2) adults generally make as stringent demands on *themselves* as they do on young people. In countries like Germany and Switzerland these latter conditions prevail, and therefore authoritarianism in home and school has few adverse effects on mental health and personality development. In New Zealand and the United States, on the other hand, authoritarianism in the home and secondary school has more serious effects because it contrasts sharply with the egalitarian and generally relaxed character of vocational and social life in the adult world (Ausubel, 1965d).

In all cultures, however, even those that are generally authoritarian, there are credible grounds for supposing that an authoritarian classroom climate would generate the same effects on thinking and problem solving as does the authoritarian personality and would lead to less effective group planning, teamwork, and self-direction. Spaulding (1963) found that punitive teachers, emphasizing shame as a technique of control, tend to inhibit pupil creativity. It also seems likely that an authoritarian and punitive classroom climate would increase the anxiety level of less able and anxious pupils and make them more defensive about exposing their inadequacies.

Partly as a reaction against traditional authoritarian practices, a small minority of schools and teachers under the influence of ultrapermissive doctrines of child rearing have instituted a laissez-faire social climate in the classroom. This approach permits pupils to do as they please, emphasizes freedom from restraint and discipline as an end in itself, strives for lack of structure and organization in school activities, and conceives of frustration as an unqualified evil to be avoided at all cost.

Under such "catch-as-catch-can" conditions, aggressive pupils become ruthless, whereas retiring children become even more withdrawn. Observation of groups in which this pattern prevails shows that it leads "inevitably to . . . confusion, insecurity, and keen competition for power among group members" (Cunningham, 1951). Pupils fail to learn the normative demands of society and how to operate within the limits these demands set, do not learn how to deal effectively with adults, and develop unrealistic expectations of the social structure of vocational life.

## Interaction among Pupils

Do pupils learn more effectively when they work individually or in groups? There is no single answer to this question, since it all depends on the nature of the task, on whether they are working *with* or merely in the presence of others, on the size and nature of the group, and on whether our criterion of superiority is a group product or the individual products of the component group members.

First, in performing simple or routine tasks requiring little or no thinking, the concomitant activity of other similar individuals seems to serve as a stimulus, generating contagious behavior and competitive striving—either when pupils work by themselves in the presence of others (Mukerji, 1940) or when they work in pairs (Myers, Travers, & Sanford, 1965). This effect is comparable to the heightened rate of activity stimulated by a pacesetter.

Second, in novel and complex problem-solving tasks where obtaining a correct solution is facilitated by generating a multiplicity of alternative hypotheses (divergent thinking), group effort is apparently superior to individual effort (M. Goldman, 1965; Klausmeier, Wiersma, & Harris, 1963;

Lorge, 1955; Marquart, 1955; Shaw, 1932; Watson, 1928). Closer analysis, however, reveals that this superiority is mostly attributable to the pooling of ideas; the total product of the group is not much better than the sum of the products of its component members. Group effort is more effective, in other words, largely because it increases the possibility of having at least one person who can arrive independently at the correct solution.

This advantage, however, is vitiated if the group is so congenial (Back, 1951; Shaw & Shaw, 1962) or if its leadership is so personal (Fiedler, 1958) that considerable group time and effort is diverted into purely social activity or pleasant conversation. Also, if the task requires evaluation or decision making, cooperative deliberation and the reaching of consensus is usually superior because it avoids the pitfalls of idiosyncratic or extreme judgment (Barnlund, 1959). Although group support undoubtedly reduces anxiety and enhances confidence in problem-solving situations, it also reduces, by the same token, individual responsibility and initiative.

The cohesiveness (congeniality) of the group may also affect the outcome of its collaborative work in a problem-solving situation. The mere presence of congenial co-workers may increase the effectiveness of cooperative effort, may enhance motivation by increasing task attractiveness, and may provide a source of mutual social reinforcement upon successful completion of the task (Lott & Lott, 1961, 1966). This, at least, appears to be the case for cohesive groups composed of high-IQ but not of low-IQ individuals (Lott & Lott, 1966).

Group size is another limiting factor in the group problem-solving situation. In a small group each individual can make a contribution and thereby increase his problem-solving skills. In a large group, on the other hand, the individual's opportunity for participation is limited not only by the number of participants but also by the fact that the more aggressive group members tend to take over and monopolize the problem-solving activity (Carter et al., 1951).

Third, if the learning product of each group member is used as our criterion of success in the former problem-solving situation, it is evident that the less able members of the group can accomplish more than they could individually, by virtue of being stimulated by and being able to adopt the ideas and strategies of the more able pupils (Gurnee, 1962). In effect, they enjoy the benefit of pupil tutors. Thus, the gain in skill is always greatest among low-ability pupils and among pupils working with superior partners (M. Goldman, 1965).

Fourth, certain tasks (for instance, the drafting of a report) requiring convergent thinking, intense concentration, and persistent attention to detail can self-evidently be performed more efficiently on an individual rather than on a group basis. This is obvious to anyone who has ever worked on a committee.

Finally, as pointed out earlier, self-paced, individualized (and programmed) instruction is a much more efficient and less time-consuming method of learning the established content of a discipline than the traditional recitation or lecture-discussion approach used in most classrooms. Discussion, on the other hand, is the most effective, and really the only feasible, method of promoting intellectual growth with respect to the less established and more controversial aspects of subject matter. It provides the best means of broadening pupils' intellectual horizons, of stimulating their thinking through cross-fertilization, of clarifying their views, and of measuring the cogency of these views against the viewpoints of others. Interaction with peers, furthermore, helps pupils overcome both egocentricity and childhood perception of adults as the absolute source of truth and wisdom with regard to all value judgments. The pupils learn the extent to which both their ideas and those of the teacher represent idiosyncratic positions along a broad spectrum of opinion whose validity is indeterminable.

## Individual Orientation to Group Experience

A brief word might be said at this point about pupils' differential personality orientations toward group experience. The child's idiosyncratic manner of relating to significant persons in the family setting has ample opportunity to become solidified long before he or she is ever permitted to venture unmonitored from the home. It is hardly surprising, therefore, that this approach to interpersonal experience with the child's earliest socializers should be generalized to other kinds of social situations. To satellizing children, the peer group provides derived status in much the same way as the parent, except that the status-giving authority resides in a corporate body to which they themselves belong. By relating to it they obtain the same spontaneous "we-feeling" experienced in the family group.

Nonsatellizers, on the other hand, cannot assume an internalized position of self-subserviency in relation to the group. The field of intragroup relations, like the home, is no place for "we-feeling"; it is just another arena in which nonsatellizers contend for earned status, prestige, power, and self-aggrandizement. They do not subordinate themselves to group interests or experience spontaneous satisfaction in gregarious activity. Every social move is carefully deliberated for the possible advantages that may accrue from it, and the currency of social interchange is supplied by the synthetic manufacture of attitudes, remarks, and behavior that can be construed as conventionally appropriate for the specifications of a given situation. These pupils are quite capable, of course, of harvesting vicarious status from identification with prestigeful membership or reference groups; but since no subservience of self is required, it bears little resemblance to the derived status of satellizers. The prestige of family, club, college, nationality, and so forth, is incorporated merely as a gratuitous form of ego enhancement or as a springboard for the realization of personal ambitions.

As already pointed out, the nonsatellizing orientation to group experience tends, on a normative basis, increasingly to characterize maturing individuals as they approach adulthood. Nevertheless, ex-satellizers continue to display satellizing-like attitudes in many group situations, particularly those that are informal and hence not directly related to their functional competence.

In harmony with the findings of previous studies, Sherif and Sherif (1964) showed that interpersonal relations within informal, spontaneously formed adolescent groups are highly patterned with respect to the roles, statuses, and reciprocal expectancies of their members. Leadership, defined in terms of "effective initiative," is correlated with but clearly differentiable from popularity. Top and bottom positions in the group emerge earlier than intermediate ranks and can also be reliably observed sooner. Observers' ratings not only agree with each other but also with the members' own appraisals of status. Leadership changes hands as the focus of activity within the group shifts, and is much more a function of the leader's commitment to group goals and of his or her ability to facilitate and coordinate group activities than of such characteristics as physical prowess or temperamental dominance.

## Competition and Cooperation

Competition ordinarily is a form of ego-enhancement motivation involving self-aggrandizing activity in which the individual vies with others for hierarchical preeminence. Cooperation, on the other hand, is a group-oriented activity in which the individual collaborates with others to attain some common goal. Nevertheless, these two activities are by no means antithetical to each other; both imply a considerable degree of interaction within the group as opposed to individual behavior that is carried on with little reference to the activities of others. Furthermore, much competition between groups occurs in the context of intense cooperation and affiliative drive within groups.

The relative prominence of cooperation and competition varies greatly with the cultural environment (Mead, 1937). Our own culture values both kinds of behavior, often inconsistently, and hence fosters much moral confusion. In general, ego-enhancement motivation has a self-aggrandizing and competitive flavor in our culture that varies from one social class to another. Although lower-class preschool children tend to be more competitive than middle-class children in play situations (McKee & Leader, 1955), the latter eventually internalize higher aspirations for academic and vocational prestige. Boys in our culture are consistently more competitive than girls during both early and later childhood (Maccoby & Jacklin, 1974; McKee & Leader, 1955).

Many activities in the peer group evoke cooperative and competitive behavior either simultaneously or alternately. Team games are competitive contests between two cooperatively organized groups. However, members of the same team may compete against each other while striving jointly for a distinctive team goal, or several teams may compete against each other in furthering a cause common to all. Some children are competitive under neutral or cooperative conditions (Ausubel, 1951), others are cooperative under competitive conditions (Stendler, Damrin, & Haines, 1951), and still others are task-oriented under any conditions (Ausubel, 1951). Thus, despite the purportedly cooperative or competitive conditions characterizing a particular enterprise, the extent to which a given child is ego-oriented, task-oriented, or group-oriented can be ascertained only by individual motivational analysis.

Competition has both desirable and undesirable effects on personality development. On the credit side it stimulates individual effort and productivity, promotes higher standards and aspirations, and narrows the gap between capacity and performance. Children of elementary-school age work harder under competitive conditions than when working anonymously (Ausubel, 1951). They also work harder for individual rewards than for group prizes (Maller, 1929; Sims, 1928). Even so, they are highly responsive to such natural competitive situations as contests between boys and girls, teams, and classrooms (Maller, 1929). By enabling individuals to obtain a more realistic estimate of their own capacities in relation to those of others, competition also exerts a salutary effect on self-critical ability. Under the stimulus of competition, children are better able to discover both their own limitations and hitherto unrealized capacities and are motivated to overcome objectionable personality traits. Competition makes group games more interesting and everyday tasks less monotonous.

On the debit side, competition may inhibit learning by arousing excessive threat and inducing undue anxiety (Shaw, 1958). When carried to unwholesome extremes, it fosters feelings of inadequacy in less able children, encourages them to withdraw from activities in which they do not excel, and unduly depresses their status in the group. Under less extreme conditions, however, it helps them to adjust to the competitive organization of our culture in which individuals must still continue striving even though they realize that preeminence is beyond their reach. It may lead to a tense, hostile, vindictive, and negative group climate (Sherif & Sherif, 1953) in which ruthlessness, unfairness, and dishonesty are condoned in the interests of emerging victorious. In such an atmosphere, the demonstration of superiority and the pleasing of authority figures become the primary goals, whereas the intrinsic value of the activity, self-expression, and creativity are de-emphasized. Finally, when excessive value is placed on superior achievement, children become obsessed with the notion of self-aggrandizement and lose sight of human values. Prestigeful attainment becomes the sole criterion of human worth and source of self-esteem; and the perceived accomplishments of others constitute a threat and a competitive challenge to the individual's sense of adequacy which must be bested or denied.

The adverse consequences of competition have undoubtedly been exaggerated, however, because of a tendency to view the matter in all-or-none terms. Competitive and noncompetitive activities are by no means mutually exclusive. A program of interscholastic athletics, for example, does not preclude in any way adequate attention to the physical education needs of the athletically less talented. Nor is it necessary to carry competition to extremes. Under experimental conditions moderate forms of competition do not lead to more negative interactions among pupils (Stendler et al., 1951), decrease group cohesiveness (Phillips & D'Amico, 1956), or increase cheating on a self-scoring test (Gross, 1946).

### Conformity and Individuality

As a reaction to overconforming tendencies in our society since World War II, it has become fashionable to decry conformity as an unqualified evil in and of itself. The issue, however, is not nearly that simple. In the first place, a certain desirable degree of conformity is necessary both for the viability of small groups and for the development and perpetuation of culture. Second, it is evident that nonconformists who deviate from the norms of their culture typically conform even more rigidly than the average person does to the norms of their particular out-group. The reasons for this will become clear shortly. Third, conformity to certain group pressures can also reinforce and support individuals in preserving their moral scruples in defiance of other negative group pressures (Milgram, 1965).

### Conformity Aspects of the Peer Culture

From the preadolescent to the adolescent period of development, as the child's dependence on and stake in the effectiveness of the peer group increases, the latter's power to exact conformity is concomitantly enhanced (Campbell, 1964; Costanzo & Shaw, 1966).

This conformity assumes exaggerated patterns, particularly relative to conspicuous aspects of behavior, such as musical tastes, fashions, and fads (Littrell & Eicher, 1973; Mussen, Conger, & Kagan, 1974), to such an extent that for the adolescent there can be no stronger argument for having or doing a thing than that "all the others are doing it." Opinions, prejudices, beliefs, likes, and dislikes are also determined by the group, and boys or girls who differ are made to feel the force of group ostracism unless they have sufficient strength to gather their peers around them (Goodenough, 1945; Stone & Church, 1973). The adolescent turns increasingly toward agemate groups and sets. "Even though his parents be loved and valued, the result is reduced emphasis on parental capability and over-estimation of the worth of age-mate capacities . . ." (Sherif, 1968, p. 157).

The tendency to conform to group opinion is greater the more attractive group membership is perceived to be (Kinoshita, 1964). In general, particularly during the adolescent period, girls are more conforming than boys (Tuma & Livson, 1960). And, as one might anticipate from the data on authoritarianism, conforming tendencies are greater among lower-class (Tuma & Livson, 1960) and religious (Fisher, 1964) adolescents.

Devereaux (1970) in his review of several studies conducted over a period of ten years states that in several samples there is "class evidence that the most peer-oriented and gang-involved children tend to come from either high permissive or high punitive homes, and that adult-conforming children tend to come from homes with optimum combinations of adequate but not smothering support, firm but not rigid control, and moderate but not excessive punishment. . . . There was also evidence that these intermediate, moderate ranges of parental behavior are related to autonomy in children" (Devereaux, 1970, p. 132).

Conformity to group standards depends, for the most part, on "the internalization of shared expectations" and of a set of norms that the group members themselves help to formulate. Overt pressures and sheer physical force are relatively minor factors (Sherif & Sherif, 1964).

> The group norms that are most binding and most consequential in the members' scheme of concerns are the ones that regulate matters of solidarity among members and that set standards of conduct in the very spheres of motivational promptings that bring them together. . . . The most tightly knit groups observed are those whose members [have] fewest stable ties with other groups and institutions, hence whose belonging [is] highly important to them (Sherif & Sherif, 1964, pp. 250, 268).

Group solidarity is, therefore, highest in low-rank neighborhoods. In all groups, however, the range of acceptable behavior exhibits least latitude for the leader and high-status members. "In matters related to the maintenance of group activities and of loyalty, the leader is expected to be the exemplar" (Sherif & Sherif, 1964, p. 179).

It is necessary, for two important reasons, that the peer group demand considerable conformity from its members. First, no institution, especially if it has status-giving functions, can exist for any length of time without due regard by its members for uniform, regular, and predictable adherence to a set of avowed values and traditions. Hence, in its efforts to establish a new and distinctive subculture and to evolve a unique set of criteria for the determination of status and prestige, the peer group must do everything in its power to set itself off as recognizably distinct and separate from the adult society that refuses it membership. If this distinctiveness is to be actually attained, widespread nonconformity obviously cannot be tolerated.

Second, conformity is also essential to maintain the group solidarity that is necessary to offer effective and organized resistance to the encroachments of adult authority. If an appeal to precedent or to a prevailing standard of adolescent behavior is to be the basis for exacting privileges and concessions from adults, a solid and united front with a minimum of deviancy must be presented to the world.

Because of the adolescent's marginality of status, the peer group is in an excellent position to demand conformity from him or her as the price of its acceptance. Much more so than children or adults, adolescents are desperately dependent on the peer group for whatever status and security they are able to achieve during these hectic years of transition. The group implicitly and explicitly makes clear that it expects conformity to its standards, interests, activities, and value systems in return for the moral support, the feeling of belongingness, the attributed status, and the opportunities for earned status that it extends. Adolescents in turn, like any people with marginal status, are excessively sensitive to the threat of forfeiting what little status they enjoy as a result of incurring the disapproval of those on whom they are dependent. Thus, to allay the anxiety from the threat of disapproval, they tend to conform more than is objectively necessary to retain group acceptance or to avoid censure and reprisal.

After adolescents win an assured place in the group, still other factors reinforce conforming tendencies. They learn that group approval brings a welcome reprieve from anxiety and uncertainty. If the group approves, these individuals can feel absolutely certain of the correctness of their position. Feelings of loyalty, belongingness, and indebtedness also influence conformity to be rendered automatically as a voluntarily assumed obligation. Finally, if these implicit group pressures and internalized restraints and dispositions are insufficient to keep an individual in line, explicit sanctions are imposed. Depending on the seriousness of the offense and the functions and nature of the group, the punishment may vary from ridicule, censure, and rebuff to physical chastisement and complete ostracism.

It is clear, therefore, that the marginality of adolescent status makes teen-agers prone to overvalue the importance of conformity and to exaggerate the degree of conformity required for acceptance by the peer group. Sociometric studies show that adolescents consistently *overestimate* the status of popular individuals and correspondingly *underestimate* the extent to which deviant or low-prestige persons are accepted by the group (Ausubel, 1955). Some evidence also points to the conclusion that apparent disregard for the group's approval tends to enhance an individual's sociometric status by making him or her appear above the need for currying favor with others (Newstetter, Feldstein, & Newcomb, 1938). Hence many perfectly safe opportunities for the expression of individuality are lost.

In the light of the structural properties of their peer group and of prevailing overconforming trends in the culture at large, it is small wonder that American adolescents tend to overvalue conformity and expediency and to avoid independent thinking and ideological commitment. In the adolescent peer culture of Prairie City, Havighurst and Taba (1949, p. 87) found that "accepting familiar stereotypes was one outstanding characteristic of most beliefs. . . . Individual positions deviating from the generally accepted code [were] feared and shunned. This was shown by hesitancy in expressing opinions contrary to common beliefs, and by approving wrong behavior if most of one's associates [were] involved in the act. There [was] a marked tendency to subordinate individually held positions to both adult and peer-group opinion even when one's own positions [were] considered morally right."

Other expressions of these same conforming tendencies include the approved attitude of "coolness" toward, and emotional detachment from, moral and controversial issues, and the low status accorded intellectuality and intellectual status in most peer groups. During the 1960s and early 1970s, however, many adolescents deviated from the norm of the culture at large and from many agemates by engaging in antiwar and civil rights movements.

### Qualifications and Positive Aspects

Lest we tend to take too dim a view of the seemingly negative features of adolescent conformity, it is important that we now consider some of the more positive aspects of this phenomenon. The transfer of allegiances from parental to peer-group standards constitutes more than an exchange of one type of slavish conformity for another. By providing a new source of values and standards, as well as experience in behaving as a sovereign person, the peer group plays an important role in devaluing parents and promoting desatellization.

In switching their basic loyalties to the peer group, adolescents take great strides toward emancipation. They find a new source of basic security to supplant the emotional anchorage to parents that had hitherto kept them confined within the dependent walls of childhood. By vesting in his peers the authority to set standards, one affirms one's *own* right to self-determination since one is patently no different from them. No longer need one implicitly subscribe to the belief that only parents and adults can determine what is right. The peer group also serves as "a bulwark of strength in combating authority. . . . By pooling their resistance in groups and throwing up barriers of one kind or another against adult . . . interference," adolescents manage to "exclude adults and protect themselves from . . . the coercions that [adults] are prone to use" (Tryon, 1944, p. 220).

The peer group's desatellizing influence also carries over into the sphere of ideas and moral values. Its norms provide the adolescent with a new and stable frame of reference for moral judgment and conduct. It furnishes relief from uncertainty, indecision, guilt, and anxiety about proper ways of thinking, feeling, and behaving. Because the peer group is never dignified by the same halo of sanctity surrounding parents, adolescents can experiment more freely with functional concepts of moral law and with a more impersonal and logical approach to value judgments. To be sure, full exploitation of this new active, independent, and critical approach to moral values is obviously limited by their marginal status and their need to conform to peer-group norms. The difference, however, is that now they conform to external standards because they consciously recognize the *expediency* of so doing rather than because they *implicitly* accept their validity.

Finally, the dreary picture of adolescent conformity must be qualified by certain limiting factors. In the first place, its existence tends to be restricted to the particular developmental requirements of the adolescent period that induce it. One of the surest signs of approaching adulthood is a resurgence in the legitimacy of deviancy. Second, along with their conforming tendencies adolescents display a "concomitant urge to be unique, to achieve individuality and 'separateness.' After the young adolescent has submerged himself in the group to the point where he cannot be criticized for nonformity, he . . . then proceeds to gain recognition for himself as an individual" (Tryon, 1944, p. 223). Adolescents must be careful, however, to keep their urge for uniqueness and creativity within the narrow framework of acceptability recognized by the group.

Finally, as we know from the history of innumerable youth movements, there is among many adolescents a vigorous strain of exuberant idealism and impatient dissatisfaction with many outmoded traditions and features of contemporary life. For example, this was reflected in dramatic ways by student activism in the 1960s. The war in Indo-China, with its accompanying draft, along with the dehumanizing pressures of a highly technological society, turned students into an independent political force. In addition, civil rights organizations in the early 1960s crystallized community action in the latter part of the decade and engaged the participation of youth. Critical of the values of a technological society, students created new lifestyles (for example, preindustrial life became fashionable); they affirmed the rights of each individual over utilitarian goals and technological efficiency (Light & Laufer, 1975); and they substituted self-fulfillment in place of a professional career. This aspect of adolescent personality, when channeled intelligently, constitutes a most strategic means for effecting social change.

*Conformity and Individuality: A Prescription for Adolescents*

Where do all of these developmental and cultural considerations regarding conformity and individuality leave us in proposing a feasible and morally defensible prescription for adolescents?

The crucial role of the peer group as a socializing agency and as a source of earned and attributed status counsels a certain minimal degree of deference to its standards during the self-limited period when such an exaggerated premium is placed on the value of conformity. During adolescence deviants are not in an enviable position. In varying degrees they all face social ridicule, abuse, and isolation. The fortunate ones achieve some measure of status and security by forming warm attachments to agemates of their own kind. Sometimes a sympathetic adult friend or teacher will offer them affection, direction, and encouragement. Often, however, they are left to flounder uncertainly, to drift further and further away from group living, to develop feelings of anxiety and inferiority, and to withdraw deeper and deeper into themselves or into a compensatory world of unreality.

As far as the wider community is concerned, the adolescent should be encouraged to adjust satisfactorily to the kind of world that currently exists, "not the kind adults wish existed but as yet have been unable to create. . . . Even while endeavoring to change them it is necessary to recognize established laws and customs, irrational or otherwise" (Partridge, 1947). This does not imply that the status quo must be implicitly accepted for what it is, but rather that a mature attitude toward social change be adopted, an attitude that does not "encourage the adolescent to batter his head against the wall of custom simply because these customs are inconsistent."

However, this minimal and desirable degree of conformity to peer-group standards and social custom is still a far cry from advocating a policy of "hunting with the hounds." Those who counsel adolescents would be remiss in their responsibility if they failed to appreciate the importance of nonconformity for the optimal differentiation of personality structure, for self-realization, and for the development of moral courage and the ability to stand alone without group support.

Counselors must also be sensitive to individual differences in the need to conform. Highly self-assertive teenagers, for example, can only restrain their individuality to a point, and introverts inevitably draw a line beyond which they refuse to participate in out-of-bounds behavior. Adolescents who have a highly developed set of moral or religious convictions may refuse to condone the practices of their group. Other individuals may have all-absorbing interests that are regarded with scorn by their agemates. Finally, as has already been pointed out, the mental hygiene dangers of nonconformity and social unpopularity have been vastly exaggerated. Even the peer group tolerates much more deviancy than the adolescent's anxiety and marginality of status lead him or her to believe.

## Adult versus Peer Group Norms

It is impossible for anyone to teach in a secondary school or college for any length of time without becoming aware of the fact that a distinct adolescent subculture exists, and that the values of this subculture are partly at variance with those of the adult community. This alienation is a source of concern for the school because it extends beyond such peripheral matters as dress and language and tends to be focused on the value of academic achievement. Adolescents accept scholastic achievement as necessary for college entrance and for the middle-class rewards of managerial and professional status, but they do not typically regard it as a legitimate basis for high status in the peer group or as a value worth striving for in its own right (Coleman, 1961; Marks, 1954). What are some of the origins of this adult-youth alienation?

Adolescents in our culture naturally have the same needs for greater earned status and volitional independence that adolescents have in more primitive and traditional cultures. But the greater complexity of our technological society necessitates an extended period of education and economic dependence on parents, prolonged vocational training, and the postponement of marriage well beyond the age of sexual maturity.

In recent years, increased technology has demanded an even longer period of preparation for the world of work, such as continuing education and postgraduate schooling. Under these circumstances, adolescents cannot experience any real volitional independence in the adult sense of the term and can obviously acquire only a token earned status outside the mainstream of the adult culture. They not only resent their exclusion from adult spheres of independence and status-giving activities, but also tend to resent such adult-controlled training institutions as the home, the school, and various youth organizations. The reason stems from the fact that these institutions conduct their training functions entirely apart from any opportunity for adolescents to exercise volitional independence or to acquire earned status within the context of the adult culture. Hence they are alienated from adult status-giving activities and from adult training institutions, and, accordingly, from adult standards as well.

This alienation from adult society, coupled with the accompanying resentment and prolonged frustration of their needs for adult volitional independence and adult earned status, has two serious consequences, namely, the generation of aggressive antiadult attitudes and the compensatory formulation of distinctive peer groups with distinctive standards, status-giving activities, and training functions of their own. The aggressive antiadult orientation not only promotes further retaliatory rejection of adult standards but also makes it more difficult for adolescents to identify with adults, to obtain any attributed status from such identification, and to accept adult values. The formation of peer groups, on the other hand, increases the existing adult-youth alienation. Precisely how it does these things deserves more detailed scrutiny.

### The Role of the Peer Group in Adult-Youth Alienation

All adolescents are in the same boat, so to speak. They share the same deprivation of their needs for adult status and independence, the same alienation from adult society, the same resentments, and the same antiadult attitudes. They may feel they are not wanted, do not belong, and are excluded from the larger scheme of things. Hence they reach out toward each other for mutual support and for providing in concert the things that they want but cannot get *individually* (Sherif & Sherif, 1964).

Thus, since the modern urban community is unable to provide youth with the kind of earned status, volitional independence, and training in social skills that they desire, the adolescent peer group is constituted to gratify, in part, these crucial needs. It is the only cultural institution in which their position is not marginal, in which they are offered earned status, independence, and social identity among a group of equals, and in which their *own* activities and concerns reign supreme.

The peer group is also the major training institution for adolescents in our society. It is in the peer group that "by *doing* they learn about the social processes of our culture. They clarify their sex roles by acting and being responded to; they learn competition, cooperation, social skills, values, and purposes by sharing the common life" (Tryon, 1944). The peer group provides regularized media and occasions for adolescents to gratify their newly acquired desires for increased social contact with the opposite sex, as well as a set of norms governing adolescent sex behavior.

By virtue of performing these essential functions, the peer group also displaces parents as the major source of attributed status during adolescence. By identifying with and acquiring acceptance in the group, by subordinating themselves to group interests, and by making themselves dependent on group approval, adolescents gain a measure of intrinsic self-esteem that is independent of their achievement or relative status in the group. This "we-feeling" furnishes security and belongingness, and is a powerful ego support and basis of loyalty to group norms.

How does all of this increase adult-youth alienation? In the first place, the very fact of membership in a distinctive peer group, with its own status-giving activities, standards, and training functions, puts adolescents in a *separate* subculture apart from adult society. Second, since the peer group is composed of *their* kind of people, and since they are largely dependent on it for their volitional independence, earned and attributed status, sense of belongingness, and opportunities to acquire social skills and practice their sex roles, adolescents accordingly tend to assimilate the group's standards. As they become progressively more responsive to group approval and disapproval, they become increasingly more indifferent to adult norms and values, to adult suggestion, and to adult approval and disapproval. Finally, the peer group's exaggerated needs for rigid conformity to its norms, as well as its power to exact conformity from its members, in return for its unique ability to satisfy their needs, further accentuate the adolescents' alienation from adult society.

But adult-youth alienation is also not an all-or-none matter. That is, operating simultaneously with the various factors causing adult-youth alienation in varying degrees, there are also two general factors within each adolescent that maintain or increase his or her identification with adult society. One of these factors stems from ultimate aspirations for the future; the other is a legacy from childhood. Both serve to counteract the severity of antiadult attitudes.

Thus we must not lose sight of the fact that at the same time adolescents, particularly those from middle-class backgrounds, are alienated from adult standards and preoccupied with achieving *vicarious* forms of adult status and independence in the peer group, they are *simultaneously* engaged in, and intensely concerned with, educational and other pursuits that serve as steppingstones to *genuine* adult status and independence and to full membership in adult society.

They know that their *ultimate* goal is not high status in the peer group but rather attainment of economic security. They realize that this attainment requires long-term striving, self-denial, postponement of immediate hedonistic gratifications, the approval of persons in authority, restraint of aggressive impulses, and avoidance of an unsavory or delinquent reputation. Furthermore, the assimilation of new peer-group values does not by any means imply complete repudiation of previously assimilated adult values.

Many middle-class adolescents today appear to have rejected the materialistic rewards of middle-class status because their elders have seemingly betrayed the underlying values (such as competence, hard work, self-fulfillment, moral uprightness, responsibility) leading to these rewards. In the process many adolescents coming from conservative families have also rejected the underlying values and have become hippies, while youngsters of liberal parents often found expression in the student activist movements (Light & Laufer, 1975). Although students of the 1970s are still concerned about these issues, their main focus is related to the uncertainty and outcome of their schooling and the possibility of obtaining a job.

Thus it greatly overstates the case to claim that adolescents are entirely oblivious of adult approval, that they completely reject adult values, standards, and aspirations, and that they manifest no feelings of moral obligation to abide by earlier assimilated norms of conduct. This much is clearly evident when we pause to consider that one of the principal functions of the peer group, in addition to providing its own distinctive set of standards, is to transmit from one generation to the next the appropriate social-class values, aspirations, motivational patterns, and character traits that adolescents are often unwilling to accept from parents and teachers, but *are* willing to accept from their agemates. It is easy, therefore, to exaggerate the existing degree of adult-youth alienation. As a matter of fact, both parties tend to perceive it as greater than it actually is (Hess & Goldblatt, 1957). Indeed, where conditions are propitious, the norms of the peer group include the same intellectual concerns and excitement that prevail among the college faculty (Newcomb, 1962).

It must be admitted, however, that the progressive moral deterioration characterizing our culture since World War II has tended to undermine the counterbalancing effect of these two factors (aspirations for genuine adult status and previously assimilated adult values) on adult-youth alienation. First, since adolescents perceive adults as being able to "get ahead" without fully exemplifying the traditional middle-class virtues, they naturally are led to believe that (1) they too can achieve the adult status and independence they crave without thoroughly acquiring these same virtues and (2) adults are not really concerned whether or not adolescents acquire these virtues. Thus, they are not as highly motivated as pre-World War II adolescents were either to develop such traits as self-restraint, willingness to work hard, a sense of responsibility, impulse control, self-denial, personal integrity, and respect for the rights and property of others, or to seek adult approval for so doing. Further, the middle-class peer group, which has the responsibility for transmitting middle-class standards to its members, can transmit only those adult standards that *actually* exist.

Second, the realization that adults do not actually live up to the standards that adolescents had implicitly accepted in childhood as axiomatically right and proper tends to undermine implicit belief in these standards and feelings of obligation to abide by them. When children become sufficiently mature to interpret adult behavior for what it actually is, they are impressed more by example than by precept.

Finally, the awareness of the grievous lack of moral courage in the adult world and of the premium that adults place on conformity and expediency furnishes adolescents with a very poor model for holding fast to their moral convictions in the face of group pressure.

## Social Sex Role and the School

The quite different social sex roles of boys and girls at all age levels have important effects on their respective adaptations to the school environment. By virtue of their differential training in the home, girls find it much easier than boys to adjust to the demands of elementary school. We have already observed that they are more intrinsically accepted by parents;

satellize more; identify more strongly with authority figures; have less insistent needs for independence, earned status, and emancipation from the home. Moreover, they are more habituated from the very beginning to docility, sedateness, conformity to social expectations, and restraint of overt physical aggression. It is hardly surprising, therefore, that boys find it correspondingly more difficult to identify with the school, with the teacher, and with classroom activities. Girls play "school" as readily as they play "house," whereas any normally robust boy would not be caught dead playing either game. Because of attitudinal changes associated with the current more militant feminist movement, however, these differences in social sex role are obviously diminishing.

It is not only that most elementary-school teachers are women, but also that feminine values prevail in the school with respect to what is taught and the kind of behavior that is expected and approved: propriety, obedience, decorum, cleanliness, tidiness, submissiveness, modesty, paying attention to what one is told, remembering, facility in handling verbal symbols, and the control of fidgetiness, curiosity, and aggressiveness. Girls also receive much more approval and considerably less scolding and reproval from teachers (Meyer & Thompson, 1956).

In terms of cultural expectations and peer-group norms, success in school is much more appropriate for the female than for the male sex role in elementary and junior high school. At this age level the higher achievement motivation of girls is largely a reflection of their greater desire for approval from authority figures and for the vicarious status that this confers. It is not at all surprising, therefore, that boys furnish a disproportionate share of the nonreaders, the underachievers, the truants, the behavior problems, the inattentive, and the dropouts.

Beginning in middle adolescence, however, cultural expectations change radically. Academic achievement becomes a more acceptable male virtue and, accordingly, the achievement gap between boys and girls begins to close. In a review of research on sex differences, Maccoby and Jacklin (1974) indicate that at about the age of 12 or 13, boys increase faster in mathematical skills than do girls. Boys with low intrinsic self-esteem and high anxiety seek more than do their female counterparts to find compensatory ego enhancement and anxiety reduction in school achievement, and gifted boys tend to maintain their high IQs better in late adolescence and adulthood.

Although girls show higher achievement in the elementary grades, they too are affected by sex-role stereotyping (Sadker & Sadker, 1972). On the one hand, school rewards feminine values but it also teaches girls about female subservience. For example, in an analysis of books for kindergarten through third grade, DeCrow (1972) found that many textbooks did not portray women outside the home, with the exception of nurses or teachers.

Girls are often depicted as fearful and dependent, whereas boys show initiative and dominance.

This form of sex bias is directly seen in the school, since elementary-school teachers are mostly female while approximately 80 percent of the principals are male (Lyon & Saario, 1973). Although males and females are similar in their intellectual potential and achievement motivation during the school years, female achievement in other than domestic areas diminishes after formal schooling (Maccoby & Jacklin, 1974). Followers of the women's liberation movement are concerned that sex typing and sex bias are damaging for both boys and girls, but especially so for girls. The current trend of changing social roles for women should lead to higher aspirations for advanced educational and professional goals.

## Social-Class Stratification and Education

The social-class membership of a pupil has important implications for his or her school achievement, aspirations for academic success, achievement motivation, and attitudes toward school. It is true, however, that social-class differences in these areas are becoming increasingly less distinct now that college education is becoming more available to and prevalent among lower-class groups (Havighurst & Neugarten, 1962). Nevertheless, there is still a moderately high relationship between socioeconomic status and school achievement (Havighurst & Breese, 1947; Havighurst & Janke, 1944; Janke & Havighurst, 1945; Pierce-Jones, 1959a, 1959b). By the time pupils reach junior-high-school age this relationship is greater than that between IQ and achievement (Kahl, 1957).

But it is important to note that the characteristic impact of social-class membership on school achievement does *not* prevail among high-ability sixth-graders (Curry, 1962), after students enter college (Washburne, 1959), or in upwardly mobile populations (Udry, 1960). Apparently the limiting effects of social class conditioning cease to operate as fully beyond certain critical ability and achievement levels. Once students exceed these levels, they seem to be influenced more by the new student subculture with which they identify than by their social-class origins.

Evidence from a nationwide survey of educational opportunity (Coleman et al., 1966) indicates a strong relationship between a student's achievement and the aspirations and educational background of other pupils in the school. Thus if a student from a minority background attends a school with classmates who come from homes that are supportive of education, his or her achievement will probably increase.

Research (Ausubel, 1965d; Hanson, 1965; Sherif & Sherif, 1964) has made it clear that young people of all socioeconomic ranks have assimilated the scholastic and vocational aspirations associated with material affluence in modern Western society. It is not the appropriate aspirations that are lacking, therefore, but rather those factors that are necessary for their implementation, namely, underlying needs and motivations for achievement, supportive personality traits, and perceived pressures and opportunities for academic and occupational success (Ausubel, 1965d; Rosen, 1964). In the first place, lower-class parents do not place the same value that middle-class parents do on education, financial independence, social recognition, and vocational success (Hess; 1970). Hence they do not really encourage to the same extent the implementation of these aspirations by voicing appropriate expectations, making unequivocal demands, dispensing suitable rewards and punishments, and insisting on the development of the necessary supportive traits (Ausubel, 1965d).

Second, lower-class adolescents are understandably dubious about the attainability of the promised rewards of striving and self-denial for persons of their status. Hence they do not develop the same internalized needs for vocational achievement and prestige. They see less point in developing, to the same degree as their middle-class contemporaries, the supportive middle-class personality traits necessary for the achievement of academic and vocational success (Davis, 1943). These supportive traits include habits of initiative and responsibility and the "deferred gratification pattern" of hard work, renunciation of immediate pleasures, long-range striving, impulse control, thrift, orderliness, punctuality, restraint of sexual and aggressive urges, and willingness to undergo prolonged vocational preparation (Davis, 1943; Havighurst & Taba, 1949; Schneider & Lysgaard, 1953).

It is hardly surprising, therefore, that lower-class children are less interested in reading than are middle-class children. Moreover, they take their schoolwork less seriously and are less willing to spend the years of their youth in school in order to gain higher prestige and social rewards as adults. Lacking the positive orientation that middle-class pupils bring to schoolwork, which preserves the attractiveness of academic tasks despite failure experience, they more quickly lose interest in school if they are unsuccessful.

Lower- and middle-class adolescents differ both in their social-value systems and in their vocational interests. Middle-class youths and their parents are more concerned with community service, self-realization, altruistic values, and internalized standards of conduct (Kahn, 1959; Stefflre, 1959). They prefer demanding, responsible, and prestigeful occupational pursuits (Pierce-Jones, 1959a, 1959b; Sewell, Haller, & Strauss, 1957). They also make higher vocational interest scores in the literary, esthetic, persuasive, scientific, and business areas than do lower-class adolescents.

The latter adolescents and their parents, on the other hand, place greater stress on such values as money, security, respectability, obedience, and conformity to authority, and tend to prefer agricultural, mechanical, domestic service, and clerical pursuits. In the school environment they respond more than middle-class pupils do to such learning incentives as praise and material rewards (Terrell, Durkin, & Wiesley, 1959; Zigler & de Labry, 1965; Zigler & Kanzer, 1962).

The working-class mother's desire for unquestioned domination of her offspring, her preference for harsh, punitive, and suppressive forms of control, and her tendency to maintain considerable social and emotional distance between herself and her children are probably responsible, in part, for the greater prevalence of the authoritarian personality syndrome in lower- than in middle-class children (Dickens & Hobart, 1959; Hart, 1957; Lipset, 1959). "The lower-class father tends to equate respect from children with their compliance and obedience to his wishes and commands" (Hess, 1970, p. 467).

Lower-class children tend to develop ambivalent attitudes toward authority figures and to cope with this ambivalence by making an exaggerated show of overt, implicit compliance, by maintaining formally appropriate social distance, and by interacting with these figures on the basis of formalized role attributes rather than as persons. Their underlying hostility and resentment toward this arbitrary and often unfair authority is later expressed in such displaced forms as scapegoating, prejudice, extremist political and religious behavior, ethnocentrism, and delinquency (Dickens & Hobart, 1959; Hart, 1957; Lipset, 1959). They are coerced in school by the norms of their peer group against accepting the authority of, and seeking the approval of, or entering into a satellizing relationship with the teacher.

Although adaptive characteristics of lower-class families remain distinct, middle-class and lower-class differences have diminished in some respects. The disillusionment with middle-class materialism, with the adaptive behavior of the "organization man," and in general with what appeared to be hypocritical adult behavior led youth in the 1960s to a reexamination of professed and practiced values. The result was a downward movement in class values and mores, particularly in regard to sex, manners, speech, and in attitudes toward school and work. Nonetheless, members of the middle class are in a better position to see the adaptive value of high aspirations for earned status, particularly in a society where educational achievement is necessitated by the demands of technological advancement and also serves as a means of control in the struggle between status groups (Collins, 1971).

### Social-Class Bias of the School

Most teachers in American schools have middle-class backgrounds, although there is currently some infusion of lower-class members and individuals from black and Puerto Rican backgrounds. But even if teachers do originate from other social-class environments, they tend to identify with the school's implicit mission of encouraging the development of middle-class values. Thus, quite apart from the issue of whether this mission is appropriate and desirable for our culture, teachers find it difficult to understand the goals, values, and behavior of pupils from other social-class backgrounds. Normal ethnocentric bias predisposes them to believe that their own class values are self-evidently true and proper and that deviations therefrom necessarily reflect waywardness.

On the other hand, since middle-class boys and girls behave in accordance with their expectations and accept the standards of the school, teachers are usually as prejudiced in their favor as they are prejudiced against children from other social strata. This tendency is further complicated by the growing trend toward school segregation between central city and suburb, causing a changing population in schools (Coleman, 1975). The majority of high schools are no longer heterogeneous, with middle-class students exerting dominant control. Most inner-city schools are composed of lower-class and minority students, whereas the greater number of their teachers have middle-class origins or outlook.

Understanding the background and values of lower-class children does not, of course, imply acceptance of their attitudes and behavior when these are in conflict with the objectives and standards of the school. It merely implies sufficient awareness of relevant socioeconomic background factors to make possible intelligent interpretation of the behavior of lower-class pupils and the avoidance of discriminatory attitudes and practices toward them.

The organization of the school in general is apt to favor middle-class behavior and penalize lower-class children. In the high-school situation, there is a tendency to favor the retention of middle-class pupils and the earlier dropping out of lower-class pupils. A disproportionate number of the latter are placed in slow-learning sections—not only on the basis of low ability and motivation but also, more informally, because of their social background (Havighurst & Neugarten, 1962; Hollingshead, 1949). Similarly, a disproportionate percentage of lower-class pupils are found in the vocational, commercial, and general high-school curriculums rather than in the college preparatory curriculum. Thus, as a result of being typed and stigmatized as members of these low-prestige groups and of enjoying relatively low scholastic morale, lower-class pupils are more disposed to drop out of school. Many urban schools, however, have specialized programs, sponsored by the United States Office of Education, to identify dropouts in order to persuade them back to school and to help lower-class students who have college potential.

The values of the dominant peer group in heterogeneous high schools are predominantly based upon middle-class norms and standards, chief of which is acceptance of the importance of getting good grades (Havighurst & Taba, 1949; Hollingshead, 1949; H. P. Smith, 1945), and evidence suggests that pupils whose behavior conforms best to the extracurricular norms and expectations of the school also do better academically (Weinberg, 1964). More important perhaps are the subtle and intangible barriers to participation in the more intimate crowds and cliques; very little crossing of social-class lines occurs in clique organization (Hollingshead, 1949). Boys and girls from lower social-class strata bitterly resent the patronizing and condescending attitudes of their more fortunate contemporaries. They feel snubbed, unwanted, and left out of things. When their situation becomes too intolerable, they often decide to leave school (Havighurst & Taba, 1949; Johnson & Legg, 1944).

## Racial Factors in Education

All of the foregoing properties of the lower-class environment also apply to the segregated black community. In spite of differential involvement in the economic structure on the part of black Americans, producing a diversity in ways of life among them, it is important to recognize that growing up black transcends status and class ranks (Deutsch, 1973; Ladner, 1971). "A disproportionate number of blacks are unemployed and poor even though there are many who are in the middle and working classes. Very few are in the upper classes. None is a member of the corporate rich. . . . Most remain in the low-income ghetto communities" (Wilkinson, 1975, p. 288). In addition, black families are characterized by a disproportionate number of illegal and loosely connected unions (M. C. Hill, 1957). Illegitimacy is very common, and it carries relatively little social stigma in the black community (Cavan, 1959).

Black families are much more unstable than comparable lower-class white families. Broken homes are even more common among black families than among white families. Fathers are more frequently absent, and a matriarchal and negative family atmosphere more commonly prevails (Dai, 1949; Deutsch, 1967; Gordon & Shea, 1967; Moynihan, 1965; Rainwater, 1966). Thus lower-class black children are frequently denied the benefits of biparental affection and upbringing. They are often raised by a grandmother or older sister while the mother works to support the family deserted by the father. One consequence of the matriarchal family climate is an open preference for girls. When compared with black children with intact families, father-absent black children feel more victimized and feel they have less control of their environment (Pettigrew, 1964).

Black family life is even more authoritarian in nature than is that of the lower social class generally. "Children are expected to be obedient and submissive" (M. C. Hill, 1957), and insubordination is suppressed by harsh and often brutal physical punishment (Dai, 1949; M. C. Hill, 1957). "Southern black culture teaches obedience and respect for authority as a mainspring of survival" (Greenberg & Fane, 1959). Surveys of high-school and college students show that authoritarian attitudes are more prevalent among blacks at all grade levels (Greenberg, Chase, & Cannon, 1957; Greenberg & Fane, 1959; C. U. Smith & Prothro, 1957).

Being black also has many other implications for the ego development of young children and adolescents that are not inherent in lower-class membership. Black children inherit an inferior caste status and almost inevitably acquire the negative self-esteem that is a realistic ego reflection of such status. Through personal slights, blocked opportunities, and unpleasant contacts with white persons and with institutionalized symbols of race inferiority (such as segregated schools and neighborhoods) they gradually become aware of the social significance of racial membership (Goff, 1949).

In addition to suffering ego deflation through awareness of their inferior status in society, black children find it more difficult to satellize and are denied much of the self-esteem advantages of satellization. The derived status that is the principal source of children's self-esteem in all cultures is largely discounted in their case since they can satellize only in relation to superordinate individuals or groups who themselves possess an inferior and culturally denigrated status. Satellization under such conditions not only confers a very limited amount of derived status but also has deflationary implications for self-esteem.

We can understand, therefore, why young black children resist identifying with their own racial group, why they seek to shed their identities (Deutsch, 1967), why they more frequently choose white than black playmates (Stevenson & Stewart, 1958), why they prefer the skin color of the culturally dominant caste (Clark & Clark, 1947; Goodman, 1952), and why they tend to assign negative roles to children of their own race (Stevenson & Stewart, 1958). Such tendencies persist at least into late adolescence and early adult life.

Several studies in the late 1960s and early 1970s yielded similar results but to a lesser degree, with some black children showing own-race acceptance and preference. Durrett and Davey (1970), after examining the research, concluded that there has been a decrease in own-race rejection by black children. These characteristic ways of adjusting have been mitigated in recent years by such movements as black militancy, black separatism, and black civil rights.

It is important to note that blacks do not represent a monolithic group. In spite of the fact that they all experience the impact of a color-based system, the variations in economic, educational, and occupational status of families breed differential aspirations, values, choices of models, and goals in life. Within the past two decades, changing social and political conditions brought alterations in role conceptions and increased political consciousness among blacks (Frazier, 1967; Wilkinson, 1975). The 1960s transformed the earlier passive resignation and placatory attitudes to a redefinition of self-conceptions and identities exemplified by the slogan "Black is Beautiful." Color distinctions, however, still affect their lives. In addition, many youths, like their elders, have assimilated the biases of the dominant group with respect to imputing cultural and intellectual significance to color (Wilkinson, 1975).

### Educational Achievement of Black Children

Partly as a result of unequal educational opportunities, black children show serious academic retardation. They attend school for fewer years and, on the average, learn much less than white children do (Ashmore, 1954; Bullock, 1950; Cooper, 1964; Osborne, 1960). On tests measuring scholastic achievement, blacks score significantly below the average for whites and Orientals. American Indians, Puerto Ricans, and Mexican-Americans score below whites but above blacks (Coleman et al., 1966). The inequality of educational facilities exists not only in the South but also in the urban North, where de facto segregation largely prevails (Pettigrew & Green, 1976; Smuts, 1957).

Some extremist black authorities relate the academic retardation of black students directly to the inferiority of black schools. Clark (1965), for example, states that there would be minimal differences in achievement between white and black students if schools in depressed areas had more effective teachers and greater educational resources. This factor, however, is not only a gross overstatement but also is not mutually preclusive with the effects of a culturally disadvantaged home. He further indicates that teachers have a negative attitude toward, and low expectations of, the educability of black disadvantaged students. In line with this contention, Rosenthal and Jacobson (1968) reported that a teacher's expectations of a student's abilities are communicated to the student in such a way as to elicit in part the expected performance. This issue, however, has aroused controversy and criticism (Snow, 1969; R. L. Thorndike, 1968) indicating a need for further research.

Even more important, perhaps, as a cause of black educational retardation is the situation prevailing in the black home. Many parents have had little schooling themselves and hence are unable to appreciate its value. Thus they do not provide active, wholehearted support for high-level academic performance by demanding conscientious study and regular attendance from their children. Furthermore, because of their large families and their own meager schooling, they are unable to provide help with lessons.

Keeping a large family of children in secondary school constitutes a heavy economic burden on black parents in view of their low per capita income and the substantial hidden costs of "free" education. The greater frequency of broken homes, unemployment, and negative family atmosphere, as well as the high rate of pupil turnover (Conant, 1961; Sexton, 1959), are also not conducive to academic achievement. In addition, the extreme intellectual impoverishment of the black home over and above its lower-social-class status reflects the nonstandard ("black") English spoken in the home and the general lack of books, magazines, and stimulating conversation.

### Educational and Vocational Aspirations

All of the factors inhibiting the development of achievement motivation and its supportive personality traits in lower-class children are intensified in segregated black children. Their overall prospects for vertical social mobility, though more restricted, are not completely hopeless. But the stigma of caste membership is inescapable and insurmountable. It is inherent in their skin color, permanently ingrained in their body image, and enforced by the extralegal power of a society whose moral, legal, and religious codes formally and proclaim their equality.

Rosen (1959) compared the educational and vocational aspirations of black boys (age 8–14) and their mothers to those of white Protestant Americans, French-Canadians, American Jews, Greek-Americans, and Italian-Americans. The mean vocational aspiration score of his black group was significantly lower than the mean scores of all other groups except the French-Canadian. Ethnicity was found to be more highly related to vocational aspirations than was social class; sizable ethnic and racial differences prevailed even when the influence of social class was controlled.

Other evidence (Hess, 1970) indicates that lower-class adolescents have higher vocational aspirations than expectations; they share the dominant values of the society but "stretch" them downward to suit their behavior, which is dictated by restricted resources. These results are consistent with the finding that white students tend to prefer "very interesting jobs," whereas black students are more concerned with job security (Singer & Stefflre, 1956).

Ellerbe (1975), reporting on more recent findings, states that career selection among black college students is changing only slightly. He cites results of the College Placement Council survey, which indicates that, for 1968–1970, "less than one percent are identified as having selected fields like medicine, dentistry, engineering and architecture. Most were in the field of education" (Ellerbe, 1975, p. 123).

Wilkinson (1975) points out that at the time of the Census Employment Survey, August 1970 through March 1971, the black youth population—16 to 24 years of age—represented nearly one-fourth of the total black population aged 16 and over in low-income areas. In October 1971 about 38 percent were unemployed, even though "significant numbers were seeking employment" (p. 288).

What is important to recognize here is that white youth of all ethnic groupings and in various socioeconomic groups never experience the culturally based handicaps and identity-negating philosophies which every black in the seventeen through twenty-four age range in America must face regardless of family social-class background. Some young blacks have expressed the view that within the economic system, they are no longer considered as instruments of production as they were during the era of slavery in America and the industrial explosion. They perceive themselves now as a stratum with a past—a heritage—which has left them outside the system of production and hence estranged from significant involvement in the economic arena. Employing a psychology of collective and defensive repudiation of a society which rejects them, many openly and actively oppose what they define as negative white patriarchal establishments and beliefs that not only deny them fair treatment and equal opportunities but inhibit their desire for self-expression and self-determination (Wilkinson, 1975, p. 289).

## Sex Differences

Girls in the segregated black community show much greater superiority over boys in academic, personal, and social adjustment than is found in the culture generally (Deutsch, 1967). They not only outperform boys academically by a greater margin, but also do so in all subjects rather than only in language skills (Deutsch, 1967). They have higher achievement needs (Gaier & Wamback, 1960; Grossack, 1957), have a greater span of attention, are more popular with classmates, show more mature and realistic aspirations, assume more responsible roles, and feel less depressed in comparing themselves with other children (Deutsch, 1967). The black female child is in many instances more assertive (Proshansky & Newton, 1968) and, when compared with white children of the same age, is less conforming to adult pressures (Iscoe, Williams, & Harvey, 1964).

Adequate reasons for these differences are not difficult to find. Black children in this subculture live in a matriarchal family atmosphere, where girls are openly preferred by mothers and grandmothers and where the male sex role is generally deprecated. The father frequently deserts the family and, in any case, tends to be an unreliable source of economic and emotional security (Dai, 1949; Deutsch, 1967). Hence, the mother, assisted perhaps by her mother or by a daughter, shoulders most of the burdens and responsibilities of child rearing and is the only dependable adult with whom the child can identfy. In this environment male chauvinism can obtain little foothold.

The preferential treatment accorded girls is even extended to opportunities for acquiring ultimate earned status. If the family pins all of its hopes on and makes desperate sacrifices for one child, it will often be a daughter in preference to a son. Even when the father is present, male identification suffers when the boy is faced with a role model while also confronted with an image of his future self (that is, his father) as an economically inadequate male (Gordon & Shea, 1967; Rainwater, 1966).

*Implications for Education*

Before blacks can assume their rightful place in a desegregated American culture, important changes in the ego structure of black children must first take place. They must shed feelings of inferiority and self-derogation, acquire feelings of self-confidence and racial pride, develop realistic aspirations for occupations requiring greater education and training, and develop the personality traits necessary for implementing these aspirations.

Such changes in ego structure can be accomplished in two different but complementary ways. First, all manifestations of the black's inferior and segregated caste status must be swept away—in education, housing, employment, religion, travel, and exercise of civil rights. This in itself will enhance the black's self-esteem and open new opportunities for self-fulfillment. Second, through various measures instituted in the family, school, and community, the black's character structure, levels of aspiration, and actual standards of achievement can be altered in ways that will further enhance his or her self-esteem and make it possible for the black individual to take advantage of new opportunities.

### Desegregation

Desegregation, of course, is no panacea for the black child's personality difficulties. In the first place, it tends to create new problems of adjustment, particularly when it follows in the wake of serious community conflict. Second, it cannot quickly overcome various long-standing handicaps that black children bring with them to school, "such as their cultural impoverishment, their helplessness or apathy toward learning, and their distrust of the majority group and their middle-class teachers." Nor can it compensate for "oversized classes, inappropriate curriculums, inadequate counseling services, or poorly trained or demoralized teachers" (Bernard, 1958, p. 158).

Yet, it is an important and indispensable first step in the reconstitution of the black personality, since the school is the most strategically placed social institution for effecting change both in ego structure and in social status. A desegregated school offers black children their first taste of social equality and their first experience of first-class citizenship. They can enjoy the stimulating effects of competition with white children and can use them as realistic yardsticks in measuring their own worth and chances for academic and vocational success. Under these circumstances, educational achievement no longer seems so pointless, and aspirations for higher occupational status in the wider culture acquire more substance.

It is also reasonable to anticipate that white children will be prejudiced and continue to discriminate against their black classmates long after desegregation accords them equal legal status in the educational system. Armor (1972) studied the effects of induced busing and desegregation in five northern cities. He reported on several studies that showed no conclusive evidence that integration had an effect on academic achievement. Bused students, however, were more likely to begin college than students who were in segregated schools. Integration increased racial consciousness and reduced opportunities for actual contact between racial groups (Armor, 1972). Furthermore, attitudes toward blacks in the South are remarkably stable, even in periods of rapid social change involving desegregation (Young, Benson, & Holtzman, 1960), and are not highly correlated with anti-Semitic or other ethnocentric trends (Greenberg et al., 1957; Kelly, Ferson, & Holtzman, 1958; Prothro, 1952).

Prejudice against blacks is deeply rooted in the American culture (Raab & Lipset, 1959) and is continually reinforced both by the socioeconomic gain and by the vicarious ego enhancement it brings to those who exhibit it (Bernard, 1958; Herr, 1959; Rosen, 1959). It is hardly surprising, therefore, that racial prejudice is most pronounced in lower-social-class groups (Westie, 1952) and that these groups constitute the hard core of resistance to desegregation (Killian & Haer, 1958; Tumin, 1958). Increased physical contact between white and black children does little to reduce prejudice (Armor, 1972; Webster, 1961), but more intimate personal interaction under favorable circumstances significantly reduces social distance between the two groups (Kelly et al., 1958; Mann, 1959; Yarrow, Campbell, & Yarrow, 1958).

### Community Action

The support of parents and of the black community at large must be enlisted if we hope to make permanent progress in the education of black children. This is the case because the character of the ghetto community largely determines what goes on in the slum school. It is therefore wholly unrealistic to contemplate significant change in the school achievement of black children without involving the black family and community (Conant, 1961).

> Whatever can be done to strengthen family life and to give the fathers a more important role in it will make a significant contribution to the development of Negro potential (Smuts, 1957, p. 462).

Working with mothers and getting them to adopt a more positive attitude toward school is an important first step in improving the educational achievement of urban black children (Conant, 1961). Enrollment of parents in adult education programs would significantly raise the cultural level of the black home and "stimulate an interest in newspapers, magazines and possibly even books. One of the troubles . . . is that when the children leave the school they never see anyone read anything—not even newspapers" (Conant, 1961, p. 25). It will also help parents to better prepare themselves for their present jobs and new work opportunities.

### Counseling

Because of current grave inadequacies in the structure of the lower-class urban black familiy, the school must be prepared to compensate, at least in part, for the deficiencies of the home; that is, it must be prepared to act, so to speak, for the parents. Teachers in predominantly black schools actually perform much of this role at the present time. In the lower grades, as a matter of fact, they are quite successful as mother surrogates. As black children approach adolescence, however, peer-group loyalties become ascendent over the affiliative drive for school achievement inspired by the substitute mother role of black teachers, and schoolwork progressively deteriorates (Conant, 1961).

It is apparent, therefore, that trained counselors must assume the role of parent substitutes during preadolescence and adolescence. They are needed to offer appropriate educational and vocational guidance, to encourage worthwhile and realistic aspirations, and to stimulate the development of mature personality traits. In view of the serious unemployment situation among black youth, they should also assist in job placement and in cushioning the transition between school and work. This will naturally require much expansion of existing guidance services in the school.

Research has shown that black children's distrust of white counselors and authority figures in general makes it extremely difficult for a white counselor to develop an interpersonal relationship with a black student such that the latter can gain appropriate insight into his problems. How can the counselor ever hope to view the personal or social worlds as his client does —as he must necessarily do if he wishes to be effective in the counseling situation—if a white person can only imagine but never really know how a black actually thinks and feels or how he perceives most personal and social problems? "The cultural lenses which are formulated from unique milieus are not as freely transferable as it is assumed, or as we are led to believe" (Phillips, 1959, p. 188).

## Motivating the Culturally Disadvantaged Pupil

We have already considered the cognitive characteristics of culturally disadvantaged pupils as well as various instructional measures that can be taken to prevent and ameliorate their educational retardation. In the present context, it is important to realize both that not all *lower-class* children are culturally disadvantaged and that cultural deprivation is not restricted to urban slum environments. Lower-class status is a necessary but not a sufficient condition for cultural deprivation. In addition, a culturally disadvantaged home is characterized by extreme intellectual impoverishment and by what Lewis (1961) calls the "culture of poverty." This implies more than economic impoverishment. It also includes attitudes of helplessness, dependency, and marginality, a highly depressed level of aspiration, and a feeling of alienation from the culture at large. Much lower-class black culture in the United States is representative of the culture of poverty. Other examples are found among migrant workers, Appalachian families, families for whom welfare is an established way of life, and families living in chronically depressed and relatively isolated rural areas.

It only remains in this section to examine some motivational considerations that apply to culturally disadvantaged pupils. The problem of reversibility is particularly salient here, inasmuch as the environment of cultural deprivation typically stunts not only intellectual development but also the development of appropriate motivations for academic achievement.

### Intrinsic Motivation[1]

The development of cognitive drive, or of intrinsic motivation for learning (for the acquisition of knowledge as an end in itself or for its own sake), is the most promising motivational strategy that can be adopted in relation to the culturally disadvantaged child. It is true, of course, in view of the anti-intellectualism and pragmatic attitude toward education that is characteristic of lower-class ideology, that a superficially better case can be made for the alternative strategy of appealing to the job acquisition, retention, and advancement incentives that now apply so saliently to continuing education because of the rapid rate of technological change. Actually, however, intrinsic motivation for learning is more potent, relevant, durable, and easier to arouse than its extrinsic counterpart.

Meaningful school learning, in contrast to most rote kinds of laboratory learning, requires relatively little effort or extrinsic incentive and, when successful, furnishes its own reward. In most instances of school learning, cognitive drive is also the only immediately *relevant* motivation, since the greater part of school learning cannot be rationalized as necessary for meeting the demands of daily living. Furthermore, it does not lose its relevancy or potency in later adult life when utilitarian and career-advancement considerations are no longer applicable.

In addition, as we know from the high dropout rate among culturally disadvantaged high-school youth, appeals to extrinsic motivation are frequently not very effective because of the prevailing social-class ideology. Among other reasons, this ideology reflects a limited time perspective focused primarily on the present, along with a character structure that is oriented toward immediate rather than delayed gratification of needs. Also present are a lack of personality traits necessary to implement high academic and vocational aspirations due to the absence of necessary family, peer-group, and community pressures and expectations and the seeming unreality and impossibility of attaining the rewards of prolonged striving and self-denial (in view of current living conditions and family circum-

[1] This and the following sections are based on Ausubel and Ausubel (1963).

stances, previous lack of school success, and the discriminatory attitudes of middle-class society).

It must be conceded at the outset that culturally disadvantaged children typically manifest little intrinsic motivation to learn. They come from family and cultural environments in which the veneration of learning for its own sake is not a conspicuous value and in which there is little or no tradition of scholarship. Moreover, they have *not* been notably successful in their previous learning efforts in school. Nevertheless, we need not necessarily despair of motivating them to learn for intrinsic reasons.

Psychologists have been emphasizing the motivation-learning and the interest-activity sequences of cause and effect for so long that they tend to overlook their reciprocal aspects. Since motivation is not an indispensable condition for short-term and limited-quantity learning, it is not necessary to postpone learning activities until pupils develop appropriate interests and motivations. Often, as pointed out above, the best way of motivating unmotivated pupils is temporarily to bypass the problem of motivation and to focus on the cognitive aspects of teaching. Much to their surprise and to their teacher's, these pupils will learn despite a lack of motivation; and from the satisfaction of learning, and thus satisfying latent cognitive drive, they will characteristically develop the motivation to learn more on the same basis.

Paradoxically, therefore, we may discover that the most effective method of developing intrinsic motivation to learn in a culturally disadvantaged pupil is to concentrate on teaching him or her as effectively as possible in the absence of motivation, and to rely on the cognitive motivation that is developed retroactively from successful educational achievement. This is particularly true when a teacher is able to generate contagious excitement and enthusiasm about the subject being taught and when he or she is the kind of person with whom culturally disadvantaged children can identify. Masculinizing the school and dramatizing the lives and exploits of minority group cultural, intellectual, and scientific heroes can also enhance the process of identification. At the same time, of course, we can attempt to combat the anti-intellectualism and lack of cultural tradition in the home through programs of adult education and cultural enrichment.

### Extrinsic Motivation

As previously indicated, the current situation with respect to developing adequate motivations for higher academic and vocational achievement among culturally disadvantaged youth is not very encouraging. But just as in the case of cognitive drive, much extrinsic motivation for academic success can be generated retroactively from the ego-enhancing experience of current success in schoolwork. Intensive counseling can also compensate greatly for the absence of the appropriate home, community, and peer-group support and expectations necessary for the development and implementation of long-term vocational ambitions.

By identifying with a mature, stable, striving, and successful male adult figure who is also of black lower-class origin, culturally disadvantaged boys can be encouraged to internalize long-term and realistic aspirations as well as to develop the mature personality traits necessary for their implementation. Hence, as a result of achieving current ego enhancement in the school setting, obtaining positive encouragement and practical guidance in the counseling relationship, and experiencing less rejection and discrimination at the hands of school personnel, they can feel that higher vocational aspirations are more realistically within their grasp.

Further encouragement to strive for more ambitious academic and vocational goals can be provided by making available educational opportunity in universities, community colleges, and technical institutes; by acquainting culturally disadvantaged youth with examples of successful professional persons originating from their own racial, ethnic, and social-class backgrounds; and by involving parents sympathetically in the newly fostered ambitions of their children.

With regard to aversive motivation, it can be argued, of course, that a long history of school failure has a demonstrably negative effect on the academic motivation and achievement of culturally disadvantaged pupils, alienates them from school and schoolwork, and increases their desire to drop out as early as possible. It is self-evident, however, that failure and fear of failure cannot motivate academic striving when pupils have never experienced any success in school, have given up hope of succeeding, have disinvolved themselves from the school situation, and have internalized no aspirations for academic success.

But the remedy does not lie in removing the threat of failure from the category of respectable motivations. Nor does it lie in the self-defeating practice of "social promotion," which fools nobody, least of all children who are ostensibly rewarded for failing to learn. To be sure, their ultimate academic achievement might be slightly higher if they move ahead to the next grade instead of repeating the same one; and they may be better adjusted socially by not being stigmatized as oversized dullards by their younger classmates. Nevertheless, they are still acutely aware of their actual failure in school, acquire unrealistic perceptions about the competence-reward relationship in the real world, and enter high school as rebellious semiliterates. The more constructive remedy is to change the preschool, classroom, family, and social environment of culturally disadvantaged children, as well as their personality structures. This way academic success not only becomes a realistic possibility for them but also becomes internalizable as a realistic aspiration. When this happens, they too will be positively motivated, as other pupils are, by desire for knowledge as an end in itself, by ego-enhancing rewards, and by aversive motivations as well.

# 14

# TEACHER CHARACTERISTICS

It seems self-evident that the teacher should constitute an important variable in the learning process. From a cognitive standpoint it should certainly make a difference, in the first place, how comprehensive and cogent the teacher's grasp of his or her subject-matter is. Second, quite independently of his or her adequacy in this regard, the teacher may be more or less able to present and organize subject matter clearly, to explain ideas lucidly and incisively, and to manipulate effectively the important variables affecting learning. Third, in communicating with pupils, the teacher may be more or less capable of translating his or her knowledge in a form appropriate for their degree of cognitive maturity and subject-matter sophistication.

Certain key aspects of the teacher's personality would also seem, on logical grounds, to have an important bearing on learning outcomes in the classroom. Theoretical considerations suggest that chief among these would be his or her degree of commitment to, or ego involvement in, the intellectual development of pupils and ability to generate intellectual excitement and intrinsic motivation for learning. Apart from these crucial cognitive and personality attributes that impinge directly on the learning process, a broad range of personal characteristics should be reasonably compatible with effectiveness in teaching.

Cognitive variables (such as teachers' degree of subject-matter preparation and achievement or level of intelligence) are only negligibly related to learning outcomes of pupils or to supervisors' ratings. It would seem, therefore, that at most these factors are limiting variables affecting pupil learning. That is, beyond a certain minimal or critical level they have no influence on teacher effectiveness. A more promising approach would be: (1) to assess the actual cogency and cohesiveness of the teacher's subject-matter knowledge, and (2) to measure his or her ability to present, explain, and organize subject-matter lucidly, to manipulate effectively the variables affecting learning, and to communicate his or her knowledge to pupils in a form that is appropriate for their level of subject-matter and developmental readiness.

Thus, selection of prospective teachers should be based more on performance in actual classroom teaching situations. This opportunity to assess aptitude for teaching is provided in the beginning sequence of field-centered performance/competency-based teacher education programs.* Similarly, teacher certification should be based more on demonstrated competence in the later sequences of student teaching and apprentice teaching. Such performance/ competency-based teacher education programs are certainly an improvement over current practices in selecting and certifying teachers because competency is not assessed on either theoretical knowledge alone or solely on pragmatic grounds unrelated to knowledge of principles of learning and teaching.

With respect to the influence of personality variables on teacher effectiveness, it appears that only two variables are significantly related to teacher effectiveness. Teacher "warmth" significantly enhances learning outcomes in pupils. This is particularly true in the case of satellizing pupils whose motivational orientation to learning exemplifies the affiliative drive and who largely relate to teachers as parent surrogates. Teacher enthusiasm, imagination, or excitement about his or her subject is the other variable that is significantly related to teacher effectiveness.

Teaching styles (including group-centered versus teacher-centered approaches, lecture versus discussion) should be adapted to the particular strengths and weaknesses of a given teacher's personality, background, and preparation. They should also vary in relation to individual differences in pupils' personalities, cognitive style, and intellectual abilities, as well as to the nature of the learning material and the particular educational objectives involved in a given learning situation.

Classroom discipline is a significant problem, especially for beginning teachers and for teachers in inner-city schools. Practical

---

* For further description of a Performance-Based Teacher Education Program, see Darcy (1971).

*instruction and guidance in appropriately democratic (as opposed to laissez-faire or overpermissive) discipline should be an important part of teacher education. This is more realistic by far than pretending that the problem is either nonexistent or is attributable solely to the faulty classroom management techniques or personality attributes of teachers.*

Despite the plethora of research data in the field very little is known about which characteristics of teachers make for success in the teaching-learning process. In part, this situation is a reflection of the difficulty of measuring the more significant teacher attributes that seem self-evidently related to pedagogic competence, and of the consequent lack of research evidence on these significant variables. In addition, it is a reflection of the emphasis that has been placed on those personality characteristics that were thought to affect the mental health and personality development of children. Clearly, since teachers deal with impressionable children and affect their personality development, they should not have unstable or destructive personalities. Nevertheless, the principal criterion in selecting and evaluating teachers should not be the extent to which their personality characteristics conform to some theoretical ideal promoting mental health or personality development, but rather their ability to stimulate and competently direct pupil learning activity.

Much of the existing research evidence in this area tends to be ambiguous, equivocal, and uninterpretable because of the absence of a satisfactory criterion against which to measure teacher effectiveness. Ratings of teacher performance are notoriously unreliable, superficial, subjectivistic, and capricious. And the achievement test scores of pupils, as we shall see in Chapter 17, are limited in depth, scope, validity and in the extent to which they measure meaningfulness, long term retention and cohesiveness of knowledge. The present research trend is observational study of teachers and pupils in interaction in the classroom.

In this chapter it will also be convenient to consider the role and impact of different styles of teaching on learning as well as the problem of classroom discipline.

## The Roles of Teachers

One approach to evaluating teachers' characteristics in terms of their relevance for teaching effectiveness is to consider the different roles that teachers play in our culture as well as the relative importance of these various roles. In recent times the scope of the teacher's role has been vastly expanded beyond its original instructional core to include such functions as parent surrogate, friend and confidante, counselor, adviser, representative of the adult culture, transmitter of approved cultural values, and facilitator of personality development. Without in any sense disparaging the reality or significance of these other subsidiary roles, however, it is nevertheless undeniable that the teacher's most important and distinctive role in the modern classroom is still that of director of *learning activities*.[1] Unfortunately, however, as viewed in retrospect by students, teachers are apparently not impressively effective in any of their roles. One sample of college students, for example, reported that only 8.5 percent of their teachers had an important influence on their intellectual or personal development; no appreciable influence in this regard was attributed to over three-quarters of the teachers in question (Allport, 1964).

One interesting study of adolescent pupils' perceptions of teachers indicates that teachers are seen as playing three major kinds of roles—as friends, opponents, and manipulators of status in learning situations (Cunningham, 1951). As friends, they are "older and wiser" persons, helpful counselors, heroes, givers of security, confidantes, and occasionally "pals." As opponents they are cast as "killjoys" who arbitrarily interfere with legitimate pleasures, as "enemies" to be "fought" and "outwitted," and as demons of power to be feared, respected, and placated. Much of this latter role obviously represents a displacement of hostile feelings from original parent targets.

Teachers also share much of the brunt of adolescents' general antiadult orientation. In the learning aspects of the school situation they are perceived as "efficient organizers" in the direction of work projects, as "necessary evils" in the acquisition of knowledge, as "steppingstones" to future status rewards, as dispensers of approval and disapproval, and as moral arbiters who can absolve from guilt as well as point the accusing finger.

## Cognitive Abilities

At first glance it might seem that the intelligence of teachers should be highly related to success in teaching. Nevertheless teacher effectiveness, as measured by pupil gains in achievement and by principals' and supervisors' ratings, is only negligibly related to teachers' intelligence (Barr & Jones, 1958; Morsh & Wilder, 1954). In all probability, therefore, intelligence operates as a limiting factor in its influence on teaching success. A certain minimal level of intelligence is obviously necessary for teaching effectively.

---

[1] In directing pupil learning activities, the teacher's chief function no longer is, or should be, the giving of information. As emphasized above, this latter function can be performed more efficiently by appropriately programmed instructional materials.

But beyond this critical point, the intelligence of teachers may not be significantly related to learning outcomes in pupils. Other, more important, cognitive and personality factors account for most of the difference in effectiveness between successful and unsuccessful teachers.

It is self-evident that teachers cannot furnish adequate feedback to students or clarify ambiguities and misconceptions unless they have a meaningful and adequately organized grasp of the subject being taught. Yet there are no really adequate measures of a teacher's actual grasp of his or her subject-matter field in terms of such crucial dimensions as comprehensiveness; cogency; stability; lucidity and precision of concepts; integration of relationships between component aspects of the field; awareness of significant theoretical issues and underlying philosophical assumptions; appreciation of methodological and epistemological problems; and so forth. Hence, although such factors presumably influence many significant aspects of the pupil's mastery of subject matter and general level of interest in and intellectual excitement about a given discipline, we know little that is definite about these important relationships.

Obviously, of course, the same difficulties that stand in the way of measuring these significant cognitive variables in teachers create obstacles in measuring corresponding learning outcomes in pupils. Actual investigation along these lines has therefore been restricted to the study of relationships between relatively formal and superficial aspects of teachers' and pupils' mastery of subject matter.

In general, degree and quality of teachers' academic preparation, as indicated by grade-point average, amount of work taken in the major field, and achievement test scores, bears only a low positive relationship to pupil learning outcomes and supervisors' ratings of success in teaching (Barr & Jones, 1958). Other studies that investigated student achievement and teachers' knowledge of subject matter also show a negligible relationship. McCall and Krause (1959) found that sixth-grade teachers' knowledge of subject matter in general was not significantly related to student achievement. Similar results were reported for the subject of English in grades 4 to 6 (Rosenshine, 1971) and for high-school physics (Rothman, Welch, & Walberg, 1969).

On theoretical grounds, however, it seems somewhat unlikely that these aspects of academic preparation are not more highly related to success in teaching than they appear to be. The empirically demonstrated low relationship may conceivably reflect in part the superficiality and low intrinsic validity of both the pupil and teacher measures of subject-matter mastery. It is also possible, of course, that academic preparation, like intelligence, may influence teaching effectiveness only when it is below a certain critical level.

Since, as one might reasonably anticipate, the provision of effective feedback depends on clarity and fluency of teacher expression, the learning of facts by pupils is significantly related to clarity and expressiveness in the teacher (Solomon, Rosenberg, & Bezdek, 1964). Consistent with this finding is the fact that ideational fluency correlates significantly with ratings of teaching effectiveness (Knoell, 1953). In a study that measured organization skills (Belgard, Rosenshine, & Gage, 1971) a positive relationship was found between student ratings for the degree with which lessons were organized and classroom achievement. In addition, research (Hiller, 1971; Hiller, Fisher, & Kaess, 1969) that measured teacher vagueness during a lecture found a negative relationship between student achievement and teacher's vagueness. Vagueness on the part of the teachers was shown to decrease as their knowledge of subject matter increased.

It stands to reason that teachers who display skill, imagination, and sensitivity in organizing learning activities and in manipulating learning variables should promote superior learning outcomes in pupils. This ability, after all, is a central feature of the teaching process and hence should be a key index of professional competence in teaching. Spaulding (1963) reported a positive relationship between orderliness in teachers and reading achievement in pupils. Pupils within a given classroom who judge the teacher as orderly and systematic in classroom management and arrangement of learning activities report greater accomplishment of work than those of their classmates who make less favorable judgments of the teacher in this regard (Cogan, 1958). Their classroom behavior is also more productive at the elementary-school level (Ryans, 1961).

Rosenshine (1971) cites several studies indicating that a teacher's achievement-oriented, businesslike behavior is positively related to student achievement. Teachers rated as superior by their principals tend to be characterized, more than are teachers rated as inferior, by a pattern of orderly, systematic, responsible, and businesslike behavior in their classroom procedures (Ryans, 1960). In addition, teachers who are adept at diagnosing learning difficulties and at appreciating the relevance of particular instructional materials for the acquisition of particular learnings are more successful than less adept teachers in terms of pupil achievement (Fattu, 1963).

Finally, the ability to adapt the communication of ideas to the pupil's level of intellectual maturity and subject-matter sophistication is an important characteristic of teacher effectiveness. Particularly at the elementary-school and less advanced levels of instruction, this ability should be significantly related to the acquisition of clear, stable, and unambiguous meanings.

## Personality Characteristics

A tremendous literature has accumulated over the past half century on the personality characteristics of teachers. Very little of it, however, is illuminating insofar as it indicates the kinds of traits that are associated with success in teaching. For the most part, the personality of teachers has been studied either as an end in itself or in relation to those aspects that influence personality development and mental hygiene in the classroom—not in relation to factors that affect learning outcomes or other criteria of teacher effectiveness. This has been the case despite the fact that many aspects of a teacher's personality may obviously influence pupils' affective response without necessarily influencing teaching effectiveness.

It is incontrovertible that pupils respond affectively to the personality characteristics of a teacher, and that this affective response influences their judgments of his or her instructional effectiveness (Hart, 1934). They not only admire teaching skill, clarity, task orientation, and good classroom control, but are also highly appreciative of fairness, impartiality, patience, cheerfulness, and sympathetic understanding. In addition they approve of teachers who are interested in pupils and who are helpful, kindly, and considerate of their feelings (Hart, 1934; Leeds, 1954). On the other side of the coin, they dislike reluctance to bestow praise, favoritism, punitiveness, irritability, fussiness, garrulousness, bossiness, and brittleness of temper. Thus, from the standpoint of simple congeniality, it can certainly do no harm and may do some good if a teacher possesses those characteristics that appeal to pupils. Nevertheless, from the standpoint of his or her principal role in our culture, it is self-evidently more important that a teacher be instructionally effective than well liked or popular.

In general, teachers' personality characteristics have *not* been highly correlated with effectiveness in teaching. The two principal exceptions to this generalization are warmth and understanding, on the one hand, and a tendency to be stimulating and imaginative, on the other. Thus, since a wide variety of personality traits appears to be consistent both with instructional effectiveness and with normal personality development and mental hygiene in the classroom, a teacher should not try to remake his or her personality to conform to the theoretically ideal cluster of characteristics in these respects—even if it were possible to do so. The more realistic and defensible course of action for teachers is to make the most effective use of those personality assets that they possess.

Teachers who are warm and understanding tend to gratify the affiliative drive of pupils. This is particularly important for the many elementary-school pupils who seek in teachers a parent surrogate and a source of acceptance and approval indicative of derived status. It becomes less important in the secondary school and university when affiliative drive constitutes a less salient motivation for learning than the growing need for ego enhancement and earned status. Warm teachers can be identified with easily by pupils. They provide emotional support, are sympathetically disposed toward pupils, and accept them as persons. Characteristically they distribute much praise and encouragement and tend to interpret pupil behavior as charitably as possible. They are relatively unauthoritarian and are sensitive to pupils' feelings and affective responses. For all of these reasons these teachers tend to score high on the Minnesota Teacher Attitude Inventory, which is keyed in this direction, and to promote more wholesome self-concepts in elementary-school pupils (Spaulding, 1963). Warm teachers tend to be rated more favorably by principals, supervisors, pupils, and other observers (Cook, Leeds, & Callis, 1951; McGee, 1955; Ryans, 1960; Solomon et al., 1964).

At all grade levels, including the elementary school, teacher warmth is less important for pupils whose motivational orientation to learning is largely cognitive or ego-enhancing rather than affiliative. For such pupils, liking of a teacher is not related to the latter's degree of warmth or to his or her score on the Minnesota Teacher Attitude Inventory (Della-Piana & Gage, 1955). In sharp contrast, pupils who *are* highly concerned with their interpersonal relationship to and feelings for a teacher tend to like teachers who are characterized by warmth (who make high scores on the Minnesota Teacher Attitude Inventory), and to dislike teachers who are not.

Another method that yields information on teacher warmth is the direct observation of classroom interaction. For example, Flanders (1970) devised a system for the analysis of student-teacher interaction in the classroom. From ten categories of classroom behavior, it was estimated that approximately 5 to 15 percent of teacher behaviors were accepting and positive while the remaining teacher-student interactions were more cognitive in orientation such as questioning and lecturing.

As a result of identifying with warm teachers, a pupil is obviously more disposed to assimilate their values. Schmuck (1966) found that when pupils perceived their teachers as being understanding, there was a more even distribution of liking and affection among classroom peers. Theoretically, also, the student should be more highly motivated to learn and thus to attain a higher level of academic achievement. But the evidence tends to be equivocal on this point (Dunkin & Biddle, 1974; Flanders, 1960; Medley & Mitzel, 1959). In any case, however, teacher warmth is significantly related to the amount of work performed by pupils (Cogan, 1958), to pupils' interest in science in general science classes (Reed, 1961), and to the "productiveness" of pupil behavior in the elementary school (Ryans, 1961).

More recent investigations on specific teacher behavior (Rosenshine, 1971) report a positive trend between a teacher's acceptance of student's ideas and classroom achievement. While there is no clear relationship between the frequency of teachers' praise and achievement, a teacher's criticism and disapproval is negatively related to students' achievement (Dunkin & Biddle, 1974; Rosenshine, 1971). In addition, Sears (1963) has presented some evidence that suggests that pupil achievement is more creative when teachers are warm and encouraging.

Ability to generate intellectual excitement and intrinsic motivation for learning is another personality characteristic of teachers that appears to have significant implications for their instructional effectiveness. Teachers who are lively, stimulating, imaginative, and enthusiastic about their subject are judged as more successful by principals and other experienced observers (Ryans, 1960). Under this kind of stimulation, pupil behavior is also more productive, both in the primary and secondary school (Rosenshine, 1971; Ryans, 1961), and greater gains in pupil comprehension are made (Solomon et al., 1964).

Perhaps the most important personality characteristic of teachers that influences their effectiveness is the extent of their personal commitment to the intellectual development of pupils. There is general agreement that this is a central component of a teacher's professional motivation. It determines in large measure whether he or she will expend the necessary effort to teach for real gains in the intellectual growth of pupils or will merely go through the formal motions of teaching. Unfortunately, however, since it is a very elusive factor insofar as reliable and valid measurement is concerned, we have no objective evidence regarding its relationship to success in teaching.

## Teaching Style

Much has been written and much pseudo-controversy has arisen about matters of "teaching style." This confusing debate, largely plagued by ambiguity in the meaning of terms, by the emotional use of slogans, and by the absence of definitive evidence, is completely unresolved and promises to yield few clear implications for teaching practice. Perhaps the most defensible conclusion that can be drawn at this point is that variability in teaching style is both inevitable and desirable.

Styles of teaching vary, in the first place, because teachers' personalities vary. What works well for one teacher may be completely ineffectual for another. Teachers should therefore adapt their instructional styles to strengths and weaknesses in their own background, personality, and preparation. This does not mean, of course, that all techniques of teaching are equally effective or that pedagogic technique is not teachable. It cannot be assumed, to begin with, that a given teacher necessarily chooses the style that is most appropriate for him or her. And beyond the assistance that can be given in making this choice, most prospective teachers can be helped to use their styles more effectively; that is, they can be provided with certain relevant techniques or shown how to use them to greater advantage.

It is also desirable for teaching styles to vary because of variability in pupil needs and characteristics. One important pupil characteristic previously stressed in this regard is the difference in learning styles between satellizers and nonsatellizers. In addition, a child's physical disability and corresponding cognitive response style can elicit a specific style of response from teachers (Hanesian, Hutchinson, Diller, & Gordon, 1973). Other important characteristics are intelligence, anxiety level, interest in subject matter, the prevailing degree of authoritarianism in the adult-child relationship that is typical of a given social-class background, and the student's degree of independence and security (Wispé, 1951). Finally, appropriate teaching style is always relative to the particular educational objective that is being striven for at a given moment. The object might be the efficient transmission of established knowledge, the generation or modification of attitudes, the improvement of problem-solving abilities, or the exploration and refinement of alternative viewpoints in controversial areas of knowledge.

### Lecture versus Discussion

Most of the discussion about teaching style has centered around the lecture versus discussion issue. Most of the studies concerned with this problem report little difference between the two methods in terms of student mastery of subject matter (Stern, 1963; Wallen & Travers, 1963). Where differences do appear they are usually in favor of the lecture method. Although there is surprisingly little direct evidence that the lecture method facilitates problem solving and the application of knowledge, Bloom (1953) reported that this method stimulates more relevant student thinking. Even when great reliance is placed on lecturing, it is evident that some discussion is necessary if students are to receive adequate feedback and if the teacher is to ascertain whether the class is comprehending the material.

The choice between lecture and discussion methods depends on administrative factors such as class size, the personality of the teacher, and on whether or not the topic in question is more or less factual or controversial. When the ratio of students to teacher is very large, the lecture method is generally used and is easily adaptable. In considering personality variables, some teachers are more capable than textbook writers of interpreting, integrating, and drawing together scattered materials from diverse sources and of presenting alternative viewpoints in a highly organized and incisive fashion, even though they may be relatively incapable of, and feel very uncomfortable about, directing discussion. Others are masterful in guiding discussion along fruitful lines or in using a Socratic type of questioning.

The unique advantages of discussion, particularly in controversial and poorly established areas of knowledge, have been described in another context. It cannot be too strongly emphasized, however, that discussion techniques cannot be expected to enhance learning outcomes in a given area unless students possess the necessary background information prerequisite for intelligent and informed discussion. When this prerequisite condition is lacking, discussion understandably amounts to little more than the sharing of ignorance, prejudice, platitudes, preconceptions, and vague generalities.

### Group-Centered versus Teacher-Oriented Approaches

Group-centered, as opposed to teacher-oriented, teaching styles place greater emphasis on student activity; on pupil participation, initiative, and responsibility in setting course objectives, in determining course content, and in evaluating learning outcomes; and on the teacher's role as a non-directive group leader. These styles of teaching apparently do not differ significantly from teacher-directed approaches with respect to student achievement or liking for subject matter (R. C. Anderson, 1959; Spaulding, 1963; Stern, 1963), but are superior with respect to such outcomes as increased group cohesion (Benne & Levit, 1953; Lippitt, 1940; Tizard, 1953), positive motivation, less dependence on the teacher (Asch, 1951; Lippitt, 1940), and improvement in group and adjustment skills (Asch, 1951; Lippitt, 1940). Democratic teaching, however, does not increase creativity or improve pupils' self-concepts (Spaulding, 1963).

In a group-centered program, care must be taken neither to confound democratic discipline with a laissez-faire approach nor to abdicate the school's primary responsibility for organizing the curriculum. Students should not be given a great deal of responsibility for structuring courses or for evaluating learning outcomes unless their background in the field is adequate and unless they have prior experience in independent study and group-centered techniques. On the whole, students who prefer nondirective approaches tend to be more secure and independent (Patton, 1955; Wispé, 1951), to be more flexible, to have more self-insight, and to be better able to cope with ambiguity (McKeachie, 1962). It is unwise for teachers to adopt a nondirective teaching style either when they feel temperamentally uncomfortable with it or when pupils are generally insecure, compulsive, or of lower-class origin.

## School Discipline

Since a certain minimal level of order and decorum is necessary for efficient school learning, discipline is a real and prevalent problem in the classroom. It is a serious concern of most teachers, especially those who are beginning their teaching careers (Eaton, Weathers, & Phillips, 1957; Ladd, 1958). It is not just a problem of the ineffectual or maladjusted teacher. Viewed in this context of relevance for classroom learning, it is evident that discipline should be as impersonal and task-oriented as possible. That is, objectionable pupil behavior should be proscribed, punished, and prevented primarily because it interferes with classroom learning, and not because it is personally distasteful or threatening. Personal punitiveness on the part of teachers leads to exaggerated pupil perceptions of the seriousness of misbehavior, less perceived teacher fairness (Kounin, Gump, & Ryan, 1961), more aggressive kinds of misconduct, more conflictful pupil attitudes about misbehavior, and less concern with learning and distinctive school values (Kounin & Gump, 1961). Thus, the student's attitude toward school and his learning achievement are influenced by the discplinary practices and classroom management of the teacher (Kaplan, 1971).

In contrast to disciplinary practices in other countries, the typical American approach to school discipline is impressively incidental. Classroom discipline in the United States does not connote explicit subjection to authority and implicit habits of obedience that are enforced by a heavy-handed set of controls and punishments. It does not imply an easily identifiable atmosphere of classroom control that the teacher maintains with much deliberate effort—in much the same sense that he or she strives to have the pupils understand and assimilate the subject matter being taught. Our teachers, rather, tend to feel that the cause of discipline is adequately served if pupils exercise sufficient self-control and observe a minimum set of rules with sufficient decorum to enable classroom work to proceed in an orderly, efficient manner. They do not, in other words, strive deliberately for discipline as an explicit goal in its own right. They assume instead that good discipline is *ordinarily* a natural by-product of interesting lessons and of a wholesome teacher-pupil relationship; that the vast majority of pupils respond positively to fair and kind treatment; and that respect for the teacher is a usual accompaniment of the latter's superior knowledge, experience, and status as a leader, and does not have to be reinforced by such artificial props and status symbols as differences in clothing, mode of address, and fear of the strap.

In line with this tendency, Kounin (1970) reported that certain specific teacher characteristics are related to students' behavior in the classroom. Based on measures of teacher behaviors taken from videotape recordings, he found that the teacher's awareness or "withitness" was positively related to student work involvement and freedom from classroom misbehavior. Teachers with good classroom control were also able to attend to more than one issue at a time ("overlapping"), maintain class activity ("momentum and smoothness"), and keep students involved ("group alerting").

### Science or Opinion

Discipline today is much less a science than a matter of opinion. It not only shifts in response to various social, economic, and ideological factors, but also manifests all the cyclical properties of fads and fashions. Objective scientific evidence about the relative merits of different types of discipline is extremely sparse. Indeed it is highly questionable to what extent valid empirical data are obtainable and even relevant in matters of discipline. Whether or not particular disciplinary practices are appropriate depends, in the first place, on the particular values, institutions and kinds of personal relationships prevailing in a given culture. Second, any definitive empirical test of appropriateness would have to be conducted over such an extended period of time that its conclusions would tend to be rendered obsolete by intervening changes in significant social conditions. For all practical purposes, therefore, the choice of disciplinary policy involves taking a rationally defensible and self-consistent position based on value preferences, on relevant considerations of child development, and on individual experience and judgment.

Because discipline cannot be placed on a largely scientific basis, however, does not mean that one position is as good as another or that no public policy whatsoever is warranted. Society is continually obliged to resolve issues of much greater moment with even less objective evidence on which to base a decision. Under the circumstances all we can reasonably expect is greater humility and less dogmatism on the part of those engaged in formulating disciplinary policy. Thus the most disturbing aspect of the entire problem is not the fact that there is precious little scientific evidence to support the disciplinary doctrines expounded in our colleges of education and educational journals and textbooks, but rather the ubiquitous tendency to represent purely personal opinions and biases as if they were incontrovertibly established findings of scientific research.

### The Definition and Function of Discipline

By discipline is meant the imposition of *external* standards and controls on individual conduct. Permissiveness, on the other hand, refers to the absence of such standards and controls. To be permissive is to "let alone," to adopt a laissez-faire policy. Authoritarianism is an excessive, arbitrary, and autocratic type of control. It is diametrically opposite to permissiveness. Between the extremes of laissez-faire permissiveness and authoritarianism are many varieties and degrees of control. One of these, to be described in greater detail below, is democratic discipline. When external controls are internalized we can speak of self-discipline; it is clear, nonetheless, that the original source of the controls, as well as much of their later reinforcement, is extrinsic to the individual.

Discipline is a universal cultural phenomenon that generally serves four important functions in the training of the young. First, it is necessary for socialization—for learning the standards of conduct that are approved and tolerated in any culture. Second, it is necessary for normal personality maturation—for acquiring such adult personality traits as dependability, self-reliance, self-control, persistence, and ability to tolerate frustration. These aspects of maturation do not occur spontaneously but only in response to sustained social demands and expectations. Third, it is necessary for the internalization of moral standards and obligations—in other words, for the development of conscience. Standards obviously cannot be internalized unless they also exist in external form; and even after they are effectively internalized, universal cultural experience suggests that external sanctions are still required to ensure the stability of the social order. Fourth, discipline is necessary for children's emotional security. Without the guidance provided by unambiguous external controls they tend to feel bewildered and apprehensive. Too great a burden is placed on their own limited capacity for self-control.

From the standpoint of school learning, as pointed out above, discipline is also necessary for the orderly regulation of classroom activities.

### Democratic Discipline

The proponents of democratic classroom discipline believe in imposing the minimal degree of external control necessary for socialization, personality maturation, conscience development, classroom learning, and the emotional security of the child. Discipline and obedience are regarded only as means to these ends, and not as ends in themselves. They are not striven for deliberately, but are expected to follow naturally in the wake of friendly and realistic teacher-pupil relationships. Explicit limits are not set routinely or as ways of showing "who is boss," but only as the need arises—when they are *not* implicitly understood or accepted by pupils.

Democratic discipline is as rational, nonarbitrary, and bilateral as possible. It provides explanations, permits discussion, and invites the participation of children in the setting and enforcement of standards whenever they are qualified to do so. Above all, it implies respect for the dignity of the individual, makes its primary appeal to self-control, and avoids exaggerated emphasis on status differences and barriers between free communication. Hence it repudiates harsh, abusive, and vindictive forms of punishment and the use of sarcasm, ridicule, and intimidation.

The aforementioned attributes of democratic classroom discipline are obviously appropriate in cultures such as ours where social relationships tend to be egalitarian. This type of discipline also becomes increasingly more feasible as children become older, more responsible, more capable of self-control and group control, and more capable of understanding and formulating rules of conduct based on concepts of equity and reciprocal obligation. But contrary to what the extreme permissivists would have us believe, democratic school discipline does not imply freedom from all external constraints, standards, and direction, or freedom from discipline. And under no circumstances does it presuppose the eradication of all distinctions between pupil and teacher roles, nor does it require that teachers abdicate responsibility for making the final decisions in the classroom.

### Distortions of Democratic Discipline

Many educational theorists have misinterpreted and distorted the ideal of democratic discipline by equating it with an extreme form of permissiveness. Fortunately, however, most classroom teachers have only accepted these distortions for examination purposes—while still in training—and have discarded them in actual practice as thoroughly unworkable.

According to one widely held doctrine, only "positive" forms of discipline are constructive and democratic. It is asserted that children must be guided only by reward and approval; that disapproval, reproof, and punishment are authoritarian, repressive, and reactionary expressions of adult hostility and leave permanent emotional scars on children's personalities. What these theorists conveniently choose to ignore, however, is the fact that it is impossible for children to learn what is *not* approved and tolerated simply by generalizing in reverse from the approval they receive for behavior that *is* acceptable. Even adults are manifestly incapable of learning and respecting the limits of acceptable conduct unless the distinction between what is proscribed and approved is reinforced by punishment as well as by reward. Furthermore, there is good reason to believe that acknowledgment of wrongdoing and acceptance of punishment are part and parcel of learning moral accountability and developing a sound conscience. Few if any children are quite so fragile that they cannot take deserved reproof and punishment in stride.

A second widespread distortion of democratic discipline is reflected in the notion popular among educational theorists that there are no culpably misbehaving children in the classroom, but only culpably aggressive, unsympathetic, and punitive teachers. If children misbehave, according to this point of view, one can implicitly assume that they must have been provoked beyond endurance by repressive and authoritarian classroom discipline. Similarly, if they are disrespectful, then the teacher, by definition, must not have been deserving of respect.

It is true, of course, that much pupil misconduct *is* instigated by harsh and abusive school discipline; but there are also innumerable reasons for out-of-bounds behavior that are completely independent of the teacher's attitudes and disciplinary practices. The misbehavior of pupils is also influenced by factors originating in the home, the neighborhood, the peer group, and the mass-media. Some children are emotionally disturbed, others are brain-injured, and still others are aggressive by temperament. And there are times when even the best-behaved children from the nicest homes develop an irresistible impulse—without any provocation whatsoever—to test the limits of a teacher's forbearance.

Both of the aforementioned distortions of classroom democracy are often used to justify the commonly held belief among educational theorists that pupils should not be reproved or punished for disorderly or discourteous conduct. One can, for example, observe classrooms where everybody talks at once; where pupils turn their backs on the teacher and engage in private conversation while the latter is endeavoring to instruct them; and where pupils verbally abuse teachers for exercising their rightful disciplinary prerogatives.

Some educators contend that all of this is compatible with wholesome, democratic teacher-pupil relationships. Other educators deplore this type of pupil behavior but insist, nevertheless, that punishment is unwarranted under these circumstances. In the first place, they assert, reproof or punishment constitutes a "negative" and hence axiomatically undesirable approach to classroom management. Second, they argue, the misbehavior would assuredly have never occurred to begin with if the teacher's attitudes had been less autocratic or antagonistic. The arguments of the second group of educators have already been answered; and to the first group it can be said that rudeness and unruliness are not normally desirable classroom behavior in any culture.

When such misconduct occurs, pupils have to be unambiguously informed that it will not be tolerated and that any repetition of the same behavior will be punished. This action does not preclude in any way either an earnest attempt to discover why the misbehavior occurred or suitable preventive measures aimed at correcting the underlying causes. But, by the same token, the mere fact that a pupil has a valid psychological reason for misbehaving does not mean that he is thereby absolved from moral accountability or rendered no longer subject to punishment. In regard to punishment Clarizio, Craig, and Mehrens (1974) reported:

> Despite the limitations associated with the technique, some psychologists today assert that negative sanctions, if properly applied, can assist in eliminating detrimental patterns of adjustment. According to the advocates of punishment, the undesirable by-products are not inherent in the technique itself but stem from faulty application (p. 576).

Still another related distortion of democratic discipline is reflected in the proposition that it is repressive and authoritarian to request pupils to apologize for discourteous behavior or offensive language. However, if we take seriously the idea that the dignity of the human being is important, we must be willing to protect it from affront. And apology is the most civilized and effective means mankind has yet evolved for accomplishing this goal. In a democratic society nobody is important enough to be above apologizing to those persons whom he or she wrongfully offends. Everybody's dignity is important—the teacher's as well as the pupil's. It is no less wrong for a pupil to abuse a teacher than for a teacher to abuse a pupil.

If apologies are to have any real significance in moral training, however, it is obvious that, even though they are explicitly requested, they must be made voluntarily and must be reflective of genuine appreciation of wrong-doing and of sincere regret and remorse. Purely formal and mechanical statements of apology made under coercion are less than worthless. Apologies are also without real ethical import unless their basis is reciprocal, that is, unless it is fully understood that under comparable circumstances the teacher would be willing to apologize to the pupils.

### What Needs to Be Done

In seeking to correct these undesirable permissive distortions of classroom democracy, it would be foolhardy to return to the equally undesirable opposite extreme of authoritarianism that flourished in this country up to thirty-five years ago and still prevails in many Western nations. Democratic school discipline is still an appropriate and realistic goal for American education; hence there is no need to throw away the baby with the bathwater. It is only necessary to discard the aforementioned permissivist doctrines masquerading under the banners of democracy and behavioral science, and to restore certain other traditional American values that have been neglected in the enthusiasm of extending democracy to home and school.

More specifically, we first have to clear up the semantic confusion. We should stop equating permissiveness with democratic discipline, and realistic adult control and guidance with authoritarianism. Permissiveness, by definition, is the absence of discipline, democratic or otherwise. We should cease instructing teachers that it is repressive and reactionary to reprove or punish pupils for misconduct or to request them to apologize for offensive and discourteous behavior.

Second, we should cease misinterpreting what little reputable evidence we have about discipline and refrain from misrepresenting our personal biases on the subject as the indisputably established findings of scientific research. The available evidence merely suggests that in our type of cultural setting, authoritarian discipline has certain undesirable effects—not that the consequences of laissez-faire permissiveness are desirable. As a matter of fact, research studies show that the effects of extreme permissiveness are just as unwholesome as are those of authoritarianism. In the school situation a laissez-faire policy, as pointed out above, leads to confusion, insecurity, and competition for power among pupils. Assertive pupils tend to become aggressive and ruthless, whereas retiring pupils tend to withdraw further from classroom participation.

Children who are handled too permissively at home tend to regard themselves as specially privileged. They fail to learn the normative standards and expectations of society, to set realistic goals for themselves, and to make reasonable demands on others. In their dealings with adults and other children they are domineering, aggressive, petulant, and capricious.

Third, we should stop making teachers feel guilty and personally responsible for all instances of misconduct and disrespect in the classroom. We do this whenever we take for granted, without any actual supporting evidence, that these behavior problems would never have arisen in the first place if the teachers involved were truly deserving of respect and had been administering genuinely wholesome and democratic discipline.

Finally, teacher education programs should provide the future teacher ample opportunity for learning disciplinary practices. This can be accomplished best through early exposure to field experiences in a performance/competency-based teacher education program. In this situation the college professor teaches in the field setting where disciplinary problems arise and need to be managed. Thus the prospective teacher can be taught more realistic propositions about the nature and purposes of democratic discipline and receive adequately supervised, down-to-earth experience in coping with classroom discipline.

# PART FOUR

# DISCOVERY
# LEARNING

# 15

# LEARNING BY DISCOVERY

*Learning by discovery has its proper place in the repertoire of accepted pedagogic techniques available to teachers. For certain designated purposes and for certain carefully specified learning situations, its rationale is clear and defensible. But learning by discovery also has its own elaborate mystique: Its legitimate uses and advantages have been unwarrantedly extrapolated to include educational goals, levels of intellectual maturity, levels of subject matter sophistication, and levels of cognitive functioning for which it is ill-adapted—and for reasons which derive from sheer dogmatic assertion; from pseudonaturalistic conceptions about the nature and conditions of intellectual development; from outmoded ideas about the relationship between language and thought; from an outmoded overempirical and "inductive" concept of epistemology; from sentimental fantasies about the nature of the child and the aims of education; and from uncritical interpretation of the research evidence.*

*The chief goal of this chapter is to distinguish between the psychological rationale and the psychological mystique of the so-called discovery method of teaching—because there is a pressing need in these troubled times to dispense with sentimental fantasy and euphoric slogans, and to get on with the realistic business of education. This means helping schools do well the kinds of jobs that schools can really do best: developing more efficient and appropriate ways of selecting, organizing, and presenting significant knowledge to students so that they can learn and retain it more meaningfully over longer periods of time—as an end in itself, as a basis for later new learning, for problem solving, and, in some cases, for creativity.*

*The discovery method is especially appropriate for learning scientific method (how new knowledge is discovered) in a particular discipline. It is also more appropriate in the preschool and early elementary-school years when more concept formation than concept assimilation occurs, and when the prerequisites for acquiring large bodies of knowledge (the availability of a large body of higher-order abstractions and transactional terms in cognitive structure and an abstract mode of assimilating ideas) are not present. Discovery methods can similarly be used for older learners in the early stages of exposure to a new discipline and at all age levels for testing, in part, whether reception learning is truly meaningful.*

*For purposes of analysis, the psychologically and educationally untenable arguments advanced in support of learning by discovery can be conveniently considered under the following twelve headings:*

*1. All real knowledge is self-discovered.*

*2. Meaning is an exclusive product of creative, nonverbal discovery.*

*3. Subverbal awareness is the key to transfer.*

*4. The discovery method is the principal method for transmitting subject-matter content.*

*5. Problem-solving ability is the primary goal of education.*

*6. Training in the "heuristics of discovery" is more important than training in subject matter.*

*7. Every child should be a creative and critical thinker.*

*8. Expository teaching is "authoritarian."*

*9. Discovery organizes learning effectively for later use.*

*10. Discovery is a unique generator of motivation and self-confidence.*

*11. Discovery is a prime source of intrinsic motivation.*

*12. Discovery ensures "conservation of memory."*

*Each of these pseudo-rationales for the use of discovery learning is subjected to detailed scrutiny, and the conclusion is reached that all of them are both logically and pedagogically invalid. Learning by discovery is simply not a feasible primary method of transmitting large bodies of subject-matter content (for learners who are capable of learning concepts and principles through expository teaching) to warrant the vastly increased time-cost it entails. It is, in fact, a repudiation of one of the most significant aspects of culture, namely, that the original discoveries of millenia can be transmitted during the course of childhood and youth, through the ingenious and mar-*

*velously efficient devices of expository teaching and meaningful
reception learning and need not be rediscovered by each new
generation.*

*A representative sample of the more significant "research" find-
ings in the field demonstrates that they are really based on empirically unsupported assertions and testimonials or that they are mostly
negative in nearly all reasonably well controlled studies. The few
research studies that do support the superiority of discovery learning tend to be methodologically defective, grossly uncontrolled with
respect to significant variables, or inapplicable to actual classroom
learning.*

## Historical Antecedents

Before attempting to set forth the rationale and mystique of the discovery
method, it might be helpful briefly to consider the more important of the
numerous educational movements and currents of thought from which it
has evolved. Some of its historical antecedents are relatively recent, whereas
others have flourished for centuries. Unfortunately, also, not all of these
precursory trends are logically compatible with each other.

The progressive education movement obviously furnished several major
strands in the design of the discovery method. One aspect of this movement
was a growing dissatisfaction with the empty formalism of much educational content in the latter part of the nineteenth century and the early part
of the twentieth century; with stultifying drill and catechism-like methods
of teaching; with the curriculum's lack of relatedness to the everyday
experience of children, their physical world, and their social environment;
and with pupils' rote verbalization and memorization of ideas for which
they had no adequate referents in experience.

Overstatement of the realities underlying this dissatisfaction constituted
the basis of the later mystique that *all* verbal learning is little more than
glib verbalism and parrotlike recitation. This led, in turn, to the exaggerated
emphasis that progressivists placed on direct, immediate, and concrete experience as a prerequisite for genuine understanding, on problem solving
and inquiry, and on incidental learning and learning in natural, uncontrived
situations. From this type of emphasis grew "activity programs" and project methods, and the credo of "learning for and by problem solving" as the
principal objective and method, respectively, of the educational enterprise.

Two final by-products of this point of view were (1) deification of the
act of discovery associated with the inductive and incidental learning methods of teaching and (2) extrapolation to the secondary-school and university
student of the elementary-school child's dependence on recent concrete-

empirical props in the comprehension and manipulation of ideas. As we shall see later, both of these developments became extremely important components of the mystique of learning by discovery.

Such modern proponents of the discovery method as Hendrix acknowledge their historical and ideological kinship to the progressive education movement, but they are quick to dissociate themselves from some of the basic assumptions made by the inductive and incidental learning approaches to instruction. Hendrix (1961, p. 296) quite rightly points out that the main fallacy of the inductive approach lies in the teacher's use of the pupil's ability to verbalize a discovery as the "criterion by which [he or she] recognizes that discovery has taken place." And in referring to the incidental learning that purportedly occurs in the course of a pupil's involvement in a project or activity program, Hendrix (1961, p. 293) correctly berates the advocates of this method because "all too often they took no responsibility for seeing that instances of the same generalization came along close enough together for the learner to become aware of either concepts or principles."

A second aspect of the progressive education movement relevant to the evolution of the discovery method was the child-centered approach to instruction that originated in the educational philosophies of Rousseau and Froebel. The adherents of this approach emphasized the importance of structuring the curriculum in terms of the nature of the child and of his or her participation in the educative process—that is, in terms of the child's current interests, endogenously derived needs, and state of intellectual and emotional readiness. According to this point of view, the educational environment facilitates development best by providing a maximally permissive field that does not interfere with the predetermined process of spontaneous maturation. Children themselves, it is asserted, are in the most strategic position to know and select those educational ingredients that correspond most closely to their prevailing developmental needs and hence are most conducive to their optimal growth.

Propositions such as these obviously make a fetish of autonomy and self-discovery. They regard as little short of sacrilege any form of guidance or direction in learning—particularly the communication of insights or generalizations by teachers to pupils. Herein lies, in part, the origin of the mystique that expository teaching is inherently "authoritarian" on developmental grounds and that self-discovered insights are uniquely and transcendentally endowed with meaning and understanding that can be achieved through no other means.

Hendrix (1961, p. 296), for example, castigates didactic exposition of generalizations as "authoritarian" and as only "satisfying to someone who is *already aware* of the ideas being presented." This same mystique also underlies the quite different educational doctrine that it is "authoritarian" (undemocratic) for a knowledgeable person to communicate his knowledge to other persons lacking his particular background of thought and study and that the latter individuals can learn more through "democratic discussion."

These two strands of the progressive education movement—emphasis on the child's direct experience and spontaneous interests and insistence on autonomously achieved insight free of all directive manipulation of the learning environment—set the stage for the subsequent deification of problem solving, laboratory work, and naive emulation of the scientific method. Many mathematics and science teachers were rendered self-conscious about systematically presenting and explaining to their students the basic concepts and principles of their field because it was held that this procedure would promote glib verbalism and rote memorization. It was felt that if students worked enough problems and were kept busy pouring reagents into a sufficient number of test tubes, they would somehow spontaneously discover in a meaningful way all of the important concepts and generalizations they needed to know in the fields they were studying.

Of course, one had to take pains to discourage students from rotely memorizing formulas and then mechanically substituting for the general terms in these formulas the particular values of specified variables in given problems. This would naturally be no less rote than formal didactic exposition. Hence, in accordance with the new emphasis on *meaningful* problem solving, students ceased memorizing formulas, memorizing instead "type problems." They learned how to work exemplars of all of the kinds of problems they were responsible for, and then rotely memorized both the form of each type and its solution. Thus equipped, it was comparatively easy to sort the problems with which they were confronted into their respective categories and "spontaneously proceed to discover meaningful solutions"—provided, of course, that the teacher played fair and presented recognizable exemplars of the various types.[1]

Similarly, as the terms "laboratory" and "scientific method" became sacrosanct in U.S. high schools and universities, students were coerced into mimicking the externally conspicuous but inherently trivial aspects of scientific method. They wasted many valuable hours collecting empirical data that, at the very worst, belabored the obvious and, at the very best, helped them rediscover principles that could easily be presented verbally in a matter of minutes. Actually, they learned precious little subject matter and even less scientific method from this procedure. The unsophisticated scientific mind is only bewildered by the natural complexities of empirical data, and learns much more from schematic models and diagrams. Following laboratory manuals in cookbook fashion, without adequate knowledge of the relevant methodological and substantive principles involved, confers

---

[1] In some instances, transferability did not even extend to a change in algebraic notation. E. L. Thorndike (1922) found that some students who could square $(x+y)$ could not square $(B_1+B_2)$.

about as much genuine appreciation of scientific method as putting on a white "lab" coat and doing a TV commercial for a patent remedy. Furthermore, the view that science is primarily a *procedure* or methodology of inquiry has its roots in Bacon's writings of 1620 and is now generally regarded as three centuries out of date (Brush, 1974; Elkana, 1970; Toulmin, 1972).

Partly as a result of the superstitious faith of educators in the magical efficacy of problem solving and laboratory methods, we have produced in the past four decades millions of high-school and college graduates who never had the foggiest notion of the meaning of a variable, of a function, of an exponent, of calculus, of molecular structure, or of electricity, but who have done all of the prescribed laboratory work and have successfully solved an acceptable percentage of the required problems in differential and integral calculus, in logarithms, in molar and normal solutions, and in Ohm's law.

One basic lesson that some modern proponents of the discovery method have drawn from this educational disaster is that problem solving in itself does not guarantee meaningful discovery. Problem solving can be just as deadening, just as formalistic, just as mechanical, just as passive, and just as rote as the worst form of verbal exposition. The types of learning outcomes that emerge are largely a function of the structure, the organization, and the spirit of the problem-solving experiences one provides. However, there is an equally important lesson that these same proponents of the discovery method refuse to draw: Because of the educational logistics involved, even the best program of problem-solving experience is no substitute for a minimally necessary amount of appropriate didactic exposition. But this minimum will never be made available as long as we adhere to the standard university formula of devoting one hour of exposition to every three or four hours of laboratory work and paper-and-pencil problem solving.

Historically, the discovery method may also be considered, in part, a revolt against the prevailing educational psychology of our time, which is largely an eclectic hodgepodge of logically incompatible theoretical propositions superimposed upon a sterile empiricism. Perhaps the most significant example of this self-defeating eclecticism has been the stubborn attempt made by various psychologists to integrate Thorndikian connectionism and a widely extrapolated neobehaviorism with the major tenets of progressive education. But the glaring contradictions that resulted from the effort to reconcile such antithetical sets of principles as the Law of Effect, drive reduction, stimulus-response and rote learning theory, the transfer of identical elements, and trial-and-error learning, on the one hand, and progressivist viewpoints regarding the understanding of ideas, active inquiry, and autonomous discovery, on the other hand, tended to alienate some of the more independent-minded educational psychologists in the progressive education camp.

Some defected to psychoanalysis, spawning a weird synthesis of Deweyism and Freudianism, whereas others were attracted by the greater emphasis on cognition and insightful problem solving that characterized such field theorists and Gestalt theoreticians as Tolman, Lewin, Köhler, Wertheimer, and Katona. Also included among the defectors were many vigorous supporters of the discovery method, who viewed the extrapolation of rote learning theory to verbal classroom learning as sufficient proof of the essentially rote nature of verbal learning and as ample justification for designing nonverbal discovery techniques of teaching.

A final current of educational thought influencing the evolution of the discovery method is the militant sentimentality underlying the currently popular educational objective of making *every* child a critical and creative thinker. This objective is, in part, a wish-fulfilling extension of our present-day preoccupation with actualizing the creative potentialities of gifted children. But it also harks back to certain conceptions within the mental measurement movement and to the official environmentalistic bias of progressive education.

### The Epistemology of Discovery

Much of the confusion regarding the value of discovery learning derives from an obsolete epistemology. Ever since the Enlightenment brought forward the power of reason and the search for laws, exemplified by the writings of Bacon and Newton in the seventeenth century, the dominant idea has been that through observation and reason man can discovery the *laws* of nature. For three centuries this epistemology held that improvement of our observations and methods for obtaining information would result in increasing precision in our laws and elucidation of immutable truths. It is in this epistemology that rampant enthusiasm for discovery learning is rooted.

With the writings of Conant (1947) and Kuhn (1962), and then a panoply of modern writing on epistemology, we have witnessed in the last decade a cascading of thought toward the view that there are no fixed truths in nature, only man's *conception* of truth.[2] Related to this view is

---

[2] One way of expressing a more relativistic brand of a belief that "absolute" truths do *in fact* exist is to say that the accretion of more valid knowledge depends on approaching through progressively closer revisions and approximations necessitated by new advances in theory and research, but never actually reaching "final" truth. This is the epistemological position taken by the senior author.

the idea that the "reality" we see is the reality framed by the concepts we hold. As Toulmin (1972, p. 35) points out:

> Man is born with the power of original thought, and everywhere this originality is constrained within a particular conceptual inheritance; yet, on closer inspection, these concepts too turn out to be the necessary instruments of effective thought.

Toulmin goes on to explain that the concepts held by an individual are the concepts obtained from his culture, albeit with idiosyncratic variation in meaning—a process to which assimilation theory is addressed. This epistemology both requires and lends support to a theory of acquisition by individuals of concepts from their culture through the process of education. Without an explanation of the latter process, serious problems arise.

> From Locke to Russell, and from Descartes to Chomsky, orthodox epistemologists have interpreted the problem of knowledge as requiring them to explain, at the outset, how an individual thinker or observer can arrive single-handed at valid ideas, truths, or grammatical forms; and this choice of priorities has given rise to grave difficulties, by distracting attention from the social character of language and the communal criteria of validity. Only recently, e.g., in the later work of Wittgenstein, has the scale tipped decisively the other way, showing us the crucial connections between concept acquisition and "enculturation" (Toulmin, 1972, p. 37).

Rooted in an epistemology based on a search for *truth*, discovery enthusiasts have nevertheless recognized that new knowledge does arise and hence they have been concerned with the heuristics of discovery. What they have failed to see is the important role that the population of concepts held by individuals of a culture at any one time plays in the selection, invention and extinction of competing concepts. Toulmin (1972) has discussed this process and it is shown schematically in Figure 15.1. This figure shows "time slices" through a segment of a culture's evolving concepts. The ellipses at each time slice represent the "population" of concepts held by individuals in the culture at any time. Some concepts are abandoned over time (occasionally because their proponents have died), new conceptual variants are advanced (as preceding time slice $t_r$ and $t_s$), and some concepts become integrated (as in the last time segment). The interplay of social, political, and conceptual factors that influence the evolution of concepts is well described by Toulmin (1972), and we commend his book to readers who wish to pursue further consideration of modern epistemology. The educational implication of this epistemology is discussed elsewhere (Novak, 1977).

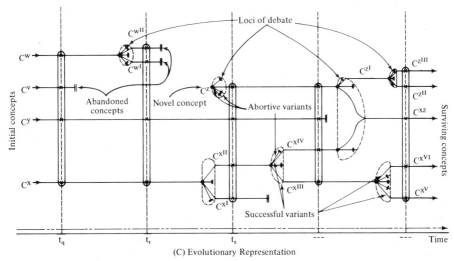

(C) Evolutionary Representation

FIGURE 15.1    Schematic view of the evolution of concepts showing "time slices" in the evolving cultural heritage. The invention of new "conceptual mutants" (a creative process), integrative reconciliation of concepts (shown in the last "time slice") and new variants (progressive differentiation) of concepts is illustrated. (From S. Toulmin, *Human understanding: Vol. 1 The collective use and evolution of concepts.* Princeton, N.J.: Princeton University Press, 1972, p. 205. Reproduced by permission.)

## Psychological and Educational Rationale of the Discovery Method

An all-or-none position regarding use of the discovery method is warranted by neither logic nor evidence. The method itself is very useful for certain pedagogic purposes and in certain educational circumstances. The objectionable aspects of the method are certain unwarranted assumptions, overstated claims, inadequately tested propositions, and, above all, some of the reasons advanced for its efficacy.

> It is evident that the young human being must receive considerable instruction but also that he should be eternally vigilant in making additional observations. His life is a complicated blending of instruction and discovery. Many facts will be handed to him outright. At the same time, during every day of his life, he will be engaged, almost unknowingly, in inductive reasoning, the process of bringing together a number of experiences and extracting from them some common factor. The issue becomes, then, not instruction versus discovery, since both are essential, but a consideration of the relative importance to be accorded each in the educational process (Stanley, 1949, p. 457).

What are some of the legitimate claims, the defensible uses, and the palpable advantages of the discovery method? In the early, unsophisticated stages of learning any abstract subject matter, particularly prior to adolescence, the discovery method is extremely helpful. It is also indispensable for testing the meaningfulness of knowledge and for teaching scientific method and effective problem-solving skills. As an adjunctive pedagogic technique it can be very useful for increasing the meaningfulness of material presented primarily by expository methods. Finally, various cognitive and motivational factors undoubtedly enhance the learning, retention, and transferability of potentially meaningful ideas learned by discovery.

Occasional use of inductive discovery techniques for teaching subject matter content is didactically defensible when pupils are in the *concrete* operational stage of cognitive development. It is true, of course, that only the availability of some concrete-empirical props are necessary to generate the semiabstract or intuitive level of meaningfulness characteristic of this stage of cognitive development. Hence, either simple verbal exposition, using concrete-empirical props, or a semiautonomous type of discovery, accelerated by the judicious use of prompts and hints, is adequate for teaching simple and relatively familiar new ideas.

When the learning task is more difficult and unfamiliar, however, autonomous discovery probably enhances intuitive meaningfulness by intensifying and personalizing both the concreteness of experience and the actual operations of abstracting and generalizing from empirical data. In these circumstances also, the time-cost disadvantage of discovery learning is relatively less serious, since the time-consuming concrete-empirical aspects of learning must take place anyway, and since a large volume of subject matter cannot be covered in any case during the elementary-school period.

In lesser degree, this same rationale also applies to adolescents and adults who are relatively unsophisticated in the basic concepts and terminology of a given discipline. The older individual, however, has the benefit of greater general cognitive sophistication and linguistic facility, as well as of past successful experience in meaningfully relating abstractions to each other without the aid of concrete-empirical props. Hence the older individual will move through the intuitive, subverbal phase of insightful understanding much more rapidly than the comparably unsophisticated child and, unlike the latter, will soon dispense with this phase entirely.

The discovery method also has obvious uses in evaluating learning outcomes and in teaching problem-solving techniques and appreciation of scientific method. There is no better way of developing effective skills in hypothesis making and testing; desirable attitudes "toward learning and inquiry, toward guessing and hunches, toward the possibility of solving problems on one's own . . . ; [and] attitudes about the ultimate orderliness of nature and a conviction that order can be discovered" (Bruner, 1960,

p. 120). As a matter of fact, this is the major rationale for laboratory work. In addition, independent problem solving is one of the few feasible ways of testing whether students really comprehend the ideas they are able to verbalize, provided that we do not fall into the trap that failure to solve related problems *necessarily* proves lack of comprehension of the ideas in question. As pointed out earlier, variables *other than* comprehension of the ideas involved affect problem-solving outcomes.

Finally, in spite of the inconclusive empirical evidence, after one has properly discounted the exaggerated claims made for the unique virtues of learning by discovery and the fanciful reasons offered for these virtues, it still seems plausible to suppose that the greater effort, motivation, excitement, and vividness associated with independent discovery lead to somewhat greater learning and retention. One might expect the advantages conferred by discovery techniques to be even greater with respect to transferability, since the experience gained from formulating a generalization from diverse distances obviously facilitates, through transfer, the solution of problems involving this generalization.

The crucial points at issue, however, are not whether learning by discovery enhances learning, retention, and transferability, but whether: (1) it does so *sufficiently*, for learners who are capable of learning concepts and principles meaningfully *without* it, to warrant the vastly increased expenditure of time it requires; and (2) in view of this time-cost consideration, the discovery method is a feasible technique for transmitting the substantive content of an intellectual or scientific discipline to cognitively mature students who have already mastered its rudiments and basic vocabulary. It is largely to an exploration of these issues that the remainder of this chapter is devoted.

## Psychological and Educational Limitations of Learning by Discovery

### All Real Knowledge Is Self-Discovered

The most general and metaphysical of the twelve propositions is the familiar assertion that to *really* possess knowledge or acquire an idea, the learner must discover it by himself or through his own insight. This proposition stems in part from the deification of the act of creative discovery in the problem-solving, activity-program approach to teaching, and from John Dewey's extreme preference for problem-solving ability, rather than ability to acquire knowledge, as the proper criterion of intelligence. It is also partly derived from the child-centered and client-centered doctrines that individuals themselves are best equipped to regulate the process of learning about themselves and their universe, and, therefore, that any tampering with this autonomy, is, by definition, detrimental to learning outcomes.

More recently a sentimental type of Rousseauan mysticism and primitivism has become fashionable, and has been superimposed upon the aforementioned ideological substrate. It is best exemplified by the following statement by Bruner:  ·

> If man's intellectual excellence is the most his own among his perfections, it is also the case that the most uniquely personal of all that he knows is that which he has discovered himself. . . . [Discovery creates] a special and unique relation between the knowledge possessed and the possessor. . . . The transition to adulthood involves an introduction to new realms of experience, the discovery and exploration of new mysteries, the gaining of new powers. This is the heady stuff of education and it is its own reward (Bruner, 1961a, pp. 22, 76).

In accordance with this conception of the true nature of genuine knowledge, Bruner formulates the objectives of education as follows:

> School should provide not simply a continuity with the broader community or with everyday experience. It is the special community where one experiences discovery by the use of intelligence, where one leaps into new and unimagined realms of experience, experience that is discontinuous with what went before. . . . Education must also seek to develop the processes of intelligence so that the individual is capable of going beyond the cultural ways of his social world, able to innovate, in however modest a way, so that he can create an interior culture of his own. For whatever the art, the science, the literature, the history, and the geography of a culture, each man must be his own artist, his own scientist, his own historian, his own navigator (Bruner, 1961b, pp. 76, 59).

It is perfectly true, of course, that one cannot simply soak up one's culture like a piece of blotting paper and expect it to be meaningful. But who advocates doing anything of the kind? The very processes of perception and cognition necessarily require that the cultural stimulus world must first be filtered through each individual's personal sensory apparatus and cognitive structure before it can have any meaning. Meaning can never be anything more than a *personal* phenomenological product that emerges when potentially meaningful ideas are integrated within an individually unique cognitive structure.

Invariably, therefore, the achievement of meaning requires translation into a personal frame of reference and reconciliation with established concepts and propositions. All of this goes on in any program of meaningful expository teaching, and is obviously a far cry from the straw-man picture of passive absorption that Bruner draws to disparage this method and thereby enhance the relative attractiveness of learning by discovery. Most of what anyone *really* knows consists of insights discovered by *others* that have been communicated to him or her in meaningful fashion.

Quite apart from its lack of face validity, the proposition that all people must discover for themselves every bit of knowledge that they *really* wish to possess is, in essence, a repudiation of the very concept of culture. For perhaps the most unique attribute of human culture, which distinguishes it from every other kind of social organization in the animal kingdom, is precisely the fact that the accumulated discoveries of millennia can be transmitted to each succeeding generation in the course of childhood and youth and need not be discovered anew by each generation. This miracle of culture is made possible only because it is so much less time-consuming to communicate and explain an idea meaningfully to others than to have them rediscover it by themselves.

> The infant is born into a logically ordered world, abounding in problem solutions accumulated during the long span of mankind's sojourn on earth, and this distilled wisdom, called "culture," constitutes his chief heritage. Were it wiped away, he would become, in all respects, a wild animal, even less well equipped to cope with nature than are the instinct-aided beasts of the jungle. An individual is sagacious in direct proportion to the facility with which he can acquire and use existing knowledge; for even the most brilliantly endowed person can make but few valuable original discoveries (Stanley, 1949, p. 455).

Within each generation, therefore, we can only expect a given individual to internalize meaningfully a reasonable fragment of the total fabric of the culture that is expounded to him or her by the various educational agencies. If we are at all concerned with the breadth of a person's knowledge, we cannot possibly expect that person to discover everything he or she is expected to know. The obligation of going beyond one's cultural heritage and contributing something new, is an obligation that applies to an entire generation, not to each of its individual members. Hence, as we shall see later, the school cannot realistically set for itself the goal of having *each* child "leap into new and unimagined realms of experience" and emerge with ideas that are "discontinuous with what went before." The school can only hope to help one child in a thousand do this, or, more likely, one child in a million.

### Meaning Is an Exclusive Product of Creative, Nonverbal Discovery

A related proposition that relies somewhat less on flat epistemological assertion, and is more naturalistically grounded, holds that abstract concepts and propositions are forms of empty verbalism unless the learner discovers them directly out of his own concrete, empirical, nonverbal experience. Another slightly different way of expressing the same idea is to say that

"Generalizations are products of problem-solving . . . and are attainable in no other way" (Brownell & Hendrickson, 1950, p. 119).

The assertion that abstract concepts and generalizations are forms of glib verbalism unless the learner discovers them himself rests, we have seen, on: (1) a misrepresentation of verbal reception learning as a passive, rote phenomenon; (2) confusion between the reception-discovery and the rote-meaningful dimensions of learning; and (3) unwarranted generalization to adolescents and adults of children's dependence on concrete-empirical props in comprehending and manipulating abstract ideas. Meaningful knowledge is not an exclusive product of creative nonverbal discovery. For potentially meaningful *presented* material to become meaningful knowledge, learners need only adopt a set to relate and incorporate its substantive import non-arbitrarily within their cognitive structure.

Discovery enthusiasts tend to confuse the act of discovery with the act of understanding. Taba (1962), for example, states that "the act of discovery occurs at the point in the learner's efforts at which he gets hold of the organizing principles embedded in any concrete instance, can see the relationship of the facts before him, understands the why of the phenomena, and can relate what he sees to his prior knowledge." Actually this is a definition of all meaningful learning irrespective of whether it is reception or discovery learning. Discovery enthusiasts also tend to deny the transition from concrete to abstract cognitive functioning. They insist rather that mature learners cannot understand an abstract verbal proposition without first relating it to concrete-empirical experience and translating it into subverbal terms. Thus Hendrix (1950, p. 337) asserts that "a cognitively sophisticated student, who is sufficiently skillful in interpreting sentence structure as well as referential symbols, can read a sentence which expresses a generalization and then construct or find enough examples of his own to make the generalization an organic part of himself—that is, to acquire the subverbal thing prerequisite to meaning of the sentence."

### Subverbal Awareness Is the Key to Transfer

We have seen, up to this point, that the reasoning underlying the mystique of discovery as a prerequisite for meaning has rested either upon bald metaphysical assertion or upon unwarranted pseudonaturalistic assumptions regarding the nature of understanding and knowledge. Hendrix tried to fill this theoretical void by constructing a more systematic and sophisticated pedagogic rationale for the discovery method than had been attempted heretofore. She did this by adapting to the problem of transfer the time-honored labeling theory of the function of language in thought. Hendrix denies that

[verbal] generalizing is the primary generator of transfer power. . . . As

far as transfer power [is] concerned the whole thing [is] there as soon as the non-verbal awareness [dawns]. . . . The separation of discovery phenomena from the process of composing sentences which express those discoveries is the big new breakthrough in pedagogical theory (Hendrix, 1961, pp. 292, 290).

The "key to transfer," Hendrix (1947, p. 200) states, is a "subverbal internal process—something which must happen to the organism before it has any new knowledge to verbalize." Verbalization, she asserts further, is not only unnecessary for the generation and transfer of ideas and understanding, but is also positively *harmful* when used for *these* purposes. Language only enters the picture because of the need to attach a symbol or label to the emerging subverbal insight so that it can be recorded, verified, classified, and communicated to others; but the entire substance of the idea inheres in the subverbal insight itself. The resulting problem then, according to Hendrix (1961, p. 292), becomes one of how to plan and execute teaching so that language can be used for these necessary secondary functions "*without* damage to the dynamic quality of the learning itself."

The principal fallacy in Hendrix' line of argument, as we have seen above, lies in her failure to distinguish between the labeling and process functions of language in thought. Furthermore, it should be self-evident that discovered generalizations are available for transfer only *if* and not until *after* they are discovered.

The unqualified generalization that verbalization of an insight prior to use inhibits transfer lacks both logical cogency and empirical support. Nonverbal understanding of principles undoubtedly exists, especially in children and unsophisticated adults, as a precursor to some verbal understandings (Hull, 1920; Luchins & Luchins, 1947). This, of course, does not mean that *nonverbal* concept meanings and propositions are actually used in the *generation* of new insights. Such a feat would be very difficult, as already explained, because ideas that are not represented by words lack sufficient manipulability to be used in any complex type of thought process. It merely suggests that a preliminary intuitive (subverbal) stage exists in the *product* of thought when the emerging new insight is not clearly and precisely refined. However, when this product is eventually refined *through* verbalization, it acquires thereby much greater transfer power. The verbalization of the insight that takes place at this point is actually a later phase of the thought process itself and is not to be confused with the still later representational process of *naming* verbalized meanings as a result of which the latter meanings become more manipulable for purposes of thought.

Thus several experiments on children's ability to solve transposition and discrimination problems (Spiker & Terrell, 1955; Weir & Stevenson, 1959) show that verbal insights are more transferable than subverbal insights. Knowledge of underlying verbal principles also enhances problem solving (Ewert & Lambert, 1932) and the learning of relevant motor skills

(Ervin, 1960b). And when distinctive verbal responses are available, they tend to facilitate concept acquisition and conceptual transfer. Verbal generalization is particularly important for concept attainment in cognitively sophisticated learners (Heidbreder & Zimmerman, 1955). In a very well-controlled experiment Gagné and Smith (1962) demonstrated the facilitating effect of verbalization on the discovery of general principles and their use in problem solving. Finally, merely informing learners verbally that previous learnings might be useful in other situations tends to increase transfer significantly (Dorsey & Hopkins, 1930).

As children enter school they encounter concepts of much greater abstractness and complexity (for instance, concepts of addition, multiplication, government, society, force, velocity, digestion) that transcend their immediate experience and language ability. Before they can hope to acquire a meaningful grasp of such abstractions directly—that is, through direct abstract-verbal exposition—they must first acquire a minimal level of sophistication in the particular subject-matter area. Then they graduate into the next higher level of intellectual development—that is, the stage of formal logical operations. In the meantime, children are limited to an intuitive, semiabstract kind of understanding of these concepts, which they often find difficult to verbalize precisely.[3] Even though convincing empirical evidence is still limited, it is reasonable to suppose that preliminary acquisition and utilization of this semiabstract level of insight both facilitates learning and transferability and promotes the eventual emergence of *full* abstract understanding (Hibbard & Novak, 1975; Nussbaum & Novak, 1976). Hendrix, of course, would say that *full* understanding was already attained in the semiabstract phase, provided that the understanding was discovered rather than presented. She would also insist that the older individual's verbalization of his or her understanding detracts from its transferability.

Now, assuming for the moment that Hendrix' (1947) experimental findings are valid, how can we explain the fact that immediate verbalization of newly acquired subverbal insight apparently renders that insight less transferable than when verbalization is not attempted? First, it seems likely that premature verbalization of nonverbal insight, before such insight is adequately clear, stable, complete, and consolidated further by extensive use, may interfere with its more adequate emergence and consolidation at

[3] It is important to differentiate between the intuitive subverbal insights of adolescents and those of elementary-school children. Because the latter use concrete-empirical props in relating potentially meaningful concepts and propositions to their cognitive structure, the initially resulting subverbal meanings are *inherently* intuitive (particularistic, semiabstract and semiprecise) on *developmental* grounds. Thus, even if they are verbalized later, they can never transcend this intuitive level. Adolescents, on the other hand, relate potentially meaningful concepts and propositions to cognitive structure without the use of concrete-empirical props; hence the subverbal meanings that initially emerge are not intuitive on developmental grounds and can be refined—in precision, clarity, explicitness, and generality—through the later process of verbalization.

this level. It also may encourage rote memorization of the marginal and ineptly stated verbal proposition. Even more important, however, is the likelihood that a verbally expressed insight—when ambiguous, unstable, unconsolidated, ineptly expressed, and only marginally competent—possesses less functional utility and transferability than the ordinarily more primitive and less transferable subverbal insight that is more adequate in these latter respects. This is particularly true in the case of children, because of their limited linguistic facility and their relative incompetence in formal propositional logic.

Drawing these various strands of argument together, what can we legitimately conclude at this point? First, verbalization does more than just encode subverbal insight into words. The use of manipulable words to represent ideas makes possible, in the first place, the very process of transforming these ideas into new insights. The verbalization of emerging subverbal insights into sentences is an integral part of the thought process that greatly enhances the precision and explicitness of its products. It therefore makes possible a qualitatively higher level of understanding with greatly enhanced transfer power.

Second, direct acquisition of ideas from verbally presented abstract propositions presupposes both that the learner has attained the stage of formal logical operations and that he or she possesses minimal sophistication in the particular subject matter in question. The typical elementary-school child, therefore, tends to be limited to an intuitive, semiabstract awareness of difficult abstractions. Older, cognitively mature individuals, however, who are also unsophisticated in a particular subject-matter area, are able to dispense with the semiabstract phase of awareness rather quickly—as soon as they attain the necessary degree of sophistication. Once they attain it, they probably short-circuit the semiabstract phase completely. Finally, premature verbalization of a nonverbal insight, when this latter insight is still incomplete, unclear, and inadequately consolidated, probably decreases its transferability. This phenomenon can be explained by means of the general developmental principle that an ordinarily higher and more efficient stage of development, while still embryonic and only marginally competent, is less functional than an ordinarily more primitive and less efficient phase of development. Running, for example, is eventually more efficient than creeping, but if a 1-year-old infant had to run for its life, the child would make better progress creeping.

Hendrix, however, comes out with somewhat different and more sweeping conclusions from the same set of data. First, she regards nonverbal awareness as containing within itself the entire essence of an emerging idea and insists that language merely adds a convenient symbolic handle to this idea. Second, she generalizes children's dependence on a preliminary semiabstract stage of understanding to all age levels, to all degrees of subject-matter sophistication, and to all levels of ideational difficulty. Actually, this semiabstract stage is highly abbreviated, both for young children learning less difficult kinds of abstractions, and for older, cognitively mature individuals working in a particular subject-matter area in which they happen to be unsophisticated; and it is bypassed completely when this latter sophistication is attained. Finally, she interprets her experimental findings regarding the inhibitory effects of immediate verbalization on the transferability of subverbal insight as providing empirical *proof* of her thesis that both the substance of an idea and the essential basis of its transfer power are present in their entirety as soon as nonverbal awareness emerges. More probably these findings merely show that a relatively clear and consolidated subverbal insight is more functional and transferable than an ambiguous, inept, unconsolidated, and marginally competent verbally expressed idea.

Unlike Hendrix, therefore, we may conclude that secondary-school and college students who already possess a sound, meaningful grasp of the rudiments of a discipline like mathematics can be taught this subject meaningfully and with maximal efficiency through the method of verbal exposition, supplemented by appropriate problem-solving experience. Moreover, we conclude, the use of the discovery method in these circumstances is inordinately time-consuming, wasteful, and rarely warranted.

Why then do discovery techniques seem to work so well in programs such as the one devised by the University of Illinois Committee on School Mathematics? For one thing, the students entering the program, being victims of conventional arithmetic teaching in the elementary schools, do *not* have a sound, meaningful grasp of the rudiments of mathematics, and have to be reeducated, so to speak, from scratch. For another, we have a very strong impression that as the program develops, the discovery element becomes progressively attenuated, until eventually it is accorded only token recognition. Finally, stripped of its quite limited discovery aspects, the UICSM approach is a much more systematic, highly organized, self-consistent, carefully programmed, abstractly verbal system of verbal exposition than anything we have known to date in secondary-school mathematics. If it proves anything, the success of this program is a testimonial to the feasibility and value of a good program of didactic verbal exposition in secondary-school mathematics—of a program that is taught by able and enthusiastic instructors and, in its early stages, makes judicious use of inductive and discovery techniques. Once again it is useful to refer to Figure 1.1 and to recognize that the rote → meaningful dimension of learning is independent of the degree of reception or discovery teaching methodology.

### The Discovery Method Is the Principal Method for Transmitting Subject-Matter Content

Educators who are convinced that abstractions are mere glib verbalisms unless independently discovered by the learner have no other logical alternative than to advocate the use of discovery techniques—in the high school and university as well as in the elementary school—as a principal method of transmitting the substantive content of subject matter. Easley (1958, 1959), for example, argues strenuously for reorganizing, in whole or in part, the curriculum of science, mathematics, and other secondary-school and college-level subjects along the lines of inductive discovery. He also insists that nonverbal understanding and application of principles should be required of and demonstrated by students before they are permitted to use them in verbal form.

From a practical standpoint, however, it is impossible to consider the pedagogic feasibility of learning by discovery as a primary means of teaching subject-matter content without taking into account the inordinate time-cost involved. This disadvantage is applicable not only to the type of discovery where learners are thrown entirely on their own resources, but also in lesser degree to the "contrived" or "arranged" type of discovery. Considerations of time-cost are particularly pertinent in view of our aforementioned developmental conclusion that the discovery approach offers no striking learning advantages except in the very limited case of the more difficult learning task, when the learner is either in the concrete stage of cognitive development, or, if generally in the abstract stage, happens to lack minimal sophistication in a particular subject-matter field.

Once students reach secondary school and university, the time-cost disadvantage can no longer be defended on the dual grounds that the time-consuming aspects of discovery learning (the need for concrete-empirical props) must take place anyway, and that in any case elementary-school pupils cannot be expected to assimilate a great deal of subject matter. Subverbal, intuitive techniques have more general applicability during the elementary-school period. But they are also more time-consuming and confer a qualitatively inferior type of understanding than does the verbal expository approach, which can be successfully employed once students reach the abstract stage of cognitive development.

Thus whereas the relatively frequent use of discovery techniques in the transmission of complex and abstract subject-matter content can be defended in the elementary school on the grounds that the acquisition and transfer of intuitive insights may possibly facilitate the later acquisition of abstract understanding, it is difficult to rationalize the same practice in high school and beyond. It is true, as already pointed out, that the utilization of subverbal insight by older individuals might be temporarily helpful in the early, unsophisticated stages of learning a difficult new discipline. Nevertheless, discovery methods are incomparably more time-consuming than didactic verbal exposition, and the cognitively mature individual does not linger very long in the unsophisticated state that is benefited by prior acquisition of such insights. Hence the use of these methods as a *primary* means of transmitting subject-matter content is as unfeasible as it is unnecessary.

If secondary school and university students were obliged to discover for themselves every concept and principle in the syllabus, they would never get much beyond the rudiments of any discipline. However, as is similarly the case in the elementary school, teachers who do not regard completely autonomous discovery as sacrosanct could greatly mitigate the time-consuming disadvantage of discovery methods by the judicious use of prompts or hints.

Some discovery enthusiasts (Bruner, 1960; Suchman, 1961) grudgingly admit that there is not sufficient time for pupils to discover everything they need to know in the various disciplines, and hence concede that there is also room for good expository teaching in the schools. In practice, however, this concession counts for little, because in the very next breath they claim that the acquisition of actual knowledge is less important than the acquisition of ability to discover knowledge autonomously, and propose that pedagogy and the curriculum be reorganized accordingly. Hence, in spite of the formal bow they make to didactic exposition, it is clear that they regard the acquisition of problem-solving ability as more basic than the acquisition of subject matter. There is, after all, only so much time in a school day. If the school takes as its principal function the development of discovery and inquiry skills, how much time could possibly remain for the teaching of subject matter?

Discovery methods of teaching are often based on the naive premise that autonomous problem solving necessarily proceeds on the basis of inductive reasoning from empirical data. Actually, even young children usually start with some preconceptions or spontaneous models derived from their own experience or from the prevailing folklore. Hence when they are supposedly discovering principles inductively, they are really attempting to use empirical experience to confirm their existing preconceptions. It is "unpromising to base a teaching program on the expectation that children can invent . . . modern scientific concepts, because their spontaneously invented concepts . . . present too much of a block." A more realistic approach "is for the teacher to *introduce* . . . modern scientific concepts . . . [and] follow the introduction with opportunities for the children to discover that new observations can also be interpreted by use of the concept" (Atkin & Karplus, 1962).

Still another disadvantage in using a discovery approach for the presentation of subject-matter content inheres in the difficulties caused by children's subjectivism and by their exaggerated tendency to jump to conclusions, to overgeneralize on the basis of limited experience, and to consider only one aspect of a problem at a time (Inhelder & Piaget, 1958; Karplus, 1962a; 1962b; Piaget, 1932). It is true that one objective of the elementary science curriculum (to enhance appreciation of scientific method) implies an effort to educate them out of these tendencies. But it is one thing to do so as part of a limited laboratory program and quite another to struggle full-time with this handicap as children are required to self-discover everything they have to learn.

It is also completely unrealistic to expect that subject-matter content can be acquired incidentally as a by-product of problem-solving or discovery experience, as, it is hypothesized, occurs in the typical "activity program" or project method. Such incidental teaching pays too little attention to graded and systematically organized content, to substantive and programmatic aspects of presentation, and to practice and feedback variables.

Finally, one might reasonably ask how many students have the ability to discover everything they need to know. Although the ability to understand original ideas worth remembering is widely distributed, the ability to generate comparably original ideas autonomously is manifested by relatively few persons—that is, by creative individuals.

In conclusion, after the elementary-school years, verbal reception learning constitutes the most effective method of meaningfully assimilating the substantive content of a discipline. Problem-solving and subverbal methods are developmentally and pedagogically unnecessary and are too time-consuming to accomplish this objective efficiently. However, the method of verbal reception learning will be restored to its rightful place in classroom instruction only when it is related to relevant but still-to-be-conducted research on the nature and conditions of long-term meaningful learning of large bodies of verbally presented material.

### Problem-Solving Ability Is the Primary Goal of Education

A fifth proposition underlying the learning by discovery thesis is the belief that the development of problem-solving ability is the *primary* goal of education. Implicit in this proposition is the assumption that the objectives involved in developing problem-solving ability, on the one hand, and in acquiring a body of knowledge, on the other, are more or less coextensive, and, therefore, that the learner somehow manages to acquire all of the important subject-matter content he or she needs to know in the course of learning how to discover knowledge autonomously. Actually, however, although these two sets of objectives are related and in a sense mutually supportive, they are far from being identical. Hence it cannot be assumed that methods promoting one objective necessarily promote the other and that the process and goal of education are "one and the same thing," as Bruner (1961a) claims they are.

In the first place, quite apart from its frequent usefulness in problem solving, the acquisition of knowledge as an end in itself must be considered the major goal of education. Despite the fact that a large proportion of what human beings learn in the course of a lifetime has no immediate utility and is not applicable to any pressing problem of adjustment, people are nevertheless strongly motivated to learn so that they can better understand themselves, the universe, and the human condition. Much of this kind of knowledge, however, would have to be dismissed as worthless if utility for problem-solving purposes was invariably considered the criterion for designating worthwhileness for learning. Hence, if we are concerned with the acquisition of knowledge as an end in itself, we cannot leave its implementation to problem-solving and discovery techniques. The use of these techniques, as already pointed out, furthers the problem-solving objective of education, but, except in the elementary school and under other special circumstances, is not very efficient for transmitting subject-matter content.

Second, the actual objective of typical problem-solving activity in most individuals is the solution of various everyday problems in living, rather than the discovery of ideas or insights sufficiently important to be included in their permanent store of knowledge.[4] For, as stated previously, although the ability to understand original ideas worth remembering is widely distributed, the ability to generate comparably original ideas autonomously is manifested by only relatively few persons, that is, by creative individuals. It is true, of course, that "arranged" or "contrived" rediscovery would require considerably less creativity; but even the use of this expedient on the part of the relatively more able (if not creative) segment of the population would be so time-consuming as to render learning by discovery an impractical method of learning everything they need to know.

In the realm of educational theory, if not in actual practice, the impact of Dewey's exaggerated emphasis on problem solving still continues to disturb the natural balance between the "transmission of the culture" and the problem-solving objectives of education. Enthusiastic proponents of the discovery method assert that "more basic than the attainment of concepts is the ability to inquire and discover them autonomously" (Suchman, 1961).

These somewhat extreme value judgments regarding the principal function of the school inspire, in turn, correspondingly one-sided proposals with respect to curriculum and pedagogy. Suchman, for example, contends that "the schools must have a new pedagogy with a new set of goals which subordinates retention to thinking. . . . Instead of devoting their efforts to storing information and recalling it on demand, they would be developing the cognitive functions needed to seek out and organize information in a way that would be most productive of new concepts" (Suchman, 1961).

The development of problem-solving ability is, of course, a legitimate and significant educational objective in its own right. Hence it is highly defensible to utilize a certain proportion of classroom time in developing appreciation of and facility in the use of scientific methods of inquiry and

---

[4] The inductive derivation of concepts and generalizations from diverse instances is an exception to this statement, but is only a conspicuous feature of concept attainment during childhood (before a really large quantity of subject matter is assimilated).

of other empirical, inductive, and deductive problem-solving procedures. But this is a far cry from advocating that the enhancement of problem-solving ability is the *major* function of the school. In addition, to acquire facility in problem solving and scientific method, it is not necessary for learners to rediscover *every* principle in the syllabus. Since problem-solving ability is itself transferable, at least within a given subject-matter field, facility gained in independently formulating and applying one generalization is transferable to other problem areas in the same discipline.

Furthermore, overemphasis on developing problem-solving ability would ultimately defeat its own ends. It would leave students with insufficient time in which to learn the content of a discipline. Hence, despite their adeptness at problem solving, they would be unable to solve simple problems involving the application of such content. Thus although actual practice in the process of formulating and testing hypotheses and in applying general principles to particular problem situations is necessary for enhancing problem-solving ability, much "teaching for problem solving" necessarily involves the efficient transmission of fundamental, widely generalizable principles that are clearly understood and can be stably retained.

"Teaching for critical thinking" and "teaching for problem solving" are really somewhat grandiose slogans, although obviously much more realistic than "teaching for creative thinking." To be sure, the critical thinking and problem-solving abilities of most pupils can be improved. But this is not the same thing as saying that most pupils can be trained to become good critical thinkers and problem solvers. Potentialities for developing high levels of these abilities are admittedly much less rare than corresponding potentialities for developing creativity. Nevertheless, there are no good reasons for believing that they are any commoner than potentialities for developing high general intelligence. Variability in genic endowment is probably responsible for more of the measured variance in critical thinking or problem-solving ability than is variability in educational experience. This conclusion is supported by a review of problem solving in mathematics (Kilpatrick, 1969).

Aptitude in problem solving involves a much different pattern of abilities than those required for understanding and retaining abstract ideas. The ability to solve problems calls for qualities (flexibility, resourcefulness, improvising skill, originality, problem sensitivity, venturesomeness) that are less generously distributed in the population of learners than the ability to comprehend verbally presented materials. Many of these qualities also cannot be taught effectively. Although appropriate pedagogic procedures can improve problem-solving ability, the number of persons who can be trained to be good problem solvers is relatively small in comparison with the number of persons who can acquire a meaningful grasp of various subject-matter fields. Thus, to ignore the latter individuals and concentrate solely on producing talented problem solvers would be educationally indefensible.

Hence a valid distinction can be drawn between "doing" and "understanding." Understanding is a necessary but not a sufficient condition for meaningful problem solving (the kind that involves genuine appreciation of underlying principles—not trial-and-error procedures or simply pragmatic rules of practice). Thus pupils can genuinely understand a proposition without being able to apply it successfully in particular problem situations, because such application requires additional knowledge, skill, ability, experience, or personality traits that are not inherent in the understanding itself. Conversely, "doing," if it is rote or mechanical in nature, does not necessarily either presuppose or enhance understanding.

Many writers (Bruner, 1961b; Carin & Sund, 1964; Easley, 1958; Hibbs, 1961; Romey, 1968; Rowe, 1973; Suchman, 1961) in the field of science education express the view that the principal objective of science instruction is the acquisition of general inquiry skills, of appropriate attitudes about science, and of training in the "heuristics of discovery." Implicit or explicit in this view is the belief either that the particular choice of subject matter chosen to implement these goals is a matter of indifference (as long as it is suitable for the operations of inquiry), or that somehow in the course of performing a series of unrelated experiments in depth, the learner acquires all of the really important subject matter he needs to know. Thus, Hibbs (1961) states: "It does not matter whether the student learns any particular set of facts, but it does matter whether he learns how much fun it is to learn—to observe and experiment, to question and analyze the world without any ready-made set of answers and without any premium on the accuracy of his factual results, at least in the field of science."

In our opinion, any science curriculum worthy of the name must be concerned with the systematic presentation of an organized body of knowledge as an explicit end in itself. Even if it is relatively superficial and organized on an intuitive basis, as it must be in the elementary school, the science curriculum should make a start in this direction and give the student a feeling for science as a selectively and sequentially organized structure. This is no less important than imparting the view that science is a method of inquiry.

Another significant difficulty with this approach is that its proponents tend to confuse the goals of the scientist with the goals of the science student. They assert that these objectives are identical, and hence students can learn science most effectively by enacting the role of junior scientist. But are the goals of research scientists and of science students really identical? Scientists are engaged in a full-time search for new general or applied principles in their field. Students, on the other hand, are primarily engaged in an effort to learn the same basic subject matter in this field that scientists learned in their student days, and also to learn something of the method and spirit of scientific inquiry.

Although it makes perfectly good sense for scientists to work full time formulating and testing new hypotheses, it is quite indefensible, in our opinion, for students to be doing the same thing—either for real, or in the sense of rediscovery. Most of the student's time should be taken up with appropriate expository learning, and the remainder devoted to sampling the flavor and techniques of scientific method.

It is the scientist's business to formulate unifying explanatory principles in science. It is the student's business to learn these principles as meaningfully and critically as possible, and *then*, after this background is adequate, to try to improve on them if he can. If a student is ever to discover, he or she must first learn; and the student cannot learn adequately by pretending to be a junior scientist. By so pretending, he or she would fail to acquire the minimal degree of subject-matter sophistication in a given discipline, much less make original research contributions to science. Moreover, most of the *scientist's* work involves the reading of relevant research studies and attempts to achieve integrative reconciliation of the concepts he or she is developing with the currently accepted concepts of a particular discipline. Technicians perform routine laboratory experiments.

It is true that some amount of training in the self-direction of learning is necessary as preparation for the years when students will no longer be in school. But knowing how to find the best material available on a given topic is not the same as discovery learning or even the same as finding and integrating all of the primary sources by oneself. For most individuals, at any stage of life, secondary sources typically present, interpret, and integrate knowledge.

### Training in the "Heuristics of Discovery" Is More Important than Training in Subject Matter

Some advocates of the discovery method favor a type of guided practice in the "heuristics of discovery" that is reminiscent of the faculty psychology[5] approach to improving overall critical thinking ability through instruction in the general principles of logic. Once the heuristics of discovery are mastered, they constitute, according to Bruner (1961a), "a style of problem solving or inquiry that serves for any kind of task one may encounter." Similarly, Suchman's Inquiry Training Program "is not proposed as a new way to teach science, but as a way of teaching basic cognitive skills . . . [that belongs] in the science program and in every other curriculum area that requires . . . reasoning and the formulation and testing of hypotheses" (Suchman, 1961).

The principal difficulty with this approach, as the faculty psychologists discovered, is that critical thinking ability can be enhanced only within the context of a specific discipline. Grand strategies of discovery, like scientific

[5] The doctrine of formal discipline is still very much alive.

method, do not seem to be transferable across disciplinary lines—either when acquired within a given discipline or when learned in a more general form apart from specific subject-matter content. This principle has been confirmed by countless studies and is illustrated by the laughable errors of logic and judgment committed by distinguished scientists and scholars who wander outside their own disciplines. The only kinds of transfer that have been empirically demonstrated in problem-solving situations are the transfer of specific skills, the transfer of general principles, and the transfer of general approach or orientation to a specified class of problems.

Hence critical thinking cannot be taught as a generalized ability. In practice it can be enhanced only by adopting a precise, logical, analytic, and critical approach to the teaching of a particular discipline, an approach that fosters appreciation of scientific method in that discipline. Also, from a purely theoretical standpoint alone, it hardly seems plausible that a strategy of inquiry that must necessarily be broad enough to be applicable to a wide range of disciplines and problems can ever have, at the same time, sufficient *particular* relevance to be helpful in the solution of the *specific* problem at hand. And from the standpoint of elementary-school children, one wonders whether principles of inquiry pitched at this level of abstraction could be meaningful enough to be used successfully in problem solving.

The rapid rate of obsolescence in science is often offered as a rationale for the heuristics of discovery approach to science teaching. Since the content of what is taught today will be obsolescent in fifteen years, the argument runs, students should be taught the process rather than the content of science. Actually the rate of obsolescence in science is vastly exaggerated. Although the specifics of science change rapidly, basic principles tend to manifest impressive longevity. This argument is also strikingly reminiscent of the objection small boys offer to washing their faces daily, namely, that they will only get dirty the next day. Obsolescence is a fact of life that must always be kept in mind; but this does not render futile the assimilation of the current content of knowledge or counsel exclusive attention to the process whereby knowledge is acquired. It merely presupposes a readiness to revise those aspects of one's knowledge that gradually become outdated. A related argument invokes the allegedly rapid rate of forgetting of school learning. Actually, however, meaningfully learned subject matter exhibits impressive longevity—even over a period of years (Kastrinos, 1965; Tyler, 1930, 1934b; Ward & Davis, 1938).

Another attempt to describe an approach or strategy for learning is Rothkopf's (1970) concept of mathemagenic activities. He defines: "Mathemagenic behaviors are behaviors that give birth to learning. More specifically, the study of mathemagenic activities is the study of the student's actions that are relevant to the achievement of specified instructional objectives" (Rothkopf, 1970, p. 325). Unlike Suchman, Cole, and other "inquiry" enthusiasts, Rothkopf emphasizes that *"mathemagenic activities are those*

*student activities that are relevant to the achievement of specified instruc-*
*tional objectives in specified situations or places"* (Rothkopf, 1970, p. 327;
italics in original). In this sense, mathemagenic activities are very much like
learning activities that foster meaningful learning as described by assimilation theory.[6]

But this is not very true in the case of mathemagenically oriented research that uses adjunct questions either before or in the body of the text
of learning passages. This is no way of knowing in such studies whether
the so-called mathemagenic effect is attributable (1) to cognitive orientation
cues that direct the learner's attention to key concepts, (2) to motivational
factors (for example, relief of boredom or separation of a long learning
passage into more manageable smaller units that appear subjectively less
difficult to master, or (3) to stimulation of retrotractive rehearsal of previously read material.

In addition the research methodology in these studies has tended to test
for verbatim (that is, rote) recall of small idea units rather than for substantive (meaningful) comprehension and retention of entire paragraphs.
As pointed out in Chapter 5, however, adjunct questions may be used to
facilitate meaningful learning of substantive comprehension and retention
tested for (Rickards & DiVesta, 1974).

Moreover, we find a confusion in Rothkopf's writings between aspects
of an instructional program and aspects of cognitive learning. At least one
review of relevant studies finds that the use of factual review questions
does not significantly influence learning of incidental information, as Rothkopf would predict (Ladas, 1973). Our conclusion is that both general
strategies of "heuristics of discovery" or general classes of mathemagenic
behavior show little promise for improvement of education.

### Every Child Should Be a Creative and Critical Thinker

Discovery methods are often rationalized in terms of the currently
fashionable slogan that the school's chief responsibility is to make every
child (or nearly every child) a critical and creative thinker. This incredible
notion is based on (1) the highly questionable assumption that all discovery
activity, irrespective of degree of originality, is *qualitatively* of one piece;

---

[6] One significant difference, however, is in the vagueness and nonspecificity of the
neologism "mathemagenic." In actual studies of "mathemagenic" behavior (typically
the use of adjunct questions) it is unclear whether the effective facilitating variable is
advance orientation, selective retrospective focusing on particular aspects of the learning passage, relief of boredom, or rehearsal of previously learned material. The tests of
learning and retention also focus on verbatim recall of discrete short phrases instead
of on substantive retention of the meanings of whole paragraphs or pages. A recent
exception to this latter practice is the research of Rickards and diVesta (1974). When
posttests tested for substantive retention, adjunct questions acted just like advance
organizers (see p. 176).

(2) a watered-down, more "democratic" definition of creativity, broad enough to include *any* type of independent discovery; (3) the belief that the very multiplicity of human abilities gives every individual a good chance, genically speaking, of being creative in at least one area; and (4) naive clean-slate conceptions of human plasticity that maintain that even if a given child has no creative potentialities, good teachers can take the place of missing genes.

Bruner is an eloquent spokesman for this point of view:

> Intellectual activity anywhere is the same, whether at the frontier of knowledge or in a third-grade classroom. What a scientist does at his desk or in the laboratory, what a literary critic does in reading a poem are of the same order as what anybody else does when he is engaged in like activities—if he is to achieve understanding. The difference is in degree, not in kind. The schoolboy learning physics *is* a physicist, and it is easier for him to learn physics behaving like a physicist than doing something else (Bruner, 1960, p. 14).

Suchman (1961) also explains that the ultimate goal of his Inquiry Training Program is for children to discover and formulate explanations that represent "the causality of a single instance in terms of broad universal principles and generalizations. This is the unification of concepts for which the scientist strives. It can, and, in our opinion, should be the ultimate goal of children's inquiry as well."

We will consider in another context (Chapter 16) the overall plausibility of this proposition. It only remains to point out here that from the standpoint of enlightened educational policy in a democracy, the school should concentrate its major efforts on teaching both what is most important in terms of cultural survival and cultural progress and what is most teachable to the majority of its clientele.

As improved methods of teaching become available, most students will be able to master the basic intellectual skills as well as a reasonable portion of the more important subject-matter content of the major disciplines. Is it not more defensible to aim at this realistic goal, which lies within our reach, than to focus on educational objectives that presuppose exceptional genic endowment and are impossible of fulfillment when applied to the generality of mankind? Would it not be more realistic to strive first to have each pupil respond meaningfully, actively, and critically to good expository teaching before we endeavor to make him or her a creative thinker or even a good critical thinker and problem solver?

We are by no means proposing a uniform curriculum and pedagogy for all children irrespective of individual differences. By all means let us provide all feasible special opportunities and facilities for the exceptional child. But in so doing, let us not attempt to structure the learning environment of the *non*exceptional child in terms of educational objectives and teaching methods that are appropriate for either one child in a hundred or perhaps for one child in a million.

### Expository Teaching Is Authoritarian

Advocates of the discovery method also take advantage of the opprobrium associated with authoritarianism in education to discredit didactic exposition and to further their own cause. In doing this, they not only rely on the straw-man technique of representing a highly exaggerated "tell'm and drill" approach as typical of expository teaching, but also assert that expository teaching is inherently authoritarian. A teacher standing in front of a classroom and presenting facts, concepts, and principles is, according to Hendrix and others, behaving in an authoritarian fashion. This is presumably so because the teacher is allegedly coercing pupils, by the prestige of his or her position and power to dispense reward and punishment, into unquestioningly accepting on faith the teacher's own version of "the truth," instead of giving the pupils an opportunity to discover it for themselves. Bruner (1961b) puts it this way: "Insofar as possible, a method of instruction should have the objective of leading the child to discover for himself. Telling children and then testing them on what they have been told inevitably has the effect of producing bench-bound learners whose motivation for learning is likely to be extrinsic to the task at hand—pleasing the teacher, getting into college, artificially maintaining self-esteem."

In the first place, this distressing picture of expository teaching is a bit overdrawn. We do not deny that schools and colleges abound in such teachers. But this characterization is certainly not true of all didactic exposition, *nor is it inherent in the method itself.* Second, there is nothing inherently authoritarian in presenting or explaining ideas to others as long as they are not obliged, either explicitly or implicitly, to accept them on faith.

Didactic exposition has always constituted the core of any pedagogic system, and probably always will, because it is the only feasible and efficient method of transmitting large bodies of knowledge. The deference to authority implied in accepting already discovered knowledge has been condemned out of all reason. If students were required independently to validate every proposition presented by their instructors before accepting it, they would never progress beyond the rudiments of any discipline. We can only ask that established knowledge be presented to them as rationally and nonarbitrarily as possible, and that they accept it tentatively and critically as only the best available approximation of the "truth."

### Discovery Organizes Learning Effectively for Later Use

We turn now to the last four propositions advanced in support of learning by discovery. These propositions were propounded by Bruner (1961a) and, taken together, may be said to constitute a proposed psychological, rather than philosophical, rationale for the discovery method. First, Bruner hypothesizes that emphasis upon discovery in learning has precisely the effect upon the learner of leading him to be a constructionist, to organize what he is encountering in a manner not only designed to cover regularity and relatedness but also to avoid the kind of information drift that fails to keep account of the uses to which information might have to be put.

However, learning by discovery, in our opinion, does not *necessarily* lead to more orderly, integrative, and viable organization, transformation, and use of knowledge. It does so only insofar as the learning situation is highly structured, simplified, and skillfully programmed to include a large number of diversified exemplars of the same principle, carefully graded in order of difficulty. But under these circumstances, one must, in all fairness, attribute these latter outcomes to the teacher's or textbook writer's organization of the data from which the discovery is to be made, rather than to the act of discovery itself.

As a matter of fact, *pure* discovery techniques, as employed by scholars and scientists, could lead only to utter chaos in the classroom. Put a young physics student into a bathtub and he or she is just as likely to concentrate on the soap bubbles and on the refraction of light as on the displacement principle that is supposed to be discovered. In the UICSM program, therefore, students are given a prearranged sequence of suitable exemplars, and from these they "spontaneously self-discover" the appropriate generalization. Elementary-school pupils in the Inquiry Training Program are similarly shown a carefully prepared demonstration film illustrative of a given principle in physics and are then permitted to ask questions answerable by "yes" or "no."

Under both of these conditions, pupils are engaging in "true" autonomous discovery in the same sense that a detective independently "solves" a crime after a benevolent Providence kindly gathers all of the clues and arranges them in the correct sequence. This type of discovery is obviously a far cry from the kind of discovery that takes place in research laboratories. As Stanley observes:

> If, as a few ultra-progressive educators seem to imply, education were solely discovery, then teachers would no longer be necessary. Usually these theorizers are thinking of classroom situations in which the process of discovery resembles an Easter-egg hunt or the piecing together of a jigsaw puzzle: the participants make discoveries that could hardly have come about without previous "structuring" of the situation. The teacher activity which is involved in setting up good learning situations is as truly a form of instruction as is direct teaching from lesson plans. Simply turning children loose without direction and expecting each of them to discover for himself important relationships, such as the fact that the first letter of the first word in every sentence is capitalized, would probably prove decidedly ineffective and wasteful of time (Stanley, 1949, p. 455).

Now in making these observations, we certainly do not wish to create the impression that we quarrel with the UICSM method of inducing discovery, or that we favor the use of raw, unselected, and unorganized data in discovery programs. We quarrel only with Bruner's interpretation that the organizing and integrative effects of learning by discovery are attributable to the *act* of discovery rather than to the structure and organization that are put there by the programmers of such curriculums as the UICSM and the Physical Science Study Committee courses in secondary-school mathematics and physics respectively.

Concern with the "structure" of a discipline is certainly not indigenous to the discovery method, as Taba (1962) seems to imply. It is also the basis of all modern approaches to expository teaching or reception learning. In fact, concern with presenting the unifying principles of a discipline is the main substantive rationale of expository teaching. The more unstructured discovery methods, on the other hand, tend to ignore the particular substantive content of a discipline as long as it can be used to further problem-solving or inquiry processes. In Suchman's Inquiry Training, for example, there is no attempt to present systematically the content of a scientific discipline. Content is largely a matter of indifference, or incidental to the process of discovery. Any kind of content is as good as any other as long as it lends itself to discovery and inquiry. Hence, unsystematic and haphazard sampling of scientific content is characteristic of his Inquiry Training Program. The same mistake was incorporated into the design of *Science, A Process Approach*, an elementary school program sponsored by the American Association for the Advancement of Science (1968).

Learning by discovery is not necessarily antithetical to programmed instruction, despite the howls of anguish that teaching machines[7] frequently elicit from discovery enthusiasts. True, the more unstructured kinds of discovery methods (for instance, the Inquiry Training Program), which demand more genuinely autonomous (unprompted) discovery on the part of the learner, are incompatible with the "ruleg" type of programming (Homme & Glaser, 1960). In the latter a verbal rule is stated at the outset, and learners are then tested on their ability to apply this rule correctly to various relevant examples.

Advocates of these kinds of discovery methods also prefer to give the learner greater scope for independent thinking than is implied in the use of closely graduated steps in programmed sequences. On the other hand, highly structured discovery methods, such as the UICSM, which lead the learner to a desired generalization through the use of carefully graded

---

[7] As stated in Chapter 10, we are advocates of "programmed" instruction in the sense that it employs the pedagogic principles (see Chapter 5) derived from assimilation theory. However, we reject completely the "teaching machine" approach that fragments knowledge into small, discrete, and meaningless bits of jumbled "facts."

problem examples, are quite compatible with a programming technique that follows the same general procedure. Similarly, Gagné and Brown (1961) conducted an experiment in which one group of learners ("guided discovery") was required to discover a principle after working a hierarchy of problems that reduced the learning task to a graduated series of sequential steps.

### Discovery Is a Unique Generator of Motivation and Self-Confidence

Bruner (1960, 1961a, 1961b) and other discovery enthusiasts (Hendrix, 1961; Suchman, 1961) perceive learning by discovery as a unique and unexcelled generator of self-confidence, of intellectual excitement, and of motivation for sustained problem solving and creative thinking. We have already acknowledged that discovery techniques are valuable for acquiring desirable attitudes toward inquiry, as well as firm convictions about the existence and discoverability of orderliness in the universe. It is also reasonable to suppose that successful discovery experience enhances both these attitudes and convictions and individuals' feelings of confidence in their own abilities. On the other hand, there is no reason to believe that discovery methods are unique or alone in their ability to effect these outcomes.

As every student who has been exposed to competent teaching knows, the skillful exposition of ideas can also generate considerable intellectual excitement and motivation for genuine inquiry, although admittedly not quite as much perhaps as does discovery. Few physics students who learn the principle of displacement from expository teaching will run half-naked through the streets shrieking, "Eureka." But then again, how many students of Archimedes' ability are enrolled in the typical physics or mathematics class? How comparable to the excitement of Archimedes' purely autonomous and original discovery is the excitement generated by discovering a general formula for finding the number of diagonals in an $n$-sided polygon after working problems one through nine in the textbook? And what happens to Archimedes Junior's motivation and self-confidence if, after seventeen immersions in the tub, he has merely succeeded in getting himself soaking wet?

Careful study of the psychological experiment cited by Bruner (1961a), by way of illustrating the allegedly unique motivational and inspirational values of discovery methods, leaves one no more convinced than one was before. Bruner describes a psychological experiment in probability learning with a two-choice apparatus in which "the payoff sequence is arranged at random and there is no pattern." Some subjects quickly begin to catch on to the fact, and rightly so in this case, that "things are happening quite by chance . . . [and] very soon revert to a much more primitive [and empirically more successful] strategy wherein *all* responses are allocated to the side that has the greater payoff." Other more trusting and optimistic souls, however, persist in believing that "there *is* some pattern to be found in the sequence . . . i.e., that regularities are discoverable," and hence keep trying one unsuccessful hypothesis after another, in each of which "the number of responses given to each side is roughly equal to the proportion of times it pays off."

"What has all this to do with the subject at hand?" asks Bruner.

> For the person to search out and find regularities and relationships in his environment, he must be armed with an expectancy that there will be something to find and, once aroused by expectancy, he must devise ways of searching and finding. One of the chief enemies of expectancy is the assumption there is nothing one can find in the environment by way of regularity or relationship (Bruner, 1961a, p. 24).

We can thoroughly appreciate the logic of this argument, but we still cannot see what relevance it has for the issue regarding the unique motivational virtues of the discovery method. All Bruner is saying here is that, in the absence of a firm conviction about the existence of discoverable regularities in a particular problem-solving situation, one will resort to simple trial-and-error behavior—just like Thorndike's cats in the puzzle box. But why should discovery methods necessarily inspire any more confidence in the existence of discoverable regularities in the universe than the method of didactic exposition, which after all is dedicated to the presentation and explication of these regularities? It is true that successful discovery experience strengthens such confidence. But unsuccessful experience has precisely the opposite effect—as demonstrated by the resurgence of magical and superstitious thinking that follows in the wake of failure to find patterns of orderliness in nature.

### Discovery Is a Prime Source of Intrinsic Motivation

A related motivational proposition put forth by Bruner (1961a) states that "to the degree that one is able to approach learning as a task of discovering something rather than 'learning about it,' to that degree will there be a tendency for the child to carry out his learning activities with the autonomy of self-reward or, more properly, by reward that is discovery itself." Bruner feels that learning by discovery frees the child from the immediate control of such extrinsic motives as high marks, desire for parental and teacher approval, and a need to conform to the expectations of authority figures. In support of this hypothesis, he cites research data showing that early "overachievers" in school tend to be conformists, to overdevelop rote abilities, and to be deficient in analytic and critical thinking ability.

In our opinion, however, there is no existing or necessary association between a discovery approach to learning and intrinsic motivation, on the one hand, and a reception approach to learning and extrinsic motivation, on the other. But because of certain cultural influences on personality development in our type of social system, we would tend to postulate precisely the *opposite* kind of relationship, namely, that discovery learning is more often associated with *extrinsic* motivation than is reception learning. Whether an individual primarily manifests intrinsic or extrinsic motivation in learning, it seems to us, is largely a function of two factors: (1) how much intrinsic self-esteem he or she possesses, and hence how great the relative need is for compensatory earned status; and (2) the strength of his or her cognitive needs in their own right, that is, the need to acquire knowledge and to understand the environment, as influenced by genic and temperamental determinants and by previous satisfactory learning experience.

On these grounds, we would think that a more plausible interpretation of Bruner's data is that it is the learner who is lacking in intrinsic self-esteem who develops an overpowering need both for such external symbols of achievement as high grades and teacher approval *and* for the glory and prestige associated with independent discovery in our culture. Hence overachievers are typically children who are deficient in intrinsic self-esteem. They rely unduly on rote memorization both because it is the surest route to the high marks and the teacher approval they crave and because (on account of anxiety and impaired self-esteem) they lack the self-confidence to improvise in novel, problem-solving test situations (Ausubel, Schiff, & Goldman, 1953). At the same time, however, to bolster their impaired self-esteem, these individuals aspire to the prestige and status that, in our culture, can be achieved only through the exercise and hypertrophy of White's so-called "competence motive," which Bruner equates with the drive to discover.

What we are suggesting, therefore, is that rather than being uniquely powered by intrinsic motives, learning by discovery, or overvigorous exercise of the drive for competence, typically reflects in our culture a lack of intrinsic self-esteem and a compensatory need to overachieve with respect to the external symbols and trappings of successful accomplishment. To be sure, there are individuals who are driven to discover principally because of a compelling need to express their individuality or creative urges, to find the answers to haunting problems, or to discharge their feelings of moral obligation to the social community. But in our particular culture with its emphasis on status, prestige, ego aggrandizement, and material rewards—especially among individuals who lack intrinsic self-esteem—such motives for discovery tend to be the exception rather than the rule.

*Discovery Ensures the "Conservation of Memory"*

In the last of his four propositions, Bruner claims unique retention advantages for material learned by the discovery method. And again he illustrates his point by citing an experiment of questionable relevance to the principle he proposes. Pairs of words are presented to 12-year-old children:

> One group is simply told to remember the pairs, that they will be asked to repeat them later. Another is told to remember them by producing a word or idea that will tie the pair together in a way that will make sense to them. A third group is given the mediators used by the second group when presented with the words, to aid them in tying the pairs into working units (Bruner, 1961a, p. 31).

The wholly predictable results were that the uninstructed children remembered least and that the "children who developed their own [mediators] for relating the members of each word pair . . . did better than the children" who were given the mediators by exposition.

Why don't these findings support Bruner's proposition regarding the beneficial influence of discovery on retention? First, the learning task in this experiment is hardly comparable to the situation where children must discover a generalization inductively and autonomously. In Bruner's experiment, the entire content of what is to be learned is *given*, and the child need only supply a mediating link from his own cognitive structure that is sufficiently inclusive to subsume both members of the word pair. Now is this not precisely the paradigm for meaningful reception learning, in which materials are presented and the learner then tries to incorporate them into his own cognitive structure by relating them to more inclusive established ideas? The superior retention of the children who used mediators, as compared to those who were uninstructed, is attributable to the facilitating effect on retention that occurs when one helps learners convert an ostensibly rote reception learning task into a more meaningful type of reception learning. The discovery variable, in our opinion, is not implicated at all in this experiment.

Second, the superior retention of the word pairs related to the *self*-constructed mediators simply reflects the value of using more stable, relevant, and familiar subsumers within cognitive structure as anchoring posts for new learning materials. Mediators that children choose themselves are obviously more relevant and familiar to them than mediators suggested to them by others. The fact that they are self-constructed is quite beside the point.

Third, even within the framework of a reception learning interpretation, we should be careful about generalizing these findings to classroom pedagogy. In a short and easy learning task dealing with familiar materials, it is quite feasible for children to construct their own organizing concepts. But one could not legitimately conclude from this experiment that it would also be feasible for them to construct their own organizers for large bodies of complex and unfamiliar learning materials in subject-matter areas where their level of sophistication is necessarily low.

### Research Evidence

We now propose to examine a representative sample of the more significant published research bearing on the discovery method. The professional literature on "learning by discovery" regrettably exemplifies, as clearly as any research in education, the all too frequent hollowness of the hallowed phase, "research shows." Careful examination of what research supposedly "shows" in this instance yields these three disheartening conclusions:

1. Most of the articles most commonly cited in the literature as reporting results supportive of discovery techniques actually report no research findings whatsoever. They consist mainly of theoretical discussion, assertion, and conjecture; of descriptions of existing programs utilizing discovery methods; and of enthusiastic but wholly subjective testimonials regarding the efficacy of discovery approaches.

2. Most of the reasonably well-controlled studies report negative findings.

3. Most studies reporting positive findings either fail to control other significant variables or employ questionable techniques of statistical analysis.

Thus, actual examination of the research literature allegedly supportive of learning by discovery reveals that valid evidence of this nature is virtually nonexistent. It appears that the various enthusiasts of the discovery method have been supporting each other researchwise by taking in each other's laundry, so to speak, that is, by citing each other's opinions and assertions as evidence and by generalizing wildly from equivocal and even negative findings.

In view of the apparently sound theoretical reasons listed earlier (under "Psychological and Educational Rationale of the Discovery Method") for predicting modest advantages in learning, retention, and transferability attributable to the use of discovery techniques, these largely equivocal and negative findings are somewhat disappointing.

In many cases, of course, findings are equivocal simply because of failure to control such other relevant variables as the rote-meaningful, the inductive-deductive, the verbal-nonverbal, and the intramaterial organization dimensions of learning while varying the reception-discovery factor. In other instances, it is quite possible that negative findings are less indicative of inadequacies in the underlying theory than of inadequacies in research design, that unfairly load the dice against the possibility of confirming hypotheses. And as far as *long-term* curriculum studies are concerned, one might anticipate that any short-term advantages accruing from the use of discovery techniques would be more than offset by its time-consuming aspects, and the consequent low rate of acquiring subject-matter content.

### Long-Term Studies

Despite their frequent espousal of discovery principles, the various curriculum reform projects have failed thus far to yield any *research* evidence in support of the discovery method. This is not to say that the evidence is negative, but rather that there just is no evidence, one way or the other—notwithstanding the fact that these projects are often cited in the "discovery" literature under the heading, "research shows."

For one thing, the sponsors of some of these projects have not been particularly concerned about *proving* the superior efficacy of their programs, since they have been thoroughly convinced of this from the outset. Hence in many instances they have not even attempted to obtain comparable achievement test data from matched control groups. And only rarely has any effort been expended to prevent the operation of the crucial "Hawthorne effect," that is, to make sure that evidence of superior achievement outcomes is attributable to the influence of the new pedagogic techniques or materials in question—rather than to the fact that the experimental group is the recipient of *some* form of conspicuous special attention; that something new and interesting is being tried; or that the teachers involved are especially competent, dedicated, and enthusiastic, and receive special training, attend expense-free conventions and summer institutes, and are assigned lighter teaching loads.

But even if the sponsors of the curriculum reform movements were all imbued with missionary research zeal, it would still be impossible to test the discovery hypothesis within the context of curriculum research. In the first place, a large number of other significant variables are necessarily operative in such programs. The UICSM program, for example, not only relies heavily on the principle of self-discovery of generalizations, but also on an inductive approach, on the problem-solving use of subverbal insight, on abundant empirical experience, on careful sequential programming, and, above all, on precise, self-consistent, unambiguous, and systematic verbal formulation of basic principles. To which variable, or to which combination of these variables and the "Hawthorne effect," should the success of this program be attributed?

For reasons enumerated earlier in this chapter, we would nominate the factor of precise and systematic verbal formulation rather than the discovery variable. (Students enrolled in the UICSM program learn more mathematics, in our opinion, *not* because they are required to discover generalizations by *themselves*, but because they have at their disposal a systematic body of organizing, explanatory, and integrative principles that are not part of the conventional course in secondary-school mathematics. These principles illuminate the subject for them and make it much more meaningful, coherent, and exciting.)

A number of long-term curriculum studies in the older literature are frequently cited as providing empirical support for the discovery method. Using basically identical research designs, McConnell (1934), Swenson (1949), and Thiele (1938) compared the so-called "drill" and "generalization" methods of teaching number facts to second-grade pupils. The drill approach emphasized rote memorization and mechanical repetition of authoritatively presented facts and rules, whereas the generalization method stressed meaningful perception of relationships and derivation of generalizations. Pupils taught by the generalization method also had the added benefit of concrete props in the McConnell study and of organized grouping of materials in the Swenson study. A well-known study by G. L. Anderson (1949) was also conducted along very similar lines, but fourth-grade pupils were used.

Needless to say, the generalization method was found to be superior in all four studies, except in criterion situations calling for immediate and automatic recall of knowledge relatively unchanged in form from that learned in the training situation. Much more salient than the discovery variable in each of these studies, however, is the *rote-meaningful* factor. Moreover, in two of the studies the differential availability to the "generalization" group of visual aids or of organized grouping of learning materials further complicated interpretation of the findings.

It should also be remembered that it is precisely in relation to this age group of young learners first entering the stage of concrete logical operations, and still completely unsophisticated in a new, difficult, and abstract subject matter, that the efficacy and feasibility of the discovery method are least disputed. The time-cost factor is relatively unimportant at this age level because time-consuming concrete-empirical props must be used in any case, because large bodies of subject matter cannot be learned through expository teaching anyway, and because the semiabstract intuitive understanding of abstract ideas at this stage of development is often facilitated by discovery learning.

However, it would be quite unwarranted to generalize from these findings that meaningful reception learning of twelfth-grade mathematics is less efficacious than learning by discovery. Preliminary findings of the Inquiry Training Program (Suchman, 1959, 1962) also fail to support the discovery hypothesis. A study in college botany using a "problem-solving" approach also failed to show superiority of this method over a conventional lecture-laboratory approach (Novak, 1958).

### Short-Term Studies[8]

The well-known Gestalt writings on insightful problem solving by Duncker (1945), Katona (1940), Köhler (1925), and Wertheimer (1959), are traditionally cited in the "discovery" literature as supportive of the discovery method of teaching. Actually, however, the Gestalt emphasis on insight deals only with the rote-meaningful dimension of problem solving and has no bearing whatsoever on the relative efficacy of the expository (reception) and discovery approaches. As pointed out earlier, both reception and discovery learning may each be rote or meaningful, depending on the conditions under which learning occurs. The Gestalt theorists merely insist that the concept of insight is more valid than the Thorndikian trial-and-error theory or the Hullian point of view in explaining problem-solving behavior that lies within an organism's verbal or subverbal reasoning ability.

Duncker's, Köhler's, and Wertheimer's monographs also do not really report research findings in the usual sense of the term. They are, rather, elaborate and sophisticated analyses of the nature and conditions of insightful problem solving from the Gestalt point of view. They use observations, informal experiments, anecdotes, and demonstrations to illustrate the principles under discussion.

Katona's studies, on the other hand, are more genuinely experimental. At the very most, however, they demonstrate that understanding of a principle, as opposed to rote memorization, leads to superior retention and transfer. One experiment in particular shows that a rotely memorized verbal principle is less transferable to new problems than is mere empirical experience with problems exemplifying the principle in question. But this indicates only that *understanding* of a principle, even when *unverbalized,* is more transferable than *rote* memorization. It does not suggest that newly emerging nonverbal awareness is *always* more transferable than verbal understanding.

This latter study by Katona is reminiscent of Hendrix' previously discussed experiment (1947), but Hendrix carried the design and argument one step further. She also included another control group of subjects, who

---

[8] The research issues related to these studies and some of the implications of the findings are discussed under the heading of "prompting and guidance" in practice (Chapter 9).

first acquired *meaningful* nonverbal awareness of a principle and then attempted immediate verbalization. She showed that her experimental subjects, who were sent out of the room while these control subjects were attempting to verbalize nonverbal awareness, were not only superior in transfer power to the control subjects who had merely learned the principle through verbal exposition, but were also superior to this other control group which had acquired nonverbal awareness *prior* to verbalization.

Hendrix interpreted her findings to mean that the full transfer power and substance of an idea are already present in the emerging subverbal insight, and that this dawning subverbal awareness, when left unverbalized, is *invariably* more transferable than when put into words. We have already explained in detail why we think that premature verbalization of insight reduces transferability, and why we believe that verbalization enhances transferability under all other circumstances. At this point, we wish only to consider methodological and statistical aspects of Hendrix' experiment.

In reporting her study, Hendrix frankly acknowledged the difficulty of devising both "a good behavioral test for the achievement of unverbalized awareness" and a suitable test of transfer. There was also the formidable problem of deciding "whether subjects were obtaining the correct answers through counting or through applying the generalization" (1947, p. 203). With respect to the maintenance of necessary controls, Hendrix freely admitted, furthermore, that it was difficult to prevent "communication and discussion among members of the different method groups in the time interval between learning and testing" and to administer the various tests and experimental procedures without revealing to the subjects that an experiment was in progress (1947, pp. 203–204).

In addition to all of these acknowledged measurement, evaluation, and control problems, only 40 subjects were available for all 3 groups, and even this relatively small number was achieved only by pooling results from three very different kinds of experimental populations, for whom a test of homogeneity of variance was not even reported. Both the small experimental population and the undetermined comparability of its three separate components rendered untenable Hendrix' assumption that random assignment of subjects to the three treatment groups equalized these groups with respect to the influence of the uncontrolled variables.

Finally, the difference on the transfer test between the "verbal exposition" group and the "nonverbal awareness group" was only significant at the .12 level, and the corresponding difference between the "nonverbal awareness" group and the group that had verbalized their nonverbal awareness was only significant at the .33 level. Neither of these levels of significance is regarded very seriously by either statisticians or educational research workers. Taking all of these factors into consideration, therefore, the experimental foundations for the far-reaching conclusions that Hendrix draws from these findings can hardly be considered impressively firm.

We come finally to a series of experimental studies in which varying amounts of *guidance* were furnished to different groups of subjects in problem-solving situations. Stacey (1949) studied the effects of directed versus independent discovery on solving a group of meaningful problems, each of which required subjects to identify the one item in a set of five that did not "belong." He found that active participation and self-discovery were more efficacious for learning than was "passive participation involving only recognition or identification of information" presented to the learner. This finding, of course, was wholly predictable, since the fostering of such complete passivity in problem-solving experience as providing the correct answer for each problem as well as the reason for same is self-evidently inadvisable and is seldom if ever practiced today. But even so, surprisingly enough, significant differences were *not* found between these extreme treatment groups on a transfer test.

Using similar kinds of material, but with college students rather than sixth-grade pupils, Craig (1956) obtained results even less favorable for the discovery method. His "directed" group, which received a brief verbal explanation of principles during the training period, learned and retained significantly more principles than did his "independent group," which had no help whatsoever in the training situation. As in the Stacey study, however, the two groups were not significantly different with respect to mean score on a transfer test.

Kittell's (1957) findings in a similar type of experiment with sixth-grade pupils were, if anything, even more damaging to the discovery cause than were Craig's. The group in his experiment that received an "intermediate" amount of guidance, but nevertheless an amount that was somewhat *greater* than that received by Craig's "directed" group (explanation of principles *plus* organization of materials) was superior in learning, retention, and transfer to groups receiving either less or more direction.

Pooling the findings of these three studies, therefore, the evidence supports the conclusion that in this type of problem-solving exercise, guidance in the form of providing information about underlying principles facilitates learning, retention, and possibly transfer, more than either the provision of less guidance or the furnishing of specific rules for each of the problems.

Haselrud and Meyers (1958) conducted a coding study, with college students, that was explicitly designed to rebut the Craig and Kittell findings. However, their subjects exhibited significantly better learning on problems where the coding rules were given than where they had to be independently derived. Furthermore, on a delayed transfer test, there was *no* difference whatsoever in the number of correct code identifications made for the problems learned originally with the rule given and the problems learned originally by independent derivation of the code. Nevertheless, on the grounds that the gain from the first to the second test was greater for those problems where the rule had been independently derived, the investigators concluded that principles that are independently derived are more transferable than principles for which the rule is given. This, in our opinion, is equivalent to saying that, of two matched race horses trained by methods A and B respectively who are tied at the end of the criterion race, the horse trained by method B is *really* superior because at the halfway mark he was one lap behind the horse trained by method A, but nevertheless caught up to him by the end of the race.

Other studies in this area by Kersh (1958, 1962) yielded results practically identical to those of Craig, Kittell, and Haselrud and Meyers on the test of original learning, but results opposite to those of Kittell on the delayed retest. By using an ingenious research design, however, Kersh was able to explain this latter finding on the basis of the greater interest and motivation, on the part of the "independent-discovery" group, to continue practicing the task during the test-retest interval. Kersh concluded that discovery experience *in itself* does *not* enhance understanding or meaningfulness.[9]

In another group of studies on the effects of varying amounts of guidance on problem solving, either no differences were found between treatment groups or a limited amount of guidance ("guided discovery") was found to be superior both to no guidance whatsoever or to complete guidance. Forgus and Schwartz (1957), Maltzman, Eisman, and Brooks (1950), Moss (1960), and Tomlinson (1962) reported no significant differences in delayed retention and transfer between "direct-detailed"[10] and "guided-discovery" types of learning groups. Ray (1957) and Rowlett (1960), on the other hand, found that guided discovery was superior to direct-detailed instruction in remembering and transferring principles of micrometer use and orthographic projection. In a study of programmed learning, Gagné and Brown (1961) reported that a small-step, guided-discovery method of programming was superior both to the "ruleg" method and to a large-step prompted-discovery procedure.[11] Corman's findings (1957) were differentiated with respect to the ability level of his subjects; highly explicit in-

---

[9] Larson (1963) found that at least part of the superior retention of Kersh's discovery group was attributable to the Zeigarnik effect—a tendency to remember more incompleted than completed tasks. Craig's (1965) findings suggest that providing *continuing* tasks and not stating the rule at the conclusion of initial learning, rather than *discovery*, enhances motivation to learn in this context.

[10] A relatively complete, explicit, step-by-step type of guidance.

[11] Ervin (1960b) used a similar "guided-discovery" approach in teaching elementary-school children the verbal principles underlying various motor performances. The children were helped by leading questions to formulate the principles from their own observations. This method of instruction resulted in greater transfer than did a nonverbal type of guidance.

structions were most effective with his more able subjects, whereas his less able subjects benefited equally from more and less explicit instructions. Grote (1960) found that the direct-detailed method was superior for high-ability students and that the guided-discovery procedure was superior for average-ability students in learning a lever principle.

The issue of expository teaching versus independent discovery in the learning, retention, and transfer of principles is still very much in doubt because of the noncomparability of the various studies, serious deficiencies in research design, and the failure to hold constant, or take into account, rote-meaningful, inductive-deductive, verbalization, ability level, cognitive maturity, subject-matter sophistication, and motivational variables.

In general the research findings support Thorndike's well-known conclusion that "refusal to supply information on the ground that the learner will be more profited by discovering the facts himself, runs the risk not only of excessive time-cost but also the strengthening of wrong habits" (1935, p. 147). Providing guidance to the learner in the form of verbal explanation of the underlying principles almost invariably facilitates learning and retention and sometimes transfer as well. *Self*-discovery methods or the furnishing of completely explicit rules, on the other hand, are relatively less effective.

The most efficacious type of guidance (guided discovery) is actually a variant of expository teaching that is very similar to Socratic questioning. It demands the learner's active participation and requires him to formulate his own generalizations and integrate his knowledge in response to carefully programmed leading questions; and it is obviously much more highly structured than most discovery methods, with the possible exception of the UICSM. Further research is needed to determine whether guided discovery is superior to simple didactic exposition in terms of relative effectiveness for the time-cost involved when such factors as cognitive maturity, subject-matter sophistication, and verbal ability are varied. To be definitive, such research must also deal with large segments of instructional material and not merely with short-term problem-solving exercises in the laboratory.

### Learning by Discovery: The Debate

In a report from a conference on "Learning by Discovery," Keislar and Shulman (1966, p. 181) concluded that the issues fell into four groups:

> At the level of classroom instruction, the question to be studied is: As I teach Johnny, should I give him a wide variety of examples and expect him to infer the underlying rule, or should I tell him what the rule is while he applies it to examples?
> At the level of curriculum development, the question involves something like the following: To what extent ought the order of subjects into which

the students inquire be determined by us, and to what extent should this order be determined by the students themselves?

At the level of psychological investigations of learning, the question becomes: What is the transfer value of statements of principles given to a subject, as contrasted with individually derived principles?

At the level of research strategy, the issue takes on a very different, yet parallel form: What is the most fruitful way to investigate the nature of instruction?

Considering the issue of classroom instruction, Keislar and Shulman (1966, p. 182) state:

> When the assertion was made at the conference that research studies had not yet produced evidence to support the hypothesis of learning by discovery, concern was expressed that the publication of this statement could have ill effects on teacher behavior. It was hinted that some teachers might go back to a learning-by-rote approach to teaching if it were implied that learning by discovery had been discredited. While no one at the conference perceived the issue in terms of this dichotomy, the importance of examining the kind of statements made to teachers cannot be ignored.

However, the conference did fail to stress the importance of *meaningful reception* learning as described in an earlier book (Ausubel, 1963) and hence floundered in confusion between the rote→meaningful and reception-discovery dimensions of school learning shown in Figure 1.1.

In the area of curriculum development, issues of epistemology arose to which we have already referred. Commenting on the work of scientists, Keislar and Shulman observe (1966, p. 189):

> Quite clearly, scientists do not spend all their time discovering. They exhibit a broad range of activities, from hypothesis-generation and model-building to listening to lectures and reading journal articles reporting someone else's research. Hence, justification of curriculum development which stresses inductive teaching on the grounds that induction is the sine qua non of scientific behavior is a half-truth, at best. Scientists do discover, it is true. That many of these are didactic or receptive in nature is apparent. . . .

Our contention is that clarification of the goals for instruction as well as instructional strategies require recognition of the importance of transmitting our evolving conceptual heritage, as well as methodologies for creating new knowledge, primarily through strategies of meaningful learning as guided by assimilation theory. We have discussed these strategies in Chapter 10.

With regard to psychological issues, Keislar and Shulman report (1966, p. 191): "Examination of both the exhaustive reviews of the literature and deliberations of the conference lead to an inescapable conclusion: The question as stated is not amenable to research solutions because the implied experimental treatment, the discovery method, is far too ambiguous and imprecise to be used meaningfully in an experimental investigation." We have noted above the primary sources of this imprecision.

Keislar and Shulman (1966, pp. 195–198) point out some of the difficulties of research in this area. Carefully controlled studies in laboratory-like settings may have methodological precision, but do the results have meaning for school learning? On the other hand, long-term classroom studies include such a complexity of interacting factors that it is difficult to isolate the effect of "discovery" strategies, even if we could agree on definitions. Keislar and Shulman (1966, p. 198) conclude in agreement with Dewey (1910) that the controversy in its present form does not appear resolvable: "Dewey maintained that controversies are resolved through redefinition and reformulation, rather than through victory of one side over another."

What we have proposed in this chapter is that assimilation theory offers an alternative view of the process of learning by discovery; in this chapter and earlier we have stressed that the problem of transfer of training, particularly to new areas of learning and problem solving, is best solved through strategies that enhance *meaningful* learning. Our "reformulation" of the problem places stress on strategies that enhance idiosyncratic acquisition of concepts, propositions and skills through the application of principles of assimilation learning theory.

## Inquiry and Process Methods of Teaching

Partly as a result of the growing awareness that "discovery" approaches to instruction were fraught with difficulties and ambiguities, a new label was applied and became popular in the 1960s; the new cry was for *inquiry* approaches to instruction. Massialus (1966), Romey (1965), Rowe (1973), Ryan and Ellis (1974), Schwab (1962), and Suchman (1960) were among the writers whose titles featured *inquiry* as a central theme.

Most of the writers who favor inquiry approaches stress the need for concrete experiences and teaching strategies for making inferences from experiences or data. Too often, however, they neglect or minimize the important role that acquisition of concepts plays in the development of "inquiry skills." Rowe (1973, p. 367), in contrast to many writers on this subject, stresses the value of concept learning in science and also emphasizes that "Teaching students how to make *better use of concepts they already know* probably represents the major task to be accomplished in inquiry training."

We have also found this to be an important issue, and much of our current research at Cornell University is centered on the question of how and why students recognize and employ relevant concepts in problem-solving situations. Inquiry strategies that transcend the traditional emphasis on inductive-deductive issues of discovery learning and place central emphasis on the acquisition and use of concepts can represent a significant advance in educational methods over the strategies traditionally advanced by "discovery" enthusiasts. Assimilation theory should be useful to resourceful educators who seek to improve inquiry methods.

During the 1960s another movement became prominent in education; in an effort to provide skills for "lifelong learning," *process education* was advocated. The goal was to design or advance programs in all subject areas that emphasized the acquisition of *skills*. "Skills may be considered to be behavioral control systems which incorporate, select, and direct different response patterns and attitudinal and behavioral tendencies and capabilities in a series of actions toward some goal" (Cole, 1973, p. 26). More ambitious than the inquiry education movement, proponents of process education seek to combine affective, social, and cognitive learning goals into one grand strategy. The now-defunct Eastern Regional Institute for Education, supported with funds from the U.S. Office of Education, took as its "mission" the implementation of *process* education in elementary schools.

Laudatory as the goals of the process education movement may be, most of the efforts that fly under this banner have encountered serious difficulty. We believe that much work is needed to improve substantially our success and accountability in cognitive learning before we can have the wisdom to advance, or to expect the public to accept, the more ambitious programs of school-wide process education.

# 16

# PROBLEM SOLVING
# AND CREATIVITY

*Both meaningful problem solving and creativity are forms of mean-*
*ingful discovery learning. Meaningful problem solving, in contrast*
*to trial-and-error learning, is hypothesis-oriented discovery learning*
*requiring the transformation and reintegration of existing knowledge*
*to fit the demands of a specified goal or means–end relationship. As*
*stated in Chapter 2 (pp. 66–67), only this aspect of problem solving*
*involves discovery learning. The comprehension of the problem*
*conditions and the assimilation of the problem solution are forms of*
*meaningful reception learning.*

*It follows, therefore, that the most important variables influencing*
*problem solving outcomes are (1) the availability in cognitive struc-*
*ture of concepts and principles that are relevant to the particular*
*problem at hand and (2) such cognitive and personality traits as*
*incisiveness, integrative ability, cognitive style, problem sensitivity,*
*flexibility, improvising ability, venturesomeness, intellectual curios-*
*ity, and frustration tolerance.*

*Language facilitates problem solving as it does concept acquisition.*
*Thus, verbal ability and general cognitive readiness (intelligence,*
*stage of development along the subjective–objective and concrete–*
*abstract dimensions) help explain both age-level trends and individ-*
*ual differences in problem-solving ability. An important task factor*
*is mastery of a given type of problem within a homogeneous setting*
*before exposing the learner to more heterogeneous samples of the*
*problem.*

565

*The ability to train problem solving is limited, as shown by the lack of generality or transferability to other kinds of problems exhibited by most training programs. It points up the importance of specific relevant ideas in cognitive structure and the genic factors that influence the cognitive and personality variables mentioned above.*

*Creativity is the highest expression of problem solving, involving novel or original transformations of ideas and the generation of new integrative (superordinate) and explanatory principles. Although creativity varies on a continuum, it is less generously distributed among learners than intelligence or problem-solving ability. The creativity of the creative person, however, differs qualitatively from the kinds of creativity exhibited by the people represented in this continuum. He or she must be able to generate original ideas in some substantive area of human endeavor that are uniquely original and significant in terms of the culture at large rather than in terms of their own individual development.*

*Thus it is clear that intelligence level and the availability of relevant ideas in cognitive structure are less important for creativity than for problem solving, and that greater weight must be placed on the genically determined cognitive and personality variables considered above. The former variables are more limiting than determining factors, particularly in the case of students at the upper end of the continuum and for the truly creative person.*

*Most available so-called tests of creativity (such as measures of divergent thinking ability) are not reliably distinguishable from tests of intelligence (that is, they intercorrelate no more highly among themselves than with IQ scores), and probably predict academic achievement largely because of this correlation with intelligence. They also do not test for potentially creative achievement in some substantive area such as a particular branch of science, art, literature, or government. Moreover, they have never been validated against later creative achievement in adult life.*

*We must conclude from the above considerations that creativity is even less trainable than problem-solving ability. The school, however, can best foster creativity both by providing appropriate opportunity for the expressions of creativity and by appropriately rewarding them.*

Problem solving refers to any activity in which both the cognitive representation of prior experience and the components of a current problem situation are reorganized in order to achieve a designated objective. Such activity may consist of more or less trial-and-error variation of available alternatives or of a deliberate attempt to formulate a principle or discover a system of relations underlying the solution of a problem (insight). When the activity is limited to the manipulation of images, symbols, and symbolically formulated propositions, and does not involve overt manipulation of objects, it is conventional to use the term *thinking*. It is clear, however, that depending on the approach taken, thinking may either employ the method of insight or may be merely an implicit variety of the trial-and-error procedure. Whether insight or trial-and-error learning is employed in the solution of a particular problem is a function of both the kind of problem involved and of the age, prior experience, and intelligence of the subject.

Problem solving, of course, involves discovery learning. The important distinction between meaningful discovery learning and meaningful reception learning has been discussed both generally, in terms of its wider implications for education, and in more explicit detail in earlier chapters. The different pedagogic ways in which these two varieties of meaningful learning can be related to each other in classroom learning, and the manner in which they are sequentially interrelated during the different phases of problem solving—in understanding or formulating the problem, in generating a solution, and in incorporating the latter solution into cognitive structure—have also been made explicit.

Thus despite the significant differences between these two kinds of meaningful learning, in terms of both underlying process and role in education, it is important to bear in mind both their interdependence and the commonalities they share in contrast to rote learning. Discovery learning is meaningful when learners nonarbitrarily and substantively relate a potentially meaningful problem-setting proposition to their cognitive structure for the purpose of generating a solution that, in turn, is potentially meaningful (relatable to cognitive structure on the same basis). It therefore implies, under these conditions, all of the essential elements that are implicated in meaningful learning generally: a meaningful learning set, a logically meaningful learning task, and the availability of relevant established ideas in the learner's cognitive structure. The distinctive and significant way in which it differs from meaningful reception learning is that the principal content of what is to be learned is not presented to the learner, but must be discovered by the learner before it can be incorporated into his or her cognitive structure and made meaningful.

## The Nature of Problem Solving

In terms of approach, two principal kinds of problem solving may be distinguished, both of which occur at all age levels. The trial-and-error approach consists of random or systematic variation, approximation, and correction of responses until a successful variant emerges. The insightful approach, on the other hand, implies a "set" that is oriented toward discovery of a meaningful means-end relationship underlying the solution of a problem. It may involve either simple transposition of a previous learned principle to an analogous new situation or more fundamental cognitive restructuring and integration of prior and current experience to fit the demands of a designated goal. Characteristically, insightful solutions *appear* to emerge suddenly or discontinuously. They are also invariably accompanied by at least some implicit appreciation of the principle underlying the solution of a problem—even if it cannot be successfully verbalized.

This understanding is demonstrated functionally both in being immediately reproducible upon subsequent exposure to the same problem and in being transferable to related problems. Hence, not only is insightful solution frequently a reflection of transfer or application of relevant established principles to new variants of the same problem, but transferability itself is perhaps the most important criterion of insight. Precisely verbalized understanding of a general principle greatly facilitates (through transfer) the solution of particular problems exemplifying it.

The utilization of hypotheses is a necessary but not a sufficient condition of insightful problem solving. However, it does not in itself provide assurance that an insightful approach is being taken toward solving a particular problem. Unless hypotheses incorporate means-end relationships, they may merely represent systematic trial-and-error elimination of available alternatives. The absence of overt trial-and-error efforts also does not necessarily imply insightful problem solving. Trial-and-error manipulation in this instance may simply be covert or implicit in thought. On the other hand, insightful solutions are not always complete, perfect, or immediate. They often appear after a protracted period of inauspicious search consumed in pursuing unpromising leads.

Trial-and-error learning is more or less inevitable in problems where no meaningful pattern of relationships exists or is discernible. Hence, it is generally characteristic of motor learning and of the solution of most mazes and complex puzzle box problems. It occurs most efficiently when subjects are aware of the direction and extent of their deviations from the desired solution and are permitted to execute the necessary correction and approximation by themselves. Copying, for example, is a much more successful way of learning to write than is tracing. This does not necessarily mean, however, that either verbal coaching (explicit pointing out of errors, suggesting more effective techniques) or drill aimed at specific disabilities (Lehman & Cole, 1928) is not efficacious in the learning of motor skills. As is true of rote discovery learning, generally, the occurrence of positive transfer in maze learning is not attributable to the application of relevant, previously learned principles, but rather to elimination of initial "warm-up" time and to such factors as general familiarity with, and orientation to, the type of approach necessary.

Insightful problem solving is obviously a type of meaningful discovery learning in which problem conditions and desired objectives are nonarbitrarily and substantively related to existing cognitive structure. It involves "going beyond the information given" (Bartlett, 1958; Bruner, 1957). It includes transforming information by analysis, synthesis, hypothesis formulation and testing, rearrangement, recombination, translation, and integration. As pointed out previously, however, it does not necessarily imply completely autonomous discovery. Typically, as a matter of fact, problem solving in the classroom constitutes a form of guided or arranged discovery.

Much that passes for meaningful problem solving is simply a species of rote discovery learning. It is exemplified by the ubiquitous "type problem" approach to the teaching of mathematics and science. There is nothing wrong, of course, with solving problems by genuinely identifying them as exemplars of a larger class to which certain principles or operations apply— provided that one understands the principles in question, why they apply to the particular case, and the relationship between the principles and the manipulative operations used in the application. All too frequently, however, this is not the case. In most mathematics and science classrooms, the solving of type problems involves little more than rote memorization and application of formulas, rote manipulation of symbols, and the use of intrinsically irrelevant cues for identifying problems as members of a class.

### Insight: Process versus Product

Insight can be thought of in terms of process or product. As product, insight refers to certain distinctive characteristics of the end result of meaningful problem solving; as process, it refers to a distinctive method of, or approach to, problem solving.

Insight as product possesses the following characteristics: (1) subjective: a pleased feeling of apt discovery, of "seeing the light" or "Eureka"; (2) objective: immediate reproducibility and transposability. In the first case we are dealing with a largely affective reaction to the learning product; in the second case we are specifying what we can do with insight once it is achieved. More significant, however, both for learning theory and educational practice, is to indicate how insight is acquired in the first place and how it differs from other types of problem solving.

Because of common misconceptions about the nature of insight, it might be helpful to summarize this discussion by specifying what it does *not* involve. First, contrary to Gestalt formulations, its emergence depends on more than just the structure of the problem task; it is by no means independent of the learner's prior experience. Second, it rarely appears abruptly and immediately—despite subjective feelings to the contrary. More commonly it follows a period of fumbling and search, of gradual emergence of a correct hypothesis. Thus the emergence of insight is reflective of a process of progressive clarification about means-end relationships in which the formulation, testing, and rejection of alternative hypotheses play a crucial and integral role in the appearance of correct solutions. Insightful problem solving—like other forms of learning—does not conform to the all-or-none paradigm. Third, a hypothesis-oriented approach, while characteristic of insightful problem solving, does not necessarily guarantee that an insightful approach is being used. Hypotheses can be generated on a purely pragmatic or empirical basis, without any intention of coming to grips with the basic cause-and-effect issues underlying a given problem. They can also lead to successful problem solving without any genuine understanding of why the solution is successful. Fourth, insightful problem solving does not in any way presuppose *completely* autonomous discovery.

In conclusion, insight, as a process of problem solving distinct from blind trial-and-error solution of a problem, implies the existence of a *set* oriented toward hypothesis generation and testing for the purpose of understanding the significant means-end relationships in a particular problem. The set is not just to vary responses by approximation and correction until a successful variant eventually appears.

Once the insight emerges, there must be conscious awareness of its existence, significance, and availability rather than mere blind advocacy of a successful variant just because it "works"—without any understanding of why. Ability to verbalize solutions undoubtedly reflects greater original completeness and clarity of insight, both of which are further refined by verbalization itself; it therefore implies greater transferability. Unreportability of insight, however, does not necessarily imply either lack of awareness or inability to transfer (Griffin & Beier, 1961).

### Logic and Thought

A commonly held position in psychology today—particularly among psychologists who have had some philosophical training—is that logic and thought are more or less coextensive, and that thought consists of the cognitive exemplification of abstract logical processes in particular individuals. It is true that by virtue of their cognitive capacities, humans have both discovered logic and have learned how to use it in drawing valid interferences from premises and data. Nevertheless, the position that logic and thought are one and the same constitutes an unwarranted superimposition of an abstract and idealized state of affairs onto the reality of cognitive functioning; that is, it equates thought itself with one of its specialized tools and products. Although Piaget (1957a) explicitly denies that logic and thought are one and the same, both his extreme emphasis upon the purely logical aspects of thought and the fidelity and symmetry with which the logical operations he identifies in children's thought parallel the formal structure of rules found in logic and mathematics imply greater perceived coextensiveness between logic and thought than he explicitly acknowledges.

Actually much thought involves very little logic. It is not illogical but *alogical*. That is, most persons can be reasonably logical about affectively neutral issues when the occasion arises for the application of logic. But in many everyday aspects of thought, the need for and the opportunity of exercising logic simply do not arise. Many of the problems with which human beings are typically confronted either cannot be reduced to terms that are susceptible to logical proof or cannot be solved merely by invoking the application of rules of inference to data. It is not implausible to suppose, therefore, that we have somewhat unrealistically oversold the role of logic and have correspondingly underestimated the role of other factors, in typical instances of human problem solving. This has been done by (1) using the mathematical or logical problem, or the scientific experiment, as the paradigm for all problem-solving tasks and (2) modeling the general operations of thought after the more formal and specialized operations that serve as rules of inference in mathematics, logic, and science. The kinds of insightful problem solving in which human beings engage are both more extensive than the paradigm allows and less abstract, formal, and rigorous than the model suggests.

### Types of Thinking

Conventional distinctions between inductive and deductive, and between divergent and convergent, thinking tend to be somewhat misleading. First, as already pointed out, it is seldom the case that an individual approaches a problem with no general hypotheses whatsoever to direct the interpretation of data. It is a gross oversimplification, therefore, to insist that when thinking inductively one proceeds from particular instances to generalizations, generating hypotheses solely from the data.

At the very most it would be warranted to claim that in inductive thinking both the initial general hypotheses that are generated and the final hypothesis that is selected are typically less familiar and less well established than in deductive thinking. Second, in most instances of problem solving, irrespective of whether it is called divergent or convergent thinking, the typical sequence of problem-solving operations involves the generation of multiple hypotheses (divergent thinking) followed by the gradual elimination of those hypotheses that are less tenable (convergent thinking).

### The Role of Cognitive Structure in Problem Solving

That existing cognitive structure plays a key role in problem solving is evident from the fact that the solution of any given problem involves a reorganization of the residue of past experience so as to fit the particular requirements of the current problem situation. Since ideas in cognitive structure constitute the raw material of problem solving, whatever transfer occurs, positive or negative, obviously reflects the nature and influence of cognitive structure variables.

The possession of relevant background knowledge (concepts, principles, transactional terms, "available functions") in cognitive structure, particularly if clear, stable, and discriminable, facilitates problem solving (Murray, 1963; Novak, 1961; Ring & Novak, 1971; Saugstad, 1955; Saugstad & Raaheim, 1960). Without such knowledge, as a matter of fact, no problem solving is possible irrespective of the learner's degree of skill in discovery learning; without it he or she could not even begin to understand the nature of the problem confronted. Still another cognitive structure source of positive transfer inheres in applicable general elements of strategy, orientation, and set that reflect prior experience with related problems. Finally, cognitive structure is related to problem solving in a repository as well as in a determinative sense: The substantive or methodological product of a problem-solving process is incorporated into cognitive structure in accordance with the same principles that are operative in reception learning.

Cognitive structure also provides an abundant source of *negative* transfer in problem solving. One type of negative transfer reflects the perseveration of inapplicable habitual sets (*Einstellungen*) derived from prior experience with similar problems (Luchins, 1946). The solution of novel problems obviously requires both improvisation and a search for new directions —a requirement that is often interfered with by a tendency to use the same approach that was found successful in previous problem-solving experience (Maier, 1930). The latter experience thus generates both helpful and interfering sets whose relative strength is a function of such factors as primacy, recency, frequency, vividness, flexibility, and level of anxiety.

A second, related source of negative transfer in cognitive structure is commonly referred to as "functional fixedness" (Chown, 1959; Duncker, 1945). This term describes an inability to conceive of other possible uses or functions of an object in problem solving because of the preemptive influence of the more conventional or established use (for instance, the failure to use a pair of pliers as a weight in a pendulum problem). Functional fixedness is increased when the conventional use of an object is experienced first rather than later in the course of a series of exposures (Yonge, 1966), and is reduced by experience with unusual uses during the training period (Flavell, Cooper, & Loiselle, 1958).

A final type of negative transfer in problem solving merely reflects the prevalence of certain general reductionistic trends found in the thinking of most persons within a given culture, for instance, conceptualizing problems in terms of single rather than multiple causality, the tendency to think in terms of all-or-none and dichotomous (either-or) propositions, and the preference for conceiving of variability in categorical, as opposed to continuous, terms.

## Language and Thought

The developmental relationship between language and thought is still a controversial and unresolved "chicken or egg" type of problem. It is clear at any rate that language and thought are not coextensive. Language can obviously be exhibited without thought and vice versa (Vygotsky, 1962).

Although simpler kinds of reasoning depend merely on relatively concrete, perceptual, and imaginal operations, and are evident in action prior to the emergence of verbal thought, the ability to think in abstract terms obviously requires the use of abstract concepts and symbols. Only the most primitive kinds of problem solving are possible without language. The role of manipulable representational symbols in facilitating the transformational aspects of thought and the role of verbalization in refining the products of thought have been discussed in another context. It is also possible that premature verbalization of insight may impair its transferability because incomplete, unclear, and unconsolidated verbalized solutions are obviously less functional for purposes of transfer than subverbal solutions that are more adequate in these respects.

Thus the role of language in the facilitation of thought is very similar to its role in concept acquisition. It not only facilitates ideational problem solving (Gagné & Dick, 1962) but also the solution of motor and perceptual problems (Egstrom, 1964; Ray, 1957). Hypotheses can be formulated and tested much more precisely and expeditiously when they are expressed in verbal form.

## Stages and Strategies of Problem Solving

As a formal description of the successive temporal stages involved in thinking, Dewey's 1910 account has not been appreciably improved upon over the past sixty-odd years. It is generally consistent with the sequence of operations and the sequential interrelationships between reception and discovery learning that have been delineated above as characterizing the successive phases of problem solving. His five stages in the order given consist of:

1. A state of doubt, cognitive perplexity, frustration, or awareness of difficulty
2. An attempt to identify the problem, including a rather nonspecific designation of the ends that are sought, the gap to be filled, or the goal to be reached, as defined by the situation that sets the problem
3. Relating these problem-setting propositions to cognitive structure, thereby activating relevant background ideas and previously achieved problem solutions, which in turn are reorganized (transformed) in the form of problem-solving propositions or hypotheses

4. Successive testing of the hypotheses and reformulation of the problem if necessary

5. Incorporating the successful solution into cognitive structure (understanding it) and then applying it both to the problem at hand and to other exemplars of the same problem.

Actually, of course, not all instances of problem solving manifest all of these stages or follow the typical sequential order. Much creative thinking, for example, short-circuits or telescopes many of the steps in this sequence. D. M. Johnson (1961) has proposed a useful distinction between the "preparatory" and "solution" phases of problem solving.

Strategies in problem solving exhibit the same characteristics as in concept formation. They reflect the influence of the type of problem involved and the conditions under which problem solving occurs, as well as idiosyncratic aspects of cognitive functioning.

## Developmental Changes in Problem Solving

Developmental changes in problem solving reflect all of the age trends described for cognitive functioning as a whole and, more particularly, those occurring in concept acquisition. Especially in the area of thinking and problem solving, it is important to distinguish between those developmental changes that are qualitative in nature and those that are merely quantitative. Despite Piaget's assertions to the contrary (Inhelder & Piaget, 1958), the weight of the evidence points to the conclusion that *some* kinds of thought processes, logical operations, and problem-solving strategies are employed at all age levels, differing principally in degree or complexity (Burt, 1919; Long & Welch, 1941a, 1941b; Welch & Long, 1943; Werner, 1948). For example, equivalence, discriminative, and eliminative logical operations seem to be qualitatively similar at all age levels once they emerge. Older children's greater competence in using these oprations largely depends on their superior ability to think abstractly and to generalize. Similarly the use of trial-and-error and insightful approaches to problem solving does not undergo qualitative change from one age level to the next. Neither approach can be said to be characteristic of children at a designated stage of intellectual development; both are found at all age levels.

The choice between the two approaches depends, mainly, on the intrinsic difficulty and complexity of the problem, on the individual's prior background of experience and general degree of sophistication in the problem area, and on the susceptibility of the problem to logical analysis and hypothesis-oriented mode of attack. It is true that older children, on the whole, tend more to use an insightful approach, but this is so only because their greater capacity for abstract thinking makes such an approach more feasible.

On the other hand, certain qualitative changes in thinking do occur with increasing age. These gradually occurring changes in *kind* emerge after a certain threshold value of change in *degree* has been reached. One such change consists of a gradual transition from subjective to objective thought, of an emergent ability to separate objective reality from subjective needs, wishes, and preferences. This trend is responsible for the striking decline that occurs during the elementary-school years in autistic, animistic, ethnocentric, magical, anthropomorphic, absolutistic, and nominalistic thinking.[1]

A second qualitative change in thought is reflective of the transition from concrete to abstract cognitive functioning and illustrates all of the characteristic features of this transition. Because preoperational children cannot meaningfully manipulate relationships between secondary abstractions, their thought processes are necessarily conducted at a low level of abstraction and also yield products at a correspondingly low level. Thus they cannot perform many significant logical operations that presuppose a capability of meaningfully manipulating relationships between secondary concepts. As a result of this developmental constraint their thought does not exhibit "conservation," and their problem-solving efforts are relatively dependent both on the overt manipulation of objects and on the internal manipulation of near images.

Concrete-operational children can meaningfully manipulate relationships between secondary abstractions and can therefore perform those logical operations reflective of this capability. However, these children are dependent in so doing on the availability of concrete-empirical props (exemplars of the abstractions). Their thought processes are thus conducted at a qualitatively higher level than those of preoperational children but are still constrained in their level of abstraction by the particularity inherent in the props used. The products of thought are therefore only intuitive and semi-abstract in nature.

Only in the stage of abstract logical operations, when relationships between secondary concepts can be meaningfully manipulated without any reference whatsoever to particular instances, does the process of thought become genuinely abstract in the fullest sense of the term. The products of such thought can therefore be refined through verbalization to yield ideas that are truly explicit, precise, abstract, and general. The individual at this

---

[1] Evidence of such thinking can, of course, be found at older age levels also, but is much less flagrant and tends to occur under more atypical conditions, such as confrontation with unfamiliar phenomena or problem areas. Evidence of the qualitative changes along the subjective–objective dimension was presented in Chapter 6. The most controversial aspect of such change is in the area of egocentricity or ability to take into account the point of view of others in disputation or in arguing from the standpoint of an arbitrary given premise. Elkind (1971) maintains that there is much evidence of egocentricity in adolescents, and Shantz (1975) argues that in the development of these latter abilities the child uses himself as a point of reference.

stage of development is capable of solving problems by formulating general principles in terms of general relationships between all possible and hypothetical combinations of abstract variables.

### Age-Level Trends in Problem-Solving Ability

The increasing ability of children to solve more complex problems with advancing age has been demonstrated both for trial-and-error learning (Munn, 1954) and for such tests of insightful learning as the double alteration problem (Gellerman, 1931; Hodges, 1954), transposition (Alberts & Ehrenfreund, 1951), other relational problems (Elkind, 1966; Heidbreder, 1928; Roberts, 1940; Wohlwill, 1960a; Yudin, 1966; Yudin & Kates, 1963), inductive and eliminative reasoning (Burt, 1919), and various tool-utilization problems (Matheson, 1931).

Younger children profit less from hints (Welch & Long, 1943) and are less able to generalize or transpose solutions to more abstract and remote situations (Spiker, 1956; Stevenson & Bitterman, 1955; Welch & Long, 1943). They have more difficulty with problems at higher levels of abstraction (Burt, 1919; Welch & Long, 1943), with more complex kinds of reasoning operations (Long & Welch, 1941b, 1942), and with problems demanding the integration of two isolated experiences (Maier, 1936). Much of the superiority of older children in these latter instances inheres in the advantages that the ability to use verbal symbols provides for the processing of generalizations, for generating hypotheses, for processing information, and for employing efficient strategies (Weir, 1964).

### Age-Level Trends in Problem-Solving Approach

With advancing age, as might readily be anticipated, the frequency of overt trial-and-error approaches to problem solving declines (Hamilton, 1916; Munn, 1954; Nelson, 1936). Hypothesis-oriented approaches become more complete (Alpert, 1928). These trends obviously reflect, in part, increasing ability to generalize and to manipulate abstract symbols. As Lewin (1954) points out, they also reflect the widening and greater differentiation of the child's "life space." In the "detour" problem, for example, older children focus less exclusively on the obtrusively obvious barrier and are better able to appreciate that the most direct route to the goal is not necessarily the shortest.

Older children are more aware than younger children of the existence of a problem when exposed to one (Heidbreder, 1928). Their plan of attack is more systematic, and their solutions tend to be more flexible and less stereotyped and perseverative (Elkind, 1966; Hamilton, 1916; Lindley, 1897; Maier, 1936; Raaheim, 1965). Since their knowledge tends to be organized in terms of more highly systematized, inclusive, and self-consistent categories, they adopt a less fragmented approach to problem solving. And because they are better able to bring prior experience to bear on a current problem (Maier, 1936), they profit more from past mistakes (Lindley, 1897).

Younger children, on the other hand, are limited by their inability to focus on more than one aspect of a problem at a time (Piaget, 1952), by the diffuseness of their thinking (Piaget, 1954b), by their low frustration tolerance, and by their reluctance to accept the immutable givens of a problem. They are more situation-bound and less able to generalize beyond a particular context (Piaget, 1950, 1954b). Their formulations are more dependent on concrete imagery and the physical presence of objects, and derive less benefit from the use of abstract symbols, higher-order concepts, and categorical propositions (Piaget, 1954b; Welch & Long, 1943). Finally, after solving a problem they are less capable of verbalizing (and hence transferring) the underlying principles (Heidbreder, 1928; Piaget, 1954b; Roberts, 1940).

### Age-Level Trends in the Objectivity of Thought

The progressive decline in the egocentricity and subjectivism of children's thought is one of the two principal aspects of cognitive development accounting for age-level changes in the quality of problem solving. Growing children become more aware of their own thought processes and are better able to distinguish between external reality and their own experiences, between "the sign and the thing signified," and between thought and the object thought about (Piaget, 1928, 1929). Logical inference becomes less a matter of subjective preference and less tied to autistic premises (Heidbreder, 1927; Piaget, 1928). The more important of these trends can be illustrated by considering changes in subjectivism associated with a child's development of notions of causality.

Considered in this light, the evidence regarding "stages" becomes less contradictory. In support of Piaget's view, children do seem to pass through gross qualitative stages of causal thinking (Dennis, 1942, 1943; Grigsby, 1932; Mogar, 1960; Russell, 1940), and rarely appreciate antecedent-consequent relationships in the adult sense of the term prior to the age of 8 to 10 (Bredderman, 1974; Cohen & Hansel, 1955; Graybill, 1975; Lacey & Dallenbach, 1940).

Even Piaget's severest critics concede that there is gradual improvement with increasing age in the quality of children's causal explanations (Deutsche, 1937; Oakes, 1947; Raven & Polanski, 1974). On the other hand, much overlapping prevails between age groups. All kinds of causal explanations are found at all age levels (Buell & Bradley, 1972; Deutsche, 1937; Grigsby, 1932; Gubrud & Novak, 1973; Lawson & Renner, 1975;

Nordland, Lawson, & Kahle, 1974; Nussbaum & Novak, 1976; Oakes, 1947). None of these facts, however, is incompatible with the existence of certain qualitative stages in children's thinking as defined earlier.

Externalization and objectification are relatively early steps in the development of ideas of causality (Piaget, 1954a). Infants must learn to distinguish between independent systems of cause and effect in the external world and effects attributable to their own volition and action. The infant begins to do this when he or she appreciates that mere volitional wishing does not satisfy one's need, that parents are mediators of need satisfaction, and that he or she is executively dependent on them (Ausubel, 1958).

Although magical thinking tends to decline with increasing age (Dennis, 1942, 1943; Piaget, 1932; Russell, 1940), it by no means disappears, even in adults (Dennis, 1943; Hazlitt, 1930; Oakes, 1947). It does, however, become less naive and more highly formalized; that is, magical properties and powers are attributed more to special words, objects, rituals, and beings, and less to wishing. Concomitantly, mechanical and naturalistic interpretations of causality increase and animistic and "artificialistic" interpretations decrease in frequency.

By animism Piaget means the "tendency to regard objects as living and endowed with will" (Piaget, 1929). The related concept of artificialism refers to a type of personification in which creative activity in nature is attributed to some human agency rather than to naturalistic phenomena. At first, according to Piaget, the child regards everything that is active, whole, and useful as alive. Later, life is attributed only to moving objects. The still more sophisticated child applies the criterion of spontaneous movement. Finally, only plants and animals, or only animals, are considered to be alive. Other investigators (Huang & Lee, 1945; Klingensmith, 1953) have shown that when children state that something is "alive," they mostly mean that it is active. They do not necessarily attribute to it the anthropomorphic characteristics of feeling, seeing, knowing, thinking, wanting, breathing, and so forth.

Animistic tendencies are also not restricted to children, but are manifested even by educated adults in our culture when required to explain events completely beyond their sphere of experience and competence (Hazlitt, 1930; Oakes, 1946). This suggests that the crucial factor in causal thinking is making a judgment of relevance between antecedent and consequent. For the unsophisticated child (or adult) antecedence in itself along with animistic, magical, and artificialistic connections between antecedent and consequent seem to be sufficient criteria of relevance (Piaget, 1932). Given the benefit of increased incidental experience and instruction, however, the same individual learns to avoid attributing causal significance to irrelevant and purely temporal antecedents of consequences and to avoid generalizing the expectation of similar consequences in all situations superficially similar to a particular cause-effect sequence (Ausubel & Schiff, 1954).

## Factors Influencing Problem Solving

Much can be learned about process factors influencing problem solving by comparing the respective performances of successful and unsuccessful problem solvers (Bloom & Broder, 1950):

1. Successful problem solvers flounder less; they are more decisive in choosing "some point at which to begin their attack." In many instances this simply reflects greater attention to and comprehension of the directions.

2. They focus more on the problem to be solved rather than on some irrelevant aspect of the problem.

3. They can better bring to bear on the problem the relevant knowledge that they possess. They perceive more clearly the implications and applicability of their knowledge to the problem at hand and are less confused by a change in wording or notation.

4. They exhibit a more active and vigorous process of search. Their approach is less passive, superficial, and impressionistic. They tend to apply solutions from previous problems less mechanically.

5. They are more careful and systematic in their approach (see also Duncan, 1964). Their efforts are less haphazard and less characterized by guesswork.

6. They tend more to follow through a line of reasoning to its logical conclusion. They are more persistent and less distractible in their performance.

7. Their attitudes toward the value of reasoning are more positive and less fatalistic.

8. They exhibit greater self-confidence in their ability to solve problems and are less discouraged by complexity.

9. Their approach to problem solving is more objective and impersonal. They are influenced less by affective and subjective considerations (see also Tate & Stanier, 1964).

10. They are able to overcome more easily the negative transfer effect of an interfering set (Duncan, 1959; McNemar, 1955).

### Task Factors

Practice with a variety of problems in a given class tends to enhance transfer in problem solving (Duncan, 1958). Heterogeneity of exemplars presumably discourages blind perseveration, forces the subject to, remain alert and attentive, and increases the generality and hence the transferability of a solution. For purposes of transfer, even the presence of irrelevant information is helpful (Overing & Travers, 1966) because it adds variety to the problem task. As pointed out previously, however, the transfer effects of heterogeneity are negative unless mastery within each problem type is achieved.

The development of problem-solving ability obviously requires long-term experience in coping with problems. For reasons already given, *some* of this experience should be autonomous or unguided. There are good grounds for believing, however, both that guidance in the form of hints facilitates problem solving (see also Burack & Moos, 1956; Maier, 1930; Maltzman, Eisman, Brooks, & Smith, 1956; Marks, 1951; Reid, 1951), and that it is pedagogically effective in developing problem-solving skills. All methods designed to improve pupils' ability to solve problems either rely on certain general hints about efficacious problem-solving techniques or provide critical feedback about the strategies employed.

Although research findings are equivocal, concreteness of the problem itself (other factors being equal) appears to be a significant facilitating factor in problem solving (Cobb & Brenneise, 1952; Gibb, 1956). Theoretical considerations suggest that concreteness makes more of a difference in the case of young children and when the problem area is particularly unfamiliar.

Prior experience with a simpler version of the problem (Hoffman, Burke, & Maier, 1963), and specific experience with objects in unrelated situations (Birch & Rabinowitz, 1951) tend to induce negative transfer. They apparently establish a perseverative, interfering set related to functional fixedness.

### Intrapersonal Factors

Intelligence is one of the most important determinants of problem-solving ability. For one thing, reasoning power is a prominent component of all intelligence tests. For another, many other intellectual abilities measured by the intelligence test (comprehension, memory, information processing, ability to analyze) affect problem solving. IQ is positively related to both trial-and-error (Munn, 1954; Nelson, 1936) and insightful problem solving (Gellerman, 1931; Harootunian & Tate, 1960; Munn, 1954). However, for those kinds of problem solving that depend on cumulative incidental experience, for example, causal thinking (Deutsche, 1937) and applications of the lever principle (Peterson, 1932), grade in school is a more significant correlate of success than either IQ or socioeconomic status.

Brightness level also affects approach to problem solving. When mental age is held constant in a categorization problem, older (and duller) children adopt a more concrete and less self-consistent approach, use more categories, and are more "immediate-minded." They also find it more difficult to shift from one basis of categorization to another (Kounin, 1943).

It cannot be emphasized too strongly that the possession of relevant background knowledge is an important determinant of problem-solving capacity. Heuristic skill is no substitute for substantive knowledge in most everyday and academic problem-solving tasks. This simple principle, however, is frequently overlooked when findings from laboratory studies are uncritically extrapolated to real-life situations. It is typically forgotten that problem tasks in the laboratory are deliberately selected on the basis of relative independence from antecedent relevant experience. Nevertheless, understanding of relevant principles and concepts, while necessary for problem solving, is not a sufficient condition; many other cognitive and personality variables are implicated (Mayer, 1975). Thus, although successful problem solving unambiguously indicates that understanding is present, unsuccessful problem solving does not prove that understanding is absent.

Other cognitive traits such as open-mindedness, flexibility, capacity for generating multiple and novel hypotheses, attentiveness, incisiveness, problem sensitivity, intellectual curiosity, and ability to integrate ideas influence problem solving in rather self-evident ways. Cognitive stye, as suggested previously, is obviously a relevant factor, particularly with respect to general strategies of problem solving. Although evidence is lacking, it seems reasonable to suppose that problem-solving ability is not a highly generalized trait within a given individual. Rather it varies on the basis of interest, experience, and aptitude in different areas of human endeavor.

Sex differences in verbal problem solving (Munn, 1954) and causal thinking (Russell, 1940) are not significant, but boys tend to surpass girls in mechanical puzzle problems (Munn, 1954), in arithmetical reasoning, and Piagetian tasks (Graybill, 1975). Motivational traits such as drive, energy level, persistence, and frustration tolerance affect problem-solving outcomes in a positive way (Alpert, 1928; French & Thomas, 1958). However, excessive drive or emotionality tends to constrict the cognitive field and to promote rigidity and perseveration (Bahrick, Fitts, & Rankin, 1952; Easterbrook, 1950).

Many temperamental and personality traits such as high kinetic level, decisiveness, venturesomeness, self-confidence, and self-critical ability (Alpert, 1928; Kempler, 1962; McKinney, 1975) facilitate problem solving when present in a moderate to high degree. But when venturesomeness or decisiveness approaches impulsiveness (Kagan, Pearson, & Welch, 1966; Meinke, George, & Wilkinson, 1975), when self-confidence borders on dogmatism or complacency, and when self-criticism becomes self-derogation, the opposite effect may be anticipated. Anxiety level, as pointed out earlier, has a negative effect on problem solving, particularly in the case of novel and difficult tasks, because of its relationship to rigidity, constriction of the cognitive field, perseveration, disposition to improvise, premature closure, and intolerance for ambiguity.

Personality variables undoubtedly interact with such situational factors as success and failure. Success experience enhances self-confidence, venturesomeness, and disposition to improvise, whereas failure experience has the opposite effect (Rhine, 1955). A mild degree of failure, however, may prove salutary by increasing drive, attentiveness, and willingness to consider other alternatives (George, 1964).

## The Trainability of Problem-Solving Skills

The issue of whether, and to what extent, problem-solving skills are trainable has a long and confused history both in psychology and education. Much of the confusion stems from failure clearly to specify the different sources of variance in problem-solving ability and to determine their relative susceptibility to training. Equally important in this regard is the tendency to extrapolate findings from fragmentary short-term laboratory studies to long-term changes in problem-solving capacity, both in academic and real-life settings. For the most part, also, investigators have tended to ignore the problem of the generality of the effects of training.

Perhaps the most widespread approach to training in problem solving is to instruct the learner in various general principles that have emerged from theoretical analysis of the thinking process and from comparative observations of successful and unsuccessful problem solvers. Such general hints include the following:

1. Formulate and delimit the problem before trying to solve it.
2. Avoid the narrowing of attention to a single aspect of the problem.
3. Go beyond the obvious.
4. Be aware of and avoid the possibility of functional fixedness and negative transfer.
5. Abandon unpromising leads and explore other alternatives.
6. Question the reliability and representativeness of your data.
7. Make explicit the assumptions underlying any set of premises.
8. Distinguish clearly between data and inference.
9. Make use of the information derived from disconfirmed hypotheses.
10. Accept with caution conclusions that agree with your own opinions.

Some success has been reported for this approach (Bloom & Broder, 1950; Maier, 1930). It must be appreciated, however, that such instruction, while having applicability to almost all problems, is so general in nature that its usefulness in any particular problem is rather limited. The aspects of problem solving that are more specific to a given discipline undoubtedly influence problem-solving outcomes more significantly than do these hints about problem solving in general.

Short-term training programs designed to develop or enhance specific kinds of thinking ability have not been generally successful (Ausubel & Schiff, 1954; Ervin, 1960b; Smedslund, 1961; Wohwill & Lowe, 1962). However, long-term and intensive training, using programmed-instruction techniques, has led to the acquisition, retention, and transfer of rather complex problem-solving skills in first-grade children (R. C. Anderson, 1965). Similarly, training in using alternative solutions has been shown to enhance positive transfer in problem solving (Ackerman & Levin, 1958; Riopelle, 1953; Schroder & Rotter, 1952). In all of those studies, of course, the generality of the transfer effect was minimal. The results, even when significant, may be suspect when we recognize that testing for problem-solving ability can produce significant differences from pretest to posttest even without intervening instruction (Lawson, Nordland, & DeVito, 1974).

More ambitious training programs striving for more generalized enhancement of thinking include Suchman's Inquiry Training Program, Abercrombie's group discussion approach, "brainstorming" techniques (Parnes & Meadow, 1959), and Crutchfield's (1966) provision of systematic, long-term practice and feedback in exercises designed to enhance productive thinking. None of these investigators, however, has been able to demonstrate any impressive degree of transfer to problem-solving situations in other contexts, disciplines, or subdisciplines. Their efforts, in other words, foundered on the improbable thesis that there is such a thing as a general heuristics of discovery.

Discredited theories in psychology, such as the doctrine of formal discipline, tend to die hard. They are periodically revived under other more palatable rubrics and slogans. B. O. Smith's (1960) approach, based on training in the logic and heuristics of particular disciplines, is more consonant with what is known about scientific method, the heuristics of problem solving, and the transferability of problem-solving skills. However, he has yet to adduce empirical support for his formulations.

The teaching of critical thinking in a generalized, *global* sense is little more than an illusory goal and a recurrently fashionable slogan in education. On both theoretical and practical grounds it can never amount to more than a critical approach to the teaching of *particular* subject-matter disciplines. Much of such teaching can be employed within the framework of an active form of reception learning supplemented by both guided discovery and more autonomous problem-solving experience. Precise definition of terms is stressed, explicit delineation of similarities and differences between related concepts is emphasized, a critical, questioning attitude is fostered, and integrative reconciliation of ideas reformulated in idiosyncratic language is encouraged.

Pupils are taught to recognize and challenge assumptions and to distinguish between hypotheses, assertions, and facts, as well as between warranted and unwarranted inferences. They are familiarized with the basic theoretical, epistemological, and methodological problems of each discipline and with its characteristic strategies of discovering knowledge. Language is used precisely and students are sensitized to "verbal magic," theoretical sophistry, and uncritical extrapolation and analogy. In furthering all of these objectives much use can be made of skillful Socratic questioning.

To summarize, the chief sources of variance in problem-solving ability are: (1) subject-matter *knowledge* and familiarity with the distinctive logic of a discipline; (2) such *cognitive* determinants as problem sensitivity, originality, and intellectual curiosity; cognitive style; general knowledge about effective problem solving; mastery of special problem-solving strategies in particular disciplines; and (3) such *personality* traits as drive, persistence, flexibility, and anxiety. In the cases of such determinants as problem sensitivity, originality, cognitive style, and personality factors, most of the variance is probably a function of genic endowment and cumulative past experience. It stands to reason, therefore, that these aspects of problem-solving ability are not very trainable. Hence the most promising approach to training in problem solving focuses on subject-matter knowledge, on the logic and strategy of problem solving in particular disciplines, and on general principles of effective problem solving.

## Creativity

Creativity is one of the vaguest, most ambiguous, and most confused terms in psychology and education today. This concept is particularly important because "teaching for creativity" has become a flourishing trend on the current educational scene.

Much of the semantic confusion regarding the term "creativity" stems from failure to distinguish between "creativity" as a trait, inclusive of a wide and continuous range of individual differences, and the "creative person" as a unique individual, possessing a rare and singular degree of this trait—that is, a degree sufficient to set him or her off *qualitatively* from most other individuals in this regard.

The same problem also exists with respect to "intelligence," but gives rise to less confusion because the term is more familiar. Everyone agrees that all degrees of intelligence exist, that even an imbecile exhibits some manifestations of intelligent behavior. But when we refer to an "intelligent person" we mean only someone who is at the upper end of the distribution of IQ scores, someone who exceeds a hypothetical cutoff point separating intelligent individuals from the general run of humans.

Thus, although creativity undoubtedly varies along a continuum, only the rare individual who makes a singularly original and significant contribution to art, science, literature, philosophy, government, and so forth, can be called a creative person. The creative person is, by definition, a much rarer individual than the intelligent person. Thousands of intelligent individuals exist for every one who is truly creative.

It is important, therefore, to preserve the criterion of unique and singular originality in designating a person as creative. All discovery activity is not qualitatively of one piece. In the course of growing older, for example, every infant inevitably discovers that objects continue to exist even when they are out of sight. This discovery, however, hardly manifests the same *quality* of creativity as Einstein's formulation of the theory of relativity. Similarly, a sixth-grade pupil may exhibit some degree of creativity in composing a song or writing a poem, but this does not mean that these accomplishments differ from Bach's and Shakespeare's merely in degree rather than in kind. The fact that it is often difficult to measure originality —and that great discoveries may frequently go unrecognized for decades or centuries—does not detract in the least from the existence of qualitative differences in creative achievement. A creative person must do more than simply produce something that is novel or original in terms of his or her *own* life history.

Truly creative individuals therefore are rare not primarily because they lack appropriate experience to develop their creative potentialities but because they are also, by definition, at such an extreme point in the distribution of creative potentialities that they are qualitatively discontinuous from persons exhibiting lesser degrees of creativity. This is not to deny the important role of the environment in the development of creativity; many potential Mozarts, for example, have spent their lives as peasants or cobblers. But even assuming an optimal environment, creative individuals would still be extremely rare. The principal determinant of creative persons, in other words, is genic. It is, however, enhanced by environmental factors.

A second source of semantic confusion regarding the concept of creativity reflects the failure to distinguish between creativity as a highly particularized and substantive capacity (a rare and unique manifestation of talent in a particular field of endeavor) and as a general constellation of supportive intellectual abilities, personality variables, and problem-solving traits. Typical of the latter conception of creativity is Torrance's definition of creative thinking as the "process of sensing gaps or disturbing, missing elements; forming ideas or hypotheses concerning them; testing these hypotheses; and communicating the results, possibly modifying and retesting the hypotheses" (Torrance, Yamamoto, Schenetzki, Palamutlu, & Luther, 1960).

These latter aspects of intellectual functioning presumably include such component traits or abilities as originality, redefinition, adaptive flexibility, spontaneous flexibility, word fluency, expressional fluency, associational fluency, and problem sensitivity (Guilford & Merrifield, 1960; Guilford, Wilson, Christensen, & Lewis, 1951; Kettner, Guilford, & Christensen, 1959). Much stress, also, is currently laid on divergent thinking as the distinctive attribute of creative thinking; and such Guilford-type tests as unusual uses, consequences, impossibilities, problem situations, and improvements (Guilford et al., 1951) have been employed to measure this ability.

However, without denying in any way the existence of general supportive abilities, it must be clarified that such abilities do not constitute the essence of creativity. It is true that they are probably more intrinsically related to creative achievement than is IQ. Genuinely creative talent, nevertheless, is a particularized intellectual-personality capacity related to the *substantive* content of a given field of human endeavor, rather than a set of general, content-free intellectual and personality traits. And with increasing age it probably becomes increasingly particularized in its expression. Creative achievement, in other words, reflects a rare capacity for developing insights, sensitivities, and appreciations in a circumscribed content area of intellectual or artistic activity.

It may sometimes happen, of course, that a single individual possesses more than one creative talent. This capacity is obviously not coextensive with any one general ability such as divergent thinking, although the possession of this latter ability, and of other supportive abilities as well, undoubtedly facilitates the actualization of particularized and substantive creativity. Arieti (1976) has made a comprehensive study of the process of creativity. He describes the creative process as a "magic synthesis"—a blending of the primitive, irrational aspects of a person's unconscious thinking with the logical, rational and cognitive aspects of his or her conscious thinking.

To summarize, creativity is a particularized, substantive capacity, whereas the commonly measured creative abilities are supportive intellectual-personality functions. These functions, such as general intelligence and capacity for disciplined concentration, help implement the expression of creativity—that is, convert creative potentialities into creative achievement. These supportive abilities are normally distributed in the population. Differences among individuals, like differences in IQ, are differences in degree rather than in kind. Varying degrees of creativity also exist, but the creative person differs *qualitatively* from individuals manifesting lesser degrees of creativity. Hence, although some supportive abilities manifest a modicum of intersituational generality (Getzels & Jackson, 1962; Kettner et al., 1959; Wallach & Kogan, 1965; Wilson, Guilford, & Christensen, 1953), there is no reason to believe that creativity *in itself* exhibits any generality of function (Anastasi & Schaefer, 1971; Eisner, 1965). Because of the implementing or enabling function of general intelligence and of general supportive traits, high scores on tests of these characteristics are more generously distributed among creative than noncreative individuals (Drevdahl, 1956; Roe, 1960). Neither type of test, however, measures creativity itself. As a matter of fact, by definition, no general test of creativity is possible. Assessments of creative potentiality can only be based on expert judgments of actual work products, suitably tempered by considerations of age and experience (Eisner, 1965).

Until these distinctions between creativity, its supportive abilities, and the creative person are clearly understood, existing semantic confusion will remain. It is claimed, for example, that an elementary-school boy behaves creatively in arithmetic when he proposes alternative approaches to the solution of problems, grasps concepts intuitively, or displays autonomy, flexibility, and freedom from perseverative rigidity in his discovery efforts (Hohn, 1961). What is actually meant, however, is not that he is manifesting even a moderate degree of mathematical creativity or that he has potentialities for becoming a creative mathematician, but, rather, that he is exhibiting some of the supportive correlates of creativity in his mathematics work.

Quite frequently also, research workers who ordinarily use "creativity" in the more "democratic" sense of the term (to refer to general supportive abilities) also imply in other contexts that the encouragement of true creativity (in the sense of original accomplishment) in every child is one of the major functions of the school. This view is implicit in Bruner's (1961b) position that the school should help all children reach discontinuous realms of experience so that they can create their own interior culture. It is also implicit in the goal that Suchman (1961) proposes for his Inquiry Training program; namely, that children should be trained to formulate the same kinds of unifying concepts in science that are produced by our most creative scientists. And it is made unambiguously explicit in the following statement by Bruner:

> A small part, but a crucial part of discovery of the highest order is to invent and develop models or "puzzle forms" that can be imposed on difficulties with good effect. It is in this area that the truly powerful mind shines. But it is interesting to what degree perfectly ordinary people can, given the benefit of instruction, construct quite interesting and, what a century ago, would have been considered greatly original models (Bruner, 1961a, p. 30).

### Creativity and Intelligence

The relationship between creativity and intelligence is exceedingly complex and is further complicated by difficult problems of measurement. Creativity measures emphasizing divergent thinking tend to correlate only moderately ($r = .25–.30$) with measures of intelligence (Cline, Richards, & Abe, 1962; Cline, Richards, & Needham, 1963; Drevdahl, 1956; Getzels &

Jackson, 1962; Guilford, 1950; Guilford & Christensen, 1973; J. L. Holland, 1961; Klausmeier & Wiersma, 1965; McGuire et al., 1961; Torrance, 1960a; Torrance et al., 1960; Yamamoto, 1964a, 1964b, 1964c). A first blush this suggests that these supportive cognitive traits associated with creativity tap a somewhat different spectrum of intellectual abilities than do traditional tests of intelligence.

However, the evidence that these supportive traits correlate just as highly with intelligence as they do among each other (Anastasi & Schaefer, 1971; Cline et al., 1962; Crockenberg, 1972; Getzels & Jackson, 1962; Ohnmacht, 1966; Piers, Daniels, & Quackenbush, 1960; Thorndike, 1963) clearly indicates that they cannot be considered representative of a common attribute of creativity that is independent of intelligence. For all practical purposes, therefore, most commonly used batteries of creativity tests measure cognitive abilities that are not reliably distinguishable from intelligence. This fact undoubtedly accounts, in part, for their positive correlation with academic achievement. Hence it is grossly misleading to distinguish on the basis of such tests between creative and intelligent individuals.

In contrast to these findings, other investigators (Flescher, 1963; Wallach & Kogan, 1965) have reported negligible correlations between intelligence and creativity. But although Flescher's battery of tests are presumably measuring some cognitive abilities that are independent of intelligence, the negligible intercorrelations among them indicate that they can hardly be considered representative of a unitary trait of creativity. Additive treatment of scores on this battery and the derivation of a composite score are therefore unwarranted. Wallach and Kogan's (1965) more homogeneous measures of creative aptitude, on the other hand, exhibit satisfactory generality over component elements and can therefore be considered reflective of a stable cognitive trait that both plays a supportive role in creative performance and is independent of intelligence.

Based on their examination of the concepts of creativity and intelligence, Anastasi and Schaefer (1971) propose that "the term 'creativity,' like the term 'intelligence' be recognized as referring to a loosely defined, broad, and many-faceted concept. Both terms will undoubtedly survive as independent concepts because they provide convenient shortcuts in designating complex behavior domains of considerable practical importance. But neither corresponds to a precisely defined or distinct entity. Each comprises a multiplicity of identifiable traits, organized in a pattern of relationships that cuts across the two domains" (Anastasi & Schaefer, 1971, p. 115).

Much more important than the relationship between intelligence and supportive measures of creativity is the relationship between intelligence and true substantive creativity. The evidence invariably shows that creative individuals in art, literature, and science are more intelligent than noncreative individuals (Barron, 1969; Drevdahl & Cattell, 1958; Hitt & Stock, 1965), and that high-IQ persons contribute much more than their share of notable and original discoveries in the various disciplines (Terman & Oden, 1959). This suggests of course that intelligence, like other supportive cognitive traits, makes possible and implements the expression of substantive creativity (Price & Bell, 1965). In other words, a certain minimal degree of intelligence above the average is necessary for the actualization of creative potentialities. But above this critical level the relationship between intelligence and true creativity is approximately zero (Barron, 1969; Drevdahl, 1956; MacKinnon, 1962; Terman & Oden, 1959). The noncreative, high-IQ individual who does very well on academic tasks and is vocationally successful, but who never generates an original idea, is a very familiar figure in our culture. Contrariwise, many highly creative individuals do not sport spectacularly high IQ's.

### Creativity and Academic Achievement

Research findings on the relationship between creativity and academic achievement tend to be contradictory. Some investigators (Cline et al., 1963; Getzels & Jackson, 1959, 1962; Torrance, 1960a; Yamamoto, 1964a, 1964b, 1964c) report that scores on Guilford- and Torrance-type creativity tests correlate just as highly with criteria of academic achievement as do intelligence test scores. They find no difference in academic achievement between high-creativity groups and high-intelligence groups despite a mean difference of about 20 points in IQ between the two kinds of groups.

High-creativity individuals are also significantly superior to low-creativity individuals on all subtests of the Iowa Test of Educational Development when the effects of intelligence are controlled statistically (Yamamoto, 1964c). Flescher (1963), however, obtained no significant relationship between creativity test scores and academic scores; and Edwards & Tyler (1965) found that a high-intelligence group of ninth-graders was superior to a high-creativity group on both achievement test scores and grade-point average.

Flescher's (1963) data provide a possible means of reconciling these contradictory findings. Since his measures of creativity were unrelated to intelligence test scores, it could be argued that the positive correlations between creativity and achievement in the other studies reflected the significant relationship between creativity and intelligence measures in these latter studies. However, this cannot be a complete explanation because when the effects of intelligence are statistically controlled, high creatives are still superior in achievement to low creatives (Yamamoto, 1964c). Another possibility, in view of the low intercorrelations among creativity tests, is that some of these tests may be positively related to achievement whereas others are not.

On purely *deductive* grounds, it seems quite unlikely that creativity should be related to academic achievement, inasmuch as mastery of a given subject-matter discipline does *not* in any way presuppose conspicuous capacity for making original or creative contributions to that discipline. As a matter of fact, since creative students tend to be nonconforming and disruptive of classroom routine and hence often irritate their teachers (Getzels & Jackson, 1962), we can anticipate a negative relationship between creativity and school grades. This is precisely what Edwards and Tyler (1965) did find when comparing ninth-grade pupils who were in the upper third of the distribution in both scholastic aptitude and creativity with pupils who ranked high in scholastic aptitude alone.

### Personality Correlates of Creativity

Considerable research has been conducted on the personality characteristics of persons who have been rated by competent judges as creative in such areas as art, architecture, literature, and science. In general, these traits are consistent with what one would expect of original and talented individuals who have achieved success and recognition in their chosen fields. On the cognitive side, creative individuals tend to be original, perceptive, insightful, independent in judgment, open to new experience (especially from within), skeptical, and verbally facile. They are flexible, open-minded, intuitive, and tolerant of ambiguity; have wide-ranging interests; and prefer complexity. They are less interested in small details and in the practical and concrete than in theoretical ideas and symbolic transformations (Barron, 1963, 1968, 1969; Drevdahl, 1956; Drevdahl & Cattell, 1958; MacKinnon, 1960, 1961, 1962).

In general they delight in paradoxes and in reconciling opposites. From a motivational standpoint they are ambitious, achievement-oriented, dominant, and have a sense of destiny about themselves. They tend to be emotionally mature, venturesome, self-sufficient, and emotionally and aesthetically sensitive. Their self-image abounds in such traits as inventiveness, determination, industry, independence, individualism, and enthusiasm. On the whole, they exhibit higher ego strength and self-acceptance, more introspectiveness, and greater femininity than noncreative individuals.

In their relations with others they are unconventional, rebellious, disorderly, self-centered, exhibitionistic, and prone to retreat to the role of observer. They tend to make deviant scores on the Minnesota Multiphasic Personality Inventory, but this is undoubtedly more reflective of complexity of personality, candor, lack of defensiveness, and openness to experience than of genuine personality distortion (Barron, 1963, 1968, 1969; Drevdahl, 1956; Drevdahl & Cattell, 1958; Hammer, 1961; MacKinnon, 1960, 1961, 1962).

Of somewhat less psychological significance are the personality characteristics associated with the supportive cognitive criteria of creativity. Wallace and Kogan (1965) found that their high creatives tended to be broad rather than narrow categorizers, to be tolerant of an unconventional type of hypothesizing about the world, and to be responsive to affective aspects of the environment. Their high-creative/high-intelligence group were high in self-confidence and self-esteem and low in defensiveness, enjoyed a high sociometric status, actively sought the companionship of others, and exhibited a high attention span and ability to concentrate. But at the same time they tended to display more than their fair share of attention-seeking and disruptive behavior.

On the other hand, high creatives who were low in intelligence exhibited the opposite set of characteristics except for attention-seeking, disruptive behavior in the classroom. Anxiety level was middling for the high-creative groups; when it was either very high or very low, it appeared to depress creativity. This suggests either that a moderate degree of anxiety is necessary to generate creative behavior or that the expression of creativity is productive of moderate anxiety.

### Identification of Creative Potentialities

It follows from our substantive conception of creativity that potentiality for creativity can be measured only in terms of capacity for sustained and highly original achievement in an important area of human endeavor. Although knowledgeable experts can reliably and validly identify creativity after it has matured and eventuated in a substantial body of work or performance, the identification of creative potential prior to actualization is a much more difficult matter. Satisfactory methods are not yet available. Self-estimates are invariably inflated and have little validity (Feldhusen, Denny, & Condon, 1965; Richards, Cline, & Needham, 1964). Teacher estimates are not much more satisfactory because they are based on generalized impressions; they exhibit low interrater reliability (Piers et al., 1960). The only feasible approach seems to lie in expert judgments of actual work products taking inexperience, immaturity, and varying rates of development into consideration (Eisner, 1965).

Some shortcomings of Guilford- and Torrance-type tests, emphasizing divergent thinking as measures of creative potential, have already been considered. In the first place, they do not exhibit an independent common quality, generally correlating as highly with intelligence as they do among themselves. Second, scores on measures of divergent thinking are indeterminably contaminated by such factors as verbal fluency and glibness, uninhibited self-expression, impulsiveness, and deficient self-critical ability. Third, these instruments have not been validated against substantive creativity in later life. Finally, on *deductive* grounds alone, they cannot possibly have high predictive validity inasmuch as they do not measure substantive creativity but rather various supportive cognitive traits.

Wallach and Kogan (1965) devised a measure of creative potential based upon the total number and uniqueness of relevant associations under conditions that maximize task orientation as opposed to ego orientation. Compared with the Guilford-type tests, this measure is more homogeneous, is more independent of intelligence, exhibits higher generality of function, and is less influenced by contaminating factors. However, the same limitations regarding validity still apply with equal force. These investigators attribute intraindividual incongruity between creativity and intelligence test scores to lack of flexibility in responding to evaluative and nonevaluative situations respectively. It seems more parsimonious, however, to attribute such discrepancy to the independence of the abilities measured by the two kinds of instruments.

Interest has been expressed in the use of curiosity as an index of creative potentiality. At the very most, however, curiosity can be regarded as a supportive motivational variable that is possibly related to creative achievement (Lazare, 1967). Evidence regarding this relationship is scant; measurement is also a difficult problem. Ratings by teachers and peers, as well as self-ratings (Maw & Maw, 1961, 1962), are of questionable reliability and validity. Generality of function is another serious problem. Even if a general factor of curiosity could be identified, it would probably have little psychological significance, since it is the level of curiosity in particular substantive areas that affects the productivity or creativity of an individual's work.

### Fostering Creativity in the Schools

Although the term "creativity" is surrounded by confusion, the school and society at large consider it a desirable quality that should be nurtured. This notion has received some indirect support from developments in the mental measurement movement. If, for example, we accept the premise that the structure of intellect can be analyzed into a multiplicity of separately identifiable cognitive abilities or factors—as many as 120 according to Guilford (1959)—the conclusion seems inescapable that, simply on the basis of probability, almost every child is destined to become a genius or a near-genius with respect to at least one factor.

The objective of "teaching for creativity," to make every child an original and creative thinker, is based on one or more of four untenable propositions. The first proposition assumes that every child, by definition, has potentialities for unique creativity, provided that he or she is not stifled by the educational system. Such potentialities, however, are rare. The second proposition is reflective of a view of human nature that asserts that even if a child has no creative potentialities, inspired and sensitive teaching can compensate for missing genes. The third proposition, ignoring the distinction between creativity and the creative individual, advances a "democratic" definition of creativity that employs an intraindividual criterion of originality and assumes that all creativity is qualitatively of one piece. By the very same token, however, if this criterion of creativity is used, the educational objective of making every pupil a creative individual becomes so watered down that it becomes virtually meaningless. The final proposition simply rests on the previously discussed assertion that the supportive creative abilities are coextensive with substantive creativity.

Research on training for originality has yielded limited success. Subjects can be trained to respond with more unusual associations, to generate more novel ideas, or to suggest more unusual uses (R. C. Anderson & Anderson, 1963; Cartledge & Krauser, 1963; Crutchfield & Covington, 1963; Freedman, 1965; Maltzman, 1960; Mednick, Mednick, & Jung, 1964). And in some instances transfer to related kinds of problem solving does take place. Such transfer, however, occurs in a very restricted range of contexts and sometimes does not occur at all (R. C. Anderson & Anderson, 1963; Maltzman, Belloni, & Fishbein, 1964).

Torrance and Torrance (1973) report on numerous experiments, training materials, and programs for teaching children to think creatively. It is important to note, however, that this kind of training implicates various supportive traits of creativity rather than substantive creativity itself. The same limitations apply to more general types of creativity training that depend on classroom milieu (Brown, 1964) or on the communication of a set of principles about how to be creative (Torrance, 1961).

Some research data are available on the school and family backgrounds of students who make high scores on the supportive aspects of creativity. The latter individuals "tend to diverge from stereotyped meanings, to move away from the model provided by teachers, to seek out careers that do not conform to what is expected of them" (Getzels & Jackson, 1962) and to challenge the opinions and assumptions of teachers (MacKinnon, 1962). The parents of these students tend to be expressive and nondominating and to work in occupations permitting much autonomy (Weisberg & Springer, 1961). They focus on such qualities as the child's openness to experience, and on the child's values, interests, and enthusiasm for life, rather than on academic success, cleanliness, good manners, and studiousness (Getzels & Jackson, 1962).

How reasonable is the goal of "teaching for creativity," that is, in the sense of singularly original achievement? A decent respect for the realities of the human condition would seem to indicate that the training possibilities with respect to this kind of creativity are severely limited. The school can obviously help in the realization of existing creative potentialities by providing opportunities for spontaneity, initiative, and individualized expression, by making room in the curriculum for tasks that are sufficiently challenging for pupils with creative gifts; and by rewarding creative achievement. But it cannot actualize potentialities for unique creativity if these potentialities do not exist in the first place. Hence the school can help only in actualizing its expression in those rare individuals who already possess the necessary potentialities. It can, of course, also help in the realization of average and less unique levels of creative potential.

> Research tells us that children and adults develop along the lines that they find rewarding. If schools are to develop the creative thinking abilities, they must find ways of rewarding this kind of thinking or achievement. . . . In the main, current school curricula at all levels of education are designed to develop and make use of the kinds of thinking abilities reflected in traditional tests of intelligence. No one is suggesting that the development of these abilities be eliminated. It is only suggested that parallel treatment be given the creative thinking abilities, as well as other abilities not adequately represented in our present tests of intelligence (Torrance, 1960b, pp. 68, 69).

How important, then, one might legitimately ask, is it to identify pupils with true creative potentialities? Persons belonging to the "genius will out" school of thought would argue that these potentialities will be actualized irrespective of what the school does or fails to do. The realization of creative potentialities, however, like the expression of any genically determined tendencies, is seldom an all-or-none proposition. It is true that in certain instances genic factors are so prepotent, or all of the relevant personality, motivational, family, peer, and cultural variables are so overwhelmingly favorable, that a successful outcome is almost inevitable. But in many other instances the influence of these variables is more equivocal, and a successful outcome hinges on the guidance, stimulation, and encouragement that is forthcoming from such agencies as the school.

The problem of creativity in relation to the school has been studied (Torrance, 1965; Torrance & Myers, 1972), with specific suggestions given for promoting creative potentialities. For example, Torrance (1965) sets forth five principles that teachers should follow to reward creative thinking: (1) respect unusual questions; (2) respect unusual ideas; (3) show students that their ideas have value; (4) provide opportunities for learning that are not evaluated; and (5) relate evaluation to causes and consequences. From a more recent review of studies designed to give information on the "teachability of creativity," Torrance and Torrance (1973) concluded, "The most successful approaches seem to be those that involve both cognitive and emotional functioning, provide adequate structure and motivation, and give opportunities for involvement, practice and interaction with teachers and other students" (p. 46).

# PART FIVE

# EVALUATION AND MEASUREMENT

# 17

# PRINCIPLES OF MEASUREMENT
# AND EVALUATION

*Measurement and evaluation are central to our concept of classroom learning: (1) because of the importance we have placed in preceding chapters on ascertaining what the learner already knows before trying to teach him further; (2) because of the importance of monitoring his ongoing learning in order to correct, clarify, and consolidate it; and (3) because of the importance of monitoring the efficacy of different teaching methods, and of different ways of organizing and sequencing subject matter (curriculum), as well as of ascertaining the extent to which their objectives are being realized. Much of the past and current opposition to the testing movement in education is a reaction to the tendency of many tests to measure the more trivial and discrete aspects of subject-matter learning, to emphasize short-term and rote learning, and to regard test scores per se as more important than the knowledge they supposedly represent. All of these shortcomings of measurement, however, are merely representative of many past and present testing procedures and objectives that are not necessarily inherent in measurement itself. That is, these shortcomings are all remediable.*

*For example, in accordance with positions taken earlier in the book, we have emphasized the importance: (1) of measuring the understanding of key concepts in every discipline; (2) of pretests and long-term posttests, as well as of ongoing and immediate posttests; (3) of mastery learning; (4) of indirectly testing knowledge of prior learning by measuring ability to learn sequentially-dependent material; and (5) of placing greater reliance on power than on speed tests. We have also advocated the use of essay tests to measure the student's organization, cohesiveness, and integration of knowledge (in addition to using multiple-choice tests to measure breadth of content) and the use of simulated real-life performance tests and of work samples (particularly in applied disciplines).*

*In order to be useful in educational practice, all tests must meet the criteria of validity, reliability, representativeness, discriminability, and feasibility. Validity refers to the extent to which a test measures what it purports to measure. It can be ascertained by the prima-facie relevance and representativeness of the content of a test for the knowledge or skills it purports to measure, by its predictive value for later subject-matter or vocational competence, and by other less significant methods. Reliability refers to the self-consistency of a test or to its generality over component items, to its stability over time (or over successive testings), and to the extent of its generality over component subtests that purportedly measure the same trait (intelligence, creativity) in different ways.*

*By representativeness we mean the extent to which the component items of a test are a fair and random sample of the trait or ability it purports to measure. The discriminability of a test depends on its ability to distinguish adequately between poor, average, and superior learners with respect to a given subject matter or skill. Finally, a good test must be feasible in terms of the significance of the information it yields, and of ease of administration, scoring, interpretation, and amenability to feedback.*

*In evaluating a student's test scores, it is important to judge him in terms of his or her own ability level, in terms of his or her relative performance among peers (norm-referenced measures), and, most important, against an absolute standard of mastery (criterion-referenced measures).*


Measurement and evaluation are integral parts of classroom learning and hence of educational psychology as well. If we are really serious about education, we must have precise ways both of measuring learning outcomes in individual students and of ascertaining whether they are consonant with our educational objectives. These measures, moreover, must do more than merely inform us whether students are actually being educated. Equally important, they must provide data that make it possible for us to monitor and thus ensure quality control over the educational enterprise. Thus, at any given point in time, they must enable us to know how effective our educational program is. And if we hope to improve learning outcomes by introducing new teaching methods, instructional materials, and ways of organizing subject-matter content and curriculum sequences, measurement and evaluation necessarily enter the picture again.

Scientific research in education, as in any empirical and experimental discipline, is completely unthinkable in the absence of reliable and valid measuring instruments and the data that they provide. It is clear, therefore, that if education is to prosper, both teachers and students must learn to welcome regular and systematic testing rather than to regard it as a threat, an intrusion, or a distraction from more important matters.

Evaluation is important at the beginning, during, and at the conclusion of any instructional sequence. First, one must decide what learning outcomes one desires to induce and then structure the instructional process accordingly. Second, it is necessary to determine the degree of progress toward the goal during the course of learning—both as feedback and motivation for the student and as a means of monitoring the efficacy of instruction. Finally, it is important to evaluate ultimate learning outcomes in relation to objectives, both from the standpoint of student achievement and from the standpoint of teaching methods and materials. With this type of feedback information we are then in a position either to modify the instructional program or to redefine our goals if we are convinced that they are unrealistic. Such evaluation is typically longitudinal or extended in nature since the effects of a curriculum on the educational product are not ascertainable immediately. These kinds of evaluative studies, therefore, involve the systematic collection of large quantities of data over many consecutive years.

In this chapter we can briefly consider only such general issues as the purposes and limitations of measurement and evaluation, the requirements that an effective measuring instrument must meet, the nature of standardized tests, the interpretation of test scores, and various informal methods of measurement and evaluation. Detailed discussion of these issues as well as particular aptitude and achievement tests, both individual and group, more properly belongs in a separate course on tests and measurements.

## The Purposes of Measurement and Evaluation

In general, the function of evaluation is to determine the extent to which various significant educational objectives are actually being attained. To evaluate is to make a judgment of worth or merit, to appraise educational outcomes in terms of whether they fulfill a particular set of educational goals. Apart from ascertaining whether such goals are being realized, any assessment of the outcomes of schooling is meaningless. No educational outcome is good or bad in and of itself. Its worth can be considered only in terms of how far it accomplishes the ends we are striving to achieve through education.

All too frequently, however, educational objectives are not clearly or explicitly formulated in advance. Thus it is small wonder that neither the instructional program nor the learning outcomes that are being evaluated bear much relation to the goals that are professed.

In recent years the schools have been criticized for outcomes in student learning, leading to investigations of educational accountability. The concept of accountability includes components such as the student's outcome goals, determining whether these goals have been achieved and at what cost, and acceptance of responsibility for results. Accountability, which has become a controversial issue, emphasizes the need for schools to be responsible for results (Good, Biddle, & Brophy, 1975). This issue ultimately reflects on the classroom teacher, who is held responsible for students' achievement. However, as discussed previously, research findings indicate that factors other than the school also influence students' learning (Coleman, Campbell, Hobson, McPartland, Mood, Weinfeld, & York, 1966; Jencks & Brown, 1975).

A current development that should help correct educational inadequacies is the growth in performance/competency-based teacher education. Elman (1972) states "In performance-based programs, performance goals are specified and agreed to in rigorous detail in advance of instruction. The student preparing to become a teacher must either be able to demonstrate his ability to promote desirable learning or exhibit behaviors known to promote it. He is held accountable, not for passing grades but for attaining a given level of competency in performing the essential tasks of teaching. . . . The emphasis is on demonstrated product or output" (p. 3).

This teaching approach identifies the outcomes of the teaching/learning process in terms of the learner's performance—cognitive, affective, and social. By specifying goals clearly and encouraging discussion and analysis, performance/competency-based teaching improves the relevance of the educational process. In this way the teacher is able to relate abstract concepts to practical life experience.

It follows, therefore, that the educational enterprise cannot be conducted efficiently unless it is directed toward the achievement of certain designated goals. Only after formulating clearly what it is we hope to accomplish through our educational efforts are we in a position rationally to determine the content and methods of instruction and to evaluate the outcomes of such instruction. It is probably true that educational objectives can be meaningfully expressed only in such behavioral terms as understandings, appreciations, capabilities, attitudes, and so forth. But if these behavioral goals are to have any real meaning and impact on education, we must go beyond a formal taxonomy of cognitive and affective objectives that mean different things to different persons and try to reach consensus on the processes underlying the behaviors in question.

The next step is to devise an appropriate instructional program that can realize the objectives we designate as important and to determine what kinds of evidence of attainment of a given objective are both theoretically defensible and subject to reliable and valid measurement. In addition to standardized testing we have to consider such methods of evaluation as essay and oral examinations, observation, ratings, and the appraisal of work products.

It is often held that the determination of educational objectives is the exclusive prerogative of educational philosophers. However, it would seem that as social scientists concerned with how knowledge is acquired, with the nature and limits of human capacities, and with developmental changes in cognitive processes, educational psychologists are in a strategic position to express a value judgment regarding the objectives of education. In the first place, they know what is realistically possible and how best to implement it. Second, educational psychologists are able to translate highly general objectives into more explicit intellectual goals. Thus, educational objectives would be developed best by the combining of multidisciplinary talents through teamwork.

### To Facilitate Student Learning

The primary purpose of evaluation is to monitor students' learning—to constitute an objective check on both their progress and ultimate achievement so that if either is unsatisfactory, suitable remedial measures may be instituted. Thus a really adequate evaluation program not only assesses the extent to which student achievement realizes educational objectives but also attempts to account for unsatisfactory achievement—irrespective of whether this inheres in unsuitable instructional methods or materials, in incompetent teaching, in inadequate student morale or motivation, or in insufficient readiness and aptitude. As a product, student learning is no different from any other significant human endeavor that society takes seriously. Considerations of efficiency and quality control presuppose systematic and rigorous assessment.

Resistance to evaluation largely reflects a long history of nonacceptance of this latter proposition in certain educational circles. In fact, two of the principal assumptions underlying the child-centered approach to education are that: (1) the *really* important objectives of education are intangible and untestable: and (2) the application of objective standards of assessment to pupils' learning is inherently repugnant to and incompatible with the ethos of a humanistic education. These arguments have been further bolstered by the assertion that genuine measurement is possible only in the physical sciences (B. O. Smith, 1938), and by calling attention to limitations and abuses of measurement in education (see below).

In our view this position stems largely from a sentimental and semi-mystical approach both to children and to the educational process. The fact that educational objectives have been vaguely stated in the past or that measurement of educational outcomes has hitherto focused on relatively trivial aspects of school learning does not mean that this must necessarily be the case. Nor does the fact that behavioral measurement cannot possibly yield data that are as precise, reliable, and valid as those in the physical sciences preclude the construction of adequately reliable and valid measuring instruments in psychology and education or their usefulness in evaluating student performance and instructional programs. In addition, the fact that any aspect of the educational program necessarily has its limitations and is subject to abuse does not mean that it should be discarded as value-less. It merely argues for intelligent and sophisticated use of measuring instruments based on awareness of their limitations and of the possibilities of abuse.

Apart from its monitoring function, evaluation facilitates student learning in many ways. In the first place, it encourages teachers to formulate and clarify their objectives and to communicate their expectations to students. Frequently, of course, examination content reflects no explicit set of teacher goals, or is even in direct conflict with professed goals. Nevertheless, nothing indicates more unambiguously what knowledge and skills teachers regard as important than the kinds of examination questions they set.

It has been shown that students distribute their study time and apportion their learning effort in direct proportion to the predicted likelihood of various topics and kinds of information being represented on the examination (Keislar, 1961). These predictions are based on the degree of explicit or implicit emphasis placed on a given topic, on examination hints, on student folklore, on the teacher's reputation, and on knowledge of or experience with previous examination questions. They include not only expectations with respect to topical coverage but also expectations regarding the kinds of mastery to be demonstrated: factual recall, evidence of comprehension, critical analysis or interpretation, application, problem solving, ability to marshal evidence and synthesize knowledge, and so forth.

It is evident, therefore, that if teachers wish to influence learning outcomes in particular ways by the kinds of evaluative devices they use, they must formulate their objectives clearly, communicate these objectives explicitly to students, and construct reliable and valid measuring instruments that test the degree to which these objectives are realized. Educational objectives, no matter how praiseworthy, simply go by the board if they do not receive representation in the scheme of evaluation. But if communicated adequately and anticipated on examinations, they can direct the kind of learning that takes place.

Second, the examination itself is a significant learning experience. It forces students to review, consolidate, clarify, and integrate subject matter in advance of being tested. It also performs a comparable review function during the course of the test. Feedback from an examination confirms, clarifies, and corrects ideas, and differentially identifies areas requiring further thought and study. Merely identifying the correct answers on a multiple-choice test significantly increases retest scores a week later (Plowman & Stroud, 1942).[1] This corrective function of feedback is extremely important since students often feel "certain" about incorrect answers (Kooker & Williams, 1959). The motivational effects of feedback have been discussed in another context.

Third, as pointed out earlier, examinations play a significant motivating role in school learning. Within limits, desire for academic success, fear of failure, and avoidance of guilt and anxiety are legitimate motives in an academic setting. It would be wholly unrealistic to expect students to study regularly, systematically, and conscientiously in the absence of periodic examinations. Frequent quizzing markedly facilitates classroom learning (Fitch, Drucker, & Norton, 1951; Kirkpatrick, 1939; Ross & Henry, 1939).

Finally, from the experience of being subjected to external appraisal, students learn how to evaluate their own learning outcomes independently. Such self-evaluation enhances school achievement (Duel, 1958) and is particularly important once students complete their formal schooling. It is also part of the long-range objective of increasing students' capacity for appraising their abilities and achievement validly and realistically.

### To Facilitate Teaching

Measurement and evaluation provide teachers with essential feedback regarding the effectiveness of their instructional efforts. They indicate how effectively teachers present and organize material, how clearly they explain ideas, how well they communicate with less sophisticated individuals, and how efficacious particular instructional techniques or materials are. Feedback from examinations identifies areas requiring further explication, clarification, and review, and is invaluable in the diagnosis of learning difficulties, both individual and group. The objective examination is also a necessary corrective against the subjectivity and impressionism of more informal methods of evaluation, which are frequently contaminated by favoritism and reward for docility and neatness (Carter, 1952).

---

[1] See Chapter 9 for a discussion of the long-term effects of feedback.

## To Appraise Curriculums and to Make Curriculum Judgments

As indicated previously, measurement and evaluation are essential for monitoring a curriculum—for assessing the merit of a particular sequence and organization of courses embracing designated subject-matter content, instructional materials, and methods of teaching. The data they furnish are also helpful in making such administrative decisions as the grade placement of subject matter and the optimal sequencing of courses. It goes without saying that research both on curriculum and on the learning process itself would be impossible without reliable and valid measures of learning outcomes.

## To Assist in Guidance, Counseling, and the Individualization of Instruction

Systematic measurement and evaluation of aptitude, achievement, motivation, personality, attitudes, and interests are necessary for individualizing instruction and for purposes of individual guidance and counseling. We must know the current aptitude levels of pupils and the current state of their subject-matter knowledge before we can "prepare curriculum materials appropriate to ability levels [and] adapt teaching methods to the learners and the content to be learned" (Adkins, 1958). In the absence of such information, intelligent decisions cannot be made about grade placement, grouping, the pacing of study, promotion, choice of courses, academic and vocational goals, and remedial work. These data, finally, are essential for reporting pupil progress to parents and for explaining to them the basis on which particular decisions are made.

## Limitations and Abuses of Evaluation and Measurement

In the long history of the measurement movement in education, many objections have been raised both to the goals of educational measurement and to the effects produced by particular techniques of measuring learning outcomes. Some of these objections do, in fact, identify palpable limitations, abuses, and shortcomings. Others are based on sentimental and semimystical conceptions of the educative process. It is important to scrutinize these objections carefully and to distinguish between those based on *inherent* limitations and shortcomings of educational measurement and those based either on correctable abuses or on attainable capabilities that are as yet unrealized.

First, it is argued that educational tests tend to evaluate the more tangible, trivial, and easily measurable as opposed to such more significant outcomes of education as genuine understanding, originality, problem-solving ability, ability to think independently, ability to retrieve information, ability to synthesize knowledge, and so forth. This criticism, however, is warranted only in relation to the early standardized tests measuring rote retention of factual information. It must be remembered that objective tests are now available that measure both comprehension of general principles and ability to interpret and apply knowledge.

Furthermore, many other kinds of measuring devices can be used to evaluate some of the more elusive outcomes of education. These include observation, self-reports, peer judgments, essay tests, oral examinations, work samples, practical examinations, research papers, and so forth. It is true that valid measures of such important traits and abilities as cognitive style, creativity, problem-solving strategy, flexibility, and problem sensitivity have yet to be devised. But there is no reason to believe that currently encountered difficulties in devising these measures will not eventually be overcome.

Second, it is frequently alleged that educational measures fail to test the attainment of objectives that are *idiosyncratic* to a particular school system, curriculum, institution, or teacher. Again this objection mistakenly regards the use of national standardized tests as coextensive with educational measurement. There is no incompatibility between using tests standardized on a broad, representative sample and tests prepared especially for a particular school system, school, curriculum, or classroom. Where advisable, both kinds of measures can and should be used.

Third, test scores and school marks often become ends in themselves, displacing in importance and presumed validity the knowledge, competencies, and scholastic achievement they are intended to sample and represent. When this happens, cognitive drive atrophies, pupils lose interest in subject matter as soon as their grades are recorded, and society places greater weight on a test score or on a diploma from a prestigious institution than on intrinsically more valid long-term evidence of scholarship and fitness to practice a profession.

This perversion of the nature and function of measurement is in a sense inevitable in a complex society where the meaning and purpose of symbols tend to get lost in time. The same persons who pay more attention to the university from which a criminal lawyer graduates and to his law school grades than to his success over the years in gaining acquittals for his clients would not dream of placing greater reliance on a spot check of ten apples in a barrel than on the evidence available from an individual inspection of every apple. Nevertheless, the solution to this dilemma is not to abolish measures of aptitude and achievement or to cease evaluating educational institutions, but to increase public sophistication about the nature of measurement and to combat test score and degree worship wherever and whenever they appear.

The tendency to regard test scores as ends in themselves and as more important than the knowledge they represent is much more a *reflection* of undesirable social attitudes about the real value of scholarship than a cause of such attitudes or an inevitable product of measurement and evaluation. Thus overemphasis on the competitive aspects of testing and on the use of test scores for creating a "meritocracy" or a pseudo-scientific rank ordering of persons tells us much more about the kind of society that sanctions such practices than about the potential abuses of measurement.

Similarly, if teachers are guided in their choice of subject-matter content solely by the desire to prepare students for standardized tests and even go to the extent of coaching them on type questions, it is more rational to blame the existing values of parents, educators, and school boards than to blame the tests themselves. Almost every aspect of culture—government, mass media, industry, commerce, recreation, sex, drugs, religion—is just as subject to abuse and perversion as are measurement and evaluation. It makes more sense, in our opinion, to prevent such abuses by increasing the level of public enlightenment about the relevant issues involved in intelligent use than by abolishing or outlawing the practice in question.

Fourth, advocates of child-centered teaching and client-oriented counseling insist that genuine learning, independent thinking, and creativity are possible only in a "nonevaluative" classroom atmosphere. They assert, furthermore, that evaluation induces tension, anxiety, excessive competitiveness, and overemphasis on extrinsic motivation. In our opinion, this position greatly overstates the case. It is true that unintelligent and authoritarian use of evaluative techniques may encourage uncritical acceptance of ideas, suppress originality, and generate undesirable levels of anxiety, competitiveness, and interpersonal tension.

Nevertheless, a reasonable degree of evaluation is still absolutely essential not only for monitoring and motivating learning but also for setting necessary and desirable standards of critical and original thinking. In a completely nonevaluative setting, creative effort is dissipated in amorphous, undirected, and undisciplined output. Freedom from anxiety is also an unrealistic goal since no significant or creative achievement is possible without some degree of anxiety. The very act of aspiring to master a body of knowledge or to create something original raises the possibility of failure and depression of self-esteem, and hence is anxiety-producing by definition.

As already pointed out, moderate emphasis on competitiveness in school facilitates achievement and self-actualization and prepares students realistically for the world of work in Western culture. Similarly, extrinsic and aversive motivation, within reason, are necessary for sustained academic effort. School marks provide students with tangible evidence of success in mastering the curriculum, are an important current source of status and self-esteem during childhood and adolescence, and indicate that progress is being made toward the ultimate achievement of vocational goals and adult status.

Fifth, evaluation has frequently been misused by teachers as a means of rewarding students for conformity and docility and of punishing them for nonconformity and independence of thought. In many schools and universities it is still employed as a weapon for controlling and intimidating students, for frightening and impressing them (as well as colleagues), and for making them feel inadequate, subservient, and deferential. It is these very same teachers who conceive of examinations as a contest in which students are to be outwitted and trapped into error. Needless to say, however, this crude abuse of evaluation hardly constitutes a valid argument for nonevaluative teaching.

Sixth, it can be claimed with some justification that good scores on achievement tests are beyond the reach of low-ability students. In a very real sense then, the imposition of absolute standards of final achievement or the use of grades based on relative standing in the class depresses their self-esteem and discourages them from putting forth their best efforts. Such detrimental effects, however, can be largely mitigated by concomitant evaluation in terms of their ability level or in terms of progress from initial levels of performance. These two different bases of evaluation are by no means mutually exclusive. We need to know how well students are progressing both in terms of their own potentialities *and* in terms of group norms. Furthermore, the negative impact of informing students that they are inferior to their peers in ability and achievement has undoubtedly been exaggerated. Realistic awareness of our relative intellectual status among our peers is a fact of life to which all of us must eventually adjust—and the sooner the better for everyone concerned. There is no profit either in sugar-coating the truth or in self-delusion.

Finally, measurement and evaluation often fail to facilitate learning or teaching because they provide no meaningful feedback. This is particularly true when only final examinations are given and when only composite scores are reported to students without comment, explanation, specification of component strengths and weaknesses, or opportunity for identifying and correcting errors. Such examinations encourage cramming, provide an unrepresentative picture of student achievement, and abet "book slamming" as soon as the grades are in. Any defensible program of evaluation therefore relies on periodic and frequent testing before, during, and at the end of instruction, uses several kinds of measures, reports scores in differential rather than composite terms, and stresses the feedback and diagnostic function of tests.

## Requirements of an Effective Test

Any effective test, irrespective of whether it is objective and standardized, on the one hand, or informal and "teacher-made," on the other, must be valid, reliable, representative, and feasible. It should also discriminate adequately between individuals or groups of individuals tested.

*Validity*

The validity of a test refers to the extent to which it measures what it purports to measure. The question of validity is always relative to the stated objectives of a test. A test that is valid for one purpose (for instance, to "screen out" gross personality deviates) is not necessarily valid for another (for example, to make precise assessments of personality status, to make a specific diagnosis of behavior disorder, to make predictions of individual outcome).

The problem of validity arises in the first place because psychological and educational measures tend to be indirect and inferential rather than based on direct behavioral samples of the trait or ability in question. An achievement test, for example, *merely assumes* that ability to answer correctly a particular set of subject-matter items is really reflective of degree of mastery of a designated discipline or subdiscipline; unfortunately, there is no more direct way of measuring knowledge. If, on the other hand, we endeavor to measure the trait of academic honesty by assessing behavior in controlled situations in which cheating on examinations can be detected unbeknown to and unsuspected by the subjects (Canning, 1956; Hartshorne & May, 1928), the question of test validity is irrelevant. The only relevant question in these circumstances is that of reliability: Will equivalent degrees of academic honesty be exhibited in a later time sample of the same situation, in different but comparable samples of the same situation, in related but different situations?

The more indirectly and inferentially a test score is related to the trait or ability it purports to measure, the more important the issue of validity becomes. Thus, although an achievement test score is admittedly not coextensive with degree of mastery of a discipline, it involves much less indirectness and inference, for example, than does an intelligence test score. In the latter situation, the trait itself is much more of a hypothetical and debatable construct, the tests used to measure it are much less homogeneous and much less self-evidently related to the trait, and there is a much greater presumption of the predictive value of the test score (of the constancy of the trait over age).

Several different types of validity have been delineated. A good test is characterized by at least one and hopefully by more than one of these types. *Content* validity is a form of face validity that is invoked for many psychological and educational tests. An achievement test, for example, may be claimed as valid on the face of things if it contains an adequate and representative sample of items—both in terms of the particular subject-matter knowledge it purports to measure and the kinds of competencies or understandings that purportedly reflect such knowledge.

*Concurrent* validity is present when test scores correlate reasonably well with some contemporaneous criterion of behavior, preferably ratings based on direct observation. Typically the question of concurrent validity arises when some shortcut method of assessment is devised to replace a more exhaustive and time-consuming measure. The difficulty in these instances is one of finding an appropriate criterion that is relevant, reliable, and valid itself.

School grades, for example, are a commonly used criterion for determining the validity of academic aptitude and achievement tests despite the fact that they are usually less reliable and less valid than the tests themselves. They are also influenced by such extraneous factors as the motivation, deportment, docility, and conformity of pupils and the personal and social-class biases of teachers. An added difficulty is the lack of comparability between the grades awarded by different schools and teachers. This is shown by the spectacular increase in the correlation between high-school and college grades when the former set of grades is rendered comparable from one school to another (Bloom, 1964b). Before any evidence of concurrent validity is applicable, it is also necessary to demonstrate that one's population is comparable in all relevant respects to the sample on which the instrument was validated.

When the criterion behavior to which test scores are related is some future measure of performance, we deal with *predictive validity*. If scholastic aptitude scores, for example, correlate reasonably well with later school grades or academic achievement scores, the aptitude test may be said to exhibit predictive validity. The problem of finding a suitable criterion still remains. A test measuring aptitude for medicine may yield scores that correlate satisfactorily with grades earned in medical school, but to what extent are these scores related to success in the practice of medicine? Not only is it very difficult to measure professional success in medicine, but there are also many different criteria of success, varying for the most part with the individual's particular career choice (general practice, specialty practice, research, teaching, writing, public health, hospital administration).

A final type of validity concerns the psychological qualities or attributes a test measures and is known as *construct validity*. The question is whether the test measures a construct or attribute for which there is no suitable criterion. Construct validity is based on logical defensible inferences from experimental or other evidence. In the case of an achievement test, the failure of a totally naive student population to obtain better than chance scores would provide one form of such evidence. Other kinds of relevant evidence would include improvement in mean test scores from one grade level to another in such hierarchically ordered competencies as reading and mathematics and a strong positive relationship between aptitude and achievement at each grade level.

### Validity in Achievement Testing

From the standpoint of meaningful verbal learning, a truly valid test of subject-matter achievement measures whether mastery of a designated body of knowledge is sufficiently stable, clear, and well organized to reflect the structure of ideas in a given discipline or subdiscipline, to make long-term retention possible, and to serve as a foundation for further learning in the same discipline. Modern achievement tests, therefore, emphasize understanding of the more significant ideas within each discipline and of the relationships among them, rather than rote mastery of discrete facts. Nevertheless, despite this laudable emphasis on genuine comprehension of a structure of ideas, these tests fail adequately to measure the functional retention and organizational strength of knowledge because they are *immediate* tests of understanding and application. Every teacher knows that any reasonably bright student can do enough cramming before an announced quarterly or final test to make a passing score, even though the same test questions would elicit only a blank stare several days later.

Thus conventional retention tests, covering previously studied material and administered at the end of a given course of instruction, are not truly reflective of the later availability of this material for new learning and problem-solving purposes. Because a short retention interval cannot adequately test the organizational strength and viability of newly acquired knowledge and because of the contaminating influence of rote memory over short time intervals, such conventional measures of retention are often misleading. They fail to distinguish adequately between the student who merely understands and retains material well enough at the moment of testing to answer rote and meaningful questions correctly and the student whose understanding and retention are sufficiently stable on a long-term basis to serve as a springboard for learning new, sequentially related material. Both individuals may frequently make identical scores on immediate tests of retention.

Problem-solving or application items provide a partial solution to this difficulty since they are less influenced by rote memory and also directly test ability to use and apply retained knowledge. But since successful problem solving also depends on many other traits (venturesomeness, flexibility, perseverance, problem sensitivity) that are unrelated to the functional availability of knowledge, success or failure on such items is as much a reflection of the influence of these latter traits as of the availability of usable knowledge.

Three other solutions to this problem of achievement test validity are available, none of which is mutually preclusive of the others or of the use of problem-solving items. First, the programmed instruction approach, which implies testing, feedback, and consolidation after each unit (topic, chapter) of subject-matter material, provides adequate safeguards for the true stability and clarity of knowledge and ensures against the dangers of cramming and rote learning. If students are given such tests weekly and quarterly, final examinations serve more of a review function and become truly valid measures of subject-matter mastery.

Second, comprehensive tests of achievement that are given six months to several years after the completion of a course also measure the functional retention of genuine knowledge as well as discourage the "book slamming" phenomenon. Such delayed tests, however, obviously become measures of cramming ability unless they are preceded by weekly, quarterly, and final examinations.

Finally, perhaps the most valid way of testing the organizational strength and viability of knowledge is not to test retention itself or to use problem-solving items but to measure retention in the context of sequential learning—in situations where ability to learn new material presupposes the availability of the old. The "transfer retention" test (Ausubel & Fitzgerald, 1962) constitutes a new approach to the problem of measuring functional retention. It attempts to do this by measuring the extent to which retained knowledge of subject matter is sufficiently stable and well organized to be available as a foundation for learning new, sequentially dependent material that could not be efficiently learned in the absence of such availability. At the same time, of course, it also provides a measure of knowledge available for problem solving because if retained knowledge is available for new sequential learning, it is reasonable to assume that it is also available for problem solving.

The transfer retention test may be administered in addition to or independently of the conventional retention test. When used for routine course examinations, the test procedure requires that students study an unfamiliar new learning passage that is sequentially related to and presupposes knowledge of the previously studied material on which they are being examined. Their scores on a test of this *new* material, called "transfer retention scores," measure the functional availability of the previously learned material for new learning.

Only valid tests of achievement can be used to evaluate the worth of a new curriculum or course of study. Thus, for the reasons given above, the ability of students to make satisfactory scores on *immediate* tests of understanding and application does not constitute proof that the material is adequately learnable, lucid, or properly programmed. It is not surprising, therefore, that when the learnability of curriculum material is assessed by conventional tests of achievement, these latter tests often give spurious and misleading impressions of genuine learnability.

Hence it is questionable how well final tests *really* measure the learnability of subject-matter content. Most adequately motivated students can "learn," for examination purposes, large quantities of overly sophisticated and poorly presented materials that they do not really understand. Unfortunately, however, in such circumstances little evidence of retention is present even a few days later. Furthermore, one of the main objectives of any new, elaborately prepared curriculum program is presumably to exceed, rather than merely to approximate, the level of academic achievement attained in conventionally taught courses.

Achievement tests also tend to lose validity if they contain items that presuppose knowledge of materials that are not ordinarily included in the scope of the discipline or subdiscipline they are designed to measure. Many teachers, for example, believe that they can discriminate more adequately between bright and average students if they use such questions. Actually the reverse is true because these items either cannot be answered correctly by any students or else measure knowledge of some *other* field of study. A good examination should emulate a good detective story in that the solution of problems should not depend on information that is unavailable to students or that they are not expected to learn.

The validity of an achievement test depends in part on how well it tests the actual competencies that are demanded of individuals in those real-life performances for which they are being trained or educated. This is the issue of concurrent or predictive validity. For example, a multiple-choice examination on "rules of the road" may exhibit good content validity, but obviously has less concurrent and predictive validity in relation to current or ultimate driving performance than an appropriate road test. It is apparent, therefore, that multiple-choice tests, valuable as they are, cannot possibly serve as complete substitutes for open-ended and practical examinations.

### Reliability

Any measuring instrument, if it is to be used with confidence, must exhibit a satisfactory degree of accuracy or reliability. That is, it must yield self-consistent scores. If a clinical thermometer on three successive determinations, for example, yielded readings of 97°, 103°, and 99.6° for the same patient, it would not be considered very reliable. Reliability, of course, is a necessary but not a sufficient condition for using a test. A highly reliable test may be totally invalid or may not measure anything that is psychologically or educationally significant.

The reliability of a single test score is expressed quantitatively in terms of the instrument's standard error of measurement. If the standard error of measurement, for example, is 2.5, we can say that there are approximately two chances in three (more precisely, 68 in 100) that the true score falls between 72.5 and 77.5 when the obtained score is 75. By definition, an unreliable test cannot possibly be valid. The necessary degree of reliability, however, depends on the use that is made of test scores. If they are used for purposes of individual assessment and guidance, a much higher degree of reliability is obviously necessary than if they are used for gross screening or research purposes.

Three types of coefficients are used to express the reliability of most psychological and educational tests. The coefficient of *equivalence* is the correlation coefficient that results when scores derived from comparable sets of items are correlated. This can be determined from "equivalent" (parallel) forms of the same test or, if only one form exists, by correlating scores derived from one randomly drawn half of the test (for example, odd items) with scores derived from the other half of the test (even items). The latter coefficient of reliability is known as "split-half reliability." It also reflects, of course, internal consistency or generality over items and is therefore often referred to as a "coefficient of internal consistency." It represents a measure of reliability in terms of the equivalence between two halves of a homogeneous test. Thus it is primarily used when a parallel form of the test is not available for determining degree of equivalence between two different sets of items purportedly measuring the same ability or behavior.

Since the split-half coefficient of reliability is obtained by correlating only half of the total number of available items in the instrument against the other half, it furnishes an underestimate of the instrument's actual coefficient of equivalence. Thus to estimate the reliability of the full-length instrument, a correction formula (Spearman-Brown) is frequently applied. Various mathematical formulas (for instance, Kuder-Richardson Formulas 20 and 21) have also been devised for arriving at a more generalized estimate of generality over, or intercorrelation among, homogeneous test items.

The coefficient of *stability*, on the other hand, measures consistency over time or short-term constancy of a trait when the same set of items is used. It is determined from successive administrations of the same test. Over short intervals of time the ability or trait being measured can be regarded as not undergoing significant change. Over longer intervals, however, a loss of stability is more reflective of developmental changes in the nature of a trait or of inconstancy in rate of growth than of test unreliability.

The coefficient of *generality* reflects the self-consistency of a test when it is composed of heterogeneous but related measures of the same trait. Tests of intelligence and of creativity, for example, typically consist of a battery of subtests, each of which measures a different facet of the trait in question. When the scores on these subtests are intercorrelated, the average intercorrelation may be taken as the coefficient of generality. Unless this coefficient is reasonably high, it is obviously unwarranted to regard the various subtests as measuring anything in common.

The length of a test is the most important single factor influencing its reliability. Obviously, the shorter a test is the more likely it is that test scores will be influenced by chance sampling or situational factors. Failure to allow sufficient time for most students to complete a test has the same effect on reliability as reducing the number of items. The reliability of a test is also decreased by inaccurate or subjective scoring and by the presence of items that lack discriminating power (see below). Moreover, inadequate or fluctuating motivation may impair test reliability. The inference that a test score actually measures true capacity rather than mere performance on a single occasion presupposes that the subject is trying his or her best. As pointed out previously, aptitude and achievement test scores are less reliable (and hence less valid) in the case of culturally disadvantaged pupils because of their unresponsiveness to speed pressure and their generally low level of test motivation.

The effect of severe anxiety on aptitude and achievement test performance is somewhat indeterminable. In general it tends to depress performance, although much depends on the novelty of test items, familiarity with testing, and the adequacy of coping mechanisms. Since high levels of anxiety can thoroughly disrupt the higher mental processes and even block any kind of response whatsoever, it is important not only to allay test anxiety as much as possible but also to regard with caution the reliability and validity of test scores that are unduly influenced by anxiety.[2] Both of these latter requirements can be taken into account by giving frequent tests instead of basing grades completely on final examinations. When students are tested frequently, they tend to be less anxious. They develop greater familiarity with the test situation, emotional desensitization to it, and the realization that their entire fate does not depend on a single score. At the same time, the availability of many scores discounts the significance of any single score that is invalidated by extreme anxiety.

### Representativeness

Almost all psychological and educational measures are based on the principle of sampling. Since it is virtually impossible, for example, to test a student for mastery of *all* of the facts, concepts, and principles in a given course of study, we typically select a sample of such content as a basis for assessing the universe from which the sample is drawn. For this procedure to be logically defensible, at least two important conditions must

---

[2] Hastings measured test anxiety by a questionnaire method as early as 1944. Since then, standardized measures of test anxiety have been developed (Sarason, Davidson, Lighthall, Waite, & Ruebush, 1960). Although "high tensions do not necessarily accompany low examination scores, nor contrariwise . . . , pupils showing higher tensions as measured by the questionnaire, at the time of an examination produce results which tend to deviate further from prediction than do the examination results of those who give evidence of lower tensions" (Hastings, 1944, p. 161). McKeachie, Pollie, and Speisman (1955) showed that "giving students an opportunity to write comments [about multiple-choice questions] aids not only in reducing the threat but also in channeling the release of anxiety" (p. 94).

be met: (1) the sample must be adequately representative of the universe, and (2) within the constraints imposed by the requirements of representativeness and significance, the sample must be randomly drawn. The reasons for these conditions are rather self-evident. If, for example, all of the examination items test knowledge of only one chapter of an assigned textbook, or if the items on each chapter cover only a restricted segment of its content, the resulting achievement test score can hardly be claimed to measure knowledge of the textbook in question. Not only would such an achievement test lack content validity, but *it* also would inevitably (and on a purely chance basis) overestimate the knowledge of some students and underestimate the knowledge of others. Nevertheless many achievement tests, particularly those that are teacher-made, do not meet these two conditions, representativeness and randomness.

Two other unfortunate practices also commonly result from failure to appreciate the nature of a test as a representative sample. Teachers who give "hints" about examination questions or who repeat the same questions year after year obviously render untenable the inference that scores on such an examination are actually representative of the students' knowledge. An even more serious error is committed by individuals who regard test scores based on a representative sample of items that are inferentially related to a given trait or ability as more valid measures of the trait or ability in question than is direct behavioral evidence over a period of years. This situation arises when test scores, degrees, or licenses are regarded as status symbols rather than as fallible sampling and inferential measures of competence. The IQ and the M.D. are two such measures that have achieved almost magical or sacred status in our culture.

*Total* evaluation is feasible for certain aspects of competence or achievement and can be used concurrently with a sampling approach. A teacher, for example, may wish to evaluate *all* of his students' homework assignments, laboratory reports, histology drawings, workshop products, or clinical performances. All other factors being equal, such measurement not only exhibits a high degree of validity and reliability but also tends to motivate students consistently to put forth their best efforts and to generate a high degree of responsibility and accountability for performance.

### Discriminating Power

An obvious attribute of an effective test is ability to distinguish maximally between individuals who vary with respect to the trait or competence being measured. In large part, of course, this attribute depends on the discriminating power of the component items and accounts for, as well as reflects, the reliability and validity of the instrument. To some extent, however, it depends on the *distribution* of the total scores and on whether the test provides adequate *ceiling* for superior persons in the group.

A *normal* distribution of scores, for example, provides maximum discrimination at both ends of the scale (where there are few scores spread out thinly) and less discrimination at the middle part of the scale (where many scores are bunched together); whereas a *rectangular* distribution of scores (an equal number of scores at all points on the scale) provides equal discrimination over the entire range. A *skewed* distribution (where a disproportionate number of scores pile up at one end of the scale), on the other hand, is most discriminating at the end where there are few scores and least discriminating at the opposite end.

An effective test must also have sufficient ceiling to permit the superior individuals in a group to stand out as such. Obviously, if an achievement test is easy enough for the average person in the group to achieve a score of 90 percent, it is accordingly impossible to distinguish between more and less knowledgeable students. Maximum discriminability generally prevails when the average score is approximately 50 percent. Adequate ceiling, however, should be provided by including a wide range of items carefully graded in difficulty, rather than depending on a criterion of speed, since the ability to answer questions quickly also reflects factors basically unrelated to superior competence or aptitude. Difficulty level can be manipulated by varying such factors as abstractness, complexity, familiarity, and degree of understanding required (mere comprehension versus application, interpretation, inference, analysis, or synthesis).

*Feasibility*

In addition to such theoretical considerations as validity, reliability, representativeness, and discriminating power, various practical matters must be taken into account before one can decide whether a proposed test is feasible. First, how significant is the information it yields, that is, how useful is it in interpreting the pupils' abilities, knowledge, and personality traits and in making educational and vocational decisions? Trivial test data are worthless irrespective of how reliable, valid, or discriminating they may be. A feasible achievement test, for example, should provide differential feedback to both students and teachers about relative strengths and weaknesses in learning and teaching, as well as suggest reasons for same. Otherwise it is useless for diagnostic and remedial purposes. Second, a feasible test should be suitable in form and content for the age range of students for which it is intended. A third practical consideration is the cost of a test and the amount of time required to administer, score, and interpret it. Fourth, how objective is the scoring and how straightforward is the interpretation of the results? Is special training required to score and interpret the test? Does the test manual provide directions for administration and scoring, a table of norms, and guidance for interpreting scores?

## The Standardized Objective Test

Objective tests, although difficult and time-consuming to construct, owe their great popularity in education to several factors. First and foremost, perhaps, is the fact that subjectivity and variability in scoring are eliminated. Precise and invariable criteria for scoring—typically a scoring key designating the correct answers—are available in advance. Second, the items are carefully and systematically selected so as to constitute a representative sample of the content to be covered and of the competencies to be evaluated. This implies precise advance specification of educational objectives —in terms both of the particular facts, concepts, principles, and applications the student is expected to master and of the ways in which such mastery is supposed to be exhibited.

Since the totality of desirable knowledge in a given area obviously cannot be tested, great care must be taken to secure a representative sample of significant (nontrivial) items that is both adequately comprehensive and places the desired relative weight on component topics. Herein lies the other great advantage of objective tests: the brevity of each item and the speed with which it can be answered permits a more comprehensive and systematic sampling of knowledge than is possible by any other means. Although the ability to recognize a correct alternative does not necessarily imply ability to recall it spontaneously, the correlation between the two abilities tends to be reasonably good (Plumlee, 1947; Tyler, 1934a).

An additional advantage in this connection is the possibility of refining the items, after initial use, for clarity and discriminability and of thus increasing test reliability and validity. Self-evidently, items that are answered correctly by all or most students are too easy to have any discriminating power; for opposite reasons the same conclusion applies to items that are answered incorrectly by all or most students. Further, a good item is obviously one that is answered correctly more freuqently by the more knowledgeable students (those making high total scores) than by the less knowledgeable students, and answered incorrectly more often by the less knowledgeable than by the more knowledgeable students.[3] Items that fail to meet these criteria are either deleted, rewritten less ambiguously, or replaced by other items.

Analysis of the relative frequency with which wrong alternatives are chosen may also reveal either ambiguities in wording or the existence of a prevalent preconception or misconception. If the latter is the case, the item serves a useful diagnostic function and should not be altered. In fact, a multiple-choice item should be deliberately written so as to contain at

[3] In practice this item-analysis function is performed by comparing the number of right and wrong responses on each item that are obtained by the upper and lower fifths or quarters of the distribution of total test scores.

least one wrong alternative that reflects a common bit of misinformation or a misconception. The adequacy of learning and teaching can then be evaluated just as validly by the good students' greater avoidance of such "sucker" alternatives as by their greater tendency to choose the correct alternative. On the other hand, if good students choose a particular wrong alternative more frequently than poor students, there are grounds for believing that the item in question is misleading or ambiguous.

Objective tests are also typically standardized with respect to the conditions of administration—the instructions, the time limit, the allowable help, the permissibility of making calculations or of marking the alternatives, and so forth, thereby ensuring comparability of scores. Finally, most standardized tests that are published provide the user with a table of norms based on a large and representative sample. This makes possible the conversion of raw scores into percentile scores or grade equivalents.

### Criticisms

Objective tests have been subjected to vigorous criticism (Black, 1963; Gross, 1962; Hoffmann, 1962), some of which is warranted but much of which is based on misunderstanding of the nature, functions, and inherent limitations of these tests. First, despite considerable improvement in this respect over the past twenty years, many objective tests still measure rote recognition of relatively trivial and disconnected items of knowledge rather than genuine comprehension of broad concepts, principles, and relationships, and ability to interpret facts and apply knowledge. Paradoxically this shortcoming of objective tests has been magnified by the programmed instruction movement, with its emphasis on small frame and step size.

Second, because of unskillful construction of test items, the correct answer is sometimes identifiable by means of unintentional hints, for example, the self-evident implausibility of the wrong alternatives, including the use of such words as "always." These deficiencies are easily correctable by using greater care in item construction, by selecting more significant test items, by stressing items that require understanding, thought, and insight, by including application and problem-solving items, and by placing greater reliance on delayed retention and transfer retention scores. The multiple-choice format minimizes the role of guessing. It should be noted, at this point, that unskillfully constructed essay and problem-solving tests may also place a premium on the regurgitation of rotely memorized knowledge and on rote application of "type problem" solutions.

Third, the correct answer in multiple-choice tests may sometimes be either arbitrary or depend on abstruse hairsplitting. In some instances it may also favor the less knowledgeable or more shallow thinker and penalize the more sophisticated student who takes into account more subtle and penetrating considerations.

Fourth, the great emphasis placed on time pressure tends to favor the glib, confident, impulsive, and test-wise student and to handicap the student who either is inclined to be cautious, thoughtful, and self-critical or is unsophisticated about testing.

Ideally, a valid test of either scholastic aptitude or academic achievement places greater weight on power than on speed (Yates, 1961). Discriminating ability is attained by providing a wide and carefully graded range of difficulty, with ample time for most students to complete the test, rather than by including twice as many items as the average student has time to answer. In our opinion, the current emphasis on speed in most standardized tests of achievement detracts from their validity by placing a premium on factors that are intrinsically unrelated to genuine mastery of subject matter.

Finally, the limitations of standardized testing must always be borne in mind. For example, mutliple-choice tests, by definition, cannot measure students' ability spontaneously to generate relevant hypotheses, to collect valid laboratory or clinical data, to marshal evidence in support of a proposition, to design an original experiment, to structure a cogent argument, or to do creative work. Other kinds of measuring devices, however, are available to test the attainment of these latter objectives.

## Interpretation of Achievement Test Scores

In general there are three different ways of interpreting achievement test scores. The first method judges a student's performance against the standard of *his or her own* ability level as determined by his or her score on an aptitude test, a pretest, a prior achievement test, or an initial achievement test in the course. This is important for both student and teacher since it indicates the extent to which normally expected progress is being made in the course. The second method assesses the adequacy of performance in relation to that of one's peers; it is necessary both for grouping, pacing, and the individualization of instruction, as well as for making important decisions about one's educational and vocational future. This is a norm-referenced measure that allows for the comparison of one individual with another (Glaser, 1963). Norm-referenced measures can compare individuals with their actual peers in the classroom situation or with a broader peer group such as a national sample. As pointed out above, both kinds of assessment are essential and neither one precludes the other. Each of these approaches is concerned with a *relative* standard of performance, but in one case the individual serves as his or her own standard and in the other an individual's performance is related to group norms. Achievement test scores furnish both kinds of measures. Raw scores or percentage scores serve as the individual's own standard of comparison, whereas percentile scores (scores indicative of the percentage of a designated population of scores exceeded by the percentile score in question) are norm-referenced measures.

In some instances, however, an *absolute* standard of performance is indicated, which is quite independent of the performance of others or of the individual's relative standing in the group. This is the case, for example, where mastery of a given topic, subject, or skill is a prerequisite for more advanced learnings, and where a certain minimal level of competence is necessary before an individual can be entrusted with certain vocational roles such as lifesaver on a beach, physician, pharmacist, secretary, railway engineer, or airplane pilot. Glaser (1963) designates such scores based upon an absolute standard of quality as *criterion-referenced* measures, in contrast to *norm-referenced* measures based upon a relative standard.

A criterion-referenced measure reveals what a student can do rather than how he or she stands in comparison to a peer group (Popham & Husek, 1969). Glaser and Nitko (1971) indicate further that a criterion-referenced measure is specifically designed to give information that can be directly interpreted in terms of an absolute criterion of performance. When criterion tests are used, students are never judged in relation to other students, and competency in a particular area is determined precisely. It should also be noted that in regard to accountability programs directed toward evaluating teaching performance, standardized norm-referenced achievement tests often lack content validity whereas criterion-referenced tests, along with other measures, are more appropriate for estimating teacher effectiveness.

In using the norms of standardized tests, it is important to make sure that they are based on a sample that is both large enough to ensure stability and adequately representative of the universe to which they purportedly pertain. The particular norms used must also be relevant in the sense that they are based on groups of individuals who are comparable to the individuals we are testing.

For example, in interpreting the achievement test scores of a particular twelfth-grade group in an American high school, we would want to use the norms of American twelfth-graders generally, plus such other differential norms that apply to our group as sex, region, state, urban or rural area, public or private high school.

If such a comprehensive analysis is not made, the interpretation can be misleading. It is possible that students from minority groups can show excellent achievement relative to their immediate peer group but show low achievement on national standardized tests. For guidance purposes (grouping, choice of courses, college application) it would also be helpful to use the local school norms as well as the cutoff scores employed by various colleges in selecting candidates for admission.

## Other Methods of Evaluation and Measurement

Because of limitations on the kinds of objectives that standardized short-answer tests can measure, other methods of evaluation and measurement are used concomitantly in most educational settings. Thoughtful teachers do not place excessive reliance on standardized objective tests.

### Essay or Discussion Questions

Essay examinations, despite their many disadvantages, have a significant place in the evaluation program of a school. They are particularly useful (1) where spontaneous recall of information and spontaneous generation of hypotheses are important aspects of the competencies being measured (for instance, formulation of diagnostic hypotheses, differential diagnosis), and (2) in less well-established areas of knowledge where there is no single "right answer." In addition, they test students' ability to organize ideas and marshal evidence, to construct cogent arguments, to evaluate ideas critically, and to express themselves clearly and convincingly. Essay-type questions also provide greater scope for original and independent thinking and give some insight into the cognitive styles, problem sensitivities, and problem-solving strategies of students. On the whole, they are better suited than short-answer questions for measuring students' grasp of the structure of a discipline.

On the other hand, they are much less satisfactory than short-answer tests for measuring knowledge of more established concepts, principles, and information in a given subject-matter field, particularly where there is no premium on ability to recall and transform ideas spontaneously. Since only a few questions can be asked on any examination, sampling of content is neither comprehensive nor representative, and scoring tends to be laborious and subjective; hence both reliability and validity are often unsatisfactory.

Further, essay examinations encourage bluffing, circumlocution, padding, and discursiveness on the part of students. They also tend disproportionately to reward those students who write neatly, excel in the mechanics of English composition (spelling, punctuation, diction, and style), and echo the views and biases of their teachers. Finally, the very ease of constructing essay examinations encourage a rather cavalier and slipshod attitude toward evaluation on the part of those who use them.

Many of the aforementioned disadvantages can be mitigated, however, by following a few simple rules. By indicating explicitly the scope and dimensions of the expected answer, much of the ambiguity and vagueness of the global discussion question can be eliminated. As a matter of fact, short essay-type questions that are relatively limited and specific in scope may exhibit considerable reliability and validity, but by the same token they may also fail to test some of the distinctive competencies that the essay examination is designed to measure. To minimize the strong chance factor in the particular questions that are selected in an essay examination, students may be given some degree of choice in questions.

It is also possible to reduce the subjectivity of scoring by using several readers and by establishing such separate explicit criteria for grading as content, organization, logic, cogency, clarity, and fluency of expression. Halo effect can be minimized by coding students' papers and by scoring, in turn, each question for all students instead of completely grading each student's paper before turning to the next paper.

Oral examinations typically enjoy the same advantages and disadvantages of the essay examination. In addition, they enable the examiner to probe more deeply when unsure of the student's knowledge or meaning and to cut short irrelevant and discursive answers. In this sense they discourage bluffing. On the other hand, they appear to evoke much more disruptive anxiety than do written examinations and to favor the verbal and socially poised individual.

### Work Samples

In most areas of education—particularly in vocational, professional, artistic, and physical training—it is possible to assess the extent to which the objectives of education are actually being attained by directly appraising a performance or work product that is self-evidently reflective of the skill being taught. Such work samples include field experiences, laboratory skills, clinical performance, drawings, themes, research reports, gymnastic or musical performance, the use of tools, art or shop products, typing and stenographic performance, and so forth. They constitute much more direct and valid criteria of the competences involved than do short-answer or discussion examinations, which can only inferentially measure the same competences. It is obviously much more important to know, for example, how well a student physician can interview, examine, diagnose, and prescribe for an actual patient than how well he or she can answer questions about the theory and practice of medicine. Such examinations also make possible direct assessments of such traits as flexibility, resourcefulness, perseverance, and creativity. Hence their value largely depends on the extent to which they are able realistically to simulate "real-life" conditions of performance.

The most serious disadvantages of these examinations are that they are time-consuming, expensive, and difficult to construct in many areas. It is also difficult to assure breadth and equivalence of sampling. If hospital cases, for example, are used as test material for students in clinical medicine, how adequately can a single case measure a student's ability, and how does one equate cases for difficulty? This argues for the desirability of appraising *all* of a student's work products in a given course of study—all of his or her laboratory drawings or clinical performances, or of using standardized (for instance, televised) case presentations that are uniform for all students.

Scoring presents still another difficulty and is no more reliable and valid than the observational and rating techniques on which it is based. These techniques can be materially improved if the dimensions on which or criteria by which the performance is to be judged are specified in advance, if discriminably different points on a rating scale can be both described and quantified, if the ratings of several trained judges are averaged, and if ratings are made concurrently rather than retrospectively. Proper training of the judges includes discussion of the nature of the trait or competence to be rated, making a trial run of ratings, comparing ratings, and deciding how ratings are to be distributed over the scale. Final ratings, of course, are made independently. "Halo effect" can be minimized by having the rater judge each item on the scale for the entire group before proceeding to the next item.

# GLOSSARY

This glossary contains only new psychological terms proposed by the authors in this textbook and its predecessor or generally accepted psychological terms that have been given special meanings.

*Abstract operational stage of cognitive development*: that stage in which the individual is capable, *without the aid of concrete-empirical props*, of acquiring secondary abstractions and of understanding, using, and meaningfully manipulating both secondary abstractions and the relations between them.

*Achievement motivation*: the motivation to achieve (typically in academic and vocational settings). In such settings it is inclusive of cognitive, affiliative, and ego-enhancement drive in varying proportions.

*Affiliative drive*: concern with achievement as a means of retaining the approval of the superordinate person or group from whom the individual obtains his or her derived status.

*Anchoring idea(s)*: an established relevant idea (proposition or concept) in cognitive structure to which new ideas are related and in relation to which their meanings are assimilated in the course of meaningful learnings. As a result of this interaction they themselves are modified and differentiated.

*Anxiety*: an actual response or a tendency to respond with fear to any anticipated situation that is perceived as a potential threat to self-esteem. In *normal* anxiety the threat is *objectively* threatening and the fear response is proportionate to the objective degree of threat involved. In *neurotic* anxiety the principal source of the threat inheres in catastrophically impaired self-esteem itself, and the response appears to be objectively disproportionate to the precipitating event. Actually it is commensurate with the subjective degree of threat experienced by the individual and arising from the damaged self-esteem.

*Applied science*: a science, such as educational psychology, that is oriented toward practical ends that have social value. It has its own independent body of theory and methodology that is just as basic as in the "pure" sciences, but is formulated in terms that are both less general and more relevant to the applied problems in its field.

*Assimilation*: the relation of a potentially meaningful idea to a relevant existing idea(s) in cognitive structure, the storing of the newly acquired meaning in linkage with the anchoring idea(s) to which it is related in the course of learning, and its subsequent reduction or loss of dissociability.

*Assimilation theory*: the theory of learning advanced in this book that stresses meaningful learning processes involving subsumption and superordinate and "combinatorial" learning, progressive differentiation, integrative reconciliation of concepts and propositions, consolidation by "mastery learning" and sequential organization of hierarchically related ideas from "the top down" in the presentation of subject matter.

*Background propositions*: relevant ideas in cognitive structure that bear on a problem-solving task as set by a problem-setting proposition.

*Cognition*: a generic term referring to such higher mental *processes* as representational learning, concept acquisition, propositional learning (comprehension of sentences), meaningful problem solving, thinking, meaningful retention, judgment, and so on; contrasted to *perception*, (which involves the generation of an immediate content of awareness from stimulus input) and to such simpler forms of learning as conditioning, rote learning, sensorimotor and discrimination learning, and so on.

*Cognitive drive*: the desire to acquire knowledge as an end in itself, that is, task-oriented motivation in learning. (See *achievement motivation*.)

*Cognitive structure*: the total content and organization of a given individual's ideas; or, in the context of subject-matter learning, the content and organization of his or her ideas in a particular area of knowledge.

*Cognitive style*: self-consistent and enduring individual differences in cognitive organization and functioning.

*Combinatorial learning*: learning the meaning of a new concept or proposition that cannot be related to any *particular* relevant idea(s) in cognitive structure but can be related to a broad background of *generally* relevant content in cognitive structure.

*Concepts*: objects, events, situations, or properties that possess common criterial attributes (despite diversity along other dimensions or attributes) and are designated by some sign or symbol, typically a word with generic meaning.

*Concept acquisition or learning*: learning the meaning of a concept, that is, learning the meaning of its criterial attributes; includes *concept formation* and *concept assimilation*.

*Concept assimilation*: the acquisition of new concept meanings through a process of reception learning; the learner is presented with the concept's criterial attributes by definition or context.

*Concept formation*: the acquisition of new concept meanings by a semi-inductive process of discovering their criterial attributes from multiple particular exemplars of the concept; characteristic of preschool children.

*Concrete operational stage of cognitive development*: that stage in which the child is capable, *with the aid of concrete-empirical props*, of acquiring *secondary* abstractions and of understanding, using, and meaningfully manipulating both secondary abstractions and the relations between them. See *secondary concept*.

*Connotative meaning*: the idiosyncratic attitudinal or affective reactions elicited by a concept name.

*Correlative subsumption*: a type of subsumptive or subordinate learning in which the new ideas in the learning task are extensions, elaborations, modifications, or qualifications of an existing relevant idea in cognitive structure.

*Creative abilities, general*: a general constellation of *supportive* intellectual traits, personality variables, and problem-solving traits (for example, flexibility, problem sensitivity, divergent thinking ability, openmindedness, venturesomeness, independence of judgment) that help implement the expression of creative potentialities but are not expressive of creativity itself (which occurs in a particular substantive area or areas).

*Creative person*: an individual possessing a rare and singular degree of originality or creativity in some substantive field of human endeavor that sets him or her off *qualitatively* from most other persons in this regard. It involves the discovery of ideas that are uniquely original in cultural history.

*Creativity*: problem-solving achievement that involves the application of knowledge to uniquely novel or remotely related problems in terms of the individual's *own* life history or the generation of corresponding problem-solving strategies; it exists on a continuum that is qualitatively continuous except at that critical point defining a "creative person."

*Cultural disadvantage*: intellectually impoverished surroudings inducing retarded intellectual development and school achievement; typically found in those lower-class settings (urban or rural) providing a paucity of patterned cognitive stimulation and characterized by attitudes of dependency, helplessness, cultural marginality, depressed levels of aspiration, and alienation from the culture at large.

*Denotative meaning*: the distinctive criterial attributes evoked by a concept name as distinguished from the correlated attitudinal or affective reactions it elicits (*connotative meaning*).

*Derivative subsumption*: a type of subsumptive or subordinate learning in which the new ideas in the learning task are supportive or illustrative of an existing relevant idea in cognitive structure.

*Derived status*: a vicarious form of status acquired through dependent identification with a superordinate figure or group.

*Discovery learning*: that kind of learning in which the principal content of what is to be learned is not given (or presented), but must be discovered by the learner before he can assimilate it into his cognitive structure. (See also *reception learning*.)

*Dissociability strength*: the extent to which an acquired meaning can be separated or retrieved from the anchoring idea(s) in relation to which it is learned and stored, that is, the extent to which it is retrievable or available as an identifiable ideational entity.

*Drive determinant*: a biological or psychological need or motive that can selectively increase an organism's responsiveness to particular forms of stimulation by inducing a drive state (that is, a multiply-determined and selectively generalized lowering of response and perceptual thresholds).

*Drive reduction*: the *immediate* reduction in the level of a drive *state* (or the elevation of selectively generalized response thresholds) following reward, as opposed to the *long-term* increase in the strength of the drive *determinant*; for example, the acquisition of a particular successful meaning or problem solution reduces the drive state induced by cognitive drive for that *particular* learning task but increases cognitive drive *generally*.

*Drive state*: a state of selectively increased motor and perceptual responsiveness to stimulation when a drive determinant (that is, a biologically or psychologically determined need or motive) is operative; it, in turn, is reflective of a selectively generalized lowering of the thresholds of elicitation of those perceptions and responses that can differentially satisfy (reduce) the need or motive in question.

*Earned status*: status that an individual earns by virtue of his or her relative degree of competence or performance ability.

*Ego-enhancement drive*: concern with achievement as a source of earned status.

*Forgetting*: a process of memorial reduction or obliterative assimilation that occurs in the course of storage (retention); as a result of this process, the dissociability strength of an acquired meaning falls below the threshold of availability and the meaning is accordingly no longer retrievable.

*Idea*: a concept or proposition relatable to cognitive structure.

*Immunizing effect of initial practice trial*: the facilitating effect that the experience of learning and forgetting on the first trial confers on the second and later trials by making the learner aware of (and thus able to circumvent) negative factors in the learning process that promote forgetting.

*Insight*: as a *process* of problem solving implies an approach that is oriented toward hypothesis generation and testing for the purpose of understanding the significant means-end relationships in a particular problem; as a *product* of problem solving it implies a subjective feeling of pleased discovery and immediate reproducibility and transposability.

*Integrative reconciliation*: part of the process of meaningful learning that results in explicit delineation of similarities and differences between related ideas.

*Intelligence*: a measurement construct designating general level of cognitive ability or scholastic aptitude.

*Learning disability*: a particular disability in one or more of the intellectual skills in an individual falling within the normal range of intelligence. It is often accompanied by distractability, hyperactivity, emotional liability, and low attention span. In the latter sense it is frequently referred to by medically-trained mental health professionals as "minimal brain dysfunction" (even if typically unaccompanied by electroencephalographic signs of minimal diffuse brain damage or by neurological signs).

*Learning shock*: the initial cognitive resistance and confusion generated by exposure to new learning material that raises the threshold of availability *immediately* after learning; the gradual dissipation of learning shock results in an *apparent* increase in retention at a later testing despite a loss in dissociability strength (i.e., the *reminiscence phenomenon*).

*Logically meaningful material*: a learning task that is sufficiently "sensible," plausible, or nonrandom to be nonarbitrarily and substantively relatable to correspondingly relevant ideas that lie within the realm of human learning capability. It does not imply empirical or logical validity in the philosophical sense of "logical."

*Maturation*: increments in capacity that occur in the demonstrable absence of specific learning experience, that is, increments that are attributable to genic influences affecting the neuroanatomical and neurophysiological substrate of behavior, perception, learning, memory, and so on, and/or incidental experience.

*Meaning*: a differentiated and sharply articulated content of awareness that develops as a product of meaningful symbolic learning or that may be evoked by a symbol or group of symbols after the latter have been nonarbitrarily and substantively related to cognitive structure.

*Meaningful learning*: the acquisition of new meanings; it presupposes a meaningful learning set and a potentially meaningful learning task (that is, a task that can be related in nonarbitrary, substantive fashion to what the learner already knows). Part of the rote→meaningful learning continuum as distinct from the reception→discovery continuum.

*Meaningful learning set*: a "disposition" on the part of a learner to relate a learning task nonarbitrarily and substantively to relevant aspects of his or her cognitive structure.

*Meaningfulness*: the relative *degree* of meaning associated with a given symbol or group of symbols as opposed to their substantive cognitive content, as measured by degree of familiarity, frequency of contextual encounter or degree of lexical substantiveness (for example, a noun or verb in contrast to a preposition).

*Nonarbitrariness*: that property of a learning task (for example, plausibility, nonrandomness) that makes it relatable to human cognitive structure in the abstract sense of the term, on some "sensible" basis.

*Organizer*: introductory material presented in advance of and at a higher level of generality, inclusiveness, and abstraction than the learning task itself, and explicitly related both to existing relevant ideas in cognitive structure and to the learning task itself; designed to promote subsumptive learning by providing ideational scaffolding or anchorage for the learning task and/or by increasing the discriminability between the new ideas to be learned and related ideas in cognitive structure, i.e., bridging the gap between what the learner *already* knows and what he *needs* to know to learn the learning material more expeditiously.

*Pacing*: the rate of introducing new subject matter as determined by the length of the time interval intervening between component task units.

*Potentially meaningful material*: a learning task that can be meaningfully learned both because it is *logically* meaningful and because relevant ideas are present in the *particular* learner's cognitive structure.

*Practice*: repeated exposure to or performance of the learning task.

*Preoperational stage of cognitive development*: that stage in which the child is capable of acquiring *primary* concepts and of understanding, using, and meaningfully manipulating both primary concepts and the relations between them.

*Primary concepts*: those concepts whose meanings an individual originally learns in relation to concrete-empirical experience—that is, those concepts whose criterial attributes, whether discovered or presented, yield *generic* meanings during learning when the attributes are *first* explicitly related to the multiple particular exemplars from which they are derived *before* the attributes alone are related to one's cognitive structure.

*Problem-setting propositions*: instructions that define the nature, conditions, and objectives of a problem-solving task. Except in research settings, they are usually acquired through reception learning.

*Problem solving*: a form of directed activity or thought in which both the cognitive representation of prior experience and the components of a current problem situation are reorganized, transformed, or recombined in order to achieve a designated objective; involves the generation of problem-solving strategies that transcend the mere application of principles to self-evident exemplars.

*Progressive differentiation*: part of the process of meaningful learning, retention, and organization that results in further hierarchical elaboration of concepts or propositions in cognitive structure from "the top downwards."

*Propositional learning*: learning the meaning of a new composite idea expressed in sentence form; acquisition of a *specific* meaning derived from two or more concepts, but constituting more than the sum of the latter because of the "semantic" properties of word order and inflection (syntax).

*Psychological or phenomenological meaning*: in contrast to *logical* meaning, the *idiosyncratic* differentiated cognitive content evoked by a given symbol or group of symbols in a *particular* learner; identical with meaning as defined above, that is, a product of meaningful learning.

*Readiness*: the existence of a *developmental* level of cognitive functioning sufficient to make a given learning task possible with reasonable economy of time and effort (as differentiated from the adequacy of specifically relevant ideas in a particular learner's cognitive structure [*subject-matter* readiness]).

*Reception learning*: that kind of learning in which the entire content of what is to be learned is presented to the learner in more or less final form. Related to the reception→discovery continuum as distinct from the rote→meaningful learning continuum.

*Reinforcement*: an increase in the availability of an idea or in the probability of response occurrence as a *direct* consequence of a lowering of the threshold of availability or elicitation; postulated by the authors to occur after reward and drive reduction only in the case of *rote* verbal learning and stimulus-response learning (for example, conditioning, instrumental learning).

*Representational or vocabulary learning*: learning the meaning of single symbols or learning what they represent; includes "naming" of particular objects, events, or ideas recognized by the learner.

*Review*: a type of practice characterized by long intervals between exposures to or performances of the learning task.

*Rote learning*: the acquisition of arbitrary, verbatim associations in learning situations where either the learning material itself cannot be nonarbitrarily and substantively related to cognitive structure (that is, does not possess "logical meaning") or where the learner exhibits a nonmeaningful learning set. (See also *meaningful learning*.)

*Satellization*: a form of dependent identification in which the subordinate party obtains vicarious or derived status from the superordinate party provided that the former is accepted and intrinsically valued by the latter.

*Secondary concepts*: those concepts whose meanings a given individual does *not* learn in relation to genuine concrete-empirical experience, that is, those concepts whose criterial attributes yield generic meaning when the attributes of the concept are related to cognitive structure *without* being first explicitly related to the *particular* exemplars from which they are derived. In the concrete stage of cognitive development, as opposed to the abstract stage, concrete-empirical props (or exemplars of the attributes) must be currently or recently available.

*Sensitizing effect of initial practice trial*: the ability of the learner on a second or later learning trial to *perceive* (that is, immediately apprehend without the benefit of a meaningful learning process) the meaning of a symbolic expression by virtue of acquiring its meaning on the first learning trial. It occurs when the meaning of an already acquired concept or proposition is encountered on a second or subsequent exposure to the substantively same material.

*Sequential dependence*: a relationship between earlier and later-appearing units of subject matter in which knowledge of the former is essential for learning the latter.

*Substantiveness or nonverbatimness*: that property of a learning task that permits the substitution of synonymous elements without change of meaning or significant alteration in the content of the task itself.

*Substrate propositions*: propositions undergoing transformation in the course or process of discovery learning or problem solving; includes *problem-setting* and *background* propositions.

*Subsumptive or subordinate learning*: learning the meaning of a new concept or proposition that can be subsumed under a relevant, *more* inclusive particular idea(s) in cognitive structure; includes *derivative* and *correlative* subsumption.

*Superordinate learning*: learning the meaning of a new concept or proposition that can subsume relevant and *less* inclusive *particular* ideas already present in cognitive structure.

*Task orientation*: intrinsic motivation for involvement in a learning task—that is, cognitive drive.

*Threshold of availability*: that critical level of the dissociability strength of a learned idea above which it is retrievable and below which it is not. It can vary as a function of attention, anxiety, competing ideas, "repression," hypnosis, criterion of retention, and so forth, without any change in dissociability strength itself.

*Transactional terms*: words (for example, conditional conjunctions, qualifying adjectives) that make possible the more efficient juxtaposition and combination of different relatable abstractions into potentially meaningful propositions and their subsequent relationship to established ideas in cognitive structure. A principal determinant of the transition from concrete to abstract functioning, along with (1) a critical mass of abstractions in cognitive structure, and (2) sufficient experience in comprehending or manipulating meaningfully expressed ideas with the benefit of concrete-empirical props so that these props are later unecessary for such processes.

*Transfer retention test*: a test that measures whether a given segment of knowledge is sufficiently stable, clear, and well-organized to serve as a basis for new sequentially related learning and problem solving by testing ability to comprehend new ideas that are sequentially dependent on previously learned material.

# REFERENCES

Aall, A. Ein neues Gedächtnisgesetz? Experimentelle untersuchung über die Bedeutung der Reproduktions-perspektive. *Zeitschrift Psychologie*, 1913, *66*, 1–50.

Abel, L. B. The effects of shift in motivation upon the learning of a sensorimotor task. *Archives of Psychology*, 1936, *29*, No. 205.

Abercrombie, M. L. *Learning to think*. New York: Basic Books, 1960.

Acker, M., & McReynolds, P. The "need for novelty": a comparison of six instruments. *Psychological Record*, 1967, *17*(2), 177–182.

Ackerman, W. I., & Levin, H. Effects of training in alternative solutions on subsequent problem solving. *Journal of Educational Psychology*, 1958, *41*, 239–244.

Adkins, D. C. Measurement in relation to the educational process. *Educational and Psychological Measurement*, 1958, *18*, 221–240.

Adorno, T. W., Frenkel-Brunswick, E., Levenson, D. J., & Sanford, R. N. *The authoritarian personality*. New York: Harper & Row, 1950.

Aebli, H. *Didactique psychologie: application à la didactique de la psychologie de Jean Piaget*. Neuchâtel, Switzerland: Delachaux & Niestlè, 1951.

Agard, F. B., & Dunkel, H. B. *An investigation of second-language teaching*. Boston: Ginn, 1948.

Aiken, L. R., Jr. Personality correlates of attitude toward mathematics. *Journal of Educational Research*, 1963, *56*(9), 476–480.

Alberts, C. A., & Ehrenfreund, D. Transposition in children as a function of age. *Journal of Experimental Psychology*, 1951, *41*, 30–38.

Aldrich, C. G., & Doll, E. A. Comparative intelligence of idiots and of normal infants. *Journal of Genetic Psychology*, 1931, *39*, 227–257.

Allen, D. C., Tyrrel, S., Schulz, R. E., & Koons, G. R. The effect of exposure-time on the relation between perceptual organization and intelligence. *American Journal of Psychology*, 1958, *71*, 573–577.

Allport, G. W. Crises in normal personality development. *Teachers College Record*, 1964, *66*, 235–241.

Allport, G. W., & Postman, L. *The psychology of rumor*. New York: Holt, Rinehart and Winston, 1947.

Alper, T. G. Task-orientation *vs.* ego-orientation in learning and retention. *American Journal of Psychology*, 1946, *59*, 236–248.

Alper, T. G., & Korchin, S. J. Memory for socially relevant material. *Journal of Abnormal and Social Psychology*, 1952, 47, 25–37.

Alpert, A. *The solving of problem situations by preschool children.* New York: Teachers College, Columbia University, 1928.

Alpert, R., & Haber, R. N. Anxiety in academic achievement situations. *Journal of Abnormal and Social Psychology*, 1960, 61, 207–215.

American Association for the Advancement of Science. *Science, a process approach.* Washington, D.C.: Author, 1968.

Amidon, E., & Flanders, N. A. The effects of direct and indirect teacher influence on dependent-prone students learning geometry. *Journal of Educational Psychology*, 1961, 52, 286–291.

Amos, R. T., & Washington, R. M. A comparison of pupil and teacher perceptions of pupil problems. *Journal of Educational Psychology*, 1960, 51, 255–258.

Amster, H. Effect of instructional set and variety of instances on children's learning. *Journal of Educational Psychology*, 1966, 57, 74–85.

Anastasi, A. Intelligence and family size. *Psychological Bulletin*, 1956, 53, 187–209.

Anastasi, A., & deJesus, C. Language development and non-verbal IQ of Puerto-Rican preschool children in New York City. *Journal of Abnormal and Social Psychology*, 1953, 48, 357–366.

Anastasi, A., & Schaefer, C. E. Notes on the concepts of creativity and intelligence. *Journal of Creative Behavior*, 1971, 5(2), 113–116.

Anderson, G. L. Quantitative thinking as developed under connectionist and field theories of learning. In *Learning theory in school situations*, University of Minnesota Studies in Education. Minneapolis: University of Minnesota Press, 1949.

Anderson, H. H. Domination and socially integrative behavior. In R. G. Barker, J. S. Kounin, & H. F. Wright (Eds.), *Child behavior and development.* New York: McGraw-Hill, 1943.

Anderson, J. E. The limitations of infant and preschool tests in the measurement of intelligence. *Journal of Psychology*, 1939, 8, 351–379.

Anderson, J. E. The prediction of terminal intelligence from infant and preschool tests. In *Intelligence: Its nature and nurture*, 39th Yearbook, National Society for the Study of Education, Part I. Chicago: University of Chicago Press, 1940.

Anderson, L. D. The predictive value of infancy tests in relation to intelligence at five years. *Child Development*, 1939, 10, 203–212.

Anderson, R. C. Learning in discussions: Resumé of the authoritarian-democratic studies. *Harvard Educational Review*, 1959, 29, 201–215.

Anderson, R. C. Can first graders learn an advanced problem-solving skill? *Journal of Educational Psychology*, 1965, 56, 283–294.

Anderson, R. C. Educational psychology. In Farnworth, McNemar, & McNemar (Eds.), *Annual review of psychology.* Palo Alto, Calif.: Annual Reviews, 1967.

Anderson, R. C., & Anderson, R. M. Transfer of orginality training. *Journal of Educational Psychology*, 1963, 54, 300–304.

Anderson, R. C., Faust, G. W., & Roderick, M. C. "Overprompting" in programmed instruction. *Journal of Educational Psychology*, 1968, 59(2), 88–93.

Anderson, R. C., & Myrow, D. L. Retroactive inhibition of meaningful discourse. *Journal of Educational Psychology*, 1971, 62(1), 81–94.

Anderson, T. A study of the use of visual aids in basket shooting. *Research Quarterly, American Association of Health, Physical Education, and Recreation,* 1942, *13*, 532–537.

Angell, D., & Lumsdaine, A. A. Prompted plus unprompted trials versus prompted trials alone in paired-associate learning. *Research Report* AIR-314-60-IR-129. Pittsburgh: American Institute for Research, October 1960.

Angell, G. W. The effect of immediate knowledge of quiz results on final examination scores in freshman chemistry. *Journal of Educational Research,* 1949, *42,* 391–394.

Annett, J. Learning pressure under conditions of immediate and delayed knowledge of results. *Quarterly Journal of Psychology,* 1959, *11,* 3–15.

Annett, M. The classification of instances of four common class concepts by children and adult. *British Journal of Educational Psychology,* 1959, *29,* 233–236.

Archer, E. J. Concept identification as a function of obviousness of relevant and irrelevant information. *Journal of Experimental Psychology,* 1962, *63,* 616–620.

Arieti, S. *Creativity: The magic synthesis.* New York: Basic Books, 1976.

Armistead, L. M. The effect of stimulus change on an exploratory drive in children. *Dissertation Abstracts,* 1961, *21,* 2190.

Armor, D. The evidence on busing. *The Public Interest,* 1972, *28,* 90–126.

Arnsdorf, V. E. An investigation of the teaching of chronology in the sixth grade. *Journal of Experimental Education,* 1961, *29,* 207–214.

Asch, M. J. Nondirective teaching in psychology. *Psychological Monographs,* 1951, *65,* 4.

Aschner, M. J. *The productive thinking of gifted children in the classroom.* Urbana: Institute for Research on Exceptional Children, University of Illinois, 1961.

Ash, P. The relative effectiveness of massed versus spaced film presentations. *Journal of Educational Psychology,* 1950, *41,* 19–30.

Asher, E. J. The inadequacy of current intelligence tests for testing Kentucky mountain children. *Journal of Genetic Psychology,* 1935, *46,* 480–486.

Ashmore, H. S. *The Negro and the schools.* Chapel Hill: University of North Carolina Press, 1954.

Atkin, J. M. Behavorial objectives in curriculum design: A cautionary note. *The Science Teacher,* 1968, *35*(5), 27–30.

Atkin, J. M., & Karplus, R. *Discovery or invention?* Urbana: University of Illinois, College of Education, 1962.

Atkin, J. M., & Wyatt, S. P. *Astronomy: Charting the Universe* (trial ed.) Urbana: Elementary School Science Project, University of Illinois, 1961.

Atkinson, R. C. Mnemotechnics in second language learning. *American Psychologist,* 1975, *30,* 821–828.

Atkinson, J. W., & Feather, N. T. *Progress and puzzles . . . A theory of achievement motivation.* New York: Wiley, 1966.

Atkinson, J. W., & Litwin, G. H. Achievement motive and test anxiety conceived as motive to approach success and motive to avoid failure. *Journal of Abnormal and Social Psychology,* 1960, *60,* 52–63.

Auble, D., & Mech, E. V. Partial verbal reinforcement related to distributed practice in a classroom situation. *Journal of Psychology,* 1953, *36,* 165–186.

Ausubel, D. P. Ego development and the learning process. *Child Development,* 1949, *20,* 173–190.

Ausubel, D. P. Prestige motivation of gifted children. *Genetic Psychology Monographs,* 1951, *43,* 53–117.

Ausubel, D. P. *Ego development and the personality disorders.* New York: Grune & Stratton, 1952.

Ausubel, D. P. The nature of educational research. *Education Theory,* 1953, *3,* 314–320.

Ausubel, D. P. *Theory and problems of adolescent development.* New York: Grune & Stratton, 1954.

Ausubel, D. P. Socioempathy as a function of sociometric status in an adolescent group. *Human Relations,* 1955, *8,* 75–84.

Ausubel, D. P. Some comments on the nature, diagnosis, and prognosis of neurotic anxiety. *Psychiatric Quarterly,* 1956, *30,* 77–88.

Ausubel, D. P. *Theory and problems of child development.* New York: Grune & Stratton, 1958.

Ausubel, D. P. Viewpoints from related disciplines: Human growth and development. *Teachers College Record,* 1959, *60,* 245–254.

Ausubel, D. P. The use of advance organizers in the learning and retention of meaningful verbal material. *Journal of Educational Psychology,* 1960, *51,* 267–272.

Ausubel, D. P. In defense of verbal learning. *Education Theory,* 1961, *11,* 15–25.

Ausubel, D. P. A subsumption theory of meaningful verbal learning and retention. *Journal of General Psychology,* 1962, *66,* 213–224.

Ausubel, D. P. *The psychology of meaningful verbal learning.* New York: Grune & Stratton, 1963. (a)

Ausubel, D. P. A teaching strategy for culturally deprived pupils: Cognitive and motivational considerations. *School Review,* 1963, *71,* 454–463. (b)

Ausubel, D. P. Adults versus children in second-language learning: Psychological considerations. *Modern Language Journal,* 1964, *48,* 420–424.

Ausubel, D. P. Some psychological aspects of the structure of knowledge. In S. Elam (Ed.), *Education and the structure of knowledge.* Skokie, Ill.: Rand McNally, 1964, 221–249.

Ausubel, D. P. A cognitive structure view of word and concept meaning. In R. C. Anderson & D. P. Ausubel (Eds.), *Readings in the psychology of cognition.* New York: Holt, Rinehart and Winston, 1965. (a)

Ausubel, D. P. The effects of cultural deprivation on learning patterns. *Audiovisual Instruction,* 1965, *10,* 10–12. (b)

Ausubel, D. P. Neo-behaviorism and Piaget's views on thought and symbolic functioning. *Child Development,* 1965, *36*(4), 1029–1032. (c)

Ausubel, D. P. *Maori youth: A psychoethnological study of cultural deprivation.* New York: Holt, Rinehart and Winston, 1965. (d)

Ausubel, D. P. Perception versus cognition in meaningful verbal learning. *Journal of General Psychology,* 1965, *73,* 185–187. (e)

Ausubel, D. P. The influence of experience on the development of intelligence. In M. J. Aschner & C. E. Bisch (Eds.), *Productive thinking in education.* Washington, D.C.: National Education Association, 1965. (f)

Ausubel, D. P. Early versus delayed review in meaningful learning. *Psychology in Schools,* 1966, *3,* 195–198.

Ausubel, D. P. A cognitive structure theory of school learning. In L. Siegel (Ed.), *Instruction: Some contemporary viewpoints.* San Francisco: Chandler, 1967, pp. 207–257.

Ausubel, D. P. *Educational psychology: A cognitive view.* New York: Holt, Rinehart and Winston, 1968. (a)

Ausubel, D. P. Symbolization and symbolic thought: Response to Furth. *Child Development,* 1968, *30,* 997–1001. (b)

Ausubel, D. P. Comment on Mischel's paper on Piagetian conceptions of motivation. In T. Mischel (Ed.), *Cognitive development and epistemology.* New York: Academic Press, 1971.

Ausubel, D. P., & Ausubel, P. Research on ego development among segregated Negro children. In A. H. Passow (Ed.), *Education in depressed areas.* New York: Teacher's College of Columbia University, 1963.

Ausubel, D. P., Balthazar, E. E., Rosenthal, I., Blackman, L., Schpoont, S. H., & Welkowitz, J. Perceived parent attitudes as determinants of children's ego structure. *Child Development,* 1954, *25,* 173–183.

Ausubel, D. P., & Blake, E. Proactive inhibition in the forgetting of meaningful school material. *Journal of Educational Research,* 1958, *52,* 145–149.

Ausubel, D. P., & Fitzgerald, D. The role of discriminability in meaningful verbal learning and retention. *Journal of Educational Psychology,* 1961, *52,* 266–274.

Ausubel, D. P., & Fitzgerald, D. Organizer, general background, and antecedent learning variables in sequential verbal learning. *Journal of Educational Psychology,* 1962, *53,* 243–249.

Ausubel, D. P., & Kirk, D. *Ego psychology and mental disorder.* New York: Grune & Stratton, 1977.

Ausubel, D. P., Montemayor, R., & Svajian, P. N. *Theory and problems of adolescent development* (2nd ed.). New York: Grune & Stratton, 1977.

Ausubel, D. P., Robbins, L. C., & Blake, E. Retroactive inhibition and facilitation in the learning of school materials. *Journal of Educational Psychology,* 1957, *48,* 334–343.

Ausubel, D. P., & Schiff, H. M. The effect of incidental and experimentally induced experience in the learning of relevant and irrelevant causal relationships by children. *Journal of Genetic Psychology,* 1954, *84,* 109–123.

Ausubel, D. P., & Schiff, H. M. A level of aspiration approach to the measurement of goal tenacity. *Journal of General Psychology,* 1955, *52,* 97–110.

Ausubel, D. P., Schiff, H. M., & Gasser, E. B. A preliminary study of developmental trends in socioempathy: Accuracy of perception of own and others' sociometric status. *Child Development,* 1952, *23,* 111–128.

Ausubel, D. P., Schiff, H. M., & Goldman, M. Qualitative characteristics in the learning process associated with anxiety. *Journal of Abnormal and Social Psychology,* 1953, *48,* 537–547.

Ausubel, D. P., Schiff, H. M., & Zeleny, M. P. Real life measures of academic and vocational aspirations: Relation to laboratory measures and adjustment. *Child Development,* 1953, *24,* 155–168.

Ausubel, D. P., & Schpoont, S. H. Prediction of group opinion as a function of extremeness of predictor attitudes. *Journal of Social Psychology,* 1957, *46,* 19–29.

Ausubel, D. P., Schpoont, S. H., & Cukier, L. The influence of intention on the retention of school materials. *Journal of Educational Psychology*, 1957, *48*, 87–92.

Ausubel, D. P., & Schwartz, F. C. The effects of a generalizing–particularizing dimension of cognitive style on the retention of prose material. *Journal of General Psychology*, 1972, *87*, 55–58.

Ausubel, D. P., Stager, M., & Gaite, A. J. H. Retroactive facilitation in meaningful verbal learning. *Journal of Educational Psychology*, 1968, *59*, 250–255.

Ausubel, D. P., Sullivan, E. V., & Ives, S. W. *Theory and problems of child development* (3rd ed.). New York: Grune & Stratton, in press.

Ausubel, D. P., & Tenzer, A. Component of and neutralizing factors in the effects of closedmindedness on the learning of controversial material. *American Educational Research Journal*, 1970, *7*, 267–273.

Ausubel, D. P., & Youssef, M. The role of discriminability in meaningful parallel learning. *Journal of Educational Psychology*, 1963, *54*, 331–336.

Ausubel, D. P., & Youssef, M. The effect of spaced repetition on meaningful learning. *Journal of General Psychology*, 1965, *73*, 147–150.

Ausubel, D. P., & Youssef, M. The effect of consolidation on sequentially related, sequentially independent meaningful learning. *Journal of General Psychology*, 1966, *74*, 355–360.

Back, K. W. Influence through social communications. *Journal of Abnormal and Social Psychology*, 1951, *46*, 9–23.

Bahrick, H. P., Fitts, P. M., & Rankin, R. E. Effect of incentives upon reactions to peripheral stimuli. *Journal of Experimental Psychology*, 1952, *44*, 400–406.

Baker, H. L. High-school teachers' knowledge of their pupils. *School Review*, 1938, *46*, 175–190.

Baker, H. V. Children's contributions in elementary school general discussion. *Child Development Monographs*, 1942, No. 29.

Baker, R. A., & Osgood, S. W. Discrimination transfer along a pitch continuum. *Journal of Experimental Psychology*, 1954, *48*, 241–246.

Baker, R. W., & Madell, T. O. A continued investigation of susceptibility to distraction in academically underachieving and achieving male college students. *Journal of Educational Psychology*, 1965, *56*, 254–258.

Baker, S. R. A study of the relationship of dogmatism to the retention of psychological concepts: A research note. *Journal of Human Relations*, 1964, *12*, 311–313.

Baldwin, A. L., Kalhorn, J., & Breese, F. H. Patterns of parent behavior. *Psychological Monographs*, 1945, *58*, No. 3 (Whole No. 268).

Ballard, P. B. Oblivescence and reminiscence. *British Journal of Psychology, Monograph Supplements*, 1913, *1*, No. 2.

Baratz, J. C. Beginning readers for speakers of divergent dialects. *Reading Goals for the Disadvantaged*, 1970, *14*, 77–83.

Barnes, B., & Clawson, E. U. Do advance organizers facilitate learning? Recommendations for further research based on the analysis of thirty-two studies. *Review of Educational Research*, 1975, *45*(4), 637–659.

Barnes, H. L. An investigation of the effects of differential instructional material on concept acquisition and transfer. (Doctoral dissertation, Michigan State University, 1972). *Dissertation Abstracts International*, 1972, *33*, 2207.

Barnlund, D. C. A comparative study of individual, majority, and group judgment. *Journal of Abnormal and Social Psychology*, 1959, *58*, 55–60.

Barr, A. S., & Jones, R. E. The measurement and prediction of teaching efficiency. *Review of Educational Research*, 1958, *28*, 256–264.

Barron, F. *Creativity and psychological health*. Princeton, N.J.: Van Nostrand, 1963.

Barron, F. The dream of art and poetry. *Psychology Today*, 1968, *2*(7), 18–23, 66.

Barron, F. *Creative person and creative process*. New York: Holt, Rinehart and Winston, 1969.

Bartlett, F. C. *Remembering*. Cambridge: Cambridge University Press, 1932.

Bartlett, F. C. *Thinking: An experimental and social study*. London: G. Allen, 1958.

Battig, W. F. Some factors affecting performance on a word formation problem. *Journal of Experimental Psychology*, 1957, *54*, 96–104.

Bayley, N. Mental growth during the first three years: A developmental study of 61 children by repeated tests. *Genetic Psychology Monographs*, 1933, *14*, 7–92.

Bayley, N. Mental growth in young children. In *39th Yearbook, National Society for the Study of Education, Part 2*. Chicago: University of Chicago Press, 1940.

Bayley, N. Consistency and variability in the growth of intelligence from birth to eighteen years. *Journal of Genetic Psychology*, 1949, *75*, 165–196.

Bayley, N. On the growth of intelligence. *American Psychologist*, 1955, *10*, 805–818.

Bayley, N. Individual patterns of development. *Child Development*, 1956, *27*, 45–74.

Bayley, N. Developmental problems of the mentally retarded child. In I. Philips (Ed.), *Prevention and treatment of mental retardation*, Part 2. New York: Basic Books, 1966.

Bayley, N. Behavioral correlates of mental growth: Birth to 36 years. *American Psychologist*, 1968, *1*, 1–17. (a)

Bayley, N. Cognition in aging. In K. W. Schaire (Ed.), *Theory and methods of research in aging*. Morgantown, W. Va.: University Library, 1968. (b)

Bayley, N. Development of mental abilities. In P. H. Mussen (Ed.), *Carmichael's manual of child psychology* (Vol. 1) (3rd ed.). New York: Wiley, 1970.

Bayley, N., & Jones, H. E. Environmental correlates of mental and motor development: A cumulative study from infancy to six years. *Child Development*, 1937, *4*, 329–341.

Bayley, N., & Oden, M. H. The maintenance of intellectual ability in gifted adults. *Journal of Gerontology*, 1955, *10*, 91–107.

Beane, D. G. A comparison of linear and branching techniques of programmed instruction in plane geometry. *Technical Report No. 1*. Urbana: University of Illinois, Training Research Laboratory, July 1962.

Beauchamp, G. A. *Curriculum theory*. Wilmette, Ill.: Kagy Press, 1961, 1968.

Bearison, D. J. Role of measurement operations in the acquisition of conservation. *Developmental Psychology*, 1969, *1*, 653–660.

Beberman, M. *An emerging program of secondary school mathematics*. Cambridge, Mass.: Harvard University Press, 1958.

Beilin, H., & Franklin, I. C. Logical operations in area and length measurement: Age and training effects. *Child Development*, 1962, *33*, 607–618.

Belgard, M., Rosenshine, B., & Gage, N. L. Effectiveness in explaining: Evidence on its generality and correlation with pupil ratings. In I. Westbury & A. A. Bellack (Eds.), *Research into classroom processes: Recent developments and next steps.* New York: Teachers College Press, 1971.

Beller, E. K. Research on organized programs of early education. In R. M. W. Travers (Ed.), *Second handbook of research on teaching.* Skokie, Ill.: Rand McNally, 1973.

Bellugi, U. Learning the language. *Psychology Today,* 1970, 4(7), 32–35.

Benedict, R. Continuities and discontinuities in cultural conditioning. *Psychiatry,* 1938, *1,* 161–167.

Benne, K. D., & Levit, G. The nature of groups and helping groups improve their operation. *Review of Educational Research,* 1953, *23,* 289–308.

Bennett, G. K., & Doppelt, J. E. A longitudinal study of the differential aptitude tests. *Educational and Psychological Measurement,* 1951, *11,* 228–237.

Bereiter, C. An academic preschool for disadvantaged children: Conclusions from evaluation studies. In J. C. Stanley (Ed.), *Preschool programs for the disadvantaged: Five experimental approaches to early childhood education.* Baltimore: Johns Hopkins University Press, 1972.

Bereiter, C., & Engelmann, S. *Teaching disadvantaged children in the preschool.* Engelwood Cliffs, N.J.: Prentice Hall, 1966.

Berkowitz, L. Leveling tendencies and the complexity–simplicity dimension. *Journal of Personality,* 1957, *25,* 743–751.

Berlin, H., & Franklin, I. C. Logical operations in area and length measurement: Age and training effects. *Child Development,* 1962, *33,* 607–618.

Berlyne, D. E. *Conflict, arousal, and curiosity.* New York: McGraw-Hill, 1960.

Berlyne, D. E. Lyuboznatel' nost' i poisk informatsii (Curiosity and the quest for information). *Voprosy Psikhologii,* 1966, *3,* 54–60. A paper presented at the 18th International Psychological Congress in Moscow.

Bernard, V. W. School desegration: Some psychiatric implications. *Psychiatry,* 1958, *21,* 149–158.

Bernard, W. Psychological principles of language learning and the bilingual reading method. *Modern Language Journal,* 1951, *35,* 87–96.

Bernstein, B. Some sociological determinants of perception: An enquiry into subcultural differences. *British Journal of Sociology,* 1958, *9,* 159–174.

Bernstein, B. Language and social class. *British Journal of Psychology,* 1960, *11,* 271–276.

Bethune, P. The nova plan for individualized instruction. *The Science Teacher,* 1966, *33*(8), 55–57.

Bettinghaus, E. P., & Baseheart, J. R. Some specific factors affecting attitude change. *Journal of Communication,* 1969, *19*(3), 227–238.

Bhatnagar, K. P. Academic achievement as a function of one's self-concepts and ego functions. *Education & Psychology Review,* 1966, *6,* 178–182.

Biel, W. C., & Force, R. C. Retention of nonsense syllables in intentional and incidental learning. *Journal of Experimental Psychology,* 1943, *32,* 52–63.

Bijou, S. W. Development in the preschool years: A functional analysis. *American Psychologist,* 1975, *30*(8), 829–837.

Binter, A. R. Two ways of teaching percent. *Elementary School Journal,* 1963, *63,* 261–265.

Birch, H. G., & Gussow, J. D. *Disadvantaged children: Health, nutrition and school failure.* New York: Harcourt, 1970.

Birch, H. G., & Rabinowitz, H. S. The negative effect of previous experience on productive thinking. *Journal of Experimental Psychology*, 1951, *41*, 121–125.

Björgen, I. A. *A re-evaluation of rote learning.* Oslo: Oslo University Press, 1964.

Black, H. *They shall not pass.* New York: Morrow, 1963.

Blank, M. A methodology for fostering abstract thinking in deprived children. In A. J. Biemiller (Ed.), *Problems in the teaching of young children.* Ontario: Ontario Institute for Studies in Education, 1970.

Bliesmer, P. Reading abilities of bright and dull children of comparable mental ages. *Journal of Educational Psychology*, 1954, *45*, 321-331.

Block, J. (Ed.) *Mastery learning: Theory and practice.* New York: Holt, Rinehart and Winston, 1971.

Bloom, B. S. Thought-processes in lectures and discussions. *Journal of General Education*, 1953, *7*, 160–169.

Bloom, B. S. *Stability and change in human characteristics.* New York: Wiley, 1964. (a)

Bloom, B. S. Quality control in education. In E. B. Page (Ed.), *Readings for educational psychology.* New York: Harcourt, 1964. (b)

Bloom, B. S. Learning for mastery. *UCLA Evaluation Comment*, 1968, *1*(2), 1.

Bloom, B. S. *Human characteristics and school learning.* New York: McGraw-Hill, 1976.

Bloom, B. S., & Broder, L. J. Problem-solving processes of college students. *Supplementary Educational Monograph*, No. 73, 1–31. Chicago: University of Chicago Press, 1960.

Bobbitt, F. *The curriculum.* Boston: Houghton Mifflin, 1918.

Boblick, J. M. Writing chemical formulas: A comparison of computer assisted instruction with traditional teaching techniques. *Science Education*, 1972, *56*(2), 221–225.

Bogden, C. A. The use of concept mapping as a possible strategy for instructional design and evaluation in college genetics. Unpublished M. S. dissertation, Cornell University, 1977.

Bolvin, J. O., & Glaser, R. Individualized instruction. In D. W. Allen & E. Seifman (Eds.), *The teachers' handbook.* Glenview, Ill.: Scott, Foresman and Company, 1971.

Bond, A. DeM. *An experiment in the teaching of genetics.* New York: Columbia University, Teachers College, 1940.

Bonney, M. E. Sociometric study of agreement between teacher judgments and student choices. *Sociometry*, 1947, *10*, 133–146.

Boreas, T. The experimental studies of memory: 2. The rate of forgetting. *Praktia. Acad. Athenes*, 1930, *5*, 382–396. In R. S. Woodworth & H. Schlosberg (Eds.), *Experimental Psychology.* New York: Holt, Rinehart and Winston, 1954.

Bostrom, R. N., Vlandis, J., & Rosenbaum, M. Grades as reinforcing contingencies and attitude change. *Journal of Educational Psychology*, 1961, *52*, 112–115.

Bourne, L. E., Goldstein, S., & Link, W. E. Concept learning as a function of availability of previously presented information. *Journal of Experimental Psychology*, 1964, *67*, 439–448.

Bourne, L. E., & Haygood, R. C. Effects of intermittent reinforcement of an irrelevant dimension and task complexity upon concept identification. *Journal of Experimental Psychology*, 1960, *60*, 371–375.

Bourne, L. E., & Jennings, P. The relationship between response contiguity and classification learning. *Journal of General Psychology*, 1963, *69*, 335–338.

Bourne, L. E., & Parker, B. K. Differences among modes for portraying stimulus information in concept identification. *Psychonomic Science*, 1964, *1*, 209–210.

Boyd, W. *A textbook of pathology* (7th ed.). Philadelphia: Lea & Febiger, 1961.

Brackbill, Y., Adams, G., & Reaney, T. P. A parametric study of the delay-retention effect. *Psychological Reports*, 1967, *20*(2), 433–434.

Brackbill, Y., Wagner, J. E., & Wilson, D. Feedback delay and the teaching machine. *Psychology in the Schools*, 1964, *1*, 148–156.

Bradway, K. P., & Thompson, C. W. Intelligence at adulthood: A twenty-five year follow-up. *Journal of Educational Psychology*, 1962, *5*, 1–14.

Braine, M. D. S. The ontogeny of logical operations: Piaget's formulations examined by nonverbal methods. *Psychological Monographs*, 1959, *73*, No. 4 (Whole No. 475).

Braine, M. D. S. On learning the grammatical order of words. *Psychological Review*, 1963, *70*, 322–348.

Brainerd, C. J. Order of acquisition of transitivity, conservation and class-inclusion of length and weight. *Developmental Psychology*, 1973, *8*, 105–116.

Brainerd, C. J. Training and transfer of transitivity, conservation and class-inclusion of length. *Child Development*, 1974, *45*, 324–334.

Braley, L. S. Strategy selection and negative instances in concept learning. *Journal of Educational Psychology*, 1963, *54*, 154–159.

Braun, J. S. Relation between concept formation ability and reading achievement at three developmental levels. *Child Development*, 1963, *34*, 675–682.

Bredderman, T. Elementary school science experience and ability to combine and control variables. *Science Education*, 1974, *58*(4), 457–469.

Briggs, L. J. Two self-instructional devices. *Psychological Reports*, 1958, *4*, 671–676.

Briggs, L. J. Prompting and confirmation conditions for three learning tasks employing the subject-matter trainer. In A. A. Lumsdaine (Ed.), *Student response in programmed instruction*. Washington, D.C.: National Academy of Sciences–National Research Council, 1961.

Briggs, L. J., & Reed, H. B. The curve of retention for substance material. *Journal of Experimental Psychology*, 1943, *32*, 513–517.

Brison, D. W. Acceleration of conservation of substance. *Journal of Genetic Psychology*, 1966, *109*, 311–322.

Brodie, T. A. Attitude toward school and academic achievement. *Personnel & Guidance Journal*, 1964, *43*, 375–378.

Bromer, J. A. A comparison of incidental and purposeful memory for meaningful and nonsense material. *American Journal of Psychology*, 1942, *55*, 106–108.

Brookover, W. B., Thomas, S., & Patterson, A. Self-concept of ability and school achievement. *Sociology of Education*, 1964, *37*, 271–278.

Brown, G. I. An experiment in the teaching of creativity. *School Review*, 1964, *72*, 437–450.

Brown, R. How shall a thing be called? *Psychological Review*, 1958, *65*, 14–21. (a)

Brown, R. *Words and things*. Glencoe, Ill.: Free Press, 1958. (b)

Brown, R., & Fraser, C. The acquisition of syntax. In C. N. Cofer & B. S. Musgave

(Eds.), *Verbal behavior and learning: Problems and processes.* New York: McGraw-Hill, 1963.

Brown, R. W. *A first language.* Cambridge, Mass.: Harvard University Press, 1973.

Brownell, W. A. Observations of instruction in lower-grade arithmetic in English and Scottish schools. *Arithmetic Teacher*, 1960, 7, 165–177.

Brownell, W. A., & Hendrickson, G. How children learn information, concepts, and generalizations. In *Learning and instruction*, 49th Yearbook, National Society for the Study of Education, Part I. Chicago: University of Chicago Press, 1950.

Brownell, W. A., & Moser, H. E. Meaningful versus mechanical learning: A study in grade III subtraction. Duke University, Research Studies in Education, 1949, No. 8.

Brownell, W. A., & Sims, V. M. The nature of understanding. In *The measurement of understanding*, 45th Yearbook, National Society for the Study of Education, Part I. Chicago: University of Chicago Press, 1946, pp. 27–43.

Bruner, J. S. Going beyond the information given. In *Contemporary approaches to cognition.* Cambridge, Mass.: Harvard University Press, 1957.

Bruner, J. S. Learning and thinking. *Harvard Educational Review*, 1959, 29, 84–92.

Bruner, J. S. *The process of education.* Cambridge, Mass.: Harvard University Press, 1960.

Bruner, J. S. The act of discovery. *Harvard Educational Review*, 1961, 31, 21–32. (a)

Bruner, J. S. After Dewey what? *Saturday Review*, June 17, 1961, 58–59, 76–78. (b)

Bruner, J. S. The course of cognitive growth. *American Psychologist*, 1964, 19, 1–15. (a)

Bruner, J. S. Some theorems on instruction illustrated with reference to mathematics. In *Theories of Learning and instruction*, 63rd Yearbook, National Society for the Study of Education, Part I. Chicago: University of Chicago Press, 1964. (b)

Bruner, J. S. *Toward a theory of instruction.* Cambridge, Mass.: Belknap Press of Harvard University Press, 1966.

Bruner, J. S., Goodnow, J. J., & Austin, G. A. *A study of thinking.* New York: Wiley, 1956.

Bruner, J. S., & Olver, R. R. Development of equivalence transformations in children. *Monographs of the Society for Research in Child Development*, 1963, 28 (Whole No. 86), 125–141.

Bruner, J. S., & Tajfel, H. Cognitive risk and environmental change. *Journal of Abnormal and Social Psychology*, 1961, 62, 231–241.

Bruner, J. S., Wallach, M. A., & Galanter, E. H. The identification of recurrent regularity. *American Journal of Psychology*, 1959, 72, 200–220.

Bruning, R. H. Effects of review and testlike events within the learning of prose materials. *Journal of Educational Psychology*, 1968, 59, 16–19.

Brush, S. G. Should the history of science be rated X? *Science*, 1974, 183, 1164–1172.

Bryan, G. L., & Rigney, J. W. An evaluation of a method for shipboard training in operations knowledge. *Technical Report No. 18.* Los Angeles: University of Southern California, Department of Psychology, September, 1956.

Bryan, J. F., & Locke, E. A. Goal setting as a means of increasing motivation. *Journal of Applied Psychology*, 1967, 51, 274–277.

Buell, R. R., & Bradley, G. A. Piagetian studies in science: Chemical equilibrium understanding from study of solubility. A preliminary report from secondary school chemistry. *Science Education,* 1972, *56*(1), 23–29.

Bullock, H. A. A comparison of the academic achievements of white and Negro high school graduates. *Journal of Educational Research,* 1950, *44,* 179–182.

Bumstead, A. P. Distribution of effort in memorizing prose and poetry. *American Journal of Psychology,* 1940, *53,* 423–427.

Bumstead, A. P. Finding the best method for memorizing. *Journal of Educational Psychology,* 1943, *34,* 110–114.

Bumstead, A. P. Distribution of effort in memorizing. *American Journal of Psychology,* 1964, *77,* 669–671.

Bunderson, C. V., & Faust, G. W. Programmed and computer assisted instruction. In N. L. Gage (Ed.), *The psychology of teaching methods.* Chicago; University of Chicago Press, 1976.

Burack, B., & Moos, D. Effect of knowing the principle basic to solution of a problem. *Journal of Educational Research,* 1956, *50,* 203–208.

Burks, B. S. The relative influence of nature and nurture upon mental development: A comparative study of foster parent–foster child resemblance and true parent-true child resemblance. 27th Yearbook, National Society for the Study of Education. Chicago: University of Chicago Press, 1928, pp. 219–316.

Burks, B. S. On the relative contributions of nature and nurture to average group differences in intelligence. *Proceedings of the National Academy of Science,* 1938, *24,* 276–282.

Burt, C. The development of reasoning in children. *Journal of Experimental Pedagogy,* 1919, *5,* 68–77.

Burt, C. The evidence for the concept of intelligence. *British Journal of Educational Psychology,* 1955, *25,* 158–177.

Burt, C. The inheritance of mental ability. *American Psychologist,* 1958, *13,* 1–15.

Burt, C. The genetic determination of differences in intelligence: A study of monozygotic twins reared together and apart. *British Journal of Psychology,* 1966, *57,* 137–153.

Burtt, H. E. An experimental study of early childhood memory: Final report. *Journal of Genetic Psychology,* 1941, *58,* 435–439.

Busch, K. Gaming techniques for concept learning: A case study. Unpublished master's thesis, Cornell University, 1973.

Butler, R. A. Incentive conditions which influence visual exploration. *Journal of Experimental Psychology,* 1954, *48,* 19–32.

Buxton, E. W. An experiment to test the effects of writing frequency and guided practice upon students' skill in written expression. Unpublished doctoral dissertation, Stanford University, 1958.

Byers, J. L. A study of the level of aspiration of academically successful and unsuccessful high school students. *California Journal of Educational Research,* 1962, *13,* 209–216.

Callantine, M. F., & Warren, J. M. Learning sets in human concept formation. *Psychological Reports,* 1955, *1,* 363–367.

Campbell, J. B. Peer relations in childhood. In M. L. Hoffman & L. M. Hoffman (Eds.), *Review of child development research* (Vol. 1). New York: Russell Sage Foundation, 1964.

Canning, R. R. Does an honor system reduce classroom cheating? An experimental answer. *Journal of Experimental Education,* 1956, *24,* 291–296.

Cantor, N. *The teaching-learning process.* New York: Dryden, 1953.

Carlow, C. D. The application of psychological theories to a curriculum project: An example. *Educational Psychologist,* 1976, *12*(1), 36—48.

Carmichael, L., Hogan, H. P., & Walter, A. A. An experimental study of the effect of language on visually perceived form. *Journal of Experimental Psychology,* 1932, *15,* 73–86.

Caron, A. J. Curiosity, achievement, and avoidant motivation as determinants of epistemic behavior. *Journal of Abnormal and Social Psychology,* 1963, *67,* 535–549.

Carr, H. A. Teaching and learning. *Journal of Genetic Psychology,* 1930, *37,* 189—218.

Carroll, J. B. Knowledge of English roots and affixes as related to vocabulary and Latin study. *Journal of Educational Research,* 1940, *34,* 256–261.

Carroll, J. B. A model of school learning. *Teachers College Record,* 1963, *64,* 723–733.

Carroll, J. B. The analysis of reading instruction: Perspectives from psychology and linguistics. In *Theories of learning and instruction,* 63rd Yearbook, National Society for the Study of Education, Part I. Chicago: University of Chicago Press, 1964.

Carter, H. D. Effects of emotional factors upon recall. *Journal of Psychology,* 1935, *1,* 49–59.

Carter, L. F., Haythorn, W., Lanzetta, J., & Mairowitz, B. The relation of categorizations and ratings in the observation of group behavior. *Human Relations,* 1951, *4,* 239–254.

Carter, R. S. How invalid are marks assigned by teachers? *Journal of Educational Psychology,* 1952, *43,* 218–228.

Cartledge, C. J., & Krauser, E. L. Training first-grade children in creative thinking under quantitative and qualitative motivation. *Journal of Educational Psychology,* 1963, *54,* 295–299.

Case, D., & Collinson, J. M. The development of formal thinking in verbal comprehension. *British Journal of Educational Psychology,* 1962, *32,* 103–111.

Case, R. Gearing the demands of instruction to the developmental capacities of the learner. *Review of Educational Research,* 1975, *45*(1), 59–87.

Cassirer, E. *The philosophy of symbolic forms.* Vol. 3 of *The phenomenology of knowledge.* New Haven, Conn.: Yale University, 1957.

Castenada, A., Palermo, D. S., & McCandless, B. R. Complex learning and performance as a function of anxiety in children and task difficulty. *Child Development,* 1956, *27,* 329–332.

Cattell, R. B. Theory of fluid and crystallized intelligence. *Journal of Educational Psychology,* 1963, *54,* 1–22.

Cattell, R. B. The theory of fluid and crystallized general intelligence checked at the 5-6 year old level. *British Journal of Educational Psychology,* 1967, *37*(2), 209–224.

Cavan, R. S. Negro family disorganization and juvenile delinquency. *Journal of Negro Education,* 1959, *28,* 230–239.

Chall, J. S. *Learning to read: The great debate.* New York: McGraw-Hill, 1967.

Chansky, N. M. Learning: A function of schedule and type of feedback. *Psychological Reports,* 1960, *7,* 362.

Chansky, N. M. Reactions to systems of guiding learning. *American Educational Research Journal,* 1964, *1,* 95–100.

Chapanis, A., & Williams, W. C. Results of a mental survey with the Kuhlmann-Anderson intelligence tests in Williamson County, Tennessee. *Journal of Genetic Psychology,* 1945, *67,* 27–55.

Chase, L. Motivation of young children: An experimental study of the influence of certain types of external incentives upon the performance of a task. *University of Iowa Studies in Child Welfare,* 1932, *5,* No. 3.

Cheyne, J. A. & Walters, R. H. Intensity of punishment, timing of punishment, and cognitive structure as determinants of response inhibition. *Journal of Experimental Child Psychology,* 1969, *7*(2), 231–244.

Chiappetta, E. L. A review of Piagetian studies relevant to science instruction at the secondary and college level. *Science Education,* 1976, *60,* 253–261.

Chomsky, N. A. *Syntactic structures.* The Hague: Mouton, 1957.

Chomsky, N. A. Review of Skinner's *Verbal behavior. Language,* 1959, *35,* 26–58.

Chomsky, N. A. *Language and mind* (enlarged ed.). New York: Harcourt, 1972.

Chown, S. M. Rigidity—a flexible concept. *Psychological Bulletin,* 1959, *56,* 195–223.

Christensen, C. C. A note on "Dogmatism and learning." *Journal of Abnormal and Social Psychology,* 1963, *66,* 75–76.

Christensen, C. M., & K. E. Stordahl. The effect of organizational aids on comprehension and retention. *Journal of Educational Psychology,* 1955, *46,* 65–74.

Clarizio, H. F., Craig, R. C., & Mehrens, W. A. To punish or not to punish. In H. F. Clarizio, R. C. Craig, & W. A. Mehrens (Eds.), *Contemporary issues in educational psychology* (2nd ed.). Boston: Allyn & Bacon, 1974.

Clark, E. V. Some aspects of the conceptual basis for first language acquisition. In R. Schiefelbusch & L. L. Lloyd (Eds.), *Language perspectives—acquisition, retardation, and intervention.* Baltimore, Md.: University Park Press, 1974.

Clark, K. B. Some factors influencing the remembering of prose material. *Archives of Psychology,* 1940, *36* (Whole No. 253).

Clark, K. B. *Dark ghetto: Dilemmas of social power.* New York: Harper & Row, 1965.

Clark, K. B., & Clark, M. P. Racial identification and preference in Negro children. In T. M. Newcomb & E. L. Hartley (Eds.), *Readings in social psychology.* New York: Holt, Rinehart and Winston, 1947.

Cline, V. B., Richards, J. M., & Abe, C. The validity of a battery of creativity tests in a high school sample. *Educational and Psychological Measurement,* 1962, *22,* 781–784.

Cline, V. B., Richards, J. M., & Needham, W. E. Creativity tests and achievement in high school science. *Journal of Applied Psychology,* 1963, *47,* 184–189.

Cobb, H. V., & Brenneise, S. H. Solutions of the Meier string problem as a function of the method of problem presentation. *Proceedings of the South Dakota Academy of Science,* 1952, *31,* 138–142.

Cocking, R. R. *Cognitive socialization: A social-learning analysis of language acquisition.* Athens, Ga.: Mathemagenic Activities Program, 1972.

Cofer, C. N. A comparison of logical and verbatim learning of prose passages of different length. *American Journal of Psychology,* 1941, *54,* 1–20.

Cogan, M. L. The behavior of teachers and the productive behavior of their pupils:

I. "Perception" analysis; II. "Trait" analysis. *Journal of Experimental Education*, 1958, *27*, 89–105; 107–124.

Cohen, I. S. Rigidity and anxiety in a motor response. *Perceptual and Motor Skills*, 1961, *12*, 127–130.

Cohen, J. The factorial structure of the WISC at ages 7-6, 10-6, and 13-6. *Journal of Consulting Psychology*, 1959, *23*, 285–289.

Cohen, J., & Hansel, C. E. M. The idea of independence. *British Journal of Psychology*, 1955, *46*, 178–130.

Cole, C. W., & Miller, C. D. Relevance of expressed values to academic performance. *Journal of Counseling Psychology*, 1967, *14*(3), 272–276.

Cole, D., Jacobs, S., Zubok, B., Fagot, B., & Hunter, I. The relation of achievement imagery scores to academic performance. *Journal of Abnormal and Social Psychology*, 1962, *65*, 208–211.

Cole, H. P. *Process education: The new direction for elementary-secondary schools.* Englewood Cliffs, N.J.: Educational Technology, 1972.

Coleman, J. S. *The adolescent subculture.* Glencoe, Ill.: Free Press, 1961.

Coleman, J. S. Recent trends in school integration. *Educational Researcher*, 1975, *4*(7), 3–12.

Coleman, J. S., Campbell, E. Q., Hobson, C. J., McPartland, J., Mood, A. M., Weinfield, F. D., & York, R. L. *Equality of educational opportunity.* Washington, D.C.: Government Printing Office, 1966.

Coleman, W., & Ward, A. H. A comparison of Davis-Eells and Kuhlmann-Finch scores of children from high and low socio-economic status. *Journal of Educational Psychology*, 1955, *46*, 465–469.

Collins, R. Functional and conflict theories of educational stratification. *American Sociological Review*, 1971, *36*(6), 1002–1019.

Conant, J. B. *On understanding science.* New Haven: Yale University Press, 1947.

Conant, J. B. *Slums and suburbs.* New York: McGraw-Hill, 1961.

Conrad, H. S., Freeman, F. N., & Jones, H. E. Differential mental growth. In *Adolescence*, 43rd Yearbook, National Society for the Study of Education, Part I. Chicago: University of Chicago Press, 1944.

Conrad, H. S., & Jones, H. E. A second study of familial resemblance in intelligence: Environmental and genetic implications of parent-child and sibling correlations in the total sample. In 39th Yearbook, National Society for the Study of Education, Part II. Chicago: University of Chicago Press, 1940.

Cook, J. O., & Spitzer, M. E. Supplementary report: Prompting versus confirmation in paired-associate learning. *Journal of Experimental Psychology*, 1960, *59*, 275–276.

Cook, W. W., Leeds, C. H., & Callis, R. *The Minnesota Teacher Attitude Inventory.* New York: Psychological Corporation, 1951.

Cooper, B. An analysis of the reading achievement of white and Negro pupils in certain public schools of Georgia. *School Review*, 1964, *72*, 462–471.

Corman, B. R. The effect of varying amounts and kinds of information as guidance in problem solving. *Psychological Monographs*, 1957, *71*, No. 2 (Whole No. 431).

Cornell, E. L. *The variability of children of different ages and its relation to school classification and grouping.* Albany: University of the State of New York, 1936.

Cornell, E. L., & Armstrong, C. M. Forms of mental growth patterns revealed by reanalysis of the Harvard growth data. *Child Development*, 1955, *26*, 169–204.

Costa, N. D. The effects of intratask similarity on learning, retention, and the transfer in connected discourse. Unpublished dissertation proposal, City University of New York, 1975.

Costanzo, P. R., & Shaw, M. E. Conformity as a function of age level. In R. E. Muss (Ed.), *Adolescent behavior and society: A book of readings*. New York: Random House, 1971. (Reprinted from *Child Development*, 1966, *37*.)

Costello, C. G. Need achievement and college performance. *Journal of Psychology*, 1968, *69*, 17–18.

Costin, F. Dogmatism and learning: A follow-up study of contradictory findings. *Journal of Educational Research*, 1965, *59*, 186–188.

Costin, F. Dogmatism and the retention of psychological misconceptions. *Educational and Psychological Measurement*, 1968, *28*, 529–534.

Cottrell, N. B., & Wack, D. L. Energizing effects of cognitive dissonance upon dominant and subordinate responses. *Journal of Personality and Social Psychology*, 1967, *6*, 132–138.

Coulson, J. E., & Silberman, H. F. Effects of three variables in a teaching machine. *Journal of Educational Psychology*, 1960, *51*, 135–143. (a)

Coulson, J. E., & Silberman, H. F. Results of an initial experiment in automated teaching. In A. S. Lumsdaine & R. Glaser (Eds.), *Teaching machines and programmed learning*. Washington, D.C.: National Education Association, 1960. (b)

Coulson, J. E., and others. Effects of branching in a computer controlled auto-instructional device. *Journal of Applied Psychology*, 1962, *46*, 389–392.

Cowen, E. L., Zax, M., Klein, R., Izzo, L. D., & Trost, M. A. The relation of anxiety in school children to school record, achievement, and behavioral measures. *Child Development*, 1965, *36*, 685–695.

Cox, J. W. Some experiments on formal training in the acquisition of skill. *British Journal of Psychology*, 1933, *24*, 67–87.

Craig, R. C. Discovery, task completion, and the assignment as factors in motivation. *American Educational Research Journal*, 1965, *2*, 217–222.

Crandall, V., Dewey, R., Katkovsky, W., & Preston, A. Parents' attitudes and behaviors and grade-school children's academic achievements. *Journal of Genetic Psychology*, 1964, *104*, 53–66.

Creager, J. G., & Murray, D. L. *The use of modules in college biology teaching*. Washington, D.C.: Committee on Undergraduate Education in the Biological Sciences, Publication No. 31, 1971.

Crewe, J. C. The effect of study strategies on the retention of college text material. *Journal of Reading Behavior*, 1969, *1*, 45–52.

Crockenberg, S. B. Creativity tests: A boon or boondoggle for education? *Review of Educational Research*, 1972, *42*(1), 27–45.

Cronbach, L. J. Issues in current educational psychology. *Monographs of the Society for Research in Child Development*, 1965, *30*, 109–125.

Cronbach, L. J. How can instruction be adapted to individual differences? In R. M. Gagné (Ed.), *Learning and individual differences*. Columbus, Ohio: Merrill, 1967.

Crowder, N. A. Automatic tutoring by intrinsic programming. In A. A. Lumsdaine & R. Glaser (Eds.), *Teaching machines and programmed learning*. Washington, D.C.: National Education Association, 1960.

Crutchfield, R. S. Teaching for productive thinking in children. Paper presented to American Psychological Association, New York City, September, 1966.

Crutchfield, R. S., & Covington, M. V. Facilitation of creative thinking and problem solving in school children. Paper presented to American Association for the Advancement of Science, Cleveland, Ohio, December 1963.

Cunningham, D. J. The retention of connected discourse: A review. *Journal of Educational Research*, 1972, 42(1), 47–71.

Cunningham, H. A. Lecture-demonstration vs. individual laboratory methods in science teaching. *Science Education*, 1946, *30*, 70–82.

Cunningham, K. S. *The measurement of early levels of intelligence.* New York: Columbia University, Teachers College, 1927.

Cunningham, R. *Understanding group behavior of boys and girls.* New York: Columbia University, Teachers College, 1951.

Curry, C. Supplementary report: The effects of verbal reinforcement combinations on learning in children. *Journal of Experimental Psychology*, 1960, *59*, 434.

Curry, R. L. The effect of socio-economic status on the scholastic achievement of sixth-grade children. *British Journal of Educational Psychology*, 1962, *32*, 46–49.

Dai, B. Some problems of personality development in Negro children. In C. Kluckhohn & H. A. Murray (Eds.), *Personality in nature, society, and culture.* New York: Knopf, 1949.

Darcy, N. T. *A performance-based undergraduate program for the education of teachers at Brooklyn College.* New York: Brooklyn College, City University of New York, 1971.

Dasen, P. Cross-cultural Piagetian research: A summary. *Journal of Cross-Cultural Psychology*, 1972, *3*, 23–40.

Davies, D. R. The effect of intuition upon the process of learning a complex motor skill. *Journal of Educational Psychology*, 1945, *36*, 352–365.

Davis, A. Child training and social class. In R. G. Barker (Ed.), *Child behavior and development.* New York: McGraw-Hill, 1943.

Davis, A. *Social class influences upon learning.* Cambridge Mass.: Harvard University Press, 1948.

Davis, O. L. Learning about time zones: An experiment in the development of certain time and space concepts. Unpublished doctoral dissertation. George Peabody College for Teachers, 1958.

Davis, W., & Phares, E. Internal-external control as a determinant of information-seeking in a social influence situation. *Journal of Personality*, 1967, *35*(5), 547–561.

Dawes, R. M. Memory and distortion of meaningful written material. *British Journal of Educational Psychology*, 1966, *57*, 77–86.

Dearborn, W. F., Johnson, P. W., & Carmichael, L. Oral stress and meaning in printed material. *Science*, 1949, *110*, 404.

Décarie, T. G. *Intelligence and affectivity in early childhood.* New York: International Universities, 1965.

DeCecco, J. P. High school: Decision making in a democracy. In J. P. DeCecco (Ed.), *The regeneration of the school.* New York: Holt, Rinehart and Winston, 1972.

DeCrow, K. Look, Jane look! see Dick run and jump! admire him! In S. Anderson (Ed.), *Sex differences and discrimination in education.* Worthington, Ohio: Charles A. Jones, 1972.

Deese, J. Meaning and change of meaning. *American Psychologist*, 1967, 22(8), 641–651.

Degnan, J. A. General anxiety and attitudes toward mathematics in achievers and underachievers in mathematics. *Graduate Research in Education and Related Disciplines*, 1967, 31, 49–62.

deGroot, A. D. The effects of war upon the intelligence of youth. *Journal of Abnormal and Social Psychology*, 1948, 43, 311–317.

deGroot, A. D. War and the intelligence of youth. *Journal of Abnormal and Social Psychology*, 1951, 46, 596–597.

Della-Piana, G. M. Searching orientation and concept learning. *Journal of Educational Psychology*, 1957, 48, 245–253.

Della-Piana, G. M. *An experimental evaluation of programmed learning: Motivational characteristics of the learner, his responses, and certain learning outcomes.* Salt Lake City: University of Utah, 1961.

Della-Piana, G. M., & Gage, N. L. Pupils' values and the validity of the Minnesota Teacher Attitude Inventory. *Journal of Educational Psychology*, 1955, 46, 167–178.

Dennis, W. Piaget's questions applied to a child of known environment. *Journal of Genetic Psychology*, 1942, 60, 307–320.

Dennis, W. Animism and related tendencies in Hopi children. *Journal of Abnormal and Social Psychology*, 1943, 38, 21–36.

Dennis, W., & Najarian, P. Infant development under environmental handicap. *Psychological Monographs*, 1957, 71 (Whole No. 436).

Detambel, M. H., & Stolurow, L. M. Stimulus sequence and concept learning. *Journal of Experimental Psychology*, 1956, 51, 34–40.

Deutsch, C. Social class and child development. In B. M. Caldwell & H. N. Ricciuti (Eds.), *Review of child development research* (Vol. 3). Chicago: The University of Chicago Press, 1973.

Deutsch, M. The disadvantaged child and the learning process: Some social psychological and developmental considerations. In A. H. Passow (Ed.), *Education in depressed areas.* New York: Columbia University, Teachers College, 1963.

Deutsch, M. Minority groups and class status as related to social and personality factors in scholastic achievement. In M. Deutsch (Ed.), *The disadvantaged child.* New York: Basic Books, 1967.

Deutsch, M., & Brown, B. Social influences in Negro–White intelligence differences. *Journal of Social Issues*, 1964, 20, 24–35.

Deutsche, J. M. *The development of children's concepts of causal relationships.* Minneapolis: University of Minnesota Press, 1937.

Devereux, E. C. The role of peer group experience in moral development. In J. P. Hill (Ed.), *Minnesota Symposia on Child Psychology* (Vol. 4). Minneapolis: University of Minnesota Press, 1970.

Dewey, J. *How we think.* Boston: Heath, 1910.

d'Heurle, A., Mellinger, J. C., & Haggard, E. A. Personality, intellectual, and achievement patterns in gifted children. *Psychological Monographs*, 1959, 73, No. 13 (Whole No. 483).

Dickens, S. L., & Hobart, C. Parental dominance and offspring ethnocentrism. *Journal of Social Psychology*, 1959, 49, 297–303.

Diekhoff, J. S. The university as leader and laggard. *Journal of Higher Education*, 1964, *35*, 181–188.

Dienes, Z. P. The growth of mathematical concepts in children through experience. *Educational Researcher*, 1959, *2*, 9–28.

Dienes, Z. P. Insight into arithmetical processes. *School Review*, 1964, *72*, 183–200.

Dillon, H. J. *Early school leavers—a major educational problem.* New York: National Child Labor Committee, 1949.

Dodwell, P. C. Children's understanding of number and related concepts. *Canadian Journal of Psychology*, 1960, *14*, 191–205.

Dodwell, P. C. Children's understanding of number concepts: Characteristics of an individual and a group test. *Canadian Journal of Psychology*, 1961, *15*, 29–36.

Dorsey, M. N., & Hopkins, L. T. The influence of attitude upon transfer. *Journal of Educational Psychology*, 1930, *21*, 410–417.

Dressel, P., Schmid, J., & Kincaid, G. The effect of writing frequency upon essay-type writing proficiency at the college level. *Journal of Educational Research*, 1952, *46*, 285–293.

Drevdahl, J. E. Factors of importance for creativity. *Journal of Clinical Psychology*, 1956, *12*, 21–26.

Drevdahl, J. E., & Cattell, R. B. Personality and creativity in artists and writers. *Journal of Clinical Psychology*, 1958, *14*, 107–111.

Drews, E. M. *The effectiveness of homogeneous and heterogeneous ability grouping in ninth-grade English classes with slow, average, and superior students.* Washington, D.C.: Government Printing Office, 1959.

Duchastel, P. C., & Merrill, P. F. The effects of behavioral objectives on learning: A review of empirical studies. *Review of Educational Research*, 1973, *43*(1), 53–69.

Duel, H. J. Effect of periodic self-evaluation on student achievement. *Journal of Educational Psychology*, 1958, *49*, 197–199.

Duncan, C. P. Transfer in motor learning as a function of degree of first-task learning and intertask similarity. *Journal of Experimental Psychology*, 1953, *45*, 1–11.

Duncan, C. P. Transfer after training with single versus multiple tasks. *Journal of Experimental Psychology*, 1958, *55*, 63–72.

Duncan, C. P. Recent research on human problem solving. *Psychological Bulletin*, 1959, *56*, 397–429.

Duncan, C. P. Induction of a principle. *Quarterly Journal of Experimental Psychology*, 1964, *16*, 373–377.

Duncan, F. M., Signori, E. I., & Rempel, H. Authoritarianism and the closure phenomenon. *Perceptual and Motor Skills*, 1964, *19*, 663–666.

Duncker, K. On problem-solving. *Psychological Monographs*, 1945, *58* (Whole No. 270).

Dunkel, H. B., & Pillet, R. A. A second year of French in the elementary school. *Elementary School Journal*, 1957, *58*, 143–151.

Dunkin, M. J., & Biddle, B. J. *The study of teaching.* New York: Holt, Rinehart and Winston, 1974.

Dunn, L. M. A comparison of the reading processes of mentally retarded and normal boys of the same mental age. *Monographs of the Society for Research in Child Development*, 1954, *19*, 8–99.

Dunn, L. M. Mentally retarded children. In C. W. Harris (Ed.), *Encyclopedia of educational research*. New York: Macmillan, 1960.

Durrett, M. E., & Davy, A. Racial awareness in young Mexican American, Negro, and Anglo children. *Young Children*, 1970, *26*, 16–24.

Dyk, R. B., & Witkin, H. B. Family experience related to the development of differentiation in children. *Child Development*, 1965, *36*, 21–55.

Easley, H. The curve of forgetting and the distribution of practice. *Journal of Educational Psychology*, 1937, *28*, 474–478.

Easley, J. A. Is the teaching of scientific method a significant educational objective? In I. Scheffler (Ed.), *Philosophy and education*. Boston: Allyn and Bacon, 1958.

Easley, J. A. The Physical Science Education Committee and educational theory. *Harvard Educational Review*, 1959, *29*, 4–11.

Easterbrook, J. A. The effect of emotion on cue utilization and the organization of behavior. *Psychological Review*, 1950, *56*, 183–201.

Eaton, M. T. *A survey of the achievement in social studies of 10,220 sixth grade pupils in 464 schools in Indiana*. Bloomington: University of Indiana, 1944.

Eaton, M. T., Weathers, G., & Phillips, B. N. Some reactions of classroom teachers to problem behavior in school. *Educational Administration and Supervision*, 1957, *43*, 129–139.

Ebbinghaus, H. *Memory: A contribution to experimental psychology—1885*. (H. A. Ruger, trans.) New York: Columbia University, Teachers College Press, 1913.

Ebel, R. L. Behavioral objectives: A close look. *Phi Delta Kappan*, 1970, *52*, 171–173.

Eckstrand, G. W., & Wickens, D. P. Transfer of perceptual set. *Journal of Experimental Psychology*, 1954, *47*, 274–278.

Edmonds, M. H. New directions in theories of language acquisition. *Harvard Educational Review*, 1976, *46*(2), 175–198.

Edwards, A. L. Political frames of reference as a factor influencing recognition. *Journal of Abnormal and Social Psychology*, 1941, *36*, 34–50.

Edwards, A. L., & English, H. B. Reminiscence in relation to differential difficulty. *Journal of Experimental Psychology*, 1939, *25*, 100–108.

Edwards, M. P., & Tyler, L. E. Intelligence, creativity, and achievement in a nonselective public junior high school. *Journal of Educational Psychology*, 1965, *56*, 96–99.

Eells, K., Davis, A., and others. *Intelligence and cultural differences. A study of cultural learning and problem-solving*. Chicago: University of Chicago Press, 1951.

Egstrom, G. H. Effects of an emphasis on conceptualizing techniques during early learning of a gross motor skill. *Research Quarterly*, 1964, *35*, 472–481.

Ehrlich, H. J. Dogmatism and learning. *Journal of Abnormal and Social Psychology*, 1961, *62*, 148–149.

Eifermann, R. R., & Etzion, D. Awareness of reversibility: Its effect on performance of converse arithmetical operations. *British Journal of Educational Psychology*, 1964, *34*, 151–157.

Eigen, L. D. High-school student reactions to programmed instruction. *Phi Delta Kappan*, 1963, *44*, 282–285.

Eikenberry, D. H. Permanence of high school learning. *Journal of Educational Psychology*, 1923, *14*, 463–482.

Eisner, E. W. Children's creativity in art: A study of types. *American Educational Research Journal*, 1965, *2*, 125–136.

Eisner, E. W. Educational objectives: Help or hindrance? *School Review*, 1967, *75*, 251–282.

Elkana, Y. Science, philosophy of science, and science teaching. *Educational Philosophy and Theory*, 1970, *2*, 15–35.

Elkind, D. The development of quantitative thinking: A systematic replication of Piaget's studies. *Journal of Genetic Psychology*, 1961, *98*, 37—48. (a)

Elkind, D. Quantity conceptions in junior and senior high school students. *Child Development*, 1961, *32*, 551—560. (b)

Elkind, D. Children's discovery of the conservation of mass, weight, and volume: Piaget replication study II. *Journal of Genetic Psychology*, 1961, *98*, 219—227. (c)

Elkind, D. Quantity conceptions in college students. *Journal of Social Psychology*, 1962, *57*, 459–465.

Elkind, D. Conceptual orientation shifts in children and adolescents. *Child Development*, 1966, *37*, 493–498.

Elkind, D. *Children and adolescents: Interpretative essays on Jean Piaget*. New York: Oxford University Press, 1970.

Ellerbe, C., Jr. Career choices of black students: The road to influential participation. *Journal of Non-white Concerns in Personnel and Guidance*, 1975, *3*(3), 121–124.

Ellis, H. C. Distribution of practice and meaningfulness in verbal learning. *Psychological Reports*, 1960, *6*, 319–325.

Ellis, N. R. Objective-quality discrimination learning sets in mental defectives. *Journal of Comparative and Physiological Psychology*, 1958, *51*, 79–81.

Ellson, D. G. Tutoring. In N. L. Gage, *The psychology of teaching methods*. Chicago: University of Chicago Press, 1976.

Elman, S. *A resumé of performance-based teacher education: What is the state of the art?* Washington, D.C.: American Association of Colleges for Teacher Education, 1972.

Endler, N. S., & Steinberg, D. Prediction of academic achievement at the university level. *Personnel and Guidance*, 1963, *4*, 694–699.

Engelmann, S. Teaching formal operations to preschool advantaged and disadvantaged children. *Ontario Journal of Educational Research*, 1967, *9*, 193–207.

Engle, T. L. High school psychology courses as related to university college courses. *Bulletin of the National Association of Secondary School Principals*, 1957, *41*, 38–42.

English, H. B., Welborn, E. L., & Kilian, C. D. Studies in substance memorization. *Journal of General Psychology*, 1934, *11*, 233–260.

Ennis, R. H. *Conditional logic and children*. Ithaca, N.Y.: Cornell Critical Thinking Project, 1969.

Entwistle, D. R. Attensity: Factors of specific set in school learning. *Harvard Educational Review*, 1961, *31*, 84–101.

Entwistle, N. J. Academic motivation and school attainment. *British Journal of Educational Psychology*, 1968, *38*, 181–188.

Epstein, W., Rock, I., & Zuckerman, C. B. Meaning and familiarity in associative learning. *Psychological Monographs*, 1960, *74* (Whole No. 491).

Ericksen, S. C. The zigzag curve of learning. In L. Siegel (Ed.), *Instruction: Some contemporary viewpoints*. San Francisco: Chandler, 1967.

Ervin, S. M. Training and a logical operation by children. *Child Development*, 1960, *31*, 555–563.

Ervin, S. M. Transfer effects of learning a verbal generalization. *Child Development*, 1960, *31*, 537–554.

Ervin, S. M., & Miller, W. R. Language development. In *Child Psychology*, 62nd Yearbook, National Society for the Study of Education, Part I. Chicago: University of Chicago Press, 1963.

Estes, W. K. An experimental study of punishment. *Psychological Monographs*, 1944, *57*, No. 3.

Estes, W. K. Learning theory and the new "mental chemistry." *Psychological Review*, 1960, *67*, 207–223.

Estes, W. K., Hopkins, B. L., & Crother, E. J. All-or-none and conservation effects in the learning and retention of paired associates. *Journal of Experimental Psychology*, 1960, *60*, 329–339.

Evans, J. L., Glaser, R., & Homme, L. E. An investigation of "teaching machine" variables using learning programs in symbolic logic. Pittsburgh: University of Pittsburgh, Department of Psychology, December, 1960. (a)

Evans, J. L., Glaser, R., & Homme, L. E. *The development and use of a "standard program for investigation of programmed verbal learning."* Paper presented at the meeting of the American Psychological Association, Chicago, September 1960. (b)

Evans, J. L., Glaser, R., & Homme, L. E. A preliminary investigation of variation in the properties of verbal learning sequences of the "teaching machine" type. In A. A. Lumsdaine & R. Glaser (Eds.), *Teaching machines and programmed learning*. Washington, D.C.: National Education Association, 1960. (c)

Ewert, P. H., & Lambert, J. F.    The effect of verbal instructions upon the formation of a concept. *Journal of General Psychology*, 1932, *6*, 400–413.

Eysenck, H. J. *Dimensions of personality*. London: Routledge, 1947.

Ezer, M. Effect of religion upon children's responses to questions involving physical causality. In J. Rosenblith & W. Allinsmith (Eds.), *The causes of behavior: Readings in child development and educational psychology*. Boston: Allyn and Bacon, 1962.

Farley, F. H. Predicting physical persistence from an unsubtle measure of "drive." *Journal of General Psychology*, 1968, *79*, 279–282.

Fast, J. *Body language*. New York: Pocket Books, 1971.

Fattu, N. Exploration of interactions among instruction, content, and aptitude variables. *Journal of Teacher Education*, 1963, *14*, 244–251.

Fawcett, H. P. Teaching for transfer. *Mathematics Teacher*, 1935, *28*, 465–472.

Feather, N. T. The relationship of persistence at a task to expectation of success and achievement related motives. *Journal of Abnormal and Social Psycholgy*, 1961, *63*, 552–561.

Feather, N. T. Level of aspiration and performance variability. *Journal of Personality and Social Psychology*, 1967, *6*(1), 37–46.

Feather, N. T. Change in confidence following success or failure as a prediction of subsequent performance. *Journal of Personality and Social Psychology*, 1968, *9*(1), 38–46.

Feldhusen, J. F., Denny, T., & Condon, C. F. Anxiety, divergent thinking, and achievement. *Journal of Educational Psychology*, 1965, *56*, 40–45.

Feldhusen, J. F., & Klausmeier, H. J. Anxiety, intelligence, and achievement in children of low, average, and high intelligence. *Child Deveolpment*, 1962, *33*, 403–409.

Feldman, K. V., & Klausmeier, H. J. Effects of two kinds of definitions on the concept attainment of fourth and eighth graders. *Journal of Educational Research*, 1974, *67*(5), 219–223.

Ferris, F. L. An achievement test report. In *Review of the Secondary School Physics Program of the Physical Science Study Committee, 1959 Progress Report*. Watertown, Mass.: Educational Services, 1960.

Festinger, L. The motivating effect of cognitive dissonance. In G. Lindsley (Ed.), *Assessment of human motives*. New York: Grove, 1958.

Fiedler, F. E. *Leader attitudes and group effectiveness*. Urbana: University of Illinois Press, 1958.

Fillenbaum, S., & Jackman, A. Dogmatism and anxiety in relation to problem solving: An extension of Rokeach's results. *Journal of Abnormal and Social Psychology*, 1961, *63*, 212–214.

Finlay, G. C. Physical Science Study Committee: A status report. *Science Teacher*, 1959, *26*, 574–581.

Finlay, G. C. Secondary school physics: the Physical Science Study Committee. *American Journal of Physics*, 1960, *28*, 574–581.

Fisher, K. M. A-T science teaching: How effective is it? *Bioscience*, 1976, *26*(11), 691–697.

Fisher, S. Acquiescence and religiosity. *Psychological Reports*, 1964, *15*, 784.

Fisher, S. C. The process of generalizing abstraction and its product the general concept. *Psychological Monographs*, 1916, *21*.

Fishman, E. J., Keller, L., & Atkinson, R. C. Massed versus distributed practice in computerized spelling drills. *Journal of Educational Psychology*, 1968, *59*, 290–296.

Fitch, M. L., Drucker, A. J., & Norton, J. A., Jr. Frequent testing as a motivating factor in large lecture classes. *Journal of Educational Psychology*, 1951, *42*, 1–20.

Fitzgerald, D., & Ausubel, D. P. Cognitive versus affective factors in the learning and retention of controversial material. *Journal of Educational Psychology*, 1963, *54*, 73–84.

Flanders, N. A. Personal-social anxiety as a factor in experimental learning situations. *Journal of Educational Research*, 1951, *45*, 100–110.

Flanders, N. A. *Teacher influence, pupil attitudes and achievement*. Minneapolis: University of Minnesota, College of Education, 1960.

Flanders, N. A. *Analyzing teacher behavior.* Reading, Mass.: Addison Wesley, 1970.

Flanders, N. A., Morrison, B. A., & Brode, E. L. Changes in pupil attitudes during the school year. *Journal of Educational Psychology,* 1968, *59,* 334–338.

Flavell, J. H. *The developmental psychology of Jean Piaget.* Princeton, N.J.: Van Nostrand, 1963.

Flavell, J. H. State-related properties of cognitive development. *Cognitive Psychology,* 1971, *2,* 421–453.

Flavell, J. H., Cooper, A., & Loiselle, R. H. Effect of the number of preutilization functions on functional fixedness in problem solving. *Psychological Reports,* 1958, *4,* 343–350.

Fleishman, E. A. Motor abilities. In R. L. Ebel (Ed.), *Encyclopedia of educational research.* New York: Macmillan, 1969.

Fleming, C. M. Class size as a variable in the teaching situation. *Educational Researcher,* 1959, *1,* 35–48.

Flescher, I. Anxiety and achievement of intellectually gifted and creatively gifted children. *Journal of Psychology,* 1963, *56,* 251–268.

Flook, A. J., & Saggar, U. Academic performance with and without knowledge of scores on tests of intelligence, aptitude, and personality. *Journal of Educational Psychology,* 1968, *59,* 395–401.

Forgus, R. H. The effect of early perceptual learning on the behavioral organization of adult rats. *Journal of Comparative and Physiological Psychology,* 1954, *47,* 331–336.

Forgus, R. H., & Schwartz, R. J. Efficient retention and transfer as affected by learning method. *Journal of Psychology,* 1957, *43,* 135–139.

Forlano, G. *School learning with various methods of practice and rewards.* New York: Columbia University, Teachers College, 1936.

Fowler, W. Teaching a two-year-old to read: An experiment in early childhood learning *Genetic Psychology Monographs,* 1962, *66,* 181–283.

Fowler, W. *Demonstration program in infant care and education.* (Final Report.) Toronto, Ontario: Ontario Institute for Studies in Education, 1971.

Frank, F. Cited by J. S. Bruner, The course of cognitive growth. *American Psychologist,* 1964, *19,* 1–15.

Frankel, E. A comparative study of achieving and under-achieving high school boys of high intellectual ability. *Journal of Educational Research,* 1960, *53,* 172–180.

Frase, L. T. *The effect of social reinforcers in a programmed learning task.* Technical Report No. 11. Urbana: Univeristy of Illinois, Training Research Laboratory, September 1963.

Frazier, E. F. *Negro youth at crossways.* New York: Schocken Books, 1967.

Freedman, J. L. Increasing creativity by free-association training. *Journal of Experimental Psychology,* 1965, *69,* 88–91.

Freedman, J. L., & Landauer, T. K. Retrieval of long-term memory: "Tip-of-the-tongue" phenomenon. *Psychonomic Science,* 1966, *4,* 309–310.

Freeman, F. N., & Flory, C. D. Growth in intellectual ability as measured by repeated tests. *Monographs of the Society for Research in Child Development,* 1937, *2,* No. 2.

Freeman, F. N., Holzinger, K. J., & Mitchell, C. B. The influence of environment on the intelligence, school achievement, and conduct of foster children. In 27th

Yearbook, National Society for the Study of Education, Part I, 1928.

Freibergs, V., & Tulving, E. The effect of practice on utilization of information from positive and negative instances in concept formation. *Canadian Journal of Psychology*, 1961, *15*, 101–106.

French, E. G., & Thomas, F. H. The relation of achievement motivation to problem solving. *Journal of Abnormal and Social Psychology*, 1958, *56*, 45–48.

French, J. W. Aptitude and interest score patterns related to satisfaction with college major field. *Educational and Psychological Measurement*, 1961, *21*, 287–294.

French, J. W. New tests for predicting the performance of college students with high-level aptitude. *Journal of Educational Psychology*, 1964, *55*, 185–194.

French, R. S. The effect of instructions on the length-difficulty relationship for a task involving sequential dependency. *Journal of Experimental Psychology*, 1954, *48*, 89–97.

Freud, A., & Burlingham, D. *Infants without families*. New York: International Universities, 1944.

Freyberg, P. S. Concept development in Piagetian terms in relation to school achievement. *Journal of Educational Psychology*, 1966, *57*, 164–168.

Frutchey, F. P. Retention in high school chemistry. *Journal of Higher Education*, 1937, *8*, 217–218.

Fry, E. G. A study of teaching machine response modes. In A. A. Lumsdaine & R. Glaser, (Eds.) *Teaching machines and programmed learning*. Washington, D.C.: National Education Association, 1960.

Fryatt, M. J., & Tulving, E. Interproblem transfer in identification of concepts involving positive and negative instances. *Canadian Journal of Psychology*, 1963, *17*, 106–117.

Fund for the Advancement of Education. *They went to college early*. New York: Author, 1957.

Furth, H. G. Concerning Piaget's view on thinking and symbol formation. *Child Development*, 1967, *38*, 819–826.

Furth, H. G. *Piaget for teachers*. Englewood Cliffs, N.J.: Prentice-Hall, 1970.

Gage, N. L. Theories of teaching. In *Theories of learning and instruction*, 63rd Yearbook, National Society for the Study of Education, Part I. Chicago: University of Chicago Press, 1964.

Gagné, R. M. The acquisition of knowledge. *Psychological Review*, 1962, *69*, 355–365. (a)

Gagné, R. M. Military training and principles of learning. *American Psychologist*, 1962, *17*, 83–91. (b)

Gagné, R. M. *The conditions of learning*. New York: Holt, Rinehart and Winston, 1965, 1970, 1977.

Gagné, R. M. Instruction and the conditions of learning. In L. Siegel (Ed.), *Instruction: Some contemporary viewpoints*. San Francisco: Chandler, 1967.

Gagné, R. M. Contributions of learning to human development. *Psychological Review*, 1968, *75*, 177–191.

Gagné, R. M. Learning hierarchies. *Educational Psychologist*, 1968, *6*, 1–3; 6; 9.

Gagné, R. M., & Briggs, L. J. *Principles of instructional design*. New York: Holt, Rinehart and Winston, 1974.

Gagné, R. M., Brown, L. T. Some factors in the programming of conceptual material. *Journal of Experimental Psychology*, 1961, *62*, 313–321.

Gagné, R. M., & Dick, W. Learning measures in a self-instructional problem in solving equations. *Psychological Reports*, 1962, *10*, 131–146.

Gagné, R. M., Mayor, J. R., Garstens, H. L., & Paradise, N. E. Factors in acquiring knowledge of a mathematical task. *Psychological Monographs*, 1962, *76* (Whole No. 526).

Gagné, R. M., & Paradise, N. E. Abilities and learning sets in knowledge acquisition. *Psychological Monographs*, 1961, *75*, Whole No. 518).

Gagné, R. M., & Smith, E. C. A study of the effects of verbalization on problem solving. *Journal of Experimental Psychology*, 1962, *63*, 12–16.

Gaier, E. L., & Wamback, H. Self-evaluation of personality assets and liabilities of Southern white and Negro students. *Journal of Social Psychology*, 1960, *51*, 135–143.

Gall, M. D., & Gall, J. P. The discussion method. In N. L. Gage (Ed.), *The psychology of teaching methods*. Chicago: University of Chicago Press, 1976.

Gallagher, J. J. Productive thinking. In M. L. Hoffman & L. W. Hoffman (Eds.), *Review of child development research* (Vol. 1). New York: Russell Sage Foundation, 1964.

Gallagher, J. J., & Lucito, L. J. Intellectual patterns of gifted compared with average and retarded children. *Exceptional Children*, 1961, *27*, 479–482.

Galperin, P. Y. An experimental study in the formation of mental actions. In B. Simon (Ed.), *Psychology in the Soviet Union*. Stanford, Calif.: Stanford University Press, 1957.

Gardner, R. A., & Gardner, B. T. Teaching sign language to a chimpanzee. *Science*, 1969, *165*, 664–672.

Gardner, R. W., Jackson, D. N., & Messick, S. J. Personality organization in cognitive controls and intellectual abilities. *Psychological Issues*, 2, No. 4. New York: International Universities, 1960.

Gardner, R. W., & Schlesinger, H. J. Tolerance for unrealistic experiences: A study of the generality of cognitive control. *British Journal of Psychology*, 1962, *53*, 41–55.

Garrett, H. E. A developmental theory of intelligence. *American Psychologist*, 1946, *1*, 372–378.

Garrett, H. E., Bryan, A. I., & Perl, R. E. The age factor in mental organization. *Archives of Psychology*, 1935 (Whole No. 175).

Garside, R. F. The prediction of examination marks of mechanical engineering students at King's College, Newcastle. *British Journal of Psychology*, 1957, *48*, 219–220.

Garverick, C. M. Retention of school learning as influenced by selective affective tone variables. *Journal of Educational Psychology*, 1964, *55*, 31–34.

Gates, A. I. Recitation as a factor in memorizing. *Archives of Psychology*, 1917, 7 (Whole No. 40).

Gates, A. I. The necessary mental age for beginning reading. *Elementary School Journal*, 1937, *37*, 497–508.

Gates, A. I., & Taylor, G. A. An experimental study of the nature of improvement resulting from practice in a motor function. *Journal of Educational Psychology*, 1926, *17*, 226–236.

Geisinger, R. W. The discovery variable: What is it? *Psychology*, 1968, *5*(1), 2–9.

Gellerman, L. W. The double alternation problem: II. The behavior of children and human adults in a double alternation temporal maze. *Journal of Genetic Psychology*, 1931, *39*, 197–226.

Gelman, R. Conservation acquisition: A problem of learning to attend to relevant attributes. *Journal of Experimental Child Psychology*, 1969, *7*, 167–187.

George, C. L'anticipation dans la résolution d'une tâche complexe. *Anné Psychologique*, 1964, *64*, 83–100.

Gesell, A. The ontogenesis of infant behavior. In L. Carmichael (Ed.), *Manual of child psychology* (2nd ed.). New York: Wiley, 1954.

Getzels, J. W., & Jackson, P. W. The highly intelligent and the highly creative adolescent: A summary of some research findings. In C. W. Taylor (Ed.), *The third University of Utah research conference on the identification of creative scientific talent*. Salt Lake City: University of Utah Press, 1959.

Getzels, J. W., & Jackson, P. W. *Creativity and intelligence: Explorations with gifted students*. New York: Wiley, 1962.

Geyer, M. T. Influence of changing the expected time of recall. *Journal of Experimental Psychology*, 1930, *13*, 290–292.

Gibb, E. G. Children's thinking in the process of subtraction. *Journal of Experimental Education*, 1956, *25*, 71–80.

Gibby, R. G. Sr., & Gibby, R. G. Jr. The effects of stress resulting from academic failure. *Journal of Clinical Psychology*, 1967, *23*(1), 35–37.

Gibson, E. J., & Levin, H. *The psychology of reading*. Cambridge: Massachusetts Institute of Technology Press, 1975.

Gibson, E. J., & Walk, R. D. The effect of prolonged exposure to visually presented patterns on learning to discriminate between them. *Journal of Comparative and Physiological Psychology*, 1956, *49*, 239–242.

Gibson, J. J. Social psychology and the psychology of perceptual learning. In M. Sherif & M. O. Wilson (Eds.), *Group relations at the crossroads*. New York: Harper & Row, 1953.

Gilbert, T. F. Overlearning and the retention of meaningful prose. *Journal of General Psychology*, 1957, *56*, 281–289.

Gilmore, J. U. The factor of attention in underachievement. *Journal of Education*, 1968, *150*(3), 41–66.

Glaser, R. Instructional technology and the measurement of learning outcomes: Some questions. *American Psychologist*, 1963, *18*, 519–521.

Glaser, R. (Ed.) *Teaching machines and programmed learning. II: Data and directions*. Washington, D.C.: National Education Association, 1965.

Glaser, R. Components of a psychology of instruction: Toward a science of design. *Review of Educational Research*, 1976, *46*, 1–24.

Glaser, R., & Nitko, A. J. Measurement in learning and instruction. In R. L. Thorndike (Ed.), *Educational measurement* (2nd ed.). Washington, D.C.: American Council on Education, 1971.

Glaze, J. A. The association value of nonsense syllables. *Journal of Genetic Psychology*, 1928, *35*, 255–267.

Gnagey, W. J. *The relationship of parental acceptance to the professional attitudes and academic achievement of students in teacher education*. Paper read before the American Educational Research Association, February 1966.

Goff, R. M. *Problems and emotional difficulties of Negro children*. New York: Columbia University, Teachers College, 1949.

Goldbeck, R. A. *The effect of response mode and learning material difficulty on automated instruction. Technical Report No. 1.* Santa Barbara, Calif.: American Institute for Research, September 1960.

Goldbeck, R. A., & Briggs, L. J. *An analysis of response mode and feedback factors in automated instruction. Technical Report No. 2.* Santa Barbara, Calif.: American Institute for Research, November 1960.

Goldbeck, R. A., & Campbell, V. N. The effects of response mode and response difficulty on programmed learning. *Journal of Educational Psychology,* 1962, *53*, 110–118.

Goldbeck, R. A., Campbell, V. N., & Llewellyn, J. E. *Further experimental evidence on response modes in automated instruction. Technical Report No. 3.* Santa Barbara, Calif.: American Institute for Research, December 1960.

Golden, M., & Birns, B. Social class and cognitive development in infancy. *Merrill-Palmer Quarterly,* 1968, *14*(2), 139–149.

Goldfarb, W. Psychological privation in infancy and subsequent adjustment. *American Journal of Orthopsychiatry,* 1945, *15*, 247–255.

Goldman, A. E., & Levine, M. A developmental study of object sorting. *Child Development,* 1963, *34*, 649–666.

Goldman, M. A comparison of individual and group performance for varying combinations of initial ability. *Journal of Personality and Social Psycholology,* 1965, *1*, 210–216.

Goldman, R. J. The application of Piaget's schema of operational thinking to religious story data by means of the Guttman scalogram. *British Journal of Educational Psychology,* 1965, *35*, 158–170.

Goldstein, K., & Scheerer, M. Abstract and concrete behavior: An experimental study with special tests. *Psychological Monograph,* 1941, *53*(2), 151.

Gollin, E. S. Organizational characteristics of social judgment: A developmental investigation. *Journal of Personality,* 1958, *26*, 139–154.

Good, T. L., Biddle, B. J., & Brophy, J. E. *Teachers make a difference.* New York: Holt, Rinehart and Winston, 1975.

Goodenough, F. L. New evidence on environmental influence on intelligence. In 39th Yearbook, National Society for the Study of Education, Part I. Chicago: University of Chicago Press, 1940.

Goodenough, F. L. *Developmental psychology.* New York: Appleton-Century, 1945.

Goodenough, F. L., & Brian, C. R. Certain factors underlying the acquisition of motor skill by preschool children. *Journal of Experimental Psychology,* 1929, *12*, 127–155.

Goodlad, J. I. Research and theory regarding promotion and nonpromotion. *Elementary School Journal,* 1952, *53*, 150–155.

Goodlad, J. I. School organization. In D. W. Allen & E. Seifman (Eds.), *The teachers handbook.* Glenview, Ill.: Scott, Foresman, 1971.

Goodman, M. E. *Race awareness in young children.* Cambridge: Addison-Wesley, 1952.

Goodnow, J. J., & Bethon, G. Piaget's tasks: The effects of schooling and intelligence. *Child Development,* 1966, *37*, 574–582.

Gordon, C., & Shea, P. D. *Self-conceptions in family structures of disadvantaged youths: An interim report for the Director of Upward Bound.* Paper presented at Sixty-second Annual Meeting of the American Sociological Association, San Francisco, Calif., August 1967.

Gordon, H. Class results with spaced and unspaced memorizing. *Journal of Experimental Psychology*, 1925, *8*(5), 337–343.

Gordon, H. Mental and scholastic tests among retarded children: An enquiry into the effects of schooling on the various tests. *Educational Pamphlets, Board of Education*, London, 1923, No. 44.

Gough, H. G. Academic achievement in high school as predicted from the California Psychological Inventory. *Journal of Educational Psychlogy*, 1964, *55*, 174–180.

Gough, P. B. (Almost a decade of) Experimental psycholinguistics. In W. O. Dingwall (Ed.), *A survey of linguistic science*. College Park: University of Maryland Linguistics Program, 1971.

Grace, G. L. The relation of personality characteristics and response to verbal approval in a learning task. *Genetic Psychology Monographs*, 1948, *37*, 73–103.

Granit, A. R. A study on the perception of form. *Journal of Experimental Psychology*, 1921, *12*, 223–247.

Grant, E. I. The effect of certain factors in the home environment upon child behavior. *University of Iowa Studies in Child Welfare*, 1939, *17*, 61–94.

Gray, S. W., & Klaus, R. A. An experimental pre-school program for culturally deprived children. *Child Development*, 1965, *36*(4), 887–898.

Gray, S. W., & Klaus, R. A. The early training project: A seventh year report. *Child Development*, 1970, *41*, 909–924.

Graybill, L. Sex differences in problem-solving ability. *Journal of Research in Science Teaching*, 1975, *12*(4), 341–346.

Green, R. F., & Berkowitz, B. Changes in intellect with age: II. Factorial analysis of Wechsler-Bellevue scores. *Journal of Genetic Psychology*, 1964, *104*, 3–11.

Greenberg, H., Chase, A. L., & Cannon, T. M. Attitudes of white and Negro high school students in a west Texas town toward school integration. *Journal of Applied Psychology*, 1957, *41*, 27–31.

Greenberg, H., & Fane, D. An investigation of several variables as determinants of authoritarianism. *Journal of Social Psychology*, 1959, *49*, 195–211.

Greenberger, E., Woldman, J., & Yourshaw, S. W. Components of curiosity: Berlyne reconsidered. *British Journal of Psychology*, 1967, *58*(3–4), 375–386.

Greenfield, P. M. On culture and conservation. In J. S. Bruner (Ed.), *Studies in cognitive growth*. New York: Wiley, 1966.

Greenwald, A. G. The open-mindedness of the counterattitudinal role player. *Journal of Expreimental Social Psychology*, 1969, *5*(4), 375–388.

Griffin, M., & Beier, E. G. Subliminal prior solution cues in problem solving. *Journal of General Psychology*, 1961, *65*, 219–227.

Grigsby, O. J. An experimental study of the development of concepts of relationship in preschool children as evidenced by their expressive ability. *Journal of Experimental Education*, 1932, *1*, 144–162.

Grodskaya, N. V. On the development of thinking of pupils in the process of mastery of homogeneous concepts. *Voprosky Psikhologii*, 1962, No. 3, 106–116.

Gronlund, N. E. The accuracy of teachers' judgments concerning the sociometric status of sixth-grade pupils. *Sociometry*, 1950, *13*, 197–225; 329–357.

Grooms, R. R., & Endler, N. S. The effects of anxiety on academic achievement. *Journal of Educational Psychology*, 1960, *51*, 299–304.

Gross, M. L. *The brain watchers.* New York: Random House, 1962.

Gross, M. M. The effect of certain types of motivation on the "honesty" of children. *Journal of Educational Research*, 1946, *40*, 133–140.

Grossack, M. M. Some personality characteristics of southern Negro students. *Journal of Social Psychology*, 1957, *46*, 125–131.

Grote, C. N. A comparison of the relative effectiveness of direct-detailed and directed discovery methods of teaching selected principles of mechanics in the area of physics. Unpubilshed doctoral dissertation, University of Illinois, 1960.

Grotelueschen, A. D. *Differentially structured introductory learning materials and learning tasks.* New York: Columbia University, 1967.

Grotelueschen, A., & Sjogren, D. D. Effects of differentially structured introductory materials and learning tasks on learning and transfer. *American Educational Research Journal*, 1968, *5*(2), 191–202.

Gubrud, A. R., & Novak, J. D. Learning achievement and the efficiency of learning the concept of vector addition at three different grade levels. *Science Education*, 1973, *57*(2), 179–191.

Guilford, J. P. Creativity. *American Psychologist*, 1950, *9*, 444–454.

Guilford, J. P. Three faces of intellect. *American Psychologist*, 1959, *14*, 469–479.

Guilford, J. P. Zero correlations among tests of intellectual abilities. *Psychological Bulletin*, 1964, *61*, 401–404.

Guilford, J. P. Intelligence: 1965 model. *American Psychologist*, 1966, *21*, 20–26.

Guilford, J. P., & Christensen, P. R. The one-way relationship between creative potential and IQ. *Journal of Creative Behavior*, 1973, *7*(4), 247–252.

Guilford, J. P., & Merrifield, P. R. The structure of the intellect model: Its uses and implications. *Psychological Laboratory Report No. 24.* Los Angeles: University of Southern California, 1960.

Guilford, J. P., Wilson, R. C., Christensen, P. R., & Lewis, D. J. A factor-analytic study of creative thinking: I. Hypotheses and description of tests. *Psychological Laboratory Report No. 4.* Los Angeles: University of Southern California, 1951.

Gurnee, H. Group learning. *Psychological Monographs*, 1962, *76*(13, Whole No. 532).

Gustafson, L. Relationship between ethnic group membership and the retention of selected facts pertaining to American history and culture. *Journal of Educational Sociology*, 1957, *31*, 49–56.

Guthrie, E. R. *The psychology of learning.* New York: Harper & Row, 1952.

Gutteridge, M. V. *The duration of attention in young children.* Melbourne: University of Melbourne Press, 1935.

Hafner, A. J., & Kaplan, A. M. Children's manifest anxiety and intelligence. *Child Development*, 1959, *30*, 269–271.

Hagen, J. W. The effect of distraction on selective attention. *Child Development*, 1967, *38*, 685–694.

Hagen, P. E. A factor analysis of the Wechsler Intelligence Scale for Children. *Dissertation Abstracts*, 1952, *12*, 722–723.

Haggard, E. A. Social status and intelligence: An experimental study of certain cultural determinants of measured intelligence. *Genetic Psychology Monographs*, 1954, *49*, 141–186.

Hall, W. F., & Demarest, R. Effect on achievement scores of a change in promotional policy. *Elementary School Journal*, 1958, *58*, 204–207.

Hambleton, R. K. Testing and decision-making procedures for selected individualized instructional programs. *Review of Educational Research*, 1974, *44*(4), 371–400.

Hamilton, C. E. The relationship between length of interval separating two learning tasks and performance on the second task. *Journal of Experimental Psychology*, 1950, *40*, 613–621.

Hamilton, G. V. N. A study of perseverance reactions in primates and rodents. *Behavior Monographs*, *3*, No. 2, 1916.

Hamilton, N. R. Effects of logical versus random sequencing of items in an autoinstructional program under two conditions of covert response. *Journal of Educational Psychology*, 1964, *55*, 258–266.

Hammer, E. F. *Creativity: An exploratory investigation of the personalities of gifted adolescent artists.* New York: Random House, 1961.

Hammond, S. B., & Cox, F. Some antecedents of educational attainment. *Australian Journal of Psychology*, 1967, *19*(3), 231–240.

Hanesian, H., Hutchinson, M., Diller, L., & Gordon, W. Response patterns in brain injured children and teaching style. *Proceedings of the 81st Annual Convention of the American Psychological Association*, 1973, *8*, 677–678.

Hanesian, H., & Regan, J. *Brooklyn College/John Jay high school cluster project.* Annual report, Brooklyn College, City University of New York, 1976.

Hanson, J. T. Ninth-grade girls' vocational choices and their parents' occupational level. *Vocational Guidance Quarterly*, 1965, *13*, 261–264.

Harari, H., & McDavid, J. W. Cultural influences on retention of logical and symbolic material. *Journal of Educational Psychology*, 1966, *57*, 18–22.

Harlow, H. F. The formation of learning sets. *Psychological Review*, 1949, *56*, 51–65.

Harlow, H. F. Learning and satiation of response in intrinsically motivated complex puzzle performance by monkeys. *Journal of Comparative and Physiological Psychology*, 1950, *43*, 289–294.

Harlow, H. F. Motivation as a factor in the acquisition of new responses. In *Current theory and research in motivation.* Lincoln: University of Nebraska Press, 1953.

Harootunian, B., & Tate, M. The relationship of certain selected variables to problem solving ability. *Journal of Educational Psychology*, 1960, *51*, 326–333.

Harris, D. B. Child development. In *Recent research and developments and their implications for teacher education.* 30th Yearbook, *American Association of Colleges of Teacher Education*, Washington, D.C.: The Association, 1960.

Harris, R. C. Concept learning as a function of type, identifiability, and variety of instructional instances. *Journal of Educational Research*, 1973, *67*, 182–189.

Hart, F. W. *Teachers and teaching.* New York: Macmillan, 1934.

Hart, I. Maternal child-rearing practices and authoritarian ideology. *Journal of Abnormal and Social Psychology*, 1957, *55*, 232–237.

Hart, J. T. Memory and the feeling-of-knowing experience. *Journal of Educational Psychology*, 1965, *56*, 208–216.

Hartley, J., & Davies, I. K. Pre-instructional strategies: The role of pre-tests, behavioral objectives, overviews, and advance organizers. *Review of Educational Research*, 1976, *46*, 239–265.

Hartogs, R. The clinical investigation and differential measurement of anxiety. *American Journal of Psychiatry*, 1950, *106*, 929–934.

Hartshorne, H., & May, M. A. *Studies in the nature of character: Vol. I. Studies in deceit.* New York: Macmillan, 1928.

Hartson, L. Does college training influence test intelligence? *Journal of Educational Psychology*, 1936, *27*, 481–491.

Hartung, M. L. Teaching of mathematics in senior high school and junior college. *Review of Educational Research*, 1942, *12*, 425–434.

Harvey, O. J. Authoritarianism and conceptual functioning in varied conditions. *Journal of Personality*, 1963, *31*, 462–470.

Haselrud, G. M. Transfer from context by sub-threshold summation. *Journal of Educational Psychology*, 1959, *50*, 254–258.

Haselrud, G. M., & Meyers, S. The transfer value of given and individually derived principles. *Journal of Educational Psychology*, 1958, *49*, 293–298.

Hastings, J. T. Tensions and school achievement examination. *Journal of Experimental Education*, 1944, *12*, 143–164.

Haveman, J. E. The effects of similarity and method of retention measurement in retroactive interference paradigms involving meaningful verbal learning. Paper presented at the meeting of the American Educational Research Association, New York, 1971.

Havighurst, R. J. Minority subcultures and the law of effect. *American Psychologist*, 1970, *25*, 313–325.

Havighurst, R. J., & Breese, F. H. Relation between ability and social status in a Mid-Western community: III. Primary mental abilities. *Journal of Educational Psychology*, 1947, *38*, 241–247.

Havighurst, R. J., & Janke, L. L. Relations between ability and social status in a Mid-Western community: I. Ten-year-old children. *Journal of Educational Psychology*, 1944, *35*, 357–368.

Havighurst, R. J., & Newgarten, B. J. *Society and education* (2nd ed.). Boston: Allyn & Bacon, 1962.

Havighurst, R. J., & Taba, H. *Adolescent character and personality.* New York: Wiley, 1949.

Haygood, R. C., & Bourne, L. E. Forms of relevant stimulus redundancy in concept identification. *Journal of Experimental Psychology*, 1964, *67*, 392–397.

Hazlitt, V. Children's thinking. *British Journal of Psychology*, 1930, *20*, 354–361.

Hebb, D. O. *The organization of behavior.* New York: Wiley, 1949.

Heidbreder, E. F. Reasons used in solving problems. *Journal of Experimental Psychology*, 1927, *10*, 397–414.

Heidbreder, E. F. Problem solving in children and adults. *Journal of Genetic Psychology*, 1928, *35*, 522–545.

Heidbreder, E. F., & Zimmerman, C. The attainment of concepts: IX. Semantic efficiency and concept attainment. *Journal of Psychology*, 1955, *40*, 325–335.

Heinonen, V. *Differentiation of primary mental abilities.* Jyvaskyla, Finland: Kusstantajat Publishers, 1963.

Hendrickson, G., & Schroeder, W. H. Transfer of training in learning to hit a submerged target. *Journal of Educational Psychology*, 1941, *32*, 205–213.

Hendrix, G. A new clue to transfer of training. *Elementary School Journal*, 1947, *48*, 197–208.

Hendrix, G. Prerequisite to meaning. *Mathematics Teacher*, 1950, *43*, 334–339.

Hendrix, G. Learning by discovery. *Mathematics Teacher*, 1961, 54, 290–299.

Henrysson, S. Gathering, analyzing, and using data on test items. In R. L. Thorndike (Ed.), *Educational measurement* (2nd ed.). Washington, D.C.: American Council on Education, 1971.

Hergenham, B. R., & Lee, P. Influence of degree of intentional learning upon the performance of an incidental task. *Psychological Reports*, 1965, *16*(3, Pt. 1), 781–785.

Herr, D. M. The sentiment of white supremacy: An ecological study. *American Journal of Sociology*, 1959, *64*, 592–598.

Herrick, V. E. Administrative structure and processes in curriculum development. *Review of Educational Research*, 1960, *30*, 258–274.

Herrick, V. E., & Tyler, R. W. Toward improved curriculum theory. *Supplementary Educational Monograph*, No. 71. Chicago: University of Chicago Press, 1950.

Hershberger, W. Self-evaluational responding and typographical cueing: Techniques for programming self-instructional reading materials. *Journal of Educational Psychology*, 1964, *55*, 288–296.

Hess, E. H. Imprinting. *Science*, 1959, *130*, 133–141.

Hess, R. D. Social class and ethnic influences upon socialization. In P. A. Mussen (Ed.), *Carmichael's manual of child psychology* (Vol. 2) (3rd ed.). New York: Wiley, 1970.

Hess, R. D. & Goldblatt, I. The status of adolescents in American society: A problem in social identity. *Child Development* 1957, *28*, 459–468.

Hess, R. D., & Shipman, V. C. Early experience and the socialization of cognitive modes in children. *Child Development*, 1965, *36*, 869–886.

Hess, R. D., & Shipman, V. C. Maternal influences upon learning: The cognitive environments of urban pre-school children. In R. D. Hess & R. M. Bear (Eds.), *Early education: Current theory, research, and action*. Chicago: Aldine, 1968.

Hibbard, K. M., & Novak, J. D. Audio-tutorial elementary school science instruction as a method for study of children's concept learning: Particulate nature of matter. *Science Education*, 1975, *59*(4), 559–570.

Hibbs, A. R. Science for elementary students. *Teachers College Record*, 1961, *63*, 136–142.

Hildreth, G. E. The difficulty reduction tendency in perception and problem solving. *Journal of Educational Psychology*, 1941, *32*, 305–313.

Hildreth, G. E. The simplification tendency in reproducing designs. *Journal of Genetic Psychology*, 1944, *64*, 327–333.

Hilgard, E. R. A perspective on the relationship between learning theory and educational practices. In *Theories of learning and instruction*, 63rd Yearbook, National Society for the Study of Education, Part I. Chicago: University of Chicago Press, 1964.

Hilgard, E. R., Edgren, R. D., & Irvine, R. P. Errors in transfer following learning with understanding: Further studies with Katona's card trick experiments. *Journal of Experimental Psychology,* 1954, *47,* 457–464.

Hilgard, E. R., Irvine, R. P., & Whipple, J. E. Rote memorization, understanding, and transfer: An extension of Katona's card trick experiments. *Journal of Experimental Psychology,* 1953, *46,* 288–292.

Hill, D. S. Personification of ideals by urban children. *Journal of Social Psychology,* 1930, *1,* 379–392.

Hill, K. T., & Sarason, S. B. The relàtion of test anxiety and defensiveness to test and school performance over the elementary school years: A further longitudinal study. *Monographs of the Society for Research in Child Development,* 1966, *31*(2).

Hill, M. C. Research on the Negro family. *Marriage and Family Living,* 1957, *19,* 25–31.

Hill, S. A. *A study of the logical abilities of children.* Unpublished doctoral dissertation, Stanford University, 1961.

Hill, W. F. Activity as an autonomous drive. *Journal of Comparative and Physiological Psychology,* 1956, *49,* 15–19.

Hiller, J. H. Verbal response indicators of conceptual vagueness. *American Educational Research Journal,* 1971, *8*(1), 151–161.

Hiller, J. H., Fisher, G. A., & Kaess, W. A computer investigation of verbal characteristics of effective classroom lecturing. *American Educational Research Journal,* 1969, *6*(4), 661–675.

Hillix, W. A., & Marx, M. H. Response strengthening by information and effect in human learning. *Journal of Experimental Psychology,* 1960, *60,* 97–102.

Hitt, W. D., & Stock, J. R. The relationship between psychological characteristics and creative behavior. *Psychological Record,* 1965, *15,* 133–140.

Hodges, A. A developmental study of symbolic behavior. *Child Development,* 1954, *25,* 277–280.

Hoffman, H. N. A study in an aspect of concept formation, with subnormal, average, and superior adolescents. *Genetic Psychology Monographs,* 1955, *52,* 191–239.

Hoffman, L. R., Burke, R. J., & Maier, N. R. F. Does training with differential reinforcement on similar problems help in solving a new problem? *Psychological Reports,* 1963, *13,* 147–154.

Hoffmann, B. *The tyranny of testing.* New York: Crowell-Collier, 1962.

Hohn, F. E. Teaching creativity in mathematics. *The Arithmetic Teacher,* 1961, *8,* 102–106.

Holaday, P. W., & Stoddard, G. D. Getting ideas from movies. In W. W. Charters, P. W. Holaday, & G. D. Stoddard (Eds.), *Motion pictures and youth.* New York: Macmillan, 1933.

Holland, J. G. Teaching machines: An application of machines from the laboratory. In A. A. Lumsdaine & R. Glaser (Eds.), *Teaching machines and programmed learning.* Washington, D.C.: National Education Association, 1960.

Holland, J. G., & Porter, D. The influence of repetition of incorrectly answered items in a teaching-machine program. *Journal of Experimental Analysis of Behavior,* 1961, *4,* 305–307.

Holland, J. L. Creative and academic performance among talented adolescents. *Journal of Educational Psychology*, 1961, 52, 136–147.

Hollingshead, A. B. *Elmtown's youth*. New York: Wiley, 1949.

Holloway, H. D. Effects of training on the SRA Primary Mental Abilities (primary) and the WISC. *Child Development*, 1954, 25, 253–263.

Holt, G. L. Effect of reinforcement contingencies in increasing programmed reading and mathematics behaviors in first-grade children. *Journal of Experimental Psychology*, 1972, 12, 362–369.

Holt, J. *How children fail*. New York: Pitman, 1964.

Holzman, P. S., & Gardner, R. W. Leveling-sharpening and memory reorganization. *Journal of Abnormal and Social Psychology*, 1960, 61, 176–180.

Homme, L. E., & Glaser, R. Problems in programming verbal sequences. In A. A. Lumsdaine & R. Glaser (Eds.), *Teaching machines and programmed learning*. Washington, D.C.: National Education Association, 1960.

Honzik, M. P. Developmental studies of parent–child resemblance in intelligence. *Child Development*, 1957, 28, 215–228.

Honzik, M. P., Macfarlane, J. W., & Allen, L. The stability of mental test performance between two and eighteen years. *Journal of Experimental Education*, 1948, 17, 309–324.

Hood, H. B. An experimental study of Piaget's theory of the development of number in children. *British Journal of Psychology*, 1962, 53, 273–286.

Horn, J. L., & Cattell, R. B. Age differences in fluid and crystallized intelligence. *Acta Psychologica*, Amsterdam, 1967, 26(2), 107–129.

Horney, K. *The neurotic personality of our time*. New York: Norton, 1937.

Horney, K. *New ways in psychoanalysis*. New York: Norton, 1939.

Horowitz, F., & Paden, L. The effectiveness of environmental intervention programs. In B. M. Caldwell & H. N. Riccuiti (Eds.), *Review of child development research* (Vol. 3). New York: Russell Sage Foundation, 1970.

House, B. J., & Zeaman, D. Positive discrimination and reversals in low grade retardates. *Journal of Comparative and Physiological Psychology*, 1959, 52, 564–565.

Houston, S. H. Reexamination of some assumptions about the language of the disadvantaged child. *Child Development*, 1970, 3, 947–963.

Houtz, J. C., & Moore, W. J. Effects of different types of positive and negative instances in learning "nondimensioned" concepts. *Journal of Educational Psychology*, 1973, 64(2), 205–211.

Hovland, C. I. Experimental studies in rote-learning theory: III. Distribution of practice with varying speeds of syllable presentation. *Journal of Experimental Psychology*, 1938, 23, 172–190.

Hovland, C. I. Experimental studies in rote-learning theory: V. Comparison of distribution of practice in serial and paired-associate learning. *Journal of Experimental Psychology*, 1939, 25, 622–633.

Hovland, C. I. Experimental studies in rote-learning theory: VI. Comparison of retention following learning to the same criterion by massed and distributed practice. *Journal of Experimental Psychology*, 1940, 26, 568–587. (a)

Hovland, C. I. Experimental studies in rote-learning theory: VII. Distribution of practice with varying lengths of list. *Journal of Experimental Psychology*, 1940, 27, 271–284. (b)

Hovland, C. I. Experimental studies in rote-learning theory: VIII. Distributed practice of paired associates with varying rates of presentation. *Journal of Experimental Psychology*, 1949, *39*, 714–718.

Hovland, C. I. A communication analysis of concept formation. *Psychological Review*, 1952, *59*, 175–182.

Hovland, C. I., Lumsdaine, A. A., & Sheffield, F. D. *Experiments on mass communication*. Princeton, N.J.: Princeton University Press, 1949.

Hovland, C. I., & Weiss, W. Transmission of information concerning concepts through positive and negative instances. *Journal of Experimental Psychology*, 1953, *45*, 175–182.

Huang, I. Experimental studies on the role of repetition, organization, and the intention to learn in rote memory. *Journal of General Psychology*, 1944, *31*, 213–217.

Huang, I., & Lee, H. W. Experimental analysis of child animism. *Journal of Genetic Psychology*, 1945, *66*, 69–74.

Hudgins, B. B., & Gore, J. Classroom recitation: The effects of interaction patterns upon learning. *Journal of General Psychology*, 1966, *75*(2), 243–247.

Huelsman, C. B. Jr. Note on absent children. *Psychological Reports*, 1968, *22*(2), 470.

Hughes, J. L., & McNamara, W. J. A comparative study of programmed and conventional instruction in industry. *Journal of Applied Psychology*, 1961, *45*, 225–231.

Hull, C. L. Quantitative aspects of the evolution of concepts. *Psychological Monographs*, 1920, *28* (Whole No. 123).

Hull, C. L. *Principles of behavior*. New York: Appleton-Century, 1943.

Hunt, J. McV. *Intelligence and experience*. New York: Ronald, 1961.

Hurlock, E. B. The value of praise and reproof as incentives for children. *Archives of Psychology*, 1924, *11*, No. 71.

Huttenlocher, J. Some effects of negative instances on the formation of simple concepts. *Psychological Reports*, 1962, *11*, 35–42.

Hyram, G. H. An experiment in developing critical thinking in children. *Journal of Experimental Education*, 1957, *26*, 125–132.

Illich, I. *Deschooling society*. New York: Harper & Row, 1970.

Inhelder, B., & Piaget, J. *The growth of logical thinking from childhood to adolescence*. New York: Basic Books, 1958.

Inhelder, B., Sinclair, H., & Banet, M. *Learning and the development of cognition*. Cambridge, Mass.: Harvard University Press, 1974.

Irion, A. L. Retention and warming-up effects on paired-associate learning. *Journal of Experimental Psychology*, 1949, *39*, 669–675.

Irion, A. L., & Briggs, L. J. Learning task and mode of operation variables in use of subject matter trainer. AFPTRC-TR-57-8, October 1957.

Iscoe, I., Williams, M., & Harvey, J. Age, intelligence and sex as variables in the conformity behavior of Negro and white children. *Child Development*, 1964, *35*, 451–560.

Israel, M. L. Variably blurred prompting: I. Methodology and application to the analysis of paired associate learning. *Journal of Psychology*, 1960, *50*, 43–52.

Iverson, M. A., & Reuter, M. E. Ego-involvement as an experimental variable. *Psychological Reports*, 1956, *2*, 147–181.

Jackson, G. B. The research evidence on the effects of grade retention. *Review of Educational Research*, 1975, *45*(4), 613–635.

Jackson, S. The growth of logical thinking in normal and subnormal children. *British Journal of Educational Psychology*, 1965, *35*, 255–258.

James, N. E. Personal preference for method as a factor in learning. *Journal of Educational Psychology*, 1962, *53*, 43–47.

Janis, I. L., & King, B. T. The influence of role playing on opinion chnage. *Journal of Abnormal and Social Psychology*, 1954, *49*, 211–218.

Janke, L. L., & Havighurst, R. J. Relations between ability and social status in a mid-Western community. II. Sixteen-year-old boys and girls. *Journal of Educational Psychology*, 1945, *36*, 499–509.

Jencks, C. S., & Brown, M. D. Effects of high schools on their students. *Harvard Educational Review*, 1975, *45*(3), 273–324.

Jenkins, J. G. Instruction as a factor in "incidental" learning. *American Journal of Psychology*, 1933, *45*, 471–477.

Jensen, A. R. Social class, race, and genetics: Implications for education. *American Educational Research Journal*, 1968, *5*(1), 1–42.

Jensen, A. R. How much can we boost IQ and scholastic achievement? *Harvard Educational Review*, 1969, *39*, 1–123.

Jersild, A. T., & Bienstock, S. F. The influence of training on the vocal ability of three-year-old children. *Child Development*, 1931, *2*, 277–291.

Jersild, A. T., & Bienstock, S. F. Development of rhythm in young children. *Child Development Monographs*, 1935, No. 22.

Jersild, A. T., Chayer, M. E., Fehlman, C., Hildreth, G., & Young, M. *Child development and the curriculum.* New York: Columbia University, Teachers College, 1946.

Jersild, A. T., & Tasch, R. J. *Children's interests.* New York: Columbia University, Teachers College, 1949.

Jester, R. E., & Travers, R. M. Comprehension of connected discourse as a function of rate and mode of presentation. *Journal of Educational Research*, 1966, *59*, 297–302.

John, V. P., & Goldstein, L. S. The social context of language acquisition. *Merrill-Palmer Quarterly*, 1964, *10*, 265–276.

Johnson, C. E., Ellison, F. P., & Flores, J. E. *A summary of the major findings at the close of the first year of the study of the development of methods and materials to facilitate foreign language instruction in elementary schools.* Urbana, Ill.: University of Illinois, 1960.

Johnson, D. M. Formulation and reformulation of figure-concepts. *American Journal of Psychology*, 1961, *74*, 418–424.

Johnson, D. W., & Johnson, R. T. Instructional goal structure: Cooperative, competitive, or individualistic. *Review of Educational Research*, 1974, *44*(2), 213–240.

Johnson, E. S., & Legg, C. E. Why young people leave school. *Bulletin of the National Association of Secondary School Principals*, 1944, *28*, 3–28.

Johnson, G. O., & Kirk, S. A. Are mentally handicapped children segregated in the regular grades? *Exceptional Child*, 1950, *17*, 65–68; 87–88.

Johnson, M., Jr. Definitions and models in curriculum theory. *Education Theory*, 1967, *17*(2), 127–140.

Johnson, M. *Intentionality in education: A conceptual model of curricular and instructional planning and evaluation.* Albany, N.Y.: Center for Curriculum Research and Services, 1977.

Johnson, R. B. The effects of prompting, practice and feedback in programmed videotape. *American Educational Research Journal,* 1968, *5*(1), 73–79.

Johnson, R. C. Linguistic structure as related to concept formation and to concept content. *Psychological Bulletin,* 1962, *59,* 468–476.

Johnson, R. C., & Zara, R. C. Relational learning in young children. *Journal of Comparative and Psysiological Psychology,* 1960, *53,* 594–597.

Johnson, R. E. Meaningfulness and the recall of textual prose. *American Educational Research Journal,* 1973, *10*(1), 49–58.

Jones, A., & McGill, D. The homeostatic character of information drive in humans. *Journal of Experimental Research in Personality,* 1967, *2*(1), 25–31.

Jones, E. E., & deCharms, R. The organizing function of interaction roles in person perception. *Journal of Abnormal and Social Psychology,* 1958, *57,* 155–164.

Jones, E. E., & Kohler, R. The effects of plausibility on the learning of controversial statements. *Journal of Abnormal and Social Psychology,* 1958, *57,* 315–320.

Jones, H. E. The pattern of abilities in juvenile and adult defectives. *University of California Publications in Psychology,* 1931, *5,* 47–61.

Jones, H. E. The environment and mental development. In L. Carmichael (Ed.), *Manual of child psychology* (2nd ed.). New York: Wiley, 1954.

Jones, H. E., & Conrad, H. S. The growth and decline of intelligence: A study of a homogeneous group between the ages of ten and sixty. *Genetic Psychology Monographs,* 1933, *13*(3), 223–298.

Jones, H. E., & Conrad, H. S. Mental development in adolescence. In 43rd Yearbook, National Society for the Study of Education, Part I. Chicago: University of Chicago Press, 1944.

Jones, M. G., & English, H. B. Notional vs. rote memory. *American Journal of Psychology,* 1926, *37,* 602–603.

Jones, R. S. *Integration of instructional with self-scoring measuring procedures.* Unpublished doctoral dissertation, Ohio State University, 1950.

Joos, L. W. *Utilization of teaching machine concept in elementary arithmetic.* Baltimore: Board of Education of Baltimore County, 1961.

Jost, A. Die assoziationfestigkeit in ihrer abhangigheit von der verteilung der wiederholungen. *Zeitschrift der Psychologie,* 1897, *14,* 436–472.

Joyce, B., & Weil, M. *Models of teaching.* Englewood Cliffs, N.J.: Prentice-Hall, 1972.

Judd, C. H. Practice and its effects on the perception of illusions. *Psychological Review,* 1902, *9,* 27–39.

Kaess, W., & Zeaman, D. Positive and negative knowledge of results on a Pressey-type punchboard. *Journal of Experimental Psychology,* 1960, *60,* 12–17.

Kagan, J. The acquisition and significance of sex-typing and sex-role identity. In M. L. Hoffman & L. W. Hoffman (Eds.), *Review of child development research* (Vol. 1). New York: Russell Sage Foundation, 1964.

Kagan, J. Reflection–impulsivity and reading ability in primary grade children. *Child Development,* 1965, *36,* 609–628.

Kagan, J., Moss, H. A., & Sigel, I. E. Conceptual style and the use of affect labels. *Merrill-Palmer Quarterly of Behavior and Development,* 1960, *6,* 261–278.

Kagan, J., Moss, H. A., & Sigel, I. E. Psychological significance of styles of conceptualization. *Monographs of the Society for Research in Child Development,* 1963, *28,* No. 2, 73–112.

Kagan, J., & Mussen, P. H. Dependency themes on the TAT and group conformity. *Journal of Consulting Psychology,* 1956, *20,* 19–27.

Kagan, J., Pearson, L., & Welch, L. Conceptual impulsivity and inductive reasoning. *Child Development,* 1966, *37,* 583–594.

Kagan, J., Rosman, B. L., Kay, D., Albert, J., & Phillips, W. Information processing in the child: Significance of analytic and reflective attitudes. *Psychological Monographs,* 1964, *78* (Whole No. 578).

Kagan, J., Sontag, L. W., Baker, C. T., & Nelsen, V. Personality and IQ change. *Journal of Abnormal and Social Psychology,* 1958, *56,* 261–266.

Kahl, J. A. Education and occupational aspirations of "common man" boys. *Harvard Educational Review,* 1953, *23,* 186–203.

Kahl, J. A. *The American class structure.* New York: Rinehart, 1957.

Kahle, J. B., & Nordland, F. H. The effect of an advanced organizer when utilized with carefully sequenced audio-tutorial units. *Journal of Research in Science Teaching,* 1975, *12*(1), 63–67.

Kahle, J. B., & Rostovac, J. J. The effect of a series of advanced organizers in increasing meaningful learning. *Science Education,* 1976, *60*(3), 365–371.

Kahn, M. L. Social class and parental values. *American Journal of Sociology,* 1959, *64,* 337–351.

Kamii, C. An application of Piaget's theory to the conceptualization of a preschool curriculum. In R. K. Parker (Ed.), *The preschool in action.* Boston: Allyn and Bacon, 1972.

Kaplan, L. *Education and mental health.* New York: Harper & Row, 1971.

Karplus, R. Beginning a study in elementary-school science. *American Journal of Physics,* 1962, *30,* 1–9.

Kastrinos, W. A study of the retention of biological facts by high-school biology students. *Science Education,* 1965, *49,* 487–491.

Katahn, M. Interaction of anxiety and ability in complex learning situations. *Journal of Personality and Social Psychology,* 1966, *3*(4), 475–479.

Kates, S. L., & Yudin, L. Concept attainment and memory. *Journal of Educational Psychology,* 1964, *55,* 103–109.

Katkovsky, W., Crandall, V. C., & Good, S. Parental antecedents of children's beliefs in internal-external control of reinforcement in intellectual achievement situations. *Child Development,* 1967, *38,* 765–776.

Katkovsky, W., Preston, A., & Crandall, V. J. Parents' attitudes toward their personal achievements and toward the achievement behaviors of their children. *Journal of Genetic Psychology,* 1964, *104,* 67–82. (a)

Katkovsky, W., Preston, A., & Crandall, V. J. Parents' achievement attitudes and their behavior with their children in achievement situations. *Journal of Genetic Psychology,* 1964, *104,* 105–121. (b)

Katona, G. *Organizing and memorizing.* New York: Columbia University Press, 1940.

Katz, J. J. *The philosophy of language.* New York: Harper & Row, 1966.

Kaufman, M. E., & Peterson, W. M. Acquisition of a learning set by normal and mentally retarded children. *Journal of Comparative and Physiological Psychology,* 1958, *51,* 619–621.

Kaufman, R. A. An experimental evaluation of the role of remedial feedback in an intrinsic program. *Journal of Programmed Instruction*, 1963, 2(4), 21–30.

Kausler, D. H. A study of the relationship between ego-involvement and learning. *Journal of Psychology*, 1951, 32, 225–230.

Kay, H. Learning and retaining verbal material. *British Journal of Psychology*, 1955, 46, 81–100.

Keislar, E. R. The development of understanding in arithmetic by a teaching machine. *Journal of Educational Psychology*, 1959, 50, 247–253.

Keislar, E. R. A descriptive approach to classroom motivation. *Journal of Teacher Education*, 1960, 11, 310–315.

Keislar, E. R. *Shaping of a learning set in reading.* Paper presented at the meeting of the American Educational Research Association, Atlantic City, February 1961.

Keislar, E. R., & McNeil, J. D. Teaching scientific theory to first-grade pupils by an auto-instructional device. *Harvard Educational Review*, 1961, 31, 73–83.

Keislar, E. R., & McNeil, J. D. A comparison of two response modes in an auto-instructional program with children in the primary grades. *Journal of Educational Psychology*, 1962, 53, 127–131.

Keislar, E. R., & Shuman, L. S. (Eds.) *Learning by discovery: A critical appraisal.* Skokie, Ill.: Rand McNally, 1966.

Keller, F. S. Goodby teacher . . . *Journal of Applied Behavioral Analysis*, 1968, 1, 79–89.

Kelley, H. H., & Stahelski, A. J. Social interaction basis of cooperators' and competitors' beliefs about others. *Journal of Personality and Social Psychology*, 1970, 16, 66–91.

Kelley, H. H., & Thibaut, J. W. Group problem solving. In G. Lindzey & E. Aronson (Eds.), *Handbook of social psychology* (Vol. 4) (2nd. ed.). Reading, Mass.: Addison-Wesley, 1968.

Kelly, J. G., Ferson, J. E., & Holtzman, W. H. The measurement of attitudes toward the Negro in the South. *Journal of Social Psychology*, 1958, 48, 305–317.

Kempler, H. L. Self-confidence and problem-solving rigidity. *Journal of Clinical Psychology*, 1962, 18, 51.

Kendler, H. H., & Kendler, T. S. Inferential behavior in preschool children. *Journal of Experimental Psychology*, 1956, 51, 311–314.

Kendler, H. H., & Kendler, T. S. Effect of verbalization on reversal shifts in children. *Science*, 1961, 135, 1619–1620.

Kendler, T. S. Development of mediating responses in children. *Monographs of the Society for Research in Child Development*, 1963, 28, No. 2, 33–48.

Keppel, G., & Postman, L. Studies of learning to learn: III. Conditions of improvement in successive transfer tasks. *Journal of Verbal Learning and Verbal Behavior*, 1966, 5, 260–267.

Kersh, B. Y. The adequacy of "meaning" as an explanation for the superiority of learning by independent discovery. *Journal of Educational Psychology*, 1958, 49, 282–292.

Kersh, B. Y. The motivating effect of learning by directed discovery. *Journal of Educational Psychology*, 1962, 53, 65–71.

Kettner, N. W., Guilford, J. P., & Christensen, P. R. A factor-analytic study across the domains of reasoning, creativity, and evaluation. *Psychological Monographs*, 1959, 73(9) (Whole No. 479).

Kight, H. R., & Sassenrath, J. M. Relation of achievement motivation and test anxiety to performance in programmed instruction. *Journal of Educational Psychology*, 1966, *57*, 14–17.

Killian, L. M., & Haer, J. L. Variables related to attitudes regarding school desegregation among white southerners. *Sociometry*, 1958, *21*, 159–164.

Kilpatrick, J. Problem solving in mathematics. *Journal of Educational Research*, 1969, *39*, 523–534.

King, R. G. *The prediction of choice of undergraduate field of concentration in Harvard College.* Unpublished doctoral dissertation, Harvard University, 1958.

Kinoshita, T. The effects of group cohesiveness and importance of the tasks upon conformity behavior. *Japanese Journal of Psychology*, 1964, *34*, 181—198.

Kinsella, P. J. A close look at preschool reading instruction. *Illinois Journal of Education*, 1965, *58*, 7–10.

Kirk, S. A. *Early education of the retarded child: An experimental study.* Urbana: University of Illinois Press, 1958.

Kirk, S. A., & Kirk, W. D. *Psycholinguistic learning disabilities: Diagnosis and remediation.* Chicago: University of Illinois Press, 1971.

Kirkpatrick, J. E. The motivating effect of a specific type of testing program. *University of Iowa Studies in Education*, 1939, *9*, No. 4, 41–68.

Kittell, J. E. An experimental study of the effect of external direction during learning on transfer and retention of principles. *Journal of Educational Psychology*, 1957, *48*, 391–405.

Klare, G. R., Mabry, J. E., & Gustafson, L. M. The relationship of patterning (underlining) to immediate retention and to acceptability of technical material. *Journal of Applied Psychology*, 1955, *39*, 40–42.

Klaus, R. A., & Gray, S. W. The early training project for disadvantaged children: A report after five years. *Monographs of the Society for Research in Child Development*, 1968, *33*(4), (Serial No. 120).

Klausmeier, H. J. Effects of accelerating bright older elementary pupils: A follow-up. *Journal of Educational Psychology*, 1963, *54*, 165–171.

Klausmeier, H. J., & Check, J. Retention and transfer in children of low, average, and high intelligence. *Journal of Educational Research*, 1962, *55*, 319–322.

Klausmeier, H. J., & Feldhusen, J. F. Retention in arithmetic among children of low, average, and high intelligence at 117 months of age. *Journal of Educational Psychology*, 1959, *50*, 88–92.

Klausmeier, H. J., Goodwin, L., & Ronda, T. Effects of accelerating bright, older elementary pupils: A second follow-up. *Journal of Educational Psychology*, 1968, *59*(1, Pt. 1), 53–59.

Klausmeier, H. J., & Loughlin, L. J. Behavior during problem solving among children of low, average, and high intelligence. *Journal of Educational Psychology*, 1961, *52*, 148–152.

Klausmeier, H. J., & Wiersma, W. The effects of IQ level and sex on divergent thinking of 7th grade pupils of low, average, and high IQ. *Journal of Educational Research*, 1965, *58*, 300–302.

Klausmeier, H. J., Wiersma, W., & Harris, C. W. Efficiency of initial learning and transfer by individuals, pairs, and quads. *Journal of Educational Psychology*, 1963, *54*, 160–164.

Kleck, R. E., & Wheaton, J. Dogmatism and responses to opinion-consistent and opinion-inconsistent information. *Journal of Personality and Social Psychology,* 1967, *5*(2), 249–252.

Klineberg, O. *Negro intelligence and selective migration.* New York: Columbia University Press, 1935.

Klingensmith, S. W. Child aninism: What the child means by "alive." *Child Development,* 1953, *24*, 51–61.

Knoell, D. M. Prediction of teaching success from word fluency data. *Journal of Educational Research,* 1953, *46*, 673–683.

Koffka, K. *Principles of Gestalt psychology.* New York: Harcourt, 1935.

Kohlberg, L. *Stages in children's conceptions of physical and social objects in the years four to eight: A study of developmental theory.* Unpublished manuscript, 1963.

Köhler, W. *The mentality of apes.* New York: Harcourt, 1925.

Kohn, P. M. Serendipity on the move: Towards a measure of intellectual motivation. *Canadian Psychologist,* 1965, *6*, 20–31.

Kohnstamm, G. A. Experiments on teaching Piagetian thought operations. In J. Hellmuth (Ed.), *Cognitive studies* (Vol. I). New York: Brunner/Mazel, 1970.

Kolb, D. A. Achievement motivation training for underachieving high-school boys. *Journal of Personality and Social Psychology,* 1965, *2*, 783–792.

Kolstoe, O. P. A comparison of mental abilities of bright and dull children of comparable mental ages. *Journal of Educational Psychology,* 1954, *45*, 161–168.

Kooistra, W. H. *Developmental trends in the attainment of conservation, transitivity, and relativism in the thinking of children: A replication and extension of Piaget's ontogenetic formulations.* Unpublished doctoral dissertation, Wayne State University, Detroit, Mich., 1963.

Kooker, E. W., & Williams, C. S. College students' ability to evaluate their performance on objective tests. *Journal of Educational Research,* 1959, *53*, 69–72.

Koran, J. J., Jr., & Koran, M. L. Differential response to structure of advance organizers in science instruction. *Journal of Research in Science Teaching,* 1973, *10*(4), 347–353.

Kounin, J. S. Intellectual development and rigidity. In R. G. Barker, J. S. Kounin, & H. F. Wright (Eds.), *Child behavior and development.* New York: McGraw-Hill, 1943.

Kounin, J. S. *Discipline and group management in classrooms.* New York: Holt, Rinehart and Winston, 1970.

Kounin, J. S., & Gump, P. V. The comparative influence of punitive and nonpunitive teachers upon children's concepts of school misconduct. *Journal of Educational Psychology,* 1961, *52*, 44–49.

Kounin, J. S., Gump, P. V., & Ryan, J. J. Explorations in classroom management. *Journal of Teacher Education,* 1961, *12*, 235–246.

Kozol, J. *Death at an early age.* Boston: Houghton Mifflin, 1967.

Krechevsky, I. "Hypothses" in rats. *Phychological Review,* 1932, *39*, 516–532.

Krechevsky, I. A study of the continuity of the problem-solving process. *Psychological Review,* 1938, *45*, 107–133.

Kreitler, H., & Kreitler, S. Crucial determinants of the attitude towards national and supranational ideals: A study of Israeli youth. *Journal of Peace Research,* 1967, No. 2, 107–124.

Krueger, L. O. The relative effect of interspersing a recall at different stages of learning. *Archives of Psychology*, 1930, *18* (Whole No. 114), 15—25.

Krueger, W. C. F. The optimal effect of recall during learning. *Archives of Psychology*, 1930, *18* (Whole No. 114), 26—34.

Krug, R. E. Over- and under-achievement and the Edwards Personal Preference Schedule. *Journal of Applied Psychology*, 1959, *43*, 133–137.

Krumboltz, J. D. Meaningful learning and retention: Practice and reinforcement variables. *Review of Educational Research*, 1961, *31*, 535–546.

Krumboltz, J. D., & Weisman, R. G. The effect of overt vs. covert responding to programmed instruction on immediate and delayed retention. *Journal of Educational Psychology*, 1962, *53*, 89–92. (a)

Krumboltz, J. D., & Weisman, R. G. *The effect of intermittent confirmation in programmed instruction.* Paper presented at the meeting of the American Psychological Association, St. Louis, September 1962. (b)

Kuenne, M. R. Experimental investigation of the relation of language to transposition behavior in young children. *Journal of Experimental Psychology*, 1946, *36*, 471–490.

Kuhlen, R. G. *The psychology of adolescent development.* New York: Harper & Row, 1952.

Kuhn, D. J. *A study of varying modes of topical presentation in elementary college biology to determine the effect of advance organizers in knowledge.* Unpublished doctoral dissertation, Purdue University, 1967.

Kuhn, D. J. A study of information acquisition in individualized instruction. *Science Education*, 1972, *56*(4), 539—545.

Kuhn, D. J., & Novak, J. D. A study of cognitive subsumption in the life sciences. *Science Education*, 1971, *55*, 309–320.

Kuhn, T. S. *The structure of scientific revolutions.* In *International Encyclopedia of Unified Sciences* (2nd ed.). Chicago: University of Chicago Press, 1962, 1970.

Kurtz, A. K., Walter, J. S., & Brenner, H. The effects of inserted questions and statements on film learning. *Technical Report SDC.269-7-16.* Pennsylvania State College, Instructional Films Research Program, September 1950.

Kurtz, K. H., & Hovland, C. I. Concept learning with differing sequences of instances. *Journal of Experimental Psychology*, 1956, *4*, 239–243.

Labov, W. The logic of non-standard English. In F. Williams (Ed.), *Language and poverty: Perspectives on a theme.* Chicago: Markam, 1970.

Lacey, H. M. Mediating verbal responses and stimulus similarity as factors in conceptual naming by school age children. *Journal of Experimental Psychology*, 1961, *62*, 113–121.

Lacey, J. I., & Dallenbach, K. M. Acquisition by children of the cause–effect relationship. *American Journal of Psychology*, 1940, *53*, 575—578.

Ladas, H. The mathemagenic effects of factual review questions on the learning of incidental information: A critical review. *Review of Educational Research*, 1973, *43*(1), 71–82.

Ladd, E. T. Perplexities of the problem of keeping order. *Harvard Educational Review*, 1958, *28*, 19–28.

Ladd, F. E. Concept learning in relation to open- and closed-mindedness and academic aptitude. *Psychological Reports*, 1967, *20*(1), 135–142.

Ladner, J. A. *Tomorrow's tomorrow. The black woman.* Garden City, N.Y.: Doubleday, 1971.

Lahaderne, H. M. Attitudinal and intellectual correlates of attention: A study of four sixth-grade classrooms. *Journal of Educational Psychology,* 1968, *59*(5), 320–324.

Lambert, P. *Schedules of reinforcement: Effects on programmed learning.* Paper presented at the meeting of the American Psychological Association, St. Louis, September, 1962.

Lambert, P., and others. Experimental folklore and experimentation: The study of programmed learning in the Wauwatosa public schools. *Journal of Educational Psychology,* 1962, *55*, 485–491.

Lantz, B. Some dynamic aspects of success and failure. *Psychological Monographs,* 1945, *59*, No. 1 (Whole No. 271).

Larson, G. L. *Comparison of acquisition, retention, and transfer among three styles of learning.* Unpublished doctoral dissertation, University of Illinois, 1963.

Larson, M. A., & Dittman, F. E. *Compensatory education and early adolescence: Reviewing our national strategy.* Menlo Park, Calif.: Stanford Research Institute, Educational Policy Research Center, 1975.

Lashley, K. S. *Brain mechanisms and intelligence.* Chicago: University of Chicago Press, 1929.

Lathrop, C. W., & Norford, C. A. Contributions of film introductions and film summaries to learning from instructional films. *Technical Report-SDC.269-7-8.* Pennsylvania State College, Instructional Films Program, 1949.

Laurendeau, M., & Pinard, A. *Causal thinking in the child: A genetic and experimental approach.* New York: International Universities, 1962.

Laurendeau, M., & Pinard, A. *The development of the concepts of space in the child.* New York: International Universities, 1970.

Lavatelli, C. *Early childhood curriculum: A Piaget program.* Boston: American Service and Engineering, 1970.

Lawrence, D. H., & Goodwin, W. R. Transfer in training behavior between two levels of speed. *USAF Personnel Center Research Bulletin,* 1954, No. AFPTRC TR, 54–70.

Lawson, A. E., Nordland, F. H., & DeVito, A. Piagetian formal operational tasks: A crossover study of learning effect and reliability. *Science Education,* 1974, *58*(2), 267–276.

Lawson, A. E., & Renner, J. W. A quantitative analysis and its implications· for curriculum. *Science Education,* 1974, *58*, 454–559.

Lawson, A. E., & Renner, J. W. Relationhip of science subject matter and developmental levels of learners. *Journal of Research in Science Teaching,* 1975, *12*(4), 347–358.

Lawton, J. P. *Effects of advance organizer lessons on children's use and understanding of the causal and logical "because."* Unpublished manuscript, University of Wisconsin, 1976.

Lawton, J. P., & Wanska, S. K. *An analytical study of the use of advance organizers in facilitating children's learning.* Unpublished manuscript, University of Wisconsin, 1976.

Lawton, J. P., & Wanska, S. K. Advance organizers as a teaching strategy: A reply to Barnes and Clawson. *Review of Educational Research*, 1977, *47*, 233–244.

Laycock, S. R., & Clark, S. The comparative performance of a group of old-dull and young-bright children on some items of the Revised Stanford-Binet Scale of Intelligence, Form L. *Journal of Educational Psychology*, 1942, *33*, 1–12.

Lazare, S. Creativity and curiosity: The overlap. *Child Study*, 1967, *29*(2), 22–29.

Leahy, A. M. Nature–nurture and intelligence. *Genetic Psychology Monographs*, 1935, *17*, 235–308.

Leeds, C. H. Teacher behavior liked and disliked by pupils. *Education*, 1954, *75*, 29–36.

Leggitt, D. Measuring progress in working skills in ninth-grade civics. *School Review*, 1934, *42*, 676–687.

Lehman, H., & Cole, L. The effectiveness of drill in handwriting to remove specific illegibilities. *School and Society*, 1928, *27*, 546–548.

Lehman, H. C. The relationship between chronological age and high level research output in physics and chemistry. *Journal of Gerontology*, 1964, *19*, 157–164.

Leifer, A. D. Teaching with television and film. In N. L. Gage (Ed.), *The psychology of teaching methods*. Chicago: University of Chicago Press, 1976.

Leighton, D., & Kluckhohn, C. *Children of the people: The Navaho individual and his development*. Cambridge, Mass.: Harvard University Press, 1947.

Lennenberg, E. H. *The biological foundations of language*. New York: Wiley, 1967.

Lennenberg, E. H. On explaining language: The development of language in children can best be understood in the context of developmental biology. *Science*, 1969, *164*, 635–643.

Lerner, J. W. *Children with learning disabilities: Theories, diagnosis, and teaching strategies*. Boston: Houghton Mifflin, 1971.

Lesh, R. A., Jr., & Johnson, H. Models and applications as advanced organizers. *Journal for Research in Mathematics Education*, 1976, 75–81.

Lesser, G. S. *Recent revisions and educational applications of the concepts of intelligence and giftedness*. Address presented at the Institute for School Psychologists, University of Wisconsin, 1962.

Lesser, G. S., Fifer, G., & Clark, D. H. Mental abilities of children from different social-class and cultural groups. *Monographs of the Society for Research in Child Development*, 1965, *30*(4), 102.

Lesser, G. S., Krawitz, R. N., & Packard, R. Experimental arousal of achievement motivation in adolescent girls. *Journal of Abnormal and Social Psychology*, 1963, *66*, 59–66.

Lester, O. P. Mental set in relation to retroactive inhibition. *Journal of Experimental Psychology*, 1932, *15*, 681–699.

Levenstein, P. *Verbal interaction project, child welfare, research and demonstration project (R-300)*. Final Report to Children's Bureau, OCD, Washington, D.C., 1971.

Leventhal, H., & Singer, D. L. Cognitive complexity, impression formation, and impression change. *Journal of Personality*, 1964, *32*, 210–226.

Levin, G. R., & Baker, B. L. Item scrambling in a self-instructional program. *Journal of Educational Psychology*, 1963, *54*, 138–143.

Levine, J., & Murphy, G. The learning and forgetting of controversial material. *Journal of Abnormal and Social Psychology*, 1943, *38*, 50–517.

Levitt, E. E. Studies in intolerance of ambiguity: I. The Decision-Location Test with grade school children. *Child Development*, 1953, *24*, 263–268.

Lewin, K. Behavior and development as a function of the total situation. In L. Carmichael (Ed.), *Manual of child psychology* (2nd ed.). New York: Wiley, 1954.

Lewis, M. M. *Infant speech: A study of beginnings of language* (2nd ed.). London: Routledge, 1951.

Lewis, O. *The children of Sanchez*. New York: Random House, 1961.

Lewis, W. D. A comparative study of the personalities, interests, and home backgrounds of gifted children of superior and inferior educational achievement. *Journal of Genetic Psychology*, 1941, *59*, 207–218.

Light, D., Jr., & Laufer, R. S. College youth: Psychohistory and prospects. In *Youth*, 74th Yearbook, National Society for the Study of Education, Part I. Chicago: University of Chicago Press, 1975.

Lightfoot, G. F. *Personality characteristics of bright and dull children*. New York: Columbia University, Teachers College, 1951.

Lillienfeld, A. M., & Pasamanick, B. The association of maternal and fetal factors with the development of mental deficiency: II. Relationship to maternal age, birth order, previous reproductive loss and degree of mental deficiency. *American Journal of Mental Deficiency*, 1956, *60*, 557–569.

Lindholm, B. W. Changes in conventional and deviation IQ's. *Journal of Educational Psychology*, 1964, *55*, 110–113.

Lindley, E. H. A study of puzzles with special reference to the psychology of mental adaptation. *American Journal of Psychology*, 1897, *8*, 431–493.

Lindsay, P. H., & Norman, D. A. *Human information processing: An introduction to psychology*. New York: Academic Press, 1977.

Lindvall, C. M., & Bolvin, J. O. Programmed instruction in the school: An application of programming principles in "individually prescribed instruction." In P. C. Lange (Ed.), *Programmed instruction*, 66th Yearbook, National Society for the Study of Education, Part II. Chicago: National Society for the Study of Education, 1967.

Linton, T. E. Dogmatism, authoritarianism and academic achievement. *Alberta Journal of Educational Research*, 1968, *14*, 49–53.

Lippitt, R. An experimental study of the effect of democratic and authoritarian group atmospheres. *University of Iowa Studies in Child Welfare, 16*, No. 3. Iowa City: University of Iowa Press, 1940.

Lipset, S. M. Democracy and working-class authoritarianism. *American Sociological Review*, 1959, *24*, 482–501.

Lipsitt, L. P. A self-concept scale for children and its relationship to the children's form of the manifest anxiety scale. *Child Development*, 1958, *29*, 463–472.

Little, J. K. Results of use of machines for testing and for drill upon learning in educational psychology. In A. A. Lumsdaine & R. Glaser, (Eds.) *Teaching machines and programmed learning*. Washington, D.C.: National Education Association, 1960.

Littrell, M. B., & Eicher, J. B. Clothing opinions and the social acceptance process among adolescents. *Adolescence*, 1973, *8*(30), 197–212.

Livson, N., & Mussen, P. H. The relation of control to overt aggression and dependency. *Journal of Abnormal and Social Psychology*, 1957, *55*, 66–71.

Livson, N., & Nichols, T. F. Social attitude configurations in an adolescent group. *Journal of Genetic Psychology*, 1957, *91*, 3–23.

Ljung, B. O. *The adolescent growth spurt in mental growth.* Stockholm: Almquist & Wiksell, 1965.

Lloyd, K. E. Supplementary report: Retention and transfer of responses to stimulus classes. *Journal of Experimental Psychology*, 1960, *59*, 207–208.

Loban, W. D. *Problems in oral English.* Champaign, Ill.: National Council of Teachers of English, 1966.

Locke, E. A. Some correlates of classroom and out-of-class achievement in gifted science students. *Journal of Educational Psychology*, 1963, *54*, 238–248.

Locke, E. A. Relationship of task success to task liking: A replication. *Psychological Reports*, 1966, *18*(2), 552–554.

Locke, E. A. Further data on the relationship of task success to liking and satisfaction. *Psychological Reports*, 1967, *20*(1), 246.

Locke, E. A. Motivational effects of knowledge of results: Knowledge or goal setting? *Journal of Applied Psychology*, 1967, *51*, 324–329.

Locke, E. A., & Bryan, J. F. Goals and intentions as determinants of performance level, task choice, and attitudes. *Ameircan Institute for Research Report*, 1967, No. R67–1.

Locke, E. A., & Bryan, J. F. Knowledge of score and goal level as determinants of work rate. *Journal of Applied Psychology*, 1969, *53*, 59–65.

Locke, E. A., Bryan, J. F., & Kendall, R. M. Goals and intentions as mediators of the effects of monetary incentives on behavior. *Journal of Applied Psychology*, 1968, *52*(2), 104–121.

Locke, E. F., Cartledge, N., Knerr, C., & Bryan, J. F. *The motivational effects of knowledge of results.* American Institutes for Research Final Report, Washington, D.C.: 1969, No. R 69–2.

Locke, E. A., Cartledge, N., & Koeppel, J. Motivational effects of knowledge of results: A goal-setting phenomenon? *Psychological Bulletin*, 1968, *70*, 474–485.

Lockhead, G. R. A re-evaluation of evidence of one-trial associative learning. *American Journal of Psychology*, 1961, *74*, 590–595.

Loevinger, J. Intelligence as related to socio-economic factors. In 39th Yearbook, National Society for the Study of Education, Part I. Chicago: University of Chicago Press, 1940, pp. 159–210.

Loevinger, J. On the proportional contributions of differences in nature and nurture to differences in intelligence. *Psychological Bulletin*, 1943, *40*, 725–756.

Long, L., & Welch, L. The development of the ability to discriminate and match numbers. *Journal of Genetic Psychology*, 1941, *59*, 377–387. (a)

Long, L., & Welch, L. Reasoning ability in young children. *Journal of Psychology*, 1941, *12*, 21–44. (b)

Long, L., & Welch, L. Influence of level of abstractness on reasoning ability. *Journal of Psychology*, 1942, *13*, 41–59.

Longstreth, L. E., & Rice, R. E. Perceptions of parental behavior and identification with parents by three groups of boys differing in school adjustment. *Journal of Educational Psychology*, 1964, *55*, 144–151.

Lorge, I. Schooling makes a difference. *Teachers College Record*, 1945, *46*, 483–492.

Lorge, I. Groupness of the group. *Journal of Educational Psychology*, 1955, *46*, 449–456.

Lott, A. J., & Lott, B. E. Group cohesiveness, communication level, and conformity. *Journal of Abnormal and Social Psychology*, 1961, *62*, 408–412.

Lott, A. J., & Lott, B. E. Group cohesiveness and individual learning. *Journal of Educational Psychology*, 1966, *57*, 61–73.

Lovell, K. A follow-up study of some aspects of the work of Piaget and Inhelder on the child's conception of space. *British Journal of Educational Psychology*, 1959, *29*, 104–117. (a)

Lovell, K. Jean Piaget's views on conservation of quantity. *Indian Psychological Bulletin*, 1959, *4*, 16–19. (b)

Lovell, K. A follow-up study of Inhelder and Piaget's "The growth of logical thinking." *British Journal of Psychology*, 1961, *52*, 143–153. (a)

Lovell, K. *The growth of basic mathematical and scientific concepts in children.* New York: Philosophical Library, 1961. (b)

Lovell, K., & Ogilvie, E. A study of the conservation of substance in the junior school child. *British Journal of Educational Psychology*, 1960, *30*, 109–118.

Luchins, A. S. Classroom experiments on mental set. *American Journal of Psychology*, 1946, *59*, 295–298.

Luchins, A. S., & Luchins, E. H. A structural approach to the teaching of the concept of area in intuitive geometry. *Journal of Educational Research*, 1947, *40*, 528–533.

Lumsdaine, A. A. Some conclusions concerning student response and a science of instruction. In A. A. Lumsdaine (Ed.), *Student response in programmed instruction.* Washington, D.C.: National Academy of Sciences—National Research Council, 1961.

Lumsdaine, A. A., & Janis, I. L. Resistance to "counterpropaganda" produced by one-sided and two-sided "propaganda" presentations. *Public Opinion Quarterly*, 1953, *17*, 311–318.

Lundin, R. W., & Sawyer, C. R. The relationship between test anxiety, drinking patterns, and scholastic achievement in a group of undergraduate college men. *Journal of General Psychology*, 1965, *73*, 143–146.

Lunn, J. C. The influence of sex, achievement level, and social class on junior school children's attitudes. *British Journal of Educational Psychology*, 1972, *42*, 70–74.

Lunneborg, P. W. Relations among social desirability, achievement, and anxiety measures in children. *Child Development*, 1964, *35*, 169–182.

Lunzer, E. A. Some points of Piagetian theory in the light of experimental criticism. *Child Psychology and Psychiatry*, 1960, *1*, 192–202.

Lunzer, E. A. Problems of formal reasoning in test situations. *Monographs of the Society for Research in Child Development*, 1965, *30*, No. 2, 19–46.

Luria, A. R. The directive function of speech in development and dissolution: Part I. Development of the directive function of speech in early childhood. *Word*, 1959, *15*, 341–352.

Lyon, C. D., & Saario, T. N. Women in public education: Sexual discrimination in promotions. *Phi Delta Kappan*, 1973, *52*(2), 120–123.

Lyon, D. O. The relation of length of material to time taken for learning and optimum distribution of time. *Journal of Educational Psychology*, 1914, *5*, 1–9; 85–91; 155–163.

Maccoby, E. A., & Jacklin, C. N. *The psychology of sex differences.* Stanford, Calif.: Stanford University Press, 1974.

MacFarlane, J. W., Allen, L., & Honzik, M. P. *A developmental study of the behavior problems of normal children between twenty-one months and fourteen years.* Berkeley, Calif.: University of California Press, 1954.

MacKinnon, D. W. The highly effective individual. *Teachers College Record,* 1960, *61,* 367–378.

MacKinnon, D. W. The personality correlates of creativity: A study of American architects. In G. S. Nielsen (Ed.), *Proceedings of the 14th International Congress of Applied Psychology.* Copenhagen, 1961.

MacKinnon, D. W. The nature and nurture of creative talent. *American Psychologist,* 1962, *17,* 484–495.

Mager, R. F. *Preparing objectives for programmed instruction.* San Francisco: Fearon, 1962.

Maier, N. R. F. Reasoning in humans: I. On direction. *Journal of Comparative Psychology,* 1930, *10,* 115–143.

Maier, N. R. F. Reasoning in children. *Journal of Comparative Psychology,* 1936, *21,* 357–366.

Maier, N. R. F., & Hoffman, L. R. Quality of first and second solutions in group problem solving. *Journal of Applied Psychology,* 1960, *44,* 278–283.

Maller, J. B. *Cooperation and competition: An experimental study in motivation.* New York: Columbia University, Teachers College, 1929.

Malmo, R. B. Activation: A neuropsychological dimension. *Psychological Review,* 1959, *66,* 367–386.

Malrieu, P. Some problems of color vision in children. *Journal de Psychologie Normale et Pathologique,* 1955, *52,* 222–231.

Maltzman, I. On the training of originality. *Psychological Review,* 1960, *67,* 229–242.

Maltzman, I., Belloni, M., & Fishbein, M. Experimental studies of associative variables in originality. *Psychological Monographs,* 1964, *78*(3) (Whole No.

Maltzman, I., Eisman, E., & Brooks, L. O. Some relationships between methods of instruction, personality variables, and problem-solving behavior. *Journal of Educational Psychology,* 1950, *47,* 71–78.

Maltzman, I., Eisman, E., Brooks, L. O., & Smith, W. M. Task instructions for anagrams following different task instructions and training. *Journal of Experimental Psychology,* 1956, *51,* 418–420.

Mandler, G. Transfer of training as a function of degree of response overlearning. *Journal of Experimental Psychology,* 1954, *47,* 411–417.

Mandler, G. From association to structure. *Psychological Review,* 1962, *69,* 415–426.

Mann, J. H. The effect of interracial contact on sociometric choices and perceptions. *Journal of Social Psychology,* 1959, *50,* 143–152.

Mannix, J. B. The number concepts of a group of E.S.N. children. *British Journal of Educational Psychology,* 1960, *30,* 180–181.

Marks, J. B. Interests, leadership, and sociometric status among adolescents. *Sociometry,* 1954, *17,* 340–349.
580).

Marks, M. R. Problem solving as a function of the situation. *Journal of Experimental Psychology,* 1951, *41,* 74–80.

Marks, P. A., & Vestre, N. Relative effects of drive level and irrelevant responses on performance of a complex task. *Psychological Record*, 1961, *11*, 177–180.

Marquart, D. I. Group problem solving. *Journal of Social Psychology*, 1955, *41*, 103–113.

Maso, N. La valeur de l'activité de l'esprit dans la fixation des idées: Contribution expérimentale a la théorie de l'école active. *Archive Psychologie Genève*, 1929, *21*, 275–292.

Massaialas, B. G. *Inquiry in social studies*. New York: McGraw-Hill, 1966.

Matheson, E. A study of problem solving behavior in pre-school children. *Child Development*, 1931, *2*, 242–262.

Matsuda, M., & Matsuda, F. The effects of motivation levels and test anxiety levels on memory learning in children. *Japanese Journal of Educational Psychology*, 1968, *16*(2), 111–120.

Maw, W. H., & Maw, E. W. Establishing criterion groups for evaluating measures of curiosity. *Journal of Experimental Psychology*, 1961, *29*, 299–306.

Maw, W. H., & Maw, E. W. Selection of unbalanced and unusual designs by children high in curiosity. *Child Development*, 1962, *33*, 917–922.

May, M. A., & Lumsdaine, A. A. *Learning from films*. New Haven: Yale University Press, 1958.

Mayer, R. E. Information processing variables in learning to solve problems. *Review of Educational Research*, 1975, *45*, 525–541.

Mayer, R. E. Some conditions of meaningful learning for computer programming: advance organizers and subject control of frame order. *Journal of Educational Psychology*, 1976, *68*(2), 143–150.

Mayeroff, M. *On caring*. New York: Harper & Row, 1971.

McCall, R. B., Hogarty, P. S., & Hurlburt, N. Transitions in infant sensorimotor development and the prediction of childhood IQ. *American Psychologist*, 1972, *27*, 728–748.

McCall, W. A., & Krause, G. R. Measurement of teacher merit for salary purposes. *Journal of Educational Research*, 1959, *53*(2), 73–75.

McCarthy, D. *The language development of the preschool child*. Minneapolis: University of Minnesota Press, 1930.

McCarthy, J. J., & McCarthy, J. F. *Learning disabilities*. Boston: Allyn & Bacon, 1969.

McClelland, D. C. Testing for competence rather than "intelligence." *American Psychologist*, 1973, *28*, 1–14.

McClelland, D. C., Atkinson, J. W., Clark, R. A., & Lowell, E. L. *The achievement motive*. New York: Appleton-Century-Crofts, 1953.

McClelland, G. *An approach to the development and assessment of instruction in science at second-grade level: The concept of energy*. Unpublished doctoral dissertation, Cornell University, 1970.

McConnell, O. L. Perceptual versus verbal mediation in the concept learning of children. *Child Development*, 1964, *35*, 1373–1383.

McConnell, T. R. Discovery versus authoritative identification in the learning of children. *University of Iowa Studies in Education*, 1934, *9*, No. 5.

McCulloch, T. L. The retarded child grows up: Psychological aspects of aging. *American Journal of Mental Deficiency*, 1957, *62*, 201–208.

McGee, H. M. Measurement of authoritarianism and its relation to teachers' classroom behavior. *Genetic Psychology Monographs*, 1955, *52*, 89–146.

McGeehee, W., & Lewis, W. D. The socio-economic status of the homes of mentally superior and retarded children and the occupational rank of their parents. *Journal of Genetic Psychology*, 1942, *60*, 375–380.

McGeoch, J. A., & Irion, A. L. *The psychology of human learning.* New York: Longmans, Green, 1952.

McGuigan, F. J., Calvin, A. D., & Richardson, E. C. Manifest anxiety, palmar perspiration-index, and stylus maze learning. *American Journal of Psychology*, 1959, *72*, 434–438.

McGuire, C. Sex role and community variability in test performance. *Journal of Educational Psychology*, 1961, *52*, 61–73.

McGuire, C., and others. Dimensions of talented behavior. *Educational and Psychological Measurement*, 1961, *21*, 3–38.

McKeachie, W. J. Psychological characteristics of adults and instructional methods in adult education. Paper presented at a Conference on "Psychological background of adult education," Syracuse University, October 1962.

McKeachie, W. J., Lin, Y. G., Milholland, J., & Isaacson, R. Student affiliation motives, teacher warmth, and academic achievement. *Journal of Personality and Social Psychology*, 1966, *4*(4), 457–461.

McKeachie, W. J., Pollie, D., & Speisman, J. Relieving anxiety in classroom examinations. *Journal of Abnormal and Social Psychology*, 1955, *50*, 93–98.

McKee, J. P., & Leader, F. B. The relationships of socio-economic status and aggression to the competitive behavior of preschool children. *Child Development*, 1955, *26*, 135–142.

McKillop, A. S. *The relationship between the reader's attitude and certain types of reading response.* New York: Columbia University, Teachers College, 1952.

McKinney, J. D. Problem-solving strategies in reflective and impulsive children. *Journal of Educational Psychology*, 1975, *67*(6), 807–820.

McLeish, J. The lecture method. In N. L. Gage (Ed.), *The psychology of teaching methods.* Chicago: University of Chicago Press, 1976.

McNeil, J. D., & Keislar, E. R. Individual differences and effectiveness of autoinstruction at the primary grade level. *California Journal of Educational Research*, 1961, *12*, 160–164.

McNeill, D. *The acquisition of language.* New York: Harper & Row, 1970. (a)

McNeill, D. The development of language. In P. Mussen (Ed.), *Carmichael's manual of child psychology* (Vol. I). New York: Wiley, 1970. (b)

McNemar, O. W. An attempt to differentiate between individuals with high and low reasoning ability. *American Journal of Psychology*, 1955, *68*, 20–36.

McNemar, Q. Lost: Our intelligence? Why? *American Psychologist*, 1964, *19*, 871–882.

McNemar, Q., & Terman, L. M. Sex differences in variational tendency. *Genetic Psychology Monographs*, 1936, *18*(1).

McTavish, C. L. Effect of repetitive film showings on learning. *Technical Report SDC. 269-7-12*, Instructional Film Research Program, Pennsylvania State College. Port Washington, N.Y.: Special Devices Center, November 1949.

Mead, M. (Ed.) *Cooperation and competition among primitive peoples.* New York: McGraw-Hill, 1937.

Mead, M. *From the South Seas*. New York Morrow, 1939.

Medley, D., & Mitzel, H. E. Some behavioral correlates of teachers effectiveness. *Journal of Educational Psychology*, 1959, *50*, 239–246.

Mednick, M. T., Mednick, S. A., & Jung, C. C. Continual association as a function of level of creativity and type of verbal stimulus. *Journal of Abnormal and Social Psychology*, 1964, *69*, 511–515.

Meehl, P. E. *Clinical versus statistical prediction*. Minneapolis: University of Minnesota Press, 1954.

Meinke, D. L., George, C. S., & Wilkinson, J. M. Concrete and abstract thinkers at three grade levels and their performance with complex concepts. *Journal of Educational Psychology*, 1975, *67*(1), 154–158.

Meister, M. Cooperation of secondary schools and colleges in acceleration of gifted students. *Journal of Educational Sociology*, 1956, *29*, 220–227.

Melaragno, R. J. Effect of negative reinforcement in an automated teaching setting. *Psychological Reports*, 1960, *7*, 381–384.

Melaragno, R. J. A study of two methods for adapting self-instructional materials to individual differences. USN ONR *Tech. Memo*, 1966, No. 2932-000-01.

Melaragno, R. J. Two methods for adapting self-instructional materials to individual differences. *Journal of Educational Psychology*, 1967, *58*, 327–331.

Melton, A. W. The science of learning and the technology of educational methods. *Harvard Educational Review*, 1959, *29*, 96–106.

Mendel, G. Children's preferences for differing degrees of novelty. *Child Development*, 1965, *36*, 453–465.

Menyuk, P. Syntactic structures in the language of children. *Child Development*, 1963, *34*, 407–422.

Menyuk, P. *Sentences children use*. Cambridge, Mass.: M.I.T. Press, 1969.

Menyuk, P. *The acquisition and development of language*. Englewood Cliffs, N.J.: Prentice-Hall, 1971.

Merrill, M. A. On the relation of intelligence to achievement in the case of mentally retarded children. *Comparative Psychology Monographs*, Vol. II, serial #10, Baltimore 1984.

Merrill, M. D. Correction and review on successive parts in learning a hierarchial task. *Journal of Educational Psychology*, 1965, *56*, 225–234.

Merrill, M. D., & Stolurow, L. M. Hierarchical preview versus problem oriented preview. *Peabody Papers on Human Development*, 1965, *3*, No. 5.

Merrill, M. D., & Stolurow, L. M. Hierarchical preview versus problem oriented review in learning an imaginary science. *American Educational Research Journal*, 1966, *3*, 251–262.

Merrill, M. D., Wood, L. E., & Starr, K. E. *Feedback and remedial instruction in learning hierarchical tasks*. Final Report, Project No. 7-8134. Contract No. OEC 4-7-078134-1660. Brigham Young University, Provo, Utah, March 1969.

Meyer, S. R. Report on the initial test of a junior high-school program. In A. A. Lumsdaine & R. Glaser (Eds.), *Teaching machines and programmed learning*. Washington, D.C.: National Education Association, 1960. (a)

Meyer, S. R. A test of the principles of "activity," "immediate reinforcement," and "guidance" as instrumented by Skinner's teaching machine. *Dissertation Abstracts*, 1960, *20*, 4729–4730. (b)

Meyer, W. J. The stability of patterns of primary mental abilities among junior high and senior high school students. *Educational and Psychological Measurement*, 1960, *20*, 795–800.

Meyer, W. J., & Bendig, A. W. A longitudinal study of the Primary Mental Abilities Test. *Journal of Educational Psychology*, 1961, *52*, 50–60.

Meyer, W. J., & Offenbach, S. I. *Effectiveness of paired verbal reinforcers as a function of task complexity.* Paper presented at the meeting of the Midwestern Psychological Association, May 1961.

Meyer, W. J., & Seidman, S. B. Age differences in the effectiveness of different reinforcement combinations on the acquisition and extinction of a simple concept learning problem. *Child Development*, 1960, *31*, 419–429.

Meyer, W. J., & Seidman, S. B. Relative effectiveness of different reinforcement levels. *Child Development*, 1961, *32*, 117–127.

Meyer, W. T., & Thompson, G. G. Sex differences in the distribution of teacher approval and disapproval among sixth-grade children. *Journal of Educational Psychology*, 1956, *47*, 385–396.

Michael, D. N., & Maccoby, N. Factors influencing verbal learning from films under varying conditions of audience participation. *Journal of Experimental Psychology*, 1953, *46*, 411–418.

Milgram, S. Liberating effects of group pressure. *Journal of Personality and Social Psychology*, 1965, *1*, 127–134.

Miller, G. A. The magical number seven plus or minus two: Some limits in our ability for processing information. *Psychological Review*, 1956, *63*, 81–97.

Miller, G. A. Toward a third metaphor for psycholinguistics. In W. B. Weimer and D. S. Palermo (Eds.), *Cognition and symbolic processes.* Hillsdale, N.J.: Lawrence Erlbaum Assoc., 1974.

Miller, G. A., & Selfridge, J. A. Verbal context and the recall of meaningful material. *American Journal of Psychology*, 1950, *63*, 176–185.

Miller, G. R., & Lobe, J. Opinionated language, open- and closed-mindedness, and response to persuasive communication. *Journal of Communication*, 1967, *17*(4), 333–341.

Miller, L. B., & Dyer, J. L. *Four preschool programs: Their dimensions and effects.* Monographs of the Society for Research in Child Development, 1975, *40*, Serial No. 162.

Millman, J., & Glock, M. D. Trends in the measurement of general mental ability. *Review of Educational Research*, 1965, *35*, 17–24.

Milner, E. A study of the relationships between reading readiness in grade one school children and patterns of parent–child interaction. *Child Development*, 1951, *22*, 95–112.

Milonas, G. T. Retroactive interference in meaningful verbal learning. *Japanese Psychological Research*, 1976, *18*, 91–104.

Mischel, T. Piagetian conceptions of motivation. In T. Mischel (Ed.), *Cognitive development and epistemology.* New York: Academic Press, 1971.

Mitzel, H. *Comparison of the effectiveness of individualized with traditional instruction in 9th year mathematics.* Paper presented at the American Educational Research Association at Atlantic City, N.J., 1962.

Mogar, M. Children's causal thinking about natural phenomena. *Child Development*, 1960, *31*, 59–65.

Montgomery, K. C. The role of exploratory drive in learning. *Journal of Comparative and Psysiological Psychology*, 1954, 47, 60—64.

Monty, R. A., Krash, R., & Taub, H. Keeping track of sequential events: Irrelevant information and paced rehearsal. *Perceptual and Motor Skills*, 1963, 24, 99–103.

More, A. J. Delay of feedback and the acquisition and retention of verbal materials in the classroom. *Journal of Educational Psychology*, 1969, 60, 339–342.

Moreira, M. A. *An Ausubelian approach to physics introduction: An experiment in an introduction college course in electromagnetism.* Unpublished doctoral dissertation, Cornell University, 1977.

Moreno, J. L. *Who shall survive?* Washington, D.C.: Nervous & Mental Disease Publishing Co., 1934.

Morphett, M. V., & Washburne, C. When should children begin to read? *Elementary School Journal*, 1931, 31, 496–503.

Morris, D. P., Soroker, E., & Buruss, G. Follow-up studies of shy, withdrawn children. *American Journal of Orthopsychiatry*, 1954, 24, 743–754.

Morrisett, L., & Hovland, C. I. A comparison of three kinds of training in human problem solving. *Journal of Experimental Psychology*, 1959, 58, 52–55.

Morsh, J. E., & Wilder, E. W. Identifying the effective instructor: A review of the quantitative studies, 1900–1952. *USAF Personnel Training Research Center, Research Bulletin*, 1954, No. AFPTRC-TR-54-44.

Moss, H. A., & Kagan, J. Stability of achievement and recognition seeking behaviors from early childhood through adulthood. *Journal of Abnormal and Social Psychology*, 1961, 62, 504–513.

Moss, J. *An experimental study of the relative effectiveness of the direct-detailed and the directed discovery methods of teaching letterpress imposition.* Unpublished Ed.D. dissertation, University of Illinois, 1960.

Mouw, J. T. Effect of dogmatism on levels of cognitive processes. *Journal of Educational Psychology*, 1969, 60(5, pt. 1), 365–369.

Moynihan, D. D. *The Negro family: A code for national action.* Washington, D.C.: United States Department of Labor, Office of Policy Planning and Research, 1965.

Mukerji, N. F. Investigation of ability to work in groups and in isolation. *British Journal of Psychology*, 1940, 30, 352–356.

Munn, N. L. Learning in children. In L. Carmichael (Ed.), *Manual of child psychology.* New York: Wiley, 1954.

Munro, B. C. Meaning and learning. *Alberta Journal of Educational Research*, 1959, 5, 268–281.

Munsinger, H., & Kessen, W. Uncertainty, structure, and preference. *Psychological Monographs*, 1964, 78, No. 9 (Whole No. 586).

Murray, D. L. *The testing of a model for the interpretation of concept formation using college biology students.* Unpublished doctoral disseration, Purdue University, 1963.

Murray, F. B. Acquisition of conservation through social participation. *Developmental Psychology*, 1972, 6, 1–6.

Mussen, P. H., Conger, J. J., & Kagan, J. *Child development and personality* (4th ed.). New York: Harper & Row, 1974.

Muus, R. E. A comparison of "high causally" and "low causally" oriented sixth grade children in respect to a perceptual intolerance of ambiguity test. *Child Development*, 1960, *31*, 521–536.

Myers, G. C. A study in incidental memory. *Archives of Psychology*, 1913, *5* (Whole No. 26).

Myers, K. E., Travers, R. M. W., & Sanford, M. E. Learning and reinforcement in student pairs. *Journal of Educational Psychology*, 1965, *56*, 67–72.

Myrow, D. C., & Anderson, R. C. Retroactive inhibition of prose as a function of type of test. *Journal of Educational Psychology*, 1972, *63*, 323–328.

Naegele, C. J. *An evaluation of student attitudes, achievement, and learning efficiency in various modes of an individualized, self-paced learning program in introductory college physics.* Unpublished doctoral dissertation, Cornell University, 1974.

Nagge, J. W. An experimental test of the theory of associative inference. *Journal of Experimental Psychology*, 1935, *18*, 663–682.

Nahinsky, I. D., & Slaymaker, F. L. Use of negative instances in conjunctive concept identification. *Journal of Experimental Psychology*, 1970, *84*, 64–68.

Nakamura, C. Y., & Boroczi, G. Effect of relative incentive value on persistence and response speed. *Child Development*, 1965, *36*, 547–557.

National Advisory Committee on Handicapped Children. *Special education for handicapped children* (First annual report). Washington, D.C.: U.S. Department of Health, Education and Welfare, 1968.

National Science Teachers Association Curriculum Committee. *Theory into action in science curriculum development.* Washington, D.C.: Author, 1964.

Naylor, J. C., & Briggs, G. E. Effects of task complexity and task organization on the relative efficiency of part and whole training methods. *Journal of Experimental Psychology*, 1963, *65*, 217–224.

Nelson, K. Structure and strategy in learning to talk. *Monographs of the Society for Research in Child Development*, 1973, No. 149.

Nelson, K., & Kessen, W. *What the child brings to language.* Lecture presented at the Jean Piaget Society Meetings, Philadelphia, May, 1974.

Nelson, V. L. An analytical study of child learning. *Child Development*, 1936, *7*, 95–114.

Newcomb, T. M. Student peer-group influence. In N. Sanford (Ed.), *The American college.* New York: Wiley, 1962.

Newell, A., Shaw, J. C., & Simon, H. A. Elements of a theory of human problem solving. *Psychological Review*, 1958, *65*, 151–166.

Newman, E. B. Forgetting of meaningful material during sleep and waking. *American Journal of Psychology*, 1939, *52*, 65–71.

Newman, H. H., Freeman, F. N., & Holzinger, K. J. *Twins: A study of heredity and environment.* Chicago: University of Chicago Press, 1937.

Newman, S. E. Student vs. instructor design of an experimental method. *Journal of Educational Psychology*, 1957, *48*, 318–323.

Newson, R. S., & Gaite, J. H. Prose learning: Effects of pretesting and reduction of passage length. *Psychological Reports*, 1971, *28*, 123–129.

Newsteter, W. I., Feldstein, M. J., & Newcomb, T. M. *Group Adjustment: A study in experimental sociology.* Cleveland: Western Reserve University, 1938.

Newton, J. M., & Hickey, A. E. Sequence effects in programmed learning of a verbal concept. *Journal of Educational Psychology*, 1965, *56*, 140–147.

Nickel, H. Untersuchungen zur Bedeutung einer erhoten Motivation fur eine einzelheitliche Auffassung in der visuellen Wahrnehmung vierjahriger Kinder. *Psychologische Rundschau*, 1968, *19*, 9–17.

Nisbet, J. Family environment and intelligence. *Eugenics Review*, 1953, *45*, 31–40.

Nissen, H. W., Chow, K. L., & Semmes, J. Effects of restricted opportunity for tactual, kinaesthetic, and manipulative experience on the behavior of a chimpanzee. *American Journal of Psychology*, 1951, *64*, 485–507.

Noble, C. E. The role of stimulus meaning (m) in serial verbal learning. *Journal of Experimental Psychology*, 1952, *43*, 437–446.

Noble, C. E. The familiarity-frequency relationship. *Psychological Review*, 1953, *60*, 80–98.

Nordland, F. H., Lawson, A. E., & Kahle, J. B. A study of levels of concrete and formal reasoning ability in disadvantaged junior and senior high school science students. *Science Education*, 1974, *58*, 569–575.

Norman, D. A. *Attention and memory*. New York: Wiley, 1965.

Northrop, D. S. Effects on learning of the prominence of organizational outlines in instructional films. *Human Engineering Report SDC.269-7-33*. Pennsylvania State College, Instructional Films Research Program, October 1952.

Northway, M. L. The influence of age and social group on children's remembering. *British Journal of Psychology*, 1936, *27*, 11–29.

Novak, J. D. An experimental comparison of a conventional and a project centered method of teaching a college general botany course. *Journal of Experimental Education*, 1958, *26*, 217–230.

Novak, J. D. An approach to the interpretation and measurement of problem solving ability. *Science Education*, 1961, *45*(a), 122–131.

Novak, J. D. The role of concepts in science teaching. In H. J. Klausmeier & C. W. Harris (Eds.), *Analysis of concept learning*. New York: Academic Press, 1966.

Novak, J. D. An approach to the interpretation and measurement of problem solving ability. *Science Education*, 1971, *48*(2), 122–131.

Novak, J. D. *Facilities for secondary school science teaching: Evolving patterns in facilities and programs*. Washington, D.C.: National Science Teachers Association, 1972.

Novak, J. D. Understanding the learning process and effectiveness of teaching methods in the classroom, laboratory, and field. *Science Education*, 1976, *60*, 493–512.

Novak, J. D. *A theory of education*. Ithaca, N.Y.: Cornell University Press, 1977.

Novak, J. D. An alternative to Piagetian psychology for science and mathematics education. *Studies in Science Education*, in press.

Novak, J. D., Ring, D. G., & Tamir, P. Interpretation of research findings in terms of Ausubel's theory and implications for science education. *Science Education*, 1971, *55*(4), 483–526.

Nussbaum, J., & Novak, J. D. An assessment of children's concepts of earth utilizing structured interviews. *Science Education*, 1976, *60*(4), 535–550.

Oakes, M. E. Explanations of natural phenomena by adults. *Science Education*, 1945, *29*, 137–142; 190–201.

Oakes, M. E. *Children's explanations of natural phenomena*. New York: Columbia University, Teachers College, 1947.

O'Donnell, R. C., Griffin, W. J., & Norris, R. *Syntax of kindergarten and elemen-*

*tary school children: A transformational analysis.* Champaign, Ill.: National Council of Teachers of English, 1967.

Oetzel, R. *Selected bibliography on sex differences.* Mimeographed report, Stanford University, 1962.

Ohnmacht, F. W. Achievement, anxiety, and creative thinking. *American Educational Research Journal,* 1966, *3,* 131–138.

Ojemann, R. H., Maxey, E. J., & Snider, B. C. Further study of guided learning experience in developing probability concepts in grade 5. *Perceptual and Motor Skills,* 1966, *23,* 97–98.

Ojemann, R. H., & Pritchett, K. Piaget and the role of guided experiences in human development. *Perceptual and Motor Skills,* 1963, *17,* 927–940.

Olsen, R. C. A comparative study of the effect of behavior objectives on class performance and retention in physical science. *Journal of Research in Science Teaching,* 1973, *10,* 271–277.

Olson, L. A. Concept attainment of high school sophomores. *Journal of Educational Psychology,* 1963, *54,* 213–216.

Olson, W. C., & Hughes, B. O. Subsequent growth of children with and without nursery school experience. *In 39th Yearbook, National Society for the Study of Education.* Chicago: University of Chicago Press, 1940.

Olson, W. C., & Hughes, B. O. Growth of the child as a whole. In R. G. Barker, J. S. Kounin, & H. F. Wright (Eds.), *Child behavior and development.* New York: McGraw-Hill, 1943.

O'Neil, H. F., Spielberger, C. D., & Hansen, D. N. Effect of state anxiety and task difficulty on computer-assisted learning. *Journal of Educational Psychology,* 1969, *60*(5, part 1), 343–350.

Osborne, R. T. Racial differences in mental growth and school achievement: A longitudinal study. *Psychological Reports,* 1960, *7,* 233–239.

Osgood, C. E., Suci, G. J., and Tannenbaum, P. H. *The measurement of meaning.* Urbana: University of Illinois Press, 1957.

Osler, S. F., & Shapiro, S. L. Studies in concept attainment: IV. The role of partial reinforcement as a function of age and intelligence. *Child Development,* 1964, *35,* 623–633.

Osler, S. F., & Weiss, S. R. Studies in concept attainment: III. Effect of instruction at two levels of intelligence. *Journal of Experimental Psychology,* 1962, *63,* 528–533.

Outhit, M. C. A study of the resemblance of parents and children in general intelligence. *Archives of Psychology,* 1933, No. 149.

Overing, R. L. R., & Travers, R. M. W. Effect upon transfer of variations in training conditions. *Journal of Educational Psychology,* 1966, *57,* 179–188.

Owen, S. G., and others previously. Programmed learning in medical education. *Postgraduate Medical Journal,* 1965, *41,* 201.

Owens, W. A. Age and mental abilities: A longitudinal study. *Genetic Psychology Monographs,* 1953, *48,* 3–54.

Owens, W. A. Effects of motivating instructions on reaction time in grade school children. *Child Development,* 1959, *30,* 261–268.

Page, E. B. Teacher comments and student performance: A seventy-four classroom experiment in school motivation. *Journal of Educational Psychology,* 1958, *49,* 173–181.

Palermo, D. S., Castenada, A., & McCandless, B. R. The relationship of anxiety in children to performance in a complex learning task. *Child Development*, 1956, *27*, 333–337.

Palermo, D. S., & Malfese, D. L. Language acquisition from age five onwards. *Psychological Bulletin*, 1972, *78*(6), 409–428.

Paradowski, W. Effect of curiosity on incidental learning. *Journal of Educational Psychology*, 1967, *58*(1), 50–55.

Parnes, S. J., & Meadow, A. Effect of "brainstorming" instructions on creative problem solving by trained and untrained subjects. *Journal of Educational Psychology*, 1959, *50*, 171–176.

Parsons, T. The school class as a social system: Some of its functions in American society. *Harvard Educational Review*, 1959, *29*, 297–318.

Partridge, E. D. Guidance of the adolescent. In E. Harms (Ed.), *Handbook of child guidance*. New York: Child Care Publications, 1947.

Pasamanick, B., & Knobloch, H. Early language behavior in Negro children and the testing of intelligence. *Journal of Abnormal and Social Psychology*, 1955, *50*, 401–402.

Pasamanick, B., & Knobloch, H. Retrospective studies on the epidemiology of reproductive causality: Old and new. *Merrill-Palmer Quarterly*, 1966, *12*(1), 7–26.

Patton, J. A. *A study of the effects of student acceptance of responsibility and motivation on course behavior*. Unpublished doctoral dissertation, University of Michigan, 1955.

Paul, I. H. Studies in remembering: The reproduction of connected and extended verbal material. *Psychological Issues*, 1, No. 2 (Whole No. 2). New York: International Universities, 1959.

Peak, H. Attitude and motivation. In *Nebraska Symposium on motivation*. Lincoln: University of Nebraska Press, 1955.

Peeck, J. Effect of prequestions on delayed retention of prose material. *Journal of Educational Psychology*, 1970, *61*, 241–246.

Peel, E. A. Experimental examination of some of Piaget's schemata concerning children's perception and thinking, and a discussion of their educational significance. *British Journal of Educational Psychology*, 1959, *29*, 89–103.

Penney, R. K. Reactive curiosity and manifest anxiety in children. *Child Development*, 1965, *36*, 697–702.

Penney, R. K., & Lipton, A. A. Children's discrimination learning as a function of reward and punishment. *Journal of Comparative and Physiological Psychology*, 1961, *54*, 449–451.

Penney, R. K., & McCann, B. The children's reactive curiosity scale. *Psychological Reports*, 1964, *15*, 323–334.

Perkins, H. V. Classroom behavior and underachievement. *American Educational Research Journal*, 1965, *2*, 1–12.

Peterson, G. M. An empirical study of the ability to generalize. *Journal of Genetic Psychology*, 1932, *6*, 90–114.

Peterson, H. A. Recitation or recall as a factor in the learning of long prose selections. *Journal of Educational Psychology*, 1944, *35*, 220–228.

Peterson, H. A., Ellis, M., Toohill, N., & Kloess, P. Some measurements of the effect of reviews. *Journal of Educational Psychology*, 1935, *26*, 65–72.

Peterson, J. The effect of attitude on immediate and delayed recall: A class experiment. *Journal of Educational Psychology*, 1916, *7*, 523–532.

Pettigrew, T. F. Negro American personality: Why isn't it more known? *Journal of Social Issues*, 1964, *2*, 4–23.

Pettigrew, T. F., & Green, R. L. School desegregation in large cities: A critique of the Coleman "White Flight" thesis. *Harvard Educational Review*, 1976, *46*(1), 1–53.

Phillips, B. N. Problem behavior in the elementary school. *Child Development*, 1968, *39*, 895–903.

Phillips, B. N., & D'Amico, L. A. Effects of cooperation and competition on the cohesiveness of small face-to-face groups. *Journal of Educational Psychology*, 1956, *47*, 65–70.

Phillips, B. N., Hindsman, E., & Jennings, E. Influence of intelligence on anxiety and perception of self and others. *Child Development*, 1960, *31*, 41–46.

Phillips, W. B. Counseling Negro students: An educational dilemma. *California Journal of Educational Research*, 1959, *10*, 185–188.

Piaget, J. *Judgment and reasoning in the child.* New York: Harcourt, 1928.

Piaget, J. *The child's conception of the world.* London: Routledge, 1929.

Piaget, J. *The child's conception of physical causality.* New York: Harcourt, 1932.

Piaget, J. *The psychology of intelligence.* New York: Harcourt, 1950.

Piaget, J. *The origins of intelligence in children.* New York: International Universities, 1952.

Piaget, J. How children form mathematical concepts. *Scientific American*, 1953, *189*(5), 74–79.

Piaget, J. *The construction of reality in the child.* New York: Basic Books, 1954. (a)

Piaget, J. Language and thought from the genetic point of view. *Acta Psychologica*, 1954, *10*, 51–60. (b)

Piaget, J. *Logic and psychology.* New York: Basic Books, 1957. (a)

Piaget, J. Logique et équilibre dans les comportements du sujet. *Études d'Epistémologie Génétique*, 1957, *2*, 27–117. (b)

Piaget, J. Development and learning. In R. E. Ripple & V. N. Rockcastle (Eds.), *Piaget rediscovered.* Ithaca, N.Y.: School of Education, Cornell University, 1964.

Piaget, J. *Genetic epistemology.* New York: Columbia University Press, 1970. (a)

Piaget, J. Piaget's theory. In P. Mussen (Ed.), *Carmichael's manual of child psychology* (Vol. I). New York: Wiley, 1970. (b)

Piaget, J. *The science of education and the psychology of the child.* New York: Orion Press, 1970. (c)

Piaget, J. *Child and reality.* New York: Grossman, 1973.

Piaget, J. *To understand is to invent.* New York: Grossman, 1974.

Piaget, J., & Inhelder, B. *Psychology of the child.* New York: Basic Books, 1969.

Pickrel, E. W. The differential effect of manifest anxiety on test performance. *Journal of Educational Psychology*, 1958, *49*, 43–46.

Pierce-Jones, J. Socio-economic status and adolescents' interests. *Psychological Reports*, 1959, *5*, 683. (a)

Pierce-Jones, J. Vocational interest correlates of socio-economic status in adolescence. *Educational & Psychological Measurement*, 1959, *19*, 65–71. (b)

Piers, E. V., Daniels, J. M., & Quackenbush, J. F. The identification of creativity in adolescents. *Journal of Educational Psychology*, 1960, *51*, 346–351.

Pines, A. L. *Scientific concept learning in children: The effect of prior knowledge on resulting cognitive structure subsequent to A-T instruction.* Unpublished doctoral dissertation, Cornell University, 1977.

Pines, M. How three-year-olds teach themselves to read and love it. *Harpers*, May 1963, *226*, 58–64.

Pinneau, S. R. The infantile disorders of hospitalism and anaclitic depression. *Psychological Bulletin*, 1955, *52*, 429–452.

Pistor, F. How time concepts are acquired by children. *Educational Method*, 1940, *20*, 107–112.

Plowman, L., & Stroud, J. B. The effect of informing pupils of the correctness of their responses to objective test questions. *Journal of Educational Research*, 1942, *36*, 16–20.

Plumlee, L. B. Comparison of problem-types in the comprehensive mathematics test. *College Board Review*, 1947, *1*, 17–31.

Popham, W. J., & Husek, T. R. Implications of criterion referenced measurement. *Journal of Educational Measurement*, 1969, *6*, 1–9.

Popp, H., & Porter, D. Programming verbal skills for primary grades. *AV Communication Review*, 1960, *8*, 165–175.

Poppleton, P. K., & Austwick, K. A comparison of programmed learning and notetaking at two age levels. *British Journal of Educational Psychology*, 1964, *34*, 43–50.

Porter, D. Some effects of year-long teaching machine instruction. In E. Galanter (Ed.), *Automatic teaching: The state of the art.* New York: Wiley, 1959.

Posner, G. J. The extensiveness of curriculum structure: A conceptual scheme. *Review of Educational Research*, 1974, *44*(4), 401–407.

Postlethwait, S. N. The use of audio-tape for a multi-faceted approach to teaching botany. *American Journal of Botany*, 1962, *49*, 681.

Postlethwait, S. N., Novak, J. D., & Murray, H. *The audio-tutorial approach to learning through independent study and integrated experience* (3rd ed.). Minneapolis: Burgess, 1972.

Postman, L. Learned principles of organization in memory. *Psychological Monographs*, 1954, *68* (Whole No. 374).

Postman, L. Repetition and paired-associate learning. *American Journal of Psychology*, 1962, *75*, 372–389.

Postman, L., & Rau, L. Retention as a function of the method of measurement. *University of California Publications in Psychology*, 1957, *8*, 217–270.

Postman, L., & Senders, V. L. Incidental learning and generality of set. *Journal of Experimental Psychology*, 1946, *36*, 153–165.

Prentice, W. C. H. Retroactive inhibition and the motivation of learning. *American Journal of Psychology*, 1943, *56*, 283–292.

Pressey, S. L. Development and appraisal of devices providing immediate automatic scoring of objective tests and concomitant self-instruction. In A. A. Lumsdaine & R. Glaser (Eds.), *Teaching machines and programmed learning.* Washington, D.C.: National Education Association, 1960.

Pressey, S. L. Basic unresolved teaching-machine problems. *Theory into Practice*, 1962, *1*, 30–37. (a)

Pressey, S. L. *New theory, no "programming," new future.* Paper presented at the meeting of the American Psychological Association, St. Louis, September 1962. (b)

Pressey, S. L. Age and the doctorate—then and now. *Journal of Higher Education*, 1962, *33*, 153–160. (c)

Pressey, S. L. Two basic neglected psychoeducational problems. *American Psychologist*, 1965, *20*, 391–393.

Pressey, S. L. "Fordling" accelerates ten years after. *Journal of Counseling Psychology*, 1967, *14*(1), 73–80.

Price, B. M., & Bell, B. G. The relationship of chronological age, mental age, IQ and sex to divergent thinking test. *Journal of Psychological Researches*, 1965, *9*, 1–9.

Probst, C. A. A general information test for kindergarten children. *Child Development*, 1931, *2*, 81–95.

Proshansky, H. M., & Newton, P. The nature and meaning of Negro self-identity. In M. Deutsch, I. Katz, & A. Jensen (Eds.), *Social class, race and psychological development*. New York: Holt, Rinehart and Winston, 1968.

Prothro, E. T. Ethnocentrism and anti-Negro attitudes in the deep South. *Journal of Abnormal and Social Psychology*, 1952, *47*, 105–108.

Provence, S., & Lipton, R. C. *Infants in institutions*. New York: International Universities, 1962.

Pufall, P. B. Induction of linear-order concepts: A comparison of three training techniques. *Child Development*, 1972, *44*, 642.

Purvis, A. W. *An analysis of the abilities of different intelligence levels of secondary-school pupils*. Unpublished Ed.D. dissertation, Harvard University, 1938.

Pyper, J. R. *The effect of simultaneous presentation of spoken and written words on the development of foreign language pronunciation habits*. Unpublished master's dissertation, University of Illinois, 1964.

Raab, E., & Lipset, S. M. *Prejudice and society*. New York: Anti-Defamation League of B'Nai B'rith, 1959.

Raaheim, K. Problem solving and past experience. *Monographs of the Society for Research in Child Development*, 1965, *30*, 58–67 (Ser. No. 100).

Rainwater, L. Crucible of identity: The Negro lower-class family. In T. Parsons & J. B. Clark (Eds.), *The Negro American*. Boston: Beacon, 1966.

Ramaseshan, R. S. A note on the validity of the mental age concept. *Journal of Educational Psychology*, 1950, *41*, 56–58.

Rambusch, N. M. *Learning how to learn: An American approach to Montessori*. Baltimore: Helicon, 1962.

Rapp, A. The experimental background of the problems of learning. *Classical Journal*, 1945, *40*, 467–480.

Rasmussen, E. A., & Archer, E. J. Concept identification as a function of language pretraining and task complexity. *Journal of Experimental Psychology*, 1961, *61*, 437–441.

Raven, R., & Polanski, H. Relationship among Piaget's logical operations, science content comprehension, critical thinking, and creativity. *Science Education*, 1974, *58*(4), 531–544.

Ray, W. E. *An experimental comparison of direct-detailed and directed discovery methods of teaching micrometer principles and skills*. Unpublished Ed.D. dissertation, University of Illinois, 1957.

Ray, W. E. Verbal compared with manipulative solution of an apparatus problem. *American Journal of Psychology*, 1957, *70*, 289–290.

Raynor, J. O. Relationships between achievement-related motives, future orientation, and academic performance. *Journal of Personality and Social Psychology*, 1970, *15*(1), 28–33.

Reed, H. B. Meaning as a factor in learning. *Journal of Educational Psychology*, 1938, *29*, 419–430.

Reed, H. B. Factors influencing the learning and retention of concepts; I. The influence of set. *Journal of Experimental Psychology*, 1946, *36*, 71–87.

Reed, H. B. Teacher variables of warmth, demand, and utilization of intrinsic motivation related to pupils' science interests: A study illustrating several potentials of variance-covariance. *Journal of Experimental Education*, 1961, *29*, 205–229.

Reese, H. W. Manifest anxiety and achievement in test performance. *Journal of Educational Psychology*, 1961, *52*, 132–135.

Regensburg, J. Studies of educational success and failure in supernormal children. New York: *Archives of Psychology*, Columbia University, 1931.

Reichard, S., Schneider, M., & Rapaport, D. The development of concept formation in children. *American Journal of Orthopsychiatry*, 1944, *14*, 156–162.

Reid, J. W. An experimental study of "analyses of the goal" in problem solving. *Journal of General Psychology*, 1951, *44*, 51–69.

Reymert, M., & Hinton, R., Jr. The effect of a change to a relatively superior environment upon the IQ's of one hundred children. In *39th Yearbook*, National Society for the Study of Education, Part II. Chicago; University of Chicago Press, 1940.

Reynolds, J. H. Cognitive transfer in verbal learning. *Journal of Educational Psychology*, 1966, *57*, 382–388.

Reynolds, J. H., & Glaser, R. Effects of repetition and spaced review upon retention of a complex learning task. *Journal of Educational Psychology*, 1964, *55*, 297–308.

Rhine, R. J. *The effect on problem solving of success or failure as a function of cue specifiicity.* Technical Report No. 8, NR 150–149. Stanford, Calif.: Stanford University, Department of Psychology, 1955.

Richards, J. M., Cline, V. B., & Needham, W. E. Creativity tests and teacher and self-judgments of originality. *Journal of Experimental Education*, 1964, *32*, 281–285.

Rickards, J. P. Processing effects of advance organizers interspersed in text. *Reading Research Quarterly*, 1975–1976, *11*, 599–621.

Rickards, J. P. Interaction of position and conceptual level of adjunct questions on immediate and delayed retention of text. *Journal of Educational Psychology*, 1976, *68*(2), 210–217.

Rickards, J. P., & DiVesta, F. J. Types and frequency of questions in processing textual material. *Journal of Educational Psychology*, 1974, *66*, 354–362.

Rickards, J. P., & Hatcher, C. W. *Meaningful learning postquestions as semantic cues for poor readers.* Unpublished manuscript, Purdue University, Department of Education, 1975.

Riesen, A. H. The development of visual perception in man and chimpanzee. *Science*, 1947, *106*, 107–108.

Riessman, F. *The culturally deprived child.* New York: Harper & Row, 1962.

Ring, D. G. *An analysis of the cognitive influence of high school chemistry in-*

*struction on college chemistry achievement.* Unpublished doctoral dissertation, Cornell University, 1969.

Ring, D. G., & Novak, J. D. The effects of cognitive structure variables on achievement in college chemistry. *Journal of Research in Science Teaching,* 1971, *8*(4), 325–333.

Riopelle, A. Transfer suppression and learning sets. *Journal of Comparative and Physiological Psychology,* 1953, *46,* 108–114.

Roberts, K. E. The ability of preschool children to solve problems in which a simple principle of relationship is kept constant. *Journal of Genetic Psychology,* 1940, *56,* 353–366.

Robins, L. N. *Deviant children grown up: A sociological and psychiatric study of sociopathic personality.* Baltimore: Williams & Wilkins, 1966.

Robinson, B. W. A study of anxiety and academic achievement. *Journal of Consulting Psychology,* 1966, *30,* 165–167.

Robinson, W. P. The achievement motive, academic success, and intelligence test scores. *British Journal of Social and Clinical Psychology,* 1965, *4,* 98–109.

Rock, I. The role of repetition in associative learning. *American Journal of Psychology,* 1957, *70,* 186–193.

Roe, A. Crucial life experiences in the development of scientists. In E. P. Torrance (Ed.), *Education and talent.* Minneapolis: University of Minnesota Press, 1960.

Roe, A. Automated teaching methods using linear programs. *Journal of Applied Psychology,* 1962, *46,* 198–201.

Roe, K. V., Case, H. W., & Roe, A. Scrambled versus ordered sequence in auto-instructional programs. *Journal of Educational Psychology,* 1962, *53,* 101–104.

Rogers, A. L. The growth of intelligence at the college level. *School and Society,* 1930, *31,* 693–699.

Rokeach, M. *The open and closed mind.* New York: Basic Books, 1960.

Romey, W. D. *Inquiry techniques for teaching science.* Englewood Cliffs, N.J.: Prentice-Hall, 1968.

Rosch, E. H. On the internal structure of perceptual and semantic categories. In T. E. Moore (Ed.), *Cognitive development and the acquisition of language.* New York: Academic Press, 1973.

Rosch, E. H. Basic objects in natural categories. *Cognitive Psychology,* 1976, *8,* 382–439.

Rosen, B. C. Race, ethnicity, and the achievement syndrome. *American Sociological Review,* 1959, *24,* 47–60.

Rosen, B. C. The achievement syndrome and economic growth in Brazil. *Social Forces,* 1964, *42,* 341–354.

Rosen, B. C., & D'Andrade, R. The psychosocial origins of achievement motivation. *Sociometry,* 1959, *22,* 185–218.

Rosenshine, B. *Teaching behaviours and student achievement.* London: National Foundation for Educational Research in England and Wales, 1971.

Rosenthal, B. G. Hypnotic recall of material learned under anxiety and non-anxiety producing conditions. *Journal of Experimental Psychology,* 1944, *34,* 368–389.

Rosenthal, R., & Jackson, L. *Pygmalion in the classroom: Teacher expectation and pupils' intellectual development.* New York: Holt, Rinehart and Winston, 1968.

Rosenthal, T. L., & Zimmerman, B. Modeling by exemplification and instruction in training conservation. *Developmental Psychology*, 1972, *6*, 392–401.

Ross, C. C., & Henry, L. K. The relation between frequency of testing and progress in learning psychology. *Journal of Educational Psychology*, 1939, *30*, 604–611.

Rossi, E. Development of classificatory behavior. *Child Development*, 1964, *35*, 137–142.

Roth, R. H. Student reactions to programmed learning. *Phi Delta Kappan*, 1963, *44*, 278–281.

Rothkopf, E. Z. The concept of mathemagenic activities. *Review of Educational Research*, 1970, *40*(3), 325–336.

Rothman, A. I., Welch, W. W., & Walberg, H. J. Physics teacher characteristics and student learning. *Journal of Research in Science Teaching*, 1969, *6*(1), 59–63.

Rowe, M. B. *Teaching science as continuous inquiry.* New York: McGraw-Hill, 1973.

Rowell, R. M. *Children's concept of natural phenomena: Use of cognitive mapping approach to describe these concepts.* Paper presented at the Annual Convention of the National Association for Research in Science Teaching, March 1975.

Rowell, R. M. *Cognitive mapping analysis of science concept development in elementary school children.* Paper presented at the 49th Annual Convention of the National Association for Research in Science Teaching, San Francisco, April 1976.

Rowlett, J. D. *An experimental comparison of direct-detailed and directed discovery methods of teaching orthographic projection principles and skills.* Unpublished Ed.D. dissertation, University of Illinois, 1960.

Rowsey, R. E., & Mason, W. H. Immediate achievement and retention in audio-tutorial versus conventional lecture-laboratory instruction. *Journal of Research in Science Teaching*, 1975, *12*(4), 393–397.

Royer, J. M., & Cable, G. W. Facilitating learning in connected discourse. *Journal of Educational Psychology*, 1975, *67*(1), 116–123.

Rudnitsky, A. M. *Content structure, cognitive structure and their relationship: A methodological investigation.* Unpublished doctoral dissertation, Cornell University, 1976.

Ruediger, W. G. The indirect improvement of mental function through ideals. *Educational Review*, 1908, *36*, 364–371.

Runkel, P. J., & Damrin, D. Effects of training and anxiety upon teachers' preferences for information about students. *Journal of Educational Psychology*, 1961, *52*, 254–261.

Russell, D. G., & Sarason, I. G. Text anxiety, sex, and experimental conditions in relation to anagram solution. *Journal of Personality and Social Psychology*, 1965, *1*, 493–496.

Russell, D. H., & Saadeh, I. Q. Qualitative levels in children's vocabularies. *Journal of Educational Psychology*, 1962, *53*, 170–174.

Russell, R. W. Studies in animism: II. The development of animism. *Journal of Genetic Psychology*, 1940, *56*, 353–366.

Rust, M. M. The effect of resistance on intelligence test scores of young children. *Child Development Monographs*, 1931, No. 6.

Ryan, F. L., & Ellis, A. K. *Instructional implications of inquiry.* Englewood Cliffs, N.J.: Prentice-Hall, 1974.

Ryans, D. G. *Characteristics of teachers.* Washington, D.C.: American Council on Education, 1960.

Ryans, D. G. Some relationships between pupil behavior and certain teacher characteristics. *Journal of Educational Psychology,* 1961, *52,* 82–90.

Ryor, J. Mainstreaming. *Today's Education,* March–April 1976, *65*(2).

Sackett, G. P. Effects of rearing conditions upon the behavior of rhesus monkeys *(Macaca mulatta). Child Development,* 1965, *36,* 855–868.

Sadker, M., & Sadker, D. Sexual discrimination in the elementary school. *The National Elementary Principal,* 1972, *52*(2), 41–45.

Sarason, I. G. Test anxiety and the intellectual performance of college students. *Journal of Educational Psychology,* 1961, *52,* 201–206.

Sarason, I. G. Test anxiety and intellectual performance. *Journal of Abnormal and Social Psychology,* 1963, *66,* 73–75.

Sarason, S. B., Davidson, K. S., Lighthall, F. F., Waite, R. R., & Ruebush, B. K. *Anxiety in elementary school children: A report of research.* New York: Wiley, 1960.

Sarason, S. B., Hill, K. T., & Zimbardo, P. G. A longitudinal study of the relation of test anxiety to performance on intelligence and achievement tests. *Monographs of the Society for Research in Child Development,* 1964, *29* (Whole No. 98).

Sarason, S. B., et al. Classroom observations of high and low anxious children. *Child Development,* 1958, *29,* 287–295.

Sassenrath, J. M. Learning without awareness and transfer of learning sets. *Journal of Educational Psychology,* 1959, *50,* 205–211.

Sassenrath, J. M. Anxiety, aptitude, attitude, and achievement. *Psychology in the Schools,* 1967, *4*(4), 341–346.

Sassenrath, J. M., & Garverick, C. M. Effects of differential feedback from examinations on retention and transfer. *Journal of Educational Psychology,* 1965, *56,* 259–263.

Sassenrath, J. M., & Yonge, G. D. Delayed information feedback, feedback cues, retention set, and delayed retention. *Journal of Educational Psychology,* 1968, *59,* 69–73.

Sattler, H. E., & Van Wagenen, R. *Empirical referents of school motivation.* Proceedings of the 75th Annual Convention of the American Psychological Association, 1967, *2,* 327–328.

Saugstad, P. Problem-solving as dependent upon availability of functions. *British Journal of Psychology,* 1955, *46,* 191–198.

Saugstad, P., & Raaheim, K. Problem-solving, past experience, and availability of function. *British Journal of Psychology,* 1960, *51,* 97–104.

Saul, E. V., & Osgood, C. E. Perceptual organization of material as a factor influencing ease of learning and degree of retention. *Journal of Experimental Psychology,* 1950, *40,* 372–379.

Sax, G. Concept acquisition as a function of differing schedules and delays of reinforcement. *Journal of Educational Psychology,* 1960, *51,* 32–36.

Sax, G., & Ottina, J. P. The arithmetic reasoning of pupils differing in school experience. *California Journal of Educational Research,* 1958, *9,* 15–19.

Sayegh, Y., & Dennis, W. The effect of supplementary experiences upon the behavioral development of infants in institutions. *Child Development*, 1965, *36*, 82–90.

Scandura, J. M. Algorithm learning and problem solving. *Journal of Experimental Education*, 1966, *34*, 1–6. (a)

Scandura, J. M. Problem solving and prior learning. *Journal of Experimental Education*, 1966, *34*, 7–11. (b)

Scanzoni, J. Socialization, achievement, and achievement values. *American Sociological Review*, 1967, *32*(3), 449–456.

Scherer, G. A., & Wertheimer, M. *A psycholinguistic experiment in foreign-language teaching.* New York: McGraw-Hill, 1964.

Schmidt, H. O. The effects of praise and blame as incentives to learning. *Psychological Monographs*, 1941, *53*, No. 3.

Schmuck, R. A. Some aspects of classroom social climate. *Psychology in the Schools*, 1966, *3*, 59–64.

Schneider, L., & Lysgaard, S. The deferred gratification pattern: A preliminary study. *American Sociological Review*, 1953, *18*, 142–149.

Schpoont, S. H. *Some relationships between task attractiveness, self-evaluated motivation, and success or failure.* Unpublished doctoral dissertation, University of Illinois, 1955.

Schramm, W. *The research on programmed instruction.* Washington, D.C.: U.S. Department of Health, Education, & Welfare, 1964.

Schroder, H. M., & Rotter, J. B. Rigidity as learned behavior. *Journal of Experimental Psychology*, 1952, *43*, 141–150.

Schrom, N. *Missouri high school English offerings reported by University of Missouri freshmen in relation to their freshman English placement scores.* Unpublished doctoral dissertation, University of Missouri, 1953.

Schuessler, K., & Strauss, A. A study of concept learning by scale analysis. *American Sociological Review*, 1950, *15*, 752–762.

Schulman, M. J., & Havighurst, R. J. Relations between ability and social status in a mid-Western community: IV. Size of vocabulary. *Journal of Educational Psychology*, 1947, *38*, 437–442.

Schulz, R. W. *The role of cognitive organizers in the facilitation of concept learning in elementary school science.* Unpublished doctoral dissertation, Purdue University, 1966.

Schwab, J. J., & Brandwein, P. F. *The teaching of science.* Cambridge, Mass.: Harvard University Press, 1962.

Schwartz, F. C. *Validation of the generalizing-particularizing dimension of cognitive style and its implications for meaningful learning.* Unpublished doctoral dissertation, City University of New York, 1972.

Scott, J. P. Implications of infra-human social behavior for problems of human relations. In M. Sherif & M. O. Wilson (Eds.), *Group relations at the crossroads.* New York: Harper & Row, 1953.

Scott, J. P. A time to learn. *Psychology Today*, 1969, *2*, 46–48; 66–67.

Scott, J. P., Fredericson, E., & Fuller, J. L. Experimental exploration of the critical period hypothesis. *Journal of Personality*, 1951, *1*, 162–183.

Scott, J. P., & Marston, M. Critical periods affecting the development of normal and maladjustive social behavior of puppies. *Journal of Genetic Psychology*, 1950, *77*, 25–60.

Scott, W. A. Attitude change through reward of verbal behavior. *Journal of Abnormal and Social Psychology*, 1957, *55*, 72–75.

Sears, P. S. Levels of aspiration in academically successful and unsuccessful children. *Journal of Abnormal and Social Psychology*, 1940, *35*, 498–536.

Sears, P. S. *The effect of classroom conditions on the strength of achievement motivation and work output in children.* Stanford, Calif.: Stanford University, 1963.

Sears, R. R. Initiation of the repressive sequence by experienced failure. *Journal of Experimental Psychology*, 1937, *20*, 570–580.

Sechrest, L., & Kaas, J. S. Concept difficulty as a function of stimulus similarity. *Journal of Educational Psychology*, 1965, *56*, 327–333.

Segel, D. *Intellectual abilities in the adolescence period.* Washington, D.C.: Federal Security Agency, 1948.

Segel, D. *Frustration in adolescent youth.* Washington, D.C.: Federal Security Agency, 1951.

Seidner, C. J. Teaching with simulations and games. In N. L. Gage (Ed.), *The psychology of teaching methods.* Chicago: University of Chicago Press, 1976.

Senesh, L. The organic curriculum: A new experiment in economic education. *The Councilor*, 1960, *21*(1), 43–56.

Serra, M. C. A study of fourth grade children's comprehension of certain verbal abstractions. *Journal of Experimental Education*, 1953, *22*, 103–118.

Sewell, W. H., Haller, A. O., & Strauss, M. A. Social status and educational and occupational aspiration. *American Sociological Review*, 1957, *22*, 67–73.

Sexton, P. C. Social class and pupil turn-over rates. *Journal of Educational Sociology*, 1959, *33*, 131–134.

Shaffer, L. H. Concept formation in an ordering task. *British Journal of Psychology*, 1961, *42*, 361–369.

Shamos, M. H. Science for citizens. *Saturday Review*, September 16, 1961, 68–69.

Shannon, D. C. What research says about acceleration. *Phi Delta Kappan*, 1957, *39*, 70–72.

Schantz, C. U. The development of social cognition. In E. M. Hetherington, J. Hagen, R. Kron, & A. H. Stein (Eds.), *Review of child development research* (Vol. 5). Chicago: University of Chicago Press, 1975.

Sharpe, J. F. The retention of meaningful material. *Catholic University of America, Educational Research Monographs*, 1952, *16*, No. 8.

Shavelson, R. J. Some aspects of the correspondence between content structures and cognitive structures in physics instruction. *Journal of Educational Psychology*, 1972, *63*, 225–234.

Shavelson, R. J. Learning from physics instruction. *Journal of Research in Science Teaching*, 1973, *10*, 101–111.

Shaw, M. C., Edson, K., & Bell, H. M. The self-concept of bright underachieving high school students as revealed by an adjective check list. *Personnel and Guidance Journal*, 1960, *39*, 193–196.

Shaw, M. C., & McCuen, J. T. The onset of academic underachievement in bright children. *Journal of Educational Psychology*, 1960, *51*, 103–108.

Shaw, M. E. A comparison of individuals and small groups in the rational solution of complex problems. *American Journal of Psychology*, 1932, *44*, 491–504.

Shaw, M. E. Some motivational factors in cooperation and competition. *Journal of Personality*, 1958, *26*, 155–169.

Shaw, M. E., & Shaw, L. M. Some effects of sociometric grouping upon learning in a second grade classroom. *Journal of Social Psychology*, 1962, *57*, 453–458.

Shay, C. B. Relationship of intelligence to step size on a teaching machine program. *Journal of Educational Psychology*, 1961, *52*, 98–103.

Sheffield, F. D. Theoretical considerations in the learning of complex sequential tasks from demonstration and practice. In A. A. Lumsdaine (Ed.), *Student response in programmed instruction*. Washington, D.C.: National Academy of Sciences, National Research Council, 1961.

Sheppard, J. L. Conservation of part and whole in the acquisition of class inclusion. *Child Development*, 1973, *44*, 380–383.

Sherif, M. Self-concept. In D. L. Sills (Ed.), *International encyclopedia of the social sciences* (Vol. 14). New York: Macmillan, 1968.

Sherif, M., & Sherif, C. W. *Groups in harmony and tension*. New York Harper & Row, 1953.

Sherif, M., & Sherif, C. W. *Reference groups*. New York: Harper & Row, 1964.

Sherman, M., & Key, C. B. The intelligence of isolated mountain children. *Child Development*, 1932, *3*, 279–290.

Shore, E., & Sechrest, L. Concept attainment as a function of number of positive instances presented. *Journal of Educational Psychology*, 1961, *52*, 303–307.

Shuey, A. *The testing of Negro intelligence* (2nd ed.). New York: Social Science Press, 1966.

Shuey, A. M. Improvement in scores on the American Council Psychological Examination from freshman to senior year. *Journal of Educational Psychology*, 1948, *39*, 417–426.

Shuttleworth, F. K. The cumulative influence on intelligence of socioeconomic differentials operating on the same children over a period of ten years. In *39th Yearbook, National Society for the Study of Education*, Part II. Chicago: University of Chicago Press, 1940.

Sieber, J. E., Kameya, L. I., & Paulson, F. L. Effect of memory support on the problem-solving ability of text-anxious children. *Journal of Educational Psychology*, 1970, *61*, 159–168.

Siegel, L., & Macomber, F. G. Comparative effectiveness of televised and large classes and of small sections. *Journal of Educational Psychology*, 1957, *48*, 371–382.

Siegel, L., & Siegel, L. C. Educational set: A determinant of acquisition. *Journal of Educational Psychology*, 1965, *56*, 1–12.

Sigel, I. E. Developmental trends in the abstraction ability of children. *Child Development*, 1953, *24*, 131–144.

Sigel, I. E. Dominance of meaning. *Journal of Genetic Psychology*, 1954, *85*, 201–207.

Sigel, I. E., Anderson, L. M., & Shapiro, H. Categorization behavior of lower and middle class Negro pre-school children: Differences in dealing with representation of familiar objects. *Journal of Negro Education*, 1966, *35*, 218–229.

Sigel, I. E., & Cocking, R. R. *Cognitive development from childhood to adoles-*

*cence: A constructivist perspective.* New York: Holt, Rinehart and Winston, 1977.

Sigel, I. E., & McBane, B. *Cognitive competence and level of symbolization among five-year-old children.* Paper presented at the meeting of the American Psychological Association, New York, September 1966.

Sigel, I. E., & Olmstead, P. Modification of classificatory competence and level of representation among lower-class Negro kindergarten children. In A. H. Passow (Ed.), *Reaching the disadvantaged learner.* New York: Columbia University-Teachers College, 1970.

Silberman, H. F. Self-instructional devices and programmed materials. *Review of Educational Research,* 1962, *32,* 179–193.

Silberman, H. F., Melaragno, R. J., & Coulson, J. E. Confirmation and prompting with connected discourse material. *Psychological Reports,* 1961, *8,* 401–406. (a)

Silberman, H. F., et al. Fixed sequence versus branching auto-instructional methods. *Journal of Educational Psychology,* 1961, *52,* 166–172. (b)

Siller, J. Socio-economic status and conceptual thinking. *Journal of Abnormal and Social Psychology,* 1957, *55,* 365–371.

Silverman, I. W., & Geiringer, E. Dyadic interaction and conservation induction: A test of Piaget's equilibration model. *Child Development,* 1973, *44,* 815–879.

Silverman, I. W., & Stone, J. Modifying cognitive functioning through participation in a problem-solving group. *Journal of Educational Psychology,* 1972, *63,* 603–608.

Silverman, R. E., & Alter, M. Note on the response in teaching machine programs. *Psychological Reports,* 1960, *7,* 496.

Simon, H. A. How big is a chunk? *Science,* 1974, *183,* 482–488.

Sims, V. M. The relative influence of two types of motivation on improvement. *Journal of Educational Psychology,* 1928, *19,* 480–484.

Singer, S. L., & Stefflre, B. A note on racial differences in job values and desires. *Journal of Social Psychology,* 1956, *43,* 333–337.

Skaggs, E. B., and others. Further studies of the reading-recitation process in learning. *Archives of Psychology,* 1930, *18* (Whole No. 114).

Skeels, H. M., & Fillmore, E. A. Mental development of children from under-privileged homes. *Journal of Genetic Psychology,* 1937, *50,* 427–439.

Skeels, H. M., et al. A study of environmental stimulation: An orphanage preschool project. *University of Iowa Studies of Child Welfare,* 1938, No. 4.

Skelton, J., & Hill, J. P. Effects on cheating of achievement anxiety and knowledge of peer performance. *Developmental Psychology,* 1969, *1*(5), 449–455.

Skelton, R. B. High-school foreign language study and freshman performance. *School and Society,* 1957, *85,* 203–205.

Skinner, B. F. *The behavior of organisms.* New York: Appleton, 1938.

Skinner, B. F. *Walden two.* New York: Macmillan, 1948.

Skinner, B. F. *Verbal behavior.* New York: Appleton, 1957.

Skinner, B. F. Teaching machines. *Science,* 1958, *128,* 969–977.

Skodak, M. Children in foster homes: A study of mental development. *University of Iowa Studies of Child Welfare,* 1939, *16,* No. 1.

Skodak, M., & Skeels, H. M. A final follow-up of one hundred adopted children. *Journal of Genetic Psychology,* 1949, *75,* 85–125.

Slamecka, N. J. Studies of retention of connected discourse. *American Journal of Psychology,* 1959, *72,* 409–416.

Slamecka, N. J. Studies of retroaction of connected discourse. *Journal of Experimental Psychology*, 1960, *59*, 104–108.

Slobin, I. Grammatical transformations and sentence comprehension in childhood and adulthood. *Journal of Verbal Learning and Verbal Behavior*, 1966, *5*(3), 219–227.

Smedslund, J. Transitivity of preference patterns as seen by pre-school children. *Scandanavian Journal of Psychology*, 1960, *1*, 49–54.

Smedslund, J. The acquisition of conservation of substance and weight in children. *Scandanavian Journal of Psychology*, 1961, *2*, 11–20; 71–87; 153–160; 203–210.

Smedslund, J. The acquisition of conservation of substance and weight in children: VII. Conservation of discontinuous quantity and the operations of adding and taking away. *Scandanavian Journal of Psychology*, 1962, *3*, 69–77.

Smedslund, J. Concrete reasoning: A study of intellectual development. *Monographs of the Society for Research in Child Development*, 1964, *29*, 1–39.

Smith, B. O. *Logical aspects of educational measurement*. New York: Columbia University Press, 1938.

Smith, B. O. Critical thinking. In *Recent research developments and their implications for teacher education*. 13th Yearbook, American Association of Colleges for Teacher Education. Washington, D.C.: The Association, 1960.

Smith, C. U., & Prothro, J. W. Ethnic differences in authoritarian personality. *Social Forces*, 1957, *35*, 334–338.

Smith, D. D. Dogmatism, cognitive consistency, and knowledge of conflicting facts. *Sociometry*, 1968, *31*(3), 259–277.

Smith, H. P. A study in the selective character of American secondary education: Participation in school activities as conditioned by socio-economic status and other factors. *Journal of Educational Psychology*, 1945, *36*, 229–246.

Smith, L. M. *Programmed learning in elementary school: An experimental study of relationships between mental abilities and performance*. Technical Report No. 2. Urbana: University of Illinois, Training Research Laboratory, August 1962.

Smith, M. E. A study of some factors influencing the development of the sentence in preschool children. *Journal of Genetic Psychology*, 1935, *46*, 182–212.

Smith, M. H., & Stearns, E. The influence of isolation on the learning of the surrounding material. *American Journal of Psychology*, 1949, *62*, 369–381.

Smith, S. Language and non-verbal test performance of racial groups in Honolulu before and after a fourteen-year interval. *Journal of General Psychology*, 1942, *26*, 51–93.

Smith, S. G., & Sherwood, B. A. Educational uses of the PLATO computer system. *Science*, 1976, *192*, 344–352.

Smock, C. D. The relationship between "intolerance of ambiguity," generalization, and speed of perceptual closure. *Child Development*, 1957, *28*, 27–36.

Smock, C. D. Perceptual rigidity and closure phenomenon as a function of manifest anxiety in children. *Child Development*, 1958, *29*, 237–247.

Smuts, R. W. The Negro community and the development of Negro potential. *Journal of Negro Education*, 1957, *26*, 456–465.

Snow, R. E. Unfinished Pygmalion. (Review of *Pygmalion in the classroom: Teacher expectation and pupil's intellectual development*, by R. Rosenthal and L. Jacobson.) *Contemporary Psychology*, 1969, *14*(4), 197–199.

Solomon, D., Rosenberg, L., & Bezdek, W. E. Teacher behavior and student learning. *Journal of Educational Psychology*, 1964, *55*, 23–30.

Solomon, R. L., & Brush, E. S. Experimentally derived conceptions of anxiety and aversion. In M. R. Jones (Ed.), *Nebraska symposium on motivation*. Lincoln: University of Nebraska Press, 1956.

Sommerfeld, R. E., & Tracy, N. H. *A study of selected predictors of success in second-year algebra in high school*. Paper presented at the meeting of the American Educational Research Association, Atlantic City, N.J., February 1961.

Sones, A. M., & Stroud, J. B. Review with special reference to temporal position. *Journal of Educational Psychology*, 1940, *31*, 665–676.

Sontag, L. W., Baker, C. T., & Nelsen, V. Personality as a determinant of performance. *American Journal of Orthopsychiatry*, 1955, *25*, 555–563.

Sontag, L. W., & Kagan, J. The emergence of intellectual achievement motives. *American Journal of Orthopsychiatry*, 1963, *13*, 175–178.

Sparks, P. D., & Unbehaun, L. M. Achievement of audio-tutorial and conventional biology students: A comparative study. *Bioscience*, 1971, *21*, 574–576.

Spaulding, R. *Achievement, creativity, and self-concept correlates of teacher–pupil transactions in elementary schools*. Urbana: University of Illinois, 1963. (Mimeographed.)

Spear, P. S. Motivational effects of praise and criticism on children's learning. *Developmental Psychology*, 1970, *3*, 124–132.

Speer, G. S. The mental development of children of feeble-minded and normal mothers. In *39th Yearbook*, National Society for the Study of Education (Part II). Chicago: University of Chicago Press, 1940.

Spence, K. W. The relation of learning theory to the technology of education. *Harvard Educational Review*, 1959, *29*, 84–95.

Spencer, R. E. *The relationship between personality anxiety and selected problem-solving processes*. Unpublished doctoral dissertation, University of Illinois, 1957.

Spicker, H. H. Intellectual development through early childhood education. In H. F. Clarizio, R. C. Craig, & W. A. Mehrens (Eds.), *Contemporary issues in educational psychology* (2nd ed.). Boston: Allyn & Bacon, 1974.

Spiegel, L. H. The child's concept of beauty: A study in concept formation. *Journal of Genetic Psychology*, 1950, *77*, 11–23.

Spielberger, C. D. The effects of manifest anxiety on the academic achievement of college students. *Mental Hygiene*, 1962, *46*, 420–426.

Spielberger, C. D., & Katzenmeyer, W. G. Manifest anxiety, intelligence, and college grades. *Journal of Consulting Psychology*, 1959, *23*, 278.

Spight, J. B. Day and night intervals in the distribution of practice. *Journal of Experimental Psychology*, 1928, *11*, 397–398.

Spiker, C. C. Experiments with children on the hypotheses of acquired distinctiveness of cues. *Child Development*, 1956, *27*, 253–263.

Spiker, C. C. Verbal factors in the discrimination learning of children. *Monographs of the Society for Research in Child Development*, 1963, *28* (Whole No. 86), 53–69.

Spiker, C. C., & Terrell, G. Factors associated with transposition behavior of preschool children. *Journal of Genetic Psychology*, 1955, *86*, 143–158.

Spitz, R. A. Hospitalism: An inquiry into the genesis of psychiatric conditions in early childhood. *Psychoanalytic Studies of the Child*, 1945, *1*, 53–74.

Spitz, R. A. The role of ecological factors in emotional development in infancy. *Child Development*, 1949, *20*, 145–155.

Spitzer, H. F. Studies in retention. *Journal of Educational Psychology*, 1939, *30*, 641–656.

Spitzer, H. F. Class size and pupil achievement in elementary schools. *Elementary School Journal*, 1954, *55*, 82–86.

Stacey, C. L. The law of effect in retained situations with meaningful material. In *Learning theory in school situations*, University of Minnesota Studies in Education. Minneapolis: University of Minnesota Press, 1949.

Stanley, J. C. The role of instruction, discovery, and revision in early learning. *Elementary School Journal*, 1949, *49*, 455–458.

Stefflre, B. Concurrent validity of the Vocational Values Inventory. *Journal of Educational Research*, 1959, *52*, 339–351.

Stein, A. H. The influence of social reinforcement on the achievement behavior of fourth-grade boys and girls. *Child Development*, 1969, *40*, 727–736.

Stendler, C. B., Damrin, D., & Haines, A. C. Studies of cooperation and competition: I. The effect of working for group and individual rewards on the social climate of children's groups. *Journal of Genetic Psychology*, 1951, *79*, 173–197.

Stephens, W. E. A comparison of the performance of normal and subnormal boys on structured categorization tasks. *Exceptional Children*, 1964, *30*, 311–315.

Stern, C. Labeling and variety in concept identification with young children. *Journal of Educational Psychology*, 1965, *56*, 235–240.

Stern, G. G. Measuring noncognitive variables in research on teaching. In N. L. Gage (Ed.), *Handbook of research on teaching*. Skokie, Ill.: Rand McNally, 1963.

Stevenson, H. W. Latent learning in children. *Journal of Experimental Psychology*, 1954, *47*, 17–21.

Stevenson, H. W., & Bitterman, M. E. The distance-effect in the transposition of intermediate size of children. *American Journal of Psychology*, 1955, *68*, 274–279.

Stevenson, H. W., & Langford, T. Time as a variable in transposition by children. *Child Development*, 1957, *28*, 365–370.

Stevenson, H. W., & Odom, R. D. The relation of anxiety to children's performance on learning and problem-solving tasks. *Child Development*, 1965, *36*, 1003–1012.

Stevenson, H. W., & Stewart, E. C. A developmental study of racial awareness in young children. *Child Development*, 1958, *29*, 339–409.

Stevenson, H. W., & Swartz, J. D. Learning set in children as a function of intellectual level. *Journal of Comparative and Physiological Psychology*, 1958, *51*, 755–757.

Stimpson, D. V. The influence of commitment and self-esteem on susceptibility to persuasion. *Journal of Social Psychology*, 1970, *80*, 189–195.

Stolurow, L. M. *Teaching by machine*. Washington, D.C.: U.S. Office of Education, 1961.

Stolurow, L. M., & Walker, C. C. A comparison of overt and covert response in programmed learning. *Journal of Educational Research*, 1962, *55*, 421–429.

Stone, L. J., & Church, J. *Childhood and adolescence: A psychology of the growing person* (3rd ed.). New York: Random House, 1973.

Stone, M. A. *The development of the intersituational generality of formal thought.* Unpublished doctoral dissertation, University of Illinois, 1966.

Stone, M. A., & Ausubel, D. P. The intersituational generality of formal thought. *Journal of Genetic Psychology,* 1969, *175,* 169–180.

Stott, L. H., & Ball, R. S. Infant and preschool mental tests: Review and evaluation. *Monographs of the Society for Research in Child Development,* 1965, *30*(3).

Stover, N. The child's learning difficulty as related to the emotional problem of the mother. *American Journal of Orthopsychiatry,* 1953, *23,* 131–141.

Strauss, A. The development and transformation of monetary meaning in the child. *American Sociological Review,* 1952, *17,* 275–286.

Strauss, S. Inducing cognitive development and learning: A review of short term training experiments. I. The organic-developmental approach to cognition. *Cognition,* 1972, *1,* 329–357.

Strictland, D. S. Black is beautiful vs. white is right. In H. F. Clarizio, R. C. Craig, & W. A. Mehrens (Eds.), *Contemporary issues in educational psychology* (2nd ed.). Boston: Allyn & Bacon, 1974.

Strike, K. A. On the expressive potential of behavioral language. *American Educational Research Journal,* 1974, *11*(3), 103–120.

Strodtbeck, F. L. Family interaction, values, and achievement. In D. C. McClelland (Ed.), *Talent and society.* Princeton, N.J.: Van Nostrand, 1958.

Strom, I. M. Research in grammar and usage and its implication for teaching and writing. *Indiana University School of Education Bulletin,* 1960, *36,* No. 5.

Stroud, J. B. The role of practice in learning. In *The psychology of learning.* 41st Yearbook, National Society for the Study of Education, Part II. Chicago: University of Chicago Press, 1942.

Sturges, P. T. Verbal retention as a function of the informativeness and delay of informative feedback. *Journal of Educational Psychology,* 1969, *60,* 11–14.

Suchman, J. R. *Training children in scientific inquiry.* Urbana: University of Illinois, College of Education, 1959.

Suchman, J. R. Inquiry training in the elementary school. *Science Teacher,* 1960, *27,* 42–47.

Suchman, J. R. Inquiry training: Building skills for autonomous discovery. *Merrill-Palmer Quarterly of Behavior and Development,* 1961, *7,* 148–169.

Suchman, J. R. *The inquiry process and the elementary school child.* Paper presented at the meeting of the American Educational Research Association, Atlantic City, February 1962.

Suedfeld, P., & Goeller, N. The effect of motivational arousal on information processing in the convergent word identification task. *Psychonomic Science,* 1967, *9,* 231–233.

Suinn, R. M. A factor modifying the concept of anxiety as an interfering drive. *Journal of General Psychology,* 1965, *73,* 43–46.

Sullivan, E. V. *An investigation into the use of different degrees of filmed verbal explanations on the activation, generalization, and extinction of conservation of substance problems in children.* Toronto: Ontario Institute for Studies in Education, 1966.

Sullivan, E. V. *Piaget and the school curriculum. A critical appraisal.* Bulletin No. 2. Toronto: Ontario Institute for Studies in Education, 1967.

Suppes, P., & Ginsberg, R. Application of a stimulus sampling model to children's concept formation with and without an overt correction response. *Journal of Experimental Psychology*, 1962, *63*, 330–336. (a)

Suppes, P., & Ginsberg, R. Experimental studies of mathematical concept formation in young children. *Science Education*, 1962, *46*, 230–240. (b)

Suppes, P., & Ginsberg, R. A fundamental property of all-or-none models, binomial distribution of responses prior to conditioning, with application to concept formation in children. *Psychological Review*, 1963, *70*, 139–161.

Swenson, C. H. College performance of students with high and low school marks when academic aptitude is controlled. *Journal of Educational Research*, 1957, *50*, 597–603.

Swenson, E. J. Organization and generalization as factors in learning, transfer, and retroactive inhibition. In *Learning theory in school situations*. University of Minnesota Studies in Education. Minneapolis: University of Minnesota Press, 1949, 9–39.

Szuman, S. Comparison, abstraction, and analytic thought in the child. *Enfance*, 1951, *4*, 189–216.

Taba, H. *Curriculum development: Theory and practice*. New York: Harcourt, 1962.

Taft, R. Selective recall and memory distortion of favorable and unfavorable material. *Journal of Abnormal and Social Psychology*, 1954, *49*, 23–28.

Tanner, J. M., & Inhelder, B. (Eds.). *Discussions on child development*. New York: International Universities, 1960.

Tate, M. W., & Stanier, B. Errors in judgment of good and poor problem solvers. *Journal of Experimental Education*, 1964, *32*, 371–376.

Taveggia, T. C. Personalized instruction: A summary of comparative research, 1967–1974. *American Journal of Physics*, 1976, *44*(11), 1028–1033.

Teeter, B., Rouzer, D. L., & Rosen, E. Development of cognitive motivation: Preference for widely known information. *Child Development*, 1964, *35*, 1105–1111.

Terman, L. M., & Merrill, M. A. *Measuring intelligence*. Boston: Houghton Mifflin, 1937.

Terman, L. M., & Oden, M. H. *The gifted child grows up: 25 years follow-up of a superior group*. Stanford, Calif.: Stanford University Press, 1949.

Terman, L. M., & Oden, M. H. *The gifted group at mid-life*. Stanford, Calif. Stanford University Press, 1969.

Terman, L. M., & Tyler, L. E. Psychological sex differences. In L. Carmichael (Ed.), *Manual of child psychology* (2nd ed.). New York: Wiley, 1954.

Terrell, G. Manipulatory motivation in children. *Journal of Comparative and Physiological Psychology*, 1959, *52*, 705–709.

Terrell, G., Durkin, K., & Wiesley, M. Social class and the nature of the incentive in discrimination learning. *Journal of Abnormal and Social Psychology*, 1959, *59*, 270–272.

Thiele, C. L. *The contribution of generalization to the learning of the addition facts*. Contributions to Education, No. 763. New York: Columbia University, Teachers College, 1938.

Thisted, M. N., & Remmers, H. H. The effect of temporal set on learning. *Journal of Applied Psychology*, 1932, *16*, 257–268.

Thomas, S., & Knudsen, D. D. The relationship between non-promotion and the dropout problem. *Theory into practice*, 1965, *4*, 90–94.

Thompson, C. W., & Margaret, A. Differential test responses of normals and mental defectives. *Journal of Abnormal and Social Psychology*, 1949, *42*, 285–293.

Thompson, G. G., & Hunnicutt, C. W. The effect of repeated praise or blame on the work achievement of "introverts" and "extroverts." *Journal of Educational Psychology*, 1944, *35*, 257–266.

Thompson, W. R., & Heron, W. The effects of restricting early experience on the problem solving capacity of dogs. *Canadian Journal of Psychology*, 1954, *8*, 17–31.

Thorndike, E. L. *The psychology of learning: Educational psychology* (Vol. 2). New York: Columbia University, Teachers College, 1913.

Thorndike, E. L. The effect of changed data upon reasoning. *Journal of Experimental Psychology*, 1922, *5*, 33–38.

Thorndike, E. L. Mental discipline in high school studies. *Journal of Educational Psychology*, 1924, *15*, 1–22; 83–98.

Thorndike, E. L. On the improvement of intelligence scores from thirteen to nineteen. *Journal of Educational Psychology*, 1926, *17*, 73–76.

Thorndike, E. L., et al. *The measurement of intelligence.* New York: Columbia University, Teachers College, 1926.

Thorndike, E. L. *Human learning.* New York: Century, 1931.

Thorndike, E. L. *The fundamentals of learning.* New York: Columbia University, Teachers College, 1932.

Thorndike, E. L. *The psychology of wants, interests, and attitudes.* New York: Appleton, 1935.

Thorndike, E. L., Bregman, E. O., Tilton, J. W., & Woodyard, E. *Adult learning.* New York: Macmillan, 1928.

Thorndike, R. L. Growth of intelligence during adolescence. *Journal of Genetic Psychology*, 1948, *72*, 11–15.

Thorndike, R. L. Methodological issues in relation to definition and appraisal of underachievement. *American Psychologist*, 1961, *16*, 46.

Thorndike, R. L. *The concepts of over- and underachievement.* New York: Columbia University, Teachers College, 1963.

Thorndike, R. L. Review of R. Rosenthal & L. Jacobsen, *Pygmalion in the classroom. American Educational Research Journal*, 1968, *5*, 708–711.

Thune, L. E. The effect of different types of preliminary activities on subsequent learning of paired-associate material. *Journal of Experimental Psychology*, 1950, *40*, 423–438. (a)

Thune, L. E. Warm-up effect as a function of level of practice in verbal learning. *American Psychologist*, 1950, *5*, 251. (b)

Thune, L. E., & Ericksen, S. C. *Studies in abstraction learning: IV. The transfer effects of conceptual versus rote instruction in a simulated classroom situation.* Nashville: Vanderbilt University, 1960. (Mimeographed.)

Thurstone, L. L. *Primary mental abilities.* Chicago: University of Chicago Press, 1938.

Thurstone, L. L., & Ackerson, L. The mental growth curve for the Binet tests. *Journal of Educational Psychology*, 1929, *20*, 569–583.

Thurstone, L. L., & Thurstone, T. G. *Tests of primary mental abilities for ages five and six*. Chicago: Science Research Associates, 1946.

Thysell, R. V., & Shulz, R. W. Concept-utilization as a function of the strength of relevant and irrelevant associations. *Journal of Verbal Learning and Verbal Behavior*, 1964, *3*, 203–258.

Tiedeman, H. R. A study of retention in classroom learning. *Journal of Educational Research*, 1948, *41*, 516–531.

Tinkelman, S. N. Planning the objective test. In R. L. Thorndike (Ed.), *Educational measurement* (2nd ed.). Washington, D.C.: American Council on Education, 1971.

Tizard, J. The effects of different types of supervision on the behavior of mental defectives in a sheltered workshop. *American Journal of Mental Deficiency*, 1953, *58*, 143–161.

Tobias, S. Effect of creativity response mode and subject matter familiarity on achievement from programmed instruction. *Journal of Educational Psychology*, 1969, *60*, 453–460.

Tobias, S., & Abramson, T. *The relationship of anxiety, stress, response mode and content difficulty in programmed instruction*. Programmed Instruction Research Project, City College, City University of New York, March, 1970.

Todd, F. J., Terrell, G., & Frank, C. E. Differences between normal and underachievers of superior ability. *Journal of Applied Psychology*, 1962, *46*, 183–190.

Tolman, E. C. *Purposive behavior in animals and men*. New York: Century, 1932.

Tomkins, S. S. An experimental study of anxiety. *Journal of Psychology*, 1943, *15*, 307–313.

Tomlinson, R. M. *A comparison of four presentation methods for teaching complex technical material*. Unpublished Ed.D. dissertation, University of Illinois, 1962.

Torcivia, J. M., & Laughlin, P. R. Dogmatism and concept-attainment strategies. *Journal of Personality and Social Psychology*, 1968, *4*(4, Pt. 1), 397–400.

Torrance, E. P. Eight partial replications of the Getzels-Jackson study. *Research Memorandum BER-60-15*. Minneapolis: Bureau of Educational Research, University of Minnesota, 1960. (a)

Torrance, E. P. Gifted children. In *Recent research and developments and their implications for teacher education*. 13th Yearbook, American Association of Colleges for Teacher Education. Washington, D.C.: The Association, 1960. (b)

Torrance, E. P. Priming creative thinking in the primary grades. *Elementary School Journal*, 1961, *62*, 34–41.

Torrance, E. P. *Education and the creative potential*. Minneapolis: University of Minnesota Press, 1963.

Torrance, E. P. *Rewarding creative behavior*. Englewood Cliffs, N.J.: Prentice Hall, 1965.

Torrance, E. P., & Myers, R. E. *Creative learning and teaching*. New York: Dodd, Mead, 1972.

Torrance, E. P., & Torrance, J. P. *Is creativity teachable?* Bloomington, Ind.: Phi Delta Kappan, 1973.

Torrance, E. P., Yamamoto, K., Schenetzki, D., Palamutlu, N., & Luther, B. *Assessing the creative thinking abilities of children*. Minneapolis: Bureau of Educational Research, University of Minnesota, 1960.

Toulmin, S. *Human understanding: Vol. I. The collective use and evolution of concepts.* Princeton: Princeton University Press, 1972.

Trabasso, T. Representation, meaning and reasoning: How do we make transitive inferences? In A. D. Peck (Ed.), *Minnesota symposia on child psychology.* Minneapolis: University of Minnesota Press, 1975.

Travers, R. M. W. (Ed.). *Second handbook of research on teaching.* Skokie, Ill.: Rand McNally, 1973.

Traweek, M. W. The relationship between certain personality variables and achievement through programmed instruction. *California Journal of Educational Research,* 1964, *15,* 215–220.

Tresselt, M. E., & Spragg, S. D. S. Changes occurring in the serial reproduction of verbally perceived materials. *Journal of Genetic Psychology,* 1941, *58,* 255–264.

Trowbridge, M. H., & Cason, H. An experimental study of Thorndike's theory of learning. *Journal of General Psychology,* 1932, *7,* 245–248.

Tryon, C. M. The adolescent peer culture. In *Adolescence.* 43rd Yearbook, National Society for the Study of Education, Part I. Chicago: University of Chicago Press, 1944.

Tulving, E. Episodic and semantic memory. In E. Tulving & W. D. Donaldson (Eds.), *Organization of memory.* New York: Academic Press, 1972.

Tuma, E., & Livson, N. Family socioeconomic status and adolescent attitudes to authority. *Child Development,* 1960, *31,* 387–399.

Tumin, M. M. Readiness and resistance to desegregation: A social portrait of the hard core. *Social Forces,* 1958, *36,* 256–263.

Tyler, F. T. Issues related to readiness. In *Theories of learning and instruction.* 63rd Yearbook, National Society for the Study of Education, Part II. Chicago: University of Chicago Press, 1964.

Tyler, R. W. What high school pupils forget. *Educational Research Bulletin,* 1930, *9,* 490–497.

Tyler, R. W. *Constructing achievement tests.* Columbus: Ohio State University, 1934. (a)

Tyler, R. W. Some findings from studies in the field of college biology. *Science Education,* 1934, *18,* 133–142. (b)

Tyler, R. W. *Basic principles of curriculum and instruction.* Chicago: University of Chicago Press, 1949.

Udry, J. R. The importance of social class in a suburban school. *Journal of Educational Sociology,* 1960, *33,* 307–310.

Uhlinger, C. A., & Stephens, M. W. Relation of achievement motivation to academic achievement in students of superior ability. *Journal of Educational Psychology,* 1960, *51,* 259–266.

Uhlman, F. W., & Saltz, E. Retention of anxiety material as a function of cognitive differentiation. *Journal of Personality and Social Psychology,* 1965, *1,* 55–62.

Ullman, C. A. Teachers, peers and tests as predictors of maladjustment. *Journal of Educational Psychology,* 1957, *48,* 257–267.

Ulmer, G. Teaching geometry to cultivate reflective thinking: An experimental study with 1239 high school pupils. *Journal of Experimental Education,* 1939, *8,* 18–25.

Underwood, B. J. Speed of learning and amount retained: A consideration of methodology. *Psychological Bulletin*, 1954, *51*, 276–282.

Underwood, B. J. Verbal learning in the educative process. *Harvard Educational Review*, 1959, *29*, 107–117.

Underwood, B. J. Ten years of massed practice on distributed practice. *Psychological Review*, 1961, *68*, 229–247.

Underwood, B. J., & Keppel, G. One-trial learning. *Journal of Verbal Learning and Verbal Behavior*, 1962, *1*, 1–13.

Underwood, B. J., Rehula, R., & Keppel, G. Item selection and paired-associate learning. *American Journal of Psychology*, 1962, *75*, 353–371.

Underwood, B. J., & Richardson, J. The influence of meaningfulness, intralist similarity, and serial position in retention. *Journal of Experimental Psychology*, 1956, *52*, 119–126.

Underwood, B. J., & Schulz, R. W. *Meaningfulness and verbal learning*. Chicago: Lippincott, 1960.

Uzgaris, I. C. Situational generality of conservation. *Child Development*, 1964, *35*, 831–841.

VanAlstyne, D. *Play behavior and choice of play materials of preschool children*. Chicago: University of Chicago Press, 1932.

VanBuskirk, C. Performance on complex reasoning tasks as a function of anxiety. *Journal of Abnormal and Social Psychology*, 1961, *62*, 200–209.

VanderMeer, A. W. The economy of time in industrial training. *Journal of Educational Psychology*, 1945, *36*, 65–90.

Vannoy, J. S. Generality of cognitive complexity-simplicity as a personality construct. *Journal of Personality and Social Psychology*, 1965, *2*, 385–396.

Vaughan, G. M., & White, K. D. Conformity and authoritarianism re-examined. *Journal of Personality and Social Psychology*, 1966, *3*, 363–366.

Vernon, P. E. Changes in abilities from 14 to 20 years. *Advances in Science*, 1948, *5*, 138.

Vernon, P. E. *The structure of human abilities*. New York: Wiley, 1950.

Vinacke, W. E. The investigation of concept formation. *Psychological Bulletin*, 1951, *48*, 1–32.

Vincent, W. S., Ash, P., & Greenhill, L. P. *Relationship of length and fact frequency to effectiveness of instructional motion pictures. Technical Report SDC. 269-7-7, Pennsylvania State College*, Instructional Film Research Program, November 1949.

vonWright, J. M. *An experimental study of human serial learning*. Helsinki: Finnish Scientific Society, 1957.

Vygotsky, L. S. *Thought and language*. New York: Wiley, 1962.

Wagman, M. University achievement and daydreaming behavior. *Journal of Counseling Psychology*, 1968, *15*(2), 196–198.

Walker, C. C., & Stolurow, L. M. A comparison of overt and covert response in programmed learning. *Journal of Educational Research*, 1962, *55*, 421–429.

Walker, C. M., & Bourne, L. E. The identifications of concepts as a function of amount of relevant and irrelevant information. *American Journal of Psychology*, 1961, *74*, 410–417.

Wallach, L., & Sprott, R. L. Inducing number conservation in children. *Child Development*, 1964, *35*, 1057–1071.

Wallach, L., Wall, A. J., & Andesron, L. Number conservation: The roles of reversibility, addition-subtraction, and misleading perceptual cues. *Child Development*, 1967, *38*, 425–442.

Wallach, M. A., & Kogan, N. *Modes of thinking in young children*. New York: Holt, Rinehart and Winston, 1965.

Wallen, N. E. & Travers, R. W. M. Analysis and investigation of teaching methods. In N. L. Gage (Ed.), *Handbook of ersearch on teaching*. Skokie, Ill.: Rand McNally, 1963.

Wallon, H. Pre-categorical thinking in the child. *Enfance*, 1952, *5*, 97–101.

Walter, D., Denzler, L. S., & Sarason, I. G. Anxiety and the intellectual performance of high school students. *Child Development*, 1964, *35*, 917–926.

Wann, K. D., Dorn, M. S., & Liddle, E. A. *Fostering intellectual development in young children*. New York: Columbia University, Teachers College, 1962.

Ward, A. H., & Davis, R. A. Individual differences in retention of general science subject matter in the case of three measurable objectives. *Journal of Experimental Education*, 1938, *7*, 24–30.

Ward, A. H., & Davis, R. A. Acquisition and retention of factual information in seventh grade general science during a semester of eighteen weeks. *Journal of Educational Psychology*, 1939, *30*, 116–125.

Ward, L. B. Reminiscence and rote learning. *Psychological Monographs*, 1937, *49*, No. 220.

Ward, W. C. Reflection-impulsivity in kindergarten children. *Child Development*, 1968, *39*, 867–874.

Washburne, N. F. Socioeconomic status, urbanism, and academic performance in college. *Journal of Educational Research*, 1959, *53*, 130–137.

Waterhouse, I. K., & Child, I. L. Frustration and the quality of performance. *Journal of Personality*, 1953, *21*, 298–311.

Waterman, C. K., & Katkin, E. S. Energizing (dynamogenic) effect of cognitive dissonance on task performance. *Journal of Personality and Social Psychology*, 1967, *6*(2), 126–131.

Watson, G. B. Do groups think more efficiently than individuals? *Journal of Abnormal and Social Psychology*, 1928, *23*, 328–336.

Watson, W. S., & Hartmann, G. W. The rigidity of a basic attitudinal frame. *Journal of Abnormal and Social Psychology*, 1939, *34*, 314–335.

Wattenberg, W. W., & Clifford, C. Relation of self-confidence to beginning achievement in reading. *Child Development*, 1964, *35*, 461–467.

Waugh, N. C., & Norman, D. A. Primary memory. *Psychological Review*, 1965, *72*, 89–104.

Webster, S. W. The influence of interracial contact on social acceptance in a newly integrated school. *Journal of Educational Psychology*, 1961, *52*, 292–296.

Wechsler, D. *The measurement of adult intelligence* (3rd ed.). Baltimore: Williams & Wilkins, 1944.

Wechsler, D. Intellectual development and psychological maturity. *Child Development*, 1950, *21*, 45–50.

Weikart, D. P. Relationship of curriculum teaching, and learning in preschool education. In J. C. Stanley (Ed.), *Preschool programs for the disadvantaged: Five experimental approaches to early childhood education*. Baltimore: Johns Hopkins University Press, 1972.

Weinberg, C. Achievement and school attitudes of adolescent boys as related to behavior and occupational status of families. *Social Forces*, 1964, *42*, 462–466.

Weiner, B. The effects of unsatisfied achievement motivation on persistence and subsequent performance. *Journal of Personality*, 1965, *33*, 428–442.

Weiner, B., Johnson, P. B., & Mehrabian, A. Achievement motivation and the recall of complete and incomplete concepts. *Journal of Educational Psychology*, 1968, *59*, 181–185.

Weiner, B., & Rosenbaum, R. Determinants of choice between achievement and non-achievement related activities. *Journal of Experimental Research in Personality*, 1965, *1*(2), 114–121.

Weingold, H. P., & Webster, R. L. Effects of punishment on cooperative behavior in children. *Child Development*, 1964, *35*, 1211–1216.

Weir, M. W. Developmental changes in problem-solving strategies. *Psychological Review*, 1964, *71*, 473–490.

Weir, M. W., & Stevenson, H. W. The effect of verbalization in children's learning as a function of chronological age. *Child Development*, 1959, *30*, 143–149.

Weisberg, P. S., & Springer, K. J. Environmental factors in creative function: A study of gifted children. *Archives of General Psychiatry*, 1961, *5*, 554–564.

Weiss, P., Wertheimer, M., & Groesbeck, B. Achievement motivation, academic aptitude, and college grades. *Educational and Psychological Measurement*, 1959, *19*, 663–666.

Welch, L. The genetic development of the associational structures of abstract thinking. *Journal of Psychology*, 1940, *10*, 211–220. (a)

Welch, L. A preliminary investigation of some aspects of the hierarchical development of concepts. *Journal of Genetic Psychology*, 1940, *22*, 359–378. (b)

Welch, L., & Long, L. Comparison of the reasoning ability of two age groups. *Journal of Genetic Psychology*, 1943, *62*, 63–76.

Wellman, B. L. IQ changes of preschool and nonpreschool groups during the preschool years: A summary of the literature. *Journal of Psychology*, 1945, *20*, 347–368.

Wender, P. H. Diagnosis and management of minimal brain dysfunction. In R. I. Sader (Ed.), *Manual of psychiatric therapeutics*. Boston: Little, Brown, 1975.

Werner, H. *Comparative psychology of mental development*. Chicago: Follett, 1948.

Werner, H., & Kaplan, B. *Symbol formation: An organismic developmental approach to language and the expression of thought*. New York: Wiley, 1963.

Wertheimer, M. *Productive thinking* (enlarged ed.; M. Wertheimer, Ed.) New York: Harper & Row, 1959.

Wesman, A. G. A study of transfer of training from high school subjects to intelligence. *Journal of Educational Research*, 1945, *39*, 254–264.

West, L. H. T., & Fensham, P. J. Prior knowledge or advance organizers as effective variables in chemical learning. *Journal of Research in Science Teaching*, 1976, *13*(4), 297–306.

Westie, F. R. Negro-white status differentials and social distance. *American Sociological Review*, 1952, *17*, 550–558.

Westinghouse & Ohio University. The impact of Head Start: An evaluation of the effects of Head Start on children's cognitive and affective development. In J. L. Frost & G. R. Hawkes (Eds.), *The disadvantaged child: Issues and innovations* (2nd ed.). Boston: Houghton Mifflin, 1970.

Wheeler, L. R. A comparative study of the intelligence of East Tennessee Mountain children. *Journal of Educational Psychology*, 1942, *33*, 321–334.

White, R. T. Research into learning hierarchies. *Review of Educational Research*, 1973, *43*(3), 361–375.

White, R. T. A model for validation of learning hierarchies. *Journal of Research in Science Teaching*, 1974, *11*, 1–3. (a)

White, R. T. Indexes used in testing the validity of learning hierarchies. *Journal of Research in Science Teaching*, 1974, *11*, 61–66. (b)

White, R. W. Motivation reconsidered: The concept of competence. *Psychological Review*, 1959, *66*, 297–333.

White, W. F. Personality determinants of the effects of praise and reproof in classroom achievement. *Proceedings of the 75th annual convention of the American Psychological Association*, 1967, *2*, 323–324.

Whitlock, G. H., Copeland, L. C., & Craig, A. M. Programming versus independent study in learning elementary statistics. *Psychological Reports*, 1963, *12*, 171–174.

Whitman, J. C. *An approach to the evaluation of selected spontaneous and scientific concepts and misconceptions of second-grade children.* Unpublished master's thesis, Cornell University, 1975.

Whorf, B. L. Language, thought, and reality: Selected writings of Benjamin Lee Whorf. In J. B. Carroll (Ed.), *Language, thought, and reality: Selected writings of Benjamin Lee Whorf.* Cambridge: Massachusetts Institute of Technology Press, 1956.

Wilkinson, D. Y. Black youth. In *Youth*. 74th Yearbook, National Society for the Study of Education, Part I. Chicago: University of Chicago Press, 1975.

Williams, J. P. Effectiveness of constructed-response and multiple-choice programming modes as a function of test mode. *Journal of Educational Psychology*, 1956, *56*, 111–117.

Williams, O. A study of the phenomenon of reminiscence. *Journal of Experimental Psychology*, 1926, *9*, 368–389.

Wilson, M., Warren, J. M., & Abbott, L. Infantile stimulation, activity, and learning by cats. *Child Development*, 1965, *36*, 843–853.

Wilson, R. C., Guilford, J. P., & Christensen, P. R. The measurement of individual differences in originality. *Psychological Bulletin*, 1953, *50*, 362–370.

Winer, G. Induced set and acquisition of number conservation. *Child Development*, 1968, *39*, 195–205.

Winterbottom, M. M. The relation of need achievement to learning experiences in independence and mastery. In J. W. Atkinson (Ed.), *Motives in fantasy, action, and society.* Princeton, N.J.: Van Nostrand, 1958.

Wiseman, S. Symposium on the effects of coaching and practice in intelligence tests: IV. The Manchester experiment. *British Journal of Educational Psychology*, 1954, *24*, 5–8.

Wispé, L. G. Evaluating section teaching methods in the introductory course. *Journal of Educational Research*, 1951, *45*, 161–186.

Witkin, H. A., Paterson, H. F., Goodenough, D. R., & Birnbaum, J. Cognitive patterning in mildly retarded boys. *Child Development*, 1966, *37*, 301–316.

Wittenberg, R. M., & Berg, J. The stranger in the group. *American Journal of Orthopsychiatry*, 1952, *22*, 89–97.

Wittrock, M. C. Set to learn and proactive inhibition. *Journal of Educational Research*, 1963, *57*, 72–75. (a)

Wittrock, M. C. Effect of certain sets upon complex verbal learning. *Journal of Educational Psychology*, 1963, *54*, 85–88. (b)

Wittrock, M. C. Verbal stimuli in concept formation: Learning by discovery. *Journal of Educational Psychology*, 1963, *54*, 183–190. (c)

Wittrock, M. C. Response mode in the programming of kinetic molecular theory concepts. *Journal of Educational Psychology*, 1963, 54, 89–93. (d)

Wittrock, M. C., & Husek, T. R. Effect of anxiety upon retention of verbal learning. *Psychological Reports*, 1962, *10*, 78.

Wittrock, M. C., & Twelker, P. A. Verbal cues and variety of classes of problems in transfer of training. *Psychological Reports*, 1964, *14*, 827–830.

Wohlwill, J. F. Absolute vs. relational discrimination on the dimension of number. *Journal of Genetic Psychology*, 1960, *96*, 353–363. (a)

Wohlwill, J. F. A study of the development of the number concept by scalogram analysis. *Journal of Genetic Psychology*, 1960, *97*, 345–377. (b)

Wohlwill, J. F. *The study of behavioral development.* New York: Acadamic Press, 1973.

Wohlwill, J. F., & Lowe, R. C. An experimental analysis of the development of the conservation of number. *Child Development*, 1962, *33*, 153–167.

Wollen, K. A. One-trial versus incremental-paired associate learning. *Journal of Verbal Learning and Verbal Behavior*, 1962, *1*, 14–21.

Wood, B. D., & Freeman, F. N. *An experimental study of the educational influences of the typewriter in the elementary school classroom.* New York: Macmillan, 1932.

Woodrow, H. The effect of type of training upon transference. *Journal of Educational Psychology*, 1927, *18*, 159–172.

Woodworth, R. S. *Experimental psychology.* New York: Holt, Rinehart and Winston, 1938.

Woodworth, R. S. *Heredity and environment: A critical survey of recently published materials on twins and foster children.* New York: Social Science Research Council, 1941.

Wooldridge, D. E. *The machinery of the brain.* New York: McGraw-Hill, 1963.

Worcester, D. A. *The education of children of above-average mentality.* Lincoln: University of Nebraska Press, 1956.

Wright, J. M., & Harvey, O. J. Attitude change as a function of authoritarianism and punitiveness. *Journal of Personality and Social Psychology*, 1965, *1*, 177–181.

Wrightsman, L. S. The effects of anxiety, achievement motivation, and task importance upon performance on an intelligence test. *Journal of Educational Psychology*, 1962, *53*, 150–156.

Wulf, F. Über die Veränderung von Vorstelbingen (Gedächtnis und Gestalt). *Psychologische Forschung*, 1922, *1*, 333–373.

Wyer, R. S., Jr. Behavioral correlates of academic achievement: II. Pursuit of individual versus group goals in a decision-making task. *Journal of Educational Psychology*, 1968, *59*(2), 74–81.

Wyer, R. S., Jr. Effects of task reinforcement, social reinforcement and task difficulty on perseverance in achievement-related activity. *Journal of Personality and Social Psychology*, 1968, *8*(3, Pt. 1), 269–276.

Wyer, R. S. Jr., & Bednar, R. Some determinants of perseverance in achievement-related activity. *Journal of Experimental Social Psychology*, 1967, *3*(3), 255–256.

Yamamoto, K. A. Role of creative thinking and intelligence in high school achievement. *Psychological Reports*, 1964, *14*, 783–789. (a)

Yamamoto, K. A. Threshold of intelligence in academic achievement of highly creative students. *Journal of Experimental Education*, 1964, *32*, 401–405. (b)

Yamamoto, K. A. A further analysis of the role of creative thinking in high-school achievement. *Journal of Psychology*, 1964, *58*, 277–283. (c)

Yarmey, A. D. Overt and covert responding in programmed learning. *Ontario Journal of Educational Research*, 1964, *7*, 27–33.

Yarrow, M. R. Campbell, J. O., & Yarrow, L. J. Acquisition of new norms: A study of racial desegregation. *Journal of Social Issues*, 1958, *14*, 8–28.

Yates, A. J. Item analysis of progressive matrices (1947). *British Journal of Educational Psychology*, 1961, *31*, 152–157.

Yoakam, G. A. The effects of a single reading. *University of Iowa Studies in Education*, 2, No. 7. Iowa City: State University of Iowa, 1924.

Yonge, G. D. Structure of experience and functional fixedness. *Journal of Educational Psychology*, 1966, *57*, 115–120.

Young, F. M. Causes for loss of interest in high-school subjects as reported by 631 college students. *Journal of Educational Research*, 1932, *25*, 110–115.

Young, R. K., Benson, W. M., & Holtzman, W. H. Change in attitudes toward the Negro in a southern university. *Journal of Abnormal and Social Psychology*, 1960, *60*, 131–133.

Youtz, A. C. An experimental evaluation of Jost's laws. *Psychological Monographs*, 1941, *53* (Whole No. 238).

Yudin, L. W. Formal thought in adolescence as a function of intelligence. *Child Development*, 1966, *37*, 697–708.

Yudin, L. W., & Kates, S. L. Concept attainment and adolescent development. *Journal of Educational Psychology*, 1963, *55*, 1–9.

Zagona, S. V., & Zurcher, L. A. The relationship of verbal ability and other cognitive variables to the open-closed cognitive dimension. *Journal of Psychology*, 1965, *60*, 213–219.

Zambelli, J. A., Stamm, J. S., Matinski, S., & Loiselle, D. L. Auditory evoked potentials and selective attention in formerly hyperactive adolescent boys. *American Journal of Psycihatry*, 1977, *134*, 742–747.

Zander, A. A study of experimental frustration. *Psychological Monographs*, 1944, *56*, No. 3 (Whole No. 256).

Zigler, E., & Butterfield, E. C. Motivational aspects of changes in IQ test performance of culturally deprived nursery school children. *Child Development*, 1968, *29*, 1–14.

Zigler, E., & Kanzer, P. The effectiveness of two classes of verbal reinforcers on the performance of middle- and lower-class children. *Journal of Personality*, 1962, *30*, 157–163.

Zigler, E., & deLabry, J. Concept switching in middle-class, lower-class and retarded children. *Journal of Abnormal and Social Psychology*, 1965, *65*, 267–273.

Zillig, M. Einstellung und Aussage. *Zeitschrift für Psychologie*, 1928, *106*, 58–106.

Zimmerman, B. J., & Rosenthal, T. L. Conserving and retaining equalities and inequalities through observation and correction. *Developmental Psychology*, 1974, *10*, 260.

# INDEX OF NAMES

715

# INDEX OF SUBJECTS